DATE DUE			

Sovereignty and Revolution in the Iberian Atlantic

Sovereignty and Revolution in the Iberian Atlantic

Jeremy Adelman

PRINCETON UNIVERSITY PRESS

PRINCETON AND OXFORD

Published by Princeton University Press, 41 William Street, Princeton, New Jersey 08540
In the United Kingdom: Princeton University Press, 3 Market Place, Woodstock,
Oxfordshire OX20 1SY

Library of Congress Cataloging-in-Publication Data
Adelman, Jeremy.
   Sovereignty and revolution in the Iberian Atlantic / Jeremy Adelman.
      p. cm.
   Includes bibliographical references and index.
   ISBN-13: 978-0-691-12664-7 (cloth : alk. paper)
   ISBN-10: 0-691-12664-X (cloth : alk. paper)
      1. Latin America—History—Autonomy and independence movements. 2. Sovereignty—
History. 3. Spain—Colonies—Administration—History. 4. Spain—Colonies—Economic
conditions. I. Title.

F1412.A34 2006
330.98—dc22

                                                                       2006024296

British Library Cataloging-in-Publication Data is available

This book has been composed in Sabon

Printed on acid-free paper. ∞

pup.princeton.edu

Printed in the United States of America

10 9 8 7 6 5 4 3 2 1

Epigraph is taken from "The Labyrinth" by Jorges Luis Borges, edited by Stephen
Kessler, copyright © 1999 by Maria Kodama; translation copyright © 1999 by Stephen
Kessler, from SELECTED POEMS by Jorge Luis Borges, edited by Alexander Coleman.
Used by permission of Viking Penguin, a division of Penguin Group (USA) Inc.

For Debbie

Zeus himself could not undo the web

of stone closing around me. I have forgotten

the men I was before; I follow the hated

path of monotonous walls

that is my destiny. Severe galleries

which curve in secret circles

to the end of the years. Parapets

cracked by the days' usury.

In the pale dust I have discerned

signs that frighten me. In the concave

evenings the air has carried a roar

toward me, or the echo of a desolate howl.

I know there is another in the shadows,

whose fate it is to wear out the long solitudes

which weave and unweave this Hades

and to long for my blood and devour my death.

Each of us seeks the other. If only this

were the final day of waiting.

—*Jorge Luis Borges, "The Labyrinth"*

Contents

Acknowledgments

This book, like the emerging countries it studies, is born deep in debt. I have benefited from the research assistance of Katie Holt, Eduardo Morales, and Hannah Tappis, and Chris Brest's cartographic skills. Many friends and colleagues read parts of the manuscript. They include Howard Adelman, Roderick Barman, Tom Bender, Claudia Goldin, Paul Gootenberg, Jonathan Israel, Patricia Marks, Arno Mayer, Gabriel Paquette, Pablo Piccato, Kirsten Schultz, Stanley Stein, Richard Turits, and Chuck Walker. I got valuable early feedback from Ken Mills, João Reis, Richard Turits, and Jack Womack, and encouraging support from John Coatsworth, Stuart Schwartz, and Rebecca Scott. Conversations with José Carlos Chiaramonte, Arcadio Díaz-Quiñones, Arno Mayer, Ken Maxwell, Jaime E. Rodríguez O., and Victor Uribe have also been important in shaping my thoughts (though they might not have known how much I was rethinking while talking). Bits and pieces of the manuscript got airings in research workshops at the Institute for Advanced Study at Princeton, Harvard, New York University, Princeton, SUNY Stony Brook, and the University of Lisbon. These were most helpful occasions. Friends and colleagues at NYU were generous enough to invite me to share no less than three chapters of the book with them, and I thank Laurie Benton, Jim Fernández, and Antonio Feros for their hospitality.

The approach to empires and revolutions adopted in this book owes a great deal to the friends and colleagues with whom I coauthored a textbook in world history. Our discussions—and arguments—compelled me to rethink the ways in which my field, Latin American history, tackles its subjects. While this book is not a "world" history, its subjects are shaped by world events in ways I once would not have seen as clearly. In particular, I want to thank Bob Tignor for the years of encouragement and collegiality, and Steve Aron for urging me to cross the conventional borders of Atlantic history.

At Princeton University Press, I am most grateful to Brigitta van Rheinberg for sage and sensible advice, and to Fred Cooper and Frank Safford for their thoughtful comments. To Frank Safford I owe deep thanks for his line-by-line suggestions and corrections.

Many friends, colleagues, and librarians and archivists of the Iberian Atlantic made this possible. This inventory of gratitude would take up pages, but to the workers and companions of the archives in Buenos Aires, Rio de Janeiro, Bahia, Bogotá, Caracas, Lisbon, and Seville let me just say what I could not say enough: thanks. In particular, Ramón Aizpurua, Guiomar Dueñas, Véronique Hébrard, João Reis, Pedro Cardim, and Jorge Pedreira were wonderful hosts and guides in the peregrinations of my research.

If people enabled me to develop this project, so did material resources. The History Department and the Program in Latin American Studies at Princeton University gave me financial help when I needed it. The former dean of the faculty at Princeton, Joe Taylor, and my former History Department chair, Phil Nord, were also very supportive in arranging leave time and research funds. I thought about and wrote this book in wonderful institutional environments, starting at the David Rockefeller Center for Latin American Studies at Harvard, at my home Department of History at Princeton, and finally the Institute for Advanced Study. I thank my friends and colleagues at all these places for their support. Finally, I wish to thank the American Council of Learned Societies and its late president, John D'Arms, for bestowing the honor of a Frederick Burkhardt Fellowship. This gave me the impetus and backing to push my thoughts into broader, if unfamiliar and challenging, intellectual frontiers.

In the end, only my sons, little daughter, and wife know the true scale of what they put up with. I thank them, especially for the things I don't even know I asked of them. Jo Jo and Sammy gave new meaning and significance to what I try to do as an intellectual. Sadie came along too late to be much more than a tantalizing distraction; but the final touches coincided with her birth. I thank my wife, Debbie Prentice, for being my companion in the labyrinth that culminated in this book. Book writing can be solitary business, but I never felt alone. It is to her that this work is dedicated.

Sovereignty and Revolution in the Iberian Atlantic

Introduction
The Labyrinth of Sovereignty

IN A FAMOUS STORY called "The Garden of Forking Paths," Jorge Luis Borges recounts the fate of a protagonist who does not know, until the very end of the tale, the reasons for his crime. At the center of the story is the mystery of a book, an endless novel where multiple futures continue to proliferate and fork. The image of the labyrinth was important for Borges; the solitary quest for deliverance inspired the poem that serves as the epigraph for this book. Tales of wandering in a labyrinth have been a common parable of Latin American history, depicting the dilemma of a region caught between a traumatic past of conquest and oppression, and a future of freedom and democracy.[1]

Parables are not literal models for history. But they nonetheless capture features of a formative moment in modern Latin American history: the passages from empire to nationhood forked in ways that required actors to make choices without knowing the certainty of the outcome. The labyrinthine image also conveys the sense of the endlessness of the process. The passage that began in the eighteenth century did not end with the triumph of something new, as so many accounts of the "transition" from colony to nation-state denote. Rather, the beginnings, middles, and ends of the epic described in this book were above all about the ways in which history remained—and remains—unresolved, and therefore political.

This book retraces the steps, beginning at the entrance, of the main actors who redrew the political, economic, and social map of the Iberian Atlantic in search of a social order in a turbulent time. Their elusive goal was to create a world governed by the notion that people who live in a civil society abide by rules to which all subjects are bound. They wanted

---

[1] Jorge Luis Borges, "The Garden of Forking Paths," in *Collected Fictions* (New York: Penguin, 1999), pp. 118–28, "The Labyrinth," in *Selected Poems* (New York: Penguin, 2000), p. 275. See also Octavio Paz, *The Labyrinth of Solitude: Life and Thought in Mexico* (New York: Grove Press, 1961), esp. pp. 204, 208.

these rules to extend to the defensible territorial boundaries of their political communities. They were struggling for sovereignty.[2]

It was sovereignty of and within empires, monarchies, nations, and republics that was at stake during the great epoch of upheaval and struggle from the middle of the eighteenth to the middle of the nineteenth centuries. What was so labyrinthine was the quest to create new foundations for social life while old rules and norms decomposed. And yet, through decades of imperial change and collapse, civil war and revolution, protagonists eventually emerged with different conceptions for the modern age. These conceptions—the ones that have shaped Latin American history to the present day—were formed, to take Borges's words, in the "severe galleries which curve in secret circles" in which reformers, rebels, and reactionaries struggled over the means to deliver societies from the endless forking paths of the beginnings of modernity.

The quest for sovereignty has had its historians from the moment the struggle began. After all, one of the propositions of the age was that a modern concept of sovereignty meant that people could make—and thus write—history anew. To a remarkable extent, it was though history writing that protagonists sought to give meanings to sovereignty. For this reason, the acts of creating and writing are hard to disentangle; part of the quest for sovereignty also involved efforts to plot narratives to evoke a sense of history of a people coming into being as they were doing so.[3] Self-rule therefore shaped and was shaped by the drive for historical self-consciousness.

If history making and history writing are entwined, this does not mean that people struck out with foresight armed with plot lines of a drive to modern futures. Rather, they used hindsight to explain how they got themselves into a present they only dimly grasped. In this fashion the birth of modern states and national historiographies were bound together, equal parts shaped and scarred by the process that sired them.

Consider a few of the first "histories" of these struggles for sovereignty. After two decades of fighting in the Andes, Simón Bolívar sat down to write a short history of Spanish Americans' struggles for sovereignty.

---

[2]Sovereignty has become a highly disputed notion in the social sciences, fueled by the contemporary debate over the limits of sovereignty of nation-states in a globalized world. See Daniel Philpott, *Revolutions in Sovereignty: How Ideas Shaped Modern International Relations* (Princeton: Princeton University Press, 2001); Stephen Krasner, ed. *Problematic Sovereignty: Contested Rules and Political Possibilities* (New York: Columbia University Press, 2001). If this book helps to keep the waters stirred, it is to insist that sovereignty was always contested, unstable, and equivocal. The quest to define it has been a motor force of international and infranational conflict.

[3]Rogers S. Smith, *Stories of Peoplehood: The Politics and Morals of Political Membership* (New York: Cambridge University Press, 2003).

En route from Lima, where he left behind a deeply fractured government, to Bogotá, where the fissures ran just as deep, the Liberator paused to compose a dispirited synthesis, "A Panoramic View of Spanish America." Bolívar's short epic began in Buenos Aires, where the revolt against Spain devolved into an "anarchic revolution": what had begun as a confrontation with Spanish cousins soon became a civil war between American brothers. Rather than leading their people to the promised land of freedom, revolutionaries unleashed "the rampant appetite of a people who have broken their chains and have no understanding of the notions of duty and law and who cannot cease being slaves except to become tyrants." This "history is that of all Spanish America." Now the formal chains of empire had been broken; but what had been freed were the passions of "unbridled ambition" once tamed by the powers of monarchy and empire. Bolívar put down his pen and resumed his own voyage, hoping to marshal his historic vision for the final prophetic act of delivering his people to freedom, only to preside over the disintegration of Gran Colombia, the secession of his native Venezuela, to die a year later, like his aspirations, in torment.[4]

Not all the protagonists in South America's independence struggles were so gloomy—or wrote such dispirited "histories." According to José da Silva Lisboa, soon the Viscount of Cairú, Brazil's history also did not dispose its subjects to a new model of political community in which kings gave way to peoples as the repositories of sovereignty. But for this Bahian jurist and writer, this was all to the good, since he did not have much affection for republican or liberal ideas. Indeed, the success of Brazilian independence, the ability to slay the demons of provincial secession, civil war, and slave revolt, lay in its ability to change so little. The fundamental principles of sovereignty—monarchy, central rule, and the ballast of an ennobled slave-owning aristocracy—remained intact even though the formal ties to Lisbon were broken. What was most important about the old regime survived, and thus prevented Brazil from getting swallowed up in civil war. This was the only major colony of all the European empires in the Americas not to splinter into parts as it proclaimed its independence. Brazil, as Cairú put it, became an integrated sovereign entity because it did *not* have a revolution. Those who struggled for Brazilian sovereignty, aware of the limitations of their subjects, knew not to take the more tempting path of relying on popular sovereignty as a way out of the maze. True to his Burkean principles, the viscount celebrated the leadership of the old regime for knowing how to guide change in order to control it.[5]

---

[4]Simón Bolívar, "A Glance at Spanish America," in David Bushnell, ed., *El Libertador: Writings of Simón Bolívar* (New York: Oxford University Press, 2003), p. 96.

[5]José da Silva Lisboa, *Constitução moral e deveres do Cidadão com exposição da moral publica conforme o espiritu da Constituição do imperio* (Rio de Janeiro: Typographia Nacional, 1824), v. 1, pp. iii–8.

Bolívar the defeatist and Cairú the triumphalist obviously differed in their politics. But they did not necessarily differ in their assumptions about Iberian empires and their South American colonies. What these accounts shared was the sense that imperial and colonial legacies endured through the struggles to dismantle them. The stamina of these legacies reflected not just what Iberian colonies were, but what they were not. They were not, in their view, colonies made up of civic-minded subjects of self-governing communities as they were idealized in the "other" America, that of English origins. Absent in the America of Iberian origins were the virtues of private citizens and the habits of representative governance. Bolívar and Cairú were not the only ones to make these kinds of assumptions. Thomas Jefferson, watching political events in Spanish America, drew some teleological conclusions of his own about "his" America in a letter to John Adams: the English colonists' owed much of their success to what they inherited from the mother country: traditions of self-government. In the Spanish colonies, Jefferson found that subjects "habituated from their infancy to passive submission to body and mind to their kings and priests" stood little chance of realizing true liberty. The people best prepared for a revolution were those least oppressed by the old regime, and those who most needed a revolution would see theirs fail.[6]

Bolívar, Cairú, and Jefferson were protagonists in events they witnessed firsthand. These "founding fathers" of new sovereign nations offered privileged retrospectives that would become the histories that lay the groundwork for grand epic writing of the nineteenth century. Their histories have come down the generations to frame the principal trajectories of the histories of the New World.

In response to the romantic emphasis on the role and limits of human will, more recently scholars have emphasized the ways in which revolutions are unintended by-products of social conflict, not the results of antecedent volition. The goal has been to disentangle intentions or motives for revolting from their results. Dismantling the past was seldom what motivated actors—a changing order was often less intended than consequential.[7]

---

[6]Cited in David Brion Davis, *Revolutions: Reflections on American Equality and Foreign Liberations* (Cambridge, MA: Harvard University Press, 1990), p. 70.

[7]Eric Hobsbawm, "The Making of a 'Bourgeois Revolution,'" *Social Research* 56:1 (1989): 5–31; Jack A. Goldstone, "Comparative Historical Analysis and Knowledge Accumulation in the Study of Revolutions," in James Mahoney and Dietrich Rueschemeyer, eds., *Comparative Historical Analysis in the Social Sciences* (New York: Cambridge University Press, 2003), pp. 41–90; Clifton Kroeber, "Theory and History of Revolutions," *Journal of World History* 7:1 (1996): 21–40.

This book seeks to illuminate the ways in which it was not at all inevitable that the people of the Iberian Atlantic considered their Spanish and Portuguese inheritances as anything less than desirable. The fact is, the Spanish and Portuguese domains, like so many others, crumbled less out of internal conflicts and more from the compound pressures of several centuries of rivalry between Atlantic powers. Social revolutions transpired when international pressures of competing sovereignties broke down state systems; it is not so easy to find a sharp boundary between internal and external dynamics of large-scale social change—in large measure because instability, not immutability, was central to sovereignty.[8] The crisis of the anciens régimes were the effects of a pan-Atlantic struggle for mercantilist control, political loyalty, and ultimately for military alliance to define the future of monarchy, aristocracy, national markets, and bonded labor across the Atlantic world.

Yet, if there is a structural backdrop to the making and remaking of sovereignty, surprisingly little is known about *how* state systems decomposed. This requires closer attention to processes of making, defending, and abandoning systems of state sovereignty—examining modern revolutions and their coeval partners in state formation, counter revolutions. When, for instance, old privileges began to face mounting pressures, some defenders of ancient entitlements sought to impose tradition on highly explosive societies. And the more there was to question about the old regime, the harder it was to contain prophecies of a new one, and the more vicious became the reaction. So, as international warfare provoked civil war within the Iberian Atlantic, the contradictory pressures of unity and secession became more difficult to resolve. At that point, the revolution—and its antithesis, the counterrevolution—tore apart the economic, social, and political foundations of the Iberian Atlantic.[9]

The challengers to, and defenders of, old ways were dealing with specific kinds of regimes: empires. This book seeks to restore the centrality of the imperial dimension to the way we think about revolutions and their national progeny, not just because they were so historically connected in the late eighteenth and early nineteenth centuries, when British, French, Portuguese, and Spanish dominions in the Americas went up in revolutionary flames, but because until then sovereignty was reflexively associated with imperium.

---

[8]Theda Skocpol, *States and Social Revolutions: A Comparative Analysis of France, Russia and China* (New York: Cambridge University Press, 1979), p. 5.

[9]Arno J. Mayer, *The Furies: Violence and Terror in the French and Russian Revolutions* (Princeton: Princeton University Press, 2000), p. 45.

Two aspects of imperial sovereignty shaped the course of events. The first involved defining the legal personality of political subjects within a state, their reciprocal obligations and rights inscribed in laws that extended to the state's borders. The second definition of sovereignty involved drawing the borders around the political community, which in the case of empires meant inscribing limits between insiders and outsiders, creating standing national "parts" out of a hitherto imperial "whole." These two dimensions were entwined since they both implied the struggle to define categories of subject, citizen, and state, and the boundaries around them. In the Americas, colonial societies made of the pluri-social peoples of the Atlantic world and mapped out since the Treaty of Tordesillas (1494), the simultaneity of the struggles for sovereignty magnified the meanings and complexities of freedom. It also made the relations between them very explosive once the legal structures that shaped centuries of exploitation, domination, and transatlantic exchange began to collapse.

This may seem self-evident. But even the majestic study by R. R. Palmer of what he called the democratic revolutions of "Atlantic civilization" treated the struggles for democracy as an epic poised against aristocracy. Personal equality, not so much state sovereignty, was the issue and quest. Sovereignty, within or outside empires, was not a casus belli worth much systematic analysis for Palmer. And yet, as anyone concerned with civil and human rights nowadays knows, defining and defending equality depended on states and their command over legal instruments. For much of the Western Hemisphere, sovereignty *was* the heart of the matter, and as the legal foundations of statehood became the source of debate and conflict, so did the social and economic practices that it upheld and legitimated.[10]

Empires have centers and peripheries, a distinction that has led to some unfortunate incisions that separate "imperial" history as European and "colonial" history as American. This book blurs the imperial-colonial distinction by referring to an Atlantic world whose history can be looked at bifocally to bring both sides of the ocean into the same visual frame of empire. The metropoles of Lisbon and Madrid and the colonies in the Americas were locked in an integrated struggle over the sovereignty of the empires. Each side constituted the other mutually, if not always amicably. Therefore, in writing about empire one principle underlies this book: empires were not about "Spain," "Portugal," or their colonies, but about the transactions and relationships between the various peoples of their domains.[11]

---

[10]R. R. Palmer, *The Age of Democratic Revolution: A Political History of Europe and America, 1760–1800*, 2 vols. (Princeton: Princeton University Press, 1959).

[11]Models of this interactive approach include Jaime E. Rodríguez O., *The Independence of Spanish America* (New York: Cambridge University Press, 1998).

These crises of ancien-régime empires did not unfold uniformly or evenly. Indeed, for decades, the empires were in trouble, but they did not collapse. What is remarkable—and worth exploring—is how they survived, or even revived, under duress. Accounting for the durability of archaic structures requires suppressing postdictive temptations to make empires appear fated to eclipse, a predilection that has always been uncomfortable for historians of Iberian worlds. We have come, perhaps due to the influence of Gibbon's 1776 masterwork, *The History of the Decline and Fall of the Roman Empire*, and the more recent grand narrative by Paul Kennedy, *The Rise and Fall of the Great Powers*, to presume that empires were—and are—doomed structures.[12] Gibbon best captured the problem with empires: they start, appropriately enough, as cities, home of the virtuous *civitas*, filled with communally minded citizens who put the general good ahead of particular reward. But their greatness leads them to expand, and as they aggrandize, the temptation to pursue private gain and abandon the virtues of the civic community is too hard to resist. So the imperium, with conquest, sows the seeds of its own decay. Kennedy compressed this story line into the synthetic term of "imperial over-stretch" in which the public costs of defending the realm exceed the private gains to those who profit—and invariably, eventually, either give way to new rivals or simply collapse.

Examined more closely, empires do not always plot themselves so neatly along curvaceous inclines and declines. Once again, a labyrinthine model better captures the ways in which subjects of empires handled imperial crises. For much of the time that the Spanish and Portuguese empires were in deep trouble, colonists did not reject the weakened hands of the metropoles when it would have been easier to declare colonial sovereignty. Not all institutional breakdowns lead to breakups. In fact, the breakdown of empires intensified proclamations of loyalty on their peripheries. If Madrid's and Lisbon's policies of recovery were oftentimes oppressive, colonists voiced some of their concerns—though almost always in the name of what was good for the empire as a whole because, in their mind's eye, sovereignty was synonymous with imperium. There was, however, a point—when the metropolitan monarchy itself was

---

[12]Edward Gibbon, *The History of the Decline and Fall of the Roman Empire* (New York: Penguin Books, 2000), originally published, though not timed to coincide with the first crisis of the British empire, in 1776; Paul Kennedy, *The Rise and Fall of the Great Powers: Economic Change and Military Conflict from 1500 to 2000* (New York: Random House, 1988). On the social science discovery of empire, see David B. Abernethy, *The Dynamics of Global Dominance: European Overseas Empires, 1415–1980* (New Haven: Yale University Press, 2000); Alexander J. Motyl, *Imperial Ends: The Decay, Collapse and Revival of Empires* (New York: Columbia University Press, 2001).

destroyed—at which imperial sovereignty went into shock. One pivotal point in this narrative involves the French invasion of the Iberian metropoles and the centrifugal effects on the peripheries. Only at this stage did imaginings of a new, postcolonial order begin to eclipse the old one.

These stages in the breakdown and breakup of empires did not lead in lockstep from one to the next: revolutions unfolded not as mechanical expressions of a self-conscious desire to "exit" empire but jostled with other, more familiar ways of coping with the decline and crisis of the world colonists knew best, "loyalty" and "voice." The options of expressions of loyalty, voice, and exit as responses to the deterioration of institutional life come closer to illuminating agents' judgments and choices that determined the fate of their empires.[13] It was the deterioration of the empires that led to the breakup of their ruling coalitions and the stirrings of revolution. Social revolutions were not the cause of imperial breakups, but their consequence.

What has been said about empires and revolutions raises some issues about nations and nationalism. It is a commonplace to argue that colonials acquired a sense of selfhood, a national identity, in opposition to empire. The assumption is, therefore, that Americans acquired a distinctive sense of self within empire. The sense of colonial apartness led colonists to repudiate imperium and to secede because they no longer felt like they belonged. The pursuit of national liberation spelled the end of imperial sovereignty in colonial lands; anticolonial nationalism spawned imperial crises; nations, with a congruent political unit, replaced empires as the dominant model of sovereignty in the Atlantic world.[14] Benedict Anderson made the case for the origins of nationalism as an alternative political community made of horizontal comradeship and held together by the circulation of print media.[15] These affective ties created proto-national identities that functioned on an entirely different level from imperial ones, so that the former supplanted the latter like distinct, separable phases in the trend lines of modernization. What Anderson, Pagden, and so many other students of nationalism have tended to presume was that "creole patriots" acquired a different sense of self as a prelude to their

---

[13]Albert O. Hirschman, *Exit, Voice, Loyalty: Responses to Decline in Firms, Organizations, and States* (Cambridge, MA: Harvard University Press, 1970).

[14]Cited in Anthony Pagden, "Identity Formation in Spanish America," in Nicholas Canny and Anthony Pagden, eds., *Colonial Identity in the Atlantic World, 1500–1800* (Princeton: Princeton University Press, 1987), pp. 91–83.

[15]Benedict Anderson, *Imagined Communities: Reflections on the Origins and Spread of Nationalism*, rev. ed. (London: Verso, 1991).

proclamations of something new. In this formulation, declarations of independence were catalysts of revolutions.

And yet as Bolívar and Cairú observed firsthand, creole nations did not predate formal announcements of their existence. Empire *or* nation? Nation *versus* empire? The dualism in fact made little sense for those whose loyalties did not break down into either or. They could feel at home imagining themselves simultaneously as Spaniards, Spanish Americans, and citizens (vecinos) of Caracas. The colonial subjects of José I, king of Portugal and the Algarves, envisioned themselves simultaneously as royal subjects and as notables in the various juntas of Rio de Janeiro.[16] After all, what made empires, especially the composite Iberian regimes, so complex was that their monarchies sheltered multiple identities under a single roof. Indeed, for decades what South Americans wanted was to be autonomous *and* to belong to a great empire, to be Americans *and* the subjects of a magnanimous monarchy; to have it as many ways as possible. There is, therefore, a big part of the story that connects empires with nations that remains untold—how colonists disidentified with empires and monarchies as a condition for identifying with something else. It is not enough, in other words, to account for the emergence of national identities in mechanical opposition to imperial ones. Much had to happen to the voices and discontents of colonial peoples before they could contribute to the makings of an alternative political identity.

Finally, a few words about the space of the Iberian Atlantic examined in this book. It was triangular, involving the connections between the Iberian peninsula, the African littoral, and South America's archipelago of ports that gave way to vast hinterlands in the interiors of the continent. These Atlantic worlds were settings for generating and apportioning spoils of trade and exploitation, in principle governed by rules made in the center and enforced in the peripheries. These terms—center and periphery—have been much maligned in recent decades, for they suggest a one-way traffic of power. In the effort to illustrate colonial or provincial autonomy or loyalty, it has become unfashionable to refer to the "centered-ness" of power itself. This is unfortunate, because the Atlantic empires *did* have centers that kept the commercial regimes going and diffused social unrest into a common political and legal vocabulary. Members of Iberian empires may have quarreled over rights and privileges (and these were at times very litigious systems), but it was rare to see these evolve into challenges to the regimes as a whole. Indeed,

---

[16]Tamar Herzog, *Defining Nations: Immigrants and Citizens in Early Modern Spain and Spanish America* (New Haven: Yale University Press, 2003).

contestants for power often draped their claims in their undying fealty to the sovereign. Membership in empire and subjecthood in monarchy did not just coincide, they reinforced each other. In turn, the monarchy and the empire over which it prevailed had a center, a capital, taproots for the systems of legitimacy that emboldened loyalty and defined personal rights within realms that could seem just while being viciously exploitative.[17]

Re-centering Iberian empires need not imply that laws, rules, and norms crossed from one (European) shore to the (American) other in only one direction. As with any monarchy, it is a mistake to infer any capacity to enforce rules and norms as they radiated from the court. What is remarkable is the degree to which peripheral agents either adapted rules to suit their purposes, or pushed back when they wanted something for themselves. The bargaining and transacting within imperial coalitions therefore also criss-crossed the Atlantic under the sovereign structures of monarchical rule. So, when the central pillars of sovereign authority—the monarchs of Madrid and Lisbon—were smashed by Napoleonic armies, centrifugal propensities ravaged the imperial worlds, setting the stage for the parts of old empires to rebuild Atlantic networks with the imperfect and contested principles of the sovereignty of nation-states and ideals of free trade.

Most of the action described in this book takes place in cities from Cartagena to Caracas and around the Brazilian bulge down to Buenos Aires—and their connections to metropolitan cities like Lisbon, Madrid, and Cádiz. The colonial gateways between the staple-producing lands of South America and African and European markets were where the politics of imperial authority, and the scope of mercantile privilege, got hammered out. Africa, in turn, furnished the crucial supplies of labor to keep the exchange networks going, flowing out of the littoral outposts from the Bight of Benin to Benguela. As we shall see, the slave trade exercised an important influence on the nature of commercial capitalism in South America, and on the calculus of loyalty, voice, and exit, when the metropolitan foundations of empire began to shake. South American colonial outposts intermediated between supply and demand of commodities and slaves across the Atlantic, even as they were the institutional homes for mediation between public authorities and powerful commercial elites that occupied an important place in the ruling coalitions with landowners, clerics, and professionals of empire. If the merchants in imperial cities occupy an important place in the narrative of this book, it is because they provided a social ballast for cross-Atlantic elites; traders were also important because of what they pumped through the sinews

---

[17] Bernard Bailyn, "The Idea of Atlantic History," *Itinerario* 20 (1996): 26, and in Spanish, "El Idea de una Historia Atlántica," *Entrepasados*, 2nd semester, 2003.

of empire: merchant capital to sustain the circulation of commodities and labor.

South America was divided by political loyalties while at the same time loosely integrated by commercial and social opportunity. As a setting for conflict and convergence between two empires, the Iberian Atlantic provides an opportunity to engage in a comparative study of imperial decline and revolution within a single geographic space over the same period of time. There are, of course, many ways to pose questions and explore them comparatively. Consider the resemblances: two monarchies sharing the same colonial and metropolitan continents, with similar social structures at the centers and peripheries; two empires locked in the same revolutionary conjuncture and facing the diffusion of ideas about representation and models of personal and political freedom; two empires occupied by the same foreign (French) army, and forced to align with the same foreign (British) power. To a large extent, what follows is a story of the demise of two analogous, though not equivalent, empires under similar constraints.[18]

The differences should not be read backward as if single unbroken lines connect the dots between primal causes and their consequences.[19] One reason it is so hard to trace the divergence of Spanish and Portuguese colonial worlds back to primal causes is because there were important regional variations within each empire. These variations were striking enough—and potent enough—to suggest that things might have gone quite differently under other circumstances. In many ways there were more affinities across the Spanish and Portuguese empires than there were within them. Several times, for instance, Pernambuco in northeastern Brazil struck out in favor of an independent republic against Lisbon and against Rio de Janeiro. Pernambucan insurgents advocated a decentralized federalist model—akin to many of the littoral provinces in the River Plate who likewise resisted Buenos Aires' and Madrid's rule. Here were remarkably similar provincial reactions to centralizing drives in two distinct political communities. Instead, Pernambucan federalists failed while those in the River Plate succeeded. In effect, at different times and places, South American outposts could have followed common trajectories. But they did not.

---

[18]For a clear statement of the comparative approach adopted here, see Charles C. Ragin, *The Comparative Method: Moving beyond Qualitative and Quantitative Strategies* (Berkeley: University of California Press, 1987); Theda Skocpol and Margaret Somers, "The Uses of Comparative History in Macro-Social Inquiry," *Comparative Studies in Society and History* 22:2 (1980): 174–97; Skocpol, *States and Social Revolutions*, pp. 36–39.

[19]Baruch Fishhoff, "For Those Condemned to Study the Past: Reflections on Historical Judgement," *New Directions for Methodology of Social and Behavioral Science*, no. 4 (1980): 79–93.

These are some of the might-have-beens that need to be understood as part of a more general appraisal. In the end, this book shies away from elegant theories premised on simplifying assumptions that gloss over how and why agents made the choices they did. If nothing else, the comparisons invoked here should illustrate the effects of strategic decisions by people who had to make judgment calls in a historic juncture in which the foundations of power were under threat at home and abroad. The choices and the conflicts they produced yielded to histories that none intended and few envisioned. Yet, in making history by groping through a labyrinth of forked paths they created the opportunity for their heirs to imagine anew the prospects for personal and political sovereignty.

1   Empires That Bleed

INTRODUCTION

In a letter to the ruler of the Portuguese empire, Dom João V, Overseas Councillor Alexandre de Gusmão, likened monarchies to bodies whose lifeblood was trade. Writing in 1748, he observed that losing trade was the "same as what happens to human bodies when blood is drained. Speaking frankly, this is where Portugal is heading, for while we struggle to extract money she is heading for poverty and, as a consequence, her Ruin." Gusmão, a powerful minister and architect of imperial policy in the middle of the eighteenth century, echoed a longstanding belief in early modern European statecraft: private wealth and public welfare were inextricably tied to commercial power.[1]

The concern about the wealth of the empire and the health of the monarchy also obsessed insiders in Madrid. José del Campillo y Cosío, minister of state, navy, war, and the Indies to Felipe V, penned similar diagnoses and prescriptions that influenced later generations of imperial thinkers and policymakers, tapping into idioms of the body to drive home a point about state power. Spain's agriculture languished, Campillo argued. Her defenses were decrepit, her education was antiquated, and her administration amounted to lethargic enforcement of obsolete regulations. But above all, Spanish commerce had become the preserve of a handful of entrenched monopolies that stifled trade and business. Campillo's *Nuevo sistema de gobierno económico para la América* (1743) called for reconstituting the monarchy not as the agglomeration of dispersed provinces bound by systems of privilege, but as the center of vast dominions teeming with competitive traders: an ideal empire. *Nuevo sistema* also drew the parallel between monarchies and bodies sustained by the circulation of commodities flowing throughout the dominions and

---

[1]Alexandre de Gusmão "Calculo sobre a perda do dinheiro do Reyno offerecido a El Rey D. João 5 no anno de 1748 por Alexandre de Gusmão," in Biblioteca Nacional de Lisboa (hereafter BNL), Coleção Pombalina (hereafter CP), Códice 473, ff. 207–9. For more on de Gusmão, see Jaime Cortesão, *Alexandre de Gusmão e o Tratado de Madrid*, 2 vols. (Lisboa: Livros Horizonte, 1984). On the body metaphor for state power, see Ernst H. Kantorowicz, *The King's Two Bodies: A Study in Medieval Political Theology* (Princeton: Princeton University Press, 1957).

converging on the heart: Spain. "Commerce," he wrote, "is what maintains the body politic like the circulation of blood in the natural body."[2] If likening monarchies to bodies was nothing new in discourses of European statecraft, what was becoming clearer in the eighteenth century was how important the circulation of commodities was in defining power politics.

The apotheosis of mercantilist empires and the heightened attention to the ties between trade and monarchies, blood and bodies, coincided with the apogee of European dynastic rivalries. Especially once the political geography of dynastic boundaries of western Europe took shape after the Treaty of Westphalia in 1648, competitors looked overseas—and especially to the Americas—in the quest for markets, materials, and military superiority. For Iberian powers, the first claimants to extensive colonies in the Americas, expansion had always brought rivalries in tow. But after 1648, the Dutch, French, and increasingly the English fixed their attention on gains in the New World to settle scores in the Old World. So it was not just that Iberians were losing trade, and therefore blood. They were losing it to their rivals. Gusmão and Campillo were therefore vexed by a historic riddle: how could Portugal and Spain, mature empires, catch up with their rivals whose body politics were more youthful, vital, and energetic?[3]

Perceptions of backwardness and vulnerable sovereignty framed the policies with which imperial rulers and magnates governed their domains. The concern to reverse the trend raised a set of thorny issues about the proper balance between public good and private interest. In general, Enlightenment thinkers promoted the idea that private interests were not just the cornerstones of public good, but enjoyed an autonomous status. If monarchies needed trade, they had to accept their dependence on members of the civitas that did the trading. Thus, the health of the regimes was tied explicitly to the privileges of private trading fortunes. Wise monarchs encouraged private interests as a way of promoting public welfare. This has become a common way to understand the origins of modern political economy and of the Enlightenment's bequest to thinking about wealth and public affairs.

---

[2]José del Campillo y Cosío, *Nuevo sistema de gobierno económico para la América* (1:43; Caracas: Universidad de los Andes, 1971), p. 70. The work circulated privately, with official blessing, until after the author's death.

[3]A fine overview of the tensions created by imperial rivalry is Peggy Liss, *Atlantic Empires: The Networks of Trade and Revolution, 1713–1826* (Baltimore: Johns Hopkins University Press, 1983). See also the first half of Tulio Halperín Donghi, *Reforma y disolución de los imperios Ibéricos, 1750–1850* (Madrid: Alianza Editorial, 1985). On the relationship among economic discourse, political power, and the origins of capitalism in early modern Europe, see David McNally, *Political Economy and the Rise of Capitalism: A Reinterpretation* (Berkeley: University of California Press, 1988), esp. chap. 2.

But the view that there was an essential primacy to the private world of property and personal interests as a condition of the commonwealth was more troublesome when it came to Europe's less dynamic flanks. Iberian rulers and their ministerial circles did not shy away from the underlying notion that public and private spheres were autonomous. But autonomy was not the same as independence. Rather, they insisted on mutual dependence of private interests and public welfare because unfettered personal drives too easily cascaded into private vice and corruption. Some public check was necessary to curb the excesses of private avarice. Good rulers had to create a centralized, more effective state to prevent private rights from backsliding into personal privileges, and then obstacles to social betterment. Merchants and monarchs shared the same fate—and the prosperity of one gave a new lease on life to the other. The art of statecraft implied creating calibrated, countervailing sources of authority to balance—indeed, to integrate more virtuously—private and public domains while respecting the autonomy of each.[4]

If one hears echoes of Montesquieu's doctrine that abuses of power or privilege required checks and balances, this chapter explores how, in the Iberian context, the concern for a new equipoise was heightened because imbalances had weakened the monarchies and left them prey to Europe's rising dynasties. For Iberians, therefore, the political economy of statecraft reflected much more than a European skill. Rather, the fates of private and public fortunes were coiled in Atlantic imperial structures. Empire was the means to realize a strong monarchy and an opulent merchant class because merchant capitalism made its fortunes through imperial ventures and empires rested on political foundations that presumed that kings were natural conveyors of godliness and affluence to the rest of the world.[5]

IMPERIAL WARS

If the Iberian Atlantic shared norms and institutions, it was nonetheless a turbulent sea of political and commercial rivalry. Warfare simultaneously integrated and fractured the legal frameworks of sovereignty for all

---

[4]Jorge Cañizares-Esguerra, "Eighteenth-Century Spanish Political Economy: Epistemology and Decline," *Eighteenth-Century Thought* 1 (2003): 295–314.

[5]J. H. Elliott, "Self-Perception and Decline in Early Seventeenth-Century Spain," *Past and Present* 74 (1977): 41–61; Laura de Mello e Souza and Maria Fernanda Baptista Bicalho, *Virando séculos: O império deste mundo, 1680–1720* (São Paulo: Companhia das Letras, 2000); Jacob Viner, "Power versus Plenty as Objectives of Foreign Policy in the Seventeenth and Eighteenth Centuries," in D. C. Coleman, ed., *Revisions of Mercantilism* (London: Methuen, 1964), pp. 61–91.

empires. Imperial warfare became, it seemed to many, a permanent state of affairs for Spain and Portugal. European rivals struggled and skirmished increasingly for commercial supremacy and carried their competition far from the seats of central power. In effect, imperial contestants displaced their conflicts over borders and alliances in the Old World, now that the legal cartographies were more or less recognized by the Treaties of Münster and Westphalia (1648) and Utrecht (1713), to fights over borderlands in the New World. These treaties may have acknowledged the sovereignty of the signatories and fastened some of the borders between states in Europe. But they also provided the interstate framework for ramped-up competition between them while displacing it overseas, creating the European architecture not for peace but for state aggrandizement and jostling for commercial supremacy through imperial warfare. Thus while national sovereignties began to take shape in Europe after 1648, imperial sovereignties became more contested than ever. "Beyond the Line," as one English saying went, "might makes right."[6]

This intensified European rivalry involved not just any kind of state. These were *imperial* states struggling for ascendancy not just within Europe but across the Atlantic world.[7] After all, what sparked the War of the Spanish Succession was Madrid's giving the *asiento* slave-trading contract to a French firm. Ten days later, fearing a French lock on the commercial networks binding Europe, Africa, and the Iberian Indies, England and Holland declared war against France and, ipso facto, Spain. Portugal, allied with England, thus got swept into the conflict. French forces took aim at Portuguese outposts. After attacking Principe, São Tomé, Benguela, and other Portuguese outposts in Africa, French troops invaded and sacked Rio de Janeiro, hoping to claim a vital corner of the Atlantic slave trade and open a French lifeline to the silver lodes in the interior of South America. Rebellions erupted in Bahia, São Paulo, and Pernambuco as colonists exploited the occasion to drive out intrusive Portuguese colonial officers. Brazil appeared to be breaking apart as its metropole got sucked into a war between rivals. Writing to Lisbon, Antônio Rodrigues da Costa noted that Brazilian riches were no guarantee that

---

[6]Stanley J. Stein and Barbara H. Stein, *Silver, Trade and War: Spain and America in the Making of Early Modern Europe* (Baltimore: Johns Hopkins University Press, 2000), p. 94; Eliga Gould, "Zones of Law, Zones of Violence: The Legal Geography of the British Atlantic, circa 1772," *William and Mary Quarterly*, 3rd ser., 60:3 (2003): pp. 479–480.

[7]There has been a slight tendency to argue that European state "systems" were, *in ovo*, clustered around urban centers and warred as they bumped up against each other to become nations. All I am arguing here is that Atlantic empire has to be located more centrally as a variable in state formation. Charles Tilly, *Coercion, Capital, and European States, AD 900–1990* (Oxford: Basil Blackwell, 1990), pp. 161–81.

Brazilian subjects would stay loyal to Portugal—or indeed any European master at all. Such were the peripheral implications of European imperial rivalry.[8]

The Treaty of Utrecht helped settle some of the boundaries between European powers, but it did little to put an end to Atlantic warfare. If anything, the relationship between interimperial warfare and transatlantic commerce got more entwined as the slave trade became a lucrative and large-scale venture binding Africa, the Americas, and Europe into an increasingly explosive, violent, and profitable knot. As part of the "peace" of Utrecht, the asiento contract was granted to the English South Sea Company, chartered in 1711, just in time to take advantage of the post-Utrecht settlement. Now English merchants could ship slaves and, more important, English manufactures tucked into holds below decks to Spanish colonies. Portugal was also fought over but collapsed more unambiguously into the British trading orbit after the 1703 trade and defense treaty between Lisbon and London. No wonder the French were so eager to stake a claim before the settlement and worked so hard to undermine English and Portuguese claims in the New World. So, while Spain and Portugal clung to their formal colonies, they themselves became informal branches for merchant capitalists in northern Europe.[9]

To make matters worse, Lisbon and Madrid tried to displace their dependency on and losses to other European powers by taking aim at each other. The Treaty of Tordesillas (1494) was supposed to inscribe legal foundations of the early modern imperial structures and define the borders of the Iberian domains. Instead, it guaranteed constant conflict around the River Plate borderlands. According to the treaty, all lands up to a line 270 leagues west of the Azore Islands fell within the Portuguese realm, and beyond that all claims were Spanish. This neat arrangement created a mess, however, when the imperial border sliced through the meandering rivers of the Platine drainage basin. Colônia do Sacramento, a small Portuguese toehold on the east bank, gave foreigners a perch on the Spanish riches descending by mule train from the great mines of Potosí in the Andes en route to the port of Buenos Aires. This was a geographic recipe for constant fighting that afflicted both sides. Alexandre

---

[8]Mello and Bicalho, *Virando séculos*, p. 61.

[9]Stein and Stein, *Silver, Trade and War*, pp. 120–21, and 131–41; Fernando A. Novais, *Portugal e Brasil na crise do Antigo sistema colonial (1777–1808)* (São Paulo: Editora Hucitec, 1979), pp. 15–28; Virgilio Naya Pinto, *O ouro Brasileiro e o comércio Anglo-Português* (São Paulo: Companhia Editora Nacional, 1979), pp. 113, 247–88; Geoffrey J. Walker, *Spanish Politics and Imperial Trade, 1700–1789* (Bloomington: Indiana University Press, 1979), pp. 206–10; H.E.S. Fisher, *The Portugal Trade: A Study of Anglo-Portuguese Commerce* (London: Methuen, 1971), pp. 32–40.

de Gusmão for one felt that Portuguese recovery in Europe should begin with peace with Spain. Rather than fight over distant possessions, draining blood from the imperial bodies, peace would allow the rivals to stand up to their more dangerous competitors, France and Britain. In 1750, he sponsored the drafting of the Treaty of Madrid (see fig. 1). This was supposed to separate the overlapping powers in the River Plate and clarify the borderlines separating the two Iberian empires so they could coexist in peace and concentrate their energies on promoting trade between the metropoles and their possessions. But suspicions die hard. The ink had barely dried on the treaty when Sebastião José de Carvalho e Melo, later the Marquis of Pombal, advised his stepbrother in Brazil to be on the lookout for the Spanish colonies belonging to a "gente de guerra e servile."[10]

Carvalho's worries were prophetic. Peace between the Iberians was futile because they each tried to overcome their dependency on England or France by trying to take advantage of the other's weakness. Spanish and Portuguese forces repeatedly violated the treaty's boundary provisions. The Seven Years War shattered the brief "peace" and was the climax of Iberian ignominy. English naval forces, with imposing artillery and outnumbering the defenders, overwhelmed Spanish colonial defenses. Two of Spain's naval bastions, Manila and Havana, fell to British forces. When the viceroy of New Spain heard the news of the fall of Havana, he braced the wealthiest of Europe's colonies for a British assault. In the end, France buckled before Spain and sued for "peace," sparing Mexico the fate of a possible British invasion. Portugal also took a beating, in spite of her alliance with the victor Britain. In 1762, Spanish troops crossed into Portugal and began marching onto Lisbon, before stalling and then withdrawing. The real fighting, as usual, took place in the colonies, where the two empires rubbed shoulders. In the River Plate borderlands, Spanish forces and their Indian allies used the occasion to drive Brazilians from the east bank.[11]

Atlantic treaties did not resolve the frictions of militarized imperialism. The Treaty of Paris (1763) was supposed to calm the waters. But relations

---

[10]BNL, CP, Códice 626, ff. 32–36, Carvalho to Mendonça, July 6, 1752. Three tributaries flowed into the River Plate, draining from Brazilian lands into a Spanish estuary. The Paraguay River starts in Matto Grosso; the Paraná drains much of Minas Gerais; the watershed of the Uruguay took from Santa Catarina and Rio Grande do Sul. All three bordered the two empires, and then flowed into the languid River Plate. For details on the treaty, see Cortesão, *Alexandre de Gusmão*, v. 2, pp. 507–40.

[11]Arquivo Histórico Ultramarino (hereafter AHU), Conselho Ultramarino (hereafter CU). Códice 235, f. 42, April 17, 1766; Kenneth Maxwell, *Conflicts and Conspiracies: Brazil and Portugal, 1750–1808* (Cambridge: Cambridge University Press, 1973), pp. 33–51. The Seven Years War also had paradoxical effects on the British empire. See Fred Anderson, *Crucible of War: The Seven Years' War and the Fate of Empire in British North America, 1754–1766* (New York: Vintage, 2001).

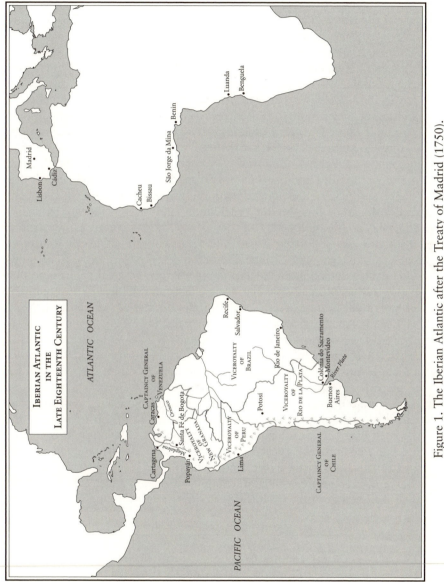

Figure 1. The Iberian Atlantic after the Treaty of Madrid (1750).

between Lisbon and Madrid remained strained. In fact, it was the blood-letting in the River Plate that prompted the government to relocate the capital of Brazil from Salvador to Rio de Janeiro in 1763 to help secure the Portuguese borders. In a tit for tat, Spain created a whole new viceroy-alty of the River Plate, with a capital in Buenos Aires, in 1776. Iberians suspended their differences long enough to sign the 1777 Treaty of San Ildefonso that—once again—was supposed to clarify the boundaries between the two empires, especially in the borderlands of the River Plate, when Colônia was finally ceded to Spanish hands. As a gesture of this new entente, the new viceroy in Buenos Aires wrote to Rio de Janeiro cel-ebrating the new "peace," and suggesting that each power turn its defenses to rounding up "delinquents, thieves and assassins." Peace would also allow them to go after the even worse scourge, *contrabandistas*, and apply their militias to "a method of delivering to each other fugitive slaves."[12]

Still, comity did not dispel competition. As long as Lisbon and Madrid fought with each other while losing ground to their northern European rivals, the job of enforcing restrictions against interlopers fell to the understaffed, ill-equipped, and corruption-ridden civilian administrators in the colonies. Applying restrictions and upholding metropolitan privi-leges in the New World therefore became a hopeless task. Reluctantly and fitfully, metropolitan authorities and many agents of peninsular mer-chants in the colonies gave up on the old system of "fleets" and fairs and let individual licensed vessels traffic among imperial ports of call.[13]

One sign of the difficulties Iberian states had in enforcing their own laws was the spread of smuggling. Always a hazard in the colonies, it became a bonanza for all sides (except for royal treasurers, who wailed about delinquents depriving the common weal of its revenues) as the eighteenth century wore on. The old nexus of the fleet system, the Panamanian isthmus, swarmed with smugglers and plunderers who launched raids and traffic along the north coast of South America, and used the Pacific side to penetrate the ports of Guayaquil and Callao. Indeed, even in times of peace, in Riohacha, Santa Marta, and the gateway port to the Magdalena River, Cartagena, illegal trade was an important source of mercantile rents and a significant means for colonists to meet their rudimentary needs. The largest commercial sluice in South America

---

[12]AHU, CU, Caixa 121, doc. 51, December 20, 1779; John Lynch, *Spanish Colonial Administration, 1782–1810* (London: Athlone, 1958), pp. 34–39; Kenneth Maxwell, *Pombal: Paradox of the Enlightenment* (Cambridge: Cambridge University Press, 1995), pp. 111–18.

[13]John R. Fisher, *Commercial Relations between Spain and Spanish America in the Era of Free Trade, 1778–1796* (Liverpool: Center for Latin American Studies, 1985), pp. 13–16; Walker, *Spanish Politics and Imperial Trade*, pp. 210–22.

was the River Plate, the crucial back entrance to the Andes. Practically from the time the Spanish began mining Potosí silver on a large scale, foreign merchants learned to ply the trails up from Buenos Aires through Tucumán to Potosí (which was why the Spanish government fought relentlessly for control of the east bank of the River Plate). Indeed, by the eighteenth century, the denizens of Buenos Aires were only too willing to join the venture as intermediaries between silver supply for Europe and colonial demand for the European manufactures.[14] Contraband in the Spanish colonies had spillover effects on Portugal's trade, whose regulators had difficulties of their own keeping traders in line. Even runaway slaves based in the hinterlands of Mato Grosso's *quilombos* made a swift business handling illegal traffic between the Brazilian littoral and the Andes—carrying contraband inland in return for silver destined for the coast. One 1785 report to Martinho de Mello e Castro, the minister in charge of the colonies, denounced the "multiplied damages, contraband, and violations across the continent, ports and coasts of Brazil ... with irreparable harm to the licit and legal trade."[15]

As the problems mounted with each war, the jeremiads about decline and decay got more of a hearing. Monarchs and ministers soon discovered, however, that they were dealing with an ageless paradox: it would have been easier to emend the empires if the resources had been more abundant and margins for error more generous. But had it been easier to

---

[14]Archivo General de la Nación Bogotá (herein AGNB), Colonia-Contrabandos, VIII, ff. 385–406, report on contraband in Panama, 1748; Lance R. Grahn, "An Irresoluble Dilemma: Smuggling in New Granada, 1713–1763," in John R. Fisher, Allan J. Kuethe, and Anthony McFarlane, eds., *Reform and Insurrection in Bourbon New Granda and Peru* (Baton Rouge: Louisiana State University Press, 1990), pp. 123–46; idem, *The Political Economy of Smuggling: Regional Informal Economies in Early Bourbon New Granada* (Boulder, CO: Westview Press, 1997), pp. 39–106. For Buenos Aires, see Zacarías Moutoukias, *Contrabando y control en el siglo XVII: Buenos Aires, El Atlántico y el espacio peruano* (Buenos Aires: CEAL, 1988). Antonio García-Baquero González, *Cádiz y el Atlántico (1717–1778)* (Sevilla: Escuela de Estudios Hispano-Americanos, 1976), v. 1, pp. 486–91; Stanley J. Stein, "Un raudal de oro y plata que corría sin cesar de España a Francia: Política mercantil española y el comercio con Francia en la época de Carlos III," *Economía y Sociedad* 2 (1989): 219–79; Paloma Fernández Pérez, *El rostro familiar de metrópoli: Redes de parentesco y lazos mercantiles en Cádiz, 1700–1812* (Madrid: Siglo XXI, 1997), pp. 4–11.

[15]AHU, CU, Códice 311, ff. 22–23, January 5, 1785; Luiza Rios Ricci Volpato, "Quilombos em Matto Grosso: Resistência Negra em área de fronteira," in João José Reis and Flávio dos Santos Gomes, orgs., *Liberdade por um Fio: Historias de Quilombos no Brasil* (São Paulo: Companhia das Letras, 1996), pp. 213–49; Dauril Alden, *Royal Government in Colonial Brazil with Special Reference to the Administration of the Marquis of Lavradio, Viceroy 1769–1779* (Berkeley: University of California Press, 1968), chap. 14.

reform, there would have been less incentive. The greater the incentive and impulse there was to change, the more imperial rulers had to contend with monumental constraints.[16]

ANATOMIES OF REFORM

It is tempting to conclude that the structural imbalance between the incentives and constraints to change locked empires into fates they could not escape. Indeed, the history of empires has been dominated by just such master narratives of the cycles of rise and inevitable decline. One of the great works of history—Edward Gibbon's *Decline and Fall of the Roman Empire*—was published just as American colonists revolted against London; political events thereby gave it a prophetic echo. Readers in Spain and Portugal and their colonies did not have to stretch their imaginations too hard to recognize themselves in Gibbon's words about Constantine's capital: "the decline of Rome was the natural and inevitable effect of immoderate greatness. Prosperity ripened the principles of decay; the causes of destruction multiplied with the extent of conquest; and as soon as time or accident had removed the artificial supports, the stupendous fabric yielded to the pressure of its own weight. The story of its ruin is simple and obvious; and instead of inquiring *why* the Roman empire was destroyed, we should rather be surprised that it had subsisted so long." Gibbon's work contributed to what was by then a gathering concern about whether it was possible to combine empire with good government at all.[17]

But despairing did not lead automatically to doomsaying. Abbé Raynal, Edmund Burke, and quite a number of Iberian thinkers devoted enormous attention to showing that empire and good government were not *necessarily* incompatible, but that sordid habits—in the terms of the day, "corruption"—could turn a virtuous arrangement into a venal one. The prince's task, imperial theorists claimed, was to extirpate the source of corruption. The problem with empires was that possession of property was so prone to becoming the owner's personal passion because the opportunity to amass was so great. Accordingly the very foundations of virtue, possession, and trade could degenerate into oligarchies of wealth

---

[16]On the difficulties of institutional sclerosis, see Mancur Olson, *The Rise and Decline of Nations* (New Haven: Yale University Press, 1982).

[17]Gibbon, *Decline and Fall of the Roman Empire*, pp. 435–36; on the historiography of empire, see Anthony Pagden, *Peoples and Empires: A Short History of European Migration, Exploration, and Conquest from Greece to the Present* (New York: Random House, 2001), pp. xvi–xxv.

and power if not watched carefully. The awareness of these intertwined dilemmas compelled the figures of the Iberian Enlightenment to try harder to show that Madrid and Lisbon could be great cities ruling grand empires.[18]

The debacle of the Seven Years War was an eye-opener. No longer could Iberian rulers cope with the costs of a militarized peace by professing neutrality in the superpower conflicts while displacing the burdens of their weaknesses by taking on their immediate neighbor. The Portuguese minister to London, Martinho de Mello e Castro, informed his government in 1764 that Portugal was caught in a spiral. He warned that Spain would try to recover some pride after the humiliation of the Seven Years War by dwelling on false grievances with Portugal. And behind Spanish complaints were French ambitions. All this only threw the Portuguese back into an unwanted defensive alliance with Britain.[19] In Spain especially, the humiliation of war increased the volume of reformist discourses, especially once Carlos III acceded to the throne in 1759. The spasm of bread riots in Madrid in 1766 only intensified the sense that reform was more than urgent; it was a condition of survival.[20]

The reforms were the offspring of a particular brand of thinking about empires. While maintaining some affinities with the philosophy of history of the Enlightenment, eighteenth-century political economists were concerned with the proper balance between the state and civil society, the capacities of domestic agriculture and foreign trade as cornerstones of greatness and wealth.[21] Spanish and Portuguese writers were distinctive mainly in the degree to which they placed empire at the center of their diagnoses and prescriptions for national revival. First, while domestic agriculture was clearly anemic, attacking its malefactors got reformers into hot water because it meant assaulting feudal vestiges. This was all

---

[18]J. G. A. Pocock, "Gibbon's *Decline and Fall* and the World View of the Late Enlightenment," in his *Virtue, Commerce, and History* (Cambridge: Cambridge University Press, 1985), pp. 143–56.

[19]BNL, CP, Códice 611, f. 213, August 21, 1764, correspondence of Martinho de Mello e Castro. See also f. 238, August 22, 1764; AHU, CU, Códice 567, ff. 10–23, "Primera carta instructiva para o Marquez de Lavradío," April 14, 1769.

[20]Pierre Vilar, "Motín de Esquilache et Crises D'Ancien Régime," *Historia Ibérica* 1 (1972): 11–34; Stein and Stein, *Silver, Trade and War*, pp. 246–54; Stanley J. Stein and Barbara H. Stein, *Apogee of Empire: Spain and New Spain in the Age of Charles III, 1759–1789* (Baltimore: Johns Hopkins University Press, 2003), pp. 84–115; Allan J. Kuethe, "The Early Reforms of Charles III in the Viceroyalty of New Granada, 1759–1776," in Fisher, Kuethe, and McFarlane, eds., *Reform and Insurrection*, pp. 19–40.

[21]Lars Magnusson, *Mercantilism: The Shaping of an Economic Discourse* (New York: Routledge, 1994), pp. 1–25; McNally, *Political Economy and the Rise of Capitalism*, pp. 66–67, for comparisons of England and France.

too clear in the Spanish nobles' resistance to agrarian reforms and thus complicity behind the 1766 bread riots.[22] Dependence on nobles also had a political logic. Iberian political discourses had deeply seated Catholic conceptions born of the reconquest of Muslim power in the peninsula that relied on regional kingdoms for spiritual, political, and ideological success. As a result, monarchs had to contend with the ingrained power of nobles, who defended their local autonomy, principles of self-governing localities, and feudal might over peasants, all rooted in a medieval structure of urban self-rule of Castilian and Portuguese Cortes. Feudal elements thereby created the conditions for their own political utility to the monarchy even as they became obstacles to social and economic change. Complex, multilayered, decentralized regimes actively promoted the idea of the monarchy as the visible image of a mystical power, and steeped themselves in the courtly rituals of deference. But they did not centralize their metropolitan dominions to the same degree as did their rivals Britain and France.[23]

In this context, accenting imperial trade as a way to bring greatness to the monarchy was not just a second-best option. It was a foundational principle of theory and history. Ascribing to empire the source of Madrid's and Lisbon's greatness, in effect, converted what was a tacit assumption about overseas trade for other European powers into a basic theory of Iberian statecraft. This meant tackling the ailments of the empires at the capillary systems that connected the heart to the body's extremities, the colonies. For Campillo, a spokesman for reform, the ties between sovereignty and empire were clear enough—and the problem was best tackled as a transatlantic phenomenon: "In America, where commerce is in complete stagnation, only sickness and political death will come." And death in the Indies posed certain demise of the metropole. But it is also important to note that Iberian political economists were also explicit about how to conceive of empire. The Portuguese and Spanish domains rested on relationships between their component parts. For rulers in Lisbon and Madrid, empire was not a political or social structure that radiated outward from a "Portuguese" or "Spanish" nation. It was not the nation that had created empires. If anything, the sources

---

[22]John Reeder, "Economía e ilustración en España: Traducciones y traductores, 1717–1800," *Moneda y Crédito* 147 (December 1978): 47–70; Miguel Artola, *Antiguo Régimen y revolución liberal* (Barcelona: Ariel, 1978); Jorge M. Pedreira, "Physiocracy and the Sterility of Commerce, Industry and Money: Political Economy, Morality and Social Thought: Some Notes from a Portuguese Viewpoint," *Economies et sociétés* 22–23:1–2 (1995): 267–95.

[23]Pedro Cardim, *Cortes e cultura política no portugal do antigo regime* (Lisboa: Edições Cosmos, 1998); Stein and Stein, *Silver, Trade and War*, p. 159, on the "poly-synodal" character of the ancien régime.

of greatness—or recovery—flowed the other way around. It would only be through vitalizing empires, insisted reformers, that Iberian nations could ensure their sovereignty in the European concert of emerging nations.[24]

Making empire the framework of sovereignty helped adapt ideas of eighteenth-century political economy to Iberian settings. But it did not make the job of reform any easier. It just redefined the historical legacies that had to be overcome. To many observers, the empires had fallen victim to the very sources that had founded them. They were decrepit products of centuries of seigniorial habits, conquistador customs, and lax policies that thrived so long as there was access to gold and silver mines, forced labor, and fertile lands stolen from oppressed Indians. The Asturian economist Pedro Rodríguez Campomanes, a follower of Campillo, warned his sovereign of what was at stake if he hung on to old ways. In 1762, as English forces stormed Spanish outposts, he finished a major treatise for the new Spanish ruler, Carlos III, called *Reflexiones sobre el comercio español a Indias*. "The evil, Señor," he wrote to the king, "lies in the body of the Nation or in the rules that until now govern the Traffic with the Indies." What ensued in the treatise was an extended analysis of the misbegotten rules that choked what should flow more freely: trade between the metropole and its possessions in the New World. Campomanes excoriated the ruling habits since the Spanish monarchy set foot in the New World. Spanish magnificence during Carlos V's reign built on the "grand conquests of Hernán Cortés and Francisco Pizarro" and consolidated "the fundamental political System of the Indies." But these were weak foundations. Campomanes cited Montesquieu's observation that "Spain saw from the start that its discovered lands were the objects of Conquest, while other more refined peoples than they recognized that their attention could be directed by the reason of Commerce." Herein lay an important distinction that informed so many Iberian imperial theorists: there were different kinds of empires. For Campomanes the distinction between empires of conquest, whose greatness was tied to the moment of conception, and empires of commerce, whose greatness was self-sustaining, helped explain what was wrong with the Spanish realm. What once made Spain great was now obsolete. The French and British newcomers devised

---

[24]Campillo y Cosío, *Nuevo sistema*, p. 70; David Brading, "La monarquía católica," in Antonio Annino, Luis Castro Leiva, and François-Xavier Guerra, comps., *De los imperios a las naciones: Iberoamerica* (Zaragoza: Ibercaja, 1994), pp. 19–43; Allan J. Kuethe and Lowell Blaisdell, "French Influence and the Origins of the Bourbon Colonial Reorganization," *Hispanic American Historical Review* 71:3 (1991): 579–607; Anthony Pagden, *Lords of All the World: Ideologies of Empire in Spain, Britain and France, c. 1500–1800* (New Haven: Yale University Press, 1995), pp. 113–24; Robert S. Smith, "English Economic Thought in Spain, 1776–1848," *South Atlantic Quarterly*, 67:2 (1968): 313.

new "fundamental political Systems" for their colonies in order to fashion even more robust nations. Campomanes likened Spain to Carthage, and Spain's rivals to Rome: "When the Roman Republic began to prepare the ruin of Carthage, it did not have to use other means than to reduce to just a few countries the navigation of Carthaginians, and thus limiting the number of Galleys of war."[25]

The distinction between empires of conquest and empires of commerce was most powerfully captured in Abbé Raynal's Enlightenment magnum opus, *A Philosophical and Political History of the Settlement and Trade of the Europeans in the East and West Indies*, a prominent work on the bookshelves of Portuguese and Spanish reformers in the latter half of the eighteenth century (until it was formally banned by Spanish censors in 1779, whereupon it became a kind of underground classic). After contrasting the various European patterns of expansion, Raynal concluded that it would be easy to seize the Spanish colonies from Spain since their defenses were weak. But controlling them was another matter: "From inclination, from laziness, from ignorance, from custom, and from pride, they are strictly attached to their religion, and their government, and will never conform to new laws. Their prejudices will furnish them with weapons sufficient to repel their conqueror; as the Portuguese, thrown into a remote corner of the earth, formerly drove the Dutch out of Brazil when they had almost entirely subdued it." Raynal, Montesquieu, and even Adam Smith confirmed what Spanish and Portuguese reformers were already preaching: the empires had to change to survive.[26]

The idea that historical events—not some basic defect of moral character—necessitated reform also had wellsprings in the colonial fringes. Over the course of the eighteenth century, merchants in the colonies grew louder and louder in their clamor for reform—in large part in response to mounting competition and contraband. Merchants in the Caribbean and the River Plate were especially alarmed by the lack of order in commercial affairs. Merchants in Santa Fé in Nueva Granada pleaded for some relaxation of trading restrictions in 1764 so that they could adapt to the competition and therefore restore the colony's wealth. This would remove obstacles to their ability to counter the illegal competition and

---

[25]Pedro Rodríguez Campomanes, *Reflexiones sobre el comercio español a Indias (1762)*, ed. Vicente Llombart Rosa (Madrid: Instituto de Estudios Fiscales, 1988), pp. 3–4, and 360; François-Xavier Guerra, "The Spanish-American Tradition of Representation and Its European Roots," *Journal of Latin American Studies* 26:1 (1994): 2–5.

[26]Campomanes, *Reflexiones sobre el comercio*, p. 361; Abbé Raynal, *A Philosophical and Political History of the Settlement and Trade of the Europeans in the East and West Indies* (Edinburgh, 1792), book eight, p. 141; Richard Herr, *The Eighteenth-Century Revolution in Spain* (Princeton: Princeton University Press, 1958), chap. 3.

thus restore some control over local markets: "Those capable of maintaining themselves in this state of complete informality and indigence, with which this principal nerve of the body politic has suffered in our republic, desire the reestablishment of our ancient and deserved splendor. We implore his royal magnificence to allow for the solid establishment of the trade of this *carrera*." What they did not state—but which authorities kept decrying—was that in the absence of better official treatment, they might resort to their own, not entirely lawful, ways of doing business.[27]

Where the colonial pressures for change were strongest can be seen in the Portuguese empire. The historic weakness of Lisbon over Brazil, combined with the greater penetration of foreign, especially British, direct trade in the colonies, gave Brazil a preexisting autonomy compared to the Spanish colonies and a more assertive role to colonial merchants in imperial business. In important ventures like the slave trade, the seat of merchant power was based much more in the colonies than in the metropoles. Indeed, Luso-Brazilian merchants had become so autonomous that they did not have to call for de jure reforms with the same sense of urgency. While Granadan merchants groused about being unable to ply their wares within their viceroyalty, Portuguese and Brazilians were busy breaking down ancient barriers to trade across continents. As Luiz Felipe de Alencastro has recently shown, there was a flourishing *atlântico fluminense* (a Rio de Janeiro Atlantic) as early as the seventeenth century, in which the eventual capital of the colony enjoyed tremendous latitude to promote its circulation of commodities and captives independent from Portugal. Brazilian merchants had become so powerful in the South Atlantic, and so instrumental in the slave trade that boosted the expansion of the staple-exporting frontier in Brazil, that they compelled the king to sign a decree in 1758 opening trade routes between Angola, the Mina Coast, and Brazilian ports. In effect, the slave trade became the thin end of a wedge opening up Iberian Atlantic commerce to merchant capitalists on both sides.[28]

---

[27]AGNB, Colonia-Consulado III, ff. 142–47; Consulado IV, ff. 1–295; Walker, *Spanish Politics and Imperial Trade*, pp. 210–14; Allan Christelow, "Great Britain and the Traders from Cádiz and Lisbon to Spanish America and Brazil, 1759–1783," *Hispanic American Historical Review*, 28:1 (1947): 2–29; Cristina Ana Mazzeo, *El comercio libre en el Perú: Las estrategias de un comerciante criollo José Antonio da Lavalla y Cortés, 1777–1815* (Lima: Pontífica Universidad Católica del Perú, 1994), pp. 76–112.

[28]The next chapter will focus on this process more directly. Arquivo Nacional Torro do Tombo (hereafter ANTT), Junta do Comércio (hereafter JC), Maço 62, Caixa 204, f. 1; Luiz Felipe de Alencastro, *O Trato dos Viventes: Formação do Brasil no Atlântico Sul* (São Paulo: Companhia das Letras, 2000), pp. 199–204, 259–62. For later in the century, see João Fragoso and Manolo Florentino, *O Arcaísmo como projeto: Mercado Atlântico, sociedade agrária e elite mercantil no Rio de Janeiro, c. 1790–1840* (Rio de Janeiro: Diadorim, 1993).

In the Portuguese empire, restrictions on imperial trade had relaxed more gradually over a longer period of time until finally the government shelved the remnants of merchant convoy systems in 1765. But there were still constraints designed to favor Lisbon as the entrepôt for imperial commerce that drew constant complaints from merchants in the colonies. In 1772 a royal decree affirmed that intercontinental traffic was licit, so long as it did not involve "foreign" merchandise and carriers sailed through Lisbon. In the words of Minister Martinho de Mello e Castro, the law was designed to curb "the pernicious consequences that arise when ships coming from Africa sail directly to Brazilian ports." The decree "requires them to return directly to the City of Lisbon from Angola without calling elsewhere and [they are] completely forbidden from selling any goods" beyond Lisbon. Merchants immediately filed for exemptions. In 1777, the owners of the *Santissima Sacramento* got permission to sail to Asia provided the carriers paid their levies at Portuguese ports. And while they could not carry foreign produce *out* of Lisbon, they got permission to make calls in foreign ports, unload "national" produce, and pick up "foreign" goods along the way. By 1784, even the metropolitan minister Mello e Castro observed that trade had leaped ahead of its legal infrastructure and that the government had to do something to catch up with private initiatives.[29]

What political economists wanted was a workable compromise that would adapt the imperial realms without challenging domestic feudal privileges within the peninsula. They also wanted to accommodate colonial demands for greater liberty to trade within empire. Looking to empire was therefore a way of resolving the obstacles to Iberian renaissance (for those who looked backward) or Iberian national sovereignty (for those who looked forward). Though this reform paradigm was by nature a compromise, it did have a fundamental goal: to "nationalize" empires that had become decentered, sprawling domains vulnerable to external predators and were failing to magnify the opulence of the metropolitan cores. The reforms were aimed at turning centrifugal regimes inside out so that resources and loyalties could flow more smoothly and amply to Lisbon and Madrid. There were important analogous efforts afoot in other Atlantic systems. Indeed, it was the centralizing, metropolitan thrust that so alienated the British North American colonists before 1776. But if this was a compromise, little could disguise the fact that it meant a change in the basic relationship between the component parts of the empire, between the colonies and

---

[29] AHU, CU, Códice 962, ff. 2–4, 59–62.

the metropoles, and within the colonies themselves to solve the problem of Iberian sovereignty.[30]

The embodiment of this effort to re-center the Spanish empire was José de Gálvez. Visitador general to New Spain from 1765 to 1771 and minister of the Indies from 1776 until his death in 1787, Gálvez sponsored policies designed to bolster the sovereignty of the Spanish empire by reconstituting it as a functioning core with functional peripheries. While in New Spain he expelled the Jesuits who challenged the authority of the state, suppressed popular uprisings that rallied to the support of the banned priests, and sent military expeditions to pacify and settle the northern borderlands of Sonora. When he moved to Madrid, he established the new Viceroyalty of the River Plate, with a capital in Buenos Aires, to enforce Spanish sovereignty, and dispatched his own paladin, Juan Antonio de Areche, as visitador general of Peru. The common feature of all these initiatives was Gálvez's determination to extend law enforcement to the territorial limits of the Spanish empire and to enhance the power of enforcers within it. Gálvez, though not a thinker with Campillo's or other political economists' originality, converted their lines of thought into policy and applied a pragmatic vocation for reform to rebuild Spanish imperial sovereignty.[31]

The epitome of Gálvez's efforts to infuse fresh blood into the empire was *comercio libre*. In the wake of the Seven Years War, the Spanish government brought down some of the old barriers to trade within the empire bit by bit until it issued a sweeping decree in 1778. Gálvez put an end to decades of wavering over the preservation of old monopolies, the fleet system, and the legality of open trade within the empire. The king's decree announced that "only a free and protected Commerce between European and American Spaniards can restore Agriculture, Industry, and Population in my Dominions to their former vigor." Fourteen peninsular ports and thirty five American ports were given rights to trade within the empire without having to apply for special permission from the privileged entrepôt, Cádiz. Only New Spain and Venezuela were exempt—though their ports were swept into the new doctrine in the late 1780s. By 1789, there was a system of open trade within the Spanish Atlantic, in which the archipelago of colonial ports could trade with each other and the ports that circled the peninsula. The idea was to increase commerce

---

[30]P. J. Marshall, "A Nation Defined by Empire, 1755–1776," in Alexander Grant and Keith J. Stringer, eds., *Uniting the Kingdom? The Making of British History* (London: Routledge, 1995), pp. 208–22; idem, "Empire and Authority in the Later Eighteenth Century," *Journal of Imperial and Commonwealth History* 15:1 (1987): 105–22.

[31]Stein and Stein, *Apogee of Empire*, pp. 69–80, on Gálvez's background; Kuethe and Blaidsell, "French Influence and the Origins of the Bourbon Colonial Reorganization," p. 594.

as a whole within the empire, and thus expand the pool of rents that could be taxed by the royal treasury. Comercio libre would thereby ensure greater transfers to the metropole and the government from the colonies by conferring them expanded rights to trade within the empire. Here was a reform model of "defensive modernization," in Stanley and Barbara Stein's words, which sought to preserve and defend ancient systems of sovereignty by reconstituting the interests of empire.[32]

By the 1770s and 1780s, it was increasingly clear that defense of the ancien régime had to make commercial policies fit the needs of state builders. But it should be stressed that this was not "free" trade as we now understand the term. Commerce with "foreign" ports remained illegal. Only the licensed ports were gateways for long-distance trade. And remnants of protection for Spanish merchandise (like clothing, wines, oils, and furniture) persisted. The point was not to make imperial subjects absolutely free to enjoy rights to trade, but to direct these contingent rights to the larger purpose of funding the monarchy's treasury. Moreover, Gálvez still thought that the one area where the empire was defeating itself the most was in the mining industry, because its yield was allowed to trickle out of the empire. This was a sector that could more directly augment the resources of the state. He wrote, "Just as mining is the origin and fount for metals which give spirit and movement to all human occupations and the universal trade of this world, by justice it therefore requires the special attention of the government." Gálvez was not necessarily equating specie with wealth; money was not an end in itself. The point, in Gálvez's view, was not just to pump precious metals out of colonial ground but to ensure that they stayed within the commercial circuitry of the Spanish empire, buoying transactions across the realm.[33]

In this sense, Gálvez remained faithful to some deeper mercantilist precepts, if not a few mercantilist policies: economic life was governed by a "circular flow" subject to discrete and distinctive laws that determined levels and movements of prices, wages, and rents. The accumulation of bullion in state coffers may have been a necessary condition for a wealthy society, especially as it gave the state the means to uphold its sovereignty. But it was not sufficient. Mining would only contribute to national wealth if trade as a whole grew and could absorb the infusion of metals, circulating it through the commercial body. Therefore, Gálvez was breaking

---

[32]Stein and Stein, *Apogee of Empire*, p. 351; Fisher, *Commercial Relations between Spain and Spanish America*, pp. 9–10, 13–15; Walker, *Spanish Politics and Imperial Trade*, pp. 223–25 passim.

[33]Cited in Brading, "La monarquía católica," p. 36; McNally, *Political Economy and the Rise of Capitalism*, pp. 28–29.

from his predecessors by shifting the focus away from *peninsular* trade and unidirectional flow of bullion to Spain, that is, an overarching concern with the empire's "balance of trade." In its doctrinal place, Madrid now emphasized *imperial* trade and the favorable balance of trade between Spain and the rest of the world. The peninsula, the heart of the nation, could be rich provided the empire were rich, which meant expanding opportunities to trade to all precincts.[34]

A similar drive to promote "national" sovereignty through re-centered empire, striking a new balance between colonies and metropoles, took root in Lisbon. The zeal for reform came a little earlier, in the 1750s, in part because it was harder to maintain the illusion that the regime could survive without change. The gold bonanza from Minas Gerais had peaked. Then the Lisbon earthquake in 1755 and the Spanish invasion of 1762 intensified the urge to defend Portuguese sovereignty by nationalizing its empire. The champion of reform was Sebastião José de Carvalho e Melo, later titled the Marquis of Pombal in recognition of his overwhelming influence. Pombal did not have Gálvez's colonial administrative experience, but he did have the supreme confidence of the king, Dom José I, who gave Pombal almost complete control over the Portuguese empire. With Dom José's death in 1777, Pombal's influence quickly waned, and he was forced out of office in disgrace. Like Gálvez, he sought to ensure that precious metals of the empire remained within its borders and did not leak out, even to "friendly" rivals. If anything, Pombal's policies were more concerted because he believed there was one important obstacle to Portuguese greatness: her "alliance" with Britain. Writing in his memoir, he later noted that "the English had firmly bound the [Portuguese] nation in a state of dependence. They had conquered it without the inconvenience of a conquest."[35]

Pombal also had to do something about relations between Lisbon and Brazil. For half a century, Portugal thrived off colonial extraction of gold and diamonds. But the euphoria waned pretty quickly in the 1750s. Exhaustion of the most accessible lodes of diamonds and gold was one reason. But officials also pointed to the inability of the imperial state to enforce its own regulations, which let precious staples leak out through commercial regulations. One report from Minas Gerais in the 1750s observed that the decline of gold and diamond production had to do with the lax enforcement of mercantilist rules, not that the rules were choking output. No one stopped colonists from creating their own industries. Instead, Brazilians were becoming self-sufficient and imported less

---

[34]Eli Heckscher, *Mercantilism* (London: George Allen and Unwin, 1955), v. 2, pp. 175–86.

[35]Cited in Alan K. Manchester, *British Preëminence in Brazil, Its Rise and Decline: A Study in European Expansion* (1933; New York: Octagon Books, 1964), p. 39.

from Portugal. This kind of reporting was music to Pombal's ministerial ears. He was only too keen to welcome intelligence that reinforced his impulse to consolidate state power over the king's dominions. No less than Gálvez, Pombal was looking for a new model of empire, effectively to place colonies at the service of the nation, to shore up an old monarchy, and to put precious metals to work to make an empire of commerce. If anything, Brazilian gold had misguided Portuguese rulers into thinking they were wealthy: "Gold and silver are fictitious riches . . . the more they are multiplied, the less is their real value." The key to vitalizing and nationalizing the empire was striking a new balance between its components: Portugal should export manufactured goods to Brazil in return for primary staples so that the two sides of the Atlantic could complement each other's commercial needs through specialization. What was new was the proposition that the colony, and its trading fortunes, had to be thriving for the metropole to export its wares. Accordingly, Pombal supported merchants who would sustain the scheme, and, where necessary, he also fostered state-chartered firms to invest in colonial commercial ventures (Grão Pará and Maranhão in 1755, and Pernambuco and Paraíba in 1759). In this fashion, not only would trade rise, it would also become more national; Lisbon would become the central clearinghouse of its empire.[36]

In both empires, therefore, reform was about creating a new pact with, and within, the Americas—in effect to make them "real" colonies of late mercantilist empires. In a fundamental respect Pombal and Gálvez were proposing to put the two empires on sounder, if not more perfect, mercantilist foundations. The old conquest model, associated with the quest for gold, silver, and preciosities, was sterile, not stimulating. It had become an end in itself. The task for reformers was not simply to bury the old obsession with the flow of precious metals to private and public coffers, but to transform imperial trade so that bullion could flow more healthily through the body's arteries. In this fashion, Spain and Portugal need not repudiate the past but simply transcend it. Doing so required taking what they conquered and placing these possessions at the service of a different model of wealth and greatness founded on commercial activity.

If this package appeared to advocate an altered course of Iberian history, there were limits to its novelty. Freedom to enjoy property rights,

---

[36]AHU, CU, Códice 311, ff. 20–21, undated report on Brazilian industries, 1750s; Pombal cited in Manchester, *British Preëminence in Brazil*, p. 40; Maxwell, *Pombal*. See also Dauril Alden, "Late Colonial Brazil, 1750–1808," in Leslie Bethell, ed., *Cambridge History of Latin America* (Cambridge: Cambridge University Press, 1985), v. 2, pp. 601–60.

especially in commercial matters, was, in important and fundamental ways, still relative. Comercio libre was contrived under a regime in which commerce served public and private interests simultaneously—and both interests were best guarded by a strong state to constrain routine excesses of self-interested individuals. Iberian reformers had to overcome a very special kind of passionate avarice—love of conquest in pursuit of treasure. To rescue the monarchy from its own weaknesses, the state, guided by a new kind of enlightened minister, had to lure, cajole, and force the leading members of the civitas to follow a new paradigm of empire. By contrast, a new spirit of economic sentiments was at work in Britain and France, one that vindicated uncertainty and made a virtue out of a "fatherless world" (in Adam Smith's words). French and British political economists observed how this order emerged from the prosaic daily activities of self-interested people. This was a conceptual move that most important thinkers and policymakers in Lisbon or Madrid could not follow. While sharing the view that trade was more than simply a zero-sum game, and conceding that self-interest could be made, under the right circumstances, to promote general interests, political economists in Spain and Portugal were committed to precepts of order, hierarchy, and stability—all knowable by the prince. More than a mere suspicion of disorder or uncertainty was involved. So too was the perception of backwardness, especially in the vortex of imperial wars in which rulers had less and less control, and more and more was at stake. Commercial discourses crystallized the aspirations of Iberian thinkers whose primary concerns were the rebuilding the foundations of regal sovereignty at the core of world empires.[37]

IMPERIAL BARGAINS

There was a rub in the prescription: building a great state was the ultimate goal, but the state was also the only agent capable of curbing private habits that deprived it of vitality. How could the state be the means to achieve greatness and the idyll at the same time?

The way out of the circular problem was an entente between political and economic power-holders—giving each room to maneuver autonomously,

---

[37]Emma Rothschild, *Economic Sentiments: Adam Smith, Condorcet, and the Enlightenment* (Cambridge, MA: Harvard University Press, 2001), pp. 223–29; for more on the subtle shifts in thinking about markets, see Albert O. Hirschman, *The Passions and the Interests: Political Arguments for Capitalism before Its Triumph* (Princeton: Princeton University Press, 1976). The term "comercio libre" was invoked by Campillo himself in 1743. See *Nuevo sistema*, pp. 146–47.

but interdependently. This solution, at first glance a matter of pragmatic balance, goes to the heart of another problem of empire. There is a tradition of explaining the nature of Spanish and Portuguese imperialism as the products of cozy pacts between ascendant monarchs and rentier elites, with vast colonial spoils as the bonding agent for an alliance of greed. Indeed, this has been a standard way of explaining European imperialism *tout court*. Lenin and Schumpeter, for all their differences, agreed that imperialism was the political outlet for social elites hungry for external profits and rulers yearning for grandeur.[38] This familiar functionalist treatment needs reconsideration. In part, it tends to convert what needs explaining—the compact between public and private power-holders—into a departure point. All-important sequencing, and thus causal linking, is reversed. At least in the case of the Iberian empires, it was the acquisition of the Americas that created the empires, and not empires and alliances of greed that conquered the Americas. The approach also exaggerates the compatibility and consonance between private and public power-holders, where there was in fact enormous strain and conflict. Indeed, the whole point of reform, as Campomanes and others insisted, was to break down private venal habits of those with entrenched stakes precisely because they undermined state power.[39]

Magnates and rulers were brought together through dependence on a specific kind of exchange between the fractious partners of the old regimes. For this reason, this book accentuates the bargaining and struggling over imperial spoils between its principal agents, which at times could be far more dysfunctional than common accounts have allowed. Here was the unstable imperial deal: Merchants enjoyed rents, returns on investment in trading activities that were protected from internal and external competition, and clustered in powerful guilds that governed the entry and exit of traders. Guilds served as self-regulating devices, with legal authority conferred by the monarchy to issue commercial licenses. They reinforced a system of privileged access to mercantile activity.[40] In return for the "legal personality" of their guilds, merchants earmarked a share of their proceeds for the imperial coffers, revenues for a cash-starved treasury. In this fashion, mercantile rents could fund the imperial

---

[38]For a useful survey of theories of imperialism, see Michael Barratt Brown, *The Economics of Imperialism* (London: Penguin, 1974), esp. chaps. 2–3.

[39]Alan Carling, *Social Division* (London: Verso, 1991), esp. pp. 15–30, for a critique of functionalist and intentionalist historical explanations. This view of empire as a consequence of expansion has been recently explored in Henry Kamen, *Empire: How Spain Became a World Power, 1492–1763* (New York: Harper Collins, 2003).

[40]Mark J. Roe, "Rents and Their Corporate Consequences," *Stanford Law Review* 53:6 (2001): 1463–94.

treasury, while rising state revenues could fund imperial defenses of mercantile property rights and their rentier machines.[41]

Interlocking relations between rulers and magnates was as true of Iberian empires as any other. There was one important nuance: the reciprocity of interests—indeed, the very definition of interests—was vulnerable to the state's chronic inability to make good on obligations to honor debts and protect rentier systems. What was lacking was not wealth but the state's credible use of power to enforce its distribution. If the state could not protect the privileges of imperial traders, rents seeped out into the hands of interlopers and free-riders. This in turn forced the imperial states to have to fight—albeit reluctantly—to defend their credibility. Fighting plunged the Portuguese and Spanish empires into a spiral of imperial warfare.

This was one circular problem. The other was that mercantile rents depended on the enforceability of merchants' instruments of exchange—promissory notes, bills of exchange—in effect the multiple ways in which merchant capital wound up in the hands of other traders and producers to release commodities into the world market. Unable to enforce these credit instruments, merchant rents would be insecure and thus eventually dwindle. And with atrophied rents, there was less capital around to flow into state treasuries. As a result, the principal threat to enforceable contracts came from the state itself, by far the largest single debtor and guardian of imperial trade. At the same time, the soaring state debt came from the need to defend imperial protection rackets from outsiders through constant war.[42]

The way out, for reformers, was through rekindling trade with the right kind of private initiative and spirit. One way to unfetter trade was to introduce greater commercial competition among "nationals" within

---

[41]Hilton Root, *The Fountain of Privilege: Political Foundations of Markets in Old Regime France and England* (Berkeley: University of California Press, 1994); John Brewer and Susan Staves, introduction, to their edited *Early Modern Conceptions of Property* (New York: Routledge, 1996), esp. pp. 1–18; Larry Neal, *The Rise of Financial Capitalism: International Capital Markets in the Age of Reason* (Cambridge: Cambridge University Press, 1990), pp. 14–16; Bruce G. Carruthers, *City of Capital: Politics and Markets in the English Financial Revolution* (Princeton: Princeton University Press, 1996), passim.

[42]This double dependence was central to the development of classical political economy. As David Ricardo would demonstrate in 1817, the price of capital, interest rates, depended on the intersection of supply and demand in the private repositories of funds—but that both supply and demand were profoundly shaped by public policies. When government consumption (especially in the form of taxes to fund wars) outpaced the growth of production in any given year, a country's stock of capital would shrink accordingly. David Ricardo, *On the Principles of Political Economy and Taxation* (Cambridge: Cambridge University Press, 1982), v. 1, p. 150. See also Tilly, *Coercion, Capital, and European States,* chap. 3.

each empire while curbing intrusions from foreigners. On the surface, this might appear to undermine merchants' privileges and free up ruinous competition. But Iberian reformers were as uninterested in pure competition as they were in absolute private property. The solution was to be found in the alchemy of a controlled, calibrated contest for shares of imperial markets. Alexandre de Gusmão felt that Portuguese sovereignty could be better ensured with an "active" model of empire. Until now, he declared to the king, we have relied on "passive trade," acting as the conduits for others to ship their manufactures and African slaves to Brazil, in return for American staples that fanned out to rival powers to consume. Meanwhile, big merchant houses rested on their easy earnings because they only had foreigners to compete with—and they dealt with that challenge by acting as the agents for foreign interests. He argued that if merchants in the metropole could be motivated to make their own commodities for export and seize a share of the slave trade, they could enhance their own fortunes, "augmenting their well earned Nobility" while stanching the efflux "of money that is extracted from our Kingdom." To accomplish this, the crown had to punish the "*gente inutil*" and reward the merchants who learned to compete with each other. What he meant by competition is perhaps more easily understood by contrast to its antonym: monopoly, especially as enjoyed by an idle few who operated as agents of shadowy foreign magnates.[43]

The antimonopoly call was especially pronounced in the prescriptions of Campomanes. For the Asturian reformer, one set of rules that supported monopoly was ruinous: the regulations that upheld the overseas trade monopoly of the port of Cádiz. From the turn of the eighteenth century, Cádiz and its powerful merchant guild claimed to control Spanish overseas trade. It cut out other peninsular ports and enforced its monopoly by colluding with the guild's satellites in Mexico and Peru. And increasingly, the French and British traders had learned to colonize the Cádiz monopoly from within, buying out Spanish houses to act as their agents to dominate the commercial sinews of the Spanish Atlantic.[44]

How to promote competition among nationals without destabilizing the rentier system as a whole? Part of the fix came from modifications to the formal decision-making and rule-enforcing bodies of the Spanish and Portuguese empires. For Pombal, administrative shuffling, especially to strengthen viceroys and governors so that they would not fall prey to private monopolists, especially foreigners, could go a long way. The State of Maranhão, for instance, was reorganized into a more centralized

---

[43]Gusmão, "Calculo sobre a perda do dinheiro do Reyno."
[44]Campomanes, *Reflexiones sobre el comercio*, p. 4.

jurisdiction (and his stepbrother dispatched as governor) and made more directly accountable to Lisbon. To cut out interlopers and, if necessary, local merchants and planters whom Pombal had always suspected of lethargic collusion with foreigners, Pombal chartered a metropolitan partnership, Companhia Geral do Comércio. This was not a state monopoly but a privately owned consortium with the rights to ship slaves, buy agricultural produce for export, and cut out foreign merchants who supposedly controlled the sale of imported manufactured goods in the region. Similar models were deployed in other regions, on the whole prying open colonial markets that foreigners had penetrated and pooling "national" merchants into coalitions to invest in empire more actively to extract sugar, tobacco, precious metals, and cotton for shipment to new Portuguese factories. This was a peculiar model of "competition" to be sure. But it conformed to Pombal's idea that making national merchants competitive meant opening more provinces for enterprise and fostering some metropolitan teamwork, all overseen by his loyal administrators, all of which was necessary to extirpate foreign monopolies.[45]

In the Spanish empire, furthering competition also meant administrative reforms, such as creating new jurisdictions (the Viceroyalty of the River Plate and the Captaincy General of Venezuela) and new tiers of bureaucracy, like intendants who would answer more directly to Madrid's policies. It also, as we have seen, meant breaking Cádiz's headlock on imperial commerce. So while creating a more centralized administrative structure, Gálvez threw open a multitude of colonial and peninsular ports so that they could trade more easily with each other, as well as weaken the corporate grip of Cádiz and the shadow interests of the foreign contingent there. The logic was less inconsistent than it might seem—centripetal bureaucracy with centrifugal trade. The former was supposed to check artificial monopolies condoned by law enforcers who had fallen prey to corrupt practices that gave some parties undue privileges. Centrifugal trade was supposed to create a larger class of merchants, into whose pools of capital the state could dip for resources on demand. Both policies were designed to re-center the empire while creating a more "national" or truly "imperial" merchant class capable of standing up to foreign competition.

To seal the deal between private merchants and the monarchies, ministers entrusted merchants' institutions to monitor the new competitive energies. The point was not to dominate private interests but to reaggregate

[45]Andrée Mansuy-Diniz Silva, "Portugal and Brazil: Imperial Reorganization, 1750–1808," in Bethell, ed., *Cambridge History of Latin America*, v. 2, pp. 478–79, 490–91. See also the classic study by Alden, *Royal Government*.

them so that private interests contributed to the common good. This was not always welcome news, especially for the holders of ancient privileges. When Lisbon merchants got wind of Pombal's new chartered companies, their Mesa do Bem Comum criticized the minister. Pombal responded by dissolving the merchant outfit, rounding up the patrician leaders, exiling some, and imprisoning others, and he told the quivering survivors that they could join new organizations—ones that would bend more easily to his model of empire. Pombal created entirely new bodies, like the Junta do Comércio (the Board of Trade) in 1755. Staffed by merchants, the junta and its network of satellites were supposed to regulate commerce, issue licenses, and dispense justice as a commercial court, thereby defining and enforcing the distinctions between licit and illicit commercial activity. Before long the junta also controlled the local Boards of Inspection that governed the pricing and quality of tobacco, sugar, and eventually cotton—and thus was a constant irritant in relations between merchants (who wanted to depress prices as much as possible) and planters (who fought for inflation). Out in the colonies, the junta eclipsed the old Mesa do Bem Comum branches, which had come under the control of landowner classes. Penalties for bad behavior included fines, embargos, prison sentences, and, most damaging, blacklisting from future commercial ventures by the omni-monitoring junta. With time, the junta formalized a system of matriculation and registration of traders. Playing by the rules allowed insiders to enjoy preferential access to colonial markets, even as they had to compete with each other for their share.[46]

This licensing system was a way of governing gentlemanly competition among imperial merchants. It should be noted that Pombal only chartered Portuguese "monopoly" trading firms where he perceived that provinces had already fallen into the clutches of the wrong kind of monopoly—one that would not serve the national interest. Charters were the exception that proved a more general rule inscribed in a royal decree of September 1765, which removed obstacles to the entry of national merchants wanting to engage in trade across the empire. Merchants could come and go as long as they complied with mercantilist rules and met the requirements stipulated by juntas. At times, this meant that the government was forced to break up collusive behavior. In early January 1769, for example, the government informed subjects that monopolies in the slave and marble trades were forbidden, and a few months later charged Domingos Dias da Silva with violating the laws of the empire by trying to restrict traffic between Angola and Lisbon. The

---

[46]C. R. Boxer, *The Portuguese Seaborn Empire, 1415–1825* (London: Hutchinson, 1969), pp. 184–86.

public decisions announced that the king "wishes to end these pernicious transgressions and help his loyal vassals." Especially where the slave trade was concerned, the government strongly encouraged competition in order to maximize the flow of captives from one side of the Atlantic to the other.[47]

There was a fine but important line to be maintained between domesticated competition and unbridled rivalry that might foster more uncertainty than opportunity. Self-regulating merchants had to be protected from excessive rivalry, all the way down the line to the most modest "retailer" operating in the very fringes of the Brazilian markets. These *comissários volantes*, itinerant hawkers, the final link in the commodity chains binding European manufacturers to their hinterland markets, operated outside the formally approved networks of merchandising. One of the difficulties in regulating them was that they were instrumental for plugging gaps where legal commerce had no, few, or simply inferior commodities to fill. At the same time they operated as legal handlers of Portuguese goods, able to maneuver in the complicated interstices of the vast market of the Brazilian hinterlands. Indeed, relying on the illegal truck and smuggling provided them with profits to make ends meet so that they could carry on the legal business. What was important for the juntas of Rio de Janeiro, Bahia, and Pernambuco was not the banning of the salesmen but controlling them, forcing them to comply with the power of the mercantile higher-ups. This was a way of shoring up the internal hierarchy within the commercial system that gave the members of the junta and the big magnates that ran it regulatory power over the capitalist pyramid underneath. It ensured that merchants from top to bottom played by rules that bridled market competition to reduce risk, ensure payments, and collect debts in the uncertain worlds of long-distance trading.[48]

In the Spanish Atlantic, merchants also acquired greater control over their own dealings, with the understanding that they would reciprocate with support for the regime. In Venezuela, in part because authorities were so incapable of controlling the smuggling from the Dutch and English islands of the Antilles, Madrid finally dismantled the Guipuzcoana Company in 1778, and in 1789, Venezuela joined the rest of South America by being thrown open to imperial trade under the mantle of

---

[47]ANTT, JC, Maço 62, Caixa 202, August 5, 1769; Real Alvará, December 10, 1765, and petition, August 13, 1776. Mansuy, "Portugal and Brazil," pp. 480–81, 489–90.

[48]ANTT, JC, Maço 10, Caixa 36, December 10, 1789; Catherine Lugar, "The Merchant Community of Salvador, Bahia, 1780–1830" (PhD thesis, SUNY Stony Brook, 1980), pp. 27–28, 32–39.

comercio libre. Now the entire Atlantic littoral was free to trade among the archipelago of imperial ports. This presented the crown with a dilemma: how to regulate the market activity of these autonomous outposts. This had conventionally fallen on the shoulders of the old monopoly guild in Cádiz, which had now lost its command over imperial commerce. For instance, in 1751, when a major Cartagena merchant, Diego Luis de Medina, died, his will was riddled with complications and burdened with debts. Cádiz dispatched two emissaries to take care of the muddle. But with comercio libre, monopoly companies and the monopoly port could no longer regulate commercial affairs. The difficulty was evident to state authorities and colonial merchants alike: commercial reforms expanded rights to trade but did little to create an enforcement mechanism for merchants to regulate competition to protect their rents.[49]

The solution responded to merchants' demands for a legal enforcement mechanism. In Venezuela, right after the Guipuzcoana Company was dismantled, and even before comercio libre extended to the region, merchants petitioned officials to create a local guild to monitor trading lest a commercial free-for-all wipe out their fortunes.[50] No sooner was the Buenos Aires market opened to imperial traders in 1778 than local merchants clamored for a system that would enable honorable capitalists "to work within the laws of Castile and the Indies." Now enjoying their newfound rights, they worried about excessive competition. Madrid's response was to approve requests to create merchant guilds, *consulados* in the main ports liberated under comercio libre. In 1792, guilds were erected in Havana, Caracas, and Cartagena; two years later Buenos Aires got its own consulado. The old control that Cádiz and its guild had over colonial trade gave way to a decentered network of guilds in the major entrepôts, with each guild in control of the business of matriculating members of the mercantile community and enforcing the commercial laws of the empire. It was now up to the colonial outposts of merchant power to monitor rent-seeking activity and to reciprocate their new relative sovereignty by expressing their loyalty to, and dividing their rents with, authorities.[51]

---

[49]AGNB, Colonia, Consulado, I, ff. 154–99; Manuel Bustos Rodríguez, *Los Comerciantes de la carrera de Indias en el Cádiz del siglo XVIII* (Cádiz: Universidad de Cádiz, 1995), 49–58.

[50]Archivo General Nacional Caracas (hereafter AGNC), Real Consulado, t. I, f. 1, July 1786.

[51]P. Michael McKinley, *Pre-revolutionary Caracas: Politics, Economy, and Society, 1777–1811* (Cambridge: Cambridge University Press, 1985), pp. 102–5; German O. E. Tjarks, *El consulado de Buenos Aires y sus proyecciones en la historia del Rio de la Plata* (Buenos Aires: Facultad de Filosofía y Letras, 1962), v. 1, pp. 48–57; González, *Cádiz y el Atlántico*, pp. 459–80.

Institutional reform—creating new centers of economic power like the Brazilian juntas or propagating old ones, like the Spanish American consulados—provided the formal means for merchants and monarchs to generate state revenues and commercial rents at the same time. Imperial authorities created institutional venues for resolving distributional contests between the state and merchant capitalists. Consider the reaction of Cartagena's merchants when they learned that royal authorities were considering reintroducing register ships. Even before they got their guild, they honed the art of joining together and petitioning the king in the supplicative voice of loyal vassals in need of—and deserving—succor. One entreaty noted that they owed their loyalty, and their fortunes, to his majesty's generosity. They were "the possessors of resources which can be abdicated for the benefit of his majesty's vassals," admitted the signatories. But they also possessed rights which, if enjoyed responsibly and faithfully, could help the region prosper for the benefit of all subjects— and of course his majesty's treasurers. So their petition went further than denouncing register ships. The merchants protested any further taxes and any more curbs on their ability to govern their own trading networks. In the interests of the province, and the empire, they had to defend their "natural liberty" and resist measures that would "annul the common good which is in great need of attending and alleviation."[52]

There is little evidence that capitalists saw themselves as absolute possessors of property rights or that public guardians enjoyed dominion over private transactions. The new discourses of freedom to trade did not counterpose individual rights against state power and vice versa; the sovereignty of property and politics in the Iberian empires were separable but not independent. There is little evidence, in short, that the steady advance of the market across the Iberian Atlantic yielded to practices and concepts that upset prescriptive mechanisms of rewards or heralded a new vision of society governed by laws of human nature determined by impersonal economic forces. Rather, imperial bargaining still rested firmly on a monarchical culture to legitimate it and the conviction that the equilibrium of life depended on the laws of man and his honorable comportment.[53] Perhaps this is why relational notions of property—with all their "feudal" connotations—have been so commonly (and too automatically) linked with anciens régimes while modern regimes have been associated with their acknowledgment of absolute and independent ideas

---

[52]AGNB, Archivo Anexo, Comercio, t. I, ff. 28–30.

[53]The contrast to the Anglo-American Atlantic is instructive. See Joyce Appleby, "Locke, Liberalism, and the Natural Law of Money," in her *Liberalism and Republicanism in the Historical Imagination* (Cambridge, MA: Harvard University Press, 1992), esp. pp. 58–60.

of property. Either way, this anachronism gets in the way of understanding the political mechanisms that pushed market revolutions into American colonies. Not long after his arrival in Brazil in 1768, the governor and captain general of Bahia, the Marquis of Lavradio, bemoaned the destitute state of his accounts and the "disanimated" condition of provincial trade. The combination "depressed" him. But he recovered, and invited "all the *homens de negocio* [merchants]" to meet with him to discuss the ways in which they might help the government. The marquis declared his intention to make it easier for traders to conduct business and capped off the entreaty for capitalist support by auctioning two tithe-collection farms. Writing to the Count of São Vicente, he applauded his own efforts. Until his arrival, there was much distrust and animosity between treasury officials and merchants. His gestures, he wrote, "have made of these people *uma bulha formidável*."[54]

What is important to appreciate is that the expansion of market forces and commercial freedoms was fully compatible with the idea of defending old empires to redouble ancient exclusions. Just as peace treaties and imperial warfare went hand in glove so too did market expansion and political control of imperial hinterlands. Promoting market activity and competition was seen as a way of supporting imperial transactions that fortified the regimes while raising the stakes of—and thus the conflict within—the expansionist game.

Profits and Patriarchs

Expanding merchants' self-regulatory bodies of the empires was one way of inducing change when the state was too hobbled to enforce its laws alone. Yet, putting these modifications to work did not rely on purely formal institutional mechanisms. Increasing the relative autonomy of the multiple nodes of merchant capitalism in the colonies reinforced informal networks of personal contacts, kinship, and credit relations that kept what Braudel famously called "the wheels of commerce" in motion. Personalized mechanisms of dependency among partners, family members, debtors, and creditors all combined the merchants of empire into transatlantic networks integrated by informal and asymmetrical bonds. Seen from afar, these networks did without a fixed center. Indeed, informal mechanisms of control and dependency reinforced the subtle shift in autonomy of colonial capitalists away from the metropoles to peripheral

---

[54]Marqués do Lavradio, *Cartas da Bahia, 1768–1769* (Rio de Janeiro: Arquivo Nacional, 1972), pp, 38–39.

nodes. This, too, was part of the compromise, though not altogether intended, between merchants and monarchs to revive imperial fortunes.[55]

Imperial trade over long distances was a diverse and risky enterprise. In an age in which insurance policies, futures markets, and long-term credit instruments—our modern, impersonal, trust-inducing techniques—were scarce or nonexistent, the magnates of the Spanish and Portuguese empires relied on tried and true personal means to handle the variety of businesses and the perils of losses. A useful way to deal with the specter of a loss in one branch of the Atlantic trade was to have lots of other branches. Consider the example of José Antonio de Lavalle y Cortés, a Peruvian-born merchant based in Lima, who exemplified the importance of diversification, not specialization, to cope with risk. And Lavalle was familiar with risk. Peruvian merchants knew only too well how volatile their fortunes could be: Madrid's decision to sever Alto Peru, and the mining districts around Potosí, from its axis with Lima and lump it into the new viceroyalty based in Buenos Aires hit them hard. No longer would the silver mines fuel their commercial ventures, as they disgorged specie into *porteño* pockets, leaving *limeños* scrambling for business. Lavalle and others had to explore alternatives. The cacao trade between Callao and Guayaquil provided a new source of income, though it was seasonal and prone to natural afflictions. Lavalle followed up then by reaching out to copper miners in Chile, and eventually after 1779 got into the slave-trade business to provide domestic servants to Peruvian notables and captives to coastal plantations and interior mines. By 1789, Lavalle had spread his energies and capital into a wide array of commodities so that he could compensate for a seasonal or yearly loss in one with returns from another trade, and to have a much more diverse "portfolio" than his predecessors who hung their fortunes on silver. Lavalle quickly rose to prominence in Lima's consulado and beyond into other official and quasi-official circles. He augmented his personal capital with political capital, helping to raise a local loan of 1.5 million pesos to fund the conflict with the Portuguese empire in 1777. The compound effects of the diversification of his personal and public business helped him win contacts and willing collaborators in the extended mercantile web radiating out of his house in Lima. Lavalle's trustworthiness gave him a reputation among his circle of investors of honoring their contributions with decent returns (up to 6 percent). Pooling funds allowed him to buy and

---

[55]Fernand Braudel, *Civilization and Capitalism, 15th–18th Century*, vol. 2, *The Wheels of Commerce* (New York: Harper and Row, 1982), pp. 134–37; see also Zacarías Moutoukias, "El crecimiento en una economía colonial del antiguo régimen: Reformismo y sector externo en el Río de la Plata (1760–1796)," *Arquivos do centro cultural Caluste Gulbenkian* 34 (1995): 772; González, *Cádiz y el Atlántico*, pp. 480–82.

sell on credit, that critical lifeline for commercial capitalism. Lavalle was one of many in the Spanish and Portuguese empires, each with his own personalized means to handle bills of exchange, discount commercial notes, and generally employ pre-corporate, pre-banking instruments to funnel the dispersed savings of the empires into credits and loans to sustain long-distance trade. Merchant houses integrated the diversity within regional economies of the empire, spurred by greater freedom to trade, under single roofs.[56]

Diversification was not restricted to branching out within a single merchant house. It also meant integration among houses, which allowed merchants to pool their capital and thus disperse risk. As well, integration meant gaining access to networks that reached into very local, particular markets, tastes, and preferences to minimize risk. Integration of merchant houses transpired through two principal means: short-term partnerships and longer-term alliances through intermarriage and mergers of kinship networks, a practice known as *parentela* or *patentesco*. Kinship was crucial for creating the organizational networks through which commodities and capital flowed. Parentela enabled branches of families to specialize within a diversified kinship network. Webs of kin relations, real and fictive, also extended informal relations into political, administrative, and even military spheres so that puissant families could ensure that the powers of the state be brought to bear on a problem—a tax, a forced loan, a deal gone sour, and even social uprisings—that might imperil the business. Consanguinity gathered loyalty, honor, and trust from the outer reaches of familial networks to their core, dominated by powerful patriarchs who knew all too well that these were the indispensable "familial capital" bases for their operations—buttressing their economic and social capital.[57]

The networks also operated, when needed, as enforcement mechanisms to ensure that payments flowed back and forth between contracting parties—and that commercial rents trickled in to the patriarch. A cousin, brother, or godson could be relied on to exercise pressure on debtors (or he himself might be a debtor) more effectively in the absence of strong

---

[56]Mazzeo, *El comercio libre en el Perú*, pp. 125–63; on Buenos Aires, see Susan Socolow, *The Merchants of Buenos Aires, 1778–1810: Family and Commerce* (Cambridge: Cambridge University Press, 1978), pp. 68–69; Jacob M. Price, "What Did Merchants Do? Reflections on British Overseas Trade, 1660–1790," *Journal of Economic History* 49:2 (1989): 273–79.

[57]Luciano Raposo de Almeida Figueiredo, *Barrocas famílias: Vida familiar em Minas Gerais no século XVIII* (São Paulo: Editora Hucitec, 1997), esp. pp. 81–103; Alida Metcalf, *Family and Frontier in Colonial Brazil: Santana de Parnaíba, 1580–1822* (Berkeley: University of California Press, 1992), pp. 87–119; Ann Twinam, *Public Lives, Private Secrets: Gender, Honor, Sexuality, and Illegitimacy in Colonial Spanish America* (Stanford: Stanford University Press, 1999), pp. 216–40.

courts, gendarmes, and states capable of compelling those in arrears to comply with their obligations. Informal enforcement powers and familial trust, the stick and the carrot, kept goods and payments flowing and provided the foundations for long-distance commercial activity touted by late mercantilist reformers. For all their rhetoric about vitalizing the empires through greater freedom to trade to strengthen the state, reformers relied on familial and paternalistic means to unblock imperial arteries. It is hard to miss the dynamic: adapting the empires redoubled the importance of traditional family-based loyalties.[58]

Membership in a prominent merchant family was the basis for membership in a whole set of other subsidiary and reinforcing networks. In the port of Cádiz, as Paloma Fernández Pérez has shown, a merchant had to marry a relative of a member of the powerful merchant guild as a condition for matriculating into the guild. In other words, family membership was the ticket to the public and quasi-public life of cities. In Cádiz, as in Lisbon, metropolitan merchant houses were open to new arrivals, foreigners and nationals alike, constantly cycling capitalists through the commanding heights of the imperial political economy.[59] The same obtained in colonial outposts. In Lima, Lavalle married into a merchant-mining-hacienda family and from there made his upward ascent. Once in the higher reaches of the mercantile elite, he made sure his sons found suitable partners from among Lima's other merchant households (two of them), and—to really diversify the network of influences—ushered the others into administrative (two more) and military (another pair) families and occupations. By the apogee of his power in Lima in the 1800s, Lavalle commanded a powerful web of loyal family allies, which he governed like a benevolent patriarch. Not only did they manage the divisions of his enterprise, but they acted as subsidiaries of his political and social dealings, raising funds to help the government

[58]Raymond de Roover, *Business, Banking, and Economic Thought in Late Medieval and Early Modern Europe* (Chicago: University of Chicago Press, 1974); Peter Mathias, "Risk, Credit, and Kinship in Early Modern Enterprise," in John J. McCusker and Kenneth Morgan, eds., *The Early Modern Atlantic Economy* (Cambridge: Cambridge University Press, 2000), pp. 15–35; Richard Grassby, *Kinship and Capitalism: Marriage, Family, and Business in the English-Speaking World, 1580–1740* (Cambridge: Cambridge University Press, 2001), pp. 413–17. Some of the issues about how historians deal with the "problem of persistence" are discussed in Jeremy Adelman, "The Problem of Persistence in Latin American History," in Adelman, ed., *Colonial Legacies: The Problem of Persistence in Latin American History* (New York: Routledge, 1999), pp. 1–14.

[59]Paloma Fernández Pérez, *El rostro familiar de la metrópoli: Redes de parentesco y lazos mercantiles en Cádiz, 1700–1812* (Madrid: Siglo XXI, 1997), pp. 124–31; Jorge M. Pedreira, "Os negociantes de Lisboa na segunda metade do século XVIII: Padrões de recrutamento e percursos sociais," *Análise Social* 116–117:2–3 (1992): 423–40.

crush the Indian insurgency in the Andes in the 1780s, pumping money into ecclesiastic endowments, and managing the Hospital of San Bartolomé. All were ways of consolidating influence, while building trust and loyalty necessary to mitigate and manage the risks presented by the backbone of his commercial fortune: long-distance imperial trade.[60]

The principal ports of the Spanish and Portuguese empires were cities dominated by closely knit, elite mercantile families, a patrician class interconnected as siblings, cousins, godchildren, and godparents, with each branch covering a domain of the business and increasingly involved in the noneconomic life of the empires. Marriage and kinship were therefore means to integrate social relations that served as the basis for integrated enterprises. But this did not necessarily mean that they were hermetically sealed networks. Nor did they inhibit social mobility—upward or downward. Indeed, faced with a major blow to the family business, a falling patriarch could bring down the whole extended network. Likewise, marriage was also a means of ascent. In the area around Rio de Janeiro, merchants clawed their way upward by marrying into local families of notables, especially landed estate owners. Not marrying strategically could slow the ascent; single merchants generally were poorer and had fewer assets—they certainly had less access to pools of investible funds in the hands of planters or even ecclesiastic estates. Sheila de Castro Faria has likened the struggle to find appropriate spouses in colonial Brazil to a relatively open marriage market that sustained commodity and credit markets. Gregório Francisco de Miranda, an immigrant Portuguese merchant of modest means, had the good fortune to find a wife, the daughter of a mill owner and former merchant, and thereby made his way up the social ladder. Small retailers, distributors, factors, and large wholesalers could be aggregated into loose familiar confederations. So, the networks were not just horizontal, integrating kinfolk within elites; they were also vertical, incorporating new members, many of whom were recent arrivals from the peninsula, into elites and ushering them upward through the ranks via marriage or fictive adoption.[61]

---

[60]Mazzeo, *El comercio libre en el Perú*, pp. 74–76; for Buenos Aires, see Socolow, *Merchants of Buenos Aires*, pp. 38–55.

[61]Sheila de Castro Faria, *A colônia em movimiento: Fortuna e família no cotidiano colonial* (Rio de Janeiro: Editora Nova Frontera, 1998), pp. 168–76, 192; Alida C. Metcalf, "Women and Means: Women and Family Property in Colonial Brazil," *Journal of Social History* 24:2 (1990): 277–98. This pattern reached even into deep hinterlands. See Liliana Betty Romero Cabrera, *José Miguel de Tagle: Un comerciante americano de los siglos XVIII y XIX* (Córdoba: Universidad Nacional de Córdoba, 1973), pp. 3–18; Ann Twinam, *Miners, Merchants and Farmers in Colonial Colombia* (Austin: University of Texas Press, 1982), pp. 72–86.

The development of the Portuguese and Spanish empires in the eighteenth century created and relied upon the consolidation of open elites across the commercial centers on both sides of the Atlantic Ocean. These elites were entrusted with managing the pressures of competition among them and investing their capital in businesses to extract staples from colonial hinterlands. They conveyed loyalty and rents to the centers of these networks ruled by patriarchs, and reciprocated with credit, protection, employment, and favors. Kinship therefore provided the foundations for capital formation in the empires. It also served as the homologue for systems of imperial power, for as these mercantile households enjoyed greater freedoms to trade and autonomy to regulate their affairs in the colonies, they reciprocated the expansion of their property rights with loyalty and revenues to the crown. As kin ties sustained the flow of influence and rents to patriarchs in the middle of mercantile networks, power and revenues flowed to the metropolitan centers of the empires through commercial hubs of coastal cities. From the patrician classes of these cities emerged the personal cornerstones of empire.

THE LIMITS OF REFORM

The model of empire inspired by the dire warnings of de Gusmão and Campomanes, and applied by Pombal and Gálvez, aimed to promote change without a violent break with established customs and hierarchies. Commercial capitalism could spread in the Atlantic world without directly undermining the feudal remnants in Europe's Iberian peninsula. To a large extent, the model made good on its promises. Overseas trade grew and diversified. Sugar, dyestuffs, cacao, coffee, cotton, hides, meat products, and many others staples flowed from the hinterlands and gathered in the principal ports to be loaded onto vessels bound for distant markets. Much of it found buyers in the peninsula, so that commercial activity in the Iberian entrepôts rose in response to the inducements to trade more freely. Even silver, the emblem of all that was wrong with the ancient model of empire, boomed. So long as war did not cut deeply into the official ledgers, rising trade and mining buoyed imperial treasuries.[62]

Where the expansion of commerce was most felt was in the colonies. There, opportunities to trade allowed planters, modest farmers, and

---

[62]Fisher, *Commercial Relations between Spain and Spanish America*, pp. 16–46; for the Portuguese empire, see Jorge Miguel Viana Pedreira, *Estructura industrial e mercado colonial: Portugal e Brasil (1780–1830)* (Lisboa: Difel, 1994), pp. 51–63; on silver, see Richard L. Garner, "Long-term Silver Mining Trends in Spanish-America: A Comparative Analysis of Peru and Mexico," *American Historical Review* 93:4 (1988): 898–935.

peasants to drive commercial frontiers deeper into colonial hinterlands like the Llanos, the Pampas, the Campos de Goitacazes, Maranhão, and the Upper Magdalena. All the way along, producers, the menial and the magnates, were encouraged by merchants and their credit to join a "market revolution" without undermining patriarchal models of organizing trade or enforcing labor systems. In important ways, the colonies thrived even more than the metropoles—for the new model of freer infra-imperial trade especially unlocked the potential for intercolonial exchanges. Freer trade made legal what had been pushed underground between South American provinces and colonies, even across the fractious divide that separated Brazil from the Viceroyalty of the River Plate. The Peruvian Lavalle, for example, placed his orders for African captives to agents in Buenos Aires, who imported them from Rio de Janeiro, the swelling entrepôt for commerce between Angola and Brazil. The circuits of commodities, captives, and credit operated autonomously from Lisbon and Cádiz, creating powerful local and regional "economic spaces" in the colonies themselves. The metropolitan hubs tolerated—indeed encouraged—this decentered arrangement so long as it reinforced the centripetal flow of loyalty and revenues to the peninsula.[63]

Just as imperial reforms aimed to adapt the anciens régimes to the pressures of ramped-up interimperial competition without challenging the fundaments of the old order in the peninsula, so too at the hither edge of the empires reform was not intended to shake up established social hierarchies or the underlying principles of capital accumulation. Commercial expansion did not clear the stage for a "bourgeoisie," which, as it matured, might set its sights on toppling ensconced aristocrats or imperial officials. The merchant class that dominated the social geography of the colonies did not self-identify as a force for change in opposition to established arrangements and loyalties. In spite of their eager responses to freer trade, their interests were firmly committed to the comforts and convenience of tradition.

However, just because there were no colonial bourgeoisies itching to break free of old mores does not mean that the transformations unleashed by imperial reform did not destabilize ancient principles of empire. The compound effects of commercial and institutional reform did run into the brittleness of colonial societies. Indeed, for centuries, the imperial systems relied on local officials to legitimate Iberian rulership by softening the most exploitive edges of colonialism. But doing more than paying lip service to the moral and material concerns of subaltern peoples

---

[63]On "economic spaces," see Carlos Sempat Assadourian, *El sistema de la economía colonial: El mercado interior, regiones y espacio económico* (Mexico: Ed. Nueva Imagen, 1983), pp. 15–16.

of the Americas stood in the way of the centripetal drive of imperial reform since it thwarted market forces from penetrating more fully into social relationships of such stratified hierarchies. The spread of merchant capitalism to the fringes of empire undermined the authority of inherited local political cultures. Therefore, the new compromises of reform in imperial capitals and entrepôts dissolved older, more archaic compromises developed over the generations since the Conquest—local arrangements that were so effective in perpetuating Iberian rulership in the Americas because they did not eviscerate the moral authority of leaders. The clash between new and old compromises of empire came to a head in the 1780s, provoking widespread unrest that eventually put a limit on how deep the reforms could shake up imperial fortunes.

The most disruptive—and frightening—responses to reform erupted in the "deepest" of colonial societies: the Andes. Up and down the cordillera, from the Comuneros of Nueva Granada to the Indians of Chayanta, complex, hybrid movements rose up against local tax collectors and merchants. What they held in common was what they disliked: the combined pressure to exact commercial rents from producers and consumers and state revenues from colonial villages to central authorities. After months of demonstrations and large assemblies centered on the city of Socorro, on June 5, 1781, 20,000 irate vecinos began marching on the capital of Nueva Granada chanting, "Death to bad government and long live the king!" Leaders like Juan Francisco Berbeo denounced in particular the policies of the regent visitor general, who had arrived in 1778 bearing instructions to apply the new reform model of commercial opening and tightened fiscal measures. Taxes rose, as did consumer prices, until colonists began to denounce openly the visitor as a "rapacious tyrant" and a violator of the moral norms of "communal" decency. The Comunero Revolt, like so many of the uprisings across the region, was not an anti-imperial movement. It simply wanted to reverse the combined fiscal burdens and commercial uncertainties. Indeed, as Berbeo explained in the *Plan de Capitulaciones*, the movement was inspired by fealty to the king and determined to keep his imperial officers governing in the interest of his subjects, the commonwealth, and therefore his majesty. Faced with administrative "tyranny" and "corruption," it fell to the vecinos themselves to defend the monarchy from the enemy within. Taxes and loans in themselves were not the problem—unjust demands were. Defending "just taxes," the *Plan* noted that "as loyal vassals we offer" to pay when called upon. "When a legitimate need of His majesty, either involving the defense of the faith or even the smallest part of his dominion, is brought to our attention and he asks for a forced loan or gift, we shall contribute with great pleasure." The protests shook the confidence of viceregal administrators, who retreated from their fiscal demands and curbed the freedoms of merchants to charge the prices they wished.[64]

Popular colonial reaction to the new imperial deals did more than fuel protest; it sparked insurrection. The fiercest reaction erupted in the lower Andes, leading to the largest Indian insurgency in the New World since the Conquest. In early 1780, a mysterious message appeared on the wall of the customs house of Arequipa one night. It announced that "the *corregidor* will die and so will the duty-collectors, court clerks and those of their faction. . . . Long live our great monarch—long live Carlos III and may all duty-collectors die." In the ensuing weeks Indians and mestizos broke down the doors to armories, customs houses, and eventually the homes of prominent officials of Arequipa, Huaraz, and Pasco, leading to a full-scale insurgency led by José Gabriel Condorcanqui, soon to be known locally as Túpac Amaru II. Insurrection spread to the Aymara-speaking peoples of Alto Peru as well, as peasants and commoners rejected the ways in which Iberian rulers relied on local mediators to perpetuate the colonial extractive system. This subaltern uprising of Indians, creoles, and even a few Spaniards of humble occupations shattered the confidence of imperial authorities in Cuzco, Lima, and beyond. Manuel Godoy, Carlos IV's minister, later wrote in his memoirs that "no one ignores that the entire viceroyalty of Peru and part of the Río de la Plata were nearly lost in 1781 and 1782." It took years to subdue the highlands and restore a precarious semblance of order. And despite the temptation to blame a few hothead agitators or venal stewards for the unrest, colonial officials did manage to conclude that their model of reform was a potentially explosive mix in such stratified and highly coercive societies. The unrest put a halt to many fiscal reforms—which left the bargain between merchant elites and ruling officials, the exchange of rents and revenues, limping on one leg.[65]

---

[64]Anthony McFarlane, *Colombia before Independence: Economy, Society, and Politics under Bourbon Rule* (Cambridge: Cambridge University Press, 1993), pp. 211–16; idem, "Rebellions in Late Colonial Spanish America: A Comparative Perspective," *Bulletin of Latin American Research* 14:3 (1983): 313–38.

[65]Pasquines que se pusieron en la ciudad de Arequipa desde el día 10 de enero de 80," in Carlos Daniel Valcarcel Esparza, ed., *Colección documental de la independencia del Perú* (Lima: Comisión Nacional del Sesquicentenario de la Independencia del Perú, 1971), v. 2, pp. 108–9; Leon G. Campbell, "Social Structure of the Túpac Amaru Army in Cuzco, 1780–81," *Hispanic American Historical Review* 61:4 (1981): 675–93; Charles Walker, *Smoldering Ashes: Cuzco and the Creation of Republican Peru, 1780–1840* (Durham: Duke University Press, 1999), p. 53 and chap. 2 for the Amaru rebellion. On the Aymara speakers, see Sinclair Thomson, *We Alone Will Rule: Native Andean Politics in the Age of Insurgency* (Madison: University of Wisconsin Press, 2002), and Sergio Serulnikov, *Subverting Colonial Authority: Challenges to Spanish Rule in Eighteenth-Century Southern Andes* (Durham: Duke University Press, 2003). For an imperial postmortem, see Archivo General de Indias (hereafter AGI), Estado, Lima, 74/57, December 31, 1781, "Relación de Audiencia de Lima sobre la rebelión del Indio José Gabriel Tupac-Amaru."

Opposition and unrest did not stop at Spanish imperial borders; colonial limits to imperial reform rose up on the Portuguese side as well. In Brazil, grievances against tax collectors and usurious merchants had been mounting since Pombal unveiled his master plan. The fissures erupted finally in Minas Gerais in early 1789, led by Joaquim José da Silva Xavier, alias "Tiradentes." A lieutenant in the colonial Dragoons, son of a treasurer in the diamond district, and part-time tooth-puller (hence the dental moniker), Tiradentes led a conspiracy to kill the governor, declare independence, and create a republic in a sui generis emulation of the United States. The plot stumbled from the start. Its leaders assumed that the local militias would join them—and they did not. More important, Tiradentes went beyond the shared dislike of policies to proclaim a whole new order. Without dismissing an underlying nativist current to the grievances, independence and republicanism were at best fantasies that appealed to few colonists; and the prospect of arming and freeing slaves horrified the rest. Not even the slaves themselves appeared to be part of the conspiracy. So the insurgency failed before its flames could feed themselves. Still, as in the Andes, Brazilian colonial officials saw that there were underlying causes to the malaise, and decided to back off the imposition of the odious *derrama* tax that had inspired the conspiracy in the first place. When the governor of Minas Gerais suspended the levy, he defused some of the tension—and deployed his considerable ring of spies and snitches to round up the plotters before they could hatch their plan. The episode, nonetheless, was a lesson in the limits of imperial policy. The turmoil of the 1780s reminded imperial authorities that their sovereignty was not only threatened by other empires but there were also local colonial limits to their sovereign power.[66]

There was more to colonial resistance than anxiety about tax collectors and merchants' greed. Late imperial reforms also ran into an ingrained political and moral order that had allowed local societies to function at arm's length from centralizing royal authorities or mercantile patriarchs. Over the centuries, in short, colonial societies had built up systems of relative self-rule within the empires, premised on local management of legitimacy and social alignments. At times these practices were inscribed

---

[66]Luciano Raposo de Almeida Figueiredo, "Protestos, Revoltas e Fiscalidade no Brasil Colonial," *LPH: Revista de História*, no. 5 (1995): 56–87; "Ofício do Secretário de Estado da Marinha e Domínios Ultramarinhos, Martinho de Melo e Castro ao Vice-Rei Luís de Vasconcelos e Sousa," March 9, 1790, in *Revista do Instituto de Histórico e Geográfico Brasileiro* 153 (375) (April–June 1992): 132–33; Maxwell, *Conflicts and Conspiracies*, pp. 116–45; Paulo Roberto Pereira, "Inconfidência Mineira: Derrota da Utopia Liberal," *Revista do Instituto de Histórico e Geográfico Brasileiro* 156 (387), (April–June 1995): 331–41.

in abstract principles of a "pact of submission," a foundational moral reciprocity between kings and subjects, with the former upholding implicit norms of the latter in return for fealty. This is why insurgents often vowed to kill "corrupt" officials even though they were simply carrying out ministerial orders, while proclaiming their undying loyalty to the king.

Most often, the moral order can be found at work in the daily, prosaic activities of governance. With all the protest, subversion, and insurrection of the 1780s, it is easy to miss the underlying, deeply entrenched resistance to imperial reform as it introduced greater autonomy to merchants and the uncertainties of market competition. In the town of Pasto, in the southern highlands of Nueva Granada, grain prices crept upward in the early 1780s. On the heels of so much unrest across the Andes, officials grew alarmed. Pasto's mayor appealed to the governor for the power to restore ceilings on prices that had been left to float as part of the shift to greater commercial freedom. Moreover, he wanted the power to force merchants to open their granaries to sell their stocks. On the surface, the local official was seeking to restore a "just price" for subsistence goods, "for the common good and for the poor." Later in the appeal what Pasto's municipal council wanted was to be able to set prices for foodstuffs in accordance with local conditions and norms, and not let prices be set by private agents. The governor acceded: "distribute them [the grains and flour stores] to support the Public, charging the prices that you consider normal to balance the needs of the *vecindario* [the citizens] as well as to ensure the regular but not excessive profits of farmers." This customary sovereignty of local colonial societies was what imperialists and merchants wanted to shake up in the name of giving new life to the Portuguese or Spanish "nation." In practice, it was much harder to replace inherited, moral vestiges with new rational foundations for the conduct of imperial affairs without undermining local, decentered but shared assumptions about sovereignty and justice.[67]

Late imperial unrest was not—with Tiradentes' foiled plot being an exception that proved a more general rule of fidelity to the ancien régime—the precursor to colonial independence. This is not to deny that creoles expressed nativist, anticolonial reactions to peninsular policies. Nor does this deny that peninsulars saw in colonial unrest a warning sign that the imperium could not count on the loyalty of its colonial parts. In the wake of the Andean revolts, José de Abalos, the intendant of

---

[67]AGNB, Colonia, Cabildos, VI, ff. 1–35 (1785); J. C. Chiaramonte, "Modificaciones del Pacto Imperial," in Annino, Leiva, and Guerra, comps., *De los imperios a las naciones*, pp. 108–11; Mario Góngora, *Studies in the Colonial History of Spanish America* (Cambridge: Cambridge University Press, 1975), pp. 170–84; Serulnikov, *Subverting Colonial Authority*, pp. 122–31.

Venezuela, warned that America's "incomparable riches generally provoke ambition and avarice, and the genius and character of its *natu-rales* . . . gives them innate proclivities and inclinations to uprisings." But readers should not assume that reactive, local processes anticipated the evolution of nativism into nationalism. Abalos went so far as to suggest that the monarch consider letting the Andean and River Plate colonies go and become independent monarchies (tied by commonwealth kinship to the Spanish throne) not because colonials wanted national rule but because they were so costly to rule. Much less should the unrest of the 1780s be seen as episodes that sowed the seeds of independence that would flower in the nineteenth century. These were not, in short, mass movements that pointed to a future alternative world. Rather, they were complex local responses to—and checks on—the peninsular model of nation building through empire. Peasants, local counselors, priests, and native chiefs warned colonial authorities of the dangers of shifting the burden of imperial adaptation to local colonial communities—and when the going got really tough, they often joined the protestors and insurgents. The warnings and the violence were important signs that Iberian efforts to reconstitute the foundations of monarchical sovereignty ran up against the delicacy of colonial compromises at the imperial fringes.[68]

CONCLUSION

Efforts to rationalize the empires to defend Iberian sovereignty fastened on a deal between imperial authorities at the center and merchants scattered across the entrepôts of the empires. In a fundamental sense, they achieved their goal of increasing the flow of commercial traffic through private hands and official revenues to the public purse. In this fashion, both Portuguese and Spanish reformers could claim, with some justification, that they had created European nations by way of empire. The metropoles of old monarchies were becoming nations—and the provinces of the old empire were on the road to becoming colonies imagined as part of Atlantic commercial orders. This process was hardly complete, and with the revolts of the 1780s, it stalled.

---

[68]"Representación del intendente de Venezuela, Jose de Abalos, dirigida a Carlos III," in *Premoniciones de la independencia de América: Las refleciones de José de Abalos y el Conde Aranda sobre la situación de la América española a finales del siglo XVIII* (Madrid: Ed. Doce Calles, 2003), pp. 59–65; Sergio Serulnikov, "Customs and Rules: Bourbon Rationalizing Projects and Social Conflicts in Northern Potosí during the 1770s," *Colonial Latin American Review* 8:2 (1999): 245–48.

Whether this was a pause or a permanent halt, we will never know since the outbreak of the French Revolution redirected the course of imperial histories. Still, reform yielded important changes. Until the 1760s, military setbacks followed by unstable treaties had undermined the confidence in Iberian monarchies as world powers. Thereafter, concerted reform did give rise to the hope that the nation could be saved because it had an empire that was potentially more lucrative, and certainly more faithful, to the monarchy, especially compared to Spain and Portugal's rivals. Centralizing pressures in the French and especially British empires braced them more effectively for large-scale warfare—but they also began to crack under the weight of the escalating clashes. There were, of course, analogous pressures and reactions in the Iberian empires, but the metropoles backed off lest colonial resistances evolve into anti-imperial revolts. What could not be doubted was that the Iberian empires were more integrated on the eve of the French Revolution than they had been at the beginning of the century.[69]

Note the emphasis on integration, not centralization, of empires. Iberian imperial reformers were more concerned with the former than the latter. To defend the realms, enlightened ministers and political economists in Lisbon and Madrid sought to aggrandize the state by recalibrating the balance of power with the dominant elements of society: the puissant merchant elites in the entrepôts. In this sense, imperial reform involved modifying the relationships and compromises that upheld the empires, not doing away with them altogether. The reforms had marked effects, especially in the commercial hubs in the colonies. From Cartagena to Rio de Janeiro and Buenos Aires, powerful merchant classes overseeing institutional and informal networks of influence and social clout pushed the capillaries of exchange deeper into the South American hinterlands. This meant that while the empires were more integrated to serve the nation, they were also decentered to the commercial hubs and merchants circles that occupied such privileged locations in the reform model. If the needs of war pushed the imperial parts closer together, the commercial dynamics unleashed by competition and freer trade began to pull them apart.

On the eve of the French Revolution, contrapuntal forces were at work within the Portuguese and Spanish empires. Balancing them could be sustained as long as the peninsular capitals stayed out of serious trouble. This would soon change. When the outbreak of revolution in 1789

---

[69]Linda Colley, *Britons: Forging the Nation, 1707–1837* (New Haven: Yale University Press, 1992); Marshall, "A Nation Defined by Empire," for contrasts with nation building in Britain.

transformed the nature of European conflict from a rivalry between imperial dynasties into an ideological contest over the concept of dynasty itself, the contrapuntal tensions within the Iberian empires widened—and threatened their negotiated harmony. But before revolutionary warfare could deliver its full effects on the Atlantic system, imperial rulers, in a fateful convergence with the merchants of empire, would put their stamp on one more major reform. If silver and gold flows had been the primary arteries of the imperial nervous systems since the Conquest, there was a traffic that was thriving in the eighteenth century, and which motivated an intensified scramble for profits of the Iberian Atlantic: the slave trade. It is to the slave trade and the effects of integrating Europe, the Americas, and Africa into a more intense, if violent and gruesome, exchange between the regional components of the Iberian empires that we now turn.

2　Capitalism and Slavery on Imperial Hinterlands

The stresses and strains of defending models of European sovereignty in the New World had profound effects on the labor systems of the Americas. The spread of market forces through empire intensified the reliance on a range of bonded labor systems, especially slavery. This combustible mixture of heightened interimperial struggles and expanded slavery decisively shaped the fates of the Iberian empires. When Spain's ruler, Carlos III, passed away on the eve of the French Revolution, he did not live to witness how the social geography of African slavery in the New World would change dramatically over the ensuing decades. Slavery and the slave trade would reach their acme, and then plunge New World societies into centuries of unresolved debate and conflict over the meanings of freedom in multiracial societies. Indeed, the hyperexpansion of slavery and the slave trade enabled colonial economies to become freer from metropoles because they were becoming more dependent on unfree labor.

The fates of slaves in the New World were intimately tied up with the fates of Europe's struggling mercantilist empires. Some accounts, like R. R. Palmer's classic, *The Age of Democratic Revolution*, skirts the slave question altogether to preserve a pristine narrative of a struggle for democracy against aristocracy.[1] Yet some historians have integrated the significance of bonded labor and the profits of the Atlantic slave trade into an analysis of the transformations of Atlantic capitalism and its institutional bulwarks. Eric Williams's classic, *Slavery and Capitalism,* aims to explain the relations between the histories of slave production with the trajectories of old empires. His much-cited phrase, "the rise and fall of mercantilism is the rise and fall of slavery," connects the history of capitalism with that of liberalism: the transformation of capitalism required slavery to generate postfeudal profits, but then unleashed technological and social changes that soon made slavery an impediment to the industrial revolution.[2]

---

[1] Palmer, *The Age of Democratic Revolution*. Palmer leaves slavery and abolition out of his analysis. Saint Domingue does not even appear in the index.

[2] Eric Williams, *Capitalism and Slavery* (Chapel Hill: University of North Carolina Press, 1944), pp. 136, 172. For a suggestive review, see Thomas Holt, "Explaining Abolitionism," *Journal of Social History* 24:2 (1990): 371–78; and Thomas Bender's introduction to Bender,

Much ink has been spilled in a debate about the relationship between the demise of slavery and the transformation of capitalism. Seymour Drescher delivered a seminal blow in 1977 with *Econocide*, taking issue with the fundamental assumption that slavery was doomed because it could not keep up. In Drescher's view, there was nothing inevitable about its demise; British slavery was abolished despite, not because of, economic forces. Yet Drescher saw *some* relationship between capitalism and the demise of slavery, but stressed the autonomy of sensibilities and social networks of actors that cannot be simply reduced to class location.[3] In a similar way, David Eltis found slavery productive and for slave traders lucrative. Indeed, as the industrial revolution shifted into high gear, so did the traffic in slaves. The slave trade "was killed when its significance to the Americas and to a lesser extent to Europe, was greater than at any point in its history."[4] In this alternative to the Williams thesis, antislavery and economic self-interest were fundamentally at odds; interests had to adjust to ideology—not the other way around.

That there was some relationship between the legal decline of the slave trade and the evolution of state systems in the Atlantic world is not in doubt. *What* the relationship was turns on two critical issues. First, the interests of merchant capital did not mold to some abstract ideal of "free markets" but the organization of profitable production based on coerced labor. It mattered how dominant classes made their fortunes, whether the traffic in slaves was integral or not to the emerging model of capitalism. But models of capitalism also depended on institutions. Specifically, political authorities capable of transforming claims into legally enforceable rights determined the course of capitalism's and slavery's evolution. The second issue therefore was the degree to which planters and merchants participated in state institutions and wielded power over imperial policy. The importance of these two variables is clear when looking at the Iberian Atlantic, where the fortunes of merchant capital and imperial authority molded to the opportunities of expanding

---

ed., *The Anti-Slavery Debate* (Berkeley: University of California Press, 1992), pp. 1–12. David Brion Davis gives more autonomy to the role of ideology. Abolitionists, in Davis's view, were ideologists of a bourgeois social order integrated by contracts, not coercion. David Brion Davis, *The Problem of Slavery in the Age of Revolution, 1770–1823* (New York: Oxford University Press, 1999).

[3] Seymour Drescher, *From Slavery to Freedom: Comparative Studies in the Rise and Fall of Atlantic Slavery* (London: Macmillan, 1999), esp. pp. 1–15, and for his reflections on Williams, see the accompanying essay, "Eric Williams: British Capitalism and British Slavery," pp. 355–78. For an important account of the primacy of ideology and state intervention, see Howard Temperley, "Capitalism, Slavery and Ideology," *Past and Present* 75 (May 1977): 94–118.

[4] David Eltis, *Economic Growth and the Ending of the Transatlantic Slave Trade* (Oxford: Oxford University Press, 1987), p. 15.

commercial hinterlands to reconstitute imperial ties by intensifying the use of bonded labor. The result was that merchant capital in the colonies acquired unprecedented voice and control over the imperial policies.

This chapter challenges one of the underlying assumptions in the debate about slavery and empire. Most accounts stress the abolition of the slave trade as a precursor to the abolition of slavery, and that this occurred fundamentally in metropolitan capitals like London.[5] Either way, the metropolitan assumption focuses on decisions made in Europe as if capitalists and abolitionists, the interested and the disinterested in slavery, were based in the imperial heartlands, not colonial hinterlands. What this chapter will show is how critical slavery and the slave trade were in restructuring the balance between colonies and metropoles, and thus reshaping the coalitions and policy regimes that dominated the empires. The peripheries, as we shall see, were hardly peripheral to the survival of the Iberian empires.[6]

THE SLAVE HINTERLANDS OF SOUTH AMERICA

Imperial fortunes were made on the backs of slaves and dependent laborers. Along the coasts of South America, following river valleys into the interiors, and even in gold and silver mines, African slavery provided the labor for the production of trade goods that flowed throughout local, regional, and transatlantic markets. Care is needed in characterizing the labor systems of the imperial hinterlands as the conditions that supported merchants and monarchs across the Atlantic. The features of slavery in South America shaped the nature of merchant capital—and the place of merchant capitalists in the broader imperial makeup. The importance of slavery did not imply ubiquitous large-scale plantations. Nor did it involve the direct exercise of metropolitan power to reproduce the slave system. In contrast to images of the "plantation complex," coercive labor systems in Latin America displayed remarkable variety, autonomy, and internal dynamism. What is more, its dynamism, rooted in autonomous commercial networks and flexible labor systems, placed the interests of expanding slavery in Portuguese and Spanish colonies in a strong position when the

---

[5]David Eltis, *The Rise of African Slavery in the Americas* (Oxford: Oxford University Press, 2000), p. 273.

[6]Christopher Schmidt-Nowara, *Empire and Anti-Slavery: Spain, Cuba, and Puerto Rico, 1833–1874* (Pittsburgh: University of Pittsburgh Press, 1999); Thomas Holt, *The Problem of Freedom: Race, Labor, and Politics in Jamaica and Britain, 1832–1938* (Baltimore: Johns Hopkins University Press, 1992); Robin Blackburn, *The Overthrow of Colonial Slavery, 1776–1848* (London: Verso, 1988).

Caribbean plantation complex began to explode in the 1790s. Indeed, in part because the Caribbean dominated European attention, South Americans could create their own slave systems based on autonomous commercial networks and fueled by colonial merchant capital. The result: the slave trade was part of a diversified commercial network from the Greater Caribbean to the River Plate. Staples included rum, tobacco, coffee, textiles, dyestuffs, hides, jerked beef, flour, and wheat, as well as raw and refined sugar, cotton, gold, and a vast array of primary goods, like cassava, for local or regional consumption. The old standbys, gold and silver, remained vital but were surrounded by ever more diverse and decentralized commercial hubs.[7]

South American slavery was a system of accumulation made up of plantations, estates, and mines within societies that included a wide spectrum of forms of bondage and dependency. It functioned within an amalgam of coercion and consent. It could be argued, drawing on Ira Berlin, that South America's expanding hinterlands were slave societies (not simply societies with slaves) where slaves were central to productive processes. Plantations existed, but they were embedded in more diversified social systems. But there is more. Slavery was central to productive processes—but it by no means was an exclusive marker; slave labor contributed to the reproduction of a hybrid system of enlisting labor. In this sense, slavery helped support rapidly commercialized, relatively diffused, and adaptive production in the South American hinterlands integrated by the flow of merchant capital. And as it did so, it helped colonies become increasingly autonomous, economically and socially, from metropolitan Spanish and Portuguese command—in contrast to "plantation" societies whose colonial ties became ever more dependent.[8]

Being part of a hybrid labor system does not diminish the significance of enslavement to colonial political economies. The expansion of slavery through the South American colonies was part of the drive to renovate the imperial pacts between colonies and metropoles, between merchants and monarchs, because slave labor was essential to invigorate the rentier-revenue machinery of the empires. One of the reasons why slavery was so important to the renovation of imperial sovereignty is because it was so adaptive to local and temporal circumstances. Consider the Captaincy General of Venezuela, whose littoral was supposed to become Spain's

---

[7]Steve Stern, "Feudalism, Capitalism, and the World System in the Perspective of Latin America and the Caribbean," *American Historical Review* 93:4 (1988): 829–72. On the plantation complex, see Philip Curtin, *The Rise and Fall of the Plantation Complex: Essays in Atlantic History* (Cambridge: Cambridge University Press, 1990), esp. pp. 11–12.

[8]Ira Berlin, *Many Thousands Gone: The First Two Centuries of Slavery in North America* (Cambridge, MA: Harvard University Press, 1998), pp. 8–9.

chief nonmining company colony in the eighteenth century producing staples for export, especially cacao and sugar. Instead, the dismantling of the Caracas Company in 1778 revealed a commercialized society of a few plantations surrounded by smaller-scale commodity production relying on mixed labor systems. In the interior *llanos*, frontiersmen ran a cattle economy rounding up feral livestock to harvest hides and cured meats. Slaves and freed colored populations fled or migrated out of the coastal range to join the plebeian workforces as both free and slave workers. They combined subsistence harvesting with contracting their labor to hacendados. By the end of the century, the llanos population was dominated by mobile and mounted *castas*, *pardos*, and blacks, for whom the frontier offered the possibility of escape from wage labor and slavery; but this frontier also used slaves alongside free workers. The hybridity of labor, however, did not stultify production for the market. On the contrary, only through the use of hybrid workforces could hacendados apply labor to the land for commodity production. As a result, the former cacao belt that dominated production until the 1780s gave way to indigo, coffee, tobacco, cotton, and sugar production, some for export, some for sale in the internal market. The large estate did not dominate rural society. Very few cacao planters had estates with over 30,000 trees; over half had fewer than 5,000. Tobacco and coffee, meanwhile, the emerging staples of the period, came from small and medium-sized estates. On all of these estates, owners relied on domestic labor, hired workers, and slaves. Late colonial Venezuela was a diversified and commercialized society dominated by a very impure form of estate-based bonded labor. In this fashion, slave, indentured, and free labor expanded the commercial frontier into the Venezuelan hinterland. The nature of this hinterland, and its market revolution, had a decisive effect on the slave trade that sustained it. Coastal estates, large and small, had to keep reinfusing slaves from Africa to compensate for the drainage of slaves to the frontier and the failure to reproduce slave stocks on the coast.[9]

Venezuela's hybrid labor systems for producing staples characterized much of hinterland South America. Moving west into the viceroyalty of New Granada, slave production sprang up along the Caribbean coast, growing more prominent from the nodules of Río Hacha and Santa Marta to the entrepôt region of Cartagena de Indias. From Cartagena, slavery expanded up the Magdalena River and especially the Cauca River. In the Occidental watershed of the Cauca, an eighteenth-century gold boom created an inland slave society such that by 1778, 60 percent

---

[9]McKinley, *Pre-revolutionary Caracas*, pp. 35–42, 46–54.

of the region's slaves worked in gold extraction. Placer gold was the viceroyalty's most important export and relied on small gangs of slaves owned by modest concessionaires who extracted alluvial deposits from scattered encampments. Slave gangs, or *cuadrillas*, seldom surpassed thirty, and very few larger-scale enterprises emerged. Prospectors combined slave and free labor in panning, crushing, washing, and very primitive refining. The Antioquian highlands and the Pacific lowland extractive centers created demand for foodstuffs and leather goods from the region, and infused some liquidity into agrarian production. Farmers and small manufacturers echoed miners' reliance on slaves to complement domestic and hired workers. The gold boom also drew attention to the potential of coastal estates: sugar, rum, and tobacco production created agrarian hinterlands around the ports, especially Cartagena. But few of these coastal estates deployed over fifty slaves. Manuel Escobar's four haciendas combined had fewer than two hundred slaves, producing molasses and aguardiente. Manuel Canabal's hacienda, San Pablo, possibly the largest sugar estate of the coast, had 101 slaves in 1780. And these were the upper-bound extremes. Otherwise, coastal estates were much more modest. Indeed, the largest estates of the viceroyalty were in the south and were owned mainly by religious orders, using a combination of indigenous workers, slaves, and creole *montañeses*.[10]

Brazilian gold mining had a similar effect, relying on scattered, modest concentrations of slave camps that commercialized an entire colony and spread slave production throughout the countryside. By the middle of the eighteenth century, Portugal's possessions had long since broken out of their northeastern littoral pockets. Moving inward created more frontier-type slave societies. Gold, as well as diamond placer mines, popped up all over Minas Gerais. Prospectors deployed fairly rustic tools to cull sludge from riverbanks or to pan the entire watercourse in search of flakes and grains of gold. Diamond mining was even more primitive, decentralized, and undercapitalized. Most of the labor was done by slaves, mainly from the Bight of Benin, and as in other frontier societies physical and social mobility prevented a slavocrat oligarchy from emerging. Frontier mining also commercialized the interior and southern flanks of the colony. To service the teeming miners and their labor forces, commercial cattle grazing and agriculture spread, artisanal industries appeared, and Portuguese settlers began to migrate into the interior. As in New Granada, many newcomers on the margins of the mining sectors

---

[10]Alfonso Múnera, *El fracaso de la nación: Región, clase y raza en el Caribe colombiano (1717–1890)* (Bogotá: Banco de la República, 1998), p. 89; Twinam, *Miners, Merchants and Farmers in Colonial Colombia,* pp. 31–44; McFarlane, *Colombia before Independence,* pp. 71–83.

themselves used slaves as complements to domestic and hired labor. So significant was the demographic and commercial effect of the gold boom that the crown relocated the colony's capital from Salvador to Rio de Janeiro in 1763. By 1800, Minas Gerais had the largest slave population of any South American province.[11]

Decentralized and household-based commercial production began to spread southward along the Brazilian littoral. Across the eighteenth century, coastal regions saw their initial cattle-grazing economies give way to arable agriculture for the production of staples for a local market. Even sugar estates (278 of them by 1783) grew up around the colonial capital of Rio de Janeiro in the Campos dos Goitacazes. Half of the Rio captaincy's population in 1789 was slave, some 82,448, and it would double in the next thirty years. Still, slave ownership was decentralized. In this conjuncture, plantations of over fifty slaves accounted for around half of all the slaves owned, and the concentration of slave production was most acute in the sugar mills. But most sugar output came not from the large *engenhos* but from smaller ones. The other half of the district's slaves worked on smaller-scale units, in the coffee farms dotting the Paraíba Valley and in market gardens producing manioc, dairy products, beans, and jerked beef for sale in nearby towns. Slavery in mines and plantations created a growing internal market for smaller-scale enterprises that soon came to employ roughly the same number of slaves as the export sectors. In these internal market-oriented sectors, mixed labor systems of domestic and slave work prevailed. In the Rio captaincy, 72 percent of farmers owned between one and five slaves in 1804 and possessed over a third of the region's slaves. Thus, in what would become the core of nineteenth-century Brazilian slavery, the old view of a bipolar society of slaves ruled by a small Portuguese aristocracy misses both the complexity of the labor systems and the local dynamism of petty slave-owning capitalism. Where slavery was most dynamic in Brazil it was not dominated by a plantation complex. One recent study of the Recôncavo, in the old sugar belt around the Bay of All Saints, shows just how diversified market production was: sugar, tobacco, cotton, and the ubiquitous cassava were all produced for local, littoral, and transoceanic markets in small, medium, and large units. Indeed, well into the recovery of sugar plantations in the eighteenth century, most Bahian

---

[11]Júnia Ferreira Furtado, *Homens de Negocio: A interiorização da metropole e do comércio nas minas setecentistas* (São Paulo: Hucitec, 1999), pp. 149–69; Kathleen J. Higgins, *"Licentious Liberty" in a Brazilian Gold Mining Region: Slavery, Gender and Social Control in Eighteenth-Century Sabaná, Minas Gerais* (University Park: Penn State University Press, 1994); A.J.R. Russell-Wood, "Colonial Brazil: The Gold Cycle, c. 1690–1750," in Bethell, ed., *Cambridge History of Latin America* v. 2, pp. 578–81.

slaves were the property of small producers, and most slave owners had fewer than five slaves. Even in the hardcore sugar county of Cachoeira, what dominated was mixed agrarian production with an assortment of landed units. Moreover, as plantations spread more thoroughly across the northwestern littoral, they grafted onto existing heterogeneous forms of organizing property relations.[12]

Slavery played a similar role in the delta of the River Plate, where local and regional markets fanned into the grasslands of the Pampas. Concentric belts of specialized production surrounded the main ports of Montevideo and Buenos Aires. Market gardening in the immediate urban environs was the business of a mosaic of small producers owning one or two slaves to supplement domestic household labor. Further afield, farming gave way to cattle grazing. Many estates combined the production of wheat, wool, hides, and beef to service local and distant markets alike. If the landed structure was heterogeneous, so too was the demand for staples, coming from local, regional, and increasingly international sources. What promoted frontier expansion was demand for hides and jerked beef for sale in the Andean interior, or to the larger slave societies of Brazil (and later the Caribbean). The exports of hides doubled between the mid-eighteenth to the end of the century, cities grew, and so did local demand for foodstuffs. The labor systems were as complex and evolving as trade networks. As with all these hinterland arrangements, they had to contend with and adapt to perpetual scarcity of workers. The largest single variable expenditure for River Plate estate owners was on labor, mainly for the employ of peons in spiked seasonal demand. But local peons were not always the most reliable of workers, especially as many had access to frontier resources for their own subsistence. Purchase of slaves gave producers a measure of labor stability. Slave and free labor worked within the same landed units, slaves often taking care of year-round work while peons took care of moments of heavy demand, like the harvest or slaughter seasons. Accordingly, slave and free labor complemented each other, rather than operated as substitutes. Combined, as in other hinterlands of South America, the form of slave labor made Pampean estates flexible and adaptive units of

---

[12]Stuart Schwartz, *Sugar Plantations in the Formation of Brazilian Society: Bahia, 1550–1835* (Cambridge: Cambridge University Press, 1985), pp. 439–51; Castro Faria, *A Colônia em movimento*, pp. 50–53; João Luis Ribeiro Fragoso, *Homens de grossa aventura: Acumulação e hierarquia na praça mercantil do Rio de Janeiro (1790–1830)* (Rio de Janeiro: Arquivo Nacional, 1992), pp. 76–117; B. J. Barickman, *A Bahian Counterpoint: Sugar, Tobacco, Cassava, and Slavery in the Recôncavo, 1780–1860* (Stanford: Stanford University Press, 1998), pp. 128–51.

production for very unstable but rapidly developing markets for staples; slaves were not obstacles to commercialized production but enabled it to flourish.[13]

Slavery supported and coexisted with several other labor forms, all of which expanded together, even where plantations were prominent features of the social landscape, such as northeast Brazil. Throughout the slave littoral then, commercial agriculture and grazing enhanced the fortunes of South American colonies. These fortunes did not rely on metropolitan investments or privileged access to metropolitan markets, unlike the British or French Caribbean colonies. Slavery afforded a highly elastic and flexible system which, depending on political events, could adapt to new commercial circumstances. Indeed, it is increasingly clear that slaves themselves contributed to the commercial vibrancy of the South American littorals. They not only worked on estates and farms, they were actively involved in farming, animal husbandry, fishing, artisanal work, and marketing on their own provision grounds or as fugitives. In Stuart Schwartz's words, slaves may have been treated like slaves, but they often behaved like commercial peasants; indeed, in many slave counties slaves blurred into peasant producers, and thus fudged the dichotomy between peasant and export agriculture. In short, there was no major South American colonial society that had plantation enclaves producing for distant markets within more general self-sufficient, autarkic societies.[14] This old dualized image of colonial societies obscures the internal dynamism within slave-based economies. It also prevents us from understanding the dynamics of merchant capitalism across the Iberian Atlantic, which enhanced the autonomy of capital accumulation within South America.

---

[13]Samuel Amaral, "Rural Production and Labor in Late Colonial Buenos Aires," *Journal of Latin American Studies* 19:2 (1987): 259–75; Juan Carlos Garavaglia, "De la carne al cuero: Los mercados para los productos pecuarios (Buenos Aires y su campaña, 1700–1825)," *Anuario del Instituto Estudios de Histórico-Sociales* 9 (1994): 61–96; idem "Las charcras y quintas de Buenos Aires: Ejido y campaña, 1750–1815," in Raúl Mandrini and Andrea Reguera, comps., *Huellas en la tierra: Indios, agricultores, y hacendados en la Pampa bonaerense* (Tandil: Instituto de Estudios Histórico-Sociales, 1993), pp. 121–146, and "La agricultura del trigo en las estancias de la campaña bonaerense," in *Huellas*, pp. 91–120; Jorge Gelman, "Sobre esclavos, peones, gauchos y campesinos: El trabajo y los trabajadores en una estancia colonial rioplatense," in Garavaglia and Gelman, *El mundo rural rioplatense a fines de la época colonial* (Buenos Aires: Biblos, 1989), pp. 48–59.

[14]Schwartz, *Sugar Plantations*, pp. 252, 328–35; idem, *Slaves, Peasants and Rebels: Reconsidering Brazilian Slavery* (Urbana: University of Illinois Press, 1992), pp. 66–84; Barickman, "A Bit of Land, Which They Call *Roça*," *Hispanic American Historical Review* 74:4 (November 1994): 653–69.

REGULATING THE SLAVE TRADE

As slave production spread through the South American hinterlands, American-based merchant capitalists increasingly formed the entrepreneurial foundations for the Atlantic slave trade. The slave trade reinforced growing, and ever more autonomous, commercial networks whose power resided in the archipelago of American port cities. These ports were the entrepôts between New World hinterlands, their export markets, and African labor supplies. Indeed, the expansion of South American production for local and regional markets helped shift control over the slave trade ever more to the fringe.

These transformations were, in a sense, the culmination of a problem posed by the legal foundations of the sovereign empires. The 1494 Treaty of Tordesillas sowed the seeds of a problem, for it reinforced an earlier ban on Spain's rights to establishing its own slaving outposts in Africa, and thus required that any economy reliant on slave labor meant dependence on cargos of Africans shipped in foreign bottoms. So long as Spain tried to thwart foreign penetration *within* its dominions, it could not fully realize the possibilities of expanding staple frontiers in the New World hinterlands because slaves had to come from *outside* them. The solution for Spain, starting in 1595, was the licensing of contracts to firms (increasingly foreign) to ship slaves from Africa straight to the colonies. For the Portuguese, of course, the problem was the converse: the treaty gave Lisbon a privileged position in the early slave trade without ensuring Lisbon's resources to control it. Thus, when Portugal decided to "liberate" Angola from Dutch occupants in 1648, the monarchy dispatched Salvador Correia de Sá to Rio de Janeiro to muster the troops, money, and vessels for the expedition. Without Brazilian merchants' support, the Portuguese would not have been able to recover Luanda and Benguela; the most important source of slaves for South America would have been in the hands of rivals. Neither metropolis could exercise its hegemony over the slave trade that was so vital for colonial expansion. The exercise of control over the slave trade for both empires was tied up with the balance of power between the metropoles and the colonies—bolstering the slave trade invariably meant ceding economic power, if not political authority, to the fringes.[15]

In fits and starts, policies governing the Iberian slave trade to the colonies sacrificed traditional mercantilist principles and adapted to the

---

[15]Walker, *Spanish Politics and Imperial Trade*, pp. 12–13; C. R. Boxer, *Salvador de Sá and the Struggle for Brazil and Angola, 1602–1686* (London: Athlone Press, 1952); Maria da Graça A. Mateus Ventura, *Negreiros Portugueses na Rota das Índias de Castela (1541–1556)* (Lisboa: Edições Colibri, 1999).

priority of promoting colonies as export zones based on African labor. Regulating the slave trade was more than just a component of imperial defense; it was a centerpiece of the effort to reintegrate the parts of the empires. More and more, as the eighteenth century unfolded, arguments about the slave trade provided the elements of a new model of empire premised on a different idea of colonialism—which made the slaving hinterlands the frontiers of Iberian revival. The commander of Spanish forces along the Cartagena coast, Antonio Narváez y la Torre, urged colonial authorities to free the slave trade from all remaining mercantilist restrictions. His urgings were prophetic. Slaves offered distinct advantages, argued Narváez, over Indians, mestizo, or creole peons. "Blacks born and raised in African, more tropical, climates have a toughness necessary for their resilience. To this is added, by their docile social nature, greater acceptance of their subjection to slavery, and in the arduous application of labor they learn and exercise their tasks with greater care and perfection. Without a daily wage, and once purchased, they do not inflict any more costs than their maintenance, which is very limited, and thus work more cheaply and are more useful." Writing in Cartagena in 1778, Narváez's model was Saint Domingue, and he pointed to the French colony as an exemplar of what the Colombian coast could become with an influx of Africans. "How much more reason does politics require . . . to facilitate by all means possible the entry of blacks, and see them as raw material among other raw materials to make America produce?"[16]

The long tradition of Spanish governance of the slave trade, founded on the contractual monopoly, the asiento, was never perfect or hermetic. At best, it was a makeshift compromise to cover for the dilemma bequeathed by Tordesillas: let only a select few foreigners partake of the slave trade to Spanish possessions. Of course, it left the colonists with an insatiable demand for more slave workers to rely on their own, often illegal devices to match supply with demand. After the middle of the eighteenth century, Spanish rulers recognized the importance of slavery to American colonial economies. Arguments that Spanish and Portuguese colonial authorities needed to liberate merchant and hacendado access to slaves dated back to the immediate post-asiento years. Once the asiento

---

[16]Antonio Narváez y la Torre, "Provincia de Santa Marta y Río Hacha del Virreynato de Santa Fé" (May 19, 1778), in Sergio Elías Ortíz, *Escritos de dos economistas coloniales* (Bogotá: Banco de la República, 1965), pp. 20–23; Jsuan Hipólito Vieytes, "Prospecto" (September 1, 1802) in his *Antecedentes económicos de la revolución de mayo* (Buenos Aires: Ed. Raigal, 1956), pp. 137–40; Jorge Palacios Preciado, *La trata de negros por Cartagena de Indias (1650–1750)* (Tunja: Universidad Pedagogica y Tecnologica de Colombia, 1973).

contract with the South Sea Company elapsed, the crown considered reissuing the deal to new bidders, but quickly abandoned the idea of slave-trade monopoly altogether. The reform of the Spanish slave trade followed the same pattern as trade policy more generally, dropping obstacles to infra-imperial trade and giving colonies access to their own means to generate commercial rents, with the objective of increasing the total traffic within the Spanish Atlantic. In 1777, around the same time that Narváez was penning his recommendations in Cartagena, in Madrid the Council of the Indies issued an important ruling designed to reverse the perceived decay in imperial trade, with an eye to promoting the development of the littoral belts. These provinces wallowed due to labor shortages, "for lack of slaves." There should be fewer obstacles to shipping slaves to these districts, the council believed.[17]

The issue was, how? Since this was the only large-scale Atlantic traffic to which Spain did not have some significant access, an opening might lure rival Europeans to exploit their participation in the slave trade to gain access to Spanish American precious metals. The solution echoed the 1765 and 1778 comercio libre decrees: let slave traders operate independently, but monitor them by licensing slave ships to enter and leave ports. Spanish and creole slavers had to obey certain restrictions—like prohibitions on carrying foreign merchandise, using only Spanish bottoms—but provided they were met, they could get permission to carry slaves into colonial ports. Moreover, since merchants had to cover the considerable costs of the enterprise (hire vessels, pay factors in Africa, and liquidate their debts), the ruling also allowed them to take New World staples out of ports. These exports could fetch cash payments or could be used in direct exchange to procure slaves on the African littoral. The ruling emphasized the role of "combined commerce"—in effect tying the export economies of the colonial littorals to the importation of African labor. Like comercio libre, the ruling was a compromise to revitalize Spanish mercantilism while at the same time conceding commercial autonomy and internal dynamism to the colonies.[18]

Slave trading within the Portuguese empire was an altogether different enterprise—thanks in large part to Tordesillas's conferring to Portugal claims to Africa, early trading posts along the Guinea coast, and deeper penetration into the hinterlands of Angola. Moreover, guild monopolies

---

[17]AGI, Estado, Americas, 86A, 14, "Dictámen leido en Consejo pleno con asistencia de su Governador en 12 de mayo de 1777 sobre el nuevo comercio de la Indias." Walker, *Spanish Politics and Imperial Trade*, pp. 215–25.

[18]Herbert S. Klein, *The Atlantic Slave Trade* (Cambridge: Cambridge University Press, 1999), pp. 38–39; Frederick P. Bowser, "Africans in Spanish American Colonial Society," in Bethell, ed., *Cambridge History of Latin America*, v. 2, pp. 362–64.

had never been enforced to the same degree within the Portuguese empire. The result: Portuguese claims along the African littoral meant that Luso-Brazilian merchants had long been participating in a vibrant slave trade in the South Atlantic. From the seventeenth century, colonial merchants had been operating across the Atlantic between Angola and Brazil—flaunting official stipulations that Lisbon be the clearinghouse for imperial trade. There was, however, little to be done. Not even the Marquis of Pombal tried to reverse colonial autonomy in the control of slave trading—indeed, in 1758, a royal order allowed direct trade between Brazil, Angola, and the Mina Coast (see fig. 2). There was, as one Lisbon merchant warned, some alarm that English, Indian, Arab, and Persian traders were making headway into Portuguese commercial bases in the Indian Ocean. The French were muscling in on Mauritius. The only way to preserve the Portuguese share of world commerce was to let the Brazilians have their way in the trade they knew best: the exchange for African slaves. By 1779, Lisbon instructed the governor of Angola to let Brazilians operate directly up and down the coast. This "freedom to trade" by colonial merchants was, the instructions noted, a legal recognition of a reality since the slave trade had "been taken over by Americans" already. As in Madrid, rulers in Lisbon aspired to promote imperial trade by expanding peripheral frontiers. The difference was a matter of degree: promoting imperial trade, when it came to trafficking in slaves, meant boosting colonial merchant capitalists.[19]

It is tempting to conclude that Lisbon and Madrid simply recognized the increasing autonomy of market forces once constrained by the Treaty of Tordesillas. There is some merit to this argument. The demise of the Iberian corner of the slave trade coincided with a change in demand and supply for slaves. Certainly, on the demand side, the imperial hinterlands relied more and more on slave laborers to produce staples destined for markets across the Atlantic world well beyond peninsular consumers. Indeed, it was not Europeans who sustained the demand for slave labor— it was Americans. Indeed, increasingly Americans acquired the means and commodities to finance their own demand. A 1782 report from Angola noted that Brazilian merchants maintained a robust business with slave

---

[19]ANTT, JC, Maço 62, Caixa 204, f. 1; AHU, CU, Código 962, ff. 137–42, "Sobre or requerimento de Ribeiro Hubens e Companhia," January 29, 1789; Código 549, ff. 2–25, "Instrucção para Joseph Gonçalo da Camara," June 22, 1779. For a superb survey, see de Alencastro, *O Trato dos Viventes*, and Joseph C. Miller, *Way of Death: Merchant Capitalism and the Angolan Slave Trade, 1730–1830* (Madison: University of Wisconsin Press, 1988). See AHU, Documentos Avulsos (hereafter DA), Caixa 121, docs. 25, 28 for sub rosa trade.

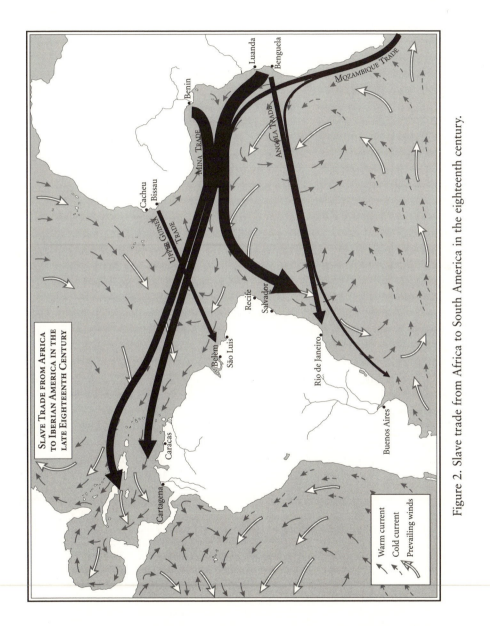

Figure 2. Slave trade from Africa to South America in the eighteenth century.

Inside the map:

SLAVE TRADE FROM AFRICA TO IBERIAN AMERICA IN THE LATE EIGHTEENTH CENTURY

MOZAMBIQUE TRADE

Luanda
Benguela

Benin

ANGOLA TRADE

MINA TRADE

Cacheu
Bissau

UPPER GUINEA TRADE

Recife
Salvador

Belém
São Luís

Rio de Janeiro

Caracas

Cartagena

Buenos Aires

Warm current
Cold current
Prevailing winds

factors simply by arriving with "wines, aguardientes, and gerebitas from Brazil which are introduced from that continent from all sorts of ports." We will see shortly how the trade goods of the South Atlantic shaped business organizations—suffice it to note here that the demand could be generated autonomously and did not depend on infusions of capital or commodities from Europe.[20]

On the supply side, there was an important shift in the locus of African trade from the Mina Coast to ports further south, especially to Angola and around the Cape to Mozambique. This coincided with a shifting balance of political forces in the African slaving frontiers. As British and French traders moved into the Dahomey districts, they pushed aside Portuguese factors who found themselves unable to compete with what they felt was more unruly, cutthroat competition. They withdrew further south into slave-harvesting territories where Luso-Brazilians could operate without rivals.[21] This was made easier by recurring warfare. The unity of the Kongo state crumbled after the Battle of Mbwila in 1665; warlords occupied the vacuum. Imbangala warrior princes thrived off the capture of villagers from the Mbundo lands south of the Kongo and the area around the Malebo pool on the Zaire River. Rising European imperial rivalry in Africa and the disaggregation of centralized monarchies into regional, feuding kingdoms released the competition to extract more chattel slaves from the interior.[22]

It would be misleading to leave the impression that peninsular rulers merely adapted to circumstances in the imperial hinterlands, as if sagacious monarchs in the capitals unilaterally unfettered market revolutions in the colonies. Dismantling the old system and replacing it with something new was, fundamentally, a response to the recomposition of ruling blocs of empires and an attempt to integrate colonial merchant classes into the political economy of Iberian rulership. What the demise of the Tordesillas order did do was reveal a powerful group of colonial merchants capable of forcing metropolitan authorities to adapt policy to their interests. In 1790, a group of merchants and planters in Pará filed a complaint with Lisbon authorities. They did not like having to rely on the licensed merchants from

---

[20]ANTT, JC, Maço 62, Caixa 202, f. date August 12, 1782; Eltis, *The Rise of African Slavery in the Americas*, p. 160.

[21]AHU, CU, Códice 255, September 22, 1758.

[22]Anne Hilton, *The Kingdom of Kongo* (Oxford: Oxford University Press, 1985), pp. 167–201; Paul E. Lovejoy, *Transformations in Slavery: A History of Slavery in Africa* (Cambridge: Cambridge University Press, 1983), pp. 73–74; Susan Herlin Broadhead, "Beyond Decline: The Kingdom of the Kongo in the Eighteenth and Nineteenth Centuries," *International Journal of African Historical Studies* 12:4 (1979): 615–50; John K. Thornton, *The Kingdom of the Kongo: Civil War and Transition, 1641–1718* (Madison: University of Wisconsin Press, 1983).

Brazil's main ports of Salvador and Rio de Janeiro since, they argued, they got the worst slaves, especially the Ladinos born in Brazil (who were disliked as "fractious and rebellious"), dumped on them. Rio and Bahia instead got the prized slaves imported directly from factories in Africa and shipped their inferior stocks to the Brazilian provinces. What Lisbon should do, the petition insisted, was open the trade completely, dispensing with licensing and special privileges for a select number of ports. Eventually they got their wish to import as they pleased directly from Africa—plus the removal of all duties on slave imports to Pará as a stimulus for agrarian production. "Deregulation" also affected metropolitan interests. In 1795, the Junta do Comércio in Lisbon informed royal ministers that "under the current circumstances it would be very convenient to alter the provisions" of the old restrictions on colonial merchants. The argument was that Lisbon could export more manufactures to Brazil if Brazil could ship more staples to and import more slaves from Africa. The junta urged that policies be adopted to promote greater intercolonial traffic between Brazil and Africa by reducing taxes and lifting stipulations that certain routes had to go through Lisbon. Authorities complied. In all, they supported the expansion of slave production as a means to promote imperial trade—even if it meant that metropolitan interests in the slave trade had to withdraw from its commercial bonanza.[23]

An even more dramatic change in policy took place in Spain's empire. It, too, involved the increasing role of colonial capitalists in the bargaining over the rules that governed the slave trade. In practice, viceroys and merchant guilds could issue special licenses for merchants—even, on occasion, foreign ones—to introduce slaves to Spanish American ports. For instance, in 1788, a partnership of Spanish, Dutch, and French merchants arranged an elaborate system for carrying slaves to Cartagena. They contracted the *Beaumont*, based in Nantes, to carry German rifles to Guinea, exchange them for slaves to be shipped to Cartagena, which would be swapped for dyewoods and brazilwood, 400 quintals of which would be unloaded in Saint Domingue before the *Beaumont* returned to Nantes. Occasionally, colonial authorities even signed contracts with specific merchants to import slaves. In 1786, officials in Cuba and Venezuela signed a deal with two Liverpool-based slavers, Peter Baker and John Dawson, to import between 5,000 and 6,000 slaves into the captaincies. But these kinds of deals required official approval and were not always tolerated, never mind encouraged. Indeed, the Baker and Dawson contract soon ran into trouble because one of the clauses allowed the British vessels to dock in the Spanish colonial ports for a

---

[23]ANTT, JC, Maço 10, Caixa 38, f. 14; AHU, CU, Códice 962, ff. 148–50.

maximum of only eight days. There was no way that the large slave cargos could be unloaded and staples could be loaded back onboard in such a short time. In due course, the contract led to litigation in Cuban and Venezuelan courts and eventually paralyzed much of the Spanish slave trade as merchants wanted to see how the dispute would be resolved.[24]

Each metropolitan solution, or concession to colonial pressure, yielded to more pressure, and thus accumulated into a sweeping new model of imperial trade: the traffic in slaves was the centerpiece to fuel merchant fortunes and to expand the commercial frontier into imperial hinterlands. In 1789, the Spanish king issued a temporary order to promote agricultural development in Venezuela, Cuba, Santo Domingo, and Puerto Rico by enabling merchants to buy slaves for sale in any port in these colonies. Slaves could be imported free of all duties, and could be paid for by exporting staples for sale in foreign ports provided the export value did not exceed the value of imported slaves. The same order permitted foreign merchants to introduce slaves to these Spanish colonial ports. Shortly thereafter, Martin Navarro, writing from London, informed the king's chief minister, Count Floridablanca, that foreign traders were interested in selling slaves to Spanish American traders, but that the opening had to be more general and durable. This was mild stuff compared to the pressure coming from the colonies that were still excluded from the order. Indeed, once it was clear that Venezuela got the concession, merchants in Montevideo, Buenos Aires, and Cartagena campaigned for inclusion in the deal. In 1784, the viceroy of the River Plate turned away a Brazilian slaver before it could unload its human cargo in Montevideo—to the consternation of the merchants who had contracted for the importation of six hundred Africans. The reason, so the viceroy's explanation went, was that the parties did not get permission beforehand. This provoked a futile uproar. So, once they got wind of the 1789 order, River Plate merchants argued that they should not be left out of favorable decrees applying to other colonies. Indeed, the viceroy was forced to admit to his superiors that his actions were not very effective since the coastal trade between the viceroyalty and Brazil was now booming beyond his regulatory oversight. He suggested that they might as well include the River Plate in the 1789 ordinance. Accordingly, in 1791 the order was extended to the Viceroyalties of the River Plate and Nueva Granada, and the concession to foreign traders extended for six more years. The Spanish policy aimed not just to promote the slave trade but also to spare officials from having to enforce pointless and infuriating rules.[25]

---

[24]AGI, Indiferente General (hereafter IG), Legajo 2822, May 26, 1788.
[25]AGI, IG, Legajo 1707, August 13, 1804; Legajo 2822, February 15, 1790; Legajo 2824, July 16, 1791, and April 30, 1791.

In the history of policymaking it is not always easy to say whether policies change practices or whether they legalize a de facto order. What can be said is that the commercial order that descended from the original division of the Atlantic world according to Tordesillas was more than exhausted. Once the prospect of expanding commercial prospects by extending slavery into imperial hinterlands dawned on metropolitan rulers and colonial merchants, it was hard to contain the pressure to dismantle the vestiges of the old Iberian systems. One of the unintended consequences was the increasing autonomy of the South Atlantic commercial exchanges. Each change in rules unblocked the pressure on these emerging networks. So when the European and North Atlantic trading networks got caught in the maelstrom of revolution and warfare, the South Atlantic was, as we shall see in the next section, functioning, indeed flourishing, on its own.

A SOUTH ATLANTIC SYSTEM

As colonial capitalists acquired more clout they reinforced a commercial system that tied the South Atlantic together. The Spanish colonies were important hinterlands for the South Atlantic system as suppliers of staples and almost insatiable consumers of African slaves. Gold dust from the Upper Magdalena and cacao and cotton from Venezuela all flowed out in exchange for European trade goods and African slaves imported by creole merchants. The most integrated and complementary Spanish American corner of the South Atlantic was the River Plate. Silver from Potosí entered the channels of the trade system from the high Andes and circulated downward into Buenos Aires and Montevideo, injecting liquidity and public revenues into the viceregal political economy. Aside from jerked beef, hides, Paraguayan tea, and other staples that were shipped up the coast to Brazil, silver also wound up in the Portuguese, Brazilian, and British trade operating out of Rio de Janeiro and, as long as it was a legal outpost, Côlonia do Sacramento. In 1770 alone, twenty-four ships entered Buenos Aires, many carrying slave cargos or manufactures picked up in Rio de Janeiro. In return for this traffic, coastal schooners made off with staples and silver for Brazil. The result was that up and down the littoral of South America, exchange networks flourished often in defiance of official rules—and increasingly forcing the rulers to adjust them accordingly.

The River Plate emerged as one of the principal hubs of the South Atlantic networks. By the 1780s, merchants on both sides of the river got increasingly involved in the coastal trade up to Rio de Janeiro, carrying cargos of staples and sometimes silver in return for manufactures and slaves. Manoel Caetano Pacheco, a merchant from Rio de Janeiro, did a swift business carrying aguardiente, rice, wood, and slaves into Buenos Aires in return for hides, jerked beef, and other staples shipped back to Brazilian ports.[26] In Buenos Aires, Domingo Belgrano Peri, Pedro Duval, Martin de Sarratea, and especially Tomás Antonio Romero emerged as coastal brokers in the contraband and slave trades. One schooner based in Buenos Aires carried hides, flour, and candles from the River Plate for Brazil, picked up slaves in Rio, and carried a combination of staples and slaves for the "French islands of the north conquered by the English [Saint Domingue]"—though this was not technically legal commerce. José Vieyra ran his brig, the *Santa Rita*, up and down the coast between Montevideo and Bahia shuffling hides and jerked beef to Brazil and slaves to the Banda Oriental (that is, until he got caught in a crackdown on contraband in 1794).[27] So extensive was the coastal trading system that creole merchants in Buenos Aires lobbied hard to be able to trade directly with "friendly" ports, and even to be able to open direct bilateral ties with Africa where, it was believed, River Plate staples would fetch decent profits and carriers could return to Buenos Aires loaded with slaves.[28]

What River Plate merchants wanted, having broken the grip of the metropolitan houses, was to cut out the dependence on middlemen operating out of Brazilian ports for access to African slaves. This was not easily effected. Brazilian-based merchants had three advantages in the mediating between African labor supplies and demand from the South American hinterlands. First, Portuguese Brazilian traders had a long tradition of direct and competitive commerce within Africa. Second, the natural currents and winds of the South Atlantic made circular trips between coastal African easier with Brazil than with the South American Spanish outlier hinterlands. Third, British manufactures entered the Portuguese trading system with much greater ease and from Brazilian stations could fan out along the littoral trade routes. These three conditions made Brazilian ports the primary gateways of the South Atlantic

[26]AGI, IG, Legajo 2824, August 14, 1791.

[27]Arquivo Nacional, Rio de Janeiro (hereafter ANRJ), Vice-Reinado, Caixa 492, pacote 2, f. 308; AHU, DA, Caixa 156, doc. 48, June 18, 1794.

[28]McFarlane, *Colombia before Independence*, pp. 90–93; Moutoukias, *Contrabando y control*. Archivo General Nacional Buenos Aires (hereafter AGNBA), Sala IX, Consulado, 29/1/1, Actas, ff. 108, 165, 201, 221; AGI, IG, Legajo 2823, October 8, 1792. On Belgrano, see Moutoukias, "El crecimiento," 792–97; Jorge Gelman, "Venta al contado, venta a crédito y crédito monetario en América colonial: Acerca de un gran comerciante del virreinato del Río de la Plata," *Jarbuch fur Geschichte von Staat Wirtschaft und Gesellschaft Latein Amerikas* 27 (1990): 101–26.

system. They preserved the most direct links to Africa and drew staples from the interiors of the South American continent. English merchants based in Lisbon and Cádiz made sure to stop over in South American ports, above all in Rio de Janeiro, en route to the Pacific around Cape Horn. Indeed, English and French whalers of the South Atlantic supplemented their quest for oil by shuffling goods and slaves back and forth across the South Atlantic. In 1797, one English ship docked in Rio carrying papers from Mauritius with a crew of Spanish, Portuguese, Bahian, African, and Macao sailors. Its regular trade drew a triangle between Africa, Brazil, and Buenos Aires. Spanish ships, too, such as the *Buenviaje*, also made the triangle trade between Buenos Aires, Brazil, and Africa. But what all these vessels shared was holding the crucial corner of the triangle in Rio de Janeiro.[29]

From 1790 to 1830, Rio de Janeiro emerged as the largest slave-importing port in the Americas, and the majority of Africans came from Luanda and Benguela (indeed, from 1780 to 1810, more slaves entered the Brazilian capital than all imports to the United States and Spanish America combined). Pernambuco also took slaves from Angola, while Bahia, Pará, and Maranhão took a significant portion from the Bight of Benin. Rio de Janeiro also served as a slave entrepôt for African shipments to Bahia. More important, Rio became an entrepôt for slave shipments southward to Montevideo and Buenos Aires. Rio-based networks even extended beyond Fortaleza to Caracas and Havana. Rio de Janeiro also became an export hub for staple shipments to Africa from the various coastal hinterlands of South America, gathering and warehousing exports before loading them on larger carriers bound for Luanda. But it also had staples of its own, like the *gerebita*, a potent brandy from sugarcane, shipped in large quantities to Africa, supplemented by gold and diamonds. As Portuguese authorities acknowledged, the scale of trade of Brazilian staples to Angola, especially gerebita, dried meat, and tobacco, was so great that they not only did not need metropolitan goods to keep up the exchange, but even British manufactures were becoming unnecessary.[30]

Rio de Janeiro was hardly the exclusive hub (see fig. 3). Salvador enjoyed a direct link to the African coast and shipped slaves up and down the coast of Bahia. But of the Brazilian ports, it was the most dependent on ties to Oporto and Lisbon. Most of its merchant community was born in Portugal, and much of the financing came from Europe. Unlike

---

[29] ANRJ, Vice-Reinado, Caixa 492, pacote 2, s.n., February 6, 1797; January 22, 1798, f. 223.

[30] AHU, CU, Códice 549, "Instrucção para Joseph Gonçalo da Camara . . . 1779," p. 19.

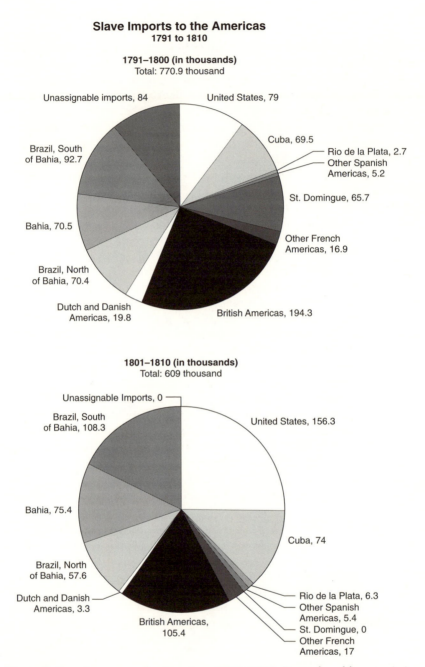

Slave Imports to the Americas
1791 to 1810

1791–1800 (in thousands)
Total: 770.9 thousand

Unassignable imports, 84

United States, 79

Cuba, 69.5

Rio de la Plata, 2.7
Other Spanish Americas, 5.2

St. Domingue, 65.7

Brazil, South of Bahia, 92.7

Bahia, 70.5

Other French Americas, 16.9

Brazil, North of Bahia, 70.4

Dutch and Danish Americas, 19.8

British Americas, 194.3

1801–1810 (in thousands)
Total: 609 thousand

Unassignable Imports, 0

Brazil, South of Bahia, 108.3

United States, 156.3

Bahia, 75.4

Cuba, 74

Brazil, North of Bahia, 57.6

Rio de la Plata, 6.3
Other Spanish Americas, 5.4

Dutch and Danish Americas, 3.3

St. Domingue, 0

British Americas, 105.4

Other French Americas, 17

Figure 3. Slave imports to the Americas, 1791–1810. Reproduced by permission from David Eltis, *Economic Growth and the Ending of the Transatlantic Slave Trade* (Oxford: Oxford University Press, 1987), p. 249.

Pernambuco, which had access to ample staples for direct trade, or Rio de Janeiro, which had staples and especially precious metals in abundance, Bahia was the poor cousin of the Brazilian entrepôts. Salvador's trade was less diverse, in content and scope, than Rio's. Still, in spite of the greater dependence on Lisbon for capital and to some extent European trade goods, Bahia traded directly with Africa, most especially the Bight of Benin, taking Nâgo-Yoruba slaves, shifting away from the Mina Coast. Pierre Verger's classic work has traced the strong and continuous links between Bahia and Benin dating back to the late sixteenth century. The principal staples included sugar, wood, and especially tobacco, and the transatlantic trade with Africa bypassed Europe, and even official colonial strictures.[31] Merchant potentates boomed in Bahia. Teodósio Gonçalves da Silva and Pedro Rodrigues Bandeira operated commercial networks spanning Brazil, Europe, Africa, and Asia, and they were quickly absorbed into the seigniorial provincial elite.[32]

By the 1790s, the slave trade along the littoral of South American colonies had evolved outside the orbit of metropolitan interests and controls. What sustained the South Atlantic system was the direct exchange between staple-producing hinterlands of the Americas and slave-harvesting hinterlands of Africa, mediated in large measure by merchants based in Brazilian ports and to some extent Spanish South American ports. Colonial merchant capital, nourished by the rapidly expanding slave trade, was breaking free of Spain and Portugal.

CREDIT, KINSHIP, AND SOUTH ATLANTIC TRADING NETWORKS

The South Atlantic trading system had features that shaped the way business was conducted. It was capital intensive and risky. High injections of merchant capital were necessary for two reasons. First, the trade relied on long-distance commodity exchanges across three continents, Europe, America, and Africa, involving manufactures, staples, and slaves and tied by credit. Nor was the trade a mere seaborne affair. Staples came from

---

[31]ANRJ, Vice-Reinado, Caixa 485, pacote 2, s.n., Ouro inspector to Conde de Rezende, August 6, 1797; Caixa 416, pacote 1, s.n., Mesa Report, April 6, 1810; JC Caixa 410, Navegação, pacote 1/12; Arquivo Publico da Bahia (hereafter APB), Seccão Colonial, Cartas Régias, doc. 60, March 8, 1799; AN, Negocios de Portugal, Ministerio da Marinha e Ultramar, Caixa 715, pacote 1, doc. 113; Pierre Verger, *Fluxo e refluxo do tráfico de escravos entre o Golfo do Benin e a Bahia de Todos os Santos dos séculos XVIII a XIX* (São Paulo: Ed. Corrupio, 1987).

[32]Lugar, "The Merchant Community of Salvador," pp. 55–66, 166–67; John Norman Kennedy, "Bahian Elites, 1750–1822," *Hispanic American Historical Review* 53:3 (1973): 415–39.

American hinterlands, manufactures from European factories, and slaves increasingly from the interior of Africa. Commodities were tied up in shipment for extensive periods and thus illiquid, with a merchant's investment literally bobbing on the high seas. Second, warehousing, ships (called *tumbeiros*, floating tombs), insurance, and defenses (especially on the African coast) implied even more sunk costs. The combination of long-distance trading and high fixed investments inflated the overhead costs of slave trading.

The vulnerability to losses compelled merchants to diversify their enterprise. They grafted the slave trade onto a business of lending and borrowing money, and trade in commodities—trying to make fortunes off a variety of transactions, not just one, in order to diminish the punishment from a loss in any one branch. If the hides went bad, or their prices dropped, or if there was a sudden glut of liquor in Benguela then earnings could be made up on other staples, like rice, dried meats, gold, or diamonds. Of course, if the whole tumbeiro were lost, as happened to the *Bellizario*, a Rio de Janeiro slaver loaded with precious metals that ran ashore off the Angolan coast in 1793, diversification was no immunity. Diversification was even more pronounced for shippers licensed to operate in the Indian Ocean. For these, as Manoel de Freitas Sylva and his partners observed, the trade to the Malabar coast and Goa allowed them to carry not only slaves back to Brazil but also Oriental preciosities. While the Junta do Comércio in Lisbon was often reluctant to let Brazilians traffic in the Indian Ocean (fearing that they would cut into the metropolitan business as they had already taken control of sizable portions of the Atlantic trade), it stipulated that Brazilians had to carry merchandise from Portugal on the trip east—magnifying the great diversity of the ports of call and commodities involved in a single trading expedition.[33]

Diversification did not flatten the hierarchy of merchants. The most successful operated on a large scale through a network of agents scattered around many trading centers in the South Atlantic, while smaller merchants had to rely on more specialized, and thus more risky and more precarious, businesses. To some extent this enhanced the concentration of merchant groups in colonial ports, as the barriers to entry were quite high and any newcomer had to join complex networks to gain access to the business. The smaller-fry merchants often stuck to the coastal trade up and down the littoral, letting the bigger traders operate the transoceanic routes.[34] This

---

[33]AHU, DA, Caixa 153, doc. 31, Caixa 154, doc. 1; CU, Códice 962, f. 2.

[34]Manolo Garcia Florentino, *Em costas negras: Una história do tráfico Atlântico de Escravos entre África e o Rio de Janeiro (Séculos XVIII e XIX)* (Rio de Janeiro: Arquivo Nacional, 1993) pp. 36, 129; Miller, *Way of Death*, pp. 318–25.

diversity with concentration gave colonial merchants a decisive edge in the South Atlantic system and buoyed their local and regional power within the colonies.

Another way to cope with uncertainties and reduce overhead expenses for individual merchants—aside from diversifying the "commodity basket" of Atlantic expeditions—was to disperse risk among agents so that, in the event of a failure, partners would share the losses. While this often flooded the commercial tribunals with lawsuits, it meant that a failed transaction did not leave one merchant bearing the entire burden of failed payments. Jacinto Fernandes Bandeira and Anastacio Gomes da Silva kept up a longstanding partnership to ship goods back and forth between Portugal, Africa, and Brazil. When they both died almost at the same time, administrators scrambled to sort out the ornate web of assets, credits, and debits scattered all over the Atlantic world.[35] In general, the pattern of partnership formation was the following: two to five merchants pooled their efforts in slave-trading transactions that could take up to seven years to close. Some went as far as issuing shares jointly to raise capital. A single partnership could thereby make several voyages while rotating different sets of investors in and out of the venture. Each partner often provided his own niche in the complicated trade, from gathering staples and specie in the American hinterlands to handling bills of exchange to owning ships and having family members posted in African ports. Thus within a partnership, a division of labor took care of the specialized tasks in the trade, pooled capital, and spread the risk that any one side of the exchange would fail. In 1793, Francisco José Leite Guimaraens formed a partnership with Sebastian Luis da Souza and created the nucleus of a network of merchants involved in manifold sides of the business from Rio Grande do Sul to Lisbon and Africa. Each associate served a special function within this broader, Rio de Janeiro–based alliance.[36]

Family relations frequently provided the foundations upon which mercantile alliances and partnerships were built. Kinship supported commercial and financial dependency by lowering the costs of transacting across long distances. Where family relations within a business enterprise scattered across a number of ports, they could be called on to enforce contractual or customary obligations where otherwise warfare and

---

[35] AHU, CU, Códice 962, ff. 1180–120.

[36] ANRJ, JC, Caixa 377, pacote 2, s.n.; for another fascinating case, see ANTT, JC, Maço 62, Caixa 203, October 14, 1799; Klein, *The Atlantic Slave Trade*, pp. 82–83; Lugar, "The Merchant Community of Salvador," pp. 136–38. See also Jeremy Adelman, *Republic of Capital: Buenos Aires and the Legal Transformation of the Atlantic World* (Stanford: Stanford University Press, 1999), pp. 145–50.

courts would have acted as enforcers. One slave-trading family straddled Angola and Brazil and shipped goods and slaves back and forth between partner-brothers. The Angolan-based brother, Luis Antonio de Souza, scorned the *arrivistes* Portuguese and English traders who new little or nothing of local customs. But he claimed there was little to fear, as Brazilian staples were coveted in Africa (though he did occasionally confess to worrying about the desire for English wares). He did warn, however, that endemic warfare in Africa was a constant cause of turmoil but also implied that slaves "can be bought at a very low price." De Souza groaned repeatedly about the sluggishness with which his local slave traders and contractors paid their debts and delivered promised slaves, inflicting chronic losses to his business. He thanked his brother for his understanding and forbearance in tolerating delays in the completion of transactions. In one gesture of gratitude, he compensated his brother-partner with the gift of a zebra shipped from Benguela to embellish his sibling's garden in São Paulo. When de Souza finally grew weary after forty years of living in Angola, he packed his belongings and returned "home" to Brazil. In Angola, he had left the African side of the family business in the hands of Alexandre de Mesquita Cardoso e Almeida, his son-in-law.[37]

Since business enterprises in colonial South American societies were often kin based, it fell to families to regulate access to and use of property rights—and indeed gave to women, siblings, cousins, and extended familial relations important managerial roles in internally diversified and geographically extended enterprises. Familial controls over loyalty, honor, and reciprocity lowered the cost of transacting within extended scale and diverse firms. Very often families had to handle the problem of accumulated debts and credits within the extended household, a constant source of friction and acrimony. For this reason, too, marital arrangements played an important function in reconstituting mercantile alliances and reconsolidating elite property. In 1779, Bento Esteves de Araujo, a prominent merchant in Rio de Janeiro, pleaded to royal authorities to absolve him of his "unhappy lot." His family was being dishonored by a scandal that, while private, threatened to tarnish his reputation as an honorable merchant as the news went public and thus to shake the local market as his debtors would renege and creditors call in their loans. A loss of reputation could therefore afflict the colonial

---

[37]AHU, CU, Códice 550, 12; Biblioteca Nacional Rio de Janeiro (hereafter BNRJ), Seção Manuscritos, Coleção Morgado de Mateus, 21/4/9, ff. 18–36. Folio 36 in particular contains an exceptional description of the Brazilian Angolan commercial system. For another example, see the case of Antonia Elena Gutierres Coutinho, in AHU, DA, Caixa 155, doc. 9.

economy more generally. The story goes as follows: Araujo married Anna da Cruz. With time he became aware of "the mystery of her infidelities." The husband ordered her into seclusion in her sister's house, but she kept escaping, allegedly to satisfy irrepressible carnal needs. Then, with the support of the governor and the bishop, in an effort to avoid "the necessary ruin of a merchant house which manages a capital base of over 200,000 cruzados," she was transferred to the Convent of Our Lady of Ajuda. What Araujo wanted was the right to have her locked up forever, for "her own good" and so that "this *homem de nego-cio* could continue to work with others from his opulent House" in the exploitation of mines and trading with "other parts of America." By locking Anna away, his five sons and two daughters could, without shame, participate in the business and find spouses to enhance the status of the family and its enterprise. Reputation was not simply important; it was everything when kinship—both real and fictive—was the foundation of confidence.[38]

Families also provided built-in enforcement mechanisms in the collection of debts. Consider the case of Luiz Coelho Ferreira, who managed a slave-trading business between Luanda and Brazil. On the Angolan side, he did most of his business with Capitão Mor Costodio Simoeno da Sylva. Ferreira based his enterprise in Bahia, but made his money by selling slaves up and down the littoral, and juggled a complex system of credits and debits. As much as he could, he relied on relatives as agents in these secondary littoral ports to sell the slaves and remit payments back to the headquarters in Bahia. His sister, for instance, was his principal agent in Pernambuco, one of his primary markets, and he leaned on her heavily to keep up prompt payments so that he could honor obligations to Simoeno. Having missed a payment in 1759, Ferreira assured Simoeno that there was no cause for alarm: his sister would be able to sell a forthcoming cargo of slaves and would expedite the transfer of funds promptly.[39]

Transatlantic credit ties integrated two distinct forms of handling the transaction costs of long-distance trade. Along coastal Africa, systems of credit depended mainly on cultural conventions of "pawnship" or debt bondage and the general fragmentation of political authority. Pawning people made promises of credit repayment for advances on imported trade goods more credible. African intermediaries, promising slave deliveries to merchants or ship captains, promised to deliver their own kin or dependencies in the event of any difficulty in slave shipments or making

---

[38]AHU, DA, Caixa 120, doc. 30.
[39]BNL, CP, 632, ff. 173–77.

payments on lapsed loans. In the Bight of Benin, a male secret society, Ekpe, organized the mechanisms to enforce the payment system. Further south, where Portuguese and Angolan merchants penetrated more deeply into the interior, a system of credit and advances tied inland communities to obligations to ship out slaves in return for imports. But these, too, molded to political and ethnic ties of dependent kin, clients, and slaves. Brazilian rum was useful, among other things, for creating altered states that favored communication with spiritual forces. Chiefs with access to the brew thus had access to gods, which reinforced their political status— while increasing their dependence on coastal intermediaries who provided the gerebita. New princes used their political resources to procure slaves and wage war, while merchants relied on financial dependency to enlarge the catchment area for slave extraction. Of course, sometimes dependency payments had a more explicitly political logic, as in the case of the Imbangala warlords who used the threat of raids to exact tributary contributions (including slaves) as a price to be paid for "peace" for those who lived in nearby Kilombos. The effectiveness of the South Atlantic business on African shores depended on the lethal combination of credit and political rivalry.[40]

In this fashion, credit and kinship interlinked and then criss-crossed the Atlantic to support a thriving slave trade. American-based kinship networks were the "trust" creating analogues to human pawnship or political clientelism in Africa. That is, personal and families ties provided a version of insurance that payments could be honored in such a risky business. On both sides of the Atlantic, personal ties then reinforced the contractual foundations of creditor-debtor relations. And where effective in generating "trust," kin fostered credit, and with the expansion of credit could go the expansion of trade.[41]

These risk-coping strategies reinforced what has already been described: the relocation of control over the South Atlantic slave trade to the European fringes, the colonies themselves. Indeed, New World partnerships replaced

---

[40]Paul E. Lovejoy, "Trust, Pawnship and Atlantic History: The Institutional Foundations of the Old Calabar Slave Trade," *American Historical Review* 104:2 (1999): 333–55; idem, *Transformations in Slavery*, pp. 124–25; Miller, *Way of Death*, pp. 128–37.

[41]Jacob M. Price, "Credit in the Slave Trade and Plantation Economies," in Barbara Solow, ed., *Slavery and the Rise of the Atlantic System* (Cambridge: Cambridge University Press, 1991), pp. 293–339; Castro Faria, *A Colônia em movimiento*, pp. 168–78; Metcalf, "Women and Means," pp. 277–98; Kennedy, "Bahian Elites," p. 423; Miller, *Way of Death*, pp. 306–10; Twinam, *Public Lives, Private Secrets*, pp. 216–40; Zacarías Moutoukias, "Réseaux personnels et autorité coloniale: Les negotiants de Buenos Aires au XVIIIe siécle," *Annales: Economies, Soicétés, Civilisations* 4–5 (July–October 1992): 889–915.

the large trading firms operating out of Europe. To be sure, they still contracted with European agents for ships and insurance, and sometimes to have other "nationals" join the contracts to enable ships to call at ports in several empires within the same extended expedition. But what they did not need, increasingly, was European capital or commodities to sustain the exchange between the Americas and Africa. Though smaller in scale than the metropolitan slave-trade companies, New World partnerships handled the capital needs and risk to make the business a lucrative one. Credit flows and kinship networks molded to the circular motion of commodities in the South Atlantic, following, very roughly, the currents and winds.

Much of the historiography on the slave trade has emphasized how the expansion of the slave frontier in the eighteenth century required traders' and merchant princes' access to trade goods and funds from Europe. There is no doubt that African traders and princes were debtors in the commercial scheme of things, and thus compelled to expand their commercial and slaving ventures to pay off obligations and ward off competitors. But the financial underpinnings did not originate just in Europe. Indeed, over the eighteenth century, credit accompanied commodities in the flow from South American ports to Africa.[42]

By the late eighteenth century, merchant capitalism in the South Atlantic was a relatively endogenous world involving diversified circuits of exchange, facilitated by personal ties of dependency and political loyalty. The slave trade was the central commercial nerve of a more complex nervous system in which staples, specie, and manufactures reinforced slave trading. The system was endogenous in the sense that extensive slave trading in turn invigorated staple and extractive economies of the South American hinterlands. Its political and personal foundations increasingly bypassed metropolitan controls. In sum, a new commercial world had emerged by the late eighteenth century held together by the variety of interests of merchant capital; this was a world made by empire but autonomous from imperial authority.

THE 1790s

By 1790, South Atlantic merchant capitalism reached a fever pitch. No sooner could colonies realize their dreams of prosperity within empire than a slave revolt erupted in the largest of all slave outposts, Saint

---

[42]Joseph Miller, "Slave Prices in the Portuguese Southern Atlantic, 1600–1830," in Paul E. Lovejoy, ed., *Africans in Bondage: Studies in Slavery and the Slave Trade* (Madison: University of Wisconsin Press, 1986), pp. 43–77, on price convergence between Rio de Janeiro and Luanda.

Domingue. News of the Caribbean uprising spread quickly across the New World. Warfare, revolution, and the diffusion of abolitionist sentiment across the Atlantic world laid bare the impermanence of slave-based prosperity of the New World, creating a dilemma for the South American economies. First, the disappearance of French competition for plantation staples was a bonanza for South American staple producers. The sugar frontier spread rapidly into new South American counties, in turn spreading demand for local inputs. Furthermore, as warfare disrupted European shipping, South American merchants could bypass metropolitan ports altogether. In the 1790s, the slave trade became the first "free trade" commercial system of the Atlantic and consolidated the channels of exchange between Africa and the Americas. Second, after 1791 panic spread across the Americas that slaves would borrow from the example of Saint Domingue's rebels. Indeed, the fear of slave uprisings was as contagious as was the lure to invest in more slaves. Merchant capitalism in South America thrived as it teetered on the knife-edge between free trade and bonded labor.[43]

European revolutions and the events in Saint Domingue set off a fever for South American staples. On the eve of the Haitian Revolution over half the North Atlantic's sugar supply came from that single colony; within a few years it was gone, creating a surge in demand from other sugar colonies. The value of Brazilian sugar exports doubled between 1790 and 1807.[44] War also strengthened demand for staples like cotton and hides. Bahia's other important staple, tobacco, reached its high point as an export, while Maranhão cotton also boomed; coffee exports soared even more. In Buenos Aires and Montevideo, merchants scrambled to the countryside asking ranchers for more hide deliveries. Hacendados, until then the lesser-ranked members of the River Plate elites, replied with demands for concessions and representation in the commercial guilds. Caracas turned to cotton as the source of a new commercial bonanza, and hacendados immediately clamored for the same rights.[45]

The staple boom in the 1790s spurred demands to liberate the slave trade altogether, intensifying the pressures on the old metropolitan mercantile system. The clamor for freer imports of slaves spread and

---

[43]Eltis, *Economic Growth*, p. 40; David Patrick Geggus, "Slavery, War, and Revolution in the Greater Caribbean, 1789–1815," in David Barry Gaspar and Geggus, eds., *A Turbulent Time: The French Revolution and the Greater Caribbean* (Bloomington: Indiana University Press, 1997), pp. 1–50, for a suggestive analysis of a pan-Caribbean crisis.

[44]Alden, "Late Colonial Brazil," pp. 631–34.

[45]AGNC, Real Consulado, Actas, 2526, ff. 76–77, April 22, 1795; 2527, t. III, f. 5, February 20, 1799, and ff. 89–90, January 24, 1800; AGNBA, Sala IX, Consulado, 29/1/1, Actas, ff. 227–35, February 7, 1797, and f. 248, March 13, 1797.

became especially pronounced in the Spanish ports of South America, the gateways to the slaving hinterlands. Colonial magnates learned a clear lesson from the executive orders of 1789 and 1791: pressure and "voice" worked. After Count Floridablanca made it easier for colonial merchants to contract with foreign shippers or travel directly to ports outside the empire in search of slaves, it was impossible to roll back the measure. Indeed, colonial merchants pushed hard for the remaining restrictions to be dropped or simply neglected.[46] By early 1794, for instance, the hacendados of the Banda Oriental were in a fit that other colonies—in particular neighboring Buenos Aires—could import their own slaves. They added that it was ridiculous to cap the amount of time a slaver could unload and load cargo in port to eight days. "Nothing will be done for agriculture in these parts if foreign ships have to leave in eight days, for they will have to depart without cargos, and will thus not return with more slaves." The crown agreed, letting Montevideo import slaves and extending the dockage time for foreigners as much as was necessary to fill the holds—so long as the export staples did not exceed the value of imported slaves. Lima's merchants and planters joined the chorus—they disliked having to rely on merchants in Buenos Aires to bring in slaves and wanted to be able to truck directly with foreigners for their own supplies. The merchant guild and the town council campaigned to be included under the umbrella of more open slave trade. A year later, in 1795, the same rights reached Lima, too; in 1798, permission was extended to foreigners to introduce slaves, and this was renewed repeatedly thereafter. In that year, the aristocratic Peruvian merchant José Antonio Lavalle, son of the Conde de Premio Real, secured the right to import 2,000 slaves to Lima from Africa. His plan was to send a small fleet from Buenos Aires loaded with staples to Angola and return to sell the bonded cargos in the Spanish viceroyalties—all this, as he put it, to cut out "the Foreigners' monopoly."[47]

The scale of the slave trade expanded dramatically in the 1790s as the barriers to trafficking fell. By the turn of the century, some began to wonder whether the slave trade had not set the stage for free trade altogether. After the intendant of Caracas signed a contract with William Robinson in 1797 enabling him to export 40,000 quintals of tobacco for sale to Tomas Eckard & Company of the Danish island of St. Thomas, some Venezuelan merchants protested. In principle, Robinson would be importing slaves whose value would match the tobacco sale to Eckard.

---

[46] AGI, IG, Legajo 2824, April 30, 1791.
[47] AGI, IG, Legajo 2822, Cedula, August 15, 1791; Legajo 2823, May 5, 1794, and September 27, 1795; Legajo 2827, February 16, 1798.

But many worried, as they watched the world's bottoms enter and leave La Guaira, whether foreigners were using the pretext of importing slaves to be able to exploit Spain's staple-producing colonies. In Buenos Aires, Viceroy Marqués de Aviles gave two important slave traders, Pedro Duval and Manuel de Aguirre, almost unlimited rights to export staples and import slaves. He conceded to Madrid that "it is possible that" this trade "will have a very damaging influence on the metropole's trade, and is becoming excessively favorable to the slave-trading merchants." Such practices were, he assured Madrid without being able to muster much cause for confidence, a business he would prevent "by necessity and by justice."[48]

As the slave trade boomed, it spawned resistance from agents who felt eclipsed by the new commercial dynamics. Cádiz merchants, for one, recognized how colonial bonanzas bypassed the old metropolitan gateway. When Tomás Antonio Romero, one of the South Atlantic's premier slave traders, began exploiting his licenses to transport large cargos of slaves and staples up and down the littorals of South America and Africa, the merchant guild in Cádiz repeatedly complained of his abuse of the Laws of the Indies. When they got wind of his 1794 license to export 250,000 pesos' worth of hides from Buenos Aires and to return with the same value of slaves, the metropolitan guild protested that Spain's interest in the empire was being forgotten. By 1804, they were still railing against the same porteño potentate, this time for his galling contract with the owners of the American bottom, the *Marrymack* out of Boston, to carry cargos across the Atlantic between Africa and South America. This protest, as in so many other cases of metropolitan appeals, yielded the same futile results when it came to controlling the slave trade. Viceroys and other colonial officials who feared that the open slave trade was corrupting the good manners of colonial merchants were no more persuasive. Neither officials nor metropolitan merchants could roll back the model of economic expansion of the South American littorals for the benefit of the empire by expanded colonial slavery.[49]

The frenzy for slaves even sparked acrimonious debate within the colonial merchant guilds by the late 1790s. These associations were normally identified with demands for more open trade. Some merchants were starting to feel that the big contracts to slavers who enjoyed privileged access to networks of credit and contacts were cutting out the smaller operators. Planters, of course, could not get enough of a good

---

[48] AGI, IG, Legajo 2827, August 29, 1797; Legajo 2825A, July 31, 1799.

[49] AGI, Consulados, Actas Sueltas, 2B, September 20, 1794; IG, Legajo 2825A, August 13, 1803.

combination: access to more export markets and more shipments of slaves. At any talk of trying to regulate colonial slave trading they rallied their forces and became, often for the first time, a potent lobby. The guilds, once halls of polite, gentlemanly agreement, became quasi-public theaters of discord over state policy. Indeed, whereas there was a general consensus a decade earlier that freer imports of slaves was a good thing, booming slave trading led to charges and countercharges of fraud and illicit monopoly. Interestingly, all sides used the defense of competition to tar their opponents. In the late 1790s, the consulado in Caracas was the scene of such a controversy. In January 1798, merchants and hacendados packed the guild hall to square off over the new slave-trading policies. A delegation of hacendados launched into a diatribe on "the causes and origins of the decadence of commercial staples." The problems stemmed from lingering controls over exports and imports, especially slaves. What the Caracas hacendados wanted was more open access to trade with North American partners, to export their staples to U.S. markets, and to import slaves. The merchant guild of Buenos Aires went through the same fracas. Cristobal de Aguirre presented a long report to the guild council in March 1797 that opened analogous controversies. For Aguirre, what was at stake was not just the wealth of the viceroyalty but that of the entire South Atlantic system, which was now so vital to the health of the empire itself. To hurt the South Atlantic exchange threatened the vitality of the monarchy. Curbs on trade menaced the ideal commercial relationship between Buenos Aires and Havana in the free circulation of meat, hides, sugar, and slaves.[50]

Like so many transformations, this one, fueled by the expansion of the slave trade, created as much friction as it did opportunity. To the consternation of Spain's commercial regulators who struggled to preserve some order to their system, concessions led to further requests to open Spanish trade. Each allowance to the slave trade turned out to be easier

[50]AGNC, Real Consulado, Actas, 2525, ff. 178–85, January 27, 1798, and 2529, ff. 167–171, October 22, 1805; Antonio Narváez y la Torre, "Discurso del Mariscal de Campo y los Rs. Exercitos D. Antonio de Narváez y la Torre sobre la utilidad de permitir el comercio libre," in Ortíz, Escritos, p. 71; José Ignacio de Pombo, "Informe del Real Tribunal del Consulado de Cartagena de Indias al Sr. Virrey" (June 2, 1800), in his reprinted collection, *Comercio y contrabando en Cartagena de Indias* (Bogotá: Nueva Biblioteca, 1986), pp. 13–16; AGNBA, Sala IX, Consulado, Actas, 29/1/1, ff. 245–60, March 13, 1797. One sugar-mill owner in Lima argued that there was not enough freedom to trade. Unable to trade freely back and forth with coastal Africa, he was forced to buy slaves from the Portuguese "at a price that they always dictate, causing infinite expenses to Spanish merchants who . . . are transporting them from Brazil, to Buenos Aires and then to Peru. Why not let us hire any foreign or creoles bottom we wish for unrestricted expeditions for slaves and cut out the Brazilians?" AGI, IG, Legajo 2826, 1802.

to make than to repeal. In 1804, the tensions over control of the slave trade came to a head. The original executive order came up for renewal. Cádiz, metropolitan merchants, and their agents in the colonies pushed for a return to the days of their centrality, restoring the slave traders to a position of having to plea for special privileges, as they did before 1789. Fifteen years later, however, they were no match for the coalition that favored the slave trade. In some respects, the outcome was foretold, as an internal report to the government argued. The slave trade had, according to the report, become the single most important component of colonial commerce. "The opulence of America, whose influence in the Commerce and Navigation among European nations [is great] ... could not exist without the slave trade." Just as the old asiento contract was useless in the promotion of colonial development, so too was any effort to restrict the slave trade to the colonies. The report urged wholesale free trade in slaves. The Junta del Estado delivered its own *memoria* at the same time, echoing the same themes, adding only that residual controls forced many colonial merchants to rely on Brazilian traders who could exploit their proximity and connections to wield monopolies in the Spanish American slave trade. It would be far better to open the slave trade to all competitors and let colonists bargain for the best deal. This in turn would reduce the cost of slaves, augment staple production, and generate more customs revenues. In effect, this report noted that free trade in slaves could make the colonies into export havens for staples that Spain could sell at great advantage to markets around the Atlantic world. Instead of Spain seeing its wealth drain away to the rest of Europe, money would flow in. As a compromise, the slave trade ordinance was renewed for another twelve years, though still falling short of "free" unrestricted slave trading.[51]

If the slave trade flourished, and in so doing increased the freedom of movement for merchant capitalists affiliated with the export sectors of the Spanish South American littorals, it took far less pressure on Portuguese authorities to yield the same outcome. The difference was that Brazilian slave traders already enjoyed considerable autonomy and had penetrated neighboring markets—and this difference had two important consequences. First, the boom in the sugar, cotton, tobacco, and cattle economies was so important to Portugal's trade balances with the rest of the world that rulers were only too pleased to strip away the remaining obstacles to slave trading. In 1798, Minister of Colonial Affairs Rodrigo de Souza Coutinho informed the viceroy, Conde de Rezende: "his Majesty has decided, for the benefit of this vast state and

---

[51]AGI, IG, Legajo 2826, August 8, 1802; 1802 "Memoria."

its colonies, persuaded that its setbacks have no other origin than the heavy weight of monopolies exercised for too many years on salt, metalware, and the introduction of slaves ... [that these and] other restrictions that are less prejudicial to the common good" shall be lifted. A year later, Souza Coutinho ordered governors in Angola to let Brazilian slave traders operate freely "on condition that they do not extract Slaves to Foreign Dominions." (They could, of course, ship them to Brazil and from there to Spanish ports.) Metropolitan merchants did not necessarily view the commercial freedom of the colonies with pleasure. Officials in Angola repeatedly asked Lisbon why Brazilian traders were allowed to take over the slave trade while offering so little business to Portuguese houses. One Portuguese trader who operated up and down the African littoral in fact requested permission to send slaves directly from Angola to Buenos Aires; once the Spanish American ports were open for business with foreign slavers, there was much interest in direct trade between Portuguese slavers and Spanish colonial buyers. This, along with most other requests of this sort, was denied as a violation of laws against trading with foreigners. In practice the ruling meant that African and metropolitan slave traders *had* to rely on Brazilian merchants and ports to gain access to the rest of the New World. Brazilian slave traders could come back and forth as they pleased, trading across the South Atlantic without metropolitan interference. Removing the legal barriers to entry now enabled Rio de Janeiro to consolidate its place as the hub of the continental slave market.[52]

Second, Brazilian merchants' access to homespun resources and networks also meant that there was far less pressure in the Portuguese colony to open the slave trade to partnerships with foreign shippers and merchants. Whereas merchants in Caracas and Buenos Aires lacked the kin, credit, and cultural contacts to procure slaves at the points of African supply, Brazilian merchants' expertise and experience effectively elbowed out foreign competitors. Indeed, if any party clamored for open trade with foreigners, it was the Portuguese slave exporters in Africa who chafed under the control of Brazilian merchants. In 1802, Portuguese merchants in Gabon pleaded for rights to trade with foreign slave buyers, especially from Spanish America and England. The petitioners complained that they were under the thumb of Brazilian merchants from Pará and Maranhão. English ships, they argued, sailed nearby, and export duties on slave shipments could contribute to the

---

[52]ANTT, JC, Maço 62, Caixa 202, October 31 1799; Maço 10, Caixa 36, f. 11; AHU, CU, Códice 962, f. 227; Códice 574, f. 45; Códice 235, ff. 69–74; Novais, *Portugal*, p. 247; AHU, CU, Códice 962, ff. 254–55.

royal treasury. And if open trade with foreign buyers was out of the question, at least the government might consider creating a monopoly firm, in which these merchants would have shares, to sell slaves to Brazilians at a "just price." This was, however, an uncommon request. For the most part, Portuguese factors feared competition from British penetration more than their subjugation to colonial merchants. Thus, in contrast to Spanish slave trading, in which open trade for creoles meant greater liberty to truck with foreigners, open trade for Brazilians affirmed their command over imperial trade policy. What was once a triangular circuit between Europe, Africa, and the New World was compressing into an oval-shaped, bilateral circuit between the hinterlands of South America and Africa.[53]

OPPORTUNITY AND ANXIETY

Opening the slave trade shifted the center of commercial gravity from the metropoles to the peripheries, and as it helped consolidate an autonomous network of exchange, merchant houses of Rio de Janeiro and around the South American entrepôts became the hubs of local capital accumulation. The colonies grew less and less dependent on Iberian capitals as they became more and more dependent on the slave trade. By the time British, American, and eventually French authorities started closing down the Atlantic slave trade in 1807, the Iberian slave trade was not just relatively immune to outside pressure; it could thrive on its own sources of supply, demand, and the entrepreneurship that bridged them. These shifts were not purely responses to the upheaval of the 1790s; they were under way beforehand and intensified as the North Atlantic shook up. In no way can there be said to have been a crisis that doomed the Iberian Atlantic before 1807. Drescher and Eltis are quite right: political acts were the catalysts for the transformation of capitalism premised on slave labor precisely because it contained within it the means to reproduce extraordinary wealth on the backs of unfree workers. What is less well known is that the colonies, and the merchant capitalists at the center of their ruling cliques, enjoyed more and more freedom to govern their own economic affairs as slavery supported the commercialization of South American frontiers.[54]

---

[53]ANTT, JC, Maço 62, Caixa 202, March 29, 1802. Occasionally, local African authorities would unilaterally condone trade with foreigners. For a case in São Tomé, see Maço 15, Caixa 169, October 31, 1803.

[54]Florentino, *Em costas negras*, p. 73; Eltis, *Economic Growth*, pp. 41–51.

If the political and economic events of the 1790s helped consolidate a South Atlantic system, they also exposed internal tensions within colonial slave societies. Caribbean crises produced contagion in other parts of the New World. The 1790s were therefore also years of spreading slave and freed black resistance, isolated uprisings and conspiracies, and thus the beginning of a more open reflection within the colonies on the meanings of slave and free labor. What made the 1790s so particular was the maturing of a contradictory system capable of yielding historically unprecedented riches, with ideological and social forces willing, seeking, and sometimes able to overthrow it. Herein lay a deep-seated ambiguity of colonial capitalism in South America: just as merchants were acquiring the power and influence to determine their own affairs vis-à-vis the metropolis, they faced much more troubling challenges to their authority from below. This ambiguity had political consequences: while commercial freedom distanced colonies from Europe, the threat from below redoubled their loyalty to metropolitan kings.[55]

Fear of what slaves might do, other than make some people rich, were not easily assuaged. Slave unrest, it turned out, was as contagious as the eagerness to buy them. In the largest slave society in the New World, conspiracies and paranoia of them spread like viruses. In 1794, Rio de Janeiro went on high alert. In late 1794, two tumbeiros entered Rio de Janeiro packed with slaves from Angola. Onboard were four Frenchmen without passports who, when grilled, explained that they had been "looking for slaves" in Africa to take to Port-au-Prince. When they heard of the upheaval in Saint Domingue, they changed their plans. And then Britain and France went to war, forcing the French traders to hide behind the Portuguese flag. This was the sort of thing that Viceroy Conde de Rezende least wanted given "the pernicious consequences of the present revolution." He subjected the four stowaways to an "escrupulozissimo" examination, then had them deported. The count subsequently informed his superiors in Lisbon that the colony was in a state of great anxiety, for there were rumors that revolutionaries lurked in closets all over Rio de Janeiro and that slaves were in cahoots with them. A cache of "the most essential and most frightening" articles had been found—including pamphlets extolling the virtue of French republicanism. Anonymous letters warning of an uprising popped up all over the city. The viceroy promptly

---

[55]Peter Linebaugh and Marcus Rediker, *The Many-Headed Hydra: Sailors, Slaves, Commoners, and the Hidden History of the Revolutionary Atlantic* (Boston: Beacon Press, 2000), p. 254. For a good survey of late colonial Spanish Amercian unrest, see Anthony McFarlane, "Rebellions in Late Colonial Spanish America: A Comparative Perspective," *Bulletin of Latin American Research*, 14:3 (1995): 313–38.

ordered a well-known literary society shut, since it was known for keeping "unlimited nocturnal hours," and had all its papers and books seized.
But what to do about the real menace: the teeming numbers of slaves
brought in daily by the hundreds of ships that sailed to and from Angola
looking for slaves "and whose trade has increased so many times over
that it is the only business going"? We live in unprecedented prosperity,
but the source of our wealth, warned the viceroy, is a great threat to our
civilization. The viceroy warned colonists that dissent would not be tolerated, and that for their own good, "passions" and "disorder" would be
suppressed without mercy.[56]

Who knows how much unrest there might have been without official
sanctions against discontents. It certainly did not put a stop to seditious
activity, the most famous of which was detected in the old sugar belt
in the northeast. In 1798 in Bahia, colonial authorities uncovered a conspiracy by mainly black and mixed-blood tailors. In August of that year,
handwritten posters appeared on public walls in Salvador praising the
idea of republicanism and freedom. Some even called upon Bahians to
arm and prepare for a violent showdown. In a city where people of color
outnumbered whites by five to one, officials immediately grew alarmed
and began mass arrests, mainly of free mulattos. One pardo tailor declared
at his interrogation that "all Brazilians would become Frenchmen, in
order to live in equality and abundance. . . . They would destroy the public officials, attack the monasteries, open the port . . . and reduce all to an
entire revolution, so that all might be rich and taken out of poverty, and
that the differences between white, black and brown would be extinguished." If the rhetoric was heated, no real subversive blueprint was
ever located and most of the detained were released. A few unlucky souls,
however, were picked out for public punishment. Some were strapped to
whipping stakes in the square of Pelourinho and flogged mercilessly.
More were banished to Angola. And three were publicly hanged, their
bodies chopped up into pieces and exhibited around the city. Behind the
idea of punishment for the "Bahian 33" was the use of exemplary violence
to strike fear in the hearts of potential subversives of the slave order and
to extinguish, as the governor proclaimed, "the infection of abominable
French principles."[57]

---

[56]AHU, DA, Caixa 157, doc. 53.

[57]Kenneth Maxwell, "The Generation of the 1790s and the Idea of the Luso-Brazilian
Empire," in D. Alden, ed., *Colonial Roots of Modern Brazil* (Berkeley: University of California
Press, 1973), pp. 118–21; Novais, *Portugal*, p. 164; APB, Secção Colonial, Cartas Régias, no.
89, doc. 11, D. Rodrigo de Souza Coutinho, January 9, 1799; Alden, "Late Colonial Brazil,"
pp. 655–57.

Rumored conspiracies followed by colonial repression were not restricted to Portuguese colonies. Seditious pamphlets and posters appeared on walls all over Spanish South America. Antonio Nariño greeted the news of the French Revolution with glee and fired up his Bogotá printing press to issue translations of the Declaration of the Rights of Man, only to have his hard work burned in public. Indeed all stamps, plates, or even manuscripts reporting on French events were banned across the Spanish empire. Colonial authorities arrested dissidents and deported men suspected of spreading the message of freedom and equality. Still, conspiracies appeared to proliferate. In Montevideo, the French captain of *The Dragon* was caught meeting with local dissidents. In Buenos Aires, a broadsheet was discovered with the bold headline, "Viva la Libertad." By 1795, the extirpation campaign was feverish, but it is hard to tell how well-founded the fears were, as most charges did not lead to definitive paper trails. Even the cabildo in the capital of Nueva Granada protested the heavy hand of paranoid rulers.[58]

The fear that popular sectors, slaves and freed people of color especially, might mobilize behind subversive principles was not entirely unfounded. Certainly, the news of the Bahian conspiracy compelled Spanish authorities in the north coast and the River Plate to monitor slave populations scrupulously. The extent to which doctrines of free labor circulated among colored artisanal sectors on the slave coast remains somewhat obscure, though some have tried to make a strong case that subaltern people of color got fired up by revolutionary ideas and examples.[59] The evidence is sporadic—but it exists. For instance, in 1799, a conspiracy among slaves to seize the Castillo de San Felipe de Barajas, overlooking Cartagena, came to light shortly before it materialized. In the days leading up to the alleged plot, several haciendas had been burned, and a few slaves were captured and accused of arson. With much concern that the burning would spread, militiamen and regular soldiers patrolled the slave cuadrillas all over the province. Then, a volunteer in the pardo militia, Sargeant Manuel Ytuzen, informed his white officers that there was a plot "to kill Whites, plunder the King's treasury, and pillage private fortunes." He accused a band of "French" slaves (probably imported from Saint Domingue) and a free black sergeant in the Spanish artillery, Jorge Guzmán, of being behind the plan. Cartagena's scare was not unique. In Maracaibo, in the same year,

---

[58]AGI, Estado, Santa Fé, 53/59, July 19, 1797; 56B, May 20, 1795; McFarlane, *Colombia before Independence*, pp. 284–93; Ricardo R. Caillet-Bois, *Ensayo sobre el Río de la Plata y la Revolución Francesa* (Buenos Aires: Facultad de Filosofía y Letras, 1929), pp. 32–104.

[59]Múñera, *El fracaso de la nación*, pp. 90–95.

authorities learned of an uprising involving slaves, mulattos, and Guajiro Indians. Indeed, the entire belt from Rio Hacha to Maracaibo was a source of regular news of cane fields being burnt, looting, slave disobedience, and widespread slave flight—which only fueled the paranoia that something was afoot in the interior where fugitives were alleged to be organizing a massive force. While this phantom army of colored sans culottes never came into sight, the coast was astir with talk of the contagion of Saint Domingue's disease. It is difficult to say whether the official vigilance simply brought unrest into the open that had always been simmering away, or whether the anxiety produced the rumors, though less often the evidence, of slave sedition. There was probably an element of both.[60]

But the fear cannot be dismissed as the mental fabrication of white officials. In Venezuela, social tensions between white and free colored folk erupted in the mid-1790s and threatened to sweep slaves into an escalating racial conflict. In the county of Coro in May 1795, the tensions finally erupted. Authorities whipped up fear of a race war as European rivalry spread warfare across the Antilles and upheaval metastasized beyond Saint Domingue. When British forces seized Trinidad in February 1797, Spanish militias and armies went on high alert lest the British begin arming freed blacks and slaves on the mainland, as they had done in Saint Domingue. Curaçao also became a British platform for intrigue, contraband, and eventually military support for insurgents in Venezuela. Vigilant authorities also exposed another conspiracy in July 1797 in La Guaira, squelching it before any toe hold could be established. Pedro Carbonell had left his home in Venezuela for Guadalupe and printed several thousand copies of the *Derechos de Hombre y del Cuidadano*. Copies of the leaflet were later found all over Venezuela, as well as lyrics to songs to be chanted by insurgents. One broadsheet urged Venezuelans to store away knives, machetes, picks, sticks, and axes, and anything from the field or kitchen that might be used as a weapon. But before the conspirators could rally their forces, the local armies began to round up suspects. When the interrogations were over, 65 men were arrested; 34 whites, 24 pardos, and seven blacks. An untold number of others fled into the interior; some of the ringleaders escaped to Trinidad (where they prepared for the next, much more serious effort in 1806). Twenty-eight of the accused were soldiers; the rest were a motley group of lawyers, merchants, farmers, and tradesmen. There was not a slave among them, and the conspirators' stance on slavery was hardly clear. None of the seditious printed material

---

[60]AGI, Estado, Santa Fé, 52/76, May 19, 1799; 52/81, July 19, 1799; 52/137, April 19, 1803; 53/77, April 30, 1799.

called for the abolition of slavery explicitly, but freedom for all was an omnipresent slogan. Known as the "Gual and España Conspiracy," Spaniards, creoles, and free men of color raised the banner of colonial emancipation and for the equality of all men. Authorities countered with the flag of racial fear. General Mateo Pérez, who took martial control of Venezuela's cities and countryside, wrote to Madrid with omens of worse to come: "it is highly likely that [rebels] will be joined by Blacks, mulattos, zambos, and even the Indians for the seduction of promises of liberty and equality." To prevent such a disaster, he argued, it was important that the king tell his colonial subjects "not to deprecate nor exasperate mulattos, zambos and Blacks with insults and mistreatment"—a tall order in a society devoted to bonded labor.[61]

The more characteristic form of slave resistance was through individuals or small groups fleeing their masters. Of course, flight was not new, and African fugitive communities in the New World were as old as European colonization. But the rumors of insurrection, fears of British backing for invasions, and free colored demands for new political rights generated sufficient perception of weakness on the part of colonial authorities to spread the impression among slaves that fugitives would not be recaptured. In the 1790s, slave flight, *petit marronage*, became pandemic. In Bahia, it did not help that most of the African arrivals came from the Bight of Benin, where new political and especially religious ferment created a more zealous oppositional culture among slaves themselves. By 1795, the residents of fugitive communities grew increasingly audacious, raiding nearby plantations for food and even captives of their own. Such military engagements evolved into guerrilla banditry. By 1808, entire Bahian counties were in a state of low-level slave ferment.[62] Mining areas of Minas Gerais were infested with fugitive slaves and quilombos who made a regular habit of raiding the camps and mule trains carrying staples and specie. Diamonds and gold allowed fugitives to get food, arms, and gunpowder for use or sale to others. Indeed, runaway slaves became important contrabandists and capitalists. They assaulted the supply routes as far away as the River Plate from quilombos based in Mato Grosso, seizing cargos from Potosí and carrying silver back into Brazil to procure illicit goods to hock in the very mining and plantation regions they had fled. Accordingly, while the slaving frontier penetrated violence and warfare deeper into Hausa and Kongo territory in Africa, the slave production frontier in Brazil in the 1790s

---

[61]AGI, Estado, Caracas, 71/2, August 23, 1797, August 30, 1797; Pedro Grases, *La Conspiración de Gual y España y el ideario de la independencia,* 2 vols. (Caracas: Academia Nacional de Historia, 1997) McKinley, *Pre-revolutionary Caracas*, pp. 121–30, 135–38.

[62]Schwartz, *Sugar Plantations*, pp. 470–482.

degenerated into simmering conflict in South America's colonial hinterlands. Even on the outskirts of Rio de Janeiro quilombos propagated up local rivers, whose inhabitants took to cultivating market gardens to sell their produce in the capital's food markets.[63]

Runaways were also a source of concern in Venezuela and Nueva Granada, where *cumbes* and *palenques* had long provided refuge for the slaves who managed to escape. Indeed, rumors of conspiracies and insurrections after 1795, while successfully exposed or dismantled, had the unintended effect of fueling slave flight even more. Members of the merchant guild of Caracas became increasingly alarmed that the plantation belt of the captaincy general would get wiped out not through slave revolution but through more banal acts of pervasive defection from the slave order. Slaves left in droves. And from their fugitive bases they did not escape beyond the plantations altogether but camped nearby, close enough to pilfer staples to sell in markets or use for subsistence. The guild raised taxes among members to create special fugitive hunting squads.[64] In the River Plate slaves also took off. Incidence of flight, fairly high on the Pampas in the best of times, escalated in the 1790s, especially once the truce accords with Indian chieftains reduced the risk that fugitive slaves would be recaptured by Araucanians. Indeed, many fugitive slaves joined indentured workers and fleeing soldiers who sought access to subsistence (feral cattle) and vacant land on a temporarily pacified grassland frontier. Pampa frontiersmen were as much free pioneers as they were slaves or indentured workers seeking freedom. Matters were worse in the Banda Oriental, where rivalry with Portuguese forces stimulated smuggling and aggravated political turmoil. Thus just as merchants beseeched hacendados for more hides, the labor force became especially unruly. Unable to maintain a dependent workforce, estate owners lobbied for state assistance. The reply came in 1797 with the creation of the Cuerpo de Blandengues (Lancers), a militia corps specifically designed to pacify and restore discipline to the rural sector, thwarting contrabandists and pilferers, and chasing down runaway slaves.[65] The duality of merchants' dependence on the slave trade and fear of slave unrest saturated debates in the merchant guilds of the Spanish and Portuguese empires.

[63]Volpato, "Quilombos em Matto Grosso", pp. 213–49; Carlos Guimarães, "Mineração, Quilombos e Palmares: Minas Gerais no século XVIII," in Reis and Gomes, *Liberdade*, pp. 139–63; Fláviodos Santas Gomes, "Quilombos no Rio de Janeiro no século XIX," in Reis and Gomes, orgs., *Liberdade*, pp. 263–90.

[64]AGNC, Real Consulado, II, f. 98, May 10, 1797; f. 121, July 28, 1797; Actas, 2525, f. 67, January 25, 1797; Actas, 2526, f. 77, April 22, 1795.

[65]Gelman, "Sobre esclavos, peones, gauchos y campesinos," pp. 73–75; Carlos Mayo and Amalia Latrubesse, *Terratenientes, soldados y cautivos: La Frontera (1736–1815)* (Mar del Plata: Universidad Nacional, Mardel Plata, 1993), esp. pp. 26, 88–93; Lucia Sala de Touron,

This dualism meant that demands for permission to import slaves were echoed by pleas to royal officials to build up local militaries, to defend against the results of their own enterprise. If anything, creoles were prepared to soften their complaints about colonial authority in order to enhance their interest in royal revenues earmarked for security. But when officials refused to siphon money that might otherwise cover Spanish military costs (for, as we will see in the next chapter, Spain was squeezing the colonies to pay for European entanglements), colonial magnates were prepared to pay their own security bills. In Caracas, the merchant guild created five patrol squadrons of twenty-four soldiers each to monitor the slave zones. One report back to guild officers noted that "blacks, sambos, and mulattos without any fixed salary or income are taking advantage of the trust" of free Venezuelans and assisting fugitive slaves. The danger, in light of Haitian events, could not be underestimated: "the consequences with time will become irremediable as we have seen in neighboring colonies in which slaves and freed people of color are deeply ingrained in these Provinces." But the danger was unavoidable: "these days it is indispensable to alter entirely the system due to the multiplication of slavery, which has almost doubled in the last ten years with the imports of blacks, as well as with those that continue to be brought in continuously as crucial and necessary for agriculture which expands prodigiously."[66]

Temptation and trepidation infused the world of printed letters. Brazil's premier political economist and translator of Edmund Burke into Portuguese, José da Silva Lisboa, argued that Brazil should follow the lead of the United States in dismantling onerous taxes and liberating trade. Given the underpopulation of the colony, however, slavery was necessary to cultivate the staples for export. At the same time, while urging freer and greater slave imports, Silva Lisboa admitted some ambivalence about the longer-term effects of slavery. Unlike the United States, whose majority population was white, Brazil's was not—indeed, "her principal population is made of slaves; the number of whites and free people is small and grows slowly. And the unfortunate law of capture and commerce along the coast of Africa makes it more difficult to attract people of European extraction, and thus is an obstacle to the creation of a more homogeneous [read: white] and compact National body." The political economist's anxieties were shared by some clerics. Fray José de Bolonha, soon to become an

---

Nelson de la Torre, and Julio C. Rodríguez, *Estructura económico-social de la colonia* (Montevideo: Ed. Pueblos Unidos, 1967), pp. 153–56; Ricardo Salvatore, "The Breakdown of Social Discipline in the Banda Oriental and the Littoral, 1790–1820," in Mark D. Szuchman and Jonathan C. Brown, eds., *Revolution and Restoration: The Rearrangement of Power in Argentina, 1776–1860* (Lincoln: University of Nebraska Press, 1994), pp. 80–81.

[66] AGNC, Real Consulado, Actas, 2526, ff. 37–38, August 8, 1794.

open abolitionist, in the 1790s began to warn authorities that "one opinion concerning slavery, which is currently spreading and being embraced, will disturb the consciences of the inhabitants of this city [Salvador] and will bring with it in the future unfortunate consequences for the conservation and survival of the colony."[67]

In general, while slave unrest worried colonists, they stood behind the system that their voice had been so effective in creating, and from which they were enjoying unprecedented fruits. Not surprisingly, abolitionism was a non-starter in both the Spanish and Portuguese empires. Thus South American slaves were deprived of potential alliances that were proving effective elsewhere in the Atlantic world. Their struggles did not echo through the broadsheets and pamphlets of free black or white humanists.

What dominated printing presses in the Spanish and Portuguese empires (when they dared or bothered to raise the issue of the legitimacy of the slave trade) was resolute defense of the capture and commercialization of Africans. José Joaquim da Cunha Azeredo Coutinho, a prominent churchman from the aristocracy of the Campos de Goicatazes in the province of Rio de Janeiro, captured the prevailing sentiment within colonial and metropolitan ruling circles. In a pamphlet circulated in 1798, he denounced the French abolitionists, Brissot and Robespierre, for condemning Saint Domingue to be "enveloped in flames, swimming on blood." He also took aim at British abolitionists and legislators who advocated the end of the Atlantic slave trade. While the Brazilian bishop argued that masters were duty-bound to treat their slaves well, slavery and the slave trade were legitimate and right. Rights, he insisted, derived from "social existence" and did not inhere in individuals naturally. Accordingly, they were relative, circumstantial, and had to conform to a general notion of what was good for society as a whole. From this, Azeredo Coutinho deduced, it was right to sell slaves in Brazil for the opulence they helped create, and capture them in Africa because a "barbarous society" with no "arts, no justice" convicted its inhabitants to the lawlessness of the jungle. By contrast, even if enslaved, the African would be uplifted by joining in a "civil society."[68] His little essay was an effort to sound reasonable and balanced in the defense

---

[67]José da Silva Lisboa, *Observações sobre a Franqueza da Industria, e Establecimento de Fabricas no Brasil* (Rio de Janeiro: Impressão Regia, 1810), pp. 11–15; Bolonha, cited in Novais, *Portugal*, p. 166.

[68]José Joaquim da Cunha Azeredo Coutinho, "Análise sobre a justiça do comércio do resgate dos escravos da Costa da Africa," in Sérgio Buarque de Holanda, ed., *Obras econômicas de J. J. Da Cunha Azeredo Coutinho* (São Paulo: Companhia Editora Nacional, 1966), pp. 233–88. For more discussion of early concerns about the slave trade and abolitionism, see João Pedro Marques, *Os sons do silêncio: O Portugal de oitocentos e a abolição do tráfico de escravos* (Lisboa: Universidade de Lisboa, 1999), esp. chap. 1.

of the slave trade. But he could not contain his vitriol when it came to dis-cussing "the philosophers of revolution." Either way, Azeredo Coutinho defended the slave trade as more than just a matter of interests. He ele-vated it to an issue of disinterested social good. This, at least until the monarchies began to shake and the pillars of Iberian sovereignty began to crumble, was overwhelmingly the prevailing discourse on slavery. In effect, it would take a political crisis, not an economic transformation, to shatter the ties within the coalitions that made up the ruling classes of the empires. This, as we shall see later, created the opportunities for expressing mean-ings of freedom that were not easily squared with a political economy dependent on slave labor.

CONCLUSION

As the eighteenth century gave way to the nineteenth, South Americans knew their futures were less than certain. But of several things they were fairly sure. There was no shared view that imperial structures were stul-tifying the colonies. Indeed, for many merchants, the dynamism and diversity of the South Atlantic economy allowed commercial capitalism to expand relatively immune from metropolitan pressures. Accumulated wealth through the South Atlantic exchange circuits reconstituted colonial elites and promoted merchant capitalists to the apex of the social strata, and as the final days of the empires loomed, South American colonies acquired the mechanisms to reproduce their own wealth. Colonies were becoming freer from metropoles because they were becoming more dependent on unfree labor.

Of one other thing they were also sure: the South Atlantic system and colonial political economies *did* depend on the survival of slavery. The justifications for slavery, even in the face of simmering rural discontent and the example of the Haitian Revolution, were not made out of self-interest but issued in the interest of the empires, which included their colonies. Whereas abolitionists in the North Atlantic had succeeded in portraying defenders of slavery as propagandists with self-interested motives, and the apostles of abolishing the slave trade as disinterested defenders of a public good, in the South Atlantic, slavery was seen as a necessary good for local and imperial welfare.[69] The claim to be arguing from disinterested motives in the Spanish and Portuguese colonies rein-forced a consensus that slavery was an institution that buoyed imperial welfare even as it served the self-interest of colonial magnates.

---

[69]Temperley, "Capitalism, Slavery and Ideology,", p. 97.

Certainty could not fully dispel anxiety. Once Haitian struggles evolved into a war not just over racial equality but national sovereignty, the stakes in social conflict appeared to rise markedly. The continued commitment to slavery, indeed its prodigious expansion after 1790, posed undeniable risks that any conflict within South America's stratified societies might escalate into an uncontrolled conflagration. The viceroy of Nueva Granada noted that "slaves don't need much incentive to conceive ideas of freedom in view of the pernicious example of those from the French colonies." Nor was this contagion a concern of just colonial officials. Even those who disliked Iberian rule had their doubts. "I confess," wrote the Venezuelan creole Francisco de Miranda in 1798, "that much though I desire the independence and liberty of the New World, I fear anarchy and revolution even more. God forbid that other countries suffer the same fate as Saint Domingue...better they should remain another century under the barbarous and senseless oppression of Spain."[70]

---

[70]Aline Helg, *Liberty & Equality in Caribbean Colombia, 1770–1835* (Chapel Hill: University of North Carolina Press, 2004), p. 84; Miranda cited in Anthony Pagden, *Spanish Imperialism and the Political Imagination* (New Haven: Yale University Press, 1990), p. 12.

3   Between War and Peace

Atlantic rivalries spawned vast new opportunities for expanding the frontiers of South American capitalism. But what about the imperial regimes that sheltered them? How did their political systems cope with escalation of conflict after the French Revolution? Certainly, the internationalization of revolutionary war had the effects of shrinking the Atlantic Ocean, drawing imperial parts closer together. Colonies became more important than ever for the survival of European powers; but the very same warfare pushed the colonies further beyond the reach of metropolitan direct control.

At the heart of these countervailing pressures on empires—increasing metropolitan dependency and waning control—was an ambiguous commercial and fiscal dynamic. At once, the 1790s gave rise to a peculiar imperial prosperity, fueled by the shocks on rival French and British Atlantic mercantile networks. Iberian colonies flourished in part because they faced less competition. As we saw in the previous chapter, the booming slave trade extended commercial frontiers deeper into imperial hinterlands. At the same time, loyalty and prosperity had to be summoned to defend empires—and their mercantilist vestiges—in the war to the death of Old World dynasties. In the end, defending the mercantilist empires put enormous strain on colonial fealty and began to provoke increasingly open questions about norms governing imperial markets. Affluence and competition therefore pulled the traditional mechanisms of handling imperial bargaining in opposite directions.

To meet the challenges of the revolutionary and Napoleonic wars, sovereigns had to activate capital in the service of imperial warfare. Getting at the lifeblood of the empire to defend it against aggressors involved opening and renegotiating the terms of the imperial pacts with merchant capitalists to identify pools of capital and transform them into revenues for the state. There were, of course, many precedents to the wrangling over money—but what characterized the years that followed 1790 was the openness of the bargaining. As elsewhere, Iberian colonists began expressing new concepts of interests, and even rights, within the framework of empires that struggled to cope with the spreading effects of revolution. Colonial elites began to push at the edges of what was permissible under the old regimes by marshaling expressions of loyalty to the monarchy that included some basic rights for his subjects. Yet, with these rights came ideas, ill-defined and inchoate to be sure, that the interests of the colonies could be separated from the metropoles for the good of the empire. What was emerging by 1805 was an image of empire that transcended the particular interests of peninsular Spain and Portugal.

INTERNALIZING WAR

The French Revolution and the intensified rivalries between European powers sucked Portugal and Spain into an Atlantic-wide confrontation. The familiar lines of European diplomacy, etched over the course of the eighteenth century, hardened radically after 1789. The quadrangle of Britain, Russia, Prussia, and Austria made for an unstable coalition—but the British remained stalwart opponents of the French. With the rise of Napoleon, the standoff grew even more momentous and stretched the canvas of war from the Middle East to the Far West. Warfare affected the ports, shipping lanes, and credit networks that held together the commercial systems of the Atlantic.[1]

In vain, Spain and Portugal struggled to remain on the sidelines. They could not, and found themselves internalizing the Atlantic-wide clashes within the peninsula. For Portugal, the history of an affiliation, if not alliance, with Britain tugged Lisbon harder into a historic orbit; refusal to join with London could invite devastating reprisals. Exposing the Luso-Brazilian world to French assaults at sea was less costly than British vengeance for refusing to play the role of client-state. Whether to be neutral or side with the British caused constant friction between several factions at the Braganza court. The rise of an overtly "English party" led by the Viscount of Balsemão and Rodrigo de Souza Coutinho tilted Portugal against France, only to plunge Portugal into the brief War of the Oranges with Spain. When Spain and France formed an alliance in 1803, Madrid began to pressure Lisbon to join the continental fraternity, shifting the fortunes to a "French party" in Lisbon. When it appeared that France was scheming to occupy Portugal, fortunes switched back to the English faction, and eventually to open war with France. European warfare therefore polarized

---

[1] D. A. G. Waddell, "International Politics and Latin American Independence," in Bethell, ed., *Cambridge History of Latin America*, v. 3, pp. 197–98; Geoffrey Bruun, "The Balance of Power during the Wars, 1793–1814," in C. W. Crawley, ed., *The New Cambridge Modern History* (Cambridge: Cambridge University Press, 1965), pp. 250–74; François Crouzet, "Wars, Blockades, and Economic Change in Europe, 1792–1815," in *Journal of Economic History* 24:4 (1964): 567–88.

and partially paralyzed the court in Lisbon, but ultimately forced the Portuguese hand to join with the British—with, as we shall see, decisive effects on metropolitan fortunes once Napoleon fastened his eyes on controlling the riches of the Iberian Atlantic.[2]

For Spain, the fear was more immediate. Proximity to France meant potential overland invasion and even more costly threats to the Spanish economy. This was clear in 1793, when Spain joined the counterrevolutionary coalition, only to get trounced by French armies. Then, humbled by the previous misalignment, Spain sided with France in 1796—provoking crippling British assaults on the colonies and on the high seas. Napoleon exploited Spain's worries, taking Louisiana under the Treaty of San Ildefonso (October 1800) in return for the creation of a "Kingdom of Etruria" in Italy for Carlos IV's daughter and son-in-law. Then, since Napoleon could not completely oust the British from the Nile delta, he enjoined Carlos IV to join in a campaign on Portugal. To secure peace with France, Spain had to turn on its western neighbor Portugal—even though both were desperate to avoid war altogether. Both wound up squaring off in the War of the Oranges, a proxy war between Britain and France that only further crippled the authority of each Iberian power. In 1805 again, France forced the insecure Spanish hand—with even more disastrous effects. The result: except for the brief peace of Amiens (1802–4) Spain was at war with one or another of the Atlantic superpowers between 1793 and 1814. These two long decades of war exhausted the commercial, financial, and eventually the political capacity of the Spanish Atlantic.[3]

Warfare in Europe, because it involved clashing empires, meant combat on the high seas. Attacking trade routes was a venerable tool in the arsenal of imperial war machinery. Indeed, for much of the eighteenth century, European powers waged their wars less in Europe itself, and more as mercantilist duels over the sea-lanes of the Atlantic. British naval forces elevated seaborne commercial warfare to an art form, blockading Iberian ports or threatening to shut them down. This old practice intensified after 1790, as naval supremacy became decisive for the continental balance. Lisbon's fleets were no match for either superpower. Thus decisions over alignments with Britain or France were often dictated by judgments of which superpower posed the greater threat to its ports. Spain, in part because it took sides against the British and its navy, was

---

[2]Valentim Alexandre, *Os sentidos do império: Questão nacional e questão colonial na crise do antigo regime Português* (Lisbon: Biblioteca das Ciências do Homem, 1993), pp. 105–37.

[3]David Brading, "Bourbon Spain and Its American Empire," in Bethell, ed., *Cambridge History of Latin America*, v. 1, pp. 434–35.

even more severely affected. In 1797, only 12 ships slunk out of Cádiz to the colonies, compared to 105 in peaceable 1796. Early that year, Cádiz merchants learned that the British navy had seized seven Spanish vessels loaded with treasure. The grim news was followed by the Battle of Cape St. Vincent, at which the pride of the Spanish navy, the *Santísima Trinidad,* was lost. Horatio Nelson, the victor of this clash, promptly blockaded Cádiz. It is said that the port's merchants would walk the city's ramparts to witness the patrolling enemy gunships. Efforts to evade the blockade were futile. In 1798 alone, the British commandeered 186 ships leaving Cádiz. Hitting Spain where it was most vulnerable was what Admiral Nelson had in mind at Cape Trafalgar in October 1805 when he sank or captured 22 French and Spanish vessels without losing a single of his. The admiral may have died in the battle, but his triumph sealed Spain off for the rest of the Napoleonic era.[4]

Heightened imperial war shook up the coalitions that dominated the Iberian Atlantic. An almost permanent state of war intensified the jostling between merchants who wanted to enhance their commercial rents while monarchs and ministers wanted more revenues.[5] The tussle over rents and revenues gave rise to new ways of dealing with conflict within empire. Most important, power devolved to the colonies themselves to work out the terms of the trade-offs between rulers and merchants, though not yet radically altering the political or economic ground rules. But as colonial merchant capitalists acquired greater powers, a new set of issues began to surface: who represents the general interest when imperial policies put the fate of the monarchy in the hands of private magnates? What is important to appreciate about the conjuncture of heightened Atlantic warfare is how much capitalists and sovereigns, merchants and monarchs, actually adapted (in contrast to longstanding views of Iberian sclerosis), and in so doing gave rise to new definitions of interests in and ideas about the reciprocal obligations tying rulers and ruled.

TRADE AND SPANISH SOUTH AMERICA

First, let us deal with the question of commercial rents and shifting notions of interest and privilege. How did merchants handle the insecurity of their commercial systems? And how did monarchs respond to

---

[4]Herr, *Eighteenth-Century Revolution in Spain,* p. 388.
[5]Root, *The Fountain of Privilege,* esp. pp. 113–38.

the threat to their sovereign domains and interests of their subjects? Though their interests were in some sense counterposed in the division of rents and revenues, royal ministers and imperial merchants became even more dependent on each other, one for revenues, the other for protection of rents. This was a dynamic of mutual dependency with heightened divergence. The Spanish king did his best to obscure this, of course, in the language of the national interest. The king's response in 1795 to a petition from Mompós merchants demonstrated this mutual dependency for the good of all. The king's benevolence was "to stimulate the seaborn circulation and traffic of my Kingdoms, ennobling with appreciable privilege those who profess their loyalty and uproot the false ideas which some persons have introduced, ignorant of the advantages to the Nation of a flourishing commerce so long as merchant families conserve themselves in this honorable profession."[6]

Shifting military alignments determined each power's choice of legal trading partners in the Atlantic. Portugal, and especially Spain, locked the decisions governing commercial policy to military and diplomatic policies. In effect, declaring war on a rival meant declaring a commercial embargo on its subjects. Trade policies therefore evolved in spasmodic fashion, leaving capitalists twisting to adjust to ephemeral rules. In 1795, Madrid allowed colonies to trade with foreign "colonies"; in 1796, merchants and ships registered in the colonies could participate in transatlantic trade (and not just the brisk coastal business), which had been the domain of metropolitan shippers. Then in 1797, colonies could trade directly with inbound "neutral" shippers, so long as outbound cargos were destined for Spain. Of course, most vessels leaving colonial ports had no intention of sailing for Spain, many foreign bottoms making for North American, Caribbean, and Brazilian ports. In 1799, under pressure from metropolitan consulados, Carlos IV revoked the neutral trade decree, though leaving enough loopholes for officials on the spot to mollify colonial merchants. The short-lived peace from 1802 to 1804 enabled officials and merchants to try to patch their yawning differences and revive old trading networks, closing down the lanes to non-Spanish ports. The resumption of war again in December 1804 put a permanent end to the Spanish mercantilist era. The following year, even before the debacle at Trafalgar, the king gave viceroys and colonial consulados considerable autonomy to handle local commercial policy and choose legal ports of call. If this sequence bewilders readers, imagine being a colonial

---

[6]AGNB, Colonia, Consulados, III, ff. 98–124; John R. Fisher, "Commerce and Imperial Decline: Spanish Trade with Spanish America, 1797–1820," *Journal of Latin American Studies*, 30:3 (1998): 459–79.

merchant trying to arrange long-distance trade deals that often took years to complete.[7]

It is hard to say what was more troublesome for the colonies: any single restriction or the constant and quite dramatic shifts in commercial policy. Either way, the flip-flopping inspired widespread discussion, debate, and eventually arguments among mercantile factions within the colonies. To make matters worse, factionalism in Spain was breaking open. During and after the palace coup in 1792, power shifted to a group led by the Count of Aranda and eventually Manuel Godoy, a clique with reactionary penchants but which feared and therefore wished to placate revolutionary France. The imperial turning point, however, was in 1796 with the outbreak of war with the British and the practical closure of trade between Spain and the New World. By 1799, it was fairly clear to most participants and observers that metropolitan policymaking had completely decomposed. Ministries fought among ministries; desperate Madrid and monopolistic Cádiz fought over priorities, and, especially within the Ministry of Finance, priorities and processes of decision making had crumbled.[8]

Faced with the breakdown of metropolitan policymaking, how did the colonies respond? It helps to distinguish between Spanish trade and Spanish American trade. If the former rose and fell with the cycles of war and peace, the latter found ways to smooth out the dips through illicit practices—and in the long run buoy wartime commerce and profits. In spite of the resultant difficulties in establishing reliable figures for Spanish American commerce, some trends are nonetheless clear. The first is the considerable diversity of the composition of commerce. While bullion remained the most prized shipment, and was especially important for vessels destined for Cádiz, commodity and slave-trade reforms began to bear fruit in the

---

[7]Donghi, *Reforma y disolución*, pp. 78–92; Fisher, "Commerce and Imperial Decline," pp. 464–68; idem, *Commercial Relations between Spain and Spanish America*, pp. 16–17; idem. *Trade, War and Revolution: Exports from Spain to Spanish America, 1797–1820* (Liverpool: Center for Latin American Studies, 1992), pp. 50–65; Javier Cuenca Esteban "Statistics of Spain's Colonial Trade, 1792–1820," *Hispanic American Historical Review* 61:3 (1981): 381–410.

[8]Richard Herr, "Hacia el derrumbe del Antiguo Régimen: Crisis fiscal y desamortización bajo Carlos IV," *Moneda y Crédito* 118 (September 1971): 37–100; Jacques Barbier and Herbert S. Klein, "Revolutionary Wars and Public Finances: The Madrid Treasury," *Journal of Economic History* 41:2 (1981): 315–39; Jacques Barbier, "The Culmination of Bourbon Reforms, 1787–1792," *Hispanic American Historical Review* pp. 57:1 (1977): 57–66; idem, "Silver, North American Penetration and the Spanish Imperial Economy, 1760–1800," in J. Barbier and Allan J. Kuethe, eds., *The North American Role in the Spanish Imperial Economy, 1760–1819* (Manchester: University of Manchester Press, 1984), pp. 6–12; Fisher, *Trade, War and Revolution*, pp. 55–61.

outpouring of agrarian staples. Indeed the new staples furnished almost half the shipments from Spanish America to Spain by the mid-1790s. Even Peru, a viceroyalty that could not shake the hegemony of silver from its trade balances, managed to diversify a little: Arequipa went through a mini-boom of textile shipments, mainly to adjacent colonies. Spanish South America's bonanza took place in the new frontiers of the Pacific rim, the pampas, and coastal Caribbean. Sluggish Nueva Granada still shipped over 90 percent of its legal exports as precious metals, though cotton from around Cartagena, cacao from around Cúcuta, as well as some dyes did grow. Venezuela was much more robust. Indigo, hides, coffee, cotton, and especially cacao boomed. The River Plate was probably the most dynamic region—exporting almost a million hides per year by the mid-1790s. Mendoza and San Juan shipped dried fruits and liquors, though they had to compete with Mediterranean products, and even some grains from Montevideo went to markets in Brazil. The offspring of the Bourbon reforms became little export engines by the end of the eighteenth century.[9] Moreover, just as the composition of trade diversified, so too did their destinations.[10]

Thus while Spain hobbled through the 1790s, Spanish South America profited. Though colonial expansion did not come at the expense of peninsular interests, it invariably affected the mood among the major metropolitan rentiers, especially in Cádiz, who fought to defend their privileged controls over imperial trade. On the eve of the French Revolution, the merchant guild in Cádiz recommended that the city consolidate itself as the gateway for trade between the Mediterranean, Africa, America, and the rest of Europe—so that it may be "a universal emporium."[11] Their grip on policymaking, however, weakened with Spain's military capacities. As a result, after 1790 the meaning of comercio libre changed sharply. In that year, the Casa de Contratación closed after 287 years of sheltering metropolitan merchants. More troublesome was the decision to

---

[9]John R. Fisher, "The Effects of *Comercio Libre* on the Economies of Nueva Granada and Peru," in Fisher, Kuethe, and McFarlane, eds., *Reform and Insurrection*, pp. 151–56; Fisher, *Commercial Relations between Spain and Spanish America*, pp. 69–75; McKinley, *Prerevolutionary Caracas*, pp. 35–39; McFarlane, *Colombia before Independence*, pp. 142–55; Juan Carlos Garavaglia, "Economic Growth and Regional Differentiations: The River Plate at the End of the Eighteenth Century," *Hispanic American Historical Review* 65:1 (1985): 51–89.

[10]Mazzeo, *El comercio libre en el Perú*, pp. 112–63; Javier Cuenca Esteban, "The United States Balance of Payments with Spanish America and the Philippine Islands, 1790–1819," in Barbier and Kuethe, eds., *The North American Role*, pp. 28–47; Javier Ortíz de la tabla Ducasse, *Comercio exterior de Veracruz, 1778–1821: Crisis de dependencia* (Sevilla: Escuela de Estudios Hispano-Americanos de Sevilla, 1978).

[11]AGI, Consulados, 2B, Actas Sueltas, f. 4, April 22, 1789.

create new merchant guilds across the archipelago of Spanish American ports. At first, Cádiz welcomed the colonial consulados, thinking they would enforce peninsular privileges in the peripheries. After the disruptions of the Seven Years War and the beginnings of the effects of comercio libre, colonial merchants clamored for their own guilds. Eventually, major outposts got their consulados: Havana, Caracas, and Cartagena in 1792, and Buenos Aires in 1794.[12]

If the expectation was that these merchant guilds would reinforce colonial participation in and subservience to imperial wishes, it became increasingly clear that what colonial merchants thought was good for the empire was not necessarily good for Cádiz. These formal, institutional changes anticipated—though they were meant to defuse—a greater degree of conflict over who got to participate in policymaking. Altering the institutions that allocated rentier rights, giving colonial merchants the voice in trade policy and practice, had unintended effects that created more, not less, friction.

Creating guilds opened deliberative assemblies at a time in which seaborne warfare aggravated the tensions between the merchants who supported Cádiz's traditional privileges (mainly importers), and those espousing trade with foreign ports (primarily exporters). So, in the name of fostering transatlantic harmony, wrangling within colonial mercantile circles came immediately to the surface. In 1794, a group of Caracas hacendados upbraided local treasury officials and the guild authorities for dereliction. Several ships loaded with staples set sail in June in an armed convoy, only to be captured. The exporters lost everything and blamed authorities for catering more to the interests of importers, many of them representing metropolitan houses, and penny-pinching by providing anemic protection for their ships. The hacendados warned that "our trade will be depressed into speculation; our staples' prices will fall to the fractional value they had in earlier wars, and for the same reason our farmers will become idle, scarcity will spread, and tithes, and export and import levies will diminish here and in Spain."[13]

These early firing shots in a war of words within merchant guilds soon became a conflict over who got voice within these guilds. In Caracas, hacendados insisted from the start that the assembly of notables should not be restricted to merchants, but that large landowners (who, by definition, were interested in promoting the exports of their staples) also represented the general interests of commerce. Royal authorities agreed

---

[12]Tjarks, *El consulado de Buenos Aires*, v. l, pp. 48–57; Fisher, "Commerce and Imperial Decline," pp. 461–62; Fisher, *Commercial Relations between Spain and Spanish America*, pp. 16–17.

[13]AGNC, Real Consulado, Actas, 2526, f. 55.

to their request to hold half the seats within the guild—to the chagrin of some of the merchants who knew full well that these exporters would not see eye to eye with importers, some of whom were leftover agents of the defunct Caracas Company. But once made, the concession stuck and set a precedent for equal representation in subcommittees to resolve disputes.[14] In addition, occasionally disputes arose over what it meant to have voice at all. Would guilds be the exclusive mouthpieces for the interests of commerce? In Cartagena, consulado officers complained to the governor about his choice of Bernardo Timoteo Alcázar to inform him on the state of regional commerce (they, of course, wanted to be the exclusive informants). This decision, they argued, was made "in spite of the courts, privileges and representation of the guild" and that such an outsider "could not represent the true merchants with honesty and dispassion."[15]

The importance of having voice became all too clear as the 1790s unfolded. In Nueva Granada and the River Plate, guild members grumbled that authorities did not do enough to compensate for the wartime restrictions on their export trades. This was especially a problem when Britain became the enemy in late 1796, as one Santa Marta shipper, Antonio Llanos, discovered. He loaded a schooner with cattle and mules and sold the livestock in Kingston, Jamaica. From there he planned to return with commercial ballast to unload back home. This business boomed as prices of clothes and especially flour rose—that is, until Llanos got caught and tried to defend himself by arguing that he was doing a service to local exporters in need of outlets for their staples.[16] In Buenos Aires, where exporters were a more powerful lot, complaints about restrictions were louder. Hacendados on both sides of the River Plate wanted restrictions eased, especially in the shipment of cattle staples, hides, and jerked beef to Brazil and the Caribbean. One prominent member of the Buenos Aires guild, Manuel Aguirre, took an active role in trying to promote freer exports. He made a point of cautioning that this would not violate the interests of metropolitan shippers who were mainly concerned with sending Spanish and European goods to the colonies. Since only specie went in sizable quantities from the River Plate to Spain, the new staples needed more relaxed trading restrictions. Besides, the River Plate itself (as opposed to the highland specie economy) produced staples

---

[14]AGNC, Real Consulado, Actas, 2525, f. 88; Adelman, *Republic of Capital*, pp. 38–40.

[15]AGNB, Colonia, Consulados, Legajo 1, ff. 1–18. For an analogous case, see AGNC, Real Consulado, t. I, f. 82.

[16]AGNB, Colonia, Contrabando, XXVIII, ff. 779–859. See also Jacques A. Barbier, "Commercial Reform and *Comercio Neutral* in Cartagena de Indias, 1788–1808," in Fisher, Kuethe, and McFarlane, eds., *Reform and Insurrection,* pp. 96–120.

for which Spain had no use but which fetched rewards in the commercial circuitry of the South Atlantic. It fell to the viceroy and consulado officers to act on the 1795 and 1797 permits to trade with friendly and neutral ports and issue permits to deserving merchants in accord with the licensing tradition of commercial guilds. This was welcomed, but it still fell short of the commercial opening that Aguirre and others had in mind—they wanted unobstructed access to non-Spanish ports, especially in Brazil and the networks that radiated from them.[17]

Creating the consulado and royal orders of 1795, 1796, and 1797 shifted authority to issue trading licenses to the colonies themselves, and made the merchant leadership responsible for enforcing laws that relaxed imperial trade but stopped short of allowing merchants to sell to whom they wished. Now the colonial potentates had to govern their own affairs—how would they deal with the hitherto thriving underground trade of the South Atlantic? By 1797, guild officers were squirming. Putting the legal onus on the rentiers themselves to enforce rules was clearly uncomfortable—it had been much easier in earlier days for everyone to agree to turn a blind eye to infractions against rules drafted and dictated far away in Spain. Finally, in March 1797, Cristobal de Aguirre stood up before the guild chamber and delivered a long speech, coming clean about the implications of exporters' demands for less obstructed trade. "While it would be more than temeritous to act against the magnificent intentions of our Sovereign," he argued, more open trade would bring bounty to the empire as a whole. "We should not just trade with French Islands ... but with all colonies and foreign settlements from any nation, whether they are islands or on the mainland ... for all is one in the intentions of His Majesty." This call for open trade was followed with an equally remarkable observation about the benefits of comparative advantage: "when this is made comprehensive, with the most immediate specialization, this will facilitate and multiply the extraction of staples and production from Buenos Aires, which is the whole purpose and final object of Our Majesty's policies." What guild members were starting to argue was that merchants should enjoy rights to trade with whom they pleased so long as their partner was not the king's enemy. Needless to say, this was not yet free trade— that would have meant dispensing with guild licensing and rentier business. But it was a dramatic case for open trade and colonial commercial sovereignty—and that this was good for "the justice, the equity, and the health of the polity." Aguirre's claims and the pressure of the export lobby validated a way of thinking about private interests and public good and led, for the next few

---

[17](AGNBA), Sala IX, Consulado, Actas, 29/1/1, ff. 138–42; ff. 221–22.

years at least, to licenses to trade more openly within and beyond the empire.[18]

A more acrimonious debate unfolded in Caracas. There, the shifting definition of what constituted personal interest and public good was more polarizing. The polarization reflected deeper schisms between creole exporters and metropolitan monopolists. But when the British seized Trinidad in February 1797 and began poking into the captaincy with support for fugitive slaves, contraband, and invasion conspiracies, the notion that exporters would want to do business with the enemy was explosive.[19] Things got more inflamed when Venezuelan exporters wanted to send their staples to non-Spanish ports throughout the Caribbean basin and the United States.[20] The rapidly changing notions of rightful commerce and autonomy of merchant capitalists to define notions of private and collective good became clear in a 1797 controversy in Caracas involving a contract with Eckard & Company of Dutch Saint Thomas to sell 40,000 quintals of Venezuelan tobacco. The intendant, desperate for revenue, sold the right to ship the tobacco to the Dutch firm. Many balked, complaining that traditional rights, the guild's autonomy, and protections of imperial trade were being violated. Other members were not so perturbed. The contract offered great "advantages" for exporters, noted some delegates. When pressed in the guild's assembly hall, a group of hacendados urged delegates to see the wisdom of open trade "with all foreign friendly colonies without any limitations with the goal of providing the Province with its needs and allowing the shipment of staples and produce, and thus also furnishing the Royal Treasury with the funds it needs to meet grave and urgent defense costs." Their presentation went on to observe how open exports would give employment to colonists, restoring their "animus," and support the "reciprocal utilities and advantages of business." What was good for planters and exporters was good for Venezuela. In the end, Eckard withdrew after shipping only 14,000 quintals. The experience suggested to some hacendados, among them a powerful coalition led by Martín Herrera, Manuel Felipe de Tovar, Martín de Aristigueta, and the Count of San Xavier, that they needn't even rely on the consulado for licenses at all, using the executive's revenue needs to press for concessions outside the guild's chambers. All four patricians would become prominent advocates of "creole" interests after 1808, and revolutionaries after 1810.[21]

---

[18]Ibid. ff. 245–60.

[19]AGNC, Real Consulado, Libro de Acta II, 2525, f. 117.

[20]Ibid. f. 203; XXXI, f. 88; McKinley, *Pre-revolutionary Caracas*, pp. 128–30.

[21]AGNC, Real Consulado, Libro de Acta II, 2525, f. 134, ff. 178–85; McKinley, *Pre-revolutionary Caracas*, pp. 130–33.

The defenders of traditional privileges, worrying that open trade would introduce greater competition in their sheltered markets, went on the counteroffensive. They, too, spoke of personal "rights" and the good of the commonwealth. The consulados of Barcelona and Cádiz warned that neutral trade and colonial concessions sacrificed "the Metropole of any benefit from possessing the said colonies." The king's chief minister, Manuel de Godoy, moaned that "all these circumstances have made me very perplexed."[22] In the colonies, the counteroffensive meant more acrimony in the guilds. Responding to the Eckard contract, four merchants (importers) lambasted the deal and the opening of the port. They warned of the "inconveniences and difficulties which this contract poses for national and foreign merchants who introduce merchandise" and the gateway this would open for "contraband" (Eckard's bottoms, they cried, would return to the port of La Guaira loaded with non-Spanish manufactures). After all, the denizens of Trinidad had become active traders to Venezuela since the island's fall to the British. The counteroffensive got more vociferous after the May 1798 royal decree ratifying neutral trade, which threw open North American ports. The agents of peninsular houses complained loudly, to little avail. Unable to get their way, this group shifted its lobbying directly to Carlos IV's ministers.[23]

Metropolitan interests decided to exercise their strength over imperial policy to restore their centrality and the old mercantilist model. By 1798, they were fed up with colonial requests for open trade. In September 1798, they got wind of a deal with the Buenos Aires slave-trading magnate Tomás Antonio Romero. Romero was licensed to import a large supply of slaves and export staples with no ceilings on the export cargos, while being exempt from a standard 6 percent levy. There was an outcry in the Cádiz guild. Their protest denounced the practice "which destroys the respective equality of rights which Justice requires among the Sovereign's Subjects." They continued, now using the very same vocabulary that colonial exporters used against metropolitans: "this privilege is a true monopoly, and as such impedes and destroys the gathering of Your Majesty's citizens to trade the very goods that are now subject to this privilege." Seven months later, under pressure from Cádiz, Minister Godoy repealed the neutral trade decree of 1797. The royal order maintained that neutral trade was intended to eliminate temporary shortages in the colonies, nothing more. While Cádiz applauded, not everyone in Spain was so happy.

---

[22]Fisher, "Commerce and Imperial Decline," pp. 465–67.
[23]AGNC, Real Consulado, Libro de Acta II, 2525, ff. 188, 205, 217; for the full debate, see ff. 134–39, 178–85, and 188–91; McKinley, *Pre-revolutionary Caracas*, pp. 130–33. For Colombian debates, see AGNB, Colonial, Contrabandos, I, ff. 931–68; and McFarlane, *Colombia before Independence*, pp. 298–99.

Finance Minister Francisco de Saavedra did not see eye to eye with his calculating peer, knowing full well that abolishing neutral trade would drive much of colonial commerce underground, out of sight of his tax collectors. When forced to choose between defending the privileges of metropolitan and colonial interests, between revenues and rampant contraband, Godoy was clearly not above pandering to the traditional mercantilist magnates of the Spanish empire.[24]

If the 1799 decision brought comfort to mercantilists, it provoked outrage in the colonies. Predictably, the fieriest reaction can be found in the archives in Caracas. Even before Spain let it be known that legal trading routes would be severely curbed, the declaration of war against Britain (November 1798) lured a swarm of British warships to the Venezuelan coasts, and therefore attacks on all vessels flying a Spanish flag. Then, when the news of the ban on trade with neutral ports (especially those in the United States) arrived, the consulado erupted. A faction within the guild complained that "merchants were experiencing irreparable damages to their interests as a result of the prohibition on neutral trade without consideration for costly impediments of free entry and unloading in the ports of this province." In an important shift in the discourse of property rights, these disgruntled capitalists insisted that "property belongs to individuals here as staple products which, under the good grace of permitted commerce, could be traded with friendly colonies." Now, they insisted, their private rights practically entitled them to violate political dictates, which came close to claiming that private property rights came before political decisions.[25] The town council of Caracas joined the ruckus, pointing out that the commercial collapse visited ruin upon urban and rural dweller alike. On October 22, 1800, the council informed the intendant and the guild that supplies of basic foods were running short, and that Venezuelans had little alternative but to buy their epicures and necessities from sources in Curaçao. "The only remedy," the report added, "now presenting us is to permit open trade with North America and Neutral Nations."[26]

Inevitably, colonial merchants defected. Expressing "voice," whether supplicative or confrontational, had clearly failed to work. "Exit" became the preferred alternative. Contraband, already widespread before the official curbs, became rampant. Ports along the shores from Maracaibo to

---

[24]AGI, Consulados, Actas Sueltas, 2B, n.n., September 15, 1798, and R.O., April 29, 1799; Fisher, "Commerce and Imperial Decline," pp. 465–67; Barbier, "Commercial Reform," pp. 109–10; idem, "Peninsular Finance and Colonial Trade: The Dilemma of Charles IV's Spain," *Journal of Latin American Studies* 12:1 (1980): 27–29; McFarlane, *Colombia before Independence*, pp. 298–302.

[25]AGNC, Real Consulado, Actas, 2527, ff. 44–45, 56, 116; Actas 2528, f. 11.

[26]AGNC, Real Consulado, Actas, 2527, ff. 162–63, 224.

Santa Marta, most especially Rio Hacha, became even more active smugglers' sieves. Schooners tacked back and forth between Nueva Granada and Jamaica—for all intents and purposes defended by the British navy. Spanish seaborne enforcers, if they poked out into open waters, made easy targets for British warships. Mule trains and carts carried imported goods overland into the hinterland. In the interior market town of San Gil, a local magistrate, José María Estengo, reported on the widespread traffic in textiles and clothing coming from Maracaibo overland via Cúcuta.[27] British, North American, and Brazilian merchants were only too happy to mock the 1799 decree. The British used bases in Jamaica and Curaçao to flood Venezuela and Nueva Granada through Maracaibo. Exporters quickly saw that smugglers made convenient partners and soon began issuing their staples in return for the contraband. By the summer of 1802, observers noted the surge in foreign cash circulating in Venezuela as a result of a rise in agrarian shipments to foreign ports—adding that while this generated private wealth it aggravated public penury.[28] In the River Plate, the main foreign contrabandists were Brazilians. With commercial authority displaced to Buenos Aires, they conducted their illegal trades under the noses of colonial authorities and often in partnership with many of Buenos Aires' most influential export merchants.[29]

The most immediate effect of the flip-flopping was to drive a great deal of colonial commerce, export and import alike, further underground—and therefore beyond officials' ability to keep track of it. Some worried that the black market had become *the* market. In the words of the Cartegenan merchant and man of letters, José Ignacio de Pombo, "honorable merchants have no other alternative: either they utterly ruin themselves at any legitimate commercial speculation, or they give in to absolute inaction, consuming their capital waiting for a new order of peace. But when will we see this?" Under these conditions, "the favor will always fall in balance to the contrabandists, for the stimulus of profit is what provides fuel for this disorder."[30] It seems likely, therefore, that official

---

[27]AGNB, Colonia, Consulado, III, ff. 585–90; II, ff. 527–640; Contrabandos, VIII, ff. 318–21.

[28]AGNC, Real Consulado, Actas, 2527, ff. 147–48; 2528, ff. 125–26; Real Consulado, Actas, 2528, ff. 178–79; AGNB, Colonia, Contrabandos, I, ff. 71–173.

[29]AGNBA, Sala IX, Consulado, 29/1/3, Actas, f. 165; Tjarks, *El consulado de Buenos Aires*, v. 1 pp. 308–12; German O. E. and Alicia Vidaurreta de Tjarks, *El comercio ingles y el contrabando: Nuevos aspectos en el estudio económico en el Rio de la Plata (1807–1810)* (Buenos Aires: N.p., 1962), pp. 3–5; and for origins of this system, see Moutoukias, *Contrabando y control*.

[30]Pombo, "Informe del real Tribunal," pp. 18–20. See also the comments in AGNB, Colonia, Consulado, II, ff. 941–72, on the state of coastal contraband after 1799; McFarlane, *Colombia before Independence*, pp. 300–304.

policy had decreasing effects on the overall balance of trade, or its partners; what it did was move the circulation in and out of legal ledgers. An
irritant to many colonials, it also pushed colonial commerce outside the
reach of tax collectors. In the end, Madrid's fiscal crisis would be the
cause of another about-face.

Brazilian Counterpoints

Merchants and power brokers in the Portuguese empire also had to handle the multiple pressures of warfare on its trade. The contrast between the
two Iberian empires illustrates how tensions over the liberty to trade
reflected yawning internal contradictions within mercantilism as it reached
old age. The greater power of colonial capital within the dominant bloc of
the empire and the military shelter afforded by the British alliance, which
reduced the fiscal burden of war, allowed Portuguese rulers and rentiers to
bargain over imperial spoils with less friction than did their Spanish
counterparts.

Commercial balances set the stage for a change in relations between
Portugal and Britain, and between Lisbon and its Brazilian possessions. In
effect, from the 1790s, Britain's trade slipped into a deficit with Luso-
Brazilian commerce, while Portugal became more dependent than ever on
Brazil. The longstanding aspirations of Portuguese state builders like the
Marquis of Pombal to wean the empire from its dependency on British
support appeared to be coming true. After the American Revolution, the
value of Portuguese exports to Britain grew faster than imports, so that by
the late 1790s, Portugal recorded surpluses. The British grew suddenly
more dependent on the Portuguese trading system in the 1790s, as North
Atlantic warfare crippled British access to European markets. Increasingly,
British exporters looked to Iberian demand as an outlet.

The flip side was increased Portuguese dependence on Brazil to earn
trade surpluses with Britain. As in Spanish South America, it was largely
from the hinterlands that Brazil projected its commercial expansion.
Brazil entered a period of stunning commercial growth in the 1790s—
reinforcing the commercial profile of the colony within the empire, and
colonial merchants in the balance between public authorities and private
interests. Cotton, sugar, and other staples shipped from Brazil accounted
for a significant share of Portuguese cargos bound for Britain. Sugar
spread south into new frontiers in Rio de Janeiro and São Paulo, especially with the construction of the *caminho do mar* (road to the sea) in
the 1780s. Coffee also began its ascent in the same regions, rising seven-
fold in exports from 1790 to 1807. In Maranhão, cotton expanded
where the old, now defunct monopoly companies had tried to introduce

the staple. Rice and cacao also expanded in newly cleared lands. But the new commercial winds also blew through the older settled staple regions, such as Bahia and Pernambuco, reviving old staples or eclipsing them by crop substitution. Tobacco and cotton folded into the commodity mix of the old northeast of Brazil.[31] By 1807, over 60 percent of all Portuguese exports came from Brazil alone. In effect, Portugal's surplus with the world implied a deficit with Brazil—a deficit that had to be arranged in bargaining with Brazilian potentates.[32]

Brazilians had a clear-eyed view of the risks and rewards posed by the new conjuncture of Portuguese dependence on its colonies, and of Britain's dependence on the South Atlantic. One report presciently concluded that this enhanced the colonial position in the empire. When the news arrived in Rio de Janeiro of the French conquest of Holland in March 1795, merchants and officials in Brazil recognized the British thirst for access to the Luso-Brazilian markets. They worried, however, that without a British alliance, British warships and merchantmen might penetrate Goa, exploit their toehold in the Cape of Good Hope, and muscle in on the South Atlantic system. It would be better to agree to a formal pact with the British to preserve the centrality of Brazilian merchant power in the Portuguese empire. Unstated was that this prospective arrangement would all but demolish the centrality of peninsular Portugal in its own empire.[33]

Aware of the stakes, Portuguese rulers struggled to stay out of the revolutionary maelstrom. The big loser in any war would be the metropolis; neutrality was good for metropolitan business. Lisbon managed to stay neutral through most of the wars until 1807—albeit with flare-ups in 1793–95 and again in the War of the Oranges ending with the Treaty of Madrid in 1801. Still, behind the neutral stance was a swing into a tighter political and military alliance with Britain. Portuguese ministers, without much guidance from an insane queen, fretted about the possibility of a Franco-Spanish alliance and invasion. After 1795, policies began to evolve quickly. When Luís Pinto de Sousa Coutinho became interim secretary of state for overseas dominions, the "English party" at the court began its general ascent. Within it a stalwart official, Rodrigo de Souza Coutinho, rose to great prominence.[34]

---

[31]Jorge Pedreira, "From Growth to Collapse: Portugal, Brazil, and the Breakdown of the Old Colonial System (1760–1830)," *Hispanic American Historical Review* 80:4 (2000): table 1, for a discussion of trade data from 1796 to 1831. Alden, "Late Colonial Brazil," pp. 628–46, 650–51.

[32]Mansuy, "Portugal and Brazil, pp. 505–6.

[33]AHU, DA, Caixa 158, doc. 23.

[34]Alexandre, *Os sentidos do império*, passim; Maxwell, *Conflicts and Conspiracies*, pp. 204–10.

The flip side of Portugal's commercial dependence on Brazil was its military dependence on Britain. Especially once it became clear that the political convulsions of the French Revolution might seep across the Pyrenees, Lisbon worried that the war might ravage the Portuguese sealanes—the arteries carrying the lifeblood of the empire. There was good reason to fret. One merchant from Maranhão, Paulo Jorge, noted that his vessels had to dodge French corsairs to get out of port, and pleaded for help to protect his property. Along the coast of Angola, French warships also attacked Luso-Brazilian vessels. France alone was a scourge; but when France allied with Spain, matters got much worse. As a neighbor, and with an impressive navy in its own right, Spain was a real threat to the Portuguese empire. One solution, designed by Rodrigo de Souza Coutinho, was to organize merchantmen into armed convoys to sail periodically from Pernambuco, Bahia, and Rio de Janeiro. Convoys had to balance between protecting Portuguese commerce against interlopers and raiders, even eager British traders, while at the same time bolstering thriving colonial commerce. And some of these convoys could be impressive, such as that escorted from Rio de Janeiro in 1802 under the escort of Francisco de Parete Leite's squadron, whose thirty-two merchantmen carried a cargo worth over 2,200,000,000 reales. Yet, given the scale of imperial business there was no way the Portuguese navy could defend its merchantmen; Lisbon had to turn to the British navy for help.[35]

In all, the revolutionary conjuncture favored the interests of the colonies. However, external pressures of European warfare alone did not determine the shift in power to the colonies. After all, Spain faced similar pressures but handled them differently. In some respects, more fundamental for explaining the transformations of the merchant empires was the *internal* balance of power and influence within the dominant bloc of the empire. In the Portuguese mercantile order, it was above all colonial magnates, tied together through credit, marriage, and opportunistic exploitation of the many loopholes of the South Atlantic economy, who conducted the business of upholding the imperial political economy. This change, under way before the 1790s, only intensified thereafter—and did not constitute a general crisis of the colonial system or the ancien régime, as has been argued by Vitorino Magalhães Godinho and Fernando Novais. Rather than a crisis, it is more accurate to call this a transformation that elevated Brazil's merchants to the center of the transatlantic

---

[35]ANRJ, Negocios de Portugal, Caixa 718, pacote 1, doc. 87, and pacote 2, doc. 36; ANTT, JC, Maço 10, Caixa 36, f. 8; Maço 64, Caixa 207, f. 1; Caixa 208, ff. 1, 2. AHU, CU, Códice 550, f. 65; 962, f. 160.

coalition that ruled the Portuguese ancien régime without ever questioning the principles of monarchy or aristocratic ennoblement.[36]

The centrality of colonial merchants became institutionalized. What was
already a difference between Spanish and Portuguese mercantilism—greater
commercial autonomy for colonial merchants in Brazil—became even more
marked after 1789. In 1755, the new Junta do Comércio, and its branches
in the colonies, took over the job of regulating commerce and stamping out
contraband. Over time, the junta served less as the instrument of imperial
merchant houses seeking to maximize the transfer of surpluses to the metropole. Rather, it became the vehicle for imposing an order designed by great
merchants of the empire—many of whom had not just outposts but headquarters for their operations in Brazil. These great merchants used the governance structure of imperial commerce, and their influence on the South
Atlantic slave trade, to uphold their control over commercial rents. In 1788,
the government expanded the junta's legal purviews and elevated it to
become the Real Junta do Comércio, Agricultura, Fábricas e Navegações
destes Reino e seus Domínios. By 1795, as one prominent Luso-Brazilian
mercantile partnership (Loureiros & Guimaraens) observed in an appeal to
the junta for rights to trade directly between Asia and Brazil, the old order
was a hollow shell of its former Pombaline self. They noted that Atlantic
warfare and the compression on long-distance trade routes, coupled with the
revenue needs of the Portuguese monarchy, meant that regulators had no
choice but to safeguard an already emerging commercial system, converting
a de facto reality into a de jure system: transferring metropolitan authority
to Brazilian ports. From Brazil, they argued, sugar, liquors, tobacco, and
other staples sold well in Asian markets, while vessels from Asia returned
with textiles and preciosities, picking up Mozambican and Angolan slaves en
route. Furthermore, balanced taxes on this trade could produce the revenues
to ensure "the dignity and independence of the Monarchy." So, like the merchants of Spain's South American ports, Brazilian merchants advocated the
recognition of a new trading system. The difference was that Brazilian magnates had the means to effect their discourses.[37]

To say that there was no crisis does not mean that imperial change
implied a frictionless adaptation to shifting material interests. To begin
with, the convoy system never insulated the South Atlantic from interlopers.

---

[36]See Alexandre, *Os sentidos do império*, pp. 54–62; Mansuy, "Portugal and Brazil,"
p. 481; José Jobson de Andrade Arruda, "Colonies as Mercantile Investments: The Luso-
Brazilian Empire, 1500–1808," in James Tracy, ed., *The Political Economy of Merchant
Empires* (Cambridge: Cambridge University Press, 1991), pp. 396–410; Vitorino Magalhães
Godinho,*O Brasil no comércio colonial* (São Paulo: Editora Atica, 1980); and Novais,
Portugal.
[37]AHU, CU Códice, 962, ff. 148–50; DA, Caixa 158, doc. 20.

Brazilian traders repeatedly violated Lisbon's official restrictions on trade with British merchants. Brazilian merchants even used Portuguese convoys, cobbled together to protect merchantmen from French warships, as cover to trade with British agents. The house of Felipe Ribeiro Filgueiras and José Francisco Loures was caught red-handed loading cotton and sugar onto their ships in Bahia destined not for imperial but British ports. Minister Souza Coutinho ordered "the most severe punishment" inflicted on these magnates and warned his deputies in the ports to be on the lookout for all foreign vessels dropping in on colonial ports, even under "the pretext of arribadão (stop overs)."[38] Still, many merchants circumvented the convoys as they pleased. In early 1798, one fleet bound for Brazil got past enemy raiders and then broke up as faster merchantmen bolted ahead of the lumbering convoy, hoping to be able to be the first to sell their wares to colonial consumers, and therefore to fetch higher prices. The leader of the naval escort had to admit to the naked opportunism of merchants and the "damage they posed to the Common Good of your Majesty's Faithful Vassals."[39]

Of course, at the same time, merchants wanted defense from French or Spanish threats. So, while defecting from Lisbon's rules they also complained about Lisbon's inefficacy. A merchant from Luanda found his Brazilian trade constantly menaced by enemies and got so fed up with interruptions and losses that he appealed to colonial authorities for them to allow the British man-of-war *Good Intention* to escort African cargos bound for Brazil. Without this protection, "there will be a great damage to the prosperity of your subjects' Commerce," with grave threats to the "Religious, Political, Civil, Economic, and Military Government of your Dominions."[40] Not suprisingly, the prophylactic goals of the convoy system only created inducements to many merchants to use the escorts to defend against enemy French warships, while at the same time violating the restrictions on any trade with willing British merchantmen seeking cargo and markets in the South Atlantic. Even Souza Coutinho admitted that the convoys were an imperfect way of reconciling competing objectives: defending metropolitan balances with Britain while letting Brazilian merchants trade with as many partners as necessary to keep the imperial boom going.[41]

The costs and benefits of the convoys were minor issues compared to official efforts to curb contraband. Smuggled commodities surged through

---

[38] APB, Secção Colonial, Cartas Regias, no. 89, doc 16, 17; ANTT, JC, Maço 64, Caixa 207, f. 1.

[39] ANTT, JC, Maço 63, Caixa 206, f. 3; ANRJ, Negocios de Portugal, Caixa 715, pacote 1, doc. 113.

[40] ANTT, JC, Maço 10, Caixa 36, f. 8.

[41] ANTT, JC, Maço 63, Caixa 206, f. 3, for an especially insightful view of the minister's dilemma. See also AHU, CU, Códice 550, f. 133.

the frontier interiors as far east as Angola and west into Minas Gerais. Benguela was a popular way station for London- and Liverpool-registered ships trying to dip into the South Atlantic economy, offering English manufactures to Brazilian merchants swapping their staples for slaves.[42] Smuggling was rampant throughout the diamond district. The general intendant of Ouro reported in 1793 that his efforts to use extreme measures of expulsions of miners and burning their mining camps yielded mixed results. No sooner did he wipe out one cluster of traders than others flooded the district. He complained, moreover, that merchants had also perfected the art of buying off his staff with bribes and kickbacks.[43] Souza Coutinho reserved his stiffest language for the enforcement of laws against contraband dealers, ordering anyone caught violating rules against foreign imports to be "severely" tried and sentenced.[44]

Not surprisingly, it was English allies, not French enemies, that posed the most severe commercial threat to Portugal's mercantile system. As far back as 1785, colonial officials were instructed to be on the lookout for English traders "seeking to penetrate the *mar do sul* and in reality against Brazil and the Spanish Dominions of these parts."[45] A decade later, Souza Coutinho informed Fernando Antonio de Noronha that in his view colonial officials had to treat the English as military friends, but "as the most threatening enemy of this Kingdom" when it came to trade. In his view, the weakest, most vulnerable channel of imperial commerce was the intercolonial business between Angola and Brazil. It was both one of the most prized and underdefended, and of course the one through which Brazilian, especially Rio de Janeiro, merchants had built an elaborate trading system—vital to the empire, but removed from metropolitan controls.[46]

Clamping down on contraband through Brazilian ports was futile because so few colonial merchants had an interest in curbing their business. As one report to the viceroy noted, every year dozens of Spanish ships passed through Rio de Janeiro from the River Plate on the way to Angola, taking staples and rude manufactures east, and returning with slaves and some European wares from Luanda. The cargos themselves were owned by Spanish and Brazilian merchants alike; the crews were ragtag groups of Africans, Spaniards, and Portuguese. Indeed, "contraband"

---

[42]ANRJ, Vice-Reinado, Caixa 492, pacote 1, s.n., report, June 21, 1796.

[43]ANRJ, Vice-Reinado, Caixa 485, pacote 2, s.n., report by Caetano Pinto de Vasconcellos Montenegro, May 3, 1793.

[44]APB, Secção Colonial, 89, doc. 17.

[45]AHU, Códice, 567, f. 11.

[46]AHU, Códice, 550, ff. 133–43; DA, Códice 574, ff. 15, 81; Códice 962, ff. 72–73; APB, Secção Colonial, 89, doc. 69.

represented, as Brazilian merchants and shippers were increasingly arguing, foreign branches on an extended South Atlantic system dominated by colonial Brazilian merchant houses. In the winter of 1794, Caetano Silvestre, a merchant based in Santa Catarina, was detained on contraband charges. Investigators found that his business consisted of trafficking in slaves procured in Rio de Janeiro, who were then shipped to Buenos Aires, and returning with hides, meat, fat, and Spanish silver, which were then shipped to other Brazilian and African ports. When they tried to slap charges, Silvestre's partners, creditors, and consumers cried foul, warning authorities that in their zeal to suppress contraband, they would undermine the commercial dynamism of the colony.[47] By the end of the eighteenth century, it was plain that English, North American, and Spanish American contraband circulating through imperial commercial circuitry may have been "foreign," but it serviced a trade run by colonial subjects and contributed, despite their violations of metropolitan regulations, to imperial prosperity.[48]

It was not long before Souza Coutinho gave up on metropolitan regulations of imperial trade almost altogether. Petition after petition came in requesting exemptions from colonial trading restrictions. In early 1801, João Rodrigues Pereira de Almeida, one of Rio de Janeiro's largest merchants, lobbied for unrestricted rights to trade with Angola. A royal letter soon followed, sent to the viceroy, giving Rodrigues and "all other merchants" of Brazil the right to import slaves and whale oil from Africa, in return for "merchandise" from Brazil.[49] To these sorts of requests to free infra-imperial trade even if it meant circumventing the metropolis Souza Coutinho buckled. Starting in late 1799, he began ordering Junta do Comércio officers along the Angolan coast to loosen constraints on the slave trade with Brazil—"only on condition that there is no shipment of Slaves to Foreign Dominions." By 1800, the Brazilian-Angolan trading system was officially exempted from metropolitan constraints. This led to a flurry of demands by other ports to join the Brazilian trade more freely. Upon hearing that Luanda and Rio de Janeiro were now free to trade, a group of merchants from Gabon sent a petition to Lisbon calling for their freedom to trade with Brazilian partners. They pointed out that the only way to defend Portuguese trade against English penetration of the slave trade was to let Brazilian merchandise and merchants work more freely along the whole African coast. "Since this Colony cannot sustain direct

---

[47] AHU, DA, Caixa 156, doc. 69, Caixa 157, doc. 53; CU, Códice 574, f. 45; ANRJ, Vice-Reinado, Caixa 492, pacote 2, s.n., June 22, 1798, and ff. 223, 308; APB, Secção Colonial, 89, doc. 69.
[48] AHU, CU, Códice 574, f. 97.
[49] AHU, CU, Códice 575, f. 186.

commerce with the Metropole, since Slaves are the principal product used to pay for merchandise [imports], and since the African coast is now open to all Nations searching for slaves, it would be most convenient for us to have the products from the country for which we draw most of our trade: Brazil."[50] Integrating the South Atlantic economy was not just vital to the empire—defending it meant cutting loose from Lisbon's merchant capitalists. What was good for the empire, and what was good for the metropole, were no longer one.

It is important to recognize that opening trade was meant to reinforce imperial commerce, not to pave the way for "free trade" in the nineteenth-century sense of the term. Imperial authorities made the defense of Brazil's commercial system the priority. They stopped short of letting colonial merchants trade with whom they pleased. When José Antonio Pereira, owner of a network of African factories from São Tomé to Angola, loaded three ships full of slaves in Luanda, he requested permission to send the vessels directly to Buenos Aires, skirting Brazil altogether. Pereira's request got a summary "no." For the most part, merchants also agreed to abide by these rules as they served their rent-seeking interests. Living within this constraint turned out to be fine by many merchants since they did not have to compete openly with British, French, or other traders. Indeed, the pressure to open commerce stopped well short of calling for free trade altogether. The self-same magnate Pereira blanched when he found out that the government of São Tomé wanted to open trade with other Europeans. It was one thing to let *him* trade with other ports in the South Atlantic economy, but quite another to let French or English traders muscle in on his world. Regulators of the Junta do Comércio agreed when he filed a protest against São Tomé: "because only the internal and external commerce which gives value to natural products and industries which encourage Agriculture and the Arts facilitating subsistence will promote the welfare of the population. The captaincies of Brazil, animated by this commerce, are iridescent proof of this truth."[51]

In both the Portuguese and Spanish empires, trade regulators struggled to reconcile increasingly fractious interests. In the Portuguese empire, there was little doubt that sovereignty over these matters had been pushed to the periphery and that in the 1790s, colonial control prevailed over imperial concerns. In the Spanish empire, matters were not quite so simple. By the late 1790s, the interests in Cádiz were up in arms about

---

[50]ANTT, JC, Maço 62, Caixa 202, n.n., March 29, 1802.
[51]AHU, CU, Códice 962, ff. 227, 245–47; AN, Vice-Reinado, Caixa 492, pacote 2, f. 223; ANTT, JC, Maço 15, Caixa 169, n.n., October 31, 1803.

colonial inroads on commercial affairs, and forced the government to reverse the course of gradual devolution—a process that sparked outrage across the empire and heated debate within much more divided mercantile circles in the colonies. In the Spanish empire, therefore, shifting decision making over commercial policy exposed deep fissures within the dominant merchant classes of the realm. In neither empire, however, did the freedom to realign interests within the ancien régime inspire any questioning of the rentier system as a whole. All agents entitled to operate within mercantilist circles, and with the kinship and credit networks to make their privileges effective, upheld the peculiar type of property created by the sovereign and enjoyed by the colonial few. Indeed, penetration into the colonial frontiers and devolution of control to the colonies themselves—even if a fitful process—only redoubled loyalty to the system. These changes therefore augmented the stakeholders in empire while increasing the plurality of "voices" engaged in the definition and allocation of imperial privileges. This was a combustible mix, not necessarily a recipe for imperial crises, which set the stage for intensified bargaining when sovereigns turned to their rentiers for revenues.

IMPERIAL FINANCES

Waging imperial war required tapping into the most liquid imperial assets. Whereas the trade issues principally involved bargaining and confrontation within merchant communities, financial issues involved bargaining between the sovereign and his subjects among the ranks of merchant capitalists. Ministers relied on taxes, mainly customs levies, and the rising rents from the commercial bonanza to buoy state revenues. In moments of more acute needs, there was a third revenue source: borrowing money from rentiers. By the 1790s, imperial authorities were beginning to explore the art of "public finance," or *crédito público*, financing emergency wartime needs by borrowing and then servicing and amortizing the debt with taxes collected during peacetime. The practice, which we now call "tax smoothing," enabled monarchs to manage the peaks and troughs of revenues and spending. In practice, managing the monarch's needs with strategic borrowing proved much more complicated. In order for merchants to invest in imperial bonds willingly, to make the tax-smoothening scheme work, they had to believe that the crown's promise to repay was credible. In the absence of credible commitments, monarchs had to make concessions: in response to the crown's revenue needs, colonial merchants pressed for more complete trade autonomy. The road of commercial change in the Spanish and

Portuguese empires twisted and turned around the mountains of imperial debts.[52]

As revenue seekers fixed their sights on agents with access to pools of capital, once again there were differences and similarities in the Iberian empires. In matters of trade, Lisbon relinquished control to Brazil, and Spain had to suffer greater discord and confusion as it let the colonial ports assume greater autonomy. In matters of finance, too, the Portuguese sovereign tilted control over revenues to the periphery with less friction. In the Spanish realm, the tensions within the dominant classes came to the fore when ministers, in dire financial straits, prepared to revise the colonial pact with its distant merchant communities—giving them greater autonomy in return for their contribution to imperial coffers. As both empires tinkered with their fiscal and financial machinery, for colonial elites, this was an opportunity, not an offense. They did not—as British colonists did—invoke imperial policies as pretexts for exiting empire. This analysis of the finances of empires shows how the peripheries and their merchant capitalists had deep vested interests in sustaining old institutions and practices. What mattered to them was control over policymaking, not polity making.[53]

The Iberian rub was that the imperial trade expansion of the 1790s generated larger rents but pooled them mainly in the colonies. At the same time the conjuncture did not create new pools of revenues in the metropolis at a time in which fiscal demands spiked with each war. One option was to tax the booming trade. Monarchs did try this. They fiddled with raising taxes on long-distance trade but tended to abandon such efforts, since it threatened to drive even more trade into illegal channels. Instead, they opted increasingly to borrow money from the merchants who made rising rents from their privileges. Thus, while colonial interests gained increasing authority over imperial policy, they also gained increasing financial stakes in its survival. The revision of the colonial pact between colonies and metropoles, between merchants and monarchs, intertwined each agent in an ever-tighter knot of mutual dependency.[54]

---

[52]For a useful survey of financial instruments in the period, see Michael D. Bordo and Eugene N. White, "British and French Finance during the Napoleonic Wars," in Michael D. Bordo and Forrest Capie, eds., *Monetary Regimes in Transition* (Cambridge: Cambridge University Press, 1994), pp. 241–73.

[53]For a comparable analysis of how archaic structures made for good business, see Stanley Stein, "Bureaucracy and Business in the Spanish Empire, 1759–1804: Failure of a Bourbon Reform in Mexico and Peru," *Hispanic American Historical Review* 61:1 (1981): 2–28.

[54]Gabriel Ardant, "Financial Policy and Economic Infrastructure of Modern States and Nations," in Charles Tilly, ed., *The Formation of National States in Western Europe* (Princeton: Princeton University Press, 1975), pp. 164–242; Root, *The Fountain of Privilege*, pp. 164–77.

Portuguese Finances

Shaping Portuguese financial evolution from 1790 was the relatively light fiscal burden imposed by war and the relative cohesion of the ruling colonial bloc that assumed greater control over trading rights. Portugal appeared to weather the storm of revolution and war before 1806 precisely because shifting control to the periphery had provoked less friction; it did not expose dividing lines within the ruling bloc. Behind the shift in Portuguese commercial policy was a strong fiscal impetus. We lack good fiscal data on Brazil from 1777 to 1805, but Brazil had never been a particularly important source of imperial revenues. Much of the income remained in the colony itself and was not remitted to the metropolis. By the late 1790s, however, the imperial treasury was in trouble. The need for revenues forced authorities to instill even more control over policymaking to where the pools of capital themselves accumulated: the colonies.[55]

One option was to increase traditional methods of tax collecting, raising tithes, and other levies on consumption. There were limits to this option, as rising food prices and perceived injustices meted out by tax collectors gripped all of South America in the 1790s. One merchant in Rio de Janeiro warned that the fiscal conventions of the salt monopoly and high import duties on iron and slaves choked private enterprise, and accounted for the "irregularities" in colonial markets. Raising old taxes was therefore rejected. In 1794, the Overseas Council in Lisbon dismissed efforts to broaden tithe collection rights in Brazil, fearing that consumers would rebel. As the 1790s saw increasing tension over food prices, the council observed "that the people are feeling these excessive burdens, and it is not worth risking more suffering due to an Execution [of a permit to increase the levy] and its natural *despezas*." These traditional means to raise revenues "only benefit the interests of particulars, and are very capable of fomenting and producing these and other ruins, as they open a grand road to malice which overwhelms the good faith of the collectors."[56]

If local consumers would not yield the required revenues, fiscal officers turned to Atlantic commerce. Indeed, the desperation to thwart contraband was driven above all by the fear that it would bleed royal revenues. Contraband was as old as the colonies themselves, but in the 1790s it became the source of official hysteria. The viceroy of Brazil informed the Overseas Council in 1795 that the opening of trade of the South Atlantic was a source of commercial bonanza, gave vitality to ports all along the

---

[55]Alden, "Late Colonial Brazil," pp. 649–50.
[56]AHU, DA, Caixa 159, doc. 23, Caixa 157, doc. 42.

Brazilian littoral, but had not yet delivered on its fiscal potential. Indeed, the opening only pushed more of the traffic out of the reach of customs officers, as "the people were accustomed" to ignoring them. The costs of imperial defenses were mounting, he warned, and the colonial population had a low threshold for additional taxes; the only solution was levies on the merchants involved in Atlantic trade.[57] By 1798, one Angolan administrator of the Junta do Comércio warned that legal commerce had declined so much that it was even worth the expense to hire British men-of-war to drive out interlopers and enforce official convoys. This would pull (or push) illicit traffic back into legal channels, within reach of tax collectors.[58]

The hullabaloo over taxes tended to lead to more consternation than revenues. By century's end, the tax system of the Portuguese empire was coming in for major criticism from all corners. José da Silva Lisboa, a prominent lawyer and deputy and secretary to the Board of Inspection of Agriculture and Commerce in Bahia, excoriated traditional efforts to regulate commerce and collect levies. The whole customs and tobacco tax-gathering business was riddled with problems and inefficacies. According to Silva Lisboa, the problem could be attributed to the persistence of local monopolies in colonial markets: the power of a handful of merchants, with the collusion of venal officers of the law, inflated the official prices of local merchandise and encouraged many smaller merchants to participate in the contraband trade to avoid taxes and sell on rampant black markets. "It's useless," he intoned, "to insist that the regulation of the market be placed in order. . . because the spirit of Service has been calumnied by the cabal of the country's rich and powerful." Silva Lisboa, as we shall see, would emerge as a significant voice for change.[59]

One option was to open colonial trade, widen the opportunities for merchants to generate more rents, and hope that this would animate state revenues. In response to João Rodrigues Pereira de Almeida's petition for unrestricted trade with Angola, the royal order made clear to the viceroy that more open trade between Brazil and Africa was to support the interests of colonial merchants and enhance their rents, but also to prop up royal revenues. "You are instructed to animate and help by all means possible these merchants, so long as this act of grace is not detrimental to My Royal Treasury."[60] Around the same time the Count

---

[57]AHU, DA, Caixa 159, doc. 60.
[58]ANTT, JC, Maço 10, Caixa 36, ff. 8, 11.
[59]APB, Secção Colonial, 87, doc. 10; AHU, DA, Caixa 156, doc. 21.
[60]AHU, CU, Códice 575, f. 187.

of Rezende removed all obstacles to the export of *cachaça* (liquor) to Africa to promote further taxable trade.[61] When the new Brazilian viceroy, Fernando José de Portugal, got his official instruction in 1800, he was reminded of his number-one priority: to continue his predecessor's efforts to promote commerce—support initiatives to bolster Caixas de Credito, moneylending, discounting notes, in fact any financial measure that might help the circulation of goods—for only by promoting mercantile rents could the state procure public revenues.[62] Merchants and ministers agreed that there was a connection between private mercantile rents and public royal revenues. And they also agreed that promoting the former was the way to enhance the latter. This was an important crystallizing moment in the history of the Portuguese ancien régime, for it made explicit a shift that had been occurring through the eighteenth century: private fortunes were the dorsal support for state finances.

The challenge of recalibrating relations between an increasingly embattled state in Europe and enriched capitalists in the colonies fell to Rodrigo de Souza Coutinho. Born in 1755, educated in law at the University of Coimbra, Souza Coutinho amassed a distinguished career as minister of the navy and overseas dominions (1796–1801), president of the royal mint and minister of finance (1801–3), and finally minister of war and Foreign Relations (1808–12). Since Pombal, there had not been a custodian so versed in the literature on political economy. He read Adam Smith's *Wealth of Nations* at twenty-three years old, and sought to apply many of the lessons he learned there and in his consumption of physiocratic texts. In an important memorandum to the crown penned in 1797, the new minister explained the importance of the colonies to Portugal, and thus the vital role that wealthy families in Brazil would play in the destiny of the monarchy. Any solution to the empire's financial troubles began, he argued, with a treatment of the overseas dominions, especially those in America, "which are, properly speaking, the base of the greatness of your august throne." He elaborated: "Your Majesty's dominions in Europe are but the capital, the center of your vast possessions. Portugal reduced to itself alone would become, in short order, a province of Spain. As long as it serves as the gathering point and the home of the monarchy which extends to the European and African islands, to Brazil, to the oriental and occidental coasts of Africa, and as far as the Royal Crown's possessions in Asia, it has, without contradiction,

---

[61]AHU, CU, Códice 574, f. 45.
[62]AHU, CU, Códice 575, f. 101.

within it all the means to figure conspicuously and brilliantly among the great powers of Europe." Portugal as the crossroads between Africa, Asia, and America was great; shorn of its colonies it was a rump. Portugal's government had to balance properly the interests of the center and those of the periphery, expressed in terms fitting for a follower of Adam Smith, not for one side but for their "reciprocal advantage." Depriving the periphery of its due threatened to alienate the colonies and would undermine "the sacrosanct principle of unity, the first base of the Monarchy."[63]

Behind Souza Coutinho's vision of imperial policy was an important doctrinal evolution. Not only did the colonies have to prosper for the empire to thrive; the center could not win at the expense of the periphery. But rulers had to accept a different model of taxation, of generating revenues out of imperial rents. Taxation had to adapt to the structure of wealth, not the other way around. Otherwise it would throttle industry, commerce, and agriculture. So, any hike in customs threatened to reduce revenues by inducing contraband. Indeed, argued Souza Coutinho, taxes on the slave trade were probably excessive already. The minister concluded that imperial policy should start by understanding what was good for capital first, what most enhanced rents as a precondition for what was good for the imperial treasury, for the crown's revenues. In effect, Souza Coutinho's views offered a double shift, simultaneously underscoring the priority—indeed the anteriority—of colonial wealth and private capital as the founts for the imperial sovereign's well-being.[64]

What obsessed Souza Coutinho above all was the state of the empire's finances—all his reflections on the colonies and good government were merely foundations for an imperial edifice built out of sound money. In this basic sense, he followed the genealogy of imperial ministers who likened commerce to the lifeline of imperial monarchies. But the revenue crunch required that Souza Coutinho trace the lines between commodities, money, and the public treasury in a way that surpassed any of his predecessors. In the 1790s, the government began issuing ever-larger ad hoc loans to cover fiscal shortfalls, payable over short terms. By 1796, however, Souza Coutinho pressed the Brazilian government to extend the maturity of loans to fifteen years, earning 4 percent interest. The government

---

[63]Rodrigo de Souza Coutinho, "Memória sobre o melhoramento dos Domínios de Sua Majestad na América," in his *Textos Políticos, Económicos e Financiaes, 1783–1811* (Lisboa: Banco de Portugal, 1993) v. 2, pp. 47–66; José Luis Cardoso, *O Pensamento Económico em Portugal nor Finais do Século XVIII, 1780–1808* (Lisboa: Editorial Estampa, 1989), pp. 128–43.

[64]Souza Coutinho "Memória sobre o melhoramento dos Domínios de Sua Majestad na América," pp. 55–61.

also approved coinage issues at the royal mint to create liquidity for trade and for merchants to buy public bills. In 1800, officials allowed the Casa de Moneda to begin minting copper coins to alleviate the currency shortage and promote trade. While this threatened to debase the value of money, "in this critical moment it is most necessary to raise public funds and dissipate the lack of confidence among the people."[65]

There were other means to cover immediate shortfalls that affected the balance between public obligations and private capacities. The treasury issued strict instructions as to how administrators should handle Bilhetes de Fazenda, treasury notes that could be used to pay any private obligation to the state. The main purpose in enabling the treasury to issue paper notes was to meet short-term official needs, thus monetizing state obligations. This was still a public resource used only occasionally so long as Souza Coutinho was on watch and the war needs were relatively modest, but as we shall see, it became a huge lever after 1812 with the eruption of revolutionary civil wars in the colonies. Here, too, was a way to inject liquidity into the commercial system because these notes could be discounted in the market. But if this was good for private interests and public institutions, the new financial regime required some strict laws. Their emission had to be handled exclusively by the Junta de Fazenda, cautiously emitted and scrupulously amortized to "ensure for the future that they, and any debt of this Captaincy, are never permitted to fluctuate uncertainly or vaguely."[66] Thus even before the outbreak of war, Souza Coutinho was confronting the nexus between the fiscal pressures on the state, the interests of merchant capital, and the creation of new kinds of money.

No sooner did the crown open trade within the empire than war with Spain erupted in February 1801. The costs of this—albeit brief—conflict sent the crown scurrying for revenues. It also finally enabled Souza Coutinho to unveil a master plan to impose some coherence on the empire's finances.[67] The war expanded and systematized the borrowing of funds—not just changing the fiscal and monetary habits of the Portuguese empire but initiating a new relationship between merchant capital and the treasury. Now, merchant capitalists became investors in the state as possessors of public bills. The minister argued that the state

---

[65]AHU, CU, Códice 573, ff. 191–92; AN, Negocios de Portgual, Caixa 718, pacote 1, f. 145; Rodrigo de Souza Coutinho, "Projecto de Alvará para abrir um empréstimo do valor de 4 milhões de cruzados" (31/1/1797), in his *Textos*, v. 2, pp. 96–103.

[66]AHU, CU, Códice 575, ff. 136–38.

[67]ANRJ, Secretária de Estado, Caixa 642, pacote 1, doc. 71; APB, Secção Colonial, 89, doc. 88. See, for instance, Rodrigo de Souza Coutinho "Projecto de carta de lei sobre o crédito público e a criação de um banco público de crédito e circulação" (c. July 1797), reprinted in his *Textos*, v. 2, pp. 105–9.

had to find a way of converting short-term debt into longer-term bonds or what he called "bank credit." The solution was the creation of an amortization fund and an authority to monitor the issuance of public bills that could also be used as legal tender. Effectively, Souza Coutinho unveiled a scheme for transforming the empire's unfunded debt, the motley collection of short-term obligations backed only by current revenues, to a "funded debt" of long-term securities (6 percent bills maturing in thirty years) backed by a special fund replenished by taxes earned on long-distance trade during years of peace. Creating such a public credit system not only bolstered public institutions, it would be good for private interests, too. The hitch was that political leaders had to make their commitment to honor the real value of these instruments credible—any sign that the state might be unable to pay the full value of the loans would immediately depreciate merchants' investments. It was clear in Souza Coutinho's plan that tapping into pools of capital meant turning to where they were largest and most accessible: Brazilian merchants. By recombining public and private interests in this way, by making *colonial* capitalists investors in the imperial state while compelling the state to live by its commitments, argued Souza Coutinho, the empire could more virtuously manage its finances. "Nothing could be more desired," he concluded, "not only so that the Royal and Public Service be conducted exactly, but also so that the state of the Royal Treasury wins all the credit that it needs, so that it could be a great base for the stability of the State and for the consolidation given by Public Opinion."[68]

The urgency to develop a funding scheme, to enlist the financial support of colonial merchants to invest in long-term securities to keep the Portuguese domain afloat, was fueled by the menace of a more widespread and drawn-out war. Unlike earlier mercantilist wars of the eighteenth century, where rivals quarreled for overseas possessions and commercial supremacy, the revolutionary wars presented the specter of a war to the death of entire regimes. Accordingly, Souza Coutinho warned, Portugal must prepare for an "energetic, powerful, and desperate Defense."[69] The war turned out to be short-lived, aborting the urgency to establish new institutions to handle the revenue needs of the imperial state. Piecemeal measures got the crown through their difficulties.

---

[68] ANRJ, Secretária de Estado, Caixa 642, pacote 1, doc. 7. The best description of this system is in Patrick K. O'Brien, "The Political Economy of British Taxation, 1660–1815," *Economic History Review* 41:1 (1988): 1–32; see also Bordo and White, "British and French Finance," pp. 345–46.

[69] Alexandre, *Os sentidos do império*, p. 131.

Non–defense spending was slashed; additional levies on staple trades in late 1801 brought in some additional funds.[70] Moreover, the government continued to rely on conventional loans from its merchants, and the treasury turned, in a pinch, to printing paper notes. By 1802, Souza Coutinho could announce that the empire was on firm fiscal footing, obviating the urgency to create a modern funding system. For the time being, the master plan of revamping the empire's fiscal and financial infrastructure was on hold.[71]

In the Portuguese empire, the booming commerce, the aborted conflict, and Souza Coutinho's financial management held the empire back from a fiscal precipice. But Portugal's financial needs did effect a change in the political economy of empire. The pressure to raise more revenues on long-distance trade and dependence on merchants for public loans altered the bargaining with merchant capitalists. Now, aware of the acute dependence of the crown on colonial capital, Brazilian merchants intensified their claims for open trade on their terms. In 1805, merchant networks in Africa and Brazil successfully won their demands to be able to trade directly with Spanish American ports. One merchant appealed for rights to ship slaves straight from Cabinda to Buenos Aires and to pick up staples there for Brazilian markets. His request was approved with the argument that "other ports along that [African] Coast are open and free to all Nations so that they may purchase slaves" and the Portuguese must be able to compete with rivals. More open trade was good for the empire as a whole, even if it meant that Lisbon was even more marginal. "In this case it is most advantageous to the national interests that the Portuguese subjects earn with this traffic [the slave trade], whose final profits reinforce the Nation . . . And whatever obstacles lie before these speculations, will only mean that this business will be conducted by Foreign Merchants, with whom we compete, and to whom we would lose to their interests at the cost of the National interest."[72] Brazilian ports and their colonial merchant capitalists now defined commercial policy on their own terms. For the time being, Souza Coutinho's plan to ask colonial merchants to shoulder the financial burdens of empire as a quid pro quo for their pride of place in imperial commerce remained on hold. Shortly, however, the feared "national war" over the existence of the regime would put the deal to the test.

---

[70]ANRJ, Secretária de Estado, Caixa 642, pacote 1, docs. 43, 60, 93.

[71]ANRJ, Secretária de Estado, Caixa 718, pacote 2, doc. 36, Caixa 642, pacote 1, doc. 71; Afonso Arinos de Melo Franco, *Historia do Banco do Brasil (Primera Fase, 1808–1835)* (São Paulo: Instituto de Economía da Associação Comercial, 1948), p. 13.

[72]AHU, CU, Códice 962, ff. 254–55.

SPANISH FINANCES

Spain could not ride the military coattails of a superpower ally like Britain. To make matters worse, being caught between seaborne threats from the British or overland threats from the French condemned Madrid to almost permanent war. The result was a much more dramatic financial challenge. At the same time, the social obstacles to reallocating funds to public coffers were more pronounced because magnates were more internally divided over the future economic model of the empire. If trade disputes revealed tensions within the colonial blocs between importers and exporters, between metropolitans and creoles, the financial impact of war pushed Madrid's authority over its provinces and colonies to its limits.

As in the Portuguese empire, Spanish monarchs turned to colonial merchants to foot the bills for national as well as imperial defense. Revenues from New Spain funneled across the circum-Caribbean to support military installations in Cuba, Nueva Granada, and Venezuela. What was left trickled into Spain. Still, as analyses of treasury accounts have shown, remittances from the Indies, above all New Spain, was the single largest source of public revenue for Madrid.[73]

There were real, political obstacles to bulking up the revenue machinery of the Spanish empire. There was only so much New Spain's taxpayers could shoulder without more unrest. After all, the wave of popular protest and rebellion in the 1780s was a stark reminder of the limits of Bourbon fiscal ambitions. After 1800, all of Spanish America was seething with more unrest from below. This meant turning to imperial merchants, appealing to them for revenues as a quid pro quo for the rents they made from capitalist expansion in the hinterlands. This was no easy task as merchants, already anxious about the insecurity posed by war, were unhappy about paying taxes and siphoning money away from the New World. In Caracas, always living with liquidity shortages and without access to mining revenues, there was some discussion of withholding the remittances to Spain from the tobacco funds so that they could be injected into the local economy.[74]

---

[73]Barbier and Klein, "Revolutionary Wars and Public Finances," p. 326; Carlos Marichal and Matilde Souto Mantecón, "Silver and Situados: New Spain and the Financing of the Spanish Empire in the Caribbean in the Eighteenth Century," *Hispanic American Historical Review* 74:4 (1994): 587–613.

[74]AGNB, Real Consulado, Actas, 2526, f. 5, Colonia, Consulados, III, ff. 307–17; McKinley, *Pre-revolutionary Caracas*, p. 69. Jacques A. Barbier, "Anglo-American Investors and Payments on Spanish Imperial Treasuries, 1795–1808," in Barbier and Kuethe, eds., *The North American Role*, pp. 134–41.

The royal treasury was then forced to explore additional taxes on commerce. Hikes in most levies on local and long-distance trade were approved across the 1790s. But the implementation yielded lackluster returns. No sooner did the doors to the consulado in Cartagena open for business than its members were asked to pay an additional 1.5 percent levy on all imports and an additional 0.5 percent levy on all exports, the so-called *derechos de avería*, exempting the trade in slaves, precious metals, and agricultural machinery. Merchants grumbled about the fiscal price tag attached to their newfound autonomy over commercial affairs. Similar reluctance was heard in Buenos Aires. In Venezuela, where the costs of defending the porous coast, and with Dutch and British vessels constantly violating Spain's sovereign waters, the captaincy general issued special decree after special decree calling for additional levies to pay for warships.[75] What is fairly clear is that the Spanish state did manage to increase revenues during tough war years, with some foot-dragging in Peru and Nueva Granada. It was less successful at channeling these revenues to central accounts in Madrid where the fiscal crunch was most dramatic.[76]

In effect, merchants were drawing the line around how much colonial rents could be siphoned into imperial Spanish revenues. The complaining among magnates grew louder as the fiscal demands rose. In 1796, tax collectors and the merchants of Nueva Granada were at each other's throats. An inspection by Juan Antonio Mon y Velarde urged local tax collectors to do something about the anemic state of the viceregal coffers. When they tried to follow up, merchants accused fiscal officers of extorting their hard-earned profits by forcing payments in specie; the latter defended themselves as officers charged with upholding "not the interests of merchants, but the Royal Treasury." As the merchants pushed back, the general superintendent of the royal treasury in the viceroyalty refused to go down without a fight. José de Espeleta Galdeano

---

[75]AGNC, Real Consulado, Actas, 2526, ff. 20, 45–46.

[76]AGNB, Real Consulado, Actas, 2526, f. 6; AGNBA, Sala IX, Consulado, 29/1/1, Actas, f. 81; Stein, "Bureaucracy and Business," pp. 14–18; John J. TePaske, "General Tendencies and Secular Trends in the Economies of Mexico and Peru, 1750–1810: The View from the Cajas of Mexico and Lima," in Nils Jacobsen and Hans-Jürgen Puhle, eds., *The Economies of Mexico and Peru during the Late Colonial Period, 1760–1810* (Berlin: Bibl. Ibero-Americana, 1986), pp. 316–29; McFarlane, *Colombia before Independence*, pp. 224–25; John Coatsworth, "The Limits of Colonial Absolutism: The State in Eighteenth-Century Mexico," in Karen Spalding, ed., *Essays in the Political, Economic, and Social History of Colonial Latin America* (Newark: University of Delaware Press, 1982), pp. 34–35; Maurice Brungardt, "The Economy of Colombia in the Late Colonial and Early National Periods," in Fisher, Kuethe, and McFarlane, eds., *Reform and Insurrection*, pp. 164–79.

pointed out that he was only complying with the stipulations of the monetary standard for taxes, that he was merely "attending to his majesty's urgencies, the exhaustion of funds, and the state in which the Royal Treasury is found."[77]

In Caracas, administrators met the same resistance. There, however, merchants did not resist the temptation to charge royal officials of duplicity: preventing merchants from trading with friendly ports, but still asking them to foot the bills for wars with enemies. By 1800, with the coffers now dried up, half the spending earmarked for imperial defenses alone, the merchant guild came clean: "the problem is the general stagnation of our trade, and moreover, since the taxes that are demanded on foreign commerce were designed in times of peace at three per cent, we can only pay now a mere one per cent." Since the abrogation of the neutral trade decree of 1797, traffic had, according to the merchants, plummeted and deprived the crown of additional revenues. One report to the captaincy general was explicit: allow us wider avenues for commerce, "the benefits of freedom to trade," and we can pay more taxes, "with attention to the considerable funds that can be contributed." That same year, the merchants of Buenos Aires wrestled with the same dilemma—and some came to the very same conclusion. After the turn of the century, enthusiasm for paying taxes was so low, some even began questioning the legal authority of tax collectors. In April 1801, merchants took off their gloves in opposition to new levies, declaring that such measures "are sufficient to alter the good reputation of your honor and to stain the dignity and disinterest with which you must proceed with the inhabitants [of these lands]." In the polite discourse of ancien-régime bargaining, these were fighting words.[78]

To the chorus of opposition to the fiscal exactions of the Spanish government was added increasingly widespread contraband. At least until 1800, merchants traded illegally in order to introduce banned merchandise or ship to prohibited markets. But after 1800, royal officers were worried that smugglers avoided inspectors not because their wares were illegal but because they were dodging taxes. Merchants themselves argued that smuggling helped reduce the cost of basic foodstuffs for urban consumers and pointed to high levies as a self-serving explanation for contraband. One astute tax collector even argued that the Spanish state might *increase* revenues by *lowering* the incidence of taxation—inducing commerce back above ground by reducing emergency

---

[77] AGNB, Colonia, Consulados, III, ff. 336–41.

[78] AGNC, Real Consulado, Actas, 2527, ff. 94, and 116, and 212; AGNBA, Sala IX, Consulado, 29/1/3, Actas 1800–1802, f. 88; Barbier, "The Culmination," p. 67.

surcharges.[79] Especially during the British wars (1797–1802, 1804–8), pools of colonial capital were now forming not just beyond the reach of the trade regulators but beyond the empire's fiscal machinery.[80]

Under the circumstances, the desperation for money shifted the financial onus to borrowing. This seemed the obvious option. After all, the practice of issuing debt to relieve short-term treasury demands was a centuries-old tradition. The question, as the eighteenth century matured, was less whether to borrow but how. The success of a regime's funding scheme was, as many have noted, a key determinant of its ability to wage war.[81] Carlos III had sought to rationalize the system in the wake of humiliating conflict with Britain and the Seven Years War. Not unlike Souza Coutinho's plan, the Spanish monarch did not pursue his financial ambitions once peacetime and the trade reforms swelled his coffers (precisely when it would have been easier). As it was, the Spanish government tried to go back to this plan when warfare returned in the 1790s, that is, when it was harder to implement it. Like ancien-régime France, just when the government had to adjust to a sustainable funding system for its credit, it had the least bargaining power with holders of capital. As in France, the fiscal drama led to financial desperation and last-ditch efforts to appeal to merchants with the means to carry the monarchy over the hump of war debt.

The financial needs of the monarchy put the merchant guilds in a bind, as they were called upon to be the agents that handled the government's debt. The guilds were already caught between desperate tax collectors who relied more and more on the consulados to enforce the collection of emergency loans and impatient merchants tired of the many "urgencies" and the flip-flopping in trade policy. The result was that the colonial guilds saw the first full-blown debate over the Spanish regime's financial policies and practices. In Caracas, the members of the merchant guild gathered in 1795 when the colonial administration called for an emergency loan of 100,000 pesos. In a packed house, the "assembled members expressed their most fervent desires to support the government with their coffers for His Majesty's service . . . but that they are found at the very same time aggrieved at being unable to be fully effective, due to the shortage of money circulating in the market." This refrain echoed across the empire. So, when war broke out again in 1796, royal credit hit an all-time low. Another emergency issue of 500,000 pesos' worth of one-year

---

[79] AGNC, Real Consulado, Actas, 2528, f. 220, 2529, f. 83.

[80] Cuenca Esteban, "Statistics of Spain's Colonial Trade," pp. 410–15.

[81] John Brewer, *The Sinews of Power: War, Money and the English State, 1688–1783* (New York: Knopf, 1989).

bonds yielding 5 percent flopped. One merchant told authorities that between the remittances already due to Spain, the obstacles to trade, and the difficulty he faced recovering his own payments, there was nothing left for the crown.[82]

The Spanish regime muddled through the late 1790s and breathed a sigh of fiscal relief during the brief peace from 1802 until 1804. It was the collapse of the Peace of Amiens that finally broke the financial spine of the Spanish empire. In September 1804, the British government, responding to the cozier relations between the Bourbon court in Madrid and the new emperor, Napoleon, in Paris, authorized assaults on Spanish vessels carrying treasure. Sure enough, a fleet leaving the River Plate, loaded with silver from Potosí, ran into British warships on the high seas. The resulting losses, followed by the declaration of war in December, followed by the quick and thorough drubbing at Trafalgar, sheared Spain from its American dominions. The return to war, coupled with the collapse of imperial trade, meant that the royal treasury faced a sudden surge in expenses while the end of legal trade wiped out revenues. Before 1802, the Spanish empire had to manage a fiscal squeeze; after 1805, it faced a crush.[83]

What was to be done? Raising taxes was clearly one option. Accordingly, a bevy of decrees summoned those with money to pay higher levies. This only sparked greater opposition to voluntary tax payments.[84] Faced with the limits on tax collecting, the crown resorted to drastic measures. The most famous policy was the remedy of forced "loans." The most infamous among them, was Manuel Godoy's consolidation and expropriation of church assets, forcing ecclesiastic authorities to sell their property and deposit receipts into special accounts in the royal treasury, for which they would earn an earmarked rate of interest.[85] The crown also borrowed from merchants. Intendants began to order ad hoc "special contributions" with increasing frequency— 20,000–50,000 pesos for the maintenance of imperial defenses. In Caracas, consulado officials warned the government to be patient, "for the distribution of this levy among the merchants of the district has made it clear that it will take much more time to meditate over the most

---

[82]AGNB, Anexo—Emprestitos, t. I, ff. 2, 9, 22; AGNC, Real Consulado, Actas, 2526, f. 64, 2525, f. 215; Mark A. Burkholder and D. S. Chandler, *From Impotence to Authority: The Spanish Crown and the American Audiencias, 1687–1808* (Columbia: University of Missouri Press, 1977), pp. 87–88.

[83]Barbier and Klein, "Revolutionary Wars and Public Finances," pp. 331–33; Barbier, "Peninsular Finance and Colonial Trade," p. 31.

[84]AGNB, Colonia, Consulados, II, f. 666.

[85]Brading, "Bourbon Spain," pp. 437–38; TePaske, "General Tendencies," p. 331; McKinley, *Pre-revolutionary Caracas*, pp. 140–41.

acceptable, and the most beneficial, form to the contributors." Money
barely trickled in. Through 1805, officials floated several 6 percent loan
requests. Merchants, however, crossed their arms and showed little interest in picking up the bonds. In desperation, in May 1806 the Buenos
Aires government announced that its emergency loans were no longer
voluntary and that consulados would be required to raise the funds from
within their ranks. Forced loans were now reaching colonial mercantile
circles.[86]

To understand the reluctance of merchants to come to the financial
rescue, we need to return to the bargaining over trade policy. As part of
the Franco-Spanish convergence, and in response to lobbying from
Cádiz, Madrid ordered the commercial reins to be tightened once more:
a royal decree issued on October 22, 1804, banned all colonial traffic
with foreign vessels and issued severe penalties. It was the disgruntled
merchants, however, who possessed the money for lending; indeed, significant sectors of colonial merchant capitalists all but boycotted calls for
emergency loans, thus exposing the limits of the crown's ability to conduct affairs. When war finally erupted late that year, local authorities
warned that the strictures would be utterly unenforceable: they would
simply drive even more commerce underground and deprive the crown
of the loyalty of the merchants it most needed. "It is now totally impossible," reported the secretary of the Caracas consulado, "to contain contraband." One group of merchants urged authorities to legalize trade
with neutrals, "for if not we will reach another evil [aside from the
scarcity of goods] of no less magnitude which is the enormous fuel given
to clandestine commerce with the cessation of legitimate trade."[87]
Colonial merchants continued to lambaste restrictions on their trade—
made all the more ridiculous since commerce with Spain itself was
impossible. As a result, Madrid issued something of a compromise: in
December 1804, the crown exempted colonial officials from the full
weight of the new decree and authorized them to restore the old neutral
trade regime if they saw fit. Finally, the government announced in 1805
that colonial authorities could exempt their provinces from the 1804
ban, hoping to placate South American merchants, embellishing the
change with some principled rhetoric: The decree "is among the great
policies adopted by civilized and flourishing nations, to make real and
effective the happiness of the State with the progress of agriculture which
produces raw materials, and commerce which puts in circulation goods

---

[86]AGNBA, Sala IX, Consulado, 29/1/4, Actas, 1802–5, f. 97; 29/1/5, Actas, 1805–10,
ff. 3, 50; AGNC, Real Consulado, Actas, 2529, f. 65.

[87]AGNC, Real Consulado, Actas, 2529, ff. 62, 83, 113, 167–68; AGNBA, Sala IX,
Consulado, 29/1/4, Actas, 1802–5, f. 92.

that make wealth ... and that the prosperity and liberty of all rights are inseparable so that farmers may realize their work and so that they do not collapse in their vital exercise for the meager utilities they derive from their tasks."[88]

The concession, it should be clear, was not the result of any paradigm shift in imperial policy, a turn to a "free trade" doctrine. Rather, trade policy was made to comply more directly with the financial needs of the state and recognized that commercial decrees had to adjust to the claims by capitalists with the deepest pockets. These were located in the colonial entrepôts with interests in commerce beyond ancient mercantilist frontiers. The captain general of Venezuela captured the essence of the 1805 concession accurately and realistically, noting that he was lifting the ban on neutral trade "to remedy the immense damages occasioned by the interruption of trade with our Metropolis," and that forbidding trade with other nations brought "ruin" to colonial agriculture, commerce, and the royal treasury. The merchants of Buenos Aires saw things the same way: opening trade arteries was a way of reducing colonial malaise and reversing the misfortunes of the royal treasury, and also secured the right to trade with neutral ports. Only in Cartagena did the authorities override the complaints of merchants who wanted more open trade, only to open the floodgates to contraband. Trafalgar effectively stripped away the rhetoric of elevated bonds between the sovereign and his capitalist subjects and laid bare the contingencies of the colonial pacts between merchants and monarchs.[89]

In the new climate, the connections between merchant trading and crown borrowing were now explicit. Positions, once convergent, were now increasingly strained. Warfare forced the monarchy to return to the imperial bargaining table with cup in hand. Colonial merchants with means—those who did not depend on trade with the peninsula—were not pleased. Indeed, they were prepared to drive a hard bargain. Therefore, the division of imperial spoils between rents and revenues—the foundation of Spanish mercantilism—grew acrimonious when the crown could least afford it. Only months after conceding to demands from merchants in the colonial ports, the crown turned to them for an "open loan," issuing voluntary 6 percent bonds. Consider the reaction in Buenos Aires, after the viceroy asked the city's mercantile magnates for money. He explicitly

---

[88] AGNBA, Sala IX, Consulado, 4/6/2, Correspondencia, f. 713; AGNC, Real Consulado, Actas, 2529, f. 62; Barbier, "Commercial Reform," p. 112; Fisher, "Commerce and Imperial Decline," p. 468.

[89] AGNC, Real Consulado, Actas, 2529, f. 112; AGNBA, Sala IX, Consulado, 29/1/5, Actas, 1805–10, f. 68; McFarlane, *Colombia before Independence*, pp. 304–6; McKinley, *Pre-revolutionary Caracas*, pp. 142–44.

pointed to the 1805 trade concession as a gesture of the government's goodwill. The reply from the consulado, conveying the lack of enthusiasm among merchants with means to invest in bonds, was not uplifting. The guild's secretary said, "I recognize and it pleases me the laudable stimulus of honor and patriotism which I observe in Your Majesty, but I must also observe that many subjects, and among them many of the most powerful of this Capital, have not answered the invitation which Your Majesty offered" of a loan. He added that "powerful subjects lack, in this critical situation, the spirit to meet the urgencies of the Monarchy when they can and must do so without any damage or risk, for they must be assured the full repayment of their capital and the most solid payment of their interests." Of the 100,000 pesos requested, Buenos Aires mustered only 18,330. If the Spanish state found it harder and harder to dip into the financial pockets of colonial merchants, its merchants had a clearer and clearer sense that what was good for peninsular mercantilism was not necessarily good for colonial business.[90]

CONCLUSION

From 1790 to 1806, the anciens régimes of the Iberian empire struggled to cope as warfare for Atlantic supremacy ramped up. The pressures of war gave rise to reform and debate about the terms of old colonial pacts. These were not years of retrenchment or backsliding on reform, as some have characterized the unfortunate reins of Carlos IV and Doña Maria I, nor of crisis of the Brazilian system. The issue was rather *how* to adapt when the interests of empire became harder and harder to reconcile. Wartime pressures shifted power within the commercial coalitions of Iberian mercantilism, notably empowering colonial exporters and traders interested in transacting beyond imperial borders. In general, the bargaining that fueled these changes was smoother in the Portuguese empire than in the Spanish empire. The integration of the Brazilian commercial elite and their sheer power in relation to metropolitan houses gave the colony and its merchants a kind of clout missing in the Spanish colonial archipelago. In the Spanish empire, this was more conflictual and incomplete, for the financial demands of war were much greater and the cohesion of colonial elites much less harmonious.

At the same time, one should not exaggerate the elasticity of the imperial regimes. Bargaining between merchants and monarchs changed the

---

[90]AGNBA, Sala IX, Consulado, 4/6/2, Correspondencia, f. 459, and Cuentas y otros, 4/8/3, "Año 1806: Empréstito y donatibo hecho a S.M."

balance of power within the empires, but it did not fundamentally change the archaic institutions that upheld mercantilist privileges to earn rents. There was clearly a limit to normal revenues from levies on trade in times of war. In light of these difficulties monarchs turned to borrowing. Some authorities recognized the merits of a more flexible, calibrated revenue machinery. If the hope was that revenues could rise during peacetime and debts could be issued during wartime, this was clearly a financial revolution beyond the state's capacity to implement. It did not help that the urgency to carry out such schemes rose during wartime when the ability of the state to make credible commitments to creditors was weakest.

For their part, colonial merchants seized upon the weakness of royal authorities to maximize their rents, bringing in contraband and shipping out staples to illegal markets. They were, without ever declaring it, "exiting" from imperial rules and norms. But colonial defection and complaint stopped short of a full-blown critique of the mercantilist system: abandoning the securities and safeguards of sheltered trade would have exposed guild merchants to greater competition. Consequently, merchant capitalists had an interest in shoring up the archaic structures of market life in the colonies. Violating imperial laws while maintaining guild-controlled trade enabled merchants to enjoy the benefits, without shouldering the costs, of empire.

This entangled shift in the needs of the state and the interests of monied men did not add up to a crisis, unstable though this was. Indeed, what deserves to be underlined is how resilient the bonds of mutual dependency were, fueled in part by a shared fear of the specter of revolution. As this chapter has shown, the imperial bargaining within elites sometimes came to bare-knuckled confrontations. But any realignment of forces in favor of a new order did not surface. The commotion did, however, give rise to some creative thinking in the colonies about property, about the state, and about their place in empire.

4   The Wealth of Empires

INTRODUCTION

If the previous chapter examined the ways in which colonists coped with
the public affairs of imperium at war, this one explores colonial anxieties
about the ways in which private agents used their privileges, and as a
consequence reconsidered the social role of the imperial state in the
colonies. These anxieties reveal some prevailing conceptions about the
ways in which ruling classes and their lettered affiliates understood
wealth, property, and their relationship to the health and prosperity of
their kingdoms. Reporting to colonial authorities in 1804, a prominent
merchant from Cartagena, José Ignacio de Pombo, opened with a collo-
quial epigram: "the rumors go by, and the money stays at home." This
little phrase, this "immoral maxim" in Pombo's words, is "too common
in practice and causes impunity among those who profess it, and reflects
on their outlook on wealth." He pointed to his fellow merchants and
accused them of unsound business practices and poor faith. This kind of
private vice could have ruinous consequences. "These countries are so corrupt, and the laws and rights of citizens so unrespected, how is it possible
to expect there to be enough candor and patriotism to express other causes
and to propose the most effective means to cut their disorder at the roots?"[1]

Pombo was ventilating a growing sentiment among elites of the
Spanish and Portuguese colonies. If imperial policies were undermining
colonial faith, colonial behavior was also responsible for the degeneration of the commonwealth. Populated by people who did not respect
rules, so felt Pombo, these realms were running the risk of being ruled by
men who could not rule. In switching his criticisms from the more familiar target of public authority to private agents, Pombo captured a concern that was becoming more widespread among many well-to-do
colonists. The upheavals in the New and Old Worlds shook some of old
convictions about what was good and right about worlds ranked by
privilege and ruled by all-knowing imperial monarchs. But they also
believed that the old orders were not doomed. It was time, therefore, for

---

[1] José Ignacio de Pombo, no title to document of March 12, 1804, in a compilation of a
few recently discovered documents, *Comercio y contrabando*, p. 49.

another round of reform—one directed less at adapting public authority than at conducing private agents to behave more virtuously. Placed in the right hands—of enlightened men capable of using reason to mold laws to enhance practical self-interest—Iberian worlds could be the homes for healthy monarchs and wealthy merchants, each looking out for the interests of the other. There was, of course, a thorny problem: how was this to come about if the dominant members of the existing order had vested interests in the status quo? This was, in a nutshell, the ambient conundrum for pamphleteers and writers in the final decades of Iberian rule in the mainland Americas.

In exploring the ways in which colonists considered personal interests and public wealth, this chapter questions some of the familiar accounts of how colonists anticipated a postcolonial order before it was born. It is often said that the origins of Latin American secession from Spain and Portugal can be traced to the men of the Enlightenment who yearned for something new in the colonies. The explanation goes as follows: colonists wanted a different, more righteous model of sovereignty but found their aspirations thwarted by officials who colluded with peninsulars to prevent any erosion of their traditional status or power. As a result, the frustrated words of late colonial men of letters conveyed the first stirrings of "Latin American" nationhood.[2] In effect, as Enlightenment precepts hit New World shores, Iberian rule, resting firmly on its premodern institutional pillars, came to be seen more and more as a corrupt system; royalty came to be seen more and more as despotism. Accordingly, the more creoles like Pombo learned to yearn for their freedom from this regime, the more Spain had to subdue them. By repressing modern aspirations, the Spanish rulers pushed creoles to take up arms. According to Simón Bolívar, the colonial system—"a government whose origins are lost in the obscurity of time," he wrote in 1814—was suffocating the aspirations of colonial subjects.[3] Worse, he wrote a year later in his "Jamaica Letter," "America was denied not only its freedom but even "an active and effective tyranny.""[4]

This common view has some strong historiographic roots. Subsequent historians have taken Bolívar, and many of the first nationalist historians

---

[2]On intellectual "origins," see Roger Chartier, *The Cultural Origins of the French Revolution* (Durham: Duke University Press, 1993), esp. pp. 193–98; Joyce Appleby, "Liberalism and the American Revolution," in her *Liberalism and Republicanism*, pp. 140–60.

[3]"Manifesto to the People of Venezuela," (September 7, 1814), in Harold A. Bierck, ed., *Selected Writings of Simón Bolívar* (New York: Colonial Press, 1951), p. 81.

[4]"Reply of a South American to a Gentleman of this Island" (September 6, 1815), in Bierck, ed., *Selected Writings*, p. 110.

of the nineteenth century, at face value. Eager to wager a myth of bold, liberal state making, men like Bartolomé Mitre and José Manuel Restrepo offered heroic narratives of nations coming into being in a struggle for modernity against premodern oppressors. In their eyes, Latin American revolutions were part of the breakup of ancien-régime Atlantic empires groaning under the pressure of accumulated enlightened demands for freedom.[5] Much later, this nineteenth-century concept of creole freedom poised against colonial tyranny provided a framework for future generations of historians, culminating in Benedict Anderson's celebrated *Imagined Communities* and David Brading's majestic *The First America*. Latin Americans had a sense, "imagined" or real, that they were different from Iberians and that they would be better served without imperial masters. What is more, in this view, such a national gestalt was already maturing before the crisis of 1807.[6]

There is much to be said for the relationship between colonial frustration and anticolonial movements. But this kind of formulation presumes that there is a direct line between colonial criticism and postcolonial struggles, that the former can be read as precursive expressions of a revolutionary movement. Recently, some historians have queried such a postdictive interpretation of late colonial sentiments. François-Xavier Guerra, José Carlos Chiaramonte, and Jaime E. Rodriguez O., for instance, have argued that the ideas of political community and personal status were still heavily shaped by premodern concepts of relations between political sovereigns and subjects. This held true even as the empires crumbled. They find colonial politics suffused with a vocabulary of representation and rights that antedated Enlightenment concepts or that were, at best, rearticulated in a newer vernacular while still bearing their Hispanic substance. According to this view, when the empires did fall apart, disgruntled creoles were arguing for a regeneration of ethical bonds between Hispanic ruler and his ruled, a restoration of an earlier pattern of filial loyalty in return for respect for the private prerogatives, privileges, and

---

[5]Bartolomé Mitre, *Historia de Belgrano y la independencia argentina*, 4 vols. (1857; Buenos Aires: Editorial Estrada, 1947), José Manuel Restrepo, *Historia de la Revolución de Colombia*, 6 vols. (1825; Bogotá: Editorial Bedout, 1969).

[6]Arthur P. Whitaker, "The Dual Role of Latin America in the Enlightenment," in his edited *Latin America and the Enlightenment* (Ithaca: Cornell University Press, 1961), pp. 3–6; Richard Graham, *Independence in Latin America* (New York: Alfred A. Knopf, 1972), chap. 1; John Lynch, "The Origins of Spanish American Independence," in Bethell, ed., *Cambridge History of Latin America*, v. 3, pp. 42–46; Anderson, *Imagined Communities*.

hierarchies of colonial subjects. They did not want a new regime so much as a restored old one.[7]

This historiography offers an important corrective to the unexamined assumptions about the Enlightenment origins of Latin American independence. It shows a more complex, ambiguous mind-set of colonial subjects, less bent on a liberal teleology in which modern institutions and beliefs supplanted premodern heritages. But in many ways, it has inverted the problem originally posed by nineteenth-century liberals who viewed creole spokesmen as harbingers of a great historic rupture and colonial writings as histories of the future. If colonists were not expressing something new, explaining the structural break in the empires winds up focusing attention on events and conflicts within the imperial centers; modernity and nationhood were Europoid exports to Iberian colonies still clinging to tradition. The colonists have become peripheral agents in their own story, so that the crisis of the empire and the diffusion of new, liberal ideas of political order are seen as exogenous developments. Whether modernity had indigenous roots in the colonies or was introduced only once the traditional structures of sovereignty were gone are important discrepant views about the formative moment in Latin American nation-states. But both schools tend to forget that the empire was made up of a set of relationships between spatially located actors who had to negotiate, sometimes violently, the terms of the pacts that kept the regimes going. It is in the relationships between the component parts of empires that modernity was made. What is remarkable is just how much creoles were willing to question the norms of empire and improvise new systems of rulership long before it was clear that rule from Lisbon or Madrid was a lost cause. In other words, it is difficult to account for the disruption in the colonies after 1807 without some understanding of the ways in which colonists were grappling with enormous uncertainty. In the uneasy years that led up to Napoleon's invasion of the Iberian peninsula, colonial thinkers were hard at work trying to devise a more workable system to rescue the monarchies from corruption and degeneration. Some of these formulations, since they were directed at members of their own communities, contained latently disruptive implications. So the Enlightenment in the peripheries of the Iberian empires was corrosive to the old regimes, even if its apostles did not intend to weaken colonial fealty; when the ancient

---

[7]François-Xavier Guerra, *Modernidad e independencias: Ensayos sobre las revoluciones hispanicas* (Mexico: Fondo de Cultura Económica, 1993), pp. 23–33; Rodríguez O., *The Independence of Spanish America*, pp. 2–5; Chiaramonte, "Modificaciones del Pacto Imperial," pp. 107–28. O. Carlos Stoetzer argues that early insurrection demands called for a restoration of the *pactum subjectionis*. See his *Scholastic Roots of the Spanish American Revolution* (New York: Fordham University Press, 1979).

principles of sovereignty were in dispute, the new terms of liberty had very polarizing effects.[8]

This chapter is part compromise between those who see creoles as protonationalists and those who see them as defenders of tradition. But it is also part challenge. While taking the influence of ideas seriously, seriously enough to treat them as forces capable of shaping the way historic agents viewed the world in which they lived, it puts class "back in" the story of colonial history. Specifically it focuses on the role of merchant capital and its organic intellectuals of the Iberian empires by exploring their utterances and ruminations within their corporate institutions, especially the guilds or juntas. Their reports, journals, and debates reflect understandings of the nascent science of "political economy" in the decades before independence. With agents and partners spread across a vast archipelago of colonial ports from Veracrúz to Buenos Aires to Luanda, this colonial class was bound by a common set of interests: to maximize the traffic along Atlantic sea-lanes, to keep out competitive interlopers, and to ensure that royal authorities supported the political fabric that made merchant property flourish in the age of mercantilism. But in the discussion about "interests," merchants and the men of letters in the colonial outposts—many of whom had intimate ties to merchant circles—began to consider much more than business affairs. Like Pombo, they began to wonder aloud about the relationships between interests, virtue, and the moral foundations of Iberian sovereignty in a way that blurred the very neat lines between premodern and modern mentalities.[9]

Second, this chapter deals with a conjuncture that is often seen to have drawn the line between premodern, Iberian, colonial worlds from the modern, national successors. Yes, for all its importance, these years remain shrouded, as the French Revolution gave way to the full breakdown of the monarchies in 1807. In this context, both empires—especially the Spanish realm—suffered from upheavals and blows that prompted colonists to explore solutions to their problems that had them imagining not so much politics but rather property in new and potentially unsettling ways. Under pressure, the monarchs resorted to ad hoc decision making, thereby testing all subjects' faith in the magnanimous and competent nature of royal authority. Squeezed by the jaws of this vice—one commercial

---

[8]Joyce Appleby has expressed similar concerns about the Neo-Whig revisionism in the Anglo-American revolutions in her *Liberalism and Republicanism*, p. 142. Some have argued that the breakdown of empire simply sparked a massive and relatively principle-less grab for power. See David Bushnell, "The Independence of Spanish South America," in Bethell, *ed., Cambridge History of Latin America*, v. 3, pp. 95–156.

[9]On the political economy of mercantilism, see Heckscher, *Mercantilism*, and a critique by Viner, "Power versus Plenty," pp. 61–91; Magnusson, *Mercantilism*; Adelman, *Republic of Capital*.

and the other fiscal—events yielded a growing sense that business methods and property rights were in peril, while undermining confidence that political authorities could be relied on to rescue propertied classes from the maelstrom of Atlantic revolutionary warfare.

From a sense of crisis merchant capitalists began to express openly concerns about the future of empire. These concerns contributed to the making of alternative visions of the balance between private interests and public obligations, and of a new concept of wealth—notions that would challenge the principles of Spanish and Portuguese colonialism. But challenging colonialism is one thing; rejecting it is another. Before 1807, merchants may have chafed under the reigning political economy and worried that imperial corruption threatened the foundations of their fortunes. They may even have begun formulating the makings of a different order. But they recoiled from advocating any great rupture—that is, until the rupture was upon them. The ideas and debates about commerce and property, virtue and corruption, did not automatically add up to a revolutionary outlook before the breakdown of Iberian sovereignty. Moreover, Enlightenment precepts were neither necessary nor sufficient "causes" for revolt—which leads us to question some common assumptions about the origins of Latin American independence and the presumption that modern aspirations were rooted in prophecies of a new order. New thinking could just as easily be put to use to defend old structures.

This does not mean that there was no connection between late colonial debates about the state of the empires and postcolonial futures. Indeed, it was the very idea that colonists could participate in the future of the empires that set the stage for strong expectations and hopeful positions when the monarchies crumbled. They saw themselves as guardians of imperial welfare—even if to extirpate sources of public corruption. This was because colonists did not see themselves as possessors of rights or senses of selfhood that were somehow violated by the metropolis. In broadsheets, pamphlets, gatherings in local cafés, scientific societies, and especially in deliberative assemblies of the merchant guilds, colonists mobilized ideas and understandings of their own ability to defend national virtue and private wealth against their malefactors. In so doing they promoted the notion that they had as much appreciation as any other of what was right for the commonwealth and sovereignty of the Iberian monarchies.

THE FOUNDATIONS OF WEALTH

The commercial transformations of Iberian colonies in the eighteenth century altered merchants' sense of belonging in imperium. If the colonial bonanzas under liberated commerce and unfettered slave trading expanded commercial horizons, they also reorganized the interests in empire into a new balance between the peripheries and the centers. These changes, the results of bargaining within and between partners in the imperial pacts, were aimed at integrating the empires by harmonizing interests.

New opportunities gave way to new visions, which in turn shaped new policies. Changing colonial commerce alerted merchants to an undeniable reality: there was more to prosperity than the precious metals that met the metropolitan eye. There was, as most reformers and their commercial backers acknowledged, a historic legacy that had to be dismantled: the centuries of reliance on the extraction of precious metals as the source of lifeblood for empire, and protection of a tight circle of oligopolistic merchants licensed from imperial ports who were supposed to invigilate the transfer of money to the peninsula. As a result, and not always by design, Bourbon and Pombaline reformers had altered the balance of private and public interests and new understandings of wealth. Without entirely disbanding the search for precious metals, political economists urged the crown to pay more attention to the agrarian basis of wealth. Furthermore, under the belief that giving greater freedom to private agents created more resources for public causes, policy changes spawned a different outlook on trade, dismantling some of the constraints on infra-imperial commerce.

What started as a concerted effort to reform the political economy of empires from centers outward had effects on colonies that soon reverberated back to the metropoles. At least until 1790, most of the change reflected a shifting understanding and focus in the centers of power. To be sure, rulers were responding to emerging interests in the peripheries, as we have seen in the case of the rules governing the slave trade. But after 1790, these interests matured and acquired distinctive expressions of their own, in part stoked by the struggles over taxation and borrowing. Indeed, by the end of the century, what were once metropolitan convictions about commerce and attention to rural sources of wealth were picked up and elevated to greater discursive prominence in the colonies. In so doing, however, the migration of ideas to the fringes had disruptive effects on the balance within colonial coalitions. Agrarianism, physiocracy, and notions of freer trade and reformist discussion provoked an even sharper reconsideration of the origins of wealth—one that would eventually lead to a fuller repudiation of the archaic mercantilist model that still struggled to siphon precious metals from the colonies. Thus what was originally envisioned as a new set of transactions between America and Europe to harmonize the two sides of the Atlantic for the benefit of both created new grounds for conflict. According to one colonial official reporting from Nueva Granada (in 1778) to the minister of the Indies, "the principal attention of our government in these countries should be to support agriculture." This manner of using New World rural resources would create new "connections, links, and reciprocal dependencies between the sides of the Monarchy." In this author's view, this new model of integrating the interests of empire, between colonial and metropolitan agents, private and public needs, would be more durable and lasting.[10] As we shall see, it was not just the formal definition of the sources of wealth that was at stake, but also the image of colonies as equal contributing partners to the broader moral enterprise of empire.

Talk of reconceptualizing wealth echoed throughout the colonies, and by the end of the eighteenth century it was a common mantra. Arguing that silver was a medium and measure of exchange and not a source of riches, and now armed with the emerging discourses of political economy—especially French translations of Adam Smith's *Wealth of Nations*, Italian physiocrats, and the Spanish *arbitristas*—colonists addressed the mercantilist foundations of empire. They wanted to make them more robust, more dynamic. According to one author, "by good fortune we have a country in which our resources are superior to our needs. Our old commerce weakened agriculture, industry, and shipping to Spain. Now we are going to turn the entire system around. With a new understanding, we will . . . begin with agriculture as the prime mover of our circulation."[11] Our author, Manuel José de Lavardén, was a prosperous merchant from Buenos Aires and frequent publicist in the decade before 1810. He was also an unabashed physiocrat—arguing that a new guiding set of principles should inform public policy. The old mercantilist model was not just sapping the metropole, it was throttling and impoverishing the colonies.[12]

Were precious metals or agrarian produce the basis of a society's wealth? This was not just a semantic debate, a dispute about rival explanations of comparative opulence from within a tight fraternity of budding economists. The attention to agriculture revealed a growing concern about the relationship between property and production, and between

[10]Narváez, "Provincia de Santa Marta y Río Hacha del Virreinato de Sta Fé," pp. 25–26.

[11]Manuel José de Lavardén, *Nuevo aspecto del comercio del Río de la Plata* (Buenos Aires: Ed. Raigal, 1953), p. 175. These essays were originally delivered at the local Sociedad Patriótica in Buenos Aires around the turn of the century. On Brazil, see BNRJ, Bahia, Corpo do Comercio, I, 32/13/14, Ambrosio Joaquim dos Reis, "Memorias sobre o comércio do Brasil" (c. 1809–10).

[12]Elliott, "Self-Perception and Decline in Early Seventeenth-Century Spain," pp. 41–61. On the influence of physiocracy and early political economy, see Maxwell, "The Generation of the 1790s," pp. 107–44; Oreste Popescu, *Studies in the History of Latin American Economic Thought* (New York: Routledge, 1997), esp. pp. 157–91.

production and exchange. Official neglect of the countryside, noted one petition from the Banda Oriental (in 1794), exposed rural proprietors to the vagaries of competition, marauders, and insolent plebeian folk. God blessed the Americas with great land, but "it is assured that her inhabitants are the world's poorest, because of the abuses committed to this bounty and the lack of a well-balanced system and administration to check nature's caprice and to make it rich."[13] Indeed, according to José Ignacio de Pombo, land, property, wealth, and moral rectitude were all bound up—bound up because the proper and enduring foundation of civic society was one that combines property with family, assuring households not just their subsistence but an opportunity to prosper. With so much land around, it made sense to imagine wealth derived less from mining and more from family agriculture. In Pombo's words (1804), "when bounty and fertility of the country, and the love of property, and for the cultivated earth and for the family are not reconciled with their new fatherland, her sons and grandsons will not be genuine Spanish Americans."[14]

For this new wealth to yield fruit, combine households with property, and recalibrate the relationship between colonies and metropoles, authorities had to take a new attitude toward markets. When Manuel Belgrano returned to Buenos Aires in 1793, after years of studying in Spain, he was appalled to find that "with a few exceptions, people knew nothing more than commercial monopolies" and exploitation. "I found that nothing would be done for these Provinces by men who, obeying their particular interests, postpone the good of all."[15] To bolster agriculture and support innovative economic activity, productive activity required new incentives, which had to come from commercial opportunity. Now as the influential secretary of the Buenos Aires merchant guild, Belgrano argued that merchants and farmers had to work together—the former buying the latter's produce and selling it where markets fetched the highest price: "The mutual dependence is such between farmer and merchant that one without the other cannot truly flourish."[16] Belgrano urged the guild's members to envision a different division of labor, one principled on a harmonious and not conflictual relationship between production and distribution. This would require, Belgrano and others repeated, a more welcoming attitude toward open markets and even competition.

---

[13] "Dos noticias sobre el estado de los campos de la Banda Oriental al finalizar el siglo XVIII," *Revista Histórica*, p. 345.

[14] Pombo, *Comercio y contrabando*, p. 89.

[15] Manuel Belgrano, *Autobiografía* (Buenos Aires: Emecé, 1942), p. 14.

[16] Manuel Belgrano, "Memoria—3," in *Escritos económicos* (Buenos Aires: Emecé, 1954), p. 99.

New thinking about markets as a way to reassemble interests in ways that made resources more productive was not restricted to Spanish colonists. José Joaquim da Cunha Azeredo Coutinho, the scion from a sugar aristocracy of Rio de Janeiro who became a prominent churchman, authored one of the most widely circulating treatises on political economy in the Luso-Brazilian world. In it he argued that more open trade would give farmers greater opportunities in the colonies and manufacturers in Portugal more opportunities to ship their wares to Brazil. The harmony of the trading relationship was, Azeredo Coutinho argued, best expressed in the demographic profile of the metropolis, "a well populated country whose provinces border the sea." It was therefore only logical that Portugal do more than comply with this natural system; it had to elevate to a guiding principle of imperialism. Azeredo Coutinho, like Belgrano, Pombo, and others, was advocating that Iberian rulers and their officials dispense once and for all with the vestiges of the old mercantilist model, which was obsessed with the balance of trade (in favor of the peninsula), and promote trade as a whole.[17]

Trade, however, was a means, not an end in itself; trade allowed agents to own property—specifically "efeitos móveis," or mobile goods. These goods could be purchased, sold, or bartered for profit. And if subjects in the colonies (or, by definition, the metropole too since Azeredo Coutinho insisted that the same principles of political economy applied to *all* parts of the empire as befitted the new universal science) could more easily make and dispose of their mobile goods, they would make better use of the resources that produced them. This brings us back to the idea of the source of wealth. Azeredo Coutinho insisted that through commerce wealth could be created, but that its fount lay in the combination of labor and land, the bases of sustenance and survival. Survival is one thing; wealth is another. For if labor and land were expected to yield more than necessities and make societies rich, they had to be activated to produce "utilities"—goods above and beyond subsistence that could be exchanged for other goods. Azeredo Coutinho then shifted his logic, in keeping with some of the basic principles of early political economy, to argue that what held for individuals likewise obtained for societies. For just as individuals producing utilities could enrich themselves, societies that shipped their utilities forth were also bound for opulence. Stifling opportunities for individuals, and for societies, would condemn both, as the common metaphors of the times would have it, to personal "barbarism" and collective "slavery." "It is necessary," he argued, "that such a

---

[17]José Joaquim de Azeredo Coutinho, *Ensaio económico sobre o comercio de Portugal e suas colónias* (1794; Lisboa: Banco de Portugal, 1992), p. 26.

State that has no commerce with other nations will be, consequently, unable to pass from its infancy and will be conserved in its primary barbarity, without arts, without luxury, and only content with the simple production of its land." Shifting back to individuals, he concluded that "the majority of its inhabitants will therefore be slaves, only living for what is absolutely necessary for subsistence while making luxuries for a small fraction of the *senhores*."[18]

We need to nuance the claim that trade was simply a mechanism to a higher end. For if trade helped motivate wealth, it was also a civilizing force. To make his case, Azeredo Coutinho invoked the example of the Indians of the Campos de Goitacazes, the area of his family's estate. If Brazil is given powers to trade, even the "savages" will join civic society. Those that live by the rivers will offer their services as fishermen. Those inhabiting the woods would hew timber for shipyards. And with cheaper wood, the Portuguese empire could expand its navy and merchant marine; and given the scale of Brazil's forests there was no limit to Portugal's maritime potential. Indians, thereby, "in the midst of absolute liberty," would recognize and enjoy the fruits of their labors and "produce marvels for an infinite progress." Natives animated to join the market and civic society could even appreciate "the necessity of learning arithmetic." And what was good for even the lowest of society would aggregate into the benefit of the whole, creating a more enduring model for "the general opulence of the State." So, in fact, the shuffling between what logically held for individuals and what obtained for societies was more than a matter of parallel logics: individual production of utilities enriched them while producing riches for the "State" or commonwealth, and a progressive commonwealth was attuned to the need to defend freedom and liberty for its subjects. Each reinforced the other, imagined as a higher-order partnership between private subjects and public authority.[19]

It is tempting—and many have not resisted such siren calls—to find in the invocations of Belgrano, Pombo, Azeredo Coutinho, and others the makings of a nineteenth-century credo. Indeed, to many, talk of a new division of labor, "free" commerce, and property rights smacks of Manchesterite "free trade" *avant la lettre*, as forerunners of a more "liberal" concept of property. What is more, historians sympathizing with the heroic liberal narrative of independence see in the celebration of local farmers and free markets a creole political economy beginning to contest metropolitan mercantilism.

This formulation should not be pressed too hard. Belgrano, the guild secretary, and Pombo, the founder of Cartagena's consulado, inhabited

---

[18]Azeredo Coutinho, *Ensaio económico*, pp. 22–31.
[19]Ibid., pp. 38–79.

an eighteenth-century, not a nineteenth-century, commercial universe. Azeredo Coutinho, while not a merchant, did not invoke Adam Smith to make his case (as some did), but he did share the Scottish philosopher's concern with the moral norms as a substrate for capitalism. Possession of property was an earned, contingent right, which could be made "perfect" (in Hume's words), though property was not conceived perfectly. It was up to good governments to ensure that rules existed so that people could trade, apply their labors, and make property more perfect. Colonists stressed the political, not the natural, aspect of economic life; the social and not atomized origins of property. They steered away from abstract universal laws governing the source of value or the cause of wealth— though for Azeredo Coutinho, Belgrano, and Pombo, the *Wealth of Nations* was familiar stuff. Echoing the physiocratic injunction to free grain prices from corporate controls, they argued for a concept of property as an extension of personhood, requiring a political system designed and oriented to encourage honest laboring and trading activity. The important point is that while there were some Lockean components in this emerging outlook (that possessive individualism was a natural state for humans), colonial writers did not treat production or trade as prepolitical activities that required "freeing" from misrule. They spoke less in a language of "rights" than in a language of "markets." When Juan Hipólito Vieytes, another porteño, argued in 1802 that centuries of experience showed that "the grade of civilization, culture and opulence" depended on the "liberty given to commerce," he was not calling for an abolition of commercial controls but better controls—controls that would allow markets to flourish and embellish the realm.[20]

Market talk did not mean leaving merchants to their own unfettered devices but exposing them to the laws of property. According to the Bahian jurist José da Silva Lisboa (who arranged for his son to translate of the *Wealth of Nations* into Portuguese), markets extended "family societies" into mutual interdependencies "for help and reciprocal security." And as more families joined the market complex, they constituted

---

[20]Juan Hipólito Vieytes, "Comercio" (October 13, 1802), in his compiled essays, *Antecedentes económicos de la Revolución de Mayo* (Buenos Aires: Ed. Raigal, 1956), p. 162. On rights talk versus market talk, see Istvan Hont and Michael Ignatieff, "Needs and Justice in the *Wealth of Nations*," in their *Wealth and Virtue: The Shaping of Political Economy in the Scottish Enlightenment* (Cambridge: Cambridge University Press, 1983), esp. p. 26. For a more extended discussion of this theme, see Hirschman, *The Passions and the Interests*. Physiocracy, it is worth saying, is not the same as traditional agrarianism, which had long flourished in the peninsula. See Pedreira, "Physiocracy and the Sterility of Commerce, Industry and Money," pp. 267–95; Robert J. Shafer, *The Economic Societies in the Spanish World (1763–1821)* (Syracuse: Syracuse University Press, 1958), pp. 94–98.

nations. In Silva Lisboa's market language, exchange was the bedrock of "civil society." Markets alone, however, were not guarantors of their existence or, more precisely, an existence capable of reconciling the particular happiness of capitalists with the happiness of society as a whole. For a society to be virtuous and opulent—one without the other lived in peril—civil society required laws to ensure that acts of self-interest aggregated into social betterment. This science of political economy, Silva Lisboa argued, was thus subject to a master axiom: to support "the security of persons and legitimately acquired property with the least amount of restrictions on each individual, regulated for the common good of the human species."[21] Commercial society was not condemned to corruption—as civic humanists might have argued—but it could slip into a Polybian spiral of decline and corruption. Nor was it bound for glory—as nineteenth-century market language would later argue—for trade could, under malign laws, compromise the commonwealth. This is precisely what began to concern merchant capitalists when their regimes began to be squeezed by Atlantic warfare.

COMMERCIAL CRISIS

Thinking about wealth, markets, and property may have been a mental process, but it took place in a material context. Indeed, it helped make sense of an unsettled material world. With normal trading channels in turmoil, Spain and Portugal watched their old mercantilist vestiges implode.[22] Let us return to the Spanish consulados and Brazilian juntas, dominated by the great merchants of the empires, to see how the magnates maneuvered between more abstract ideas about markets and practical effects of the commercial turbulence of crumbling mercantilism. Members of these communities were given the responsibility of drafting recommendations to foster trade, industry, and agriculture, guild principles that gathered relevance and force in the absence of strong metropolitan guidance. Accordingly, within the meeting halls of the guilds, we find evidence of a not-quite-public debate that suggests divergent understandings of what kinds of interests were best poised to support the empires. At times poignant, often acrimonious, merchants queried the government's policies and wrestled over the legal boundaries separating

---

[21]José da Silva Lisboa, *Principios de economia política* (Lisboa: Impressa Régia, 1804), pp. 112–16.

[22]Josep Fontana Lázaro, "Colapso y transformación del comercio exterior español entre 1792 y 1827," *Moneda y Crédito* 115 (December 1970): 3–23; Fisher, "Commerce and Imperial Decline," pp. 459–79.

legal and illegal business practices. Charges of corruption were soon on everyone's lips.[23]

When Spain went to war with Britain in October 1796, the commercial effects sparked a full-blown argument in colonial consulados. After defeating the Spanish fleet at Cape St. Vincent, Admiral Nelson began blockading Cádiz. Colonial merchants, deprived of ships to handle their export staples and without legal imports of manufactures or slaves, began calling for special emergency measures and leaned on local authorities to alleviate their suffering. Despite the outcries of Cádiz houses (who saw their grip on colonial commerce disappear), one by one local intendants and guilds began to allow foreign traders to do business in Spanish ports. The crown—again to the consternation of Cádiz capitalists—made it easier to do business with non-Spanish, neutral ports. Foreign ships—North American in the Caribbean, British and Brazilian in the River Plate and the north coast of South America—poured into Spanish colonial entrepôts. But the vital interests of *peninsular* mercantilism could not countenance such concessions to colonial autonomy and Cádiz houses compelled an ever-weaker monarch to revoke the concession in April 1799. What this flip-flopping dramatized was not just the weak hand at the helm of the imperial tiller, but the internal divisions lurking within the Spanish merchant class.[24]

When confidence in the imperial order trembled, it destabilized consensus within merchant classes of the colonial archipelago. In Caracas—where merchants were more beholden to agrarian interests—the pressure mounted to open the port to any takers of the region's exports. The hacendados welcomed the opening of 1797, and then decried the closure of the port in 1799. Merchants, however, were divided. Those who lived off the export trade lined up with the hacendados while those who relied on imports sympathized with Cádiz and worried about potential foreign competition. In the end, the consulado created a special "junta" of merchants and producers to devise an emergency solution.[25] Some merchants—like the patrician Ramón de Valdespino, wealthy vecino of Caracas and owner of a vast estate in the Valley of Güigue, who combined importing and exporting—felt the discomfort from both ends.[26] By mid-1797,

---

[23]Barbier, "The Culmination," pp. 51–68.

[24]There were some minor—if ignored—qualifications to the royal order of November 18, 1797: mainly, neutral ships were supposed to sail to Spain with American cargos. This was largely a sop to angry Cádiz merchants and was, as far as I can tell, utterly unenforceable in colonial ports. For a longer discussion, see Fisher, *Trade, War, and Revolution*, pp. 50–57.

[25]AGNC, Consulado, t. II, f. 177.

[26]AGNC, Consulado, Actas, t. 2525, f. 53.

Caracas merchants were in the throes of an internal debate over trade with non-Spanish ports, ending with a resolution urging the intendant to curb unwanted imports but to allow open exports of cacao "and the general extraction of vendible staples of this country." This solution did not hold: when the house of Eckard & Company of Saint Thomas agreed to carry 40,000 quintals of tobacco (a massive and lucrative haul for hacendados), import merchants bristled. Eckard's vessels, they claimed, threatened to flood the port with cheap imports and their own slaves. The conflict came to a head in early 1798. On January 27, witnesses packed the consulado's hall to watch the intendant hear each side's position. The hacendado delegation, represented by the Conde de San Javier, Martín de Herrera, and Manuel Felipe de Tovar presented a lengthy summary of "the causes and origins of the decadence of our staples." Brandishing a detailed assault on colonial controls, they urged practical opening of the port to restore prosperity to the Province of Caracas. More open trade, the delegation concluded, would yield to "reciprocal utilities and advantages to all businesses." The guild president, however, wanted compromise between the two sides. He lamented "the unfortunate and contrary disunion, [which is] most prejudicial to this body's real interests." After much debate, with no amicable solution in sight, the meeting was postponed to mid-February—by which time discord mutated into bitterness. A group of hacendados blasted the merchants associated with the Cádiz houses (especially the factor of the Real Compañia de Filipinas), "and showed our sense of offense which has grown in response to the libelous infamy which gravely offends [the hacendados], while the behavior of other merchants hurts everyone's conduct."[27] The dispute endured until May, with charges and countercharges, until the intendant announced that it would be legal to trade with neutral parties. What landed and exporting interests loudly proclaimed was that more open trade was good for the empire because it was good for the colonies. While some individuals may lose their particular riches, society would gain in wealth. For the time being at least, this position had the ear of colonial authorities.

Buenos Aires saw a similar debate—although here merchants were more autonomous from landed interests and the Cádiz-linked houses were more powerful. Still, this did not prevent one merchant, Manuel Aguirre, from making the case for more freedom to export staples. His appeal to the porteño guild met with the same response as in Caracas: open commerce would be injurious to the privileges of "Spanish" trade, claimed the critics of neutral commerce. Aguirre's detractors argued that

---

[27]Ibid., ff. 178–90.

"free trade would open the way for fraud and indirect commerce by foreigners, in visible detriment" to imperial trade. But as appeals for rights to trade with neutral ports increased, so did the pitch of the debate within the consulado. As in Caracas, the dispute culminated in a pro-Cádiz defense against the gathering demands for commercial openness. And as in Caracas, Buenos Aires producers responded to the big recalcitrant merchants, accusing them of betraying the health, and wealth, of the empire. In the words of one frustrated guild member: "What similarity there is in the relationship between the agriculture of Buenos Aires and Spain, and the fall of the Roman Empire! . . . Rich are then cities and impoverished are the fields; while merchants, interested only in their profits . . . accustomed to lucrative speculation and economy, pay attention only to the advance of their business."[28] As we shall see shortly, the parallels between Spain's emporium and its classical predecessors became more and more explicit as the concern about corruption and decay intensified.

When the monarch buckled to Cádiz merchants and revoked the neutral shipping decree in 1799, the debate erupted once more. This time, however, the oligopolistic merchants linked to Cádiz had clearly gained the upper hand. No longer could the exponents of more open trade invoke the sympathy of their sovereign. Keeping the ports sealed to "foreign" commerce hardly resolved the problem from any side's vantage point. It simply redirected it onto another plane. As the legal channels of commerce closed off, illegal ones flourished. While the Iberian empires were never hermetic systems and foreign traders plied their wares with varying degrees of immunity, by the 1790s, what was once a leaky system had given way to rampant porosity. Contraband boomed—and it is probable, though we will never know for sure, that illegal trade was larger than legal trade in the last two decades of Spanish rule in the Americas. The same may well be true of Brazil, where Lisbon houses compelled authorities to clamp down on unlicensed traders. One vessel belonging to the Bahian house of Felipe Ribeiro Figueiras and José Francisco Loures was impounded while loading a cargo of sugar and cotton bound for England, and the merchants were subjected to "the most rigorous punishment."[29]

---

[28] AGNBA, Sala IX, Consulado, 29/1/1, Actas, ff. 238–49.

[29] APB, Secção Colonial, 89, doc. 16, Dom Rodrigo de Souza Coutinho, January 13, 1799; for other cases, see docs. 60 (March 8, 1799) and 69 (April 5, 1799). Zacarías Moutoukias, "Redes, autoridad y negocios: Racionalidad empresaria y consenso colonial en Buenos Aires (segunda mitad del siglo XVIII)," unpublished paper in author's possession. See also his "El crecimiento en una economía colonial del antiguo régimen," pp. 771–813.

Thriving contraband only fueled the wrangling within the guilds over legal business definitions and allegations of corruption. Oligopoly merchants, using the rhetoric of "corruption" of proper commercial mores, wanted authorities to repress rogue competitors; defendants argued that they were simply providing local markets with necessities at more "just" prices. One judge from San Gil (in Nueva Granada) revealed his dilemma when he tried clamping down on the illegal clothing filtering in from contrabandists in Maracaibo: "let me know," he asked the Cartagena guild that controlled the import-export nexus of the colony, "if it is admissible to permit all traffic and commerce in these regions, [for consumers] to get it faster and cheaper, so that, to get the most utility, they may procure their purchases where convenient."[30] Defining just prices, a matter of concern among political economists concerned with the social effects of modern money economy, became a matter of dispute for merchants and regulators of empire: were prices determined before goods entered markets, shaped by agreements over market shares and dressed up as moral imperatives? Or did prices reflect what markets could bear, stabilizing in the long run, as supply met demand? The answer depended on what was deemed legitimate supply. Nueva Granada was in fact a colonial sieve of contraband. A longstanding problem given the string of ports—like Rio Hacha, Santa Marta, and Portobelo—contraband trade easily avoided the pseudo-controls of Cartagena's monopoly (in fact, Cartagena's denizens were as skilled at evasion as anyone along the leaky Caribbean coast). But wars opened the floodgates; Maracaibo became a major black market—with, according to one observer, hundreds of carts trundling out of the port loaded with illegal imports, with traders brandishing false permits, *guías*, issued by corrupt officials. Consulado officials sent constant missives around the colony urging strict application of regulations. According to Manuel de Pombo (José Ignacio's brother), "it is evident throughout the kingdom that there is a vast and stealthy flow of contraband, which has reduced legitimate commerce with the Metropolis to one tenth of what it should be."[31] In Buenos Aires, the guild ordered its officers and local port officials to enforce controls without flinching, "to avoid the damages which result from laxity, both to personal as well as the public cause." A few years later, the guild members

---

[30]AGNB, Colonia, Consulados, II, f. 531.
[31]AGNB, Colonia, Consulado, II, f. 948. On Maracaibo, see AGNB, Colonia, Contrabandos, VIII, ff. 318–21; Narváez, "Discurso del Mariscal de Campo y los Rs. Exercitos D. Antonio Narváez y la Torre," pp. 69–75. On the long history of contraband in Colombia, see Grahn, *The Political Economy of Smuggling*. On Brazilian comments, see José da Silva Lisboa, *Observações sobre o commercio franco no Brasil*, pp. 97–98.

voted unanimously that illegal commerce "is prejudicial, obnoxious and induces inevitable criminal abuses."[32]

Consternation over scarcities, just prices, and charges of malfeasance and corruption also afflicted Brazilian ports, where colonial merchants could operate with greater latitude from Lisbon and metropolitan merchants. The market power of colonial merchants, however, put them at odds with officials who worried more about the gap between just and real prices, or as the town council of the Brazilian capital intoned, "the rising prices and the formal sterility which threatens the people." Town after town issued petitions to viceregal authorities to do something about (as one delegation put it) "the nefarious activities of some businessmen and profiteers selling at excessive prices, while exporting to Pernambuco and other ports foodstuffs of the first necessity while the people of this city are squeezed by hunger." Complaints prompted a judge in Rio de Janeiro, Baltasar da Silva Lisboa (no relation to the Bahian jurist), to take action in 1793. On the heels of unrest in the Portuguese colonies, the local magistrate argued that Brazil was facing enormous shortages of basic necessities. He blamed merchants who were busy shipping staples out of Brazil for profits—especially the slave traders who were loading their tumbeiros with wares to sell in Africa. To make matters worse, contrabandists and other merchants were hoarding goods to drive up prices. In an effort to keep the peace and stop local food prices from rising, Silva Lisboa ordered his deputies to board seven slave-trading vessels loaded with provisions bound for Africa and seize any unlicensed cargos that might have exceeded the legal exporting limits. "Always on the lookout for my jurisdiction," he wrote to the minister of overseas dominions, Martinho de Mello e Castro, "and the fear of a public calamity, not to mention the violence that endangers it, it is necessary that Your Majesty take account of the legality of what I have done . . . to remedy such an imminent public ruin!"[33] The seizures led to public turmoil on the Largo de Palacio and local beaches as crowds gathered to witness the forced unloading, hoping to get first dibs on the cargos. Shippers and merchants flooded Minister Martinho de Mello's mail with appeals and pleas—and demands that the magistrate himself be charged with actions "prejudicial to business interests" and "encumbrances to commerce" that menace the interests of everyone.[34] In the end, the minister ordered an investigation, which led to a report to the Overseas Council in Lisbon that catalogued

---

[32]AGNBA, Sala IX, Consulado, 29/1/3, Actas, f. 147 (October 15, 1800); 29/1/4, Actas, f. 92 (January 21, 1805). On the River Plate, see Moutoukias, *Contrabando y control*.

[33]AHU, DA, Caixa 153, March 23, 1793.

[34]See, for instance, the appeal by Francisco Pinheiro Guimarens in AHU, DA, Caixa 154, no. 10, July 28, 1793.

the "faults and misdeed" of Silva Lisboa, and found that the assaults on Rio de Janeiro's notables damaged the harmony of the city. The council then urged the Prince Regent to put an end "to the labyrinth of constant disorder" and name a successor "to make the people tranquil."[35] This episode filled the tea salons and state courtrooms with chatter, but it also exposed the growing divergence about the place and autonomy of private interests in the maintenance of the public good. If in the Spanish colonies we have seen how the specter of competition gave rise to charges and countercharges of corruption and abuse of public faith, in Brazil, explicit profit seeking was seen as a potential menace to local harmony. Either way, as the old mercantilist structures were crumbling, no one was making the case for an absolute free trade order and the complete independence of mercantile interests to conduct business free from public concerns.

Some traders and exporters, however, did not take charges of illegality and corruption lightly. In Brazil, the defendants against Baltasar da Silva Lisboa's actions made the case for the need to protect their private property. The deluge of contraband exemplified how capitalists, if not voting with ballots in the guilds, were certainly voting with bills of exchange. In Caracas, in the wake of the 1799 revocation of trade with neutral ports, one group of merchants complained about "the irreparable damages visited upon merchants' interests with this prohibition on neutral commerce and without consideration for the entry and unloading of cargo in the ports of this province and the expeditions which are supposed to return . . . whose property belongs to individuals from this place as products of their export staples which was, in good commercial faith, permitted with friendly ports."[36] From all corners of the empire, merchants, producers, and even local officials mourned the decline in legitimate business, the depletion of revenues, and hinted that recourse to illegal and corrupt practices was unfortunate but, under the circumstances, understandable. The cabildo of Caracas informed the intendant and guild in October 1800 that blockades and legal port closures meant that it was "necessary that agriculture be completely ruined and public revenues be condemned to absolute decadence." Worse, for "without hope . . . of some legitimate commerce this brings inevitable consequences: first contraband that provides necessary goods, more difficulty guarding our shores, and very attractive and advantageous profits."[37]

---

[35] AHU, DA, Caixa 155, no. 13, October 20, 1793.

[36] AGNC, Real Consulado, Actas, 2527, f. 56 (September 25, 1799).

[37] Ibid., ff. 162–63 (October 27, 1800). For general discussion, see Barbier, "Commercial Reform," pp. 96–120; McKinley, *Pre-revolutionary Caracas*, pp. 132–34; Moutoukias, "El crecimiento en una economía colonial del antiguo régimen."

If the big merchants opposed to foreign competition labeled interloping traffic as private cheating and failure of public enforcement as "corruption," many other merchants and officials seemed willing to violate metropolitan strictures and business norms.

In the Spanish Atlantic before 1802, the language of corruption and charges of commercial skulduggery flourished as traders linked to the big metropolitan houses associated with Cádiz tried to impose order—and legal norms—on small and large traders who violated mercantilist principles. Corruption rhetoric was a critical weapon in the arsenal of oligopoly merchants' war against what they deemed "illegal" competition. From the competitors' vantage point, of course, they were simply giving outlets to local producers and furnishing imports for local consumers—respecting the material needs of colonists. In Brazil, merchants that stood in the way of freer-flowing necessities (including slaves) also risked being tarred for malfeasance by depriving the commonwealth in favor of personal enrichment. At the same time there was a limit to public officials' powers to rule over merchants as the dustup over Baltasar da Silva Lisboa's actions demonstrate.

If merchants began to lose confidence in the 1790s, nothing prepared them for the maelstrom provoked by resumed war in 1804—first against Britain, then against France. Between 1802 and 1804, trade between Spanish and Spanish American ports soared. Then came the news of renewed war. Colonial capitalists' mood sank to all-time lows when they heard of the British surprise capture of a loaded treasure fleet from Montevideo. Then the news of the defeat at Trafalgar turned concern into panic. Napoleon's Continental System, meanwhile, also ravaged the traffic from Lisbon, since the Portuguese capital aligned with Britain. The colonies were, for most commercial intents and purposes, on their own.[38] The rancor of merchants' debates in the 1790s now burst into open confrontation within the genteel world of the guilds. It is worth noting the inversion, now, of the anticorruption, countercontraband crusade. Used earlier to upbraid the contraband practices of unlawful subjects, corruption rhetoric became a weapon of some merchants and colonial exporters against the "monopolistic" practices of the metropolitan-linked merchants. The Bahian merchant and lawyer José da Silva Lisboa accused merchants who warned that foreigners would monopolize colonial commerce of hypocrisy: "Those merchants accusing foreigners of monopoly

---

[38]Fisher, *Trade, War and Revolution*, p. 67. For an appraisal of the commercial effects on Spain, see Cuenca Esteban, "Statistics of Spain's Colonial Trade," pp. 381–428; and on the British position, Dorothy Burne Goebel, "British Trade to the Spanish Colonies, 1796–1823," *Hispanic American Historical Review* 43:2 (1938): 288–320.

projects are those that plead for the Government to give them this monopoly, against the interests of the Sovereign, and damning all fellow citizens." Agents of a "pernicious monopoly" with "privileges to buy and sell to those without the same rights" threaten "good order and the progressive opulence of nations."[39] Colonial merchants turned the tables, accusing metropolitan traders of corruption and even treason. When the consulado in Caracas gave Francisco Caballero Sarmiento (the factor for the Marquis of Poranchiforte) an exclusive flour-importing concession, other merchants issued a sharp rebuke: "these provinces will, from this day forward, experience the detestable effects of Monopoly by the declared exclusion of Don Francisco Caballero Sarmiento." Some guild members openly admitted that they "cannot control their behavior, for it is indispensable that we follow any news to avoid damaging the interests of the public and the State." The outpouring concluded that this concession "would inflict atrocious and tragic scenes upon Caracas on a scale of suffering not less than that of the Bengali inhabitants at the hands of Lord Clive."[40]

Other ports followed a similar pattern, but their anger was more muted. In Cartagena, merchants simply gathered and voted to declare the city open to trade with neutrals, sending its resolution to political authorities in the name of "saving these provinces from total ruin." But here, too, guild members distinguished between the rights of the few concessionaires and the good of commerce as a whole. Their petition argued that partial palliatives of more generous individual concessions would not work, adding that "this would not only not be enough, but such measures principally favor the merchant and not trade, which Your Excellency knows are very different things." Concession would create "semi-monopolies shared among one or two *vecinos*."[41] In Buenos Aires, many merchants also warned that restoring old privileges would damage commerce as a whole and impose shortages on consumers.[42]

As ports began to open up, and once Britain became an ally in 1808, the leaky world of mercantilist trading collapsed. Merchants now had to

---

[39]Silva Lisboa, *Observações sobre o commercio franco no Brasil*, p. 113. Some Bahian merchants did not welcome this position—defending empire and religion against "gente ecterodoxa [sic]." See BNRJ, Bahia, Corpo do Comercio, I, 31/28/26 (1808).

[40]AGNC, Real Consulado, Actas, 2530, ff. 36–39. For a comparable argument from Bahian tobacco exporters, see ANRJ, JC, Caixa 416/1, s.n. April 26, 1809, petition to the consulado comercial to let their staples sail more freely. Written from the area around Cachoeira, their complaints were directed against privileged Salvador merchants. For an analogous critique from sugar growers, see Caixa 378/3, s.n., September 7, 1809.

[41]AGNB, Colonia, Consulado, I, f. 509.

[42]AGNBA, Sala IX, Consulado, 29/1/5, Actas, f. 48. For complaints about British competition, see f. 180. In Brazil, see APB, Secção Colonial, 87, doc. 10, José da Silva Lisboa, March 27, 1799.

contend with a whole new order, one that spilled well beyond the confines of the guild: unbridled competition. Consider the following case from Popayán in 1807 involving the debate about just prices. The local deputy of the viceregal consulado, Ignacio del Campo, reported on a clash between the local mayor and a merchant. The merchant wanted to offer goods at a lower price (probably contraband, though this is unclear from the document) while other merchants charged him with "undermining" conventional commercial practices, the "just price" determined by prior agreements. The nub of the conflict was the merchant's right to charge a clearing price for his wares—a violation of existing ordinances for some products (like flour), "for each good must have a certain and assured price," noted del Campo, "which cannot be reduced. This point," he continued, "at first appearance favors merchants, but in reality after hurting the public and the good of the *vesindario*, it turns out not to be helpful to all individual merchants, especially in these thieving [*ratero*] places, where we can no longer speak of formal commerce." In the old days of galleons and the Portobelo Fair, local merchants depended on an established, oligopolistic network of wholesalers, prices did not float, and commerce was a regulated, stable enterprise. At the hither edge of mercantilism, retailers passed on prices, prices dictated not by competition but by mutual agreement within the self-regulated world of merchant capital. Now, warfare and contraband were shredding the fabric of this system. "In Quito, Popayán, Caly, Buga, Honda, Santa Fe, and other places where there is no more merchandising of this nature, but where many traders have relied on Cádiz and Cartagena for their supplies, how will it be possible for shopkeepers to live off their interests if they do not retail and hock by any way possible?" Now, selling goods in Popayán was becoming a cutthroat operation—shopkeepers "are offering to buyers thousands of *gracias* to attract their business."[43] The defenders of the old commercial order, the "monopolists" who wished to keep trade flowing through hermetic channels of their own invention, were becoming the agents of corruption and crisis in the view of this commercial spirit. In the words of Manuel José de Lavardén, "if we listen to the exhausted maxims of the tyranny of monopoly, one would think that the Americas were exclusively the domain of precious metals and other natural preciosities; that they are occupied by ancient *naturales*, and that their prosperity could furnish proportions as mere exemptions of our domain."[44]

---

[43]This fascinating document, written in 1807, can be found in AGNB, Colonia, Consulados, III, ff. 432–55.

[44]Lavardén, *Nuevo aspecto del comercio*, p. 172.

What Is To Be Done?

This commercial turmoil recast market language in the colonies. On one level, the idea and practice of greater freedom to participate in market life acquired ever more salience in the debate over imperial policy. By issuing shock waves in a world in which property and power were supposed to be the prerequisites of virtue and authority, the climacteric forced colonial merchants to broadcast market language with ever more urgency. At the same time, greater autonomy of commercial agents to conduct business free from the scrutiny of public authorities (or even their own regulatory guilds) implied greater uncertainty and the prospect that not all interests could be harmonized in civil accord. The mercantilist culture of empire rested on the idea that trade brought people together in an atmosphere of polite bargaining. Montesquieu's notion of *doux commerce* was not just an idyll. In practice, dispassionate exchange between agents, abiding by the rules of Iberian guilds, was supposed to enable producers to apply their labors while calibrating a system that conveyed needed consumer goods to the colonies while South America's staples to were shipped to faraway buyers. Whether this model operated in such a seamless fashion is not the issue. The problem was that the basic institutions and practices, whatever the ideal, of Iberian mercantilism left the custody of this order to the internal controls of guilds and the external defense of sea-lanes. In such a fashion, virtue of traders and the responsibility of public authorities combined to sustain a massive imperial enterprise. This was now a system in deep trouble. If the transformation prompted merchants to break their norms and customs of business in pursuit of personal interests, it also kindled concern about the "corruption" of colonial subjects and the "degeneration" of ties to the sovereign.[45]

The turbulence of imperial trade and the consternation within commercial circles was increasingly seen as a crisis that jeopardized the foundations of colonial wealth with disastrous social consequences. One obsession was not just the wealth but the very health of the countryside. After decades of rural prosperity—in the sense that production and population rose markedly—the 1790s ushered in years of trouble. All around, commentators worried about the shadow cast over the American countryside by the Atlantic commercial crisis. Repeated demands to allow exports of staples were followed by warnings of dire effects on rural fortunes.[46] Weak agriculture, elites feared, would in turn weaken work habits.

---

[45]J. G. A. Pocock, "The Mobility of Property and the Rise of Eighteenth-Century Sociology," in his *Virtue, Commerce and History*, pp. 103–23.

[46]AGNC, Real Consulado, Actas, 2525 (1797), ff. 98–99; 2528 (1802), f. 11; 2529 (1807), ff. 28–30.

In Caracas, estate owners moaned that general idleness taught bad habits: most of the city's indigent are people who would rather beg than work, complained one group. Make them work, the city's elite cried, "with orders that they go back to their ranches and farms which need them, but with the special recommendation that they be treated humanely, and that they be instructed with care to love work which, although in the beginning they will react with horror, in just a few days will allow them to grow accustomed to the utility that results from effort."[47] According to Buenos Aires' Juan Hipólito Vieytes, the rural population "these days are to be found concentrated in the most reprehensible inactivity, only content with getting their basic food with the minimum of effort and diligence. But these very lazybones . . . would emerge from their lethargy and idleness once the bait of utility is found to inflame them, which surely no man would ignore just out of indigence." For Vieytes, the ability of commerce to restore order and revive wealth in the Americas rested entirely on the ability of commerce to operate at all. Azeredo Coutinho feared that benefiting a few privileged capitalists would impoverish the majority of colonists, driving a greater wedge between the privileged minority and the rest, "who by comparison find themselves almost without work."[48]

Waning work habits threatened the entire system when they struck at the labor system of many colonies: slavery. After the Haitian revolution, Iberian colonies shivered with apprehension. Bahian officials uncovered a "conspiracy" of black tailors. The "Gual and España" plot of 1796 exposed raw paranoid nerves in Caracas. Venezuelan merchants warned of the menacing effects of the "backwardness and stagnation in which the agriculture of this province is stuck." A province afflicted by slave flights and depredations of cacao, indigo, and sugar stocks was causing "damages to hacendados in particular and the state in general, and even to the slaves themselves due to the corruption of their morals." "Negroes, sambos and mulattos with no fixed wage are courting the dangerous confidence of such contemptible subjects."[49] For Silva Lisboa, commerce was *the* social glue: "the true spirit of commerce is social." And without it, the social fabric threatened to fall apart, with calamitous consequences

---

[47]AGNC, Real Consulado, Actas, 2528, f. 6.

[48]Vieytes, *Antecedentes económicos*, p. 161. For echoes elsewhere, see the report to the Audiencia in Santa Fé de Bogotá (September 1808) on the effects of the economic crisis after 1803: AGNB, Colonia, Cabildos, VIII, ff. 417–525; Azeredo Coutinho, *Ensaio económico*, p. 22.

[49]AGNC, Real Consulado, Actas, 2526 (1794), ff. 29, 38. On the conspiracy, see Grases, *La Conspiración de Gual de España y el ideario de la independencia*; AGNC, Real Consulado, Actas, 2525 (1797), ff. 67, 99.

for one of the world's largest slave societies. Indeed, Silva Lisboa, Edmund Burke's Portuguese translator, reserved nothing but venom when it came to the French Revolution—an occasion for "lots of phrases and few ideas."[50]

Some commentators even began to speculate whether the proprietary pillars of colonial society could hold up the imperial edifice. So long as the commercial order remained prone to external menaces, the internal makeup of the colonies would always tremble. Once again, it is in the slave colonies that we find the causal links between proliferating "vicious" commercial habits and potential social turmoil most neatly drawn. José Ignacio de Pombo actually wondered whether the colonies ought to abandon slave property altogether and colonize land with "Catholic farmers," prohibiting "the impolitic and barbarian commerce in blacks," creating a "new system to extinguish slavery in order to save and preserve America. We should promote, by all means possible, the meeting and mixing of the various castes which inhabit it so that there be no more than one class of citizens in the common order." Consider Saint Domingue, he warned, where "seventy thousand French troops, capable of conquering a European Kingdom, have been victims or have received the law of Santo Domingo's blacks.... This new empire, difficult if not impossible to destroy, will soon make tributaries out of European and American nations, as it has already in Africa. The English in Jamaica will be the first to reap the rewards," Pombo noted sarcastically, "for their current help [in the Haitian struggle against France] and avarice. How often does cane juice flow in their sugar mills, along with the blood of these miserable people?"[51]

The concern about the uncoupling of commercial wealth from social health was not just an obsession in plantation belts. It also concerned elite colonists in slave societies more generally. In the River Plate, a slave society (not just a society with slaves) where the line between free and unfree labor was not always easy to detect, idleness, restlessness, and general decay of social norms also became keynotes of contemporary writers. Restoring the foundations of wealth meant putting commerce into perspective, emphasizing that commerce was not an end in itself, but a means. According to Belgrano, "as long as the land is not completely populated...and as long as men have not established a sustained and firm method of agriculture and labor, we should not contemplate giving exclusive protection to any other branch." These are significant words, coming from the secretary of Buenos Aires' merchants' guild, but they

---

[50]Silva Lisboa, *Observações sobre o comercio franco no Brasil*, pp. 17, 41.
[51]José lgnacio de Pombo (1804 untitled doc.), in *Comercio y contrabando*, pp. 57, 88.

did not imply ignoring commerce altogether: "we should not abandon the protection of healthy and useful [*utilísimo*] commerce, which animates, and gives life and value to agrarian production."[52]

How was commercial property supposed to exercise its moralizing functions if commerce could itself not operate according to proper manners? It is hard to find any evidence of demands for a return to pristine mercantilist days, except perhaps in the metropole itself. Even the minority of merchants tied to Cádiz desisted from arguing that authorities should simply clamp down on all wayward commerce and restore the old rule of oligopolists. What they did want was insulation against "foreign" competition to keep their grip on the rest of the colonies' mercantile matrix. If not the old order, then what?

Public morality and the absence of corruption depended on the behavior of individuals and the ways in which they disposed of their property. Pombo's injunctions to authorities to do something about contraband, a commerce that not only violated laws and customs but corrupted public officials and merchants themselves, saw these crimes as an expression, not a cause, of the crisis. The problem, in fact, lay in ourselves, Pombo observed: "Men, whose first behavioral maxim is to possess the vilest of passions associated with the lowest of souls, will these be good fathers of families, faithful subjects, friends of the public good and assiduous judges with integrity? Their example, their connections, their influence, and their interest in corrupting others, how much damage will they have committed to all classes and orders of the State?"[53] It is not that men are bad, but that in the colonies they had been subjected to bad laws. From Bahia, Silva Lisboa observed that men could succumb to vice or propagate virtue. As carriers of natural inclinations to trade and generate personal wealth, men of money will pursue self-interests above all. The challenge was to create a legal framework to allow capitalist activity to support, not undermine, a social order, especially one deeply divided by social class and property. Indeed, it was this very preoccupation that compelled Silva Lisboa to draft a modern commercial code in 1798 to support healthy competition and "capitalists [against the] terrible monopoly over other citizens which is paralyzing National industries."[54] Citing Adam Smith, Pombo saw these bad laws as the brainchildren of beneficiaries of "exclusive commerce." Better laws would enable traders' inclinations to flourish aboveboard, in the daylight of legitimate commerce,

[52]Belgrano, March 10, 1810, in *Escritos económicos*, p. 118.

[53]Pombo (1804 untitled doc.), in *Comercio y contrabando*, p. 102.

[54]Silva Lisboa, *Observações sobre comercio franco no Brasil*, pp. 169–89; idem, *Princípios de Dereito Mercantil e Leis da Marinha* (Lisbon: Officina Typografica, 1789), p. 51.

enjoying more unobstructed access to commodities and consumers. Legalized, the very same commerce could exercise civilizing powers. In a colonial context, the familiar dichotomy between interests and passions was rehearsed as a conflict over the personality of merchant capital in the age of revolution.

Rather than tame the human passions of greed and avarice, colonial commerce unbridled them by driving trade into sub rosa channels, outside the monitoring powers of the guild and beyond the taxing purview of an increasingly indebted state. What upset the creole merchants was this sense that distant power-wielders held their enterprise, their interests, in disdain. Tarred as corrupt contrabandists in the 1790s for violating imperial orders and seeking out markets for their staples or catering to unmet colonial demand, after the turn of the century creole merchants accused the monopolizers and excluders of corrupting otherwise healthy market activity. In 1801, Manuel José de Lavardén issued a poetic lament against the venal rich, the monopolists, "nobles," whose greed contrasts with the humble, honest merchant.

> El bien común. No es cierto,
> Que es la única base
> Sobre que funda el noble
> Todas sus veleidades?
> Pues, quién será más útil,
> Dime noble arrogante,
> Tus ocios, tus locuras
> El útil Comerciante,
> Que paga sus tributos,
> Que arriesga sus caudales,
> Que trata, compra, vende,
> Que el dinero reparte
> Poniendo en acción todos
> Los Oficios, las Artes?[55]

> The common good. Is it not well-known,
> That it is the only base
> Upon which the noble bases
> All his frivolities?
> What, then, would be more useful,
> Tell me, you arrogant noble,
> Your vices, your flights
> Or the useful Merchant

---

[55]Lavardén, "Oda" (April 8, 1801), in *Nuevo aspecto del comercio*, p. 55.

Who pays his dues,
Who risks his rewards,
Who trades, buys, and sells,
So that money might spread
To put in motion all
The Professions and Arts?

As Albert Hirschman has noted of eighteenth-century political economists, the dividing line between the indulgence of unruly passions and the application of healthy interests was never easy to identify. The distinction did come into sharper view as commerce and credit angled for greater autonomy from venal aristocratic exploits. When commercial changes spread through the ports and hinterlands of the Iberian colonies, it prompted an analogous evolution of market language to that seen in Europe. But it was not identical. In these outposts of Atlantic empires, it was less the struggle between old landed property and new commercial property that created the material basis for an intellectual exchange, but rather a clash between two models of commerce warring within Iberian mercantilism. The first was the progeny of an old idea of exclusive oligopoly protected by a monarch's defense against rivals—what Barbara and Stanley Stein have called a Hapsburg paradigm of twining metropolitan mercantile wealth and monarchical power. The second, always nestled in the interstices of the first, was a Bourbon product: new merchant capitalists thriving off colonial exports and increasingly handling the quasi-legal commodities of a dawning commercial age. In the words of one colonist, it was not that passions were natural to Americans but that the interests of the colonies were at odds with an older set of policies; thus the conflict between private behavior and public legal norms: "the course of men's passions, while they might exceed necessary limits ... offer a thousand advantages to society, and without it, society will not be opulent. The extremes are well known: public scandal, insubordination before legal authorities, and harm to honor, health...these being everything that we must impede."[56]

In this political climate, it would have been hard to point to the sovereign as the malefactor without incurring the wrath of the gendarmes and viceroys. The result was to point especially to the private agents who had done so well off within the older, "Hapsburg" model as the retardant agent in Iberian prosperity. Still, shifting the critique to subjects themselves did not exempt the sovereign from all responsibility for the fate of his "possessions," the colonies. If individual merchants had to handle their own

---

[56]Lavardén, *Nuevo aspecto del comercio*, p. 178; Hirschman, *The Passions and the Interests*.

property with the proper ethical sense, so too rulers had to treat their property—the colonies—with a code of reason and morality. Here are José Ignacio de Pombo's 1807 words: "it is very important that the government, to avoid and cure this terrible affliction, with respect both to customs and public morals, as well as the public treasury, as well as to honorable citizens that rely upon legitimate commerce," open the ports to active trade.[57] Petition after petition warned authorities that they had a moral obligation to stamp out the causes of colonial malaise.

For the most part, requests that the sovereign attend to his colonial subjects were framed as requests that he uphold ancient obligations to his subjects. It is this language that recent revisionists see as evidence of a colonial commitment to an ancient constitutional tradition, not proof of modern enlightened convictions. It is true, the frustration of colonial merchants and producers with imperial policy is palpable, but it is muted in the conventions of supplicative royal language of subjects petitioning for favors. We should avoid, however, diminishing the compound effects of the strain exercised upon Portuguese and especially Spanish mercantilism. For what was potentially disruptive was the sense that colonial subjects—or at least the enlightened magnates in the fringes—also harbored passions that could be converted into virtuous interests, and that these should not be sacrificed for the sake of any other particular group within the empire. Azeredo Coutinho exemplified the new model of imperial equipoise that emerged from colonial understandings of political economy. Portugal, he argued, stood to be among the leaders of civilization, the envy of her rivals. Her possessions in Asia, Africa, and especially the Americas gave her the potential to rearrange the modern world into a crafted balance of regions producing for and trading with each other as partners in a higher imperial venture designed for the benefit of all the parts, not just the center. Critical here was the special place not of the metropole, but of Brazil. "Brazil is located in the eastern most part of America, almost in the middle of the world almost reaching Africa, with one foot on land, the other in the sea, with her arms extended, one to Europe the other to Asia." What America offered was to be part of a more truly universal empire, a monarchy that was more than just European. But for this to flourish the sovereign had to appreciate that Portugal was one—albeit with some privileges—among several components of the empire, but whose ancient interests could not stand in the way of a new, greater imperial synthesis. "The metropole," continued

---

[57]Pombo, "Informe de Don José Ignacio de Pombo del Consulado de Cartagena sobre asuntos económicos y fiscals," in Ortíz, *Escritos*, p. 157; for a similar direct appeal to policymakers, see Belgrano's "Memoria" to the consulado of July 1796 in *Escritos económicos*, p. 74.

Azeredo Coutinho, "is therefore like a mother, who must give the colonies, like her sons, all the good treatment and help necessary to defend and ensure their lives and their welfare." For Portugal to be more than just a great power—but a virtuous one capable of realizing all the promise of the new science of political economy—she had to see the metropole and the colonies in a different way. "It is therefore necessary that the interests of the metropole become linked to those of the colonies, and that these be treated without rivalry. For when all the subjects are richer, the sovereign will be even more so." Thus, to be more than just another great power meant recasting the empire as a partnership between the colonies and the metropole, between the interests of the peripheries and those of the old centers.[58]

Azeredo Coutinho's essay therefore resolved the tensions that were mounting in the Iberian empires by reassembling their parts. His project in fact exemplified the growing chorus of many other colonial political economists. But this effort to project a different model of empire, to rescue it from internal vice and external threats, was not so easily squared with the longstanding commitment to adapt the Spanish and Portuguese empires along the lines envisioned by Bourbon and Pombaline architects— who still had in mind a vision of defending metropolitan sovereignty. To be sure, in the accent on trade and interests as the lifeblood of imperial welfare there were some undoubted continuities between peninsular reformers before 1789 and colonial advocates thereafter—and thus colonial words appeared less disruptive than it might appear.

But the prospect of a new imperial balance did run into difficulties when confronted with old imperial habits. The potentially abrasive features of colonial political economy erupted into the open the instant Bourbon and Braganza authority shook in 1807–8. Decades of contention came to a head when metropolitan authority imploded. When João VI sailed into Salvador da Bahia, there was José da Silva Lisboa waiting with a blueprint for freer exchange, a framework for "genuine principles of sociability." The emperor's first measure was to declare the ports open to friendly nations, followed by a decree mandating Silva Lisboa to draft an exposition of the realm's governing principles of political economy.[59]

---

[58]Azeredo Coutinho, *Ensaio económico*, pp. 91–102.

[59]Silva Lisboa worked with D. Fernando José de Portugal, one of João's key ministers, fine-tuning the decree, and later joined the emperor's inner circle. Silva Lisboa, *Observações sobre a prosperidade do Estado pelo Liberales principios da Nova Legislação do Brasil* (Rio de Janeiro: Impressão Regia, 1810), pp. ii, 8; Oliveira Lima, *D. João VI no Brasil*, 3rd ed. (Rio de Janeiro: Topbooks, 1996), pp. 131–36.

The Brazilian shift was relatively peaceable compared to Spanish America's, where frustration was evolving into downright anger. Upon hearing the news of Napoleon's invasion of Spain and capture of the Bourbon king, colonists fretted over how to handle the shock. After some months of great uncertainty, some creoles seized the opportunity to call for a new regime. With Ferdinand VII jailed in France, the Supreme Junta of Seville beckoned to the merchants and hacendados of the colonies to yield patriotic funds to support the struggle against French armies. Not unlike the Thirteen Colonies half a century earlier, propertied sectors of the colonies shot right back. Connecting revenue with representation, colonial patriciates argued that they deserved a say in policies that governed their fortunes. They would pay taxes, merchants agreed, so long as they enjoyed freer rein to trade. The Cartagena guild members did not mince a word in their communiqué to Seville in November 1808: "there is an urgent necessity for prudent rules and good policy, to give honest occupation to the thousands of individuals who, directly or indirectly, subsist from commerce and trade; let us say this just once to save this State which, as a material edifice, is collapsing because its mortar is destroyed—made of agriculture, industry, commerce and all traffic; we demand in the name of all justice, a general remedy, swift and rigorous, and applied without partiality and without concern." "Open our ports," cried the missive, "to all friendly or neutral nations of America, and let us also go freely to yours."[60] These were the opening verbal salvos, shaped by the precepts of colonial political economy, in a war of words that soon cascaded into a full-blown civil war.

CONCLUSION

Pombo, trained in philosophy and law and a successful trader in Nueva Granada, founded the merchant guild and signed a declaration in December 1810 recognizing the Spanish Cortes (Parliament). A year later he was elected to the Constitutional Convention in Cartagena, only to be politically crushed in the civil war that ensued, dying in 1815, his family's fortunes lost and Nueva Ganada in counterrevolutionary flames.

---

[60]AGNB, Colonia, Consulado, I, f. 505; AGNBA, Sala IX, Consulado, 4/6/10, "Copiador de Correspondencia," November 14, 1809. This language calling for a policy aimed at the colonies and less at the metropole is perhaps best exemplified in Mariano Moreno, "Representación a nombre del apoderado de los hacendados de las campañas del Río de la Plata dirigida al excmo: Señor Virrey Don Baltasar Hidalgo Cisneros" (September 30, 1809), in his *Escritos políticos y económicos* (Buenos Aires: Cultura Argentina, 1915), pp. 111–79.

Belgrano, at the other end of South America, followed a similar path. Scion of a powerful merchant household in Buenos Aires, trained in law, a prominent voice in the merchant guild, signed on as an intellectual beacon when the River Plate rejected the Spanish regency's commands. He also died, much of the family's property wiped out in the wars, his political designs in tatters, in 1820. Pombo, Belgrano, and dozens of other enlightened spokesmen of the merchant class of the Spanish empire struggled to make sense of the world around them as it crumbled. Their fates—and fortunes—were personal and public concerns. From this combined sense of being both capitalists and *letrados*, they began to express alternative foundations for emerging political economies.

Pombo, Belgrano, and their colleagues tried to navigate the political revolutions of 1810 according to a constellation shaped by their colonial status and class interests. They wanted a greater measure of local control wrested from the metropole. And they wanted it to ensure the application of policies that would better serve merchant capital—freer (not "free") trade with other ports and greater attention to the potential for vast new staple industries of the Americas. They won and lost. One by one the colonies seceded from Spain. And one by one, the political revolution evolved into a social revolution, followed by nearly a half century of civil war. The turbulence of civil war in turn ravaged the power of merchant capital. What took centuries to nourish—an apparatus to channel incalculable riches to the coffers of European dynasts and their commercial epigones in metropolitan ports—was now wreckage.

Brazil stands as something of a contrast to the Spanish American pattern. Its rupture with metropolitan authority did not involve a clash of armed forces; its political revolution demoted the crown to constitutional constraints, steering away from any republican path. The merchants, as Silva Lisboa argued in a sustained output of royalist pamphlets, retained control of the economic helm of the realm—even of an independent Brazil. Brazilian statehood enabled, among other things, Brazilian merchants to command unrivaled status in the most lucrative Atlantic exchange of all: slaves. The braided continuity of merchant capital and monarchical rule was the product of unforeseeable contingencies, like the flight of João's court from Lisbon in 1807. But it was also the product of decades of policy and trading adaptation that shifted greater authority over commercial affairs away from the peninsula to the colony. Men like Silva Lisboa never had to face the choice of a rupture with old ways, which is why, as the Brazilian historian Sérgio Buarque de Holanda has argued, Silva Lisboa could champion market language while defending a stratified slave society; he could champion the cause of change in order to preserve the virtues of tradition.[61]

This chapter has tried, however, to challenge Brazilian "exceptionalism." Brazil, like the Spanish colonies, had to contend with strictures of empire under which it chafed, and under which a generation of colonial letrados would sharpen critiques of the old regime. Market language gave colonists a framework to chastise metropolitan controls, while imagining a social order capable of promoting "opulence" while assuring the virtuous behavior of subjects. What is more, the critique and the alternative were forged in the heat of a growing commercial crisis of both empires. Brazilian denizens did not invoke the ancient constitution of Hispanic pacts, nor did they rely on the language of civic humanism, the alleged framework for the critique of British capitalism and colonial rule. This is why this chapter has tried to describe the uses of the term "corruption," for it was not invoked to call for the restoration of an earlier pristine age of self-governing moral communities or rule by an ethical Catholic monarch. Instead, colonial critics rebundled various components of eighteenth-century political economy to make specific claims against what they felt were violations of liberties to realize a more perfect form of property.

More than personal property was at stake. So too was the nature of empire. Indeed, what is so novel about these colonial deliberations is the way in which private interests and public welfare were reassembled to reimagine the relationship between capitalism and empire. Colonial urgings did not challenge the capitals of empire but were aimed at the empires' capitalists. By nurturing a new concept of property—one capable of improving labor, bringing prosperity, and providing rulers with an even sounder foundation for "public credit"—colonial capitalists presented themselves as possessors of a fundamentally different kind of property than metropolitan capital. And with this difference in property flowed a difference in personality. Charges of monopoly and corruption were rhetorical means to degrade the personality of metropolitan traders while presenting colonial merchants as more virtuous and capable of shaking empires out of their "lethargy" and "indolence."

What market language did not do, however, was recombine the relationship between private property and political representation. Emerging ideas of capitalist property may have called for revised laws to safeguard

---

[61]For Buarque de Holanda, this provides evidence of Brazil's lack of a true modernizing bourgeoisie. Sérgio Buarque de Holanda, *Raízes do Brasil* (São Paulo: Companhia das Letras, 1995), p. 85.

virtuous commerce, but they did not generate a political economy for new ideas of rulership. Rights to property did not lead automatically to, or harken back to, rights to representation. Colonial injunctions did not include political demands, and if they did, they were couched not as "rights" for themselves but as claims that were good for the sovereign that ruled both sides of the Atlantic. In this sense they were concerned not with who ruled, but how they ruled the empires. And at no point did any of the letrado vindications accuse the sovereign of public corruption. There is little evidence of Anglo-American republicanism shaping Iberian Atlantic thinking; colonial criticism did not unfold into a fuller indictment of the principles of imperial sovereignty. Instead, patrician classes in colonial outposts had to imagine a new legal order when the old one was already in shambles.

5 Spanish Secessions

The Foundations of Secession

In the summer of 1806, the Venezuelan creole Francisco de Miranda led an expeditionary force to the shores of his native land with the goal of liberating it from the Spanish yoke. Counting on British support, he hoped that his little army of white, black, and mulatto patriots would start a revolution to free a continent. In preparation, not only did Miranda bulk up on weapons and uniforms, but he also transported a newer technology of liberation, a printing press (which the colony did not have), to issue thousands of copies of revolutionary proclamations. The daring escapade was, however, a fiasco. A Spanish man-of-war spotted the small flotilla and forced two of the schooners aground, depriving Miranda of the element of surprise. Spanish soldiers paraded the captured sailors through Puerto Cabello, hanged ten of them before a crowd, and sent the rest to face trials in Spain. Several months later Miranda returned, and this time landed a force of 1,500 men. He took the town of Coro with the following proclamation: "the time and the conjuncture are perfectly favorable for us to carry out your designs, and the many people who compose this army are your friends and compatriots, resolved to give their lives if necessary for your liberty and independence under the auspices and protection of the British navy." Some Indians and mulattos joined him. But otherwise the townsfolk fled or stayed indoors. After dawdling for ten days wondering what to do, Miranda learned that royal troops—some 1,200 infantrymen, plus 600 freed black militiamen—were marching from Caracas. Miranda withdrew before the two multiracial forces could clash.[1]

Miranda had his reasons for backing off. He later observed that while Venezuelans yearned for "Civil Liberty," they did not know how to grasp

---

[1] AGI, Gobierno, Caracas, Legajo 458, September 13, 1806, Manuel de Guevara Vasconcelos to Principe de la Paz; September 5, 1806, Francisco Cavallero Sarmiento to Principe de la Paz; Estado/Caracas, 71/9, November 8, 1808, "Informe de Secretaría á S.M. sobre el asunto de Miranda"; Francisco de Miranda, "Todo Pende de Nuestra Voluntad," in his *America Espera* (Caracas: Biblioteca Ayacucho, 1982), p. 356; AGNC, Real Consulado, Actas, 2530, f. 143, March 11, 1808. Karen Racine, *Francisco de Miranda: A Transatlantic Life in the Age of Revolution* (Wilmington, DE: Scholarly Resources Press, 2003).

and protect it. They needed a liberation that would introduce virtuous laws and institutions, instructing Venezuelans in the art of modern politics, eclipsing old venal and violent habits through sheer volition. This was why the printing press, a portable factory of words about historical oppression, liberty, and sovereignty, was such a decisive instrument of change: its output would induce people to join the cause as an act of collective will. But this is also why British support was so crucial in Miranda's eyes—because the show of might would tilt the scales so much than no one would resist change. Without the fuller backing of the Royal Navy and the illuminating power of enlightened ideas, the war of words would falter and give way to a war that threatened the goal of replacing bad laws with good ones with a minimum of friction. "If we have to use *force*," warned Miranda, "in whatever form that might be, the result will be opposition and internal divisions." His sentiments would turn out to be prophetic.[2]

If this was the case in 1806, a few years later conditions had changed dramatically. In 1810, one by one colonies demanded sovereignty within empire. A year later, some colonists were calling for secession from Spain. Thus, what appeared so far-fetched in the summer of 1806 was much more plausible four years later. In the interim, models of rulership created and refined over centuries had collapsed. With the collapse of imperium colonists had to improvise a new system. In the debating that ensued, the isolated voices of liberation acquired a valence that they could only have wished for a few years earlier. Indeed, after 1810 more and more colonists converted the loyalism of 1806 into calls to secede from empire altogether. Thus, from 1806 to 1812, the Spanish colonies of South America swung from expressions of loyalty to increasing "voice" to "exit" as responses to collapsing imperial institutions.[3]

The response to the sovereignty crisis in Spain was to intensify a process that Bourbons had been seeking for decades: re-center the parts of the imperial monarchy into an integrated "nation" through reform from its revitalized center. Though there was some disagreement among loyalists over which reforms would best re-center the empire, there was much less disagreement over the fundamental objective.

But reconstituting the Spanish empire as a "nation" did not sit well with all its parts. When loyalists in the center and their minions in the peripheries attempted to reassert power over increasingly autonomous

---

[2]Francisco de Miranda, "Exhaustivo y documentado alegato por la emancipación de Colombia" (January 10, 1808), in *America Espera*, p. 368.

[3]Hirschman, *Exit, Voice and Loyalty*; idem, "Exit, Voice and the German Democratic Republic," in his *Propensity to Self-Subversion* (Cambridge, MA: Harvard University Press, 1995), pp. 12–14.

colonies, they invigorated colonial reactions and "voice," which soon came to articulate quite a different model of sovereignty—though resting on some of the same principles, such as the idyll of the nation, as those championed by loyalists. In effect, colonial subjects acquired anticolonial identities not because they harbored deeply gestating grievances that suddenly erupted at the opportune moment. Rather, anticolonial identities emerged in response to the ways in which loyalists handled the crisis of imperial sovereignty. Colonial identity formation was a reactive process, responding to external political pressures that forced the issue of who got to speak for the general interest in the absence of a king; new identities did not precede and motivate political change. From this conflict over group interests emerged intergroup conflict and eventually in-group identities. In this fashion, anticolonialism and its corollary, nationalism, were the effects, not the causes, of a broader imperial collapse. The process was profound enough to enable Miranda to lead the creation of a sovereign system out of a colony in 1811—a chimerical idea in 1806.[4]

INTERNATIONAL JUNCTURE

Spanish American conflicts were part of what the Spanish statesman and reformist Gaspar Melchor de Jovellanos called "a civil war within an international one." Atlantic warfare, intensifying during the 1790s, became a war to the death after Napoleon's coronation. The struggle for Atlantic supremacy culminated in the smashing of the Spanish monarchy at its core, and sparked a conflict across its imperial possessions over how to fill the political vacuum posed by the collapse of ancient sovereign structures. In the four years between 1804 and 1808, the centralizing legal pillars of the world's biggest empire crumbled.

The crisis of sovereignty was first of all sparked by external, not internal, forces. Spain struggled to stay out of the Franco-British conflict, to no avail. To force Spain to stop supporting France, the Pitt government ordered the Royal Navy to attack Spanish vessels. After losing several ships carrying bullion from the River Plate, Spain finally declared war on Britain on December 12, 1804. At the Battle of Trafalgar, Spain lost most of its fleet, and what was left of its navy straggled into Cádiz. Finally, in November 1806, Spain formally adhered to Napoleon's Continental System, sealing itself off from maritime contact with any enemy of France,

---

[4]Henri Taifel and John C. Turner, "The Social Identity Theory of Intergroup Behavior," in S. Worchel and W. G. Austin, eds., *Psychology of Intergroup Relations* (Chicago: Nelson and Hall, 1986), pp. 7–24.

and thus ensuring British attack on anything flying a Spanish flag. Later, when Napoleon tried to take over the peninsular empires directly, Spanish rulers switched sides and aligned with the British. But whichever super-power Spain joined, the metropole was cut off from its colonies and plunged into a costly and ruinous war at home that would last until 1814.

International warfare aggravated the paralysis within the court in Madrid. From 1802 onward, the court's main opposition came from Carlos IV's own son, the Prince of Asturias, Ferdinand. The high nobil-ity and old aristocracy aligned with Ferdinand out of impatience with Charles's Minister Godoy, the "Prince of Peace." What Ferdinand and the nobility shared was a desire to rescue a royal dynasty they felt was crum-bling at the top. In an effort to placate Napoleon, Charles signed the Treaty of Fontainbleau in October 1807, which allowed French troops to cross Spain en route to occupying Portugal. This only intensified the palace intrigue until Ferdinand finally staged a coup at the Aranjuez Palace on March 19, 1808. But while the destruction of Godoy's ministry was wildly popular, the crisis of the Bourbon monarchy converted the French military invasion (in the few months after Fontainebleau, Napoleon flooded Spain with 100,000 soldiers) into an occupation. Thus, when the new king entered his capital to be greeted by celebrating crowds, the shadow of French power already loomed over Madrid. Invited to Bayonne to convene with the French emperor, Ferdinand left behind a junta to rule in his expected short absence. The French emperor welcomed the ill-advised Ferdinand, put him under house arrest, and forced him to abdicate.[5]

One might think that Napoleon's efforts to annex Spain would have resolved the crisis of Spanish sovereignty. After all, many Spaniards (and some colonists) thought the future would prosper under a French pro-tectorate. But it did not. Instead of co-opting a compliant Bourbon regime to fold Madrid's empire into the French orbit, Napoleon unwit-tingly brought down the pillars of Spanish sovereignty. To be sure, he placed his brother Joseph on the Spanish throne and there were many Spanish reformers who supported the new regime, feeling that this was the ticket to pushing through the oft-thwarted modernization efforts. Many Spaniards were less welcoming. As it became clear that the French forces were more than just itinerants and planned to become occupants, the unconsulted hosts began to resist the Napoleonic plan. Stoked by conservative aristocrats and churchmen, who had their respective reasons

---

[5]Timothy E. Anna, *Spain and the Loss of America* (Lincoln: University of Nebraska Press, 1983), pp. 21–27; Brian R. Hamnett, *La política española en una época revolu-cionaria, 1790–1820* (México: Fondo de Cultura Económica, 1985), pp. 57–67.

for disliking the new reform era, the peninsula seethed with insurrection. Epitomized by the famous uprising in Madrid on May 2, a new coalition protested against the French occupation. The *levée en masse* redistributed political and military power to the provinces and municipalities that armed and manned the ensuing guerrilla war. Province after province created juntas to rule in the place of a single king. All the centrifugal forces of Spanish regionalism came to the fore. About the only thing local forces could agree on was that now Spain should align with Britain to resist the French occupants. The alliance of local guerrilla chieftains with a British expeditionary force would eventually prove effective enough to bleed Napoleon's army to death. As his forces got bogged down in a Vietnam-like war, Napoleon would groan about his "Spanish ulcer."

Guerrilla warfare in the peninsula might have been effective against the French, but it could not resolve the problem of what to do about a rapidly fragmenting empire. To prevent a complete breakup, Spanish notables enlisted the provincial juntas to form a Junta Central. This body, led by the eighty-year-old Count Floridablanca, was wracked by continuous infighting. To make matters worse, French armies swept into Madrid in December 1808, forcing the Junta Central to withdraw to Seville. When Andalusia fell to French forces in early 1810, the Junta Central retreated to the port city of Cádiz. Feeling that a complete Napoleonic takeover was impossible to avoid, some in the Spanish government made plans to flee, as the Braganza dynasty had done from Lisbon, for the dominions in the New World (see chapter 6).[6]

The power vacuum became an almost permanent state of affairs that not even the intervention of great powers could resolve. If international contests led to the crisis of Spanish sovereignty, the tug-of-war between centralizing and centrifugal forces in the Spanish Atlantic posed problems for international combatants. Consider the dilemma for the British. In 1806 the British were only too happy to hammer at Spain's sprawling empire, supporting Miranda in Venezuela, and most audaciously occupying Buenos Aires in an effort to seize the silver sources flowing from the Andes. Since Napoleon severed British merchants from their European markets, they looked to Iberian colonies as commercial compensation. When Spain flipped sides and aligned with Britain against France, the British had to call off all their adventurers and more aggressive merchants. London now needed a viable Spanish regime to pin down French forces and prevent them from preparing for an invasion across the English Channel. This was no easy task. The beleaguered Perceval ministry sunk scarce men and money into the

---

[6]Miguel Artola, *La España de Fernando VII* (Madrid: Espasa, 1999).

protracted peninsular campaign.[7] London also disclaimed any support
for the colonial cause and repudiated their earlier role in Buenos Aires
and Caracas. This is why Miranda was so disenchanted by British policymakers, at first conspiring with and then abandoning him. When
the Venezuelan patriot met with the languid foreign secretary, Richard
Wellesley, to enlist support for the colonists in 1809, he walked away
concluding that the British "have abandoned us, sacrificing us without
the least remorse."[8]

Here was a case in which the Spanish state was too strategic to abandon but too weak to exploit. As both the French and the British governments sought to annex the Spanish empire by trying to bolster rivals
in the peninsula, the colonies drifted without central control. Indeed,
since both superpowers sought to bring the Spanish empire into their
respective orbits through the old metropolis, neither France nor Britain
could support the colonial causes (for fear of driving Spain to the
enemy) or squelch them (for fear of losing the colonies to the enemy).
So, the fall of Spain and the capitulation of the Bourbon monarchy may
have been just the moment that secessionists were waiting for, but it did
not mean that they could count—as the rebels of the Thirteen Colonies
had done with the help of the French and Spanish governments—on
outside help.

Thus, the nature of the international war, the meltdown of the
Westphalian interstate system, and the contingencies of the Spanish sovereignty crisis created a power vacuum across the empire. The absence,
therefore, of either a powerful metropolitan force or an international one
to counterbalance the vacuum at the center deprived those who struggled
to resolve the sovereignty crisis of the Spanish empire of any galvanizing
alternative to internecine feuding. In this context, spoilers, even well-
meaning ones, could command greater voice than their numbers would
otherwise have suggested.[9]

---

[7]Richard Wellesley to George Canning, August 15, 1809, in Richard Wellesley, *The Dispatches and Correspondence of the Marquess of Wellesley K.G. during His Lordship's Mission to Spain* (London: John Murray, 1828), p. 24. A useful account of the war in Spain is David Gates, *The Spanish Ulcer: A History of the Peninsular War* (London: DaCapo Press, 2001).

[8]Francisco de Miranda, "Diario," January 26, 1809, in Miranda, *America Espera*, p. 386; AGI, Estado, Caracas, 63/33, December 10, 1810, Esteban Varela to Secretaria del Estado; 63/31, f. 5, May 27, 1809, Canning to Apodaca; AGI, Estado, Americas, 87/1, August 10, 1810, "Instrucciones al General Apodaca."

[9]William W. Kaufmann, *British Policy and the Independence of Latin America, 1804–1828* (New Haven: Yale University Press, 1951), esp. pp. 47–48; AGI, Estado, Americas, 87/4, June 16, 1810; John Street, *Gran Bretaña y la independencia del Río de la Plata* (Buenos Aires: Paidós, 1967), pp. 110–27.

Public Opinion

Getting voice in the context of a deep political crisis involved dramatic changes in the practices of politics. These changes accentuated the differences among imperial parties. Atlantic rivalry and warfare only account for part of the dynamics of imperial breakdown. International factors may be causes, but they do not explain *how* empires break down. Coincident with modern war across the Atlantic was the emergence of another political force: public opinion, as well as the circulation of newspapers, broadsheets, and pamphlets claiming to represent or at least inform it. Francisco de Miranda's faith in his printing press was not simply the reflection of an idealist's stock in the printed word; it exemplified the rapid transformation in the conduct of politics and a new way to sway political subjects, one which he had seen at work in other revolutionary settings in Philadelphia, London, and Paris.

So just as the Atlantic wars intensified, rulers had to contend with a force that held them to certain standards of conduct and legitimacy. In fact, ramped-up war and publicity were not simply coincident factors; they intertwined and shaped each other's sustenance. At times the press served rulers well, drumming up support (and money) for patriotic causes. At other times it could be merciless in its attention to losses at war and defaults and "depravity" at home. Indeed, the language of the entwined concerns with virtue and corruption we analyzed in the previous chapter were broadcast far and wide in large part because Atlantic warfare augmented the domestic profiles of rulers as champions of a patriotic, "national" cause, and as more burdensome users of peoples' money. In this basic respect, the imagined features of nationhood, disseminated through the press and instruments of print capitalism so provocatively captured by Benedict Anderson, were grounded in a more fundamental legitimacy crisis of empire. Indeed, it would be hard to understand the makings of modern nationhood in the Iberian Atlantic without coming to terms with the anterior politics of empire and the ways in which the latter gave shape to the former.

To say that war and publicity were causally linked does reduce one to the other. Just as Atlantic wars had their own dynamics, so too did the public force of the printing presses. Either way, the public's opinion thrived with a measure of autonomy from dynasts and rulers. Pioneering works from Bernard Bailyn to Jürgen Habermas have shown the potency of this political force, though they have perhaps not fully appreciated the degree to which the struggle for public opinion thrived off broader battles for European and Atlantic supremacy; news of military triumphs could make or break political careers.[10]

---

[10]Bernard Bailyn, *The Ideological Origins of the American Revolution* (Cambridge, MA: Harvard University Press, 1967); Keith M. Baker, "Politics and Public Opinion under

One common assumption about the role of public opinion should be qualified. This sphere of political activity need not lean toward a new model of integration and consensus making. In the case of the Spanish Atlantic caught in the vortex of a sovereignty crisis, it would become clear that public opinion and new spheres of political mobilization did re-center public affairs from courts and aristocratic dealings to a more popular and inclusive mode of reconciliation—which one might have expected given the metropolitan blows to the ancien régime. François-Xavier Guerra and others have pioneered studies of how the press erupted on the public stage on both sides of the Spanish Atlantic to play an important role in the formation of public opinion just as the accepted structures of politics were themselves thrown into crisis. The press, public assemblies, and salons became important spaces for conducting public affairs in the absence of formal "political" mechanisms of representation within the state. But if public opinion helped drive the transformations of regimes elsewhere, the Iberian Atlantic presents important wrinkles to anyone tempted to generalize a pan-Atlantic theory of political change. The "public" was the subject (what had to be *created* in order for any legitimate ruler to rule) and object (that which *decided* a ruler's legitimacy) of politics. The Venezuelan journalist and jurist Miguel José Sanz argued that public opinion was indeed the only true force capable of counterbalancing political passions and ensuring that good laws got passed. Good laws, after all, are the only ones that patriots can love. "The state and political force of law is the result of this opinion," he noted in late 1810. But this opinion was still fractured and irresolute.[11]

Before 1810, there was not much of a free press. To be sure, there were weeklies, such as Buenos Aires' *Telégrafo Mercantil* or the *Semanario de Agricultura*. But their circulation was limited and words caged. There were also occasional outbursts of seditious leaflets and graffiti, like the banners that appeared mysteriously one night in Quito with oracular slogans like "LYBERY, STO, FELYCY7A7EM, E7, GLORIAM, CONSEQUENTO." This sort of nocturnal crypticism only reinforced the point that the colonies did not have an open public sphere tolerant of dissent and capable of

the Old Regime: Some Reflections," in Jack Censer and Jeremy Popkin, eds., *Press and Politics in Pre-Revolutionary France* (Berkeley: University of California Press, 1987), pp. 204–46. On the public sphere more generally, see Craig Calhoun, ed., *Habermas and the Public Sphere* (Cambridge, MA: MIT Press, 1992).

[11]Miguel José Sanz, "Politica 1810," in *Pensamiento político de la emancipación venezolana* (Caracas: Biblioteca Ayacucho, 1988), p. 89; François-Xavier Guerra and Annick Lempérière, introduction to Guerra and Lempérière, eds., *Los espacios públicos en Iberoamérica: Ambigüedades y problemas. Siglos XVIII–XIX* (México: Fondo de Cultura Económica, 1988), pp. 5–21.

aggregating sentiments into public causes. When Manuel Belgrano returned to Buenos Aires from his studies in Europe in the early 1790s, he was flush with the ideas and fervor of the French Revolution. What he found in the colonial outpost was a stifling world where dissent and debate did not leak out of the few salons, and where the limited press steered clear of any open discussion of the public issues of the day.[12]

The breakdown of the central regime opened the space for newspapers and broadsheets across the empire. As they flourished in the political vacuum, the editors did not shirk from openly scrutinizing decisions taken by interim governments. Indeed, in some cities, the press campaigning gave way to a one-sided pamphlet war against perceived injustices in Spain. In early 1810, the *Diario de Comercio* published a list of complaints to the viceroy Cisneros and it included an article called "Origen de la grandeza y decadencia de los imperios." The essay, Belgrano recalled, drew historical contrasts with other empires, most notably Rome, and did not veil observations that Spain was following the same course. Francisco José de Caldas's *Semanario del Nuevo Reino de Granada* was founded in late 1807. A year later the first newspaper appeared in Caracas; the local government finally admitted the importation of a printing press, hoping to bolster its own legitimacy in part aware that Miranda's seditious pamphlets could just as easily recirculate. Paradoxically, while the Venezuelan government enabled printers to share the news of the world with readers, the young lawyer who had been dispatched to interrogate the prisoners of Miranda's ill-fated expedition for the government, Juan Germán Roscio, would soon become one of the most prominent editorialists for secession. Indeed, it did not take much time for papers in Santa Fé and Caracas to become less elliptical, bolder, and more audacious in criticizing the stand-in authorities in Spain. By late 1810, the *Gazeta de Caracas* and its cousin in the River Plate, the *Gazeta de Buenos Aires*, were reprinting articles published in London's new *El Colombiano*, another Miranda brainchild, which urged readers to measure good government by its ability to deliver peace and "common happiness" to all its people, not to the privileged few.

The advent of this new political instrument, and the speed with which it became more and more partisan, can be seen in Caldas's *Semanario*.

---

[12]Belgrano, *Autobiografía*, p. 14; AGI, Estado, Santa Fe, 53/55, November 19, 1794. For a pioneering study of the late colonial press, see Renán Silva, *Prensa y revolución a finales del siglo XVIII* (Bogotá: Banco de la Republica, 1988); Victor Uribe Uran, "The Birth of a Public Sphere in Latin America during the Age of Revolution," *Comparative Studies in Society and History* 42:2 (2000): 425–57. On the importance of oral communication, See Rebecca Earle, "Information and Disinformation in Late Colonial New Granada," *The Americas* 54:2 (1997): 167–84.

In the very first issue of the *Semanario*, the paper restricted itself to an extended description of the climate and physiology of the country, believing that "geographic knowledge is the thermometer with which one measures the learning, commerce, agriculture and prosperity of the people. Its stupidity and barbarity is always proportionate to its ignorance of these facts. Geography is the fundamental base of any political speculation." While hardly a direct salvo against imperial rule, the New Granadan writer was making more explicit what physiocrats had intimated in earlier years: Spanish policies had not exactly harnessed the colony's potential. Caldas ended thus: "Maybe the day will come in which a stronger and better populated colony will be active from its center to its extremities, and that it will be necessary to lift the cover for countries that now see us from afar and with indifference." Within a year, the editor was becoming even more explicit about the limits of imperial governance, cast in the vernacular of scientific and economic betterment. One example of the "ruin" of "public greatness and happiness" was the failure of the government to open the colony's arid belts up for the manifold bounty of cochineal farming.[13]

The newfound voice of newspapermen and editors even reached Lima, though it took a bit more time. The Peruvian viceroy, José Fernando de Abascal, could assure his government in 1810 that he had kept seditious literature like subterranean copies of *El Colombiano* from the circulating. Abascal was adept at using public spaces, like the theaters, cafés, and print media, to promote fidelity to Spain. But even a stalwart defender of the old censorious order like Abascal had only so many fingers to stick in the leaky dikes; the press did not always abide by his authority. By 1812, the Peruvian viceroy grumbled about the recent insubordination of the limeño press. *El Peruano*, for instance, was a thorn, for it promised to inform its readers of their rights as "free men" and challenge all arbitrary uses of authority. Accordingly the paper was "a safe asylum for the innocent and an exterminating sword for all sorts of misdemeanors which in previous times were committed constantly and with impunity, but which today, thanks to the liberal principles of the Cortes, can be proclaimed and taught with a public judgment before the tribunal of public opinion."[14]

---

[13]Belgrano, *Autobiografía*, pp. 27–28; Renán Silva, *Los ilustrados de Nueva Granada, 1760–1808* (Medellin: Fondo Editorial Universidad Eafit, 2002); McFarlane, *Colombia before Independence*, pp. 310–11; McKinley, *Pre-revolutionary Caracas*, pp. 164–65.

[14]*Semanario del Nuevo Reino de Granada*, December 8, 1807, and December 15, 1809; AGI, Estado, Lima, 74/17, May 23, 1812, José Fernando de Abascal to Secretaria del Estado; Víctor Peralta Ruiz, *En defensa de la autoridad: Política y cultura bajo el gobierno del Virrey Abascal, Perú, 1806–1816* (Madrid: Consejo Superior de Investigaciones Científicas, 2002), pp. 48–49, 70–78, for fascinating details on Peruvian censorship; Racine, *Francisco de Miranda*, p. 199.

The birth of public opinion and the limitations on state authority were not simply new practices. Principles were also at stake. Indeed, in many ways it was the crumbling regime that extolled the role of public opinion as a way of redoubling loyalty to it. So what was becoming a de facto reality in many colonial outposts became law when, in November 1810, the Cortes declared freedom of the press, thus releasing publishers from censors. If the idea was to reinforce loyalty, the expansion of printed material became a major force in the conduct of public affairs, broadened "voice," and ultimately shaped the outcome of politics—all the more so as the contending sides appealed to splintered and increasingly polarized "public opinion."[15] Indeed, the editors of these papers would emerge not just as public figures in the revolution but in many instances leaders of the movements. The press in the colonies reported ceaselessly on the gap between peninsular rhetoric of common nationhood and equality, and fanned the flames not of a unified public opinion but of secession. The sudden change in colonial politics soon acquired the means to define the colonies as structurally different and inevitably separable from the metropole. In the causal spiral of conflict within the Spanish Atlantic, the press played a decisive role in constructing group identities—the identity of both the colonists and metropolitan rulers.

Loyalty and Voice

Fueled by an alarmist press, many colonists figured that Spain was doomed, that the Spanish armies and guerrillas were no match for the French occupants. But the catalyst to come up with a new order came less from Napoleon's sword than from his pen. The French emperor hastened to legitimize his regime in Madrid. On the heels of Ferdinand's abdication, Napoleon summoned his version of the Spanish Cortes (an ancient, if defunct, representative body made up of delegates from the various kingdoms). In an effort to lure colonial loyalty to his regime, Napoleon included six Americans among the delegates. On June 6, 1808, his brother Joseph became king of Spain as José I. Nine days later, the Cortes hurried to approve a constitution, which created a new parliament replete with delegates from the colonies. What is more, America and Asia were given more than rights to representation; they got freedom of agriculture and industry, and eventually trade. The hope was that constitutional representation and voice for all the components of the Spanish

---

[15]Margarita Garrido, *Reclamos y representatciones: Variaciones sobre la política en el Nuevo Reino de Granada, 1770–1815* (Bogotá: Banco de la República, 1993), esp. chap. 4.

empire would embolden it to the new European order with its unequivocal center in Paris.[16]

If exporting constitutional modernity to the Spanish empire was supposed to help legitimate Napoleon's claim to lordship over the Iberian Atlantic, the French conqueror instead set off a process that led to the collapse of the Spanish empire. The Napoleonic regime in Madrid forced two issues: the relative freedom of colonies to pursue their own affairs, and the rights to representation in imperial assemblies. Together, these issues acknowledged a model of sovereignty that broke with Hapsburg and Bourbon practice. The hobbled Spanish government had to respond with something at least as appealing. From its base in Seville and later Cádiz, the government reached not forward but backward, and resuscitated the following ancient doctrine: in the absence of the monarch sovereignty reverted to the people. It had not been heard for many generations; it seemed more than suitable, however, to the circumstances. The junta leaders did this to claim higher moral ground than their competitors in Madrid.

While this old idea of sovereignty appeared to have deeper, "Hispanic" taproots, it begged more questions than it answered. Who constituted the people of this sprawling imperium? How were they to choose their representatives?

The interim government grappled with the sovereignty crisis with several sweeping decrees to all members of the Spanish realm, first concerning the status of the colonies in the empire, and then regarding the composition of a general deliberative body to create a new order. These were momentous shifts. A young lawyer in Nueva Granada, José Manuel Restrepo, recalled the day when the Junta Central's envoy arrived in the viceroyalty with the news of French victories and bearing the retreating Andalusian-based government's plea to Americans to stay loyal (and fund the peninsular wars). The junta's envoy announced "that the Spanish dominions in America are not colonies, but an essential and integral part of the Monarchy." This language was meant to generate colonial enthusiasm for sending delegates to a Spanish parliament, the Cortes, with the express aim of thwarting the Napoleonic regimes in Madrid's appeal to colonists. With membership in the political community came representation. In this fashion, the ancient repository of sovereignty, the Cortes, reclaimed its centrality in the body politic with the unprecedented concession that gave colonies formal rights to choose their own representatives. These were powerful words and immediately inflated expectations

---

[16] A. F. Zimmerman, "Spain and Its Colonies, 1808–1820," *Hispanic American Historical Review* 11:4 (1931): 439.

of respect and representation for colonists. But it is important to recall that it was the French menace that had forced events. The fear that the empire would dissolve without a single overarching government finally compelled authorities in Cádiz to dissolve the junta in January 1810. In its place a "Regency" (an executive branch of five men) was created that would then summon deputies from around the "provinces" of the empire to augment the powers of the Cortes (legislative branch). "Dear and beloved subjects, Spanish Americans," went the call for delegates, "you enjoy the same rights and prerogatives and those of the Peninsula, as an essential part of these Dominions of the Spanish Monarchy." It followed with a ringing declaration of the end of bad times: "you are now elevated to the dignity of free men from the yoke that oppressed you with avarice, ignorance and arbitrariness of a few rulers of the old Government." The hope was that this new language of membership, and a parliament to uphold it, would provide the foundations for political legitimacy of a new order by reconciling modern practices of representation with imperium.[17]

To this point, the struggle to resolve Spain's sovereignty crisis could still be seen as a traditional reaction. Some historians have argued that even the acknowledgment of American membership in the political community was still consistent with early understandings of "Spain" as a composition of multiple kingdoms, bound by its own natural law tradition.[18] This may be true as ideas and possibly intentions go, but convening the Cortes had powerful disruptive implications. This assembly did something very new at its outset and converted its legal, political démarche into a proclamation. Its "Opening Decree" announced that sovereignty resided in the nation and the people that composed it, and for whom it alone could deliberate and decide. What was new was the replacement of the monarchy with the nation as the essential framework of membership in the political community. As in France, creating the opportunity for representation and public voice to legitimate a wobbly regime had unintended consequences that were as difficult to foresee as they were impossible to reverse: shifting sovereignty from monarchs to citizen to shore up an old order wound up ushering in a new one.[19]

---

[17]Restrepo, *Historia de la Revolución de Colombia*, v. 1, p. 105; Hamnett, *La política española*, pp. 73–101; Rodríguez O., *The Independence of Spanish America*, pp. 82–91.

[18]See most recently the important work by Rodríguez O., *The Independence of Spanish America*, pp. 75–81; José Carlos Chiaramonte, "El principio del consentimiento en la gestación de las independencias Ibero y Norteamericanas," *Anuario del Instituto de Estudios Histórico Sociales* 17 (2002): 21–33.

[19]AGI, Estado, Americas, 86A/24, July 1810, "Real Decreto convocando Cortes Extraordinarios y Generales."

The familiarity of the principle of monarchy as the bedrock for the Spanish political community had dispelled at least some of the equivocal features of sovereignty. Not so the "nation," for with it went the right to "voice" and deliberation over public affairs. From the moment it was convened, the Cortes ran into trouble managing its own foundational principles of "representation" and the scope of voice. There was immediate debate over the Opening Decree itself. American delegates wanted to add a line to the principle of "national sovereignty" stipulating explicit support for "American subjects'" equality within the nation. Two problems surfaced, became harder to sidestep, and eventually marred the business of the Cortes. First, what population participated in the election of delegates? Did this include people of color, and thus incorporate the 15–17 million people in the colonies, in contrast to the 10.5 million peninsulars? Or did Spanish mean white, of *sangre pura*? Second, the original formula for representation tied the number of delegates to territorial units of provinces, viceroyalties and captaincies. However one sliced it, the idea that capitals in each unit should elect their delegate could not obscure the fact that there were many more peninsular provinces than colonial ones. The arithmetic devised to calibrate representatives to regions and populations became an immediate sore point. The share of deputies from the colonies never rose and constituted at best an active minority.[20]

Once the delegates convened in September 1810, the Cortes proceeded to try to buttress the regime by deliberating over and finally approving a liberal constitution in 1812. The alternative to the crumbling autarky of the ancien régime was a constitutional monarchy—centralized, and modeled in part on the French 1791 Constitution. Unfortunately, by the time the new constitution rolled off the printing press, South America was in revolt. Several colonies, like New Spain and Peru, formally adhered to the new regime. But in most of South America colonists (and not a few Spaniards who pushed for provincial autonomy) were dismayed to read about a new unified, unicameral, centralized regime concocted in Cádiz, one that the Bourbons only dreamed of using to brace the Spanish Atlantic world together under one roof. And what the king himself would feel about being tied to constitutional limitations would become clear when he returned to Madrid in 1814.[21]

---

[20]Josep María Fradera, "Raza y ciudadanía: El factor racial en la delimitación de los derechos de los americanos," in his *Gobernar Colonias* (Barcelona: Ed. Península, 1999), pp. 51–70; John F. King, "The Colored Castes and American Representation in the Cortes of Cadiz," *Hispanic American Historical Review* 33:1 (1953): 35–36; Manuel Chust, *La cuestión nacional americana en la Cortes de Cádiz* (Valencia: Fundación Instituto Historia Social and Universidad Nacional Autónoma de México, 1999), esp. pp. 36–41.

[21]Anna, *Spain and the Loss of America*, pp. 63–65; idem, "Spain and the Breakdown of the Imperial Ethos: The Problem of Equality," *Hispanic American Historical Review* 62:2

Rather than reuniting the empire, declarations that sovereignty resided in the nation, and that Americans were equal to peninsulars, divided it. The Cortes ushered in an era of deliberative activity resting on principles of association, but these self-same principles could mean different things to different peoples—and since the expression of voice was integral to legitimacy, these differences became public. The reinvention of formal politics, coinciding with the sudden emergence of public spaces of assembly and debate, soon embroiled public opinion in the polarization within the Cortes. One of the delegates from the Indies got up in the parliament to declare America's "equality in all rights enjoyed by Spaniards, in the same graces, the same liberty, and the same part of the constitution.... It is necessary, Sir, to remember that Americans are nothing other than Spaniards."[22] Assertions of colonial voice such as this one immediately appeared in American broadsheets and newspapers and became the talk of colonial salons, markets, commercial congregations, and local assemblies. So too were the rebuffs coming from peninsular delegates who wanted American loyalty but did not like what Americans were saying.

VOICE OR LOYALTY?

All of this—the crisis of sovereignty in Spain, the creation of a new vocabulary of membership in the political community, and the sudden invention of new forms of politics—set the stage for the first rupture across the South American colonies. What is important about what happened in 1810 was both the way in which new politics was conducted as well as its substance: not just *how* rulers would rule, as had been the concern until then, but *who* would rule. The colonies wanted the same rights to govern themselves through loyal juntas as did the Spanish provinces, claiming common rights as subjects of the monarchy to constitute local assemblies. And the Spanish rhetoric of equality of all subjects and rights to representation only seemed to reinforce the legitimacy of the colonists' position. After all, ensuring colonial loyalty required the expression of voice. However, as this section will show, equal representation based on common rights was not exactly what peninsular forces had in mind when they convoked the Cortes—and so their recalcitrance when dealing

(1982): 256–58; Brian R. Hamnett, "Spanish Constitutionalism and the Impact of the French Revolution, 1808–1814," in H. T. Mason and W. Doyle, eds., *The Impact of the French Revolution on European Consciousness* (Gloucester: A. Sutton Publications, 1989), pp. 64–80.
[22]Christina M. Duffy Burnett, "The American Delegates at the *Cortes de Cádiz*: Citizenship, Sovereignty, Nationhood" (M.Phil thesis, Cambridge University, 1995), p. 21.

with colonial demands appeared to violate their own promises. Spain's officials within the colonies, old envoys from Bourbon days, were even less inclined to let colonial voice sway their policies. "Voice" then gave way to expressions of "disloyalty," not so much to Spain as to Spain's rulers.

It was the struggle over loyalty that set off the first sparks. There was no real constitutional rupture in the colonies until early 1810; if anything the more pressing fear was of a French takeover. The news of the Junta Central's invitation to the colonies to send delegates (early 1809), followed by the news of the fall of Andalusia (early 1810) and the government's retreat to Cádiz, provided a series of shocks to colonial confidence in imperium. And when viceroys and colonial governors—usually stout defenders of the old regime who suspected the interim Spanish government of being too soft—often refused to accede to colonial requests for concessions, the abrasion mounted. In Quito, where colonists and peninsulars had been scuffling over who best could uphold the city's loyalty, colonists deposed the president of the audiencia and established their own junta in August 1809—and the news spread to Santa Fé, Lima, and beyond. The Peruvian viceroy dispatched troops and magistrates to squelch the *quiteños,* culminating in a violent showdown. Events in Quito only enflamed passions in neighboring Nueva Granada where colonists and authorities alike watched developments, one side with sympathy, the other alarmed. So when the Quito junta leaders were shackled and some of their followers executed, colonists in Santa Fé were outraged. The viceroy in Nueva Granada, whose own popularity was debatable, took a hard line against the sympathizers. He arrested Antonio Nariño, a radical publicist who wanted to prevent royal troops from being sent from Santa Fé to crush Quito's creoles; he ordered the army to crush other upstarts. Charges of betrayal flowed from the words of another publicist, Camilo Torres, whose "Memorial de Agravios" catalogued grievances against imperial authorities for having violated the principles of their existence. He insisted that Americans were not "strangers within the Spanish nation" but sons, "descendants of those who spilled their blood to acquire new dominions for the Spanish crown." What is more, it was the colonists who made Spain great: Americans "were those that extended Spain's frontiers and gave her a representation in the political balance of Europe that she alone could not have attained." Instead of gratitude and recognition, Americans were now getting the opposite. After denouncing the Spanish governor, Torres trumpeted "equality, sacred right of equality; justice that rests on you and gives what belongs to each of us, may you inspire European Spain with these sentiments of Spanish America." And he concluded ominously: "Oh, may heaven prevent other less liberal principles and ideas from producing the loathsome effects of an eternal separation!"[23]

Rather than assuage colonial concerns, peninsular events animated them, peninsular officials irritated them, and finally peninsular policies enraged them. At first the news of the fall of Spain's junta and the creation of the Regency provoked fears that it would govern as an executive authority with even less counsel from the New World than the defunct Bourbon king ever did. Indeed, in the words of the Venezuelan lawyer Juan Germán Roscio, the *only* mandate the Regency had was to convoke the Cortes because in the absence of the king, sovereignty reverted to its original and ancient repository: the people. And the people enjoyed constitutional rights to send their delegates to the Cortes who would rule in the monarch's stead. What the Regency symbolized was a "new oligarchy" determined to usurp the natural rights of Spanish citizens.[24]

Thus even before colonists began to consider how to send delegates to the Cortes, some were inclined to see the Regency and its officials in the colonies as trampling on the natural rights of members of the Spanish nation on both sides of the Atlantic. What was paradoxical was that the junta and Regency had, if anything, shifted power away from old colonial officers like viceroys and audiencias to local assemblies, especially town councils (cabildos or *ayuntamientos*) charged with choosing delegates to the Cortes, relocating constitutional authority from the executive to the legislative branch. This is one reason why old imperial officials were often at odds with municipal assemblies. So, between the affronts of local officials and the fears of the distant Regency, the perception of illegitimate exercise of authority was strong enough to compel colonists to rebel against both. By mid-June, Santafesinos openly began to debate whether or not to topple the imperial officials to authorize the cabildo to name replacements. Between July 14 and 26, 1810, the cabildo of Santa Fé elected to depose the viceroy and the audiencia, repudiated the Regency, and created a Junta Suprema to rule. The Junta Suprema immediately enlisted Nariño, recently released from prison, to author a manifesto to the people of the viceroyalty. It should be clear what this was: an elite coup that transferred authority from one body of the state to another—within

---

[23]Camilo Torres, "Memorial de Agravios," in José Luis Romero and Luis Alberto Romero, comps., *Pensamiento político de la emancipación* (Caracas: Biblioteca Ayacucho, 1977), pp. 29–42; Restrepo, *Historia de la Revolución de Colombia*, v. 1, pp. 125–33. For a summary of these events, see Frank Safford and Marco Palacios, *Colombia: Fragmented Land, Divided Country* (New York: Oxford University Press, 2002), pp. 83–86.

[24]Juan Germán Roscio, "Vicios de la Regencia de España," *Gaceta de Caracas*, June 29, 1810.

the framework of the patched-together empire, and still loyal to the absent king. Indeed, the coup was justified in the name of the king and for the health of the empire.[25]

Spain's two Regency commissioners to Nueva Granada watched these events, impotent, but with more empathy for colonists than anything expressed by deposed authorities. At the end of August they reported back to Cádiz that the problem was that colonists loved Spain, but they did not like their government. One of the commissioners noted that "combined with all the distrust and exasperation of the Pueblos, many people looked at me as one more instrument of tyranny who'd come to trick them and restore their chains." He urged Cádiz to learn a lesson "from this revolution." It was up to the government in Spain to restore confidence using "kindness, conciliation and politics, and the utmost prudence—these are the only means that H.M. can adopt." This means a "liberal, wise government which respects that these people are equal to those of the Peninsula, that the Colonial System is forgotten and destroyed, that it is a by-gone era, and that bad faith and arbitrariness have disappeared forever from the Ministries." Above all it is important to avoid policies that might "cause a war between Brothers and subjects of the very same King." The Spanish government was therefore well informed of the risks of mishandling the crisis. It had envoys on the ground who urged more, not less, conciliation. This is important to recall, for claims that that the Spanish government was simply out of touch or careless do not square with the evidence. At the same time, it is a mistake to assume that all metropolitan authorities advocated the same, hard line; empire did not collapse because its parts were structurally irreconcilable but due to contingent frictions between competing models of legitimacy.[26]

In Caracas and Buenos Aires, the sequence was more or less the same. Each bit of news deepened the sense that the metropole was imploding. And yet each instruction from the junta or the Regency enhanced the scope of voice within the empire, while transferring political power to the colonies and within the colonies. The press openly celebrated the rapid changes, and soon proclaimed for itself a privileged role as the conveyor of public opinion to colonial leaders. The result was explosive: the more colonial officials dragged their feet, the more illegitimate they became. On April 19, 1810, Caraqueños sent the intendant packing and created the Junta Conservadora de los Derechos de Fernando VII.

---

[25] AGNB, Colonia, Cabildos, II, ff. 770–853; McFarlane, *Colombia before Independence*, pp. 336–44.

[26] AGI, Estado, Santa Fé, 53/79, August 19, 1810.

The junta sent a delegation that included the young Simón Bolívar and *homme de lettres*, Andrés Bello, to London to make the case for legitimate rights of colonial autonomy in the absence of a ruling monarch—and to curry the favor of a powerful patron in Caracas's showdown with the Spanish government. One of the less intended effects of this mission, despite instructions to prevent this, was that Francisco de Miranda could not sit out the revolution of his homeland. If the Caracas junta feared the old rebel's propensity to create enmities, the junta was even more adamant that it was not seceding from Spain but simply declaring sovereignty within the empire. Still, the headstrong Bolívar broke his own orders and issued the entreaty for Miranda to take over the command of the local government; Miranda was only too eager to accept the "invitation." Meanwhile, the *Gazeta de Caracas* proclaimed that in the absence of the monarch public opinion recovers its "empire"—and that it was bound to "resist all despotism." What was "public" remained openended. At least at the outset, the junta incorporated both peninsular and colonial elite representatives, and it never confused the distinction between *public* and *popular* spheres. A month later, on May 25, 1810, Buenos Aires' municipal body did the same to the viceroy and the audiencia, and founded its own Primera Junta. Toppling old imperial officials and creating local juntas spread like wildfire across the colonies; what was common was that these first juntas aimed to shore up the empire, not dismantle it. Within most colonial juntas were hybrid coalitions of peninsulars and creoles, merchants and lawyers, conservative royalists and voluble renegades. For the most part, the defense of natural rights of all Spaniards and the integrity of the empire—albeit now united under the roof of public opinion—provided the justification for creating these loose—and unstable—alliances capable, they felt, of ruling more legitimately through local juntas and assemblies.[27]

From the start, the coalitions were subject to the pressures from a precocious press. Recent events and the multiplying stories of abuse by Spanish officials provided the elements for narrating a drama whose fate could be foretold. The *Diario Político de Santafé de Bogotá* serialized an account of the brutality of the repression in Quito in August 1809 a year after the fact. What had circulated through rumor was now "news" that added up to a narrative of self-sacrifice and struggle for higher ends. It had a beginning (the invasion of Spain and the promise of equality), a middle (betrayal of these principles at the hands of "ruthless and cunning"

---

[27]Véronique Hébrard, "Opinión pública y representación en el congreso constituyente de Venezuela (1811–1812)," in Guerra and Lampérière, eds., *Los espacios públicos*, pp. 198–201; Adelman, *Republic of Capital*, pp. 78–79.

colonial officials), an apogee (an assertion of self-rule), and a tragic conclusion (the repression). Called "la historia de nuestra revolución," the articles went into lugubrious detail about the "despotism" of the "tyrants,"
the "barbarous assassinations," and the skulls on pikes decorating the
city. As a result, the decision to topple the viceroy in July 1810 was a
legitimate act "by the brave people of Santa Fé" to reverse the recent history of illegitimate abuse. What is interesting about these essays is not
just their vilification of the overthrown officials, but that recent events
could be folded so quickly into narratives of oppression and alienation
of "American" rights.[28]

The government in Spain knew what was going on in the colonies—of
the high degree of instability of local ruling coalitions and the increasing
polarization of public opinion within the colonies. By October 1810,
colonists had clearly ventilated their dislike of imperial officials and mistrust of the peninsular government. They did not, however, revoke their
loyalty to Spain. In effect, what drove the colonies and the metropolis
apart was not the end of the ancien régime. That was dead. The wedge
was the struggle over the definition of the new regime.

Whose Voice

It took the quarreling over representation in the Cortes and Cádiz's insistence on upholding old mercantilist privileges to sway the voices from
exclamations of loyalty to the fallen king to questioning the legitimacy
of interim rulers and, finally, to advocating exit. The rise of the exit
option in turn shifted the balance within coalitions in the colonies away
from those wanting to work within the system.

First, consider the quarreling over representation. The instructions to
choose delegates to the Cortes contained within them the ingredients of
a problem that only grew as time passed between 1810 and 1812.
Immediately the colonial minority pushed the Cortes to honor the rhetoric of equality, with representation based on populations of "all free
inhabitants." Such a body count would have tilted the assembly to favor
colonists on the basis of one delegate per 50,000 inhabitants (which was
becoming the accepted formula for choosing deputies). Part of the issue
was the arithmetic of equality; the other part was more principled. In the
stirring words of one New Granadan deputy, José Mejía Lequerica,
the Cortes should "grant equality to all free castes [that is, free people
of African descent]. . . . The blood of colored men is red, and so is that of

---

[28]*Diario político de Santafé de Bogotá*, September 25, 1810.

warriors of healthy men: pure and noble blood." But when numbers and principles came together, the claim had even greater political punch. Mejía warned his fellow deputies that denying rights to nonwhites would favor the cause of the more rebellious assemblymen in the colonies: "The juntas established in America have won this class [of people] to their side, granting them the equality for which they yearn. We must win them back with a similar declaration."[29]

That the math could cut both ways was not lost on delegates. There were its champions. But some (albeit rare) colonial delegates were squeamish about broadening the suffrage; giving rights to nonwhite subjects threatened basic norms of political hierarchy back home. Certainly, the politics of complexion was also clear to peninsulars. What made the color bar more troublesome was their mistrust of Americans: conservatives found them colonial upstarts; liberals worried that colonials were knee-jerk conservatives. Many wanted to defer the matter; wrangling over it now only got in the way of the urgent need to come up with a new order. Agustín de Argüelles, a major peninsular figure in the Cortes and a liberal, insisted that time not be wasted on the particularist demands of the colonists. He pushed the assembly to get on with the pressing business of writing a constitution to secure "the liberty and security of the Spanish nation." Conservatives and liberals agreed to squash the promises that Americans were equal members of the nation and to code citizenship along color lines that confined the "active" (that is, voting) possessors of rights in the colonies to fewer active citizens than peninsular Spaniards. For a time, a compromise seemed possible. On October 15, the Cortes issued a decree that ratified the principle of equality of all "natives" of all Spanish dominions (*naturales originarios*); a compromise that relied on the deliberate ambiguity of the definition of native. Indians and mestizos counted, according to the Laws of the Indies; but the legal status of "castes" implicitly excluded them because they were not "naturales." According to one delegate from New Spain, this vague concession was meant to suggest to caste populations that they possessed rights when in fact the purpose of the decree was to exclude them. What was becoming clear was that many peninsulars felt that representation was a privilege that had to be merited by an obvious ability to conduct oneself as an active, reasonable citizen, whereas for many Americans, it was a right belonging to all subjects of the monarchy—the difference meant pushing around the line between those included and

---

[29]King, "The Colored Castes and American Representation," p. 41; Marie Laure Rieu-Millan, *Los diputados americanos en las Cortes de Cádiz* (Madrid: Consejo Superior de Investigaciones Científicas, 1990), pp. 146–48.

excluded from the political community reconstituted as a "nation." As the news trickled back to the colonies that American demands that their rights to representation premised on equality were getting short shrift, it only kindled suspicions that their problems might not have been simply attributable to corrupt officials. The problem, suspected more and more colonists, might be "Spain's" refusal to give up old ways.[30]

There were also plenty of local ways in which the new language of "the people" and equality shaped politics and authority in the colonies that made it difficult to contain efforts to imagine a very different model of sovereignty. As the Cortes delegates debated the rights of Indians and people of African descent, so did municipal assemblies in the urban outposts of the empire for precisely the same reason. In order to reconstitute legitimate order, many felt, it had to be a more inclusive one for all free people. In Cartagena, where free people of color were the majority, it was hard to issue the clarion call for local sovereignty without admitting *pardo* rights. The city's creole elites, in an effort to buttress their own political careers against old colonial authorities, reached out to pardos. In May 1810, the cabildo launched its offensive against the Spanish governor and began enlisting support from commoners' neighborhoods. Pedro Romero, a pardo artisan from the working-class area of Getsemaní, soon became an important coconspirator with local creole elites. By the end of the year, this developing cross-racial alliance inscribed in its local electoral the principle that "all parishioners, whites, Indians, mestizos, mulattos, *zambos* and blacks, as long as they are household heads and live from their own work, are to be summoned for elections." In Venezuela and Buenos Aires also, the political line between black and white people was increasingly washed out as creole elites sought allies to contest the petty rule of Spanish officials. In effect, while Spanish parliamentarians were struggling to provide a new overarching structure for representation for the empire, across its colonial parts subjects were reconstituting the fundamental practices and principles of local sovereignty that were increasingly at odds with metropolitan purposes.[31]

It is hard to say what the majority in the Cortes thought the colonies would feel when Americans learned that their representational demands

[30]Fradera, "Raza y ciudadanía," pp. 53–55; Anna, "Spain and the Breakdown of the Imperial Ethos," pp. 257–58; Chust, *La cuestión nacional*, p. 55; Duffy Burnett, "The American Delegates at the *Cortes*," pp. 17–23; King, "The Colored Castes and American Representation," p. 45.

[31]See the pioneering article by Marixa Lasso, "A Republican Myth of Racial Harmony: Race and Patriotism in Colombia, 1810–1812," *Historical Reflections* 29:1 (2003): 54–57; Helg, *Liberty and Equality*, pp. 122–28.

had been rejected point blank. It did not take long for them to get the message back. The American printing presses responded with outrage at both the Regency and Cortes for betraying their own principles. An anonymous writer in Buenos Aires exclaimed in 1811 that "we possess the basic rights to build our own house, and we will work on our own fate as we can, for good or for ill, so that our achievement will fit our ideal rather than that of a distant power."[32] The *Gazeta de Caracas* justified the creation of the city's own junta by denouncing the Regency's decision to convoke the Cortes with a formula that stacked the numbers of delegates against Americans: "we have expressed our objections directly to the Council of Regency concerning the disproportion of the numbers of Deputies with the population of America . . . and our lack of confidence that the people can place in elected individuals under the immediate influence of their oppressors."[33] *El Argos Americano* applauded some of the Cortes's "liberality," freeing the press, holding public meetings, and relocating the source of sovereignty to the nation. But at the same time, the paper accused Spanish delegates of betraying the principles framing the invitation to participate in the assembly in the first place: "We were seduced by such exalted ideas, and we believed that the rays of the dawning of a happy regeneration were beginning to shine." It argued that, under these circumstances, the colonies reserved the right to secede temporarily. The call for delegates had constitutional substance, and so the violation of the principle of equality delegitimated the assembly. The conclusion: "a distant government cannot ensure the happiness of its people, and therefore we recognize it only as an *interim sovereignty while one is constituted legally according to the principles which have been proclaimed, and in the meantime we always reserve interior administration and economic policy for this Province*" (emphasis original). Spain was using one hand to fight France, "shedding blood to defend its liberty," while using the other hand to "hold the whip aloft against those who cannot tolerate their chains." Cartagena responded to peninsular policies by severing its ties with Spain altogether. Well before inking the details on the new charter for the Spanish regime, the whole process of devising constitutional foundations for Spanish sovereignty on both sides of the Atlantic branded it with the stigmata of tyranny.[34]

---

[32] Cited in Eduardo Martiré, *1808: Ensayo histórico-jurídico sobre la clave de la emancipación hispanoamericana* (Buenos Aires: Instituto de Investigaciones de Historia del Derecho, 2001), p. 16.
[33] Cited in Chust, *La cuestión nacional*, p. 39.
[34] *El Argos Americano*, Buenos Aires v. November 18, 1881.

Diverging Interests

If voice yielded to discord, the Cádiz government only worsened transatlantic relations with its economic policies, which often made Americans feel they were nominally equal "provinces" treated like subaltern colonies. It could be argued—as colonists did increasingly—that Spanish insensitivity could be reduced to racism or simply imperial habits. These elements no doubt shaped peninsular attitudes. But there was also a significant degree of financial and commercial urgency to keeping the colonies as colonies—and thus undermining the principle of equality. Since the sovereignty crisis was the result of interimperial struggle and war, it shattered Spain's precarious finances. The effort to reverse Spanish penury forced peninsular power-holders to issue new taxes and call for new loans. Moreover, as the Spanish government backed into Cádiz it fell almost literally into the arms of merchants who had been arguing that commercial concessions to the colonies and the loss of their privileges were depriving Spain of its economic rents. The Cádiz merchants knew that their only salvation was to preserve the metropolitan port's traditional privileges, and the fiscal dependency of the regime gave them the bargaining power to push hard for preserving Cádiz's privileges. In the colonies, the combination of fiscal and commercial grievances only reinforced the perception that the rhetoric of equality was empty; far from being provinces, the colonies were just that: colonies. Defending the natural rights of all Spaniards to be equal no matter where they lived, many colonists raised the flag of secession from Spain.

Without colonial remittances the Spanish government was more dependent than ever on Cádiz merchants. When Spain aligned with France again in 1805, its finances immediately deteriorated. Juan Escolano even warned the Cádiz consulado in mid-1805 that a return to war would be devastating because the Spanish treasury had become more and more dependent on transfers from the Americas, and warfare threatened this fiscal lifeline. War would therefore dry up remittances and force the metropolitan government to lean more heavily on its peninsular merchants. In turn, rising state debt "will make impossible any repayment of the loans, and there will therefore be even fewer funds to help meet the urgencies of the crown." By early 1806, Escolano informed the guild that *vales reales* (akin to treasury bonds secured on American bullion) were trading at a mere 42 percent of their face value. This was not good news for any holder who treated these bonds as semi-liquid assets. When the government approached merchants for another loan in early April 1808, the merchants appealed to the consulado of Cádiz, pleading for some relief from the constant exactions. This was all to no avail: the Junta Central came back at them for more "donativos" for "the just cause of defending the Nation." By early 1811, the Cortes effectively made the consulado of Cádiz a vital source of revenue for the state—asking it to raise a loan among Spanish merchants—and empowered it to inform all civil, ecclesiastic, and commercial authorities that loans and donations would flow through the merchant guilds of the empire. The international war therefore wrapped the same austere noose around the necks of governors and merchants in Cádiz.[35]

It would be hard to underestimate the severity of the fiscal drama. As the French tightened their grip on the peninsula, the war losses mounted—as did the expenditures. Money was so tight by 1813 that the Cortes authorized English guineas to circulate as legal tender for one year since Spanish currency was worthless. Still, the new Cortes struggled mightily to manage the empty public credit system. In September 1811, it created the Junta del Crédito Público to monitor the bond issues and to introduce some budgeting. In July the next year, this junta launched a scheme to rationalize the debt, paying off the most urgent and politically sensitive obligations, deferring those that could be delayed, and imposing some stricter guidelines on the Spanish budget to set aside amortization monies. By the time this junta actually figured out how much the Spanish government owed its creditors in 1814, the sums were: 5.7 billion pesos inherited from before 1806, and another 5.1 billion accumulated since. The report concluded rather gloomily that the Spanish state was for all intents and purposes bankrupt. The only way out was to begin to sell off state property and lands in a hurry, and to ensure "the transfers from Overseas which, unfortunately, we cannot count on right now."[36]

While the Cádiz government's efforts to impose a fiscal system were more inflammatory than effectual, there were reasons for its policies: the implication drawn by the junta, the Cortes, and its debt overseers was that Spain could not afford *not* to squeeze resources from the colonies. The reasons why address some of the basic principles underlying fiscal systems of the anciens régimes. Central revenue collectors pursued the most liquid sources of capital—and thus fixed their eyes on pools generated by trade and in the coffers of merchant capitalists. This simple practice underlay the fates of European states through the early modern period, and the success of tapping into these repositories determined the relative capacity of states to wage wars, centralize authority, and curb the power of aristocracies whose own fiscal autonomy depended on

---

[35]AGI, Consulados, Legajo 257, Juan Escolano to Cádiz, May 3, 1805, and Legajo 258, Escolano to Cádiz, January 14, 1806; Consulados, 2bis, April 28, 1808; November 29, 1809; IG, Legajo 1576, September 29, 1808; IG, Legajo 2320, February 3, 1811.

[36]AGI, Consulados, Legajo 4, July 27, 1813; IG, Legajo 1708, June 1, 1814.

agrarian wealth. Solving ancien-régime fiscal needs depended not only on discriminating between different kinds of capital by the size and liquidity of its pools. Political factors also determined the choice of whom to tap for money. Revenue seekers preferred soaking agents who posed fewer political costs to the regime, and issued stronger commitments to honor obligations to those agents with greater political influence. It mattered, therefore, that who got squeezed either enjoyed less voice or could force revenue seekers to make good on their promises to respect commitments to uphold their claims. This was the setting for the mess that Louis XVI got into when he summoned the Estates General: to get revenues he had to concede voice to its sources. In Spain, as the government stumbled to Cádiz, the one thing it could not afford to do was to alienate the economic magnates in the port that fiercely defended its legal dominion over colonial trade. As one report noted in mid-1810, the government therefore had to balance between saving the empire by making concessions to Americans while saving the metropole by squeezing the colonies. But as the colonies were less "visible" and had less voice in Cádiz, the temptation to milk them for more remittances was too hard to pass up.[37]

Just as the crisis unleashed centrifugal political forces, Cádiz pushed hard to restore centripetal economics. Cádiz merchants used the opportunity to try to restore their hegemony over colonial trade. A handful of Cádiz's most influential merchants sent a report to the government in June 1809, urging it to close all the loopholes on the Atlantic trade. All openings for foreigners to trade in the colonies had to be repealed, and colonial merchants caught trading with non-Spanish ports should be severely punished. They even went as far as urging a restoration of the defunct fleets, the Carrera. By 1814, the guild in Cádiz was even insisting that it be the sole conduit for channeling funds raised by loans in the colonies into the Spanish treasury, thereby preserving the government's dependency on the peninsular magnates and cracking the whip over the heads of colonial guilds that did not keep up their subventions to the state.[38]

Cádiz's efforts to restore some, if not all, of its bygone commercial privileges flew right in the face of colonists' longstanding demands for more commercial autonomy. After Trafalgar, colonial guilds began to dismantle mercantilist policies; those that refused saw their merchants

---

[37]AGI, Consulados, 2bis, October 1, 1808; Estado, Americas, 86A/26, July 27, 1810, "Oficio de Esteban Fernández de Leon"; John M. Veitch, "Repudiations and Confiscations by the Medieval State," *Journal of Economic History* 46:1 (1986); 31–36; Carruthers, *City of Capital*; Michael D. Bordo and Forrest Capie, Introduction to Bordo and Capie, eds., *Monetary Regimes in Transition*, pp. 1–12.
[38]AGI, Consulados, 2bis, July 6, 1809; AGI, IG, Legajo 2320, August 23, 1814.

dismantle them de facto. In the case of Buenos Aires, open trade came in the wake of the short-lived British occupation of 1806–7. After porteño militias drove out the intruder, the Buenos Aires merchant guild issued a circular on September 5, 1807, celebrating open trade as the recipe for the "accumulation of damages" to trade with Spain. The circular made clear that colonial freedoms were necessary for the empire's well-being: "we have arrived, though belatedly, at the recognition that free trade with Foreigners, that the piety of the King has conceded to us out of his benevolence . . . is the only instrument powerful enough to pull the empire back from the threshold of its ruin." While the metropole might complain, the circular noted, its merchants had to appreciate that the kingdom's health and wealth depended more on the trade of the colonies than that of Cádiz. At stake are the "Interests which need to be repaired, for the monarchy as a whole," not just the metropolis. What is more, added Manuel Belgrano in 1809, Buenos Aires had little choice *but* to trade with Spain's crucial ally, the British, and that as far as many merchants of the viceroyalty were concerned, what was good for the colonies was good for Spain, and what was good for the colonies was strong ties with Britain. Mariano Moreno made a similar case in a direct appeal on the part of the hacendados of Buenos Aires: what is good for rural producers is good for the monarchy—and access to markets was the cornerstone of rural prosperity. He added that without opportunities, the countryside would backslide into lethargy, bad habits, and unruliness. Civilization, good manners, and habits all depended on the government's ability to keep the countryside industrious. Trading would uplift the colonists and make them even more worthy subjects of His Majesty. Echoing themes explored by Montesquieu, of the taming and domesticating properties of commerce—doux commerce—Moreno warned of the corrupting and debasing effects of fetters on trade.[39]

So by the time the news of the collapse of the Spanish regime arrived, the colonies were already forming a coherent, self-regarding view as economies and societies with distinctive histories, plights, and needs over the issue of trade. Trade, moreover, meant much more than expanding particular rights; it reinforced the virtuous fabric of the empire as a whole. Hitherto, these ideas stopped short of explicit political assertions or claims. But after 1805, the views of property and the autonomy of private rights acquired a more explicit political edge. In some cases, colonists were already asserting that commercial freedom of the imperial parts was good for the whole; it was Cádiz's demands that were particularist

---

[39]AGI, Consulados, Legajo 343, October 11, 1809; Moreno, "Representación a nombre del apoderado de los hacendados de las campañas del Río de la Plata," pp. 111–79.

claims. The good of the monarchy was identified with the colonial interests. In the minds of many colonists, then, loyalty to the crown meant putting colonial concerns ahead of Spain's.[40]

The response was the same in other ports. In early 1808, the Caracas consulado got wind of the invasion and opening of Buenos Aires' port, raised it as a model of free trade in slaves and staples, and urged Venezuelan authorities to be as enlightened as those in the River Plate. By 1809, the tensions within the consulado and between the consulado and the government had led to some heated debate over free trade. The intendant confessed to his superiors that he finally decided to allow more open trade "for the tranquility of his majesty's subjects, for order and justice, and to conserve and defend his dominions." A completely open slave trade in particular was "an absolute necessity." This was mid-1809. Even the viceroy of Nueva Granada, Antonio Amar y Borbon, argued in August 1807 that these provinces could be wealthy like the Pampas of Buenos Aires if there were more incentive for farmers and ranchers to produce and more inducements to trade. (Characteristically, though, he stopped short of endorsing freer trade, which he consistently loathed. What he did yearn for was a vibrant metropolitan market—a pipe dream under the circumstances.) Undaunted, the consulado in Cartagena pushed hard for less restrictive trading rights. The guild excoriated the viceroy for having shut the ports and driven otherwise licit commerce underground—echoing the porteño rhetoric about the importance of thriving colonial trade for the well-being of the empire. The guild's accountant reminded the viceroy that "reciprocal utilities," that is, the benefits to dominions on both sides of the Atlantic, had to be the cornerstone of his policy, to enhance trade, boost revenues, and thus "conform to the General Interest."[41]

If colonial interests became the foundations of the monarchy's general interest, and peninsular, Cádiz, interests seen as simply particular, colonists added to their verbal arsenal by denouncing the mercantilist strictures as the instruments of monopoly. The Cartagena consulado voted unanimously on a resolution requesting that the viceroy rescind his outlawing of free trade, wrapping their demands as freedom from oppressive and stultifying monopolies. Policies, the merchants argued,

---

[40]AGI, Consulados, Legajo 342, September 5, 1807; McKinley, *Pre-revolutionary Caracas*, pp. 142–44; Jacques Barbier, "Colonial Reform and Comercio Neutral in Cartagena de Indias, 1788–1808," in Fisher, Kuethe, and McFarlane, eds., *Reform and Insurrection*, pp. 114–15.

[41]AGNC, Real Consulado, Actas 2530, ff. 150–150v, March 28, 1808; AGI, IG, Legajo 1707, August 6, 1807; Gobierno, Caracas, Legajo 917, June 10, 1809; Gobierno, Santa Fe, Legajo 960, f. 1388, April 16, 1807; AGNB, Colonia, Consulado, I, 1808, ff. 504–6.

"had to be for trade and not just for a trader—and these are, as you know, very distinct things, although many confuse them." Without freedom to trade, "there will emerge semi-monopolies between one or two traders in Rio Hacha, three or four in Santa Marta, and eight or ten in Cartagena . . . and this would cause great harm to the public cause, to all consumers, to the treasury and to agriculture." Demolishing monopoly was the finest way "to constitute the property of the State in general, and the comfort or at least the well-being of each particular person." The same antimonopoly rhetoric charged the debate in Caracas, with the same implications: pandering to a few monopolists in the colonies and Spain choked trade and would "damage the interests of the public and the State."[42]

What made colonial merchants even more upset were the recurring requests, followed by demands, for money to be loaned or donated to the imperial treasury. In late 1807, a group of Cartagena merchants wrote to the viceroy complaining that they had complied with a loan request of 88,200 pesos, had been subjected to the capricious opening and closing of the port, and now wanted to be paid back. The policies of the Spanish government were undermining their confidence in the system, they warned. "This process appears to us as impolitic and very contrary to the interests of the King, the State, and to public service which requires the utmost trust of subjects." Ominously, they admonished that the loss of credibility "will also depress the authority and personhood [*persona*] of the Chief [*Jefe*] himself." They concluded with the following underlined passage: "*the real Interest of the State is to conserve its credit with private agents. Not complying with solemn words weakens justice, and compromises this Tribunal [the guild] to whose authority you approached and appealed for this loan.*" Still, in spite of the mounting grievances, colonial ports bundled up their donations and loans and remitted them to Cádiz as they could. In July 1810, Cartagenans sacrificed gold, diamonds, and jewelry that belonged to private subjects, packed their preciosities in a chest, and remitted them to the Spanish treasury.[43]

As in Spain, colonial sources of capital, wracked by the paralysis of Atlantic commerce, began to dry up. To make matters worse for the central tax and loan collectors, each colonial junta also faced fiscal pressures. Given the proximity and the greater political dependency of merchants on local juntas to uphold commercial rules—and order—they

---

[42]AGNB, Colonia, Consulado, I, pp. 509–10, 1808; AGNC, Real Consulado, Actas, 2530, f. 37, February 17, 1807.

[43]AGI, Gobierno, Santa Fe, Legajo 960, ff. 659–745. See in particular letters of April 30, and September 3, 1807.

honored the colonists' demands for funds over the peninsular appeals. It
did not take much time for all fragments of the regime to be wallowing
in debt and unable to fund their basic functions. Merchant capitalists on
both sides of the Atlantic grew increasingly dependent on revenues just
as capitalists' rents dwindled. This brought in the predictable pleas for
exemptions and reprieves. One small merchant in Cartagena pointed out
his dilemma: authorities asked for more and more money, but the war
meant less and less trade, and "in the meantime I am struggling to meet
the needs of my large family."[44]

As the pressure mounted in the colonies and the security of the metropolitan regime grew more precarious, one by one the viceroys and
intendants gave into the colonial merchants' demands for more open
trade. What clinched the case was merchants' clear linking of the freedom of trade with the ability to generate revenues and lend money to the
treasury. Some authorities, fearing that they might be toppled, even
refused direct orders from the peninsula to clamp down on foreign trade.
On January 10, 1809, the intendant of Caracas got instructions to repeal
his concession. He shrugged it off. A few months later, the consulado and
the cabildo got together to give instructions to the newly elected deputy
to the Cortes. He was ordered to make clear that there was a close tie
between the loyalty of the colonies and their happiness, and that happiness depended on their rights to do business with fewer obstructions. In
Cartagena local merchants browbeat authorities to throw the port open
or face an even worse situation: traffic would go everywhere *but* Nueva
Granada unless the vicreroyalty were put on the same footing as Cuba,
Venezuela, and the River Plate. When the viceroy came back to the merchants of Cartagena for a 100,000-peso loan, they snapped back that his
ban on trade with neutral or friendly parties only drove commerce
underground, beyond the reach of tax collectors. You want the revenues
to support the colonial state? Then give us the rights to do business. In
the end, the governor of Cartagena, Blas de Soria, threw open Cartagena
to non-Spanish ports, admitting that his intentions were primarily fiscal.
He could not allow Cartagena to remain sealed up while traffic boomed
in Venezuela and authorities in Santa Fé de Bogota were busy dispensing
money they did not have to put down rebellions. So, across the colonies,
a new deal was in the making before 1810: in the quest for revenues,
local rulers allowed merchant capitalists to enjoy more rights to seek

---

[44]For remittances, see AGI, IG, Legajo 1576, 1809–10 from Cartagena, and the squab-
ble with Panama over the donation burden in AGI, Gobierno, Santa Fe, Legajo 961,
Informe, January 30, 1811. On the fiscal crisis of the fledgling colonial juntas, see AGNB,
Anexo, Emprestitos, I, 51, March 10, 1813, and the undated petition by Juan Josef Gaona.

rents through open trade. This was the potential making of a new imperial pact—taking care of the fiscal crisis of the regime and earning it some legitimacy in the eyes of frustrated colonial elites. This possibility is worth emphasizing because it was not a foregone conclusion that the fiscal crisis of the Spanish state necessarily doomed the ancien régime.[45]

It is important to appreciate the momentous shift in power and authority that these decisions made in the colonies and what they implied for the imperial order. For one, they signified the degree to which officials became aware that their—and their regime's—survival required the support of the colonists more than that of the crumbling metropole. Second, bodies like the cabildo and the consulado were becoming more deliberative (though not public in the sense that citizens elected representatives and could watch proceedings) assemblies for the colonial elites. Third, a new discourse of competition, opportunity, and equality served to justify the appropriation of sovereignty and the demand that political authorities acknowledge and uphold the interests of rights-holders. Finally, the agreement to let colonies trade with neutral and friendly powers meant, above all, the right to trade with the British. This was a bonanza for the merchants who wanted to export staples and even to take over the slave-trade routes abandoned by British merchants. But it was a devastating blow to peninsular houses accustomed to being able to ship manufactures in their bottoms without having to face competition. If the wars were not destructive enough of the old mercantilist trade routes, the opening of colonial ports certainly was. Effectively, by 1810, without any formal declaration, South America became a free trade partner with Britain.

The incipient deal flew in the face of Cádiz's predicament. They had mouthpieces in the colonies; some merchants representing peninsular houses operating in the periphery protested open trade. Miguel Fernández de Agüero, the Cádiz envoy to Buenos Aires, blamed the empire's economic woes on the decision by the viceroy to allow freer trade and accused him of "a scandalous betrayal committed against our commercial laws." Referring to the consulado of Buenos Aires' majority urgings that trade open up, he noted that "I am appalled that these informing bodies [the guild] support the free entry and trade of these ports for English merchandise without the slightest consideration of the damages that the realization of this project will cause." It will hurt "the entire Nation," Spanish merchants in particular. The English, moreover, now secured what they

---

[45]AGNB, Colonia, Consulados, IV, 1808–9, ff. 777–803; Consulados III, 1809, ff. 832–49; AGNC, Real Consulado, Actas, 2531, f. 41, May 5, 1809; f. 43, May 10, 1809; AGI, Consulados, Legajo 343, October 11, 1809.

had always wanted: Spanish "GOLD." "Their sole objective is to enrich themselves with our treasures depriving us of all our silver and gold produced in these rich provinces." And when the news of Buenos Aires' open ports reached Peru, Lima's Cádiz envoy was shocked. "Speaking out of innocence, I never imagined that such a measure might be written by a Spanish Chief."[46]

But the main resistance came from Cádiz itself—and gathered political strength as the Spanish government leaned on peninsular merchants for income. Faced with the colonies' unilateral announcements of open trade, the merchant guild in Cádiz formed an extraordinary junta to discuss and decide what the metropolitan authorities should do. In September 1810, the committee issued its report to the rest of the members. The report put the blame squarely on opportunistic foreigners who were taking advantage of Spain's weakness, in cahoots with a handful of disloyal subjects who put their own personal interests ahead of the monarchy's. All this got started with the concession to neutral trade back in 1797. And in the current war, this mésalliance was all the more pernicious. Now "foreign monopolists" contracted with local "smugglers" to deprive the monarchy of its fiscal foundations and swipe upstanding Spanish merchants of their rightful due as law-abiding subjects. (The fact that colonial merchants were actually obeying the laws and paying taxes was a nuance the magnates chose to overlook.) "At what stage," the report asked, "do we cut off the interests of a few particulars to reunite with great advantage the national relations between each of the hemispheres?" It concluded, "if Americans are given the permission, even temporarily, to engage in trade with neutral or friendly foreigners . . . and if we let the rules and regulations be so abused, very soon and easily we will arrive at the complete extinction of metropolitan commerce, as well as all the reciprocity of relations. For it will give them such an abundance of resources to do what they will, that in just a few days they will not need Spain at all."[47]

Cádiz merchants inverted the discourse about particular versus general interests—it was the peninsula that embodied the latter and a few malcontents in the colonies that pursued the former. The very same language of interests—particular versus general, usurping versus rightful—was polarizing each side of the Atlantic: for one side, freer trade and the interests that would rescue the empire, while for the other these "freedoms" meant monopoly for strangers and thus spelled doom for the economics of the ancien régime.

---

[46]AGI, Consulados, Legajo 343, November 18, 1809; Legajo 344, January 13, 1810.
[47]AGI, Consulados, 2bis, September 29, 1810.

When trade policy came up in the Cortes, the war of words about interests, freedom, and monopoly got ramped up. There, the mutual dependence of the merchants on the assembly to restore the old mercantilist rules and the assembly on the merchants for political and financial support conspired to aggravate Atlantic relations. The American deputies pushed to have their hemisphere's concerns addressed. But the majority would not budge. It upheld a position laid out by the Cádiz consulado in a published manifesto in 1811. According to the guild, when it first heard that the assembly was going to entertain an American proposal for open trade, it was incumbent to defend "the common happiness of all the people of the Spanish Monarchy." The pamphlet charged the American delegates with being dupes or conspiring to bring down the regime, with "sending an exterminating blow to our very existence." Indeed, the guild argued, the colonies—"our brothers"—could not be entrusted with these matters as they evidently did not know what was good for them, especially as they were isolated from their traditional tutors. The colonies' lack of sense of imperial welfare reflected their immaturity: these are "nascent agrarian peoples, whose industry is nothing more than mediocre, and whose majority population barely knows the difference between necessity and luxury, and in which only a sixth asks for the help of foreigners." To cap things off, the guild argued—in keeping with a patronizing use of family metaphors—more than the fate of the empire was at stake; so too was that of the child-colonies themselves. Free trade would orphan the colonies, who would fall prey to foreign usurpers. Since the Conquest, the manifesto concluded, Spain has been responsible for the colonies, and especially now when the siren calls of false parents echo across the Atlantic from other ports. The manifesto was signed by twenty-five of Cádiz's richest merchants.[48]

From Voice to Exit

Napoleon's Iberian invasion smashed the pillars of Spanish sovereignty. Leaders on both sides of the Atlantic tried to reassemble a new set of foundations out of the fragments, creating mechanisms for voice in the press and in deliberative assemblies to establish legitimacy for a new political order. The paradox was that the means for rebuilding sovereignty drove the imperial sides apart, not together. It needs to be stressed that *loyalty* to the crown and to Spain was not in doubt when the colonies

---

[48]AGI, Indiferente General, Legajo 2320, "El comercio de Cádiz Representado Legitimamente, Recurre segunda vez a S.M."

created their self-governing bodies and juntas. Deciding who would govern and how they would govern did not necessarily imply disloyalty to Spain, just to its governors; and this certainly did not inexorably lead to exit. But once flourishing, the media of voice conveyed to the colonies a less mystified sense of what they were: colonies in an empire that was collapsing, and not equal subjects at the empire's peripheries. Indeed, it was all too evident that the metropole needed the colonies to be more subservient than ever to rescue itself from French domination. By 1812, therefore, each side of the Atlantic was more polarized than ever. Under the circumstances, it was hard for colonists to put up with the peninsular abuses that the press in the colonies enjoyed sensationalizing.

Events moved extremely quickly. In 1810, the colonies pronounced themselves in control. Mariano Moreno authored a public proclamation on behalf of the Buenos Aires junta to the rest of the population of the viceroyalty. He reminded his readers of the Spanish junta's original—now betrayed—words: "From this moment forth, Spanish Americans, you have been elevated to the dignity of free men; you are not the same as before, looked upon with indifference, vexed by greed, and destroyed by ignorance; your destiny no longer depends on Ministers, Viceroys, or Governors. It is in your hands." For Moreno, who would become a central figure within the local ruling coalition, all that porteños were doing was upholding these principles, not declaring a revolution. "Be aware," he warned, "of the features of independence or insurrection, for they are irreconcilable with our principles." Self-rule in Buenos Aires was declared, rather, to preserve what Spain could not: "if it is not a special crime in America to follow the models that we have been imitating from the peninsula; and if the people of these immense territories are free and with rights to vote; and if at least they are not beasts submitted to bear the yoke which their lords want to impose . . . then there is nothing illegitimate about respecting and obeying the superior authority of our junta." Each resistance from the metropole pushed Moreno and his partners in the home-rule coalition to adopt an increasingly aggressive stance. Moreno urged the colonists to replace the defunct regime with a constitution. Without a monarch, and unable to rely on the Spanish Cortes to respect the principle of equality of all subjects, the colonies were effectively headless, acephalous but sovereign entities. In calling for a constitutional congress, Moreno was not calling for full independence from Spain (that had to wait until 1816). He was repudiating Spain's model of re-creating political authority in favor of a temporary exit from imperial rules in order to preserve colonial order. As long as Spain "could only sustain its own legitimacy with the décore of domination," the colonies had to secede and create their own regimes. In the years that followed, the juntas and assemblies of Buenos Aires accepted this premise—that they could no longer rely on Spanish authority to provide the spine of political order.[49]

Some colonies went further than temporary secession from the Spanish government. Others embraced outright independence from Spain. Caracas was the first to go. By the end of 1810, reading circles, cafés, and public spaces of all sorts were alive with political debate. Each bit of news coming from Spain sparked another wave of discussion and open discord. The press, like the *Gaceta de Caracas*, the *Semanario*, and the *Mercurio*, played up the weakness and abuses of the Spanish government. The most famous political club of all, the Sociedad Patriótica, opened its doors as the government lifted controls on political activities. Modeled in part on Jacobin organizing in Paris, the Sociedad aggressively advocated a full break with the metropole and issued its own publication, *El Patriota de Venezuela*. When Miranda returned to Caracas, he immediately became an active member of the radicalizing Sociedad Patriótica and in the local colonial ruling alliance. As public sentiment in the city began to polarize, the coalition that had deposed the government and declared sovereignty within empire became deeply fractured. Some wanted to stay the middle course, others were growing fearful and wanted a restoration of the status quo ante, while others pushed for a break with Spain. In March 1811, the junta had given way to a full-scale Constitutional Assembly, tilting the center of political gravity to more radical colonists. On July 5, 1811, the Venezuelan assembly voted to declare independence. Several weeks later, Juan Germán Roscio penned a manifesto to the world explaining the reasons why the assemblymen voted to secede. It began with the following lines: "America, condemned to three centuries of having no other existence than to serve and augment the political power of Spain, without the least influence or participation in its greatness, would have . . . become the guarantor and victim of the disorder, corruption and conquest which has disorganized *la nación conquistador*, were it not for the instinct of its own security that dictated to Americans that the moment had arrived to pick the fruit of three hundred years of inaction and patience." Roscio was also looking over his shoulder. Aware that a more radical break with Spain might alienate too many Venezuelans, he began to worry that independence might

---

[49]Mariano Moreno, "Manifesto de la Junta Provisional Gubernative de las Provincias del Rio de la Plata . . . (23 de julio, 1810)," in his *Escritos*, p. 107; idem, "Sobre la mision del Congreso convocado en virtud de la resolucion plebescitaria del 25 de mayo," in his *Escritos*, p. 279, 290.

solve the problem of sovereignty only to plunge the freed colony into civil war.[50]

Nueva Granada followed suit. In Santa Fé, colonists raised the flag of secession (though not yet full independence) in March 1811, animated by the same sense of injustice as cousins in Buenos Aires and Caracas. Santa Fé was rebaptized Santa Fé de Bogotá and soon simply Bogotá, expurgating the remnants of Spanish colonialism. Nariño echoed Roscio and Moreno. What they wanted was variations of home rule to preserve a political order, not a revolution at home. Cartagena followed the same logic but went further than Bogotá. In the coastal port, where federalism ran deep, the press beat the drums of "voice" so loudly, upbraiding the misdeeds of colonial officials with such energy, that the city and its province soon took a stance against all authorities that threatened the port's sovereignty. Cartagena found itself on the verge of seceding from the empire *and* the viceroyalty. In late 1811, the Cartagena cabildo issued a set of principles of its own: the Spanish nation is independent; all citizens, without mentioning race, enjoyed equal rights; constitutional powers were now divided; the legislature was to meet in public sessions; the executive was to convoke deputies to draft a constitution; and cabildos would hold open elections. In effect, the peninsular efforts to create a new model of legitimacy for the empire offered to the colonies the means to claim rights to secede. *El Argos Americano* noted that the Cartagena manifesto of November 11 got its legitimacy from the recent history of conflict with Spain: "A while back a general disgust erupted over the recognition we get in Spain. The tyrannical behavior that the government of this nation applied to us, in spite of our moderation, raised the spirits . . . for the repeated demands for a declaration of OUR ABSOLUTE INDEPENDENCE." What is more, observed the paper, these abuses were not completely new. Retrieving a discourse reserved for Spain's Atlantic rivals, the Colombian paper accused Spain of meting colonists with "three hundred years of vexations, misery and suffering of all kinds." Paradoxically, it was the merchant guild's press, normally used to issue edicts of metropolitan commercial decisions, that printed this paper. Nor was this sentiment restricted to white elites alone; an anonymous pardo issued his own condemnation of Spanish rule in a pamphlet

---

[50]Carole Leal Curiel, "Tertulia de dos ciudades: Modernismo tardío y formas de sociabilidad en la provincia de Venezuela," in Guerra and Lempérière, eds., *Los espacios públicos*, pp. 180–83. On Roscio's text, see "Manifiesto que hace el mundo la Confederación de Venezuela en la America Merdidional" (July 30, 1811), in Roscio, *Obras* (Caracas: Secretaría General de la Décima Conferencia Interamericana, 1953), v. 2, p. 41; Sanz, "Acta de la Independencia," in *Pensamiento político*, pp. 134–40.

called "Political and Moral Reflections of a Descendant of Africa to His Nation, in which he Manifests his Amorous Lamentations to his American Brothers." In it, he called any violation of pardo citizenship and equality as unchristian and unjust—and that Cádiz's lawmakers were both.[51]

The rhetoric of the Black Legend, which other Europeans used to justify attacking Spain and its possessions, was now being used by Spain's possessions against the metropole. The invented tradition of being "American" quickly became entangled with a historical self-representation as perpetually subordinated and oppressed people to Spain. With the exercise of the "exit" option came the flourishing of a potent antipeninsular worldview. But more than that, Venezuela's declaration of independence, redolent with a newborn historiography of deep-seated oppression, argued that colonial subjects were not just deploying natural rights they always possessed but never exercised as Spaniards. They were also using these rights to rescue Spain from its own imperial vices. According to Roscio, one of the declaration's authors, a free Venezuela was destined to become a more perfect Spain by being a more virtuous monarchy (indeed, declaring independence did not mean embracing republicanism at all—and Roscio was a fervent monarchist until he lost all faith in the Bourbon dynasts). If the conquest of America gave rise to commercial, cultural, and scientific greatness in "Europe" through the "oppression and bondage" of "America," the emancipation of America would enhance Europe's achievements through liberty. "In this way," he argued, "geography, shipping, astronomy, industry and commerce, perfected by the discovery of America, and to its peril, can now be converted into much greater means to accelerate, consolidate, and perfect the happiness in both worlds." Departure from the peninsular mold was defended as the exercise of natural rights that the peninsular government violated because "Spain" had become so degraded that it had fallen into the clutches of despotic and corrupt interests that trampled on the commonwealth. Indeed, the foundational charters for self-rule agreed: the colonists would secede from Spain because they were Spaniards, blessed with rights they possessed by virtue of their membership in the monarchy, a monarchy that was as much destroyed by outside aggressors as by venal usurpers from within.[52]

---

[51]*El Argos Americano*, November 18, 1811. A good summary can be found in Rebecca A. Earle, *Spain and the Independence of Colombia, 1810–1825* (Exeter: University of Exeter Press, 2000), pp. 36–39; Lasso, "A Republican Myth of Racial Harmony," pp. 60–61.

[52]Roscio, "Manifiesto," pp. 41–42.

From Exit to Civil War

Breaking away from Spain to defend natural rights was one thing. Creating a new legitimate order in the empire's stead was quite another. Having declared their exit *from* Spain, what were the colonists going to be loyal *to*? Dealing with this question, it turned out, was much more vexatious than the secessionist coalitions anticipated. Differences surfaced once sovereignty shifted to the people, whose political identities got vaguer and vaguer once the monarchy and "Spain" lost their integrative powers. Even the most "loyal" of colonies, Peru, where home-rule movements never took flight, had to contend with internal discord. In effect, the same centrifugal forces that hit the empire as a whole also struck each colony; the burdens of false promises and the pressures of unpopular taxes and trade policies that broke up imperial coalitions soon shattered coalitions in the colonies.

What was remarkable was how quickly colonial spaces fragmented into smaller, contentious parts. In Bogotá's and Cartagena's decisions to vote themselves out of the Spanish constitutional arena, we find immediate evidence of the problem confronting colonial coalitions. Cartagena's junta had as much legal right to be a sovereign body for its province as Bogotá did for Cundinamarca. The conflict was that colonists in Bogotá presumed that other Granadan provinces would accept the legal powers of the old viceregal capital over the secondary towns and provinces. By early 1812, the territories of the newly independent, if ironically named United Provinces of New Granada, were at war with each other. Cundinamarca disliked Cartagena's declaration of decentralized autonomy; and the secessionists were hounded by royalist strongholds in Pasto, Popayán, and Santa Marta. By early 1813, Nariño's centralist forces had gained the upper hand over federalists. But no sooner were patriots at each other's throats than their common enemies gathered strength. Cartagena was soon at war with the coastal royalists in Santa Marta; Cundinamarca had to fight a rearguard defense against conservatives in Popayán and Pasto. Refugees scattered from the towns and got caught between rival causes until civil conflict soon began to consume the rebels that started it. Nariño, after a botched effort to drive royalist armies from the south, beat a hurried retreat but was captured and sent in chains back to Cádiz, where he would languish in prison until 1820.[53]

The same happened in the River Plate, where Montevideo so disliked Buenos Aires' centralism that it opted to remain loyal to Spain, in spite

[53]Earle, *Spain and the Independence of Colombia*, pp. 44–53.

of the humiliations meted out in Cádiz. Better to live with tyranny from a distance than with one from across the river. When Manuel Belgrano, quickly elevated to commander of armies, led expeditions to Paraguay and the Andes, local forces drove him back, unwilling to substitute Buenos Aires' rule for that of Spain. By 1812, Buenos Aires' "United Provinces" were also reduced to a fissiparous band of mini-states around the mouth of the river—and the ancient axis between the Andes and the port was broken for good. Moreno, in a desperate effort to secure financial and political backing from the British to rescue his government from collapse, boarded a vessel in early 1811. He never reached the other side, perishing mysteriously in the Atlantic. Within two years of declaring home rule in Bogotá and Buenos Aires, colonial coalitions were tearing themselves apart in civil wars.[54]

In the independent "American Confederation of Venezuela" things fell apart with equal speed. Some of the colony's provinces dithered about whether to align with Caracas; others, like Guayana, Coro, and Maracaibo, stayed loyal to Cádiz. Miranda took charge of the military campaign to liberate the town of Valencia—which he did after some initial setbacks. While Valencians were not wiped out with the repression that some historians of the First Republic and Miranda-bashers have exaggerated, it is true that the government did not deal with dissent with a light hand—rounding up the opposition leaders and ordering their followers to get their "patriotic education." Loyalists were not the only recalcitrant forces. Members of the secessionist coalition proved incoherent once they ceased power. The assembly had declared the country free. Crowds tore down the portraits of Carlos IV and Ferdinand VII. There was much fanfare in the capital. Months later, in a fit of voluntarism, the government also abolished the slave trade—a powerful blow to the merchant and planter classes that the local rulers desperately needed for social ballast and financial support. Whatever creole elite support still survived was taxed even further when fighting broke out across Venezuela. When Miranda aimed to enlist soldiers to his cause, he offered freedom to any slave that joined the patriotic army. Merchants and landowners were horrified. Soon the republican treasury was threadbare. Eventually, merchants, planters, conservatives, and those just worried about the potential of impending anarchy defected to the loyalist cause. This unholy alliance was scarcely more coherent than the secessionist one. But as the Miranda government radicalized and splintered, its opposition gathered strength. Also, what the loyalist coalition had was the support of local military officers led by Domingo Monteverde. Monteverde made

---

[54]Safford and Palacios, *Colombia*, pp. 87–91; Adelman, *Republic of Capital*, pp. 78–83.

life miserable for the republicans, marauding rebel towns and humiliating local commanders like Bolívar.[55]

The Venezuelan "republic" lasted only a year, collapsing in the summer of 1812. Amid the first anniversary of Venezuelan independence on July 5, news reached the capital that royalists had defeated Bolívar's hold of the fortress near Puerto Cabello. This was a final turning point. Bolívar's military loss spelled personal doom for his patron. Miranda, now elected "dictator" to be able to defend the revolution without the constraints of constitutional niceties he once vaunted, reverted to the way he responded to the debacle in 1806. Rather than fight, and risk losing everything, he chose to withdraw. Miranda took it upon himself to negotiate a deal with royalists. He worried that what precious "civil liberty" survived in Venezuela would get destroyed in the spiral of violence. Miranda agreed to an armistice with loyalists, allowing his allies to retreat, set sail from La Guaira, and avoid capture. Just before the flotilla was to set sail under a British escort (for they, too, wanted stability above all), Miranda's allies betrayed him and let Monteverde take him away in chains. Meanwhile, the embittered survivors, Bolívar among them, escaped. Eventually, Spanish authorities shipped Miranda to Cádiz's La Carraca prison. He finally died in 1816, his country ravaged by civil war and a brutal Spanish counterrevolution.[56]

As the empire fragmented, so too did old territorial units of the colonies. The dynamic unfolded as the unifying symbol of legitimacy for holding the empire together—the monarchy—was gone, and no recourse to ancient principles could fill the void of sovereignty. Colonial leaders in the capitals, having seceded from Spain, watched provinces secede from capitals. The critical issue here was that the process started at the core: it was the crown and metropolitan authority that imploded. Left behind were vacuums. The crisis of the metropolis created opportunities in the peripheries—but it did not mean that stable and solid coalitions were in place to fill the vacuums. Secession opened up bickering among provinces in the colonies—and soon quarreling within the colonial coalitions themselves. As power shifted to the imperial fringe, and then within colonial coalitions to factions advocating secession and outright independence, the actual ruling bloc became narrower and narrower, representing a tinier fragment of the population.

[55]Caracciolo Parra-Pérez, *Historia de la Primera República de Venezuela* (Caracas: Biblioteca Ayacucho, 1992).

[56]Gerhard Masur, *Simón Bolívar* (Albuquerque: University of New Mexico Press, 1969), pp. 104–5; AGI, Estado, Caracas, 71/9, No. 15, August 7, 1810; AGI, Estado, Caracas, 63/38, November 22, 1812.

Faced with the internal fragmentation of the old colonial spaces and the shrinking coalitions in power, secessionists began to tout antidemocratic means to consolidate their political orders. That these revolutions were launched to defend the equal rights of Spanish subjects did not mean that all subjects were positioned to defend the revolution. The Sociedad Patriótica in Caracas urged the assembly to create a Tribunal de Seguridad Pública "to suffocate the pernicious germs of division and seduction, punishing disturbers and malicious seducers, and showing to each incautious and simple citizen what their real interests are, and protecting the innocents from the traps of malevolents." It was this Jacobinist logic that compelled the assembly to give Miranda the dictatorial powers he then used to surrender unilaterally. The same logic obtained elsewhere. Moreno himself authored a blueprint to get the government of Buenos Aires through the transitional period before unveiling a new constitution. He invoked the past: "the ancient and modern history of revolutions instructs us completely on the deeds that must be pursued to consolidate our system, for I am proud of what we have accomplished thus far, but I fear, to tell you the truth, that if we do not control the order of events with the necessary energy . . . our building will collapse. Because man, in certain moments, is the son of rigor and force, and we will realize nothing with benevolence and moderation." His plan included censoring the press, locking up dissidents, and widespread espionage, all in the name of securing the regime against opposition. "Moderation," he wrote, "is a weakness when a system is adopted in circumstances that do not require it. Never in a revolution have moderation and tolerance been adopted with success." In a gruesome passage outlining the practicalities of securing the revolution, he advocated "cutting heads, spilling blood and sacrificing at all costs, even when it means adopting means that look like the customs of cannibals and Caribs."[57]

How did colonial rebels finesse the discrepancy between the democratic cause and the authoritarian means? One formulation can be found in the views advanced in *Martir o Libre*, a Buenos Aires paper that promoted the creation of a "dictatorship" to fill the political vacuum. Sovereignty, it is true, lies with the people, and the people want independence. But having declared oneself politically independent—expressed one's loyalty, exercised one's voice, and decided to exit—the people are still the same. They have rights. But they also inherited the bad and venal

---

[57]Restrepo, *Historia de la Revolución de Colombia*, v. 2, p. 270; Moreno, "Plan de operaciones que el gobierno provincial de las Provincias Unidas del Rio de la Plata debe poner en practica para consolidar la grande obra de nuestra libertad e independencia (30 Aug., 1810)," in his *Escritos*, p. 306, 307, 311.

habits of old ways. Civil society was wracked by disunion, the government by discord, because Spain never let its people learn the ways of self-government and self-improvement. They did not form a community of learned citizens but of egotists incapable of considering the public good. "As a result, it is necessary to fix a plan capable of combining security and order . . . to prescribe political tranquility among a people who are now free, but who are accustomed to being slaves." Freedom among those who did not know what to do with it was dangerous—and had to be made to conform to a "general will." Citing Rousseau to explain the meaning of false freedom—that there is a distinction between "liberty and unchecked license"—the paper argued that the fledgling state had to make sure that what ruled was the general will, not the sum of licensed individuals.[58] Bernardo Monteagudo, a founder of *Martir o Libre* and Buenos Aires' Sociedad Patriótica, expanded on the notion that colonial subjects were not prepared for their newfound freedom. The problem for Monteagudo was that colonists were culturally disabled to live together in the civitas because centuries of Spanish rule never helped subjects transform their personal passions into virtues. Passions served "to sustain the monarch on the throne." Now, "everyone knows that America, due to its political circumstances . . . [and] subject to the most depressing and humiliating colonial system for three centuries already, cannot flatter itself for having left its infancy behind." People more "accustomed to the yoke of servitude" were prone to the "seductions" of the enemies of progress. The people may now be nominally free possessors of rights but, for their inherited traits, exercise their liberties against those who have liberated them. The result was less a counterrevolution than anarchy. "A people that rapidly passes from slavery to LIBERTY runs the risk of plunging itself into a state of anarchy and sliding back into a state of slavery."[59]

This brings us back to the dilemma posed by the apostles of public opinion. The emergence of a modern, reasoned politics was supposed to guide the making of a new order. But it was not exactly an instrument that was born of old practices. Public opinion, therefore, had to be "created" and was expected to "create" a reasonable citizenry. What prevailed instead were multiple voices that agreed, although scarcely, on the principle of negating imperial centralism—but not much else. The *Gaceta de Caracas*, after extolling the role of public opinion in the making of good laws, warned Venezuela against undermining its own freedom by

---

[58]*Martir o Libre*, April 6, and 20, 1812.

[59]Bernardo Monteagudo (December 27, 1811, January 10 and 24, 1812), in his *Escritos Políticos* (Buenos Aires: N.p., n.d.), pp. 36, 46, 57.

letting popular opinions flourish in a new political setting. The need to create a singular public opinion, guided by revolutionary leaders, justified silencing dissidents and muzzling the recently liberated press. Moreno, Nariño, and the firebrands of the new order believed that they were the defenders of a unitary force, the "people." Their task was not to convey or even represent a popular will but to organize it in the first place and apply it as an instrument of politics for the creation of a virtuous order.[60]

The year 1812 leaves us with a conundrum: the Spanish regime imploded and prompted the colonies to take matters into their own hands. But once colonists took power, they found that it was much easier to overthrow a collapsing regime than to build a new one. As they looked back on their dismantling of the political and economic structures of empire, and their failure to create something viable in its place, they pointed to the persistence of the old regime's cultural legacies. The same justifications for secession—to break with the Spanish past—provided narratives to support their dismay about the future. The despondent views of the liberated people that flowed from the pens of the liberators justified adopting ever more repressive and dictatorial methods. Vanguards in the capitals justified the necessity of autocratic means to create democratic ends. As they did so, their feeble coalitions of merchants, planters, and colonial thinkers fell apart. They made a critical political mistake: assuming that their coalitions were as unanimous about their vision of the new order as they were about the one they rejected. And from that mistake, they drew lessons that were destined to shape future struggles. Simón Bolívar escaped Venezuela and sailed to Cartagena where he would join the ultimately failed defense of that city. When he arrived, he shared his views of why he and his cohorts had fared so miserably at home. He blamed the use of paper money and forced loans that alienated the merchants. He felt the short-lived federal constitution sapped the central government of any strength. And he concluded that all this flowed from the naïveté of colonial leaders who failed to understand just how bereft colonials were of the prerequisite condition for political participation: virtue. Instead, they "imagined republics out of air, presupposing the perfectibility of this human lineage." But without virtue to start with, freed peoples fell prey to the political charms of demagogues and opportunists who peddle passion and sedition where order and compliance with laws were necessary.[61] For better

---

[60]Hébrard, "Opinión pública y representación," pp. 198–224.

[61]Simón Bolívar, "Memoria dirigida a los ciudadanos de la Nueva Granada por un Caraqueño," in *Pensamiento político de la emancipación*, ed. José Luis Romero and Luis Alberto Remero (Caracas: Biblioteca Ayacucho, 1977), p. 198.

or worse, Bolívar took this particular lesson to heart and applied it in the next round of struggle. If appeals to civic virtue would not work to help break with the past and move into the future, perhaps a call to arms would.

CONCLUSION

War and occupation within Europe kicked the legs out from under the Bourbon throne and subjected those who tried to fill the political vacuum with the costs of fighting the invader and defending the colonies, while backing into the arms of a merchant class that wanted to reverse rather than adapt to new circumstances. Between 1807 and 1810, the Spanish rulers created mechanisms for voice to bolster their legitimacy through more active participation of the dispersed elites of the empire. But in promising equality for all the provincial corners of the domain as a way to re-centralize it, peninsular governments not only crafted a rhetoric they could not live up to, they soon had to face the disenchantment with their authority in the very organisms of "voice" that they endorsed for their salvation.

Voice alone did not lead automatically to disloyalty and exit. Secession of the colonies required political choices to be made where power was most concentrated, if weak: Cádiz. The Cortes's deliberations shaped the fate of the empire in the absence of a king. But in trying to reunite the regime, they could not prevent colonial representatives from calling for proportional representation and for the end of Spanish mercantilism. Deliberated in assemblies and publicized in periodicals and newsprint, the choices made in Cádiz accomplished the opposite of what they were supposed to do and reinforced the centrifugal propensities in an empire that had lost its moral and political center.

The Spanish Atlantic changed suddenly in 1807 and created the opportunity for transforming voice into exit for Francisco de Miranda and colonists elsewhere in South America. The sense of contributing to saving the empire from the French—being loyal by sending donations and loans—but being affronted by Spain's imperial centralism fueled the drive to repudiate the authority of the Cortes and to secede from the peninsula. This decision was justified in roundly historical terms: colonies, born of conquest, endowed with rights but untutored in the act of practicing them, suddenly being asked to carry the burden of supporting Spain while degraded to an unequal status were casting off the yoke of centuries of oppression.

But moving from a repudiation of bad rulers to creating something new was a more difficult feat. Where did sovereignty now lie if not with the monarchy or Spanish nation? Viceroyalties, provinces, cities? To solve this riddle, the recently invented history of the colonies *as* colonies was no help, for what was shared was something distinctively negative: empire. What was not shared, by the very logic of Spanish imperialism, was the making of something new before the empire collapsed: an invented history of local communities as distinct nations coming into being. In effect, the political conflict and process of imagining a historical self got stuck in the complex chains of events in which ancien-régime empires gave way to liberal nation-states. It is this fundamental political transformation at the heart of creating a new model of sovereignty organized around "nations" that were supposed to fill the gap left by collapsing empires that is missing from Benedict Anderson's account of modern nationalism.

Faced with this quagmire, colonial leaders adopted, not unlike the Cortes in Cádiz, unpopular measures to preserve traditional political formations of viceroyalties in the face of regional and provincial movements that aspired to local sovereignty. So, like the decomposition of the empire, the decomposition of "freed" colonies evolved out of the challenge of constructing models of authority where there was no consensus. Rogers Smith has recently observed that historical narratives—what he calls "stories of peoplehood"—gave moral content and boundaries to nascent political communities, enabling people to tell themselves stories about their coming into being, and thus possessing moral claims to sovereignty. If so, this chapter has shown that narratives can cut several ways; efforts to integrate political subjects by constructing shared stories can also polarize and thus disintegrate. What cannot be forgotten are the political contingencies, and cascading reactions, inherent in the struggle to refashion models of sovereignty in deep crisis.[62]

The breakdown of the Spanish empire in South America did not begin in the peripheries. It started in its core and issued its shockwaves outward. This sequence affected how colonies grappled with the crisis of sovereignty because nascent political communities emerged *because* not *before* the Spanish empire imploded. Colonists began inventing histories of themselves as distinctive political communities only once the ancien régime was defunct. American secession was a reaction to the metropolitan effects of Atlantic warfare, and not the expression of accumulated colonial grievances that spawned a separate political identity. South American colonies had seceded when Spain was least able to subject the colonies to old ways. As we shall see in future chapters, this decisively shaped the regimes they created out of civil war.

---

[62]Smith, *Stories of Peoplehood.*

6   Brazilian Counterpoints

INTRODUCTION

In 1807, Rio de Janeiro was a thriving hub of a booming Atlantic colony. A city of some 40,000 inhabitants, its markets were clearinghouses for agricultural and mining staples destined for markets around the Atlantic world. It was also a magnet for slaves. Since 1790, some 10,000 Africans were unloaded every year onto the city's wharves and channeled through its auction houses en route to agrarian hinterlands. Brazil occupied a special place in Rodrigo de Souza Coutinho's vision of a "Great Empire" because it was indispensable to the metropolis that centered the Portuguese imperium. However, within months, Rio de Janeiro's place in empire would change dramatically from indispensable outpost to new center. As French troops marched across the Iberian peninsula, the fate of the monarchy hung in the balance, and eventually led to the exodus of the Braganza dynasty from Lisbon to its colony, where it would plant New World roots. Relocating the center of empire to American peripheries set in motion an alternative, enigmatic trajectory of imperial breakdown—one that inverted the Portuguese empire's geographic foundations in order for it to endure the storm of revolution.

This inversion has prompted the question: "Why was Brazil different?"[1] As this chapter shows, there were important contrapuntal features of the ways in which the Portuguese empire handled the more general process of imperial and revolutionary upheaval of the late eighteenth and early nineteenth centuries. At the same time, Brazil did not simply step out of the temporalities of the Atlantic world. Indeed, one of the beguiling aspects of the age of revolution is how it shook dynasties without demolishing most of them. Landed magnates, conservative religious leaders, and ruling households who reinvented themselves as paternal guardians of ancient "nations" rebuilt the pillars upon which the roof of anciens régimes rested. So, for all the upheaval, underlying structures proved their durability; Brazil may have been "different" but it was not necessarily

---

[1]Kenneth Maxwell, "Why Was Brazil Different?" in his *Naked Tropics: Essays on Empire and Other Rogues* (New York: Routledge, 2003), pp. 145–68.

exceptional.[2] In some respects, the revolutions on both sides of the Atlantic gave rise to even firmer commitments to and greater coherence of traditional social forces. It took the upheavals of the age of revolution to create its antithesis, conservativism. There would have been no Edmund Burke, whose *Reflections on the Revolution in France* so powerfully repudiated the idea that governments were supposed to protect natural rights, but rather were a "contrivance of human wisdom to provide human *wants*" without the eruption, and disruption, of rights talk. This is one of the reasons why Arno Mayer has argued that no tale of revolution is logically or empirically complete without an account of counter revolution, and the struggle, violence, and terror that necessarily envelop the two.[3]

But persistence is not fate; the past is not literally ageless. Institutional durability requires the reproduction of inherited elements in new historic contexts; it requires adaptation. Persistence is a process. It was part of Burke's genius to recognize this when he observed that "a state without the means of some change is without the means of its conservation."[4] If durability is a process, it is also political with a context. Protagonists of the old regime struggled to save what they could of their models of sovereignty and privilege, but they did so through imperial adaptation to the pressures of international warfare. Colonies may have been located at the margins of the empires, but they were not marginal to the survival of Iberian dynasties. Rather, the overseas dominions were as essential to dynastic stamina as they were instrumental to dynastic origins. So, just as empire was the structure for a set of long-distance relationships between spatial parts, it was also the setting for ongoing transactions between constituents.

Similar to the previous chapter, this one's examination of how the Portuguese regime responded to the same crisis of empire accents the adaptive struggle to survive and in so doing to evolve into something else. Imperial dynamics and the survival of dynasties differed in Portugal and Spain because of the discrepant ways in which ruling blocs handled the

---

[2]Arno J. Mayer, *The Persistence of the Old Regime: Europe to the Great War* (New York: Pantheon, 1981), esp. pp. 4–9; for a nuanced take on persistence in the Iberian Atlantic, see Stanley J. Stein and Barbara H. Stein, *The Colonial Heritage of Latin America: Essays on Economic Dependence in Perspective* (New York: Oxford University Press, 1970).

[3]Burke, *Reflections on the Revolution in France* (New York: Penguin, 1969), pp. 150–51, emphasis in the original; Palmer, *Age of Democratic Revolution*; Hannah Arendt, *On Revolution* (London: Penguin, 1963), pp. 28–29; Mayer, *The Furies*, pp. 6–7.

[4]Burke, *Reflections*, p. 106; Olson, *Rise and Decline of Nations*; Charles Tilly, *Durable Inequality* (Berkeley: University of California Press, 1998), esp. chap. 6. I have explored some of the ways in which Latin American historians have grappled with this dilemma in "The Problem of Persistence."

relations between the struggling metropoles and the American colonies. Two variables were important: the deals with European powers and bargains with colonists as prices for the defense of sovereignty. The Portuguese empire navigated (literally) the stormy waters of the Napoleonic Wars differently than did the Spanish empire and arrived at a new model of sovereignty designed and implemented by a group whose most important member was Rodrigo de Souza Coutinho. The minister's death in early 1812 brought closure to a period of imperial adaptation to a profound crisis of the monarchy at its core. Souza Coutinho's achievements remapped the geography of the Portuguese empire, the price for which would be expressed in a new balance of regal dependency on European allies and colonial elites.

Precursors

When the Napoleonic commander General Junot marched into Lisbon, precipitating a crisis in late 1807, he was seeking to take control on behalf of France of a vast empire with a track record of instability and loose control the further one went from the metropolis. Napoleon's Continental System and the threat of French corsairs slashed trade off the African coast and in the River Plate delta. Indeed, the entire pan-European payments systems of interlocking bills of exchange and partnerships that supported the Portuguese commercial system had begun to paralyze in 1805. While some historians have concluded that the empire was doomed and have proffered structural explanations for its demise, it is more likely that the slump reflected short-term difficulties of war. As we saw in previous chapters, before the breakdown of the Peace of Amiens there was a commercial bonanza fueled in large part by an expanding slave trade. Still, it was a slump nonetheless and was already on the minds of Lisbon's rulers even before the tempest hit in 1807.[5]

Brazil, the lifeline for Portugal, was also becoming more politically frangible. Starting in the late 1780s, calls—real and perceived—for a new political and social order could be heard more frequently. Despite the hypervigilance of colonial officials, plotting, conspiracy, and rumors of revolt would not go away. Worse, as the French Revolution washed up on the Caribbean, the fear of a full-fledged slave uprising spread throughout the slaving belts of the Portuguese colony. When two slave ships unloaded their human cargo from Angola in 1794, four Frenchmen were found aboard. Evidently, part of the cargo was meant for transshipment to

---

[5]Alexandre, *Os sentidos do império,* esp. p. 54.

Port-au-Prince. But the Frenchmen summarily found themselves in shackles, like the slaves. The local authorities explained their actions as efforts to root out "the pernicious consequences of the present revolution" and announced in their report that they subjected the sailors to an *escrupolizissimo* examination. The viceroy appended a longer report to the Overseas Council about the recent findings of French revolutionary evidence around the capital. One literary society was known for its gatherings for "unlimited nocturnal hours," and incendiary papers and books were found all over the city. Anonymous letters warned of a pending social explosion. When the prominent merchant Jeronimo Teixeira Lobo got his copy, he promptly turned it over to the worried viceroy.[6]

Bahia was the centerpoint of paranoia. A decade after Tiradentes' conspiracy in Minas Gerais, a similar fate befell a group of tailors in Salvador. This conspiracy differed mainly in the racial composition of the rebels, free blacks, who extolled not just republicanism but abolitionism to the dissenting mix. Thus calls for a "Democratic, Free, and Independent" government in 1798 were all the more worrying in the slave belt around the Bahia de Todos os Santos. Authorities meted out an even more gruesome punishment, scattering chopped up body parts of some of the insurgents around the provincial capital. In 1807, a group of slaves from a Hausa tribe were likewise caught plotting revolution. Thus, even before Napoleon's invasion, Brazil had seen its share of—albeit easily suppressed—challenges to imperial authority in the name of a political alternative.[7] The much-maligned Juiz de Fora of Rio de Janeiro, Baltasar da Silva Lisboa, noted in the wake of the Minas Gerais conspiracy that there was more and more evidence of the spreading revolutionary doctrine—"wherever the name of Liberty appears it is adored and loved"—and warned of its siren calls.[8]

The legitimacy of the crown's administrators in the periphery began to obsess the ruling elite. The viceroy, the Count of Rezende, informed Lisbon in 1795 that the Campos de Goitacazes, an important commercial agrarian district outside the capital, reeked with nepotism, corruption, and favoritism perpetrated by local officials who cared little about their popularity among the subject population. The region's magistrate in particular was "dominated by his passions." The count warned that the recent population growth, expansion of the agrarian frontier, and

---

[6] AHU, DA, Caixa 157, doc. 53.

[7] Alden, "Late Colonial Brazil," pp. 654–57; Maxwell, *Conflicts and Conspiracies,* 116–39, 218–29; Roderick Barman, *Brazil: The Forging of a Nation, 1798–1852* (Stanford: Stanford University Press, 1988), pp. 30–38.

[8] For the paper trail of Silva's Lisboa's administrative vitae, see AHU, DA, Caixa 154, docs. 10, 33; Caixa 153, doc. 21, Caixa 155, doc. 13, Caixa 157, doc. 53.

spreading disorder pushed colonists "too far from the forces that would make them obey," with the consequential "rise in intrigues, and clamor of the same population with irremediable dangers and damages to the spirit of Laws." Throughout the 1790s, officials in Minas Gerais had warned that the root cause of the unrest of 1789 continued to be "maladministration."[9]

All this noise in the streets, courthouses, and taverns did not, however, add up to a crisis of the ancien régime. Trouble, yes; potential for collapse, no. What is important to appreciate is that even as imperial ministers had to confront French soldiers in the heart of the metropolis, they had to confront a colonial subject population with some experience at pushing back the intrusions and perceived injustices of metropolitan or local elite demands. Not only was the economy generally prospering, but whatever attractions the French Revolution held out for free colonists, they paled as the 1790s unfolded into Parisian Terror and the slave revolt in Saint Domingue. What is more, the reforms under the ministry of Rodrigo de Souza Coutinho after 1796 (see chapter 3) eased some of the pressure on the state's fiscal agents—the perennial source of popular umbrage. But it was clear that imperial adaptation to new emergencies was not infinitely elastic and could not count on the unquestioned loyalty of colonial subjects to the empire and to the crown. Brazil was a prosperous but brittle bastion of the Portuguese emporium. So, while rulers relied on empire to salvage the dynasty, they could not presume a solid, unflinching colonial loyalty immune from the contagion of conspiracy and revolution that was ravaging other corners of the Atlantic world.

DELIVERANCE

No European empire charted its history alone. The cycles of rise, apogee, and crisis of empire were entwined with analogous cycles of rivals and allies in the scramble for power in the Atlantic world. Portugal's imperial fate was simply an extreme example of the porosity—for nationalists this would be its "vulnerability"—of its frontiers and framework. Accordingly, the difficulty of managing the Portuguese empire got entangled with the impossible task of handling the conflict between the British and French empires.

---

[9]AHU, DA, Caixa 159, doc. 86; Caixa 153, doc. 10; AN, Vice-Reinado, Caixa 485, pacote 2, s.n., report by Caetano Pinto de Vasconcellos Montenegro, the intendant general of Ouro.

The cycle of Portuguese dependency on Britain, inscribed in treaties since the duke of Braganza gave concessions in return for protection in the 1640s, came to a head in 1807. For some members of the ruling clique, the prospect of a Napoleonic victory over Britain presented Portugal with a historic chance. Here was an opportunity to reverse the cycle of dependency on London by aligning with France. The French government knew this and issued its entreaties to join the Continental System. Britain, represented by the shrewd Lord Strangford, tried to combat such a temptation. When he feared that Prince Regent João (his mother, Maria I, had been deemed mentally incompetent to rule since 1792) was close to succumbing, Strangford warned of retaliations. So it was that the court in Lisbon grew increasingly divided over how to handle each blow to its sovereignty. One faction was pro-French, led by Antonio de Araujo de Azevedo. The pro-English rival faction had Rodrigo de Souza Coutinho at the helm. The former ousted the latter after 1803 when Spain signed a neutrality treaty with France. Araujo assured the prince that the French would leave the Braganza house alone with the presumption that Napoleon simply wanted the Iberian powers *not* to align with Britain. This turned out to be a miscalculation since Napoleon needed more than Iberian passivity. He wanted access to the immensely more important bounty: Iberian imperia. Araujo was able to keep the court on his side, playing on the Braganza fear of Franco-Spanish threats while obfuscating their motives.

However, imperial sovereignty could not be resolved within the court itself; Araujo's campaign did not settle alignments. The tension mounted after Spain abandoned its neutrality and allied with France against Britain—and thus against Portugal. The Braganza court was torn between two powers and two polarizing factions: should it side with France or with Britain, knowing that siding with either guaranteed an invasion or assault by the other? Once Napoleon declared his continental blockade, and once the news that a Franco-Spanish force was amassing in October 1807, it was impossible for Araujo to portray France as neutral. Still, the royal family dithered. The court was so indecisive that it came close to plunging Portugal into a war with both superpowers at the same time, if only because it could not decide with which to align. It is difficult, as a result, to make a strong case for the inevitability of the fate of the Portuguese empire.[10]

Just because the cost of doing nothing was rising did not make the choice any easier. At the time, it was not at all clear who would win the

---

[10]For a superb reconstruction of the internal debate, see Alexandre, *Os sentidos do império,* pp. 137–59.

struggle for supremacy of the Atlantic world. Rodrigo de Souza Coutinho, the architect of fiscal and financial policy before 1803, had anticipated the possibility of a direct confrontation—and even occupation—by France. He viewed Portugal's empire as a delicate balancing act, with Lisbon as the center of a sprawling domain but whose extensions, Brazil above all, were more important than the center. Accordingly, the ex-minister drafted a plan for the migration of the court to Rio de Janeiro. In his plan, Souza Coutinho observed that any alliance of Paris and Madrid would inevitably doom Lisbon's world, as the partners would inevitably fix their eyes on occupying the Portuguese metropolis and claiming its imperium, an easy feat for Spain since Madrid's possessions had military resources that could be deployed on Brazil's borders. If necessary, the court should migrate to Brazil, Portugal's prize possession. For it was more important to keep Brazil out of French clutches than Portugal itself. The latter could always be brought back; but Brazil, once lost, might never be recovered. This would permanently cripple, if not destroy, the empire and therefore the Braganza dynasty itself. Even if it meant complete alignment with the British, whose navy and money would be necessary to defend and escort the court across the Atlantic, the price of the dynasty's sovereignty was worth paying. Needless to say, for Souza Coutinho's rivals, ruminations and warnings of this sort only made a French occupation of Portugal all the more likely as Napoleon would thereby accelerate his rush to seize Lisbon. They could also argue plausibly that a compromise was always possible with France, and that France posed no threat to Portuguese sovereignty so long as Lisbon abided by the Continental System (which was not technically a declaration of war against the British). The real menace to Portugal was the British. Either way, after 1805 neutrality was not an option. The issue was which was the lowest price to pay to defend imperial sovereignty.[11]

The more the prince vacillated, the more the French pressured Portugal to join the Continental System, thus forcing Napoleon's hand and weakening Araujo's. What Lisbon did not know was just how vulnerable it had become to the personal aspiration of Manuel Godoy, who had grand ambitions for himself as an Iberian potentate once the axis of Madrid and Paris consolidated. French and Spanish forces gathered momentum for an occupation. The threat of invasion began to tilt the balance in the court in favor of Rodrigo de Souza Coutinho, who, at Prince João's beckoning, returned to the Council of State but did not get a ministerial portfolio back until

---

[11]"Parecer sobre as difíceis circunstâncias do momento presente" (June 21, 1798), in Souza Coutinho, *Textos*, v. 2, pp. 77–89; Alexandre, *Os sentidos do império*, pp. 161–63; Manchester, *British Preëminence in Brazil*, pp. 54–55; Barman, *Brazil*, pp. 42–43.

early 1808. His brother, Domingos de Souza Coutinho, the Portuguese envoy to London, welcomed Foreign Secretary George Canning's secret promise to protect the Portuguese government, but warned that this would surely induce a French attack. This was as late as September 1807. It was not until Lord Strangford brandished a threat that the British navy would bombard Lisbon if the court did not accept the offer to escort the royal family out of the capital that Souza Coutinho got his way. On November 19, Marshal Andoche Junot's advance forces crossed the border from Spain into Portugal. With French troops barely five days from Lisbon, Dom João accepted Souza Coutinho and Lord Strangford's plan to flee, escorted by a British squadron, to Brazil. It took three days for the court—its retinue, treasury, archives, and thousands of staff and hangers-on—to pack and load the thirty-vessel fleet amid torrential rainfall. For good measure, a printing press, the royal jewels, dishes, and even a vast book collection were thrown into the cargo. On the morning of November 29, 1807, hours before Junot's advance troops entered the capital, the immense flotilla weighed anchor and sailed out the mouth of the Tagus River. Their destination was Rio de Janeiro. French troops swept into the vacated capital and began to set up an occupation regime.[12]

After the nail-biting exodus from Lisbon, British leaders breathed a sigh of relief. They were confident in Souza Coutinho and applauded his ability to work with Strangford on shuffling the court out of the imperial capital. But they still worried that the Braganza circle could slip back into the French orbit. Indeed, when rumors of Souza Coutinho's declining health began to circulate in late 1809, London immediately reacted with alarm, lest the British lose their darling minister and watch the Braganza court swing beyond its control. *The Times* of London celebrated the role that Souza Coutinho could play, keeping Portugal's critical resources out of French hands. "What a pity it would be if such base and light-headed men should again have the possibility of ruining one country [Portugal] as they have the other [Spain]!" Warning that a "cabal" might take advantage of Souza Coutinho's ill health, the paper spoke ominously: "These men have already formed their plans to be the instruments of artfull Communications from France; and to undermine here as they did in Portugal, the British interest."[13]

---

[12]ANTT, Ministerio de Negociaçoens Estranjeiros (hereafter MNE), Correspondencia das Caixas, Caixa 726, n.f.; Leslie Bethell, "The Independence of Brazil," in Bethell, ed., *Cambridge History of Latin America*, v. 3, pp. 168–70; Kirsten Schultz, *Tropical Versailles: Empire, Monarchy and the Portuguese Royal Court in Rio de Janeiro, 1808–1821* (New York: Routledge, 2001), pp. 79–80; Maxwell, *Conflicts and Conspiracies*, pp. 236–38; BN, CP, Códice 651, ff. 268–69.

[13]AHU, DA, Caixa 245, doc. 85, handwritten transcription of an article in *The Times*, October 29, 1809.

In the crossing, and during the first few months of the court's life in the New World, Souza Coutinho unveiled a much larger plan of reform and restructuring of the Portuguese Atlantic, adapting it to the perceived interests of Brazil and expressed interests of Britain. From the point of view of the British, whatever was good for Brazil could more easily be made to be good for Britain. This, at least, was the idea at the outset. In a short tract published in May 1808 in Brazil, Souza Coutinho, soon to be made the Count of Linhares, outlined the guiding principles of the new imperial order for the next four critical years. The migration of metropolitan power to the periphery was a deliverance of nearly biblical proportions. It afforded a historic opportunity for the monarchy to regenerate and revitalize itself guided by modern principles of governance. For the monarchy could now reconstitute its pact with subjects on both sides of the Atlantic by attending to their enlightened self-interests. In this fashion, the Portuguese monarchy could reveal to the world the mendacious claims by revolutionaries that only a country ruled by the people could be a country for the people. The manifesto, discussed and ratified by the Council of State, began with a condemnation of France, for "incommensurable ambition without limits." "The Court of Portugal," he declared, "will raise its voice from the breast of its new empire which it will create; with authentic and true achievements, displayed with singularity and moderation, it will make known to Europe, and to its own vassals, all that it has just suffered." The French Revolution, through bad faith and sheer ambition, threatened the pillars of European virtue, monarchy and the family of European empires.[14] Deliverance to Brazil would restore, indeed redeem, them.

Managing the monarchy from its principal colony produced a new set of problems. As it turned out, Souza Coutinho could count on Portugal's loyalty to the monarchy more easily than he could the provinces of Brazil. In effect, a major threat to the stability of the realm was the difficulty in crafting Brazil's own sovereignty, now constituted as a New World center of an Old World empire. Difficulties soon arose in the southern borderlands, fueled by the clash of rival imperial designs for the ever nettlesome River Plate region. Since it was technically

---

[14]Rodrigo de Souza Coutinho, "Manifestou, ou exposição fundada, e justificativa do procedimento da Corte de Portugal a respeito da França desde o princípio de revolução até à epoca da invasão de Portugal," in his *Textos*, v. 2, pp. 335–43. There was a great deal of talk and speechifying about a new era of splendor and civilization in the wake of the crown's arrival. See Schultz, *Tropical Versailles*, pp. 67–87, for a description of how defenders of the ancien régime transformed the tragedy of exile into a triumph of a new reason of state.

a joint Franco-Spanish force that took Portugal, Portugal was at war with Spain, which escalated tensions on the frontiers with the River Plate and Guyana. To make matters worse, the unrest in the River Plate, described in the previous chapter, seeped into the territories of Rio Grande do Sul, worrying Rio de Janeiro that this might inspire a popular uprising, with perilous consequences for the slavocracy of Brazil. The ruling circles in Rio de Janeiro responded with a combination of opportunistic aggression to settle old territorial scores in the borderlands, as well as fear of a revolutionary wildfire from the Pampas. Ultra-royalists in Montevideo appealed to Rio de Janeiro for support against rebellious Buenos Aires—and against the incipient rural insurgency in the Banda Oriental. The Brazilian monarchy was only too happy to cooperate. In mid-1811, Souza Coutinho ordered a large expeditionary force to the region in support of the Montevideo faction. When it arrived, commanders found themselves embroiled in a withering war with Buenos Aires' armies and the guerrilla fighters of José de Artigas. It would take almost two decades for Brazil to fully extricate its forces from the region—after huge material, human, and financial costs.[15]

The regime in Rio de Janeiro did not just get sucked into the maw of borderland war; it tried to take advantage of it. Members of the court in Rio de Janeiro were eager to recover some of their sullied prestige after the narrow escape from Lisbon. The yawning power vacuum in the Spanish colonies appeared to give them their opportunity. Accordingly, Portuguese expansionists fastened on the unruly but lucrative River Plate. However, far from filling the vacuum, intervening in the southern borderlands brought the conflict to the heart of the court itself. João and his ambitious wife, Joaquina Carlota, sister of the imprisoned Ferdinand, each had different plans to annex the borderlands. So long as Buenos Aires rejected the Cádiz government, Carlota nurtured hopes of becoming queen of the River Plate and thus restoring Bourbon grandeur. Quarreling within the royal family only intensified each side's eagerness to lay claim to the southern borderlands as a way to tip the scales in favor of their project, much to the dismay of some. As far away as London, the envoy Domingos de Souza Coutinho groaned that "Rio de Janeiro must be very careful" when it came to dealing with "the spirit of insurrection" in Buenos Aires. Both the vacuum in the River

---

[15]The next chapter will go into this war in much more detail. For a discussion of its causes, see Adelman, *Republic of Capital*, pp. 80–91; and Alexandre, *Os sentidos do império*, pp. 244–58.

Plate and the power vacuum in the Brazilian capital sucked both sides into a crippling war.[16]

For the Count of Linhares, entering the southern borderlands with a show of force satisfied several goals to fit his master plan for revitalizing the Portuguese monarchy. The court's chief minister proposed to resolve the feuding between João and Carlota with a royalist, counterrevolutionary alliance between the Braganza throne and the Cádiz government. Brazilian armies would force Buenos Aires back into the Hispanic fold, ensuring Cádiz's sovereignty over the River Plate. As a quid pro quo, Cádiz would recognize a member of the Rio de Janeiro royalty, Carlota ("Prinzesa Nossa Senhora"), as the ruler of a joint monarchy. This would "ensure the principles of Monarchical Government." This was an audacious plan; Linhares could never be accused of not thinking big. But there were, as with all grand designs, all sorts of devils in the details. There is no evidence that Cádiz embraced the idea. Indeed, the interim Spanish government hoped that Buenos Aires would rejoin the metropolitan fold when it could approve a constitution (which rolled off the printing presses in 1812). For their part, the British government was deeply skeptical. Since the age of Philip II, London had remained resolved to scupper an Iberian fusion. The grand notion of an Iberian alliance went nowhere—but it nonetheless revealed the scale upon which power-holders in Rio de Janeiro were now reimagining the Iberian Atlantic as a model for a world restored to the triadic harmony of monarchy, slaveholding, and aristocracy.[17]

THE LIMITS OF SURVIVAL

The migration of the Portuguese court to the New World delivered it from the kind of crisis that befell the Bourbon regime in Spain. It also presented an opportunity to resolve some of the inherited senses of weakness, dependency, and even decay by becoming even more splendid in a new environment. Souza Coutinho was clearly prone to this kind of yearning. The regime did survive, but warfare and the constraints on using Brazilian resources to fund its ambitions soon drove it headlong into a new cycle of dependency on Britain and therefore, eventually, into a new balance with Brazilian society.

---

[16]*Gaceta do Rio de Janeiro*, November 6, 1809; ANTT, MNE, Caixa 729, August 29, 1810; Neill Macauley, *Dom Pedro: The Struggle for Liberty in Brazil and Portugal, 1798–1834* (Durham: Duke University Press, 1986), pp. 40–41.

[17]ANTT, MNE, Legação de Portugal em Londres, Caixa 37, doc. 8.

If lofty aspirations could not resolve conflicts within the Braganza court, they did exacerbate relations with the British, with whom the government was immediately tied up in difficult negotiations over trade and financial matters. Domingos de Souza Coutinho informed British foreign secretary Wellesley that his government was organizing a "Noble Confederation" to replace the spreading republican revolution and restore order to Buenos Aires. A great expedition was en route from Rio de Janeiro to the south. Wellesley, who had his hands full trying to keep the feeble Spanish government afloat, was not at all pleased. He did not want two important allies fighting each other as desperate acts to bolster their reputations. Lord Strangford, who had also migrated to the Brazilian capital to keep tabs on Britain's ally, got instructions from London to try to intercede. He tried to mediate among the rivals, Rio de Janeiro, Montevideo, and Buenos Aires, hoping to defuse the war, to open markets for British trade, and to prevent the emergence of a single hegemon in the region. By 1812, he secured a short-lived withdrawal of Brazilian armies from the Banda Oriental. But relations remained strained nonetheless.[18]

Peace in the borderlands was not the only thing on Strangford's mind. The British government had its own headaches back home. The handling of the war in Europe was not going well; some urged the cabinet to let Spain go. The British economy, severely affected by the Napoleonic blockade, slumped just as it was called upon to support a large war effort. After the Peace of Tilsit, Sweden, Denmark, and eventually all of Iberia joined the Continental System. British exports plummeted, manufacturers went broke, and unemployed textile workers smashed the machines they blamed for their malaise. All this compelled the British government to ensure that South American markets stay open—if possibly with preferential access—to British business. George Canning rejoined the British cabinet and took charge of foreign affairs, and he craftily handled the fissiparous South American colonies. His bargaining power grew after the hurried flight of the Braganza court from Lisbon, as this placed the Portuguese government more squarely in a position of dependency.[19]

For the Brazilian-based monarchy, reliance on the British economy was also a necessity. Now that the colonial periphery was the center of the Portuguese empire, the traditional triangular relationship between Brazil,

---

[18]ANTT, MNE, Caixa 730, January 18, 1811, July 8, 1811; Alexandre, *Os sentidos do império*, pp. 257–61; Waddell, "International Politics and Latin American Independence," pp. 201–4; Manchester, *British Preëminence in Brazil*, pp. 118–44.

[19]Bruun, "The Balance of Power during the Wars," pp. 267–69; Patrick K. O'Brien, "The Impact of the Revolutionary and Napoleonic Wars, 1793–1815, on the Long-Run Growth of the British Economy," *Review* 12:3 (1989): 335–95.

Portugal, and Britain had to be overhauled to permit more open exchange between Brazil and Britain. The issue was, what terms would underlie this new bilateral order with the Portuguese entrepôt out of the picture? From a very early stage, the British seized the negotiating lead and managed throughout to hold the most powerful cards. As early as September 1807, the foreign secretary advised Domingos de Souza Coutinho that his government would be willing to protect the Braganza throne and escort the royal refugees to Rio de Janeiro, and offered furthermore a commercial treaty "entre le gouvernement Portuguais transplanté au Brésil et le gouvernement Brittanique." Included in the draft were stipulations that the Portuguese monarch agree to clamp down and eventually close the slave trade in the dominions of the empire. Indeed, even as early as April 1807, scarcely three weeks after Parliament approved a bill to outlaw the slave trade in the British empire, the Foreign Office urged Lisbon to do the same. The Portuguese envoy had a clear-eyed view of the stakes. He thanked the foreign secretary but advised that any such treaty might be viewed by some sectors in Portugal as prejudicial to their manufactures. Worse, an end to the slave trade would hurt Brazilian mercantile interests and might push public opinion in Rio de Janeiro to favor the solicitous French, who, it did not need reminding, had reinstated slavery and promised to promote the slave trade.[20]

British merchants joined the pressure to open Portuguese imperial—that is, Brazilian—markets. They sent a petition to Souza Coutinho with promises of widespread support on the part of Britain's finest capitalists for the Portuguese monarchy in its time of need. But they could not resist adding a little dig, an elliptical warning of what might happen without more gratitude and cooperation on the part of the government in Rio de Janeiro. Stocks of "Portuguese" staples—sugar, coffee, tea, tobacco, and cocoa—had been sitting idle in British ports waiting for unloading. Without a treaty, the signatories added, "we have only to add that it would be of very serious consequence to our constituents, at least until the final disposal of their detained property, and that we submit the measure with confidence to Your Excellency's acknowledged zeal and to the liberality of His Majesty's government." The bottom of the letter included such magnates as Baring Brothers, Gorman Brothers, Gordon Murphy, Thomas Nash, Burmeister and Son, Menzies, White & Company; in effect the luminaries of an emerging international financial class. João's decision to leave Lisbon, in the end, forced the issue, and negotiations over several treaties finally began. Details

---

[20]ANTT, MNE, Correspondencia das Caixas, Legação de Portugal em Inglaterra, Caixa 726, unnumbered files, dated September 12, 23, November 30, 1807; Manchester, *British Preëminence in Brazil*, pp. 71–81.

were hammered out in London between Domingos de Souza Coutinho and the Foreign Office, and in Rio de Janeiro between Lord Strangford and Domingos's brother, the Count of Linhares. The final bundle of treaties and secret articles were finally signed in February 1810 by Linhares and Lord Strangford in Rio de Janeiro. The Treaty of Alliance and Friendship revealed all the imbalances in bargaining power between the parties, and specifically bound the Portuguese monarchy to cooperate with London's campaign "for bringing about the gradual abolition of the slave trade." British pressure reduced Brazilian tariffs on their merchandise to 15 percent. Here was an emerging order accepted as the necessary price to be paid for the monarchy's sovereignty. Strangford assured the Foreign Office that England would now enjoy "undoubted Superiority" and "acquire a still stronger claim to the Title of Protector and Friend of Brazil."[21]

While backroom negotiations aimed to ensure that the fate of the Spanish monarchy and its empire would not befall the Portuguese, the court dismantled the vestiges of Portuguese mercantilism. But in this case, too, adjustments for sovereignty took their toll. As the flotilla crossed the Atlantic in late 1807, the royal ministers agreed that the Prince Regent had to arrive in Brazil with a great concession to embolden the loyalty of colonial subjects. It was the key ministers, Rodrigo de Souza Coutinho and Fernando José de Portugal, who agreed that commercial restrictions on colonial commerce had been thorns worth removing from the colonial side. When the royal flotilla arrived in Bahia in late 1807, a local lawyer and political economist of some distinction, José da Silva Lisboa, whose work we discussed in chapter 4, joined the ministerial circle. At Silva Lisboa's urgings, on January 28, 1808, João pronounced Brazilian ports henceforth open to trade with friendly nations. The Carta Regia was announced amid much fanfare and official theatrics for the consumption of Bahian spectators. They were told that exports were free to flow where they found markets and all imports had to pay 24 percent ad valorem levies without regard for port of origin. While the Prince Regent issued this famous declaration as a reflection of his magnanimity, he in fact had few options. With Portugal occupied and British merchants bearing down for open markets, it would have been hard to imagine how the government might have upheld rules that protected metropolitan interests. Souza Coutinho himself skipped the official hoopla, for he had already left for the new capital, Rio de Janeiro, to prepare for the rest of the retinue and cabinet.[22]

---

[21]ANTT, MNE, Correspondencia das Caixas, Legação de Portugal em Inglaterra, Caixa 727, letters of Domingos de Souza Coutinho to George Canning, January 16–17, 1808; Caixa 729, Souza Coutinho to Forjaz, June 27, 1810; Manchester, *British Preëminence in Brazil*, p. 82.

[22]Lima, *D. João VI*, pp. 128–38; Manchester, *British Preëminence in Brazil*, pp. 69–71.

More reforms followed in the wake of the open port decree. Their compound effect was supposed to "free" colonial commerce and its agents from old restrictions. In April 1808, the court announced the end to all prohibitions on establishing industries in the colonies; several months later levies on the imports of goods carried on national bottoms were slashed to promote a national merchant marine. Trade liberalization brought down most of the longstanding obstacles to entrepreneurial activity not just in Brazil but across the Portuguese possessions from the Azores to Angola, freeing all vassals, as one communiqué noted, to establish manufactures. This included lifting all restrictions on shipping slaves from Angola to Brazil by either Portuguese "nationals" or foreigners. The court applauded its own deeds in the rhetoric of royal goodness. In early 1810, the prince assured his colonial subjects that "maritime commerce has been since remotest Ages to the most recent times that which promises and supports the solid Wealth of People who exercise it." Easing commerce "is the principal objective of My Paternal Decrees, to Abbreviate the Shipment and Trade, and also to Alleviate My Faithful Vassals of burdensome levies."[23]

The celebratory tone that accompanied the reforms was meant to neutralize some of the complaints about the 1810 treaty with Britain. One of the ironies of the period was that the perception of British mercantile advantage fueled Brazilian debates and discussions about ideas of political economy that had been adapted from Scottish and English writings. The vocabulary of political economy came to prominence in the public sphere just as newspapers, pamphleteering, and the shaping of public opinion were becoming powerful arenas for conducting politics. Indeed, proclamations about commercial virtues coincided with the arrival of Brazil's first printing press along with the court. The definition of interests, therefore, became part of the contest to legitimate the new commercial order and thus shape the reasons of state. Count Linhares, despite some personal reservations about the treaty, defended the accord he had negotiated as a reversal of historic inequalities. Portuguese shippers, argued the minister, had to endure restrictions applied on all foreign operators working in British markets while British shippers enjoyed the status and privileges afforded to Portuguese nationals within the Portuguese system. The 1810 treaty, he claimed, put both sides on equal footing. Accusing the treaty's critics, especially the *Correio Brasiliense*'s editor, Hipólito José da Costa, of "miserable and incoherent rhapsodies," Linhares observed that the treaty ended special protections and privileges "which were for many

---

[23]AHU, CU, Códice 551, ff. 35–36; AHU, DA, Caixa 246, doc. 20; Miller, *Way of Death*, p. 365; Alexandre, *Os sentidos do império*, p. 212.

centuries the prestige of great and enlightened nations." The old world of privilege was giving way "to the beautiful system of freedom of thought, which is the solid basis of the happiness on which nations depend.... They also comprise the base, and removal of all obstacles against, the natural level achieved from the free activity of all those who operate the foundations of national wealth." With these words, the Count of Linhares extolled the prince for his liberal principles, penned one of his last writings, and several months later died. He passed away relieved that he had been the handmaiden of a new economic system while keeping—indeed in order to keep—the monarchy intact.[24]

The voice of the new political economy, and leading defender of the agreement with the British, was José da Silva Lisboa. Born in Bahia, Silva Lisboa completed his legal studies at the University of Coimbra in 1779, and became the deputy and secretary of the Board of Inspection of Agriculture and Commerce in Bahia. In this capacity he wrote several works advocating a reform of Portugal's commercial code and a series of pamphlets about political economy—and in 1808 joined the Count of Linhares' ministry as the deputy to the Royal Council of Trade in Rio de Janeiro. Eventually he went on to become the Bahian delegate to the Constitutional Assembly and later a senator of the empire, by which time he earned a noble title as the Viscount of Cairú for his services to the monarchy. Silva Lisboa argued that political economy was a science subject to abstract, objective principles, whose understanding can guide policymakers. In his 1804 pamphlet, *Princípios da economia política*, he inscribed a maxim he believed could serve as the leitmotif for a revitalized monarchy: "The security of people and legitimately acquired property," he wrote, "with the least possible restriction on the liberty of each individual, regulated by the common wealth of the human species and circumstances specific to the territory and state of each nation." The state, he believed, had the prime function of protecting property rights and extending the reach of the market as far as possible so that "commercial agents" could circulate commodities and help the provinces of the empire produce that which they are fittest to produce. No sooner was the open ports decree announced than Silva Lisboa reeled off a short pamphlet dedicated to the prince, assuring him that he would go down in history as "THE LIBERATOR OF TRADE." Indeed, the decree was more than a political expedient, it was "the constitutional law of Commercial Nations" because it maximized the extent of the market and created opportunities for reciprocal exchange and sociability among agents. Trade would beget

---

[24]Rodrigo de Souza Coutinho, "Apontamentos em Defesa do Tratado de Comércio de 1810," in his *Textos*, v. 2, pp. 398–400.

opulence, and Brazil would cease to be a colony subjected to the anti-quated rules of metropolitan mercantilism. With commercial freedom, Brazil would become a sovereign nation within a glorious empire.[25]

For all the appeal to reasoned self-interest as a means to transform private passions, Silva Lisboa's interventions contributed to a one-sided debate. It is difficult to say just how fortunate Brazilian subjects felt about the prince's announcements given the absence of a widespread and free press. Indeed, one of the differences between the two Iberian systems was the relative lack of unfettered "public" debate in the new Portuguese capital. The court had introduced the first printing press to Brazil, but it kept a tight hold on its heavily censored usage. There were salons, reading groups, and even more formal gathering points, but there was no contestatory press, as we saw explode in Spanish cities after 1808. As chapter 8 will show, a battle of words began to erupt in the Brazilian provinces only after 1816, and in the capital after 1820, which cascaded into what one Brazilian historian has called a war of "printed insults." For the time being, as we shall see shortly, the dissonance took place outside the still diminutive public sphere.

Yet what began as an effort to invoke a dispassionate discourse in the service of imperial renovation evolved into an impassioned defense of the new commercial order. Silva Lisboa portrayed the court's critics—and there were few in Brazil who had access to printing presses, while the disgruntled voices mainly found room in the London-based *Correio Brasiliense*—as defenders not just of a bygone era but as apostles of barbarism. He enlisted the writings of "eminent authors" to lambaste all those who wanted to thwart Brazil's common progress and protect the interests of particular agents, especially wielders of traditional privileges. Like Linhares, Silva Lisboa counterposed the protectors of particular privileges against liberators of the common good. Only more access to trading rights would allow all subjects to participate in productive and uplifting commercial activity. Expanding trade would thereby correct the misrepresentations of Brazil as a land of uncivil, barbaric folk, and replace it with a more charitable image of a people with healthy personal drives aligned with the "civilized" societies of the Atlantic world. But commercial opportunity could do yet more for the new center of the empire. He quoted

---

[25]Silva Lisboa, *Principios da economia política*, pp. 115–23; idem, *Observações sobre commercio Franco*, p. li. For some general discussion of the viscount's life and works, see António Almodovar, "Introdução," in José da Silva Lisboa, *Escritos económicos Escolhidos* (Lisboa: Banco de Portugal, 1993), v. 1, pp. xiii–xv; Antonio Penalves Rocha, "Economía política e política no periódo Joanino," in Tomás Szmrecsányi and José Roberto do Amaral Lapa, orgs., *História económica da independência e do império* (São Paulo: Ed. Hucitec, 1996), pp. 27–43.

Montesquieu's famous axiom about the wonders of doux commerce: "where there is commerce there is *doçura* of customs, and where there is *doçura* of customs there is commerce." Montesquieu's trope about how trade could calm private passions and convert them into reasoned interests was summoned here to argue that not only would colonists become better subjects, but freer trade would allow subjects of the empire to make the dominions more virtuous environments for a new civic, and therefore political, culture. To deny trading rights to Brazilians, as Silva Lisboa mis-leadingly represented the concerns of the regime's critics, was a recipe for disaster. Obstacles to commerce and fetters on entrepreneurial activity would sow vice and corruption. What is worse, Brazil would lose the free-doms necessary to guarantee its prosperity and sovereignty, and would fall prey to particular interests at the expense of the common weal. In his entreaty, Silva Lisboa invoked a venerable tradition—spawned by Machiavelli—of lumping the reasons of state, *ragione di stato*, with per-sonal *interesse*.[26]

This new synthesis was only conceivable by relocating the monarchy and the center of the empire to its periphery, free of the old interesse vested in monopoly and exclusion. In a sense, the survival of the dynasty required its exodus, but deliverance gave it a new lease on life, enabling it to imagine a more virtuous combination of reasons of state and private interests. Indeed, the Brazilian ecclesiastic, José Joaquim da Cunha Azeredo Coutinho, penned a dedication to Prince João in the 1811 reis-sue of his famous 1794 treatise, *Ensaio económico sobre o comercio de Portugal e suas colónias*. His short inscription pushed the logic of João's deliverance a step further. Here, he claimed, was a historic opportunity. Civilization, the churchman argued, developed in stages. First Egypt civi-lized Greece, then withdrew to become Greece's "first state." Then Greece civilized Italy, only to recede as Rome became the center of civilization. Italy did the same to the rest of Europe, and Europe carried the same civ-ilizing process on to America. The uplifting concatenation meant that now "America will realize the virility of its civilization" as a matter of destiny. But destiny could be betrayed—as the dark menace of Saint Domingue showed, which not only severed its ties with empire but over-threw a natural social order premised on the historic necessity of slavery. It was up to Brazil to show the world the virtues of a new model of empire

---

[26]José da Silva Lisboa, *Refutação das declamaçõens contra o commercio inglez extrahida de escritores eminentes* (Rio de Janeiro: Impressão Regia, 1810), p. iv; for a more developed sense of his views, see *Estudos do bem comum e economía política ou ciência das leis naturais e civis de animar e dirigir a geral industria e promover a riqueza nacional e prosperidade do estado* (Rio de Janeiro: Impressão Regia, 1819); Schultz, *Tropical Versailles*, pp. 197–207. Hirschman, *The Passions and the Interests*, p. 33.

and redeem it by becoming its new center. "How different would be the destiny of an empire founded on justice and virtue! Agriculture, the arts, science and commerce, animating the shadow of peace, would dispel from its midst laziness, ignorance and misery. The sovereign of the state would protect the different orders, and would be adored." Everything the prince had done since his deliverance suggested that he was up to the historic mission of rescuing civilization, not from primitive barbarism, but from an even more malicious threat: revolution.[27]

THE PRICE OF SOVEREIGNTY

How did the possessors of interesse view this emerging political economy? Official discourse freighted the fortunes of the monarchy on the fact that imperial merchants actually experienced the commercial transformations as doctrines predicted. Unfortunately for those like Linhares, Silva Lisboa, and Azevedo—whose restorationist dreams depended on a notion of particular subordination to the commonwealth—it was not always easy for merchants to cope with mounting expectations. Between a costly war in the south and the series of changes in commercial policy, sovereignty was coming at a price that they were being asked to pay. The crisis of Portuguese sovereignty inevitably destabilized the coalition between merchants and monarchs that held the ancien régime afloat in better times.

The reciprocity that supported the old regime—bolstering rents by curbing competition, in return for revenues for the treasury—was already under stress before Lisbon fell. Even before Junot's invasion of Portugal, the government had to deal with merchants who were defecting from the arrangement by illegally buying stocks of manufactured goods left behind by the British when they withdrew from Buenos Aires. But once the metropolis fell to France, the rent-for-revenue exchange fell apart as fiscal needs soared and traditionally protected markets were thrown open. To this point, the government dealt with "economic" policy as if the chief problem was contraband, the temptation by a few rogue subjects and mainly greedy interlopers to violate the basic rules of commerce. The government, prodded by merchants who did play by the rules and paid their taxes, issued injunction after injunction against "dishonorable" violators of imperial regulations. However, once British merchants were deprived of their European markets and fastened their eyes on Iberian America, government efforts to keep out interlopers were rather like trying to whistle in a storm. When the British vessel *Holy Star* sailed into Rio de Janeiro in

---

[27] Azeredo Coutinho, *Ensaio económico*, pp. 5–8.

June 1807, a Portuguese warship was sent to inspect the vessel and to interrogate the crew. There was plenty of merchandise all ready for sale. There was also a ship captain waving written orders from the most prominent houses in Rio de Janeiro replete with quantities and prices of requested contraband. The viceroy concluded his disconsolate report exclaiming that "almost all the Inhabitants of this country are contrabandists or their protectors!" They were also the merchants with whom the relocated monarchy had to conduct business to put the mercantile-monarchical pact back together.[28]

Difficulties mounted after the fall of Lisbon—indeed because of the fall of Lisbon—for the costs of deliverance and sustenance of the court that once rested on metropolitan shoulders now rested on Brazilian ones. Bringing the imperial regime in close quarters with powerful private agents in the colony did not make for a more intimate, frictionless combination; quite the contrary. The conflict in the southern borderlands aggravated relations between the court and Brazilian magnates, who were as dismayed to hear of personal ambitions of royal family members in the south as were the British. After all, they had sustained a brisk, lucrative, and stable coastal and slave trade between Pernambuco and Buenos Aires through thick and thin so long as the centers of power were still in Iberia. But as the question of defining imperial sovereignty evolved, raising the ante on the territorial extensions of the colonial possessions, colonial capitalists found that the autonomy they once enjoyed by virtue of their distance from the metropole and its dynastic troubles was now compromised and eventually challenged. As early as July 1807, after the British debacle in Buenos Aires, agents in Rio de Janeiro began to worry about the River Plate's stability and the effects on trade. Not the least of merchants' worries was the effect of the complete opening of the Buenos Aires market to British manufactures, reversing the historic flow of merchandise through the entrepôt of Rio de Janeiro. "It is impossible," noted one observer, "to overlook the imminent danger to the commerce of our colony from the Provinces of the River Plate, which are beginning to fall to English domination." Santa Catarina was aflood with smuggled goods. By 1812, the standards of coastal commerce, with the magnates of Rio de Janeiro playing the role of financiers and clearinghouses of the South Atlantic economy, were coming undone.[29]

The flood of British manufactures was one problem, assaults on Atlantic trade routes another. Consider the case of the giant merchant house of José Dias da Silva Guimaraens, when faced with a complaint by a smaller

---

[28]AHU, DA, Caixa 239, docs. 20, 24.
[29]AHU, DA, Caixa 240, doc. 49.

River Plate merchant, José Francisco da Costa, who claimed that the Brazilian had failed to pay for a shipment of hides. The resulting investigation of Silva Guimaraens, one of the large merchants operating a business emporium between Pernambuco, Bahia, Lisbon, Angola, and the River Plate, revealed how an entire webwork of credit, merchant bills, and contracts were now threatened by the political havoc ripping through the trading system. This *carioca* potentate had amassed enormous credits—and debts—and managed to keep his ledgers in the black so long as merchandise moved, payments flowed, and accounts cleared. The problems started with the Napoleonic blockades, mounted as French warships targeted sea-lanes off Africa and ravaged business when warfare erupted across the River Plate borderlands. When some of his clients, such as the Pernambucan trader José Baptista Ferreira, reneged on payments, Silva Guimaraens found himself overexposed and began to suspend payments on his own debts. Even worse was the wiping out of Lisbon's traders, who vanished with the Napoleonic occupation, taking their substantial debts to Silva Guimaraens with them. This plunged the Rio merchant from insolvency into bankruptcy, and whiplashed merchants all along the South American littoral. One of Silva Guimaraens's business associates based in Bahia, Anselmo José Antunes, informed the investigators that "all these disorders have thrown our commerce into convulsion, not only due to the general prohibition on the departures of our ships from America to Europe, because they cannot leave, nor load cargos ... at all." He pleaded to the Commercial Tribunal to uphold, in these difficult times, "the essential confidence of trade between merchants who have always lived in harmony with each other."[30]

Magistrates could not defend merchant honor from the upheavals. Another one of Rio de Janeiro's largest merchant families ran afoul of their partners. When the house of João Francisco de Lima, established in 1719 and run by "one of the principal Noble families in the same city of Rio de Janeiro which has always operated with much honor, seriousness and splendor," collapsed, its failure sent riptides across the South Atlantic trading system. Indeed, sorting out the confusing latticework of debts and credits taxed the patience of all involved. The house of de Lima tried to defend its honor and reputation against merchants who dragged them to the Commercial Tribunal. Pushed to the wall, the defendants threatened to disclose to the magistrates a pattern of endemic fraud and contraband long practiced by many of the merchants with which the house did regular business. The threat to expose creditors as malfeasants might force them to

---

[30]ANRJ, JC, Comerciantes, Caixa 377, pacote 3, s.n. case of José Francisco da Costa (1812).

back off their charges. It did not appear to work—and the ruin to the house of de Lima spread a contagion of distrust throughout the merchant community of Brazil.[31]

If fictive kinship networks holding the mercantile trust system together began to unravel under political and economic pressures of occupation and war, real kin ties also fell victim to the convulsion. When the Pernambucan merchant José Esteves de Aguiar and his brother, Julião Gervasio de Aguiar, based in Lisbon, decided to dissolve their partnership amicably in mid-1807, the mutual trust, and debts, got shredded by war. When it came time to settle their accounts, Marshal Junot controlled Lisbon, and Julião's trading network was cut off by the Continental System. José, in the meantime, had payments of his own to make and protested to the courts that his brother was withholding transfers. So much for merchants' harmony, never mind brotherly love. The entire imperial system, founded on fairly stable prices and robust trading networks across the South Atlantic, in fact turned out to be vulnerable. One set of minor defaults—never mind the ruin to metropolitan merchants— could set off a destructive chain reaction. When major magnates began to tremble, the coastal and transatlantic system felt the reverberations. Bad news in turn prompted many merchants to call in their loans and demand payments. Political insecurity thus hammered a once thriving system that rested on conventional systems of trust and merchant capital and that had raised merchant capital to colonial preeminence.[32]

INTERESTS AGAINST REASONS

The end of Portuguese metropolitan sovereignty shook up the links built up over centuries connecting Africa to South America and Europe. While the Count of Linhares tried to rescue the court from Europe, he could not contain some of the multiplier effects of European imperial warfare. He could not attenuate the damage visited upon the Atlantic trade routes, the mainstays for the fortunes of the merchant capitalists of the South Atlantic economy. Indeed, the count's efforts to restore monarchical grandeur in Rio de Janeiro only aggravated an already dire situation. Saving the ancien

---

[31]AHU, DA, Caixa 239, doc. 7.

[32]AN, JC, Caixa 378, pacote 3, doc. 12; AHU, CU, Códice 577, f. 211. Dozens of Lisbon merchants appealed for passports to leave Portugal and resettle in Brazil but in their petitions pleaded that they also be given clemency to protect them against Brazilian creditors who would file cases against them upon setting foot in the "colony." See AHU, DA, Caixa 242, doc. 55, Caixa 245, doc. 25.

régime came at a price—one that would be settled in the complicated bargaining between colonial merchants and the monarchy.

The restored empire still rested on a series of transactions. Early signals from merchant capitalists—those who were meant to be the prime beneficiaries of the new "liberal" order—reveal less enthusiasm for state policies than did the celebratory words that rolled off the official printing presses. This did not mean that grumbling was a low-volume challenge to the more abstract theories of modern political economy, nor even that grumblers questioned the legitimacy of regime. But the official justifications for public policies could not mask their private toll. To begin with, Britain enjoyed unobstructed access to Portuguese colonies, but Portuguese and Brazilian traders did not have reciprocal rights in British colonies. Another asymmetry was that British goods entering Brazil would face an ad valorem duty of 15 percent—lower than the levy issued even on Portuguese goods as a means to raise revenues (the going rate was 24 percent). Others, including Silva Lisboa himself, worried that falling tariffs on British trade would deprive the state of customs revenues. But these were mainly technical considerations buried deeper in the text of the treaty. What irked many Brazilian merchants was the immediate effect of competition by British traders in local markets and the increasing pressure by the British government on Brazilian slave traders. After so many generations of being able to contain market competition and regulate risks through colonial juntas' licensing systems, "free" trade felt like a perilous proposition.[33]

Predictably, metropolitan industrialists in Portugal took the biggest hit, first from the Napoleonic occupation and the enforcement of the Continental System, and then by their loss of preferential access to colonial markets after 1810. But their voices, while plenty and frantic, got little reception and made less difference. At best they got short-lived promises that the government would not apply the Commercial Treaty provisions immediately—which only inspired critical reprisals from London that the court was backsliding on its legal promises.[34] Ambrozio Joaquim dos Reyes sent the prince a series of memoranda from London warning of the dire consequences that would strike Portuguese trading from opening the imperial markets to British competition. Without an aggressive effort to promote imperial trading interests through a network of "Consulates"—a reconstituted Board of Trade—to defend the empire's shares of Atlantic

---

[33]Alexandre, *Os sentidos do império*, pp. 217–19; Lima, *D. João VI*, pp. 136–39.

[34]For a sample of the ways in which the court tried to defend metropolitan protections, see AN, JC, Caixa 361, pacote 1, doc. 19, pacote 2, doc. 20; ANTT, MNE, Caixa 729, n.n., file dated June 27, 1810. The contentious issues were the application of Article V on customs on British imports and the persistence of some metropolitan monopolies.

markets, Brazilian and metropolitan commercial capital would be overrun by the new competition. Free and reciprocal trade was fine; dos Reyes did not question the principles of the emerging order. But imperial capitalists needed stronger state backing to square off against their arrivistes rival capitalists. He noted that free trade did not mean that the government had no role in promoting prosperity. Jabbing at those who defended the new commercial order with high-minded principles, he added that "it is not necessary to resort to abstract doctrines of political economy, and it is enough to take a look at the history of industry in different European nations ... whose prosperity, wealth and power advanced when a merchant marine and a progressive state are united."[35]

Merchants in the colonies were also worried about the risks of the new order. They, too, questioned the verities of official rhetoric. Some worried that local distributors would be eclipsed by British importers and agents. Others worried about the advantage that British merchants had in modern business practice—echoing dos Reyes's concerns that the sudden dismantling of centuries of protection left Luso-Brazilian merchants unprepared for a trading system for which they had not been advocating. One appeal by a group of Bahian merchants urged the prince not to allow foreign merchants to set up shop in Brazil. In particular, if outsiders start to handle Brazil's staple trades, the empire will be doomed. The letter warned about the insidious penetration by "Gente Ecterodoxa." "Trade," the authors insisted, "to be equal must be merchandise for merchandise.... But the English do not want equal trade; they want to use all their advantages to receive less than a thousand in merchandise as they introduce ten thousand of theirs, wanting everything, and payable in gold." They concluded that opening the ports would end up "restricting the utilities that favor your faithful vassals."[36]

The opposition to trade opening did not come just from merchants in Bahia. Those in Rio de Janeiro also protested, as a petition from a group of merchants in the capital in late 1809 to the prince attests. It yielded to an exchange that exposed how little the merchant capitalists of the empire felt they controlled policymaking, and thus resented not being partners in the deal-making behind a restored empire. The petitioners applauded the monarchy's desire to promulgate good laws, obeying the norms of royal solicitation. But their supplicative preface was brief, giving way to a sharper text, informing the monarch of the "great shortage of Commerce, which

[35]ANTT, JC, Maço 51, Caixa 169, f. 2; MNE, Legação de Portugal da Inglaterra, Caixa 728, see entire case; also in BNL, I/32/13–14. For an analysis of how the changing commercial order affected metropolitan fortunes, see Pedreira, *Estructura industrial e mercado colonial*, pp. 307–26.

[36]BN, Bahia, Corpo de Comercio, I/31/28, 26.

due to the general upheaval of the universe has put the petitioners in complete decline, reduced for the most part only to the business of handling English merchandise." "There are," they added, "a large number of people who, contrary to the common utility of commerce … are infesting this Court, while publicly selling in the streets and private establishments all sorts of merchandise." They don't pay taxes; they don't respect the commercial customs of the country; and they undersell the upstanding members of the realm. The Royal Board of Trade should promote "the common good of Commerce" and must expunge "that type of person" from our midst. One of the prince's aides replied, denying their request, observing that "this request is impermissible, as it is contrary to the liberal principles of the freedom of trade and industry adopted at this time." The merchants did not take kindly to this response. When they received notification of the January 1808 decree throwing the ports open, "it appeared that the old system of restrictions had been virtually derogated." This was fine. What was not was the prospect that commerce might be enthralled to those who considered personal interests above the commonwealth. "We thought that the letter and spirit of this new liberal system of Economic Administration had the Royal intention to restore the natural justice of civic contracts [*contratos civis*]." Surely the goal of the court's policy was "to promote the common good of your vassals, to facilitate the means to live well off their useful labors which they loyally apply." So the problem was not so much reform in principle but the lawlessness of commerce, its rule by those unbound by common concerns and respect for the familiar traditions of the Luso-Brazilian mercantile world. Here were merchants who applauded Montesquieu's image of doux commerce but for whom the new order unleashed the unruly passions of individualists. In effect, what they advocated was reform—not dismantling—of the old mercantile regime, letting the existing Brazilian magnates enjoy their property as sovereign possessors of assets. This meant getting rid of lingering metropolitan restrictions, not creating competition from a new metropole based in London.[37]

To make matters worse, Brazilian magnates did not feel the effects of a dismantled order just at home. They also felt it in the backbone of the South Atlantic trading system: the slave trade. To be sure, Brazilian and Portuguese officials wanted to keep the slave trade clear of treaty negotiations. But the British government insisted, having recently abolished the slave trade within its trading orbit, that other nations follow suit. Accordingly, Article 10 of the 1810 treaty committed both countries to cooperate in abolishing the slave trade. As the Braganza dynasty was doubly dependent—on British support and on the lifeline of Atlantic

---

[37]Arquivo Nacional, JC, Caixa 379, pacote 1, s.n.

commerce and the slave trade—it was caught in a difficult squeeze. In the main, governments until 1851 formally agreed to phase out the slave trade while doing nothing—keeping an arm's length between promises and practices of curbing the slave trade.[38]

But official foot-dragging could not immunize Brazilian merchants from the effects of the new trading order on their slave trade. Brazilian merchants had to suffer the indignities of their slave vessels being seized, their cargos impounded, and fines levied off the coast of West Africa. When the Bahian merchant Ignacio Antunes Guimaraens saw his big slaver, *Providencia*, seized off the Mina Coast in 1813, 417 captives were released and an entire cargo lost (the tobacco rolls alone were worth 5.5 million reales). His total estimated losses were 50 million reales—and his plea to the Royal Board of Trade was futile. Others, like Francisco Joaquim Carneiro, had his new tumbeiro, *Triumphante*, meant to carry almost 650 slaves, taken in 1812 after it was cornered in Ajudá. The list of captured vessels grew longer—as did the inventory of dismayed merchants whose own government stepped back from defending their property. One of the biggest traders between Bahia and Benguela, Joaquim José de Andrade e Silva Menizes, not only lost part of his fortune when French troops took Portugal, but when he lost several vessels off the Mina Coast he was forced to declare bankruptcy, initiating a complex embargo on his assets and paralyzing part of the province's trade.[39]

When the curbs on slave traders dovetailed with the penetration of British wares into Portuguese commercial channels, the challenge for Brazilian merchants got even more daunting. British merchants may have dropped the slave trade, but they turned to Africa, as they had to Iberian America, to compensate for their losses in Europe and proceeded to ply the African coast in search of markets for their manufactures, finding the thriving slave-exporting emporia of the Mina and Angola Coasts a needed market for their wares. The problem for Brazilians was that this cut into their bilateral commerce of Brazilian staples, like tobacco, sugar, foodstuffs, and hides, in return for captives. Increasingly, they were asked by African traders to buy their slave cargos with precious metals that the African middlemen could then use to pay for British manufactures. Five Pernambucan merchants appealed to the prince to do something about "os Inglezes" who had taken away their African agents with their own merchandise, thus making it difficult to sustain the staples-for-slaves exchange. The governors

---

[38]For a good review of the issue, see Leslie Bethell, *The Abolition of the Brazilian Slave Trade* (Cambridge: Cambridge University Press, 1971).

[39]Arquivo Nacional, JC, Navegação, Caixa 410, pacote 1, docs. 8, 12, pacote 2, doc. 3; Comerciantes, Caixa 378, pacote 1, n.n., dated September 1812; Consulados Comerciais, Caixa 416, pacote 3, n.n., dated May 25, 1816.

of São Tomé and Principe informed the court in 1813 that the entire Mina Coast was infested with British traders, and that the customary commerce between Brazil and Africa, for which the islands served as way stations and provisioners, was under threat of extinction. They urged the government to open new slave-trading links beyond the routes of British frigates, and to promote some kind of Brazilian competition to sell to African merchants lest they lose complete control over the trade. Even as far south as Angola, where the British penetration was late in reaching, the commercial networks were disrupted severely enough to provoke a tumult within the Board of Merchants in 1810. Traders on the coast accused many factors in the interior of defecting on the customs of warehousing and organizing commercial fairs, "conducting themselves with notable criminal abuse of good faith, which is inseparable for contracts and gives confidence." As factors let British goods circulate in the Angolan interior, it depressed the terms of exchange for Brazilian staples and thus hiked the price of slaves. Coastal slave exporters to Brazil advocated the restoration of a regime "in which there were no impediments, and no serious motives, against the disposition of their Property."[40]

These complaints should not imply that the new commercial regime was choking the slave trade. The pressures tended to be localized, especially to Pernambuco and Bahia on one side of the Atlantic and the Mina Coast on the other. In these provinces, slave prices began to rise, and the commercial links began to break. The central channel between Rio de Janeiro and Angola thrived. Not only did it lie outside the routes of royal naval squadrons, but Rio could increase its entrepôt business, becoming almost the monopoly importing port from Africa. In 1808, 765 slave-trading vessels entered Rio de Janeiro; by 1810, the figure was 1,214. More broadly, between 1801 and 1839, fully 570,000 slaves entered Rio de Janeiro alone, by far the most important destination for African slaves in the world. What the griping suggests is a growing tension between the monarchy and merchant capitalists born as a result of the disruption of the endogenous circuits of accumulation generated over the course of the eighteenth century, and which upheld the mercantilist coalition. It was paradoxical that while the scale of the slave trade expanded in the decades after 1808, many slaving magnates nonetheless perceived that the court was not exactly their protector as the South Atlantic adapted to an emerging free trade regime. This would be a source of friction when the monarchy turned to merchants for financial support.[41]

---

[40]Arquivo Nacional, JC, Mesa de Inspecção, Caixa 179, pacote 1, doc. 4; Correspondencia y Consultas, Caixa 361, pacote 1, doc. 16, pacote 2, doc. 28; AHU, CU, Códices 551, ff. 35–36.

[41]Florentino, *Em costas negras*, pp. 31–51.

SOVEREIGNTY AND SOLVENCY

The drama of the Portuguese ancien régime began with the occupation of the metropole and evolved with the Americanization of the monarchy and the government's commercial policies from 1808 to 1810. It culminated with a fiscal crisis of the empire and a clash with merchants over the crown's desperate need for revenue. This brings us full circle to some unintended effects of the convergence between the regime and its former colonies, to which they now had to turn to cover the costs of restoring sovereignty. Ever since the unrest of the 1780s, Lisbon knew it had to be careful about tightening financial and fiscal screws on the colony. Perforce, that now changed, and was all the more urgent when the government plunged into warfare in the River Plate borderlands. Americanization of the monarchy did not resolve but simply relocated the underlying difficulties of the ancien régime. It placed the tensions over the rents-for-revenue transactions directly inside the hubs of South Atlantic merchant capitalism.

Even before the outbreak of war in the south, the crown had its fair share of fiscal problems. The costs of the war against the French, the evacuation, and setting up shop in Rio de Janeiro introduced a bevy of high bills to pay at a moment in which normal revenues declined precipitously with the closure of trade to Portugal. In response, six new taxes rolled off the statute books between 1808 and 1810, and officials were instructed to apply existing levies with energy and diligence. The customs levies and collecting systems were harmonized with an eye toward generating revenues and not protecting industries, especially in the metropole. Export taxes, for instance, flattened to an even 6 percent on all staples in July 1809; as of 1810, adult slave imports carried a levy of 200 reales, children, 100. Also, to cover immediate needs, the government invited merchants to make voluntary contributions. The court was so desperate for resources it took revenue payments in kind. Sacks of flour or rice were accepted through the first year of the court's life in Rio de Janeiro. The court also accepted special contributions to pay for the rescue of Portuguese subjects caught in Algeria.[42]

Raising basic revenues, however, was easier decreed than done. From the lofty heights from which the court viewed the world, especially one to which it had been so recently introduced, the prince was unaware of just how much the state structure had been destroyed by the Napoleonic occupation, and how thin the administrative apparatus of the colony had been on the eve of his arrival. The Brazilian state may have been placed on the

---

[42] Arquivo Nacional, JC, Mesa de Inspecção, Caixa 178, pacote 2, n.n.; JC, Correspondencia y consultas, Caixa 361, pacote 3, doc. 17; BNRJ, Secção Manuscritos, II, 34, 26, 19, "Representação dos proprietários, . . . a S.A.R., "December 1811; *Gaceta do Rio de Janeiro*, October 14, 1808, November 24, 1810.

course to its own sovereignty, but there was not much of an administrative system to secure its solvency. Upon arriving in Brazil, the court scrambled to allocate positions to the officials who accompanied the massive retinue, but of course immediately ran into the dilemma of how to pay for its cadre of bureaucrats without a revenue base. Indeed, having issued the call for more money, the court had to enlist collectors. After the first few tax decrees, the president of the royal treasury advised the prince that he lacked the personnel to expedite the job and conceded that he would have to auction positions as tax collectors.[43]

Merchants, faced with rapidly changing commercial rules, losses from the collapse of the metropolitan corner, and conflicts with former trading partners especially in the south, did not find the cluster of revenue demands easy to absorb. Five merchants from Pernambuco pleaded that their personal rents had so contracted that they could not oblige the crown's new taxes. In particular, they had to face rising competition: "the damage caused by the intrusions made by the English . . . and now the unloading of goods in unknown ports and beaches, deprecating the public markets where we are accustomed to conduct our shipping," made it impossible to pay higher taxes. Meanwhile, in Bahia tobacco producers and shippers also pleaded penury. While they thanked the prince for his goodwill, they enclosed a long list of grievances from the high levels of taxes to the poor prices earned on their staples. Bahian sugar magnates issued an identical appeal at the very same time. The protests were not restricted to provincial ports. In January 1810, fifty-three powerful merchants from Rio de Janeiro signed a collective petition to the prince. They acknowledged their "indisputable dependence" on the crown, but "under the current circumstances in which the general interest in shipping has declined due to the interruption of trade with Europe, and as we are more burdened with taxes and must spend inordinate time dealing with the disruptions and inconveniences of trips," hardship is the order of the day. In conclusion, although they acknowledged the importance "of the good of the State and the attention to the public cause," these merchants "cannot but proclaim themselves opposed to the particular and arbitrary impositions."[44]

Facing a hobbled state, it was fairly easy for merchants to protect their own rents by resisting the court's revenue demands. In so doing merchants created a solvency crisis to compound the state's sovereignty crisis. As the

---

[43] Arquivo Nacional, JC, Topographica, Caixa 770, pacote 2, doc. 23; AHU, DA, Caixa 243, docs. 3, 37; Barman, *Brazil*, p. 47.

[44] Arquivo Nacional, JC, Mesa de Inspecção de Pernambuco, Caixa 179, pacote 1, doc. 4; JC, Consulados Comerciais, Caixa 416, pacote 1, n.n., appeal, April 26, 1809; JC, Comerciantes, Caixa 378, pactoe 3, n.n., appeal, September 7, 1809; AHU, DA, Caixa 246, doc. 20.

prince grappled with the challenges of restoring the imperial commercial system, urging his merchants to reclaim their positions in the trade with Africa and Asia, one of his aides reminded him that merchants would not even contribute to pay for warships to defend the sea-lanes. The prince responded with a futile order to raise funds to pay for an armed escort for a large tobacco shipment from Bahia to Macau. A customs official, tired of being snubbed by those who were supposed to pay their dues, complained to the royal treasury about the "tremendous laxity and indolence, and above all the sordid interest with which the Royal Revenues and principal bases of the political economy are viewed." Merchants had little respect for public custodians, he lamented. The Count of Linhares wrote to his brother Domingos in London, telling him that the royal treasury had been "plundered."[45]

Linhares was despondent. His efforts to defend monarchy pushed it to the edge of insolvency. Still, he never lost his vision of public policy, building on his readings in political economy, to map state institutions and policies onto social and economic realities shaped by freely operating market forces (chapter 3). In this sense, he inverted a longstanding mercantilist tradition, including Pombal's, which sought to have private practices and habits conform to a grander state design. Now, giving such autonomy to private interests from the reasons of state may have complied with modern intellectual precepts. But it also dramatized the dependence of the state on private fortunes over which it was now giving up even more authority. In one of his final reports to the prince, the dying minister informed the ruler that the entire fiscal edifice of the regime was at risk. Was it up to the task to rescue itself by embracing modern principles and making them practice? More pressingly, how would the state make up for its revenue needs in order to reform? The count's concerns inevitably led him to the issue of money and debt. As he had been insisting for almost two decades, the minister called for a funding system that would be able to convey the treasury through good times and bad. To ensure that spending be supported through ups and downs, the state should be able to borrow money in lean years (so that taxes would not have to rise when subjects were least able to afford hikes) and repay in abundant ones (when subjects could afford to pay taxes). In the long run, with proper management, Brazil's trade would flourish enough to generate the customs revenues to liquidate existing loans and put the treasury on a path to solvency. The short-run cornerstone was the creation of an amortization fund and a proper monetary institution to handle the emission

---

[45]AHU, DA, Caixa 245, doc. 2; BNRJ, Mesa de Inspecção, Caixa 178, n.n., report, April 28, 1810; ANTT, MNE, Caixa 730, n.n., doc. November, 30, 1811.

of paper notes—thus showing creditors that the state was committed to earmarking future revenues to pay off the loan while printing more money to meet the immediate shortfall. To manage this "public credit" system, a public bank was "necessary to consolidate the fluctuating debt which is in arrears in all captaincies, and which has until now enriched many usurers, impoverished the Royal Treasury, and robbed from unfortunate creditors who make cruel sacrifices on their property which has often been taken from them violently for the Royal Treasury."[46]

In theory, therefore, this funding scheme was supposed to refashion state finances and make it comply with the interests and capacities of private agents—and not to force merchant capitalists to mold to the reasons of state. But it did not automatically make the proposal more compelling to those who had to fund it. On August 4, 1808, Rio de Janeiro's elite merchants gathered to commit themselves to contributing to a metallic money base that would operate as the backbone of a bank owned by private shareholders. On October 12, 1808, the government issued a decree announcing the birth of the Banco do Brasil. The preamble to the decree did not mince words about the relationship between the privately owned bank and the crisis of the ancien régime: in light of the royal mint's inability "to realize the funds upon which the Monarchy depends for its maintenance," this "public bank" was created to "facilitate the means and resources to cover the State's expenses and the public's needs." This was of course a compromise between private and public interests. But framed in this fashion, the bank's own twenty-year charter created something of a dilemma that would plague the final years of the ancien-régime empire. Would the bank cater to the private needs of financiers or the public demands of borrowers?[47]

Part of the problem of the new Banco do Brasil lay in its design; part of the problem was the context in which private agents were being asked to have confidence in the state bank. The travails of the Banco do Brasil show how difficult it was to reconstitute imperial sovereignty when the magnates who were supposed to foot the bill were still wary of the regime's credibility. The bank had a twofold mandate. First, it was to create a monetary base—out of paper money—that would alleviate chronic scarcity of tender

---

[46]Souza Coutinho, "Representação a S.A.R. o Príncipe Regente sobre o restablecimento da fazenda real" (September 7, 1811), in his *Textos*, v. 2, pp. 360–62. It is worth noting that this tension within the bank's mandate had been anticipated, but not resolved, in Souza Coutinho's initial proposals. See ANRJ, JC, Secretaria de Estado, Caixa 642, pacote 1, doc. 2, undated memo, R. de Souza Coutinho to the prince. He did insist that for such an enterprise to work, it needed the full confidence of the merchant class—and accordingly had to be run by "an Assembly of Businessmen." For more documents and some discussion, see Pinto de Aguiar, *Bancos no Brasil colonial* (Bahia: Livraria Progresso, 1960).

[47]De Melo Franco, *Historia do Banco do Brasil*, pp. 15–26.

for private transactions. Second, it had to handle the funds of the royal treasury and discount public bills, in effect mediating between private pools of capital and the state's resource needs. Meeting these two objectives while having to scramble for investors would have been a feat in itself. But to accomplish this when the relationship between the state and local capitalists was so strained was a major obstacle to the bank's becoming Linhares's dream of an effective agent to smoothen the revenue bulges while creating a new credible monetary system. The prince ordered his ministers in early 1809 to "convoke the corps of merchants and to explain to them the general and private advantages of the existence of this bank." Still, three years after its inauguration, only 126 shares (of 1,200 initial issues) found investors. In desperation, by September 1813, the crown offered royal titles and honors to anyone who bought more than three shares. The Banco do Brasil did not really acquire the capital necessary to begin handling public bills or operating commercially until 1817. In the first years of activity, therefore, bank directors printed paper notes without the backing of reserves. Between 1810 and 1815, the supply of banknotes in circulation soared from 160,000 to 1.2 million, yielding to creeping inflation. This only reinforced the image among many merchants that the bank's and the government's commitments to fiduciary stability and financial security were not credible.[48]

In spite of the Count of Linhares's high standing, merchants never saw his financial proposals as much more than a burden. Indeed, the invitation for merchants to place their deposits and to purchase shares in the new bank while at the same time having to shoulder rising taxes was hardly a confidence-building combination. But when the court began defaulting on its own obligations to local capitalists who had assumed earlier debts, merchants practically began boycotting official decrees. Miguel Pareiro observed that "the new system" did introduce some improvements, but that something was needed to replace the bankrupt old financial regime. The arrears in the payment on bills "to different peoples at convenient points" were beginning to breed unrest among Rio de Janeiro's investors. In early 1812, Rafael da Cruz Guerreira shared his sober views with the Count of Funchal, noting the deterioration of the monarchy's finances. What worried him most was "the difficulty between the Bank of Brazil and this Administration in light of the [dismal] news ... about the state of the Royal Treasury, and in view of the news the British Government has probably received from their own agents here." This news added up to "imperial orders of forced seizures, which I confess I do not admire, and which

---

[48]Ibid., pp. 24–34; Harold B. Johnson, Jr., "A Preliminary Inquiry into Money, Prices, and Wages in Rio de Janeiro, 1763–1823," in Alden, ed., *Colonial Roots of Modern Brazil*, p. 244.

is repugnant to the British Government as it enters into new Contracts for new Loans."[49]

Thus, in the first three years of the monarchy's life in the New World, it was still bereft of basic monetary and fiscal machinery, while its commercial policies had been devised without consulting or warning merchants and the costs of defending the realm's sovereignty were rising. The combination put enormous strains on the alliance of merchants and monarchs that once held together the Luso-Atlantic world. Looming insolvency began to threaten the sovereignty of the regime. While merchants did not quite express disloyalty to the monarchy, they certainly did not comply with financial demands and rules the monarchy had devised for its own survival.

The New Dependency

Unable to get Brazilian magnates to bankroll its operations, and seeing what monetary emissions were doing to inflation in Brazil, the court turned to external, British sources of money. Foreign sources, the prince's advisors hoped, would solve the twin problems of sovereignty and solvency. Their hopes for external financial salvation were reinforced by the activities of a clutch of British business magnates in London, members of the Brazil Society, who advocated closer economic ties between Brazil and Britain. In early 1809, the court announced that it secured a loan of 600,000 pounds sterling in Britain, while it was also negotiating the Commercial Treaty. Indeed, the desperation for immediate funds forced the Brazilian government to make the trade concessions that were so uncomfortable to Portuguese subjects on both sides of the Atlantic. The trade-off was, in the view of the Count of Linhares, a lamentable necessity. In May 1809, he admitted to his brother Domingos, the London point man in both negotiations, that the timing was most unfortunate. It was clear that London could threaten to withhold money to force Brazilian trade negotiators to sweeten the commercial deal. Domingos discovered that the Brazil Society may have promoted his country's interests in Britain—but it was also urging the British government to press hard for maximal trade concessions, knowing that Rio de Janeiro was desperate for money and would go to great lengths to secure a loan. It seems quite likely, therefore, that the unequal treaties of 1810 bore a price the government was willing to pay for its financial survival—a price

---

[49]ANTT, MNE, Caixa 37, doc. 5; Caixa 731, n.n., April 7, 1812. This was also the view as far as London; see Domingos de Souza Coutinho's own private views in MNE, Caixa 729, n.n., Rodrigo de Souza Coutinho to Domingos de Souza Coutinho, May 9, 1810.

that would have to be paid when the foreign loan came due, a classic case of securing the present at the expense of the future.[50]

Negotiations over money and granting more trade concessions in return for a loan got caught up in the spiral of the regime's weakening position. To start with, the bulk of the foreign loan was intended to pay off older British debts and to pay for the costs of the peninsular war against French troops—not to cover immediate spending in Brazil. This was about all the British were willing or able to invest in; they had their own war effort to finance. But the monarchy in Rio de Janeiro still held out for more money to consolidate itself in its new environment. Appeals for more money faltered. Domingos noted to his brother that British investors were growing increasingly queasy as the news of Brazil's financial troubles filtered in to London. British investors who had sunk their money into Portuguese bonds were now crying foul as the court accumulated arrears. The Count of Linhares, aware of how time was *not* on his side, urged his colleagues to hurry up and approve the Commercial Treaty so that they could remove one source of anxiety. Indeed, the longer the treaty, and thus the new loan, got postponed "the more I consider the urgent necessity of some sort of extraordinary pecuniary help to pay for our armies."[51] He breathed a huge sigh of relief when the signed treaty was dispatched to London to arrive in July 1810—in time, he hoped, to kindle interest among British financiers in a loan to Rio de Janeiro.

Time was not on his side. No sooner did news of the treaty reach London than mayhem broke out across the remnants of the Spanish empire. In August 1810, when the news arrived in London of the uprisings in Caracas and Buenos Aires, British authorities grew even more alarmed at the state of affairs in South America and the prospects of looming anarchy among Britain's allies and critical markets for its merchandise. This only fueled the Count of Linhares's eagerness to send an army into the River Plate to pacify the region and dispel foreign alarm. Seizing and consolidating the possession of the southern borderlands and the lucrative River Plate, the minister hoped, might also bolster the monarchy's appeal to foreign investors. While launching an armed assault in mid-1811, Linhares suggested to the Count of Funchal that the government should pursue secret negotiations with the Spanish Cortes in Cádiz, leading to the fusion of both Iberian powers in the war against Napoleon. Not only would this display a common resolve and reduce the costs of fighting the

---

[50] ANTT, MNE, Caixa 728, n.n., Rodrigo de Souza Coutinho to Domingos de Souza Coutinho, May 10, 1809.

[51] ANTT, MNE, Caixa 729, n.n., Rodrigo de Souza Coutinho to Forjaz, June 27 and August 29, 1810.

French foes, thereby winning favor from the British government, it would secure the fate of monarchy in Iberian lands—thus making them more enticing for the foreign investor. In fact, the British saw the excursion into the River Plate as a waste of money and a consolidated Iberian regime as a potential monolith. In any event, the Count of Linhares deeply miscalculated Cádiz's own resolve to defend the status quo. His own brother had to warn the Brazilian government that the "spirit of insurrection," especially in Buenos Aires, was damaging for all Iberian sides.[52]

This was the context in which Domingos de Souza Coutinho tried to enter into serious negotiations with Wellesley for a guarantee from the British government to make such a sizable loan (the prince wanted 1.5 million pounds) acceptable to London financiers. Under pressure from Wellesley, the Brazilian regime agreed to a temporary cease-fire in the River Plate and acceded to demands to use the funds only for the original obligations to pay British financiers. The foreign secretary also got Rio de Janeiro to agree to cooperate more eagerly in the suppression of the Atlantic slave trade (which irritated Brazilian magnates even more). The Foreign Office still refused to guarantee a large private loan, and simply propped the ailing Braganza regime with increments of "subsidiary aid" mainly to cover the costs of the peninsular military campaign.[53]

The Brazilian regime finally abandoned hopes of a British government guarantee and went, cap in hand, straight to the financiers. The Count of Funchal met with Alexander Baring to talk about a small loan of 130,000 pounds. Baring made it clear that such a credit would be unlikely, despite its modesty. It could only be guaranteed on Lisbon's revenues, where "it must produce at least as great an effect in draining the peninsula of specie as could result from any other operations from hence for which our means are more extensive and more varied." Lisbon by this time (late 1812) was free of French soldiers, but it was utterly penurious. And the plausibility of any further lending depended wholly on the strength of Brazilian revenues. With the conflict in the River Plate draining Rio de Janeiro's finances, Baring did not see how a loan on Brazilian revenues would inspire any more confidence. For all the concessions and pleas, no significant private money was forthcoming. The notion that a large foreign loan would make up for the lack of merchant confidence in the regime did not materialize. As the Count of Linhares passed away in early 1812, the regime to which he had devoted decades of public service

---

[52]ANTT, MNE, Caixa 729, n.n., Domingos de Souza Coutinho to Rodrigo de Souza Coutinho, May 9, August 13 and 29, 1810, Domingos de Souza Coutinho to Forjaz; Caixa 37, doc. 8.

[53]ANTT, MNE, Caixa 730, n.n., Domingos de Souza Coutinho to Wellesley, January 18 and July 15, 1811; Caixa 731, Funchal to Galveas, August 4 and December 5, 1812.

may have been delivered from French armies, but it still hung on the edge of insolvency and turmoil along its Brazilian frontiers.[54]

CONCLUSION

Five years after the deliverance of the Portuguese monarchy from the center of its empire its survival was not in doubt, but its sovereignty was still in question. Hounded by French occupants, severed from its metropolitan roots, and at odds with much of the colonial merchant class, the prince and his ministers maneuvered to enlist external—that is, British—military and financial support. To keep Brazil out of the French orbit, British forces were willing to defend the Braganza dynasty, which was enough to keep the monarchy intact even though the peninsular-centered empire was dashed. By contrast, the Spanish regime's refusal to cut metropolitan ties preserved the centrality of the peninsula to the empire but weakened the regime's sovereignty in the colonies.

The conjuncture opened by the Napoleonic occupation of Portugal thus appeared to usher in a structural break that differed from Spain's, but a break nonetheless. The Americanization of the monarchy and the empire forced the regime to adapt to a new world. Ports were opened to the rest of the world; treaties lowered trade barriers; old licensing practices that restricted trading rights vanished. Legally, nothing stood between the industrial revolution of northwest Europe and the vast staple-producing hinterlands of Brazil. All this was dressed in the finery of "political economy." Indeed, the prince's advisors launched a rhetorical campaign to legitimate royal decrees in terms of a rupture with tradition and an embrace of modern economic doctrine. Idealist convictions no doubt helped give these changes a patina of enlightened inspiration, but it is hard to resist concluding that there was a measure of spinning a virtue out of necessity. Deep-seated commercial reform was also a survival measure to earn British favor and enlist the support of Brazil's merchant elites precisely because the monarchy's metropolitan foundations were so shaken.

Emphasis on the survival or even "persistence" of the dynasty should not obscure important changes. The most important was that the regime was brought into more intimate contact with the sources of social and economic power in its former colonies—which occasioned adaptations and frictions. "Free" trade and restrictions on the slave trade were irritants, but they also helped restructure without revolutionizing Brazilian capitalism. For starters, the trade in unfree Africans remained the bulwark

---

[54]ANTT, MNE, Caixa 733, n.n., Funchal to Galveas, November 18, 1812.

of its economy. Rio de Janeiro had been the largest slave-importing port in the New World before 1807; thereafter, shipments rose even more. No port in history imported as many slaves as the Brazilian capital did when it became the center of the Portuguese empire. A boon to local planters and merchants, this was a constant annoyance to the British. After meeting with the new foreign secretary, Lord Castlereagh, who warned that the Royal Navy was going to step up its patrols, Count Funchal lamented that the British government did not choose to apply modern political economy to this business, as it did with all others. Instead, they viewed the slave trade "with a blindness and ardor which equals other times of Religious Fanaticism, whether sincere or affected!" On the other hand, having failed to secure the demise of the traffic in unfree laborers, the British did triumph in unlocking markets in Brazil. Irritants and disruptions from changes to commercial regulations did not destroy but forced an adaptation and subsequent flourishing of the underlying model of commercial accumulation based on staples and slaves.[55]

The adaptation of merchant capitalism provided an important bulwark of stability in Brazil, but it also put merchant classes in much closer, frictional contact with the core of political power. Until the deliverance, colonial merchants operated at an important degree of remove from the monarchy. Largely self-regulating, colonial merchants dominated their own autonomous circuits of exchange in the South Atlantic without much metropolitan intrusion, almost sheltered from a state it did little to fund. Crowding the two, merchants and monarchs, into the same new center, Rio de Janeiro, had ambiguous effects that would continue to unfold until the final caesura with Lisbon. One immediate effect was abrasion. Revenue demands, exposure to foreign competitors, and the creeping instability of paper money deepened a wedge between merchants and the monarchy. Conflict was not the only consequence. The dependence of the monarchy on the support of Brazilian merchant magnates was now transparent. So when it came to deciding state policy and designing the institutional makeup of Brazil's new political economy, merchants could—and soon would—have unrivaled access to the corridors of courtly power. The struggle for control of state policy in the new empire became a means by which Brazilian merchants compensated for the sense of uncertainty posed by the market experience.

The costs of deliverance also compelled adaptation of a regime that was now expected to live by different norms, norms inscribed in its own rhetoric. Silva Lisboa, the most prolific of the prince's coterie of enlightened

---

[55]ANTT, MNE, Caixa 733, n.n., Funchal to unknown, April 1, 1813; Florentino, *Em costas negras*, pp. 51–52; Fragoso, *Homens de grossa aventura*, pp. 79–83.

ministers and aides, argued relentlessly that the monarchy survived because of the depth of the metropolitan crisis. Coming to Brazil delivered the dynasty from the scourge of revolution—and opened the ruling family's eyes to the true potential of rule of enlightened monarchs. In the New World, free of the legacies of feudalism and exempt from the siren calls of revolution stoked by the misery of industrial cities, property owners could practice "the genuine principles of sociability"—trading, investing, polite commercial sociability. For Silva Lisboa, the source of instability for anciens régimes in Europe—monarchy's dependence on privileged but fickle aristocrats—was reconstituted in Brazil as a harmony of enlightened rulers and patricians. Out of the crisis of sovereignty could emerge a more perfect empire and a more solid monarchy—slavocrat salvation for an Atlantic world engulfed in revolution.[56]

Translating norms into practices involved a new relationship with society, not just with the urban magnates with whom arrangements were supposed to be so mutually beneficial. Such a restoration, however, was incomplete and precarious. It was also subject to contingencies shaped by events beyond Portuguese imperial borders. What the rulers in Rio de Janeiro could not imagine would be how the wars that were now spreading across Spanish South America would eventually push a shaky Portuguese monarchy to the edge of its own revolution.

---

[56]José da Silva Lisboa, *Observações sobre a Prosperidade do Estado pelos Liberales Principios da Nova Legislação do Brasil* (Rio de Janeiro: Impressão Regia, 1810), p. 8; idem, *Observações sobre o comercio franco no Brasil*, pp. 97–107.

7 Dissolutions of the Spanish Atlantic

INTRODUCTION

With Napoleon's defeat a reactionary spirit began to sweep the Old World. Ruling classes and dynastic regimes agreed to set aside old rivalries and expunge the forces of instability within Europe. In 1814, the king of Spain, Ferdinand VII, reclaimed his throne in Madrid and vowed to restore Spanish grandeur. This was the moment in which Spanish South Americans had to choose between folding back into a restored imperium or forging ahead beyond empire, in isolation. The choice was sobering, made worse by the recognition that this would be not just a fight against distant Spain but, as Simón Bolívar noted in a manifesto to Venezuelans in September 1814, a conflict among cousins at home. Faced with this confusion and potential carnage, even Bolívar's resolution faltered, "for even as Justice warrants the boldness of undertaking [our cause], the impossibility of its accomplishment only reflects the inadequacy of the means."[1] It looked as if Ferdinand could put an end to home-rule movements in the colonies. Yet, this is exactly what did not happen. Spanish restoration transformed a struggle over local sovereignty within empire into a civil war, and thence into a revolution that shattered Spanish sovereignty in the Atlantic world.

Sorting out the steps from the breakdown of metropolitan sovereignty to the breakup of empire requires an approach that does not presume their inevitability. We have for too long presumed a teleological appeal of colonists' desire for exit from colonialism. Imperial breakdown challenged colonists to reimagine the conditions of their subject-hood, but for the most part still within imperium. It did not predict a breakup of empire. Indeed, imperial endurance was more than a possibility; for many dominions, the European convergence after Napoleon's defeat eliminated a principal source of the crisis: imperial rivalry.[2]

---

[1]Simón Bolívar "Manifesto to the People of Venezuela" (September 7, 1814), in Bierck, ed., *Selected Writings*, v. 1, p. 81.

[2]Lawrence Stone, "Theories of Revolution," *World Politics* 18:2 (1966): 159–176; Michael S. Kimmel, *Revolution: A Sociological Interpretation* (Oxford: Polity, 1990), pp. 9–10.

As a condition for understanding imperial breakup, we need to account for the failure of restoration, the fate of loyalism, and how a struggle over home rule became a revolution—in effect, how the crisis of the ancien-régime empire led to revolutions and not the reverse order of events. Two immediate factors were crucial transformers, both of which contributed to colonists' reappraisal of the loyalties that had once inspired them to exercise a "voice" in favor of empire and eventually an option of "exit" from empire. The first was the decision on the part of metropolitan authorities to stamp out secessionism repressively; the Spanish Atlantic went through a counterrevolutionary process before there was a real revolution: reaction preceded, indeed spawned, the revolution. In so doing, the Spanish monarchy alienated the very subjects it wanted to reintegrate into the empire. The second was partly a result of the metropolitan reaction, the irremediable break in the cohesion of ruling blocs of the empire, especially the composition of merchant capital that held the Iberian commercial systems together. The combination of counterrevolutionary violence and the shattering of ruling blocs diminished the appeals of loyalism and the opportunity costs of the exit option, breaking away in favor of something new.

THE STALEMATE

Before Ferdinand's return to Madrid to restore his pseudo-absolutist regime, the secessionist cause was on the run. Most secessionists had been defeated or were on their heels. The rest were at odds with each other. This enabled loyalists to recover ground. Indeed, by 1812, only a few outposts around the River Plate, the eastern parts of Venezuela, and a few provinces in Nueva Granada lingered in the hands of secessionists. It looked as if loyalist domains, like Viceroy Abascal's command over an enlarged and stoutly royalist "Peru" (which now extended its might from Quito to Potosí), anticipated a more general restoration of imperium in South America.

Yet, the upheavals of imperial breakdown did leave deep scars and contoured future restorations. The struggle for sovereignty militarized politics that culminated less in a decisive victory for any side than a protracted stalemate. The nature of the war shaped some short- and long-term effects. For both sides, "holding the line," defending and consolidating a position against the enemy, was extremely difficult. Given the power vacuum and the absence of authority on either side, a victory in one corner meant exposure to the enemy from other corners; gaining control of Caracas left Maracaibo open; seizing Cartagena left Santa Marta to the enemy; Buenos Aires went secessionist and Montevideo stayed loyalist. The result

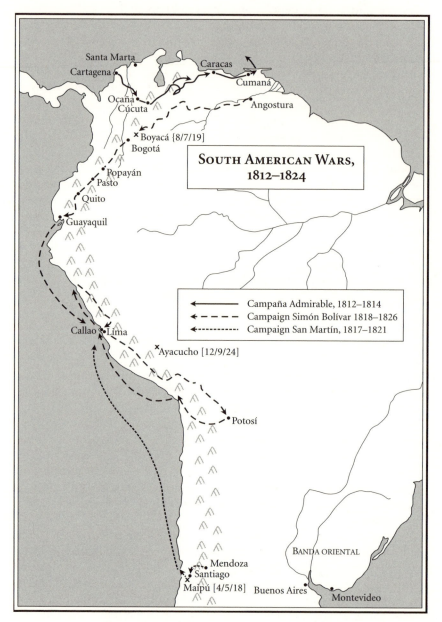

Figure 4. South American wars, 1812–1824.

was inconclusive seesawing across plains and valleys. Furthermore, in the absence of professional standing armies, a different kind of fighting force emerged. Covering such large terrains and maintaining mobility meant that slow-moving infantry and artillery were handicapped tools in the see-saw war of position. Especially in rainy seasons, these prominent features of European warfare became a military liability in South America's skir-mishing, getting bogged down on steep mountain slopes or in the mire of the Llanos or Pampas, which turned into gluey swamps with a downpour. Military advantage tilted to smaller, agile, and faster units of mounted fighters, the so-called *montoneras*. This form of fighting aggravated the inconclusiveness not of battles but of war since the enemy could be beaten, but not into submission. Enemies could therefore withdraw to engage another day, at another crossroads.

In the long run, the stalemated war transformed the social structures of political control: it militarized public authority, shifting control from magistrates, viceroys, and the civilian patriotic leadership to officers who rose up through the ranks of loyalist and rebel cavalries, often from the ranks of plebeian fighters themselves. This kind of militarized politics also shifted the theater of political struggle from traditional centers in cities to the countryside, where the recruits, and increasingly the resources neces-sary for sustaining the war, were concentrated. Whereas cities like Buenos Aires, Caracas, Cartagena, and Quito were the nodal points of the vac-uum in 1810, the struggle vaporized into rural backlands where vying for territory and cities raged—and as it did so, civil wars then evolved into countrywide revolutions.[3]

Colonial spaces, once integrated and dominated by urban civilian authorities, fragmented. The largest of the viceroyalties, the River Plate, was perhaps the most dramatic example—though not the most violent—of decomposition. The coalition that deposed the viceroy in Buenos Aires quarreled endlessly within itself. Still, one thing the porteño patriciate did agree on was that the port city had to keep a grip on the outlying provinces to keep the city's fortunes intact. To ensure compliance with decisions made in Buenos Aires, the vanguard dispatched military expe-ditions to far-flung provinces to "liberate" them from officers who still obeyed Cádiz. But instead of meeting crowds delighted to be freed, each one of the expeditions ran into fierce resistance, and left the viceroyalty irremediably fractured.[4]

[3]Christon I. Archer, "Setting the Scene for an Age of Warfare," in Archer, ed., *The Wars of Independence in Spanish America* (Wilmington, DE: Scholarly Resources, 1999), pp. 8–31.

[4]Juan Canter, "El año XII, las Asambleas Generales y la Revolución del 8 de octubre," in Ricardo Levene, ed., *Historia de la nación Argentina* (Buenos Aires: El Ateneo, 1941), v. 5:2, pp. 403–511; Adelman, *Republic of Capital*, pp. 84–91.

For the leaders in Buenos Aires the critical link was to the Andes. Preserving the ancient axis between the sources of silver and Atlantic markets was the lifeline for any future—within imperium or not. Silver flows were the main sustenance for revenues to finance the fledgling regime, as well as for rents to support the mercantile magnates in the capital. Accordingly, the first "Liberating Army" under Juan José Castelli, a follower of Mariano Moreno and the radicals, marched out of Buenos Aires in mid-1810. After winning the Battle of Suipacha in November, the small army marched on to "free" Potosí, abolishing Indian tributes and forced labor schemes along the way. But even before the Buenos Aires forces reached the altiplano, a royal judge from Chayanta warned the retreating authorities that Indians were already gathering to elect their representatives to the new assemblies. Rumors swirled that Ferdinand had been killed in Europe, and local villagers proclaimed that they would accept no pretenders in his place. Irate mine owners grumbled about the Buenos Aires leaders who, they felt, had been overwhelmed by Enlightenment delirium and a Rousseauian fit to restore the "natural" dignity of indigenous folk. By the time Castelli's force reached Lake Titicaca, it was overstretched, surrounded by furious Spaniards and creoles, and no match for the seasoned Andean royal army perched in the highlands to prevent a repeat of the 1780s Indian uprising. On June 20, 1811, Spanish forces crushed the patriots and drove them back to Tucumán. Subsequent expeditions to restore the silver axis in 1813 by Manuel Belgrano, no longer a political economist but a revolutionary general, and by José Rondeau in 1815 were decimated by royalist soldiers. This was, as *La Prensa Argentina* noted in Buenos Aires, a turning point in the war, severing the port from the Andean hinterland, spreading gloom, and intensifying the feuding within Buenos Aires itself.[5]

If the link to the highlands broke, the unity of the colonial space around the River Plate delta also splintered. In some measure, the breakdown of the viceroyalty at the mouth of the river had its origins in the rivalry between the two dominant ports, Buenos Aires and Montevideo, over the spoils of the South Atlantic commercial systems. Now there was less reason for Montevideo to recognize the power of Buenos Aires than Cádiz, which was powerless to assert its authority anyway. Montevideo, insisting that it was equal to Buenos Aires, emerged therefore as its nemesis, elevating its governor, Francisco Elío, now to be *the* viceroy defending the Regency government and metropolitan policy, and thus

---

[5]*La Prensa Argentina*, April 9, 1816, in *Biblioteca de Mayo: Colección de obras y documentos para la historia Argentina* (Buenos Aires: Senado de la Nación, 1960), v. 7, p. 6083; Ricardo R. Caillet-Bois, "La revolución en el Virreinato," in Levene, ed., *Historia*, v. 2, pp. 118–51.

what porteños would soon call "the counterrevolution." By February 1811, both sides declared open war against the other, and as Buenos Aires and the rural armies encircled Montevideo, Elío reached out to the Portuguese armies in Brazil for help. This worked—forcing Buenos Aires to sue for a brief peace. But the stalemate did not end, as rural militias took over the fight. As a result, from 1812 to 1814, Montevideo was effectively besieged. Protracted war between cities soon meant that each one lost control of its immediate provincial hinterlands, letting rural armies invent politics on their own.[6]

By 1814, Buenos Aires ruled over an increasingly rebellious domain, engulfed in a chronic and indecisive war between cities, between the countryside and cities, and between Spanish and Portuguese armies. Some, like the guerrilla leader from the Andes, Martín Güemes, and the chastened Manuel Belgrano, argued for a new monarchy, possibly of an Inca descendant so that the genealogy would be authentically American, to restore order. Others argued for a more genuine republic. Still others dedicated themselves to the political causes that would most enhance their own personal ambitions. Many, Belgrano included, worked hard to strike an accommodating deal with Spain to avoid an escalation of the war. One Buenos Aires envoy to Spain, Bernardino Rivadavia, was fully prepared to exceed the instructions he had been given in order to stave off what he feared was inevitable: a full-scale Spanish reconquest. Either way, it was hard to be optimistic when assemblymen gathered in Tucumán to declare independence from Spain on July 9, 1816. A few months later *La Crónica Argentina* celebrated the decision, but reminded readers that two enemy armies—from the Andes and Brazil—threatened the fledgling republic, and that the exhausted and divided patriotic forces had no foreign support whatsoever. Buenos Aires was free; but it was also prey.[7]

Along the Caribbean coast of South America, the stalemate was equally widespread. There, too, the standoff led to protracted jostling between rival factions—each side proclaiming fidelity to one or another crumbling cause. In Venezuela, the fall of Miranda's republic gave way to two years of mayhem. His main enemy, Captain Domingo de Monteverde, appeared to have triumphed over the republicans. What Monteverde did not realize was that his victory was due less to his own leadership, or the trust in Cádiz's rule, than to the ineptitude of the rebels. He was also bereft of political acumen, letting Bolívar and others escape, then flaunting many of the provisions of the 1812 Cádiz constitution. Instead of trying to patch up

[6]Tulio Halperín Donghi, *Historia argentina: De la revolución de independencia a la confederación rosista* (Buenos Aires: Paidós, 1989), pp. 68–79.

[7]*La crónica Argentina*, November 2, 1816, in *Biblioteca de Mayo*, v. 7, p. 6353.

the differences, he alienated many creoles by taking their property (including Bolívar's estates), thus ensuring that the creole elites would not put down their weapons. Finally, Santiago Mariño opened a rebel front in eastern Venezuela, and Bolívar, who had fled to Cartagena, returned with his "Admirable Campaign" from the west—determined, among other things, to take back his family's properties. But the spiral continued. Vowing to wage "a War to the Death," Bolívar only aggravated the conflict, which descended into a war of terror on all sides, with recriminatory massacres of civilians and captured soldiers. By August 6, 1813, Bolívar was back in the capital, Caracas, where the Municipal Council, a little prematurely, gave him the title "El Libertador." Before the Caracas Assembly in January 1814 he declared, "I will act as the trustee of supreme authority until . . . peace reigns throughout the Republic." The assembly replied by giving him dictatorial powers.[8]

The Liberator's bloody tactics and personal accumulation of power only deepened the Venezuelan fissures. Rather than unifying a new order, Bolívar became a polarizing force. This revolt was, from the point of view of many country folk, an elite, urban escapade, which promised to subject them to more exploitation without the king's royal benevolence. Bolívar's promise to purge Venezuela of peninsular blood—including that of middling and plebeian folk from Spain—made clear that his "liberation" would not be for everyone and would, many suspected, yield to a new regime of privilege, this time for creole plutocrats of the cities. It did not help that one of Miranda's laws in 1811 promised to take the open grasslands and divide it up among private landowners, curbing the open range of rural folk known as the *llaneros*. Venezuelan llaneros rallied in sizable numbers to the royalist cause. Drawing strength from the countryside ultimately tilted political fortunes toward the royalists who, led by the Asturian sailor and erstwhile smuggler José Tomás Boves, soon drove the rebels into the sea. Boves and his "Legion of Hell" especially appealed to the frontier plebeian peoples—whites, mestizos, and pardos—who resented the elite creole regime in Caracas, by promising to hear their gripes and to dispense property to his followers as a reward for their efforts. With time, Boves also offered freedom to slaves who joined the royal cause—much to the chagrin of imperial authorities. Ramón Piñero, a Venezuelan slave, joined Boves "with arms in hand" to defend "with much love and faithfulness my King."[9]

---

[8]Simón Bolívar, "Address before the Caracas Assembly" (January 2, 1814), in Bierck, ed., *Selected Writings*, v. 1, p. 64.

[9]Bolívar, "Manifesto to the People of Venezuela," pp. 81–82. For details on early slave responses and the quote from Piñero, see Peter Blanchard, "The Language of Liberation: Slave Voices in the Wars of Independence," *Hispanic American Historical Review* 82:3 (2002): 510.

This civil war, Venezuela's Vendée, had horribly uncivil features. Violence and terror were intrinsic to the standoff between two sides that were better at checking their opposition than installing a more enduring order. Taking no prisoners and releasing all constraints on fighting was an effective, if not very orderly, way of feeding the fighting machines. Boves used the pillage of creole property as a way to pay his followers and leave nothing for his enemies. The fighting was gruesome: when Francisco Rosete took the city of Ocumare in February 1814, his troops butchered the inhabitants, slicing off noses, ears, breasts, and sexual organs, leaving the town littered with body parts as a deterrent to rebels. One instrument of terror involved tying suspected dissidents, with their heads recently shaved, to stakes in the central plazas and letting them bake to death in public. On June 15, 1814, Boves trounced the combined armies of Bolívar and Mariño at the Battle of La Puerta, driving the final stake in the second republican experiment. When Boves then turned on Valencia, the city capitulated to avoid a fight but could not avoid a massacre, followed by a morbid ball to which Boves invited the widows and orphaned girls of his creole victims. Ultimately, Boves died near year's end in mop-up skirmishes with a lance through his chest. Still, Bolívar retreated steadily eastward, with a bedraggled army and 20,000 refugees in tow. The Liberator, eventually forced to flee again, shared his dismay in a "Manifesto to the People of Venezuela," in which he lamented that what started as a promise of freedom had become a civil war. This had become an intractable fight because he had tried to free "men who have been debased by the yoke of servitude and reduced to brutishness by the doctrine of superstition." They had to be forced to be free—for left to their own devices they naturally inclined to Spanish tyranny and "a government whose origins are lost in the obscurity of time." The next day (September 8, 1814) he set sail again for Nueva Granada, searching for a less helpless cause.[10]

He did not find it. When he disembarked in Cartagena, Nueva Granada was no less fractured than was the River Plate or Venezuela. Different parts of the coast split loyalties: Santa Marta sided with royalists and Cartagena went with the rebellion. Valley people also disagreed with each other and found themselves exchanging skirmishes. Around Cúcuta, royalists and rebels fought constantly until the royalist Remigio Ramos drove the young rebel commander Colonel Francisco de Paula Santander from the region. The southern city of Pasto in particular became a bastion of peninsular

---

[10]German Carrera Damas, *Boves: Aspectos socio-económicos de su acción histórica* (Caracas: Ministerio de Educación, 1968), esp. pp. 31–53. Bolívar, "Manifesto to the People of Venezuela," in Harold A. Bierck, ed., *Selected Writings of Bolívar* (New York: The Colonial Press, 1951), v. 2. p. 68.

loyalty and fended off armies from the north and south. Finally, to make matters worse, the revolutionary coalition was more deeply split in this area than in any other viceroyalty—Cartagena embraced the revolutionary cause but rejected Santa Fé de Bogotá's centralism. By the time the armies agreed to a truce, the port was infested with plagues, Bolívar's own force was reduced to 1,200 starving soldiers, 300 of whom lay on the ground infirm. This "unity" was too feeble and certainly too late. No sooner did the two sides sign a pact on April 30, 1815, than they learned of the imminent arrival of an expeditionary force from Spain. By then, massive loyalist forces were also gathering in Venezuela and Peru, with the intention of smashing the weakling authorities in Nueva Granada. Bolívar, exasperated by the internal feuding, finally abandoned Nueva Granada in May 1815 and sailed for Jamaica to resign (so it is often thought) from the revolutionary cause for good. Cartagena, once a thriving port, sat isolated, waiting for the onslaught.[11]

By 1814, what had started out as a buoyant assertion of local sovereignty in the absence of a king in 1810 had collapsed. Some rebellious leaders gave up all hope. *La Prensa Argentina* suggested to its readers that their liberty was doomed. The fate of "America" was up to Americans, a people who showed little capacity for self-rule. "The first obstacle that presents itself," the editors argued, "is the habit of blind obedience, for three hundred years, the most arbitrary domination which, degrading human nature makes men insensitive to their interests to the point of being persuaded that their abject state is a natural duty."[12] The most famous document capturing the forlorn disposition came from the pen of the Liberator as he pondered his future in Jamaica, known as the "Jamaica Letter." Spanish tyranny, beginning with the killing of Montezuma and Atahualpa, created a legacy "that America was denied not only its freedom but even the most active and effective tyranny." Spanish Americans, unable to govern their own affairs, unable to enjoy property, and encumbered by "galling restrictions" on their private freedoms, were frozen in a state of "permanent infancy." He invoked Montesquieu's observation that it is harder "to release a nation from servitude than to enslave a free nation." Accordingly, "there is no reasonable probability to bolster our hopes." While not every colonist agreed with Bolívar's ways, many were resigning themselves to the diagnosis that the rebellion had failed from within.[13]

---

[11]Restrepo, *Historia de la Revolución de Colombia,* v. 1, pp. 367–86, v. 2, pp. 6–51, esp. pp. 12–17; David Bushnell, *The Making of Modern Colombia: A Nation in Spite of Itself* (Berkeley: University of California Press, 1993), pp. 39–45.

[12]*La Prensa Argentina,* September 19 1815, in *Biblioteca de Mayo,* v. 7, p. 5921.

[13]Simón Bolívar, "Reply of a South American Gentleman of This Island," (September 6, 1815), in Bierck, ed., *Selected Writings,* v. 1, pp. 105–27.

Between 1812 and 1814, the colonies were cast adrift. Neither side could vanquish the other, in part because neither side was especially strong. The central government in Spain was weak—and the local administrations in the colonies were even weaker. Even among the stoutest loyalists in Lima, capitalists disagreed over how to cope with an acephalous empire. The Peruvian jurist José de Baquíjano quipped in May 1814 that the government in Cádiz was wasting colonial fealty because it listened more to metropolitan magnates than to the vast numbers of loyalists in America: "the Consulado of Cádiz [was] the absolute dictator of the resolutions of the Regency and Cortes" because they exercised "prideful power acquired by means of a paltry loan of twelve or fifteen million pesos, which deprived the Motherland of an annual revenue of thirty-five million," which the treasury could have earned simply by treating American merchants as equals.[14] Indeed, in many provinces it was only the fragility of the metropolitan cause that allowed rebels to survive.

In this stalemate, popular loyalties crossed all ways and for a variety of reasons. In highland Pasto and grassland llanos, loyalty to Spain and the crown was fierce; along the slave-plantation belts of Cartagena and among the gauchos of the Banda Oriental, creole autonomy could mean popular sovereignty. More often plebeians fought plebeians. If Boves enlisted the subalterns and slaves to his side in the llanos, Mariño and the mulatto Manual Piar reached out to slaves and runaways in eastern Venezuela. What was happening was the shakeup of traditional colonial vertical authority. Indeed, even in coastal Peru, where the forces for change were relatively weak, slaves fled plantations and fugitive communities of bandits and *bandoleros* took special aim at royalist property; Tacna (1811 and 1813), Huánuco and Huamanga (1812), and Arequipa (1812) erupted with mini-revolts of their own.[15] Still, while social stratification in the colonies was shaking, it is impossible to depict the struggle before 1814 as a simple class war of subalterns seeking to overthrow centuries of injustice. Nor was this a pan-creole alliance rallying behind a nationalist revolt. The stalemate sliced through class, race, and national classifications.[16]

---

[14]Patricia Marks, "Power and Authority in Late Colonial Peru: Viceroys, Merchants and the Military, 1775–1821" (PhD thesis, Princeton University, 2003), p. 226. For an analysis of the internal skirmishing within the *limeño* merchant class, see pp. 208–29.

[15]Alberto Flores Galindo, *Aristocracia y plebe: Lima, 1760–1830* (Lima: Mosca Azul, 1983), pp. 120–21, 144–48.

[16]Brian Hamnett, "Popular Insurrection and Royalist Reaction: Colombian Regions, 1810–1823," in Fisher, Kuethe and McFarlane, eds., *Reform and Insurrection*, pp. 292–326; Joel Chassin, "Lima, sus elites y la opinión durante los últimos tiempos de la colonia," in Guerra and Lampérière, eds., *Los espacios públicos*, pp. 243–44 and Alberto Flores Galindo, "Bandidos de la Costa," in Carlos Aguirre and Charles Walker, eds., *Bandoleros, abigeos y montoneros* (Lima: Pasado y Presente, 1990), pp. 57–68.

The Reaction

The quarrel over the meanings of sovereignty had degenerated into a series of concentric rebellions within rebellions, a stalemate that appeared to be unresolvable without a major external shift. That came in 1814 with the restoration of Ferdinand to the throne and the liberation of Spain from French occupation. At this stage it seemed as if—with the exception of only a few hamlets—the secessionist cause might collapse as the dispersed provinces rallied behind the restored monarchy and reintegrated themselves as parts of the empire. This is not what transpired. Ferdinand, for reasons we shall see, decided to put an end to secessionist movements by reimposing the old order on the colonies. His actions condemned his regime to a vortex of violence across Spanish South America. And in escalating the lethality of the stalemate in the colonies, he destroyed the prospects of a political ground on which people might harbor loyalties to empire while enjoying their relative sovereignty in the colonies—which had been part of the political and legal discourse since 1808. Colonists, literally, were forced to choose between more and more polarized sides, between imperium and something else.

The circumstances of the king's restoration, and his own personal inclinations, help explain the decision to mount a counterrevolution against enfeebled secessionists. On December 11, 1813, the Treaty of Valençay provided for his return to Madrid, signed by him unilaterally without consulting either the Cortes or the Regency. Even before arriving in Madrid he ordered, with the full backing of the Duke of Wellington, the closure of the parliament and concentrated power among his military leaders. In effect, he tore up the Constitution of 1812, which had been drafted in large part to legitimate imperial claims in the absence of the king. Ferdinand was determined to roll back whatever political powers had been stripped from the monarchy and to restore or, more accurately, to create the image of a regime of impregnable strength. Desperate to appear less feckless than his father, Ferdinand elected to maximize his freedom of action by avoiding compromises with all parties and even reducing his ministers to incoherent and constantly rotating impotence. But if he thought amassing personal power would be a source of strength, he crippled the lines of authority in his administration and created a chaotic and confusing structure for decision making. Ironically, what he wanted to achieve by rolling back the clock could not have been more ill timed. To call the fiscal conditions of the imperial treasury parlous would be a monumental understatement. There was no money in the coffers, and one of the main sources of revenues, charges on colonial commerce, had vanished. Spain owed a fortune to London for the war effort. To this was added the utter ruination of the peninsular merchant classes, who were anxious to claw back their access to Atlantic commerce.[17]

Under these circumstances, the Spanish monarch and peninsular merchants saw eye to eye on one important thing: it was essential to get the state of the empire back to where it was before the troubles began. If Ferdinand was not going to brook any deals with liberals in Spain, he was certainly not going to be sympathetic to those calling for reforms—commercial, civic, political—in the colonies. The merchants could not agree more with his revanchist spirit, less for ideological reasons than instrumental ones. In March 1815, the Cádiz commercial guild petitioned the king, urging him to establish "order" in the colonies. Preying on the ruler's insecurities, the memo read: "No one knows better than Your Highness how vehement have been, and are, the desires of the European Maritime Powers to gain possession of the commerce of the Spanish Indies since the days of the conquest." They spread "sedition" among colonists and with the promise of reforms have reduced the empire "to the unfortunate state we now see." The king should swiftly "reestablish order and a system of public administration" as "a good father would treat his peoples." If paternal love was supposed to rebind the monarch to his colonial subjects, the goal must be to restore the old trading order for "Commerce, Sir, must be considered as the foundation of the universal prosperity of all States." As far as the peninsular merchants were concerned, the problem was natural to the people the king had to subdue: for colonists, like children, were vulnerable to passions and could not appreciate the superiority of interests—interests, they added, that dignified the state and commonwealth over personal gains. "General History, and our own experience, show how inherent human weaknesses and disorderly passions, which we see in all Kingdoms and Republics, allow just a few perverted men to bring disgrace on all... by seducing and demoralizing the majority." Thus, what was good for Cádiz was by definition also good for the health of the imperium. Urged by the merchants, the king sent a decisive message to the colonies: no reforms would be tolerated that did not add to the neo-absolutist principles of his government or that would deprive Cádiz of its rightful place as the gateway of Spain's commercial emporia.[18]

The idea of metropolitan restoration had its champions in the fringes. One area that the king did not have to worry about was Peru, at least as he

---

[17]Hamnett, *La política española*, pp. 174–202; Anna, *Spain and the Loss of America*, pp. 115–22.

[18]AGI, IG, 2320, March 7, 1815, Consulado to Secretario de Estado; see also August 23, 1814, "Expediente sobre la exacción en América del derecho llamdo de Subvención de Guerra."

understood it. From Peru came signals to Spain that a restoration of the old order was not just possible, but might be easy. The viceroy, José Fernando de Abascal, was a powerful and adept figure in Andean politics, far more skilled than his peers in the other provinces. In most ways, the Peruvian viceroy's skills almost compensated for his king's debilities. Writing to authorities in Spain, even as they were drafting the new constitution in 1812, he claimed that only force "would make these men come to their senses." From the start, he resisted and blunted the spread of liberalism and was a consistent advocate of coercive means to deal with dissent. For all intents and purposes, the 1812 constitution had little effect on Peru and the provinces that Abascal annexed (Quito, Alto Perú); Abascal proudly announced that any domain over which he ruled would remain faithful to the "antiguo Gobierno."[19] Abascal had never liked the ways in which the Spanish juntas and Regency had given new rights to colonists and had to cope with many of the disruptive effects of local electioneering. Several Peruvian cities were hosts to increasing tension and occasional fighting between peninsulars and creoles. The local press, to the viceroy's chagrin, badgered him with charges of foot-dragging on new rights and liberties.[20]

Abascal tended to see this sort of activity as marginal expressions of craven subjects. Accordingly, he dealt with agitators harshly, and once they were defeated he depicted them as authors of their own fate. This did not exactly encourage subtle or moderate thinking. In late 1812, Abascal ordered a royal army to march on Quito and move north to reinforce the loyalist holdouts in Pasto. The repression was violent enough to compel the Spanish government to wonder whether excessive force had been used—a charge the restored Quito president, Joaquín de Molina, refuted, claiming that the region was on the verge of something far worse than another Tupac Amarú revolt.[21] In 1813, Abascal snuffed out efforts to establish constitutional autonomy in Chile. He threw all affordable resources at the defense of Alto Perú against the expeditions from Buenos Aires. Once Belgrano had been driven back to the River Plate, Abascal informed Spain that across the Andes, his armies "have broken the chains that have oppressed us from the dissidents of Buenos Ayres" and that in due course his government will start "shipping the minerals from Potosí."[22] While there might have been qualms about

---

[19]AGI, Estado, Lima, 74:8, May 23, 1812, José Fernando de Abascal to Secretario de Estado. For a magnificent study of Abascal, see Peralta Ruiz, *En defense de la autoridad.*

[20]John Fisher, "Royalism, Regionalism, and Rebellion in Colonial Peru, 1808–1815," *Hispanic American Historical Review* 59:2 (1979): 242–44.

[21]AGI, Estado, Lima, 74/51, January 25, 1813, Marqués de la Concordia to Secretario. de Estado; 74/72, July 23, 1813, Joaquin de Molina to Consejo de Regencia.

[22]AGI, Estado, Lima, 74/8, October 13, 1812 Abascal to Secretario de Estado.

Abascal's method, the promise of reviving silver flows must have been a frisson to metropolitan restorers.

If Abascal preferred to attribute the insurgency to a few rabble-rousers and show that they could be defeated with a show of force, he left out any analysis that suggested that many colonists were disinclined to toe his line. In the provinces of Huamanga and Tarma conspiracies flourished; in other districts violence had erupted. After the Cádiz Constitution reached Lima, it fired up a great deal of discussion, especially in Cuzco. Peninsular authorities resisted change. Mateo García Pumacahua, the *cacique* of Chincheros and an alleged descendant of the Incas but who had fought against Tupac Amarú in the 1780s and helped repress dissidents again in 1811, could not be called disloyal. But when Abascal and his officers refused to abide by many of the 1812 reforms (including the abolition of some of the onerous burdens on Indians), Pumacahua was squeezed between loyalty to the viceroy and fealty to the new constitutional regime celebrated by *cuzqueño* liberals in the municipal cabildo. The showdown culminated in a revolution in August 1814, hatched by liberals, but which soon swept in Pumacahua himself. The rebels demanded that the 1812 constitution be implemented (ironically almost at the same time that Ferdinand was tearing it up) and rallied a coalition of Indians and poorer creoles to rise up in Puno, La Paz, Huamanga, and Huancavelica—thus threatening the precious silver routes as well as Abascal's reactionary convictions. Pumacahua's revolt came close to fusing with the persecuted holdouts in the *republiquetas* of Alto Perú. The viceroy, furious, threw his armies—helped now by reinforcements from the peninsula—at the Indians, mestizos, and creoles who defied him, and eventually chased down Pumacahua. In May 1815, the old Indian cacique was executed publicly before his followers.[23]

The Peruvian counterrevolution affected perceptions of what was possible from Madrid. It reinforced—or was conjured to reinforce—Ferdinand's belief that it was not necessary to compromise or even negotiate when dealing with colonial demands. Colonial home rule and imperial sovereignty were simply oxymoronic. Order was best secured with force; the reactions of colonists to the concessions of the previous decade provided ample proof that giving in to peripheral demands only led to more demands.

---

[23]Peralta Ruíz, *En defensa de la autoridad*, pp. 149–75; David Cahill and Scarlett O'Phelan Godoy, "Forging Their Own History: Indian Insurgency in the Southern Peruvian Sierra, 1815," *Bulletin of Latin American Research* 11:2 (1992): 125–67; John R. Fisher, "The Royalist Regime in the Viceroyalty of Peru, 1820–1824," *Journal of Latin American Studies* 32:1 (2000): 59–60; Walker, *Smoldering Ashes*, pp. 98–104.

To drive the message home, Ferdinand assembled a huge restorationist army to subdue all who ever thought that constitutionalism might have served as the new foundation of sovereignty. From the time of the king's return to Madrid, his advisors were concerned less with whether to reconquer the colonies than with how. The Count of Vistaflorida laid out in minute detail the means to "pacify" the colonies. The problem, he felt, began with the French invasion (which created "anarchy") and worsened when surrogate governments of the Regency and Cortes created liberties to vote and trade all over the empire, "with scandalous doctrines which circulated without shame and only increased the lack of confidence and excused all errors." The concept that the people were in any sense sovereign was the root of the evil. To make matters worse, mulattos, blacks, and Indians added to the "damage" by treating themselves as citizens with equal rights. All this had to be extirpated by the crown with the same zeal as the Inquisition before it, by force of arms if necessary where it most deeply burrowed. The Council of the Indies finally put together its recommendations to the king in October 1814, echoing these sentiments, and agreeing that getting rid of a few *malvados* inspired by foreign models would restore the natural hierarchy of the empire. The circle around Ferdinand agreed on the principles of what would become in the twentieth century a textbook counterinsurgency, concocted out of a mixture of wishful thinking and amnesia. The only real matter to debate was which colony to subdue first. Feeling that Abascal's restoration of royal control in the Andes would eventually hem in the rebels of Buenos Aires, and exaggerating the endurance of loyalists in Montevideo, Ferdinand chose to send his expeditionary army to Venezuela. From Venezuela, his army could then move into Nueva Granada and thence down the cordillera, crushing resistors along the way.[24]

Designing a strategy to pacify the Americas was one thing, actually implementing it exposed the king's worst deficiencies. He combined a personal intransigence with a deep misconception about the ease of the enterprise and its costs into one self-defeating mix. The expedition was impressive but flawed from the start. In August 1814, Ferdinand named a seasoned commander, a professional who had risen through the ranks from modest beginnings, Field Marshal Pablo Morillo, as the new captain general of Venezuela. By February 1815 he set sail with forty two transports, five escorting warships, and an army of more than 10,000 veteran fighters. From the start morale was low, with constant desertions

---

[24]AGI, Estado, 87/31, May 31 1814, Informe Vistaflorida; see also 87/39, May 22, 1814, Oficio del Conde de Puñonrostro al Duque de San Carlos; AGI, IG, 1568, October 8, 1814, "Consultas del Consejo de Indias."

and unrest. Indeed, the ultimate destination of the expedition had to be kept secret for fear that the troops would rebel or flee en masse if they knew they were bound for Venezuela, where the reputation for brutal warfare was already legendary in Spain. The troops learned only once they were seaborne. The problems were portentous—and indeed Morillo wound up, in the five years he fought in South America, spending almost as much energy keeping his troops in line as he did fighting the enemy. To make matters worse, Morillo did not get full instructions until March 1816, long after his arrival in the Americas. The political aspects of his mandate were unclear. Were, for instance, royal officials supposed to resume their duties, or were they subordinate to military commanders? No less clear was the military mandate. Did military pacification mean complete defeat of the rebels, or tactical victories coupled with promises of amnesties to demilitarize the conflict? On both the military and political fronts, Morillo had to improvise as he went along—with the sole mandate to make military reconquest a condition for political reintegration in the pacification scheme.[25]

Venezuela, in fact, did not require reconquering. Bolívar and others had been routed not once but twice, and the Liberator had all but given up hope. Boves and his successors had done almost all the dirty work by the time Morillo's army arrived, as Morillo discovered when he approached the coast. Mishaps plagued the expedition from the start and forced the commander to try to restore the fictive status quo ante in a hurry. The expedition's largest vessel, the *Pedro Alcántara*, loaded with munitions and coffers (with one million pesos) to pay the troops, accidentally burned in the harbor of Coche. This immediately forced Morillo to have to turn to Venezuelan merchants to lend him money. Still, the region seethed with unrest, and Morillo had to leave half his force in situ before marching on Nueva Granada. Here began a series of strategic mistakes born of the fallacy that Spanish South America's natural state was as submissive colonies. Morillo, fearing that it would be harder to govern Venezuela with the remnants of Boves's popular armies than without them, disbanded them so that regular troops could take over the military occupation. This meant that while he had only half his peninsular fighters with him, he demobilized llaneros who could not resist the temptation to join the other side, if only to continue the acquired preference for pillaging towns and estates. None of these problems would have been intractable if he could rely on reinforcements and cash transfers from Spain. However, despite his recurring—and increasingly desperate—pleas for

---

[25]Margaret L. Woodward, "The Spanish Army and the Loss of America, 1810–1824," *Hispanic American Historical Review* 48:4 1968: 586–90.

money, he got none. It became essential for Morillo to inflict a sudden and decisive victory over the rebels.[26]

To understand why the counterrevolution failed, it is important to distinguish among a tactical military victory, pacification, and restoration of the ancien régime, and between battles for territory and the struggle for loyalty. Meeting the first objective, beating the rebels in the battlefield, was hard enough, but it was accomplished with some consistency. Morillo was, if nothing else, a fine commander and a shrewd tactician. The rebels usually did not possess his combined skills. But what they did not lack—some popular support in the cities and countryside—made it harder to pacify colonists and restore the ancien régime. Insurgents also could open up more fronts, especially once the war became a classical guerrilla operation, than Morillo could possibly defend.

As the pacification campaigns ground on, Morillo started to lose the war for loyalty. In Venezuela he had been conciliatory and lenient; but the reconquest of Nueva Granada saw him adopt an ever more coercive stance when faced with even the mildest of opposition because he was so pressed for time. Cartagena, home of South America's biggest Spanish fortress and the nerve center of coastal commerce and gateway for the Magdalena trading system, was rife with internal feuding. In some ways, the city had fallen already. Knowing Morillo's flotilla was approaching, many Cartagenans swore fidelity to Ferdinand to avoid recriminations. Others, like José Francisco Bermúdez, tried to fire up black troops to defend the city and their newfound rights: "Remember, above all you men of color, how this conflict began; it can only call more strongly on your gratitude, your self-interest, and your honor."[27] But if the colonists hoped for leniency, Morillo disabused them of the fiction that the reconquest would be soft. On August 20, 1815, Morillo besieged the port—and stopped all traffic in and out for 106 days. Horses, oxen, and dogs became the only food for the city. On October 25, his artillery began its bombardment. Six thousand people, one-third of the population, died during the siege from the shelling, disease, and starvation, until finally the remnants of the defenders succumbed and invited General Morillo into the city on December 6. The night before, knowing that Morillo did not intend to deal kindly with the rebels, 2,000 fugitives escaped the city aboard light corsairs. Many drowned in the effort, others were captured,

---

[26]Laura F. Ullrick, "Morillo's Attempt to Pacify Venezuela," *Hispanic American Historical Review* 3:4 (1920): 535–65; Stephen K. Stoan, *Pablo Morillo and Venezuela, 1815–1820* (Columbus: Ohio State University Press, 1974), pp. 134–46; Earle, *Spain and the Independence of Colombia*, pp. 70–3.

[27]Cited in Lasso, "A Republican Myth of Racial Harmony," p. 61.

and those who got through the blockade joined the thousands of other patriots across the Caribbean diaspora. Morillo disembarked in a demolished city, reeking from the stench of death. As he made his way through the streets, he was horrified by the sight: "The city offered the most horrendous spectacle to our eyes. The streets were littered with cadavers which infested the air, and the majority of inhabitants were inert from hunger." Cartagena would, thereafter, be an occupied city until 1821, becoming the last of the South American Caribbean ports to be liberated, its once powerful commercial class, like the city itself, in ruins. With the fall of Cartagena, other constitutionalist holdouts also collapsed. The valleys around Cucutá succumbed. Bogotá, practically defenseless, awaited Morillo as he traveled up the Magdalena River to the capital.[28]

On the evening of May 26, 1816, Morillo entered the capital and immediately imposed a draconian system on the city's inhabitants. He ordered that all seditious people be rounded up and incarcerated; he created a military tribunal—much to the chagrin of civil justices who clamored for a restoration of their authority—to extirpate the viceroyalty's insurgents. The Purification Council—another innovation—was designed to deal with non–capital punishment cases. And the Junta de Secuestros handled the seizure of properties belonging to the hundreds of detainees—effectively to auction off the holdings to the highest bidder. For six months the city endured the spectacle of public executions of men who had dominated the political stage since 1810—including Camilo Torres, Joaquín Camacho, José Gregorio y Frutos Gutiérrez, Cristiano Valenzuela, Miguel Pombo, and Francisco José de Caldas, the distinguished philosopher and mathematician. In sum, three hundred of the colony's leading lights perished. After shooting them, Marillo's forces transported their cadavers to outposts across the viceroyalty to dangle from posts. Heads were jammed onto stakes or, as in the case of Camilo Torres, locked inside a cage to rot, publicly, in the center of the capital. These were not the atrocities of battle or part of a pillaging campaign; Morillo used the display of force to terrorize bystanders in the pursuit of the restoration of an imperiled past. Morillo's terror was part of a logic unleashed out of frustration and desperation. For while he was executing his version of justice in Nueva Granada, news began to filter in about recrudescent uprisings in Venezuela and the open jealousies and disagreements among Spanish commanders. All this added to Morillo's determination to deliver swift, violent justice and pull out.[29]

---

[28]See Múñera, *El fracaso de la nación*, pp. 211–14, Morillo quote on p. 212; Restrepo, *Historia de la Revolución de Colombia*, v. 2, pp. 77–125; Earle, *Spain and the Independence of Colombia*, pp. 62–64.

[29]Restrepo, *Historia de la Revolución*, v. 2, pp. 134–57; Earle, *Spain and the Independence of Colombia*, pp. 78–85; Bushnell, *The Making of Modern Colombia*, pp. 45–7.

Finally, Morillo was upholding a strategy that wound up creating enemies out of neutrals and friends. Just before reaching Bogotá, Morillo got his final instructions from Madrid—which included giving him "unlimited faculties" to accomplish the pacification. Whatever means necessary were justified to accomplish the ends. He was also told to restore old institutions once the pacification was complete, "without introducing dangerous innovations." From Morillo's standpoint, rebuilding institutions had to wait until his war was over. This was not inconsistent with the king's instructions—but it created all kinds of problems on the ground, especially among those who desired the reconquest precisely because it promised to restore some institutional stability. Many merchants were furious at the auctioning of patriots' properties, especially since many owed sizable debts to the merchants, or were partners. Worse, the Junta de Secuestros allocated these assets without proper procedures according to commercial law. Local officials, in turn, disliked ceding their jurisdictions to army officers. Many clergymen, even those who accused the patriots of ungodliness, had serious qualms about seeing so many body parts hanging from high places.[30]

The concerns of loyal colonists soon got back to Madrid and sparked a controversy among Ferdinand's advisors—a controversy Ferdinand resolved in a way that removed any possibility of restoring the ties between the colonies and the metropolis. Juan Lozano de Torres wrote to Secretary of State Martín de Garay—one of the few moderates within the king's circle—sharing his impressions of the catastrophic conditions of the regions occupied by Morillo's armies. And as more news trickled in, Garay consulted the secretary of war, suggesting that they propose to the king that he name a viceroy immediately and recall General Morillo. This would restore institutional life to the colonies and bring an end to "the deplorable state" of the colonies and "the arbitrariness of the officers and lesser commanders." The Spanish government received a thick dossier cataloguing testimonials of the "violence committed by the expeditionary troops." A less absolutist regime might have grown alarmed, or at least flinched. This was not the case in Madrid. Ferdinand's military commanders, upon whom he had relied a great deal to restore his power in Spain, stood behind the reconquest model for South America. Across the board, the military establishment argued that the enemy's savagery warranted the repressive means; counterrevolutionary terror was not just spasmodic and impulsive, it was historically necessary.[31] Finally, in November 1817, the Council of the

---

[30] AGI, Estado, Santa Fe, 57/35, March 10, 1816, "Oficio de Martín de Garay," for a full list of Morillo's instructions; Earle, *Spain and the Independence of Colombia*, pp. 85–90.

[31] AGI, Estado, Santa Fe, September 2, 1817, Juan Lozano de Torres to Martín De Garay; January 29, 1818, Minuta del Oficio del Secretario de Estado.

Indies began to probe the allegations of abuse but wound up exonerating the general on constitutional grounds: he had been given unlimited powers to do what he considered necessary to accomplish the pacification. Finding him guilty would have condemned instructions coming from the king himself.[32]

If the king's ambition to reestablish a full-blooded absolutist system sowed confusion in Madrid, and thus made it impossible to either recall Morillo or change his ways, it meant that Morillo's actions in the colonies alienated colonists for good. In effect, the ends and means of restoration pushed colonists—even those who had once hung onto their Spanish loyalties, especially to the reforms of 1812—to rally behind a cause that promised to break the Atlantic chains altogether. Out of what was once an incoherent and weak rebellion in 1810, which was sputtering by 1814, peninsular counterrevolution created revolutionary armies. Note the spiral: rebellion led to counterrevolution, which then spawned the revolution. The patriotic stragglers, fearing persecution, rekindled their struggle and took refuge in the plains. The news of the horror of Cartagena and Bogotá inspired many disenchanted colonists scattered in their Caribbean diasporas to return and take up the fight once more. By mid-1816, having learned of the coincidental brutality in Nueva Granada and uprisings in Venezuela, the previously despondent Bolívar returned to Venezuela, which was starting to crumble in Morillo's absence, and began his long road to the "Third Republic." He would never leave South America again. Thus, as Morillo pounded cities into submission, the countrysides of Venezuela and Nueva Granada became the havens for guerrilla strikes against Spanish divisions. Indeed, the wars in the two theaters bled into each other, converging into a massive insurrection against royal authority where it had once imploded of its own inconstant volition. The more Morillo won battles, the more he was losing the war. The more he was besieged, the more he turned to unsavory practices. And the more the armies of reaction struggled to pacify the colonies the more unlikely was a restoration of the ancien régime.[33]

REVOLUTIONS

As counterrevolution sired a revolution, the cycle of violence gave the secessionist cause a decidedly military personality. In 1810, the patriotic coalitions were dominated by civilian urbanites: lawyers, prominent merchants,

---

[32]AGI, Estado, Santa Fe, 57/35, October 17, 1817, "Consulta de Consejo de Indias"; Earle, *Spain and the Independence of Colombia*, pp. 29–33.
[33]Hamnett, "Popular Insurrection," pp. 302–15.

clergymen, and notable vecinos of colonial cities. And their styles of action and media of mobilization reflected the public spaces they had dominated: the press, literary salons, local assemblies, parishes, and gatherings in the streets. By 1815 these men were not so much sidelined as folded into an increasingly militarized brand of politics as the perimeter of the revolutionary coalition expanded, especially to include rural agents. Indeed, some of the 1810 figures shed their civilian skins altogether and donned martial ones to blend into the new complexion of the movement. As politics became militarized, the decisive spheres of collective action shifted from the urban spaces, which flourished in the final days of the empire, to new "associational" mobilization: armies. In this phase, with the colonial response to metropolitan reaction, the final bloody and chaotic denouement of empire was the historic breeding ground for actors who would populate the postimperial age in South America.

Mass mobilization to conduct the revolution was not of a piece. Indeed, we are accustomed to think more conceptually of the role of armies in political history as exercising centripetal influences, due in large part to models of state formation governed by interstate violence.[34] In the context of a revolution born of civil conflict—infrastate violence over internal sovereignty—the dynamics are different. A Weberian model of state formation—where states incrementally acquire the monopoly over the legitimate use of violence—steps aside in favor of a much more Hobbesian one—in which it is the sovereign who creates law by delivering subjects from a state of nature. In the case that concerns us here, the ancien régime was demolished from within, not because a party (Mao) or an army (Cromwell) asserted an alternative and established its hegemony through the application of centralized force, but because the political vacuum of an imperial crisis unleashed the centrifugal furies of multiple fighting machines.

In most regions, the mobilization was widespread yet the most effective fighting units were highly mobile. Where guerrilla warfare was most intense, it created dispersed, decentralized ties between local chieftains and clients. This was precisely the fighting force that proved so frustrating for the Spanish expeditionary armies. No sooner did Morillo leave Nueva Granada to try to restore order in Venezuela in 1817 than Indians, led by the priest Ignacio Mariño, formed guerrilla bands and rose up across the Casanare plains. Peasants in the Cauca Valley also took up arms, and their example spread to Socorro and Tunja. Pretty soon the capital, Bogotá, was a royalist island in a sea of guerrillas. General Juan Sámano, the Spanish commander, ordered a series of public

---

[34]See, for instance, Tilly, *Coercion, Capital, and European States.*

executions on November 14 as a desperate display of force—outraging the llanero and peasant formations in the countryside, who prepared to close in on the city. Spanish and royalist families, when they learned of the imminent attack by the unwashed guerrillas, frantically began to pack their belongings and flee.[35]

Guerrilla warriors aggregated into an indomitable force across northern South America, operating from the hinterlands against royalist outposts. This enemy also reshaped the claims of the revolutionaries. In Venezuela, the seesaw wars so disrupted the social stratification of plantations, estates, and urban castes with the pillaging, seizures, and destruction that many plebeians fled to remote corners and devoted themselves to protecting newfound freedoms. Slaves and free blacks from the plantation valleys of Cuiepe, Capaya, and Guapo had long since evacuated their bondage and joined both sides—often winding up fighting each other. Other times, as in the valleys and coasts of Barlovento and up the valleys of Santa Lucía, blacks formed their own nonpartisan battalions, devoted principally to defending their personal freedom and looting property. After 1815, faced with royalist consolidation and the prospect of reincorporation (which to many meant re-enslavement), increasing numbers felt better able to protect hinterland livelihoods by throwing in their lot with local patriotic chieftains. Critical to the guerrilla strength, and to the ability of patriotic commanders to channel it to larger political purposes, was translating promises of freedom to indentured workers and slaves who would join their ranks into an actual program.[36]

The most important Venezuelans to appeal to plebeians were the mulatto Manuel Piar and the mestizo José Antonio Páez, son of an employee of a state monopoly firm from the western outpost of Barinas. Piar was instrumental in churning up the eastern lowlands, while Paez's influence, especially in the western llanos, forced the patriots and loyalists to adapt to his form of fighting and the substance of his cause. Páez rose up through the ranks of the patriotic forces, honed his equestrian skills, and refined a populist appeal to ever more devoted troops. Páez filled in the void vacated by the death of the royalist Boves, and like Boves offered personal freedom, property, and loot as compensation to any man who followed him into battle. As Páez liberated western towns in the piedmont

---

[35]Restrepo, *Historia de la Revolución de Colombia*, v. 2, pp. 158–71; Earle, *Spain and the Independence of Colombia*, pp. 78–81.

[36]Blanchard, "The Language of Liberation," pp. 512–18; Marixa Lasso, "Haiti as an Image of Popular Republicanism in Caribbean Colombia: Cartagena Province (1811–1828)," in David Geggus, ed., *The Impact of the Haitian Revolution in the Atlantic World* (Columbia: University of South Carolina Press, 2001), pp. 176–91.

and Llanos, he doled out lands belonging to Spanish loyalists and freed the slaves, adding recruits to his swelling armies. Among those flocking to his side were Cunaviche Indians, who rallied to the promise of freedom from colonial tribute. From this amalgam in the interior, guerrillas harassed royal troops stationed near or in the larger cities and along the coast, and picked them apart when they dared pursue their tormentors.[37]

Rural guerrillas forced the war to conform to their terms. Rebel forces were so costly to the royal regime that Morillo had to abandon his original plans to move down the Andes, and return to Caracas to reorganize the defenses in early 1817. Bolívar, watching this war unfold, was inspired to add social substance to political liberation. He proclaimed that all slaves that fought for liberty would win their personal emancipation as he worked over the eastern end of Venezuela. This was not his initiative; local guerrilla commanders had been doing this for years, and even the interim captain general of Venezuela, José Ceballos, had urged the Spanish secretary of state to give special benefits and rights to "caste" peoples to win them over. Indeed, the war for the loyalties of Venezuelan commoners grew so intense that Pablo Morillo himself defied the king's instructions not to destabilize the social order and issued abolitionist promises to slaves who joined royalist ranks. At first Morillo got rapped on the knuckles, but when he pointed out that black rebel troops were among the most effective fighting units, the king gave him permission in December 1818 to free slaves who fought for the monarchy. By then it was too little, too late. Nominal commitment to the abolition of slavery and rights of commoners were cardinal ingredients of what it meant to belong to free political communities—free, that is, from Spain.[38]

The formation of popular armies, whose commanders carried programs of social liberation under their arms, ultimately made it extremely difficult for Spanish armies to win the war. Even where loyalists were militarily indomitable, as in the highlands of Peru and Upper Peru, the republiquetas and guerrilla fighters had also made the transition from resisting Spanish rule to challenging social hierarchies and renegotiating

---

[37]R. B. Cunninghame Graham, *José Antonio Páez* (New York: Cooper Square Publishing, 1970).

[38]John Lynch, *The Spanish American Revolutions, 1808–1826* (New York: Norton, 1986), pp. 212–14; Hamnett, "Popular Insurrection," pp. 311–15; James F. King, "A Royalist View of the Colored Castes in the Venezuelan War of Independence," *Hispanic American Historical Review*, pp. 526–33; Aline Helg, "Simón Bolívar and the Spectre of *Pardocracia*: José Padilla in Post Independence Cartagena," *Journal of Latin American Studies* 35:3 (2003): 447–71; Camilla Townsend, "'Half My Body Free, the Other Half Enslaved': The Politics of the Slaves of Guayaquil at the End of the Colonial Era," *Colonial Latin American Review* 7:1 (1998): 105–28.

terms of social inclusion in market life. Many, in the course of fighting, dismantled estates and the holdings of *corregidores* and dispersed them to villagers, both as compensation for support and as part of an emerging ideological shift in the war. Horizontal ethnic and class affiliations in Ocongate and Marcapata not only helped dismantle the residues of the old colonial establishment, but even challenged the conventions of indigenous stratification that tied villagers to the tributary order.[39]

Perhaps the most striking example of popular mobilization to wage militarized politics turned out to be a struggle not just against Spanish absolutism but against the prospect of domination by merchant capital—even creole leaders of the patriotic cause. The Banda Oriental, squeezed between Brazil and Buenos Aires, exemplified the shift from demands for local sovereignty to a social revolution that shook up property relations. José Gervasio Artigas, the leader of the *orientales*, rose up from fairly modest beginnings through the ranks of a rural militia force, the Blandengues (Lancers), in the colonial era. When the upheaval between loyalists in Montevideo and patriots in Buenos Aires erupted, Artigas did not demur and joined the latter cause. In the ensuing years, he captivated the countryside, which mobilized for war against the monied men in Montevideo who schemed with Cádiz for a counterrevolution and had beckoned to Portuguese armies to move in and drive out the rebels. His popular armies blocked further incursions from Portuguese expansionists and throttled the loyalists in Montevideo. This was decisive for the survival of the rebellion in Buenos Aires, which hovered on the precipice of collapse by 1814. It is hard to clinch the counterfactual, but it is likely that without Artigas's mobilization of the Oriental countryside into a mass popular army Buenos Aires might have imploded in the same way Venezuelan and Nueva Granadan revolts had before the Spanish counterrevolution.[40]

In the course of war, Artigas vowed to inscribe a new convenant for the Oriental peoples. Influenced from the start by an amalgam of revolutionary writings of the porteño Mariano Moreno, especially declarations of freedom from colonial burdens on Indians and the works proclaiming the virtues of decentralized federations of sovereign people, Artigas appears also have been influenced by foreign writers (like Rousseau) and foreign models (like Jefferson's notion of modest settler capitalist societies in the hinterlands). His thought cohered in 1813 in an

---

[39]Luis Miguel Glave, "Antecedentes y naturaleza de la revolución del Cuzco de 1814," in Scarlett O'Phelan Godoy, comp., *La independencia del Perú* (Lima: Instituto Riva-Agüero, 2001), pp. 77–97; Cahill and Godoy, "Forging Their Own History," pp. 134–61.

[40]John Street, *Artigas and the Emancipation of Uruguay* (Cambridge: Cambridge University Press, 1959), esp. pp. 118–55.

address to the Congress of Peoples' Provincial Deputies, imploring them to uphold the principles expressed by the foot soldiers of his armies in the broader constitutional deliberations over the future of the viceroyalty. The assembly also read the draft of a constitution for the province, declaring it "free, sovereign and independent." There, the combination of federalism, so that state structures could more perfectly mold to the social and cultural topography of the "pueblo," and the redistribution of estate lands fused into one bold, revolutionary démarche. Oriental leaders created the institutional bases of their federal, republican political economy: elected local magistrates, municipal councils, provincial control of taxation, and a tribunal to seize property and allocate it to producers. Finally, in September 1815, Artigas issued his "Reglamento Provisorio," which gathered many of these initiatives into a revolutionary plan firmly committed to personal freedom, property ownership by households, bans on the accumulation of financial debts, and a program of widespread property distribution. Article 6 specifically identified "Free Blacks, Sambos of the same Class, Indians, and poor Creoles" as entitled to a plot of land (a suerte de estanica), "if with their labor and proper conduct (*hombría de bien*) they contribute to their happiness and that of the Province."[41]

In this fashion, Artigas gathered around him a multi-ethnic and multiracial army to defend a radical model of republicanism. By April 1813, the Indians around Yapeyú had arisen and joined the insurrection. The northern caciques of Guaycurú and Abipon began to send their subjects to Artigas as soldiers and as settlers. The republican political economy especially appealed to the Guaraní Indians, who for centuries had to wage a defensive struggle against Portuguese planters and slave hunters, as well as Spanish authorities wanting to impose levies on villages. Guaranís became an important cohort of fighters and officers in Artigas's armies. Deep behind the province's defensive lines, commanders parceled land from the estates of Francisco Albín, Miguel de Azcuénaga, Manuel Rollano, Juan Francisco Alvarez, Francisco Martínez, and many others, Spaniard and creole alike, as rewards for Artigas's soldier-settlers. Indeed, as the war unfolded it became harder and harder to untangle the

---

[41]Lucia Sala de Touron, *Nelson dela Torre, and Julío C. Rodriguez, Artigas y so revolución agraria, 1811–1820* (Montevideo: Ediciones Pueblos Unidos, 1967), pp. 114–53; Agustín Beraza, *La economía en la Banda Oriental, 1811–1820* (Montevideo: Ed. Banda Oriental, 1964), pp. 33–54; Pablo Blanco Acevedo, *El federalismo de Artigas y la independencia nacional* (Montevideo: N.p., 1939), pp. 46–47; Ariosto D. González, *Las primeras formulas constitucionales en los Paises del Plata* (Montevideo: Barreiro y Ramos, 1962), pp. 347–48.

compensatory function of expropriating estates from the goal of a social transformation of the region's capitalist base.[42]

The social revolution at the center of the political clash came to a head in 1816. Artigas's movement was simply too incendiary to be tolerated by powerful neighbors. The prospect of converting the borderlands into a heartland for a radically different propertied and cultural order altered the diplomatic balance between Brazil and Buenos Aires. Brazilian magnates, dedicated to expanded slaveholding and fearing insurrection on its southern flank, bristled when news spread about the plebeian groundswell. For Buenos Aires, any concession to provincial autonomy and federalism at the mouth of the River Plate, the gateway to the Atlantic world, threatened to deprive the central government in Buenos Aires of the monopoly of trading rents and revenues; it, too, turned against Artigas and his followers. Thus, when the Portuguese invaded the Banda Oriental again to pacify its southern flank and take the opportunity to annex territories, Buenos Aires turned a blind eye and did not rush to the support of Artigas, who had been so decisive in destroying royalist threats from Montevideo years earlier. Oriental envoys pleaded, but Argentine troops stood by while Brazilian naval and ground forces slowly crushed Artigas's revolution. In the ensuing years, federalist guerrillas fought large powerful units of cavalry, infantry, and artillery. The warfare was as awful as the battling in Venezuela and Nueva Granada. The physical infrastructure, social relations, and the entire fabric of one of Spain's most dynamic colonies were pulverized by three Brazilian army divisions and a squadron of warships that traveled up the Uruguay River to bombard riverine towns.[43]

The organization of popular fighting machines was crucial for the struggle against the defenders of the ancien régime. By appealing to commoners, popular military leaders tilted the balance of power in favor of patriots, who recovered or gained whatever legitimacy creole rebels could not claim in 1812. In the words of Francisco Estrada, a slave from the Banda Oriental who joined the insurgency, "we chose then the generous system of the patria; we sang the hymns of freedom; and uniting our desires and our hearts with the holy sentiments of the just system of liberty, we once and for all renounced indignantly that hard, miserable, and disorganized government that degraded men and did not permit

---

[42]Sala de Touron, *Artigas*, pp. 208–12; Eduardo Azcuy Ameghino, *Historia de Artigas y la independencia argentina* (Montevideo: Ed. Banda Oriental, 1993), pp. 214–28; Patricia S. Pasqualí, "La expansion artigüista 1813–1815: Objetos y accionar," *Res Gesta* 22 (July–December, 1989): 150–53.

[43]Blanco Acevedo, *El federalismo*, pp. 164–71; Street, *Artigas and the Emancipation of Uruguay*, pp. 294–321.

those who are called slaves to claim the rights of humanity."[44] No doubt, it was important that Spanish officers in Caracas, Montevideo, and Lima had rejected or demobilized popular armies, worried that giving arms to Indians, blacks, mulattos, pardos, and subaltern whites was too risky. It left a massive constituency, frequently armed anyway, capable of providing the muscle and blood to win not just battles, but also the war. Local patriotic chieftains created a form of popular affiliation and vindicated rights as free men that were not originally part of the secessionist vocabulary in 1810 and would shape the postrevolutionary order.[45]

Páez, Piar, and Artigas also pinned down counterrevolutionary forces long enough to bleed the Spanish (and even the Portuguese) of resources and buy time for the revolution's leaders to build a parallel source of military strength: organized standing armies. Consider Artigas again. His armies not only helped vanquish Spanish royalists in Montevideo and the first Portuguese occupants. They also enabled Buenos Aires to revamp its Andean strategy; by tying up royalists on the east bank of the River Plate, Artigas allowed Buenos Aires to muster resources to open a new front on the west, aiming once more to "liberate" the Andes, this time via Chile and up the Pacific coast. A campaign of this sort required a real army, capable of fighting a more conventional war for territorial gain while at the same time being mobile and able to survive off more than just the resources it could soak from local popular folk. While the littoral went up in flames, Buenos Aires threw its fate in the hands of an experienced creole officer, José de San Martín, who had seen plenty of action fighting French armies in Spain. San Martín not only brought tactical and strategic skills, he also had organizational abilities. Based in Mendoza, the Argentine government named him the governor of Cuyo, and he used the position to siphon revenues gradually into the task of building a modern army. San Martín assembled his "Army of the Andes" of 5,000 trained, systematized, and ranked soldiers with a real chain of command. Moreover, San Martín knew that as the expedition would venture far from its home base, it had to bring with it the resources to spare itself endless and vulnerable supply lines and to avoid tapping into liberated communities for money and materiel, which might compromise its welcome. By early January 1817, the expeditionary force began its long trek through the several Andean passes and began driving back Ferdinand's troops until Chile declared its independence in February 1818. The final main Chilean battle took place at the plains of Maipú in April 1818, where San Martín brilliantly outmaneuvered a seasoned

---

[44]Cited in Blanchard, "The Language of Liberation," p. 518.
[45]Archer, "Setting the Scene for an Age of Warfare," pp. 8–16.

army of 6,000 men sent from Peru. It was one of the decisive battles of the long war—and showed how the Argentine commander mastered the techniques of war and used them against those who had trained him. Thereafter, San Martín, now joined with Chilean resources and reinforcements, began to prepare the naval assault on coastal Peru.[46]

In northern South America, mass militarization also rolled back the reconquest, shifted the balance of power within the patriotic forces, and spawned a revolution. Páez's guerrillas made life miserable for the Spanish forces in Venezuela and forced Morillo to abandon Bogotá, diluting the Spanish counterrevolutionary armies across the region. At La Mata de la Miel, Páez's mounted guerrillas overwhelmed a superior Spanish force during a night battle, killing 400 soldiers, taking another 500 prisoner, and making off with more than 3,000 horses—precisely the kind of victory that ravaged Morillo's morale and allowed the guerrillas to live on. Later, at Mucuritas, Páez's llaneros encircled a Spanish detachment of 4,500 cavalry and infantry, took up a windward position and set fire to the grasses, and then plunged into the choking royalists with their lances and sabers. In none of these battles did Páez definitively crush the Spanish forces, but they did inflict heavy losses. With each crippling skirmish, the guerrillas shifted the political balance to the patriots, even if they could not stand as decided victors on the battlefields.[47]

Getting from resistance to vanquishing the royalists required a fusion of fighting forces and styles between guerrilla insurgents and standing armies. The blend depended on the type and scale of royalist retrenchment as well as the strength of grassroots military formations. The balance varied from region to region. In the area around the Banda Oriental, revolutionary forces tilted more toward formations of smaller fighting units capable of quicker strikes, but San Martín's campaign across the Andes resembled more the movements of a large standing army. Hence, in the River Plate two kinds of military forces emerged: one to fight in the east and the other in the west, dependent upon each other but separate. By contrast, across the llanos guerrilla and standing forces fused into hybrid combat units because there a powerful occupying army was much harder to dislodge and could, as late as 1819, still successfully hold its own on the battlefield and thus controlled much of the coast and the major cities. The fate of the revolution hinged, therefore, on the combination of standing and guerrilla fighting units to win more than battles but the actual war.

---

[46]AGI, Estado, Lima, José María de Alós to Secretario de Estado, 20/12/19; Lynch, *Spanish American Revolutions*, pp. 133–43.

[47]Graham, *José Antonio Páez* pp. 99–102, 116–19.

Ultimately the combination was the handiwork of Simón Bolívar, who gathered the fighting factions under the umbrella of a "Liberating Army." This was not an easy coalition. Bolívar himself had been reluctant to cede too much strategy, tactics, and substance to the popular guerrilla leadership, especially since he yearned to liberate the coastal cities and his hometown, Caracas. But all his frontal assaults had ended disastrously. After 1816 he had run into a succession of defeats while Páez expanded his raiding across the western plains. Bolívar accepted that his only way of liberating the Venezuelan heartland was by more effectively bonding with fighters from the hinterlands: he appealed to Páez and other *guerrilleros*, promising the grassland commanders rank, property, and a place in the leadership of the emerging nation. Bolívar adapted to the mobile, light-skirmishing llanero fighting style as much as he channeled it into a permanent machine capable of moving far from its home base to liberate, province by province, delivering more decisive blows to the enemies with more extended and eventually frontal engagements.[48]

With time, Bolívar's leadership acquired, like San Martín's from Buenos Aires, constitutional authority, vitalized by the notion that political communities should rest on some legal foundations that recognize all subjects as members of new nations. At Angostura in early 1819, Bolívar celebrated the multi-ethnic, poly-class, hybrid nature of the societies that were being liberated. Diversity was not what doomed the revolution, as the pessimists of 1812 argued, and as Bolívar himself had suggested in his "Jamaica Letter". It rescued it. And while he articulated deep concerns about the peoples' ability to live in ideal liberty, he made clear that the future of any republic depended on its ability to accommodate all colonists within the political community. Political equality was the foundation of the new state, even if political virtues were unevenly spread. What was crucial about Angostura was that a republican congress with representatives from seven liberated provinces conferred authority, with wellsprings of legitimacy, on Bolívar as commander in chief to fight the last stage of the war, enabling him to muster the necessary resources and carry the struggle to distant lands. Bolívar was given a mandate to liberate Nueva Granada and move southward down the Andes, under the pretext that Venezuelans could not be free unless its neighbors were, too.[49]

The fusion of civic and military leadership, and of the two fighting styles, began to pay dividends in 1819, and the balance of the struggle

---

[48]Restrepo, *Historia de la Revolución de Colombia*, v. 3, pp. 258–59; David Bushnell, *Simón Bolívar: Liberation and Disappointment* (New York: Longman, 2004), pp. 87–91.

[49]Simón Bolívar, "Address Delivered at the Inauguration of the Second National Congress of Venezuela in Angostura" (February 15, 1819), in Bierck, ed., *Selected Writings*, pp. 180–83.

began to tilt irrevocably to the patriotic forces. The Battle of Boyacá, on August 7, 1819, featured the combination of setpiece maneuvers in open battles for bridges and roads, while lightning charges and swift retreats by llaneros sliced up the royalist wings. In all, it lasted but two hours and cost the patriots only thirteen casualties. But it was brilliant, decisive, and exemplified the effectiveness of the military amalgam that took so long to germinate but finally vanquished the royal armies of central Nueva Granada. Bogotá was now open for the taking. The viceroy, disguised as an Indian, escaped to the Magdalena River; three days later Bolívar entered the weary capital and took possession of the royal "treasury." Morillo, tied down in skirmishes with Venezuelan llaneros, moaned when he got the news of Boyacá: "On a single day Bolívar destroys the fruit of a five-year campaign, and in one battle wins back all that we have gained in countless engagements."[50]

As the weight of Spanish power rested so much on its military leg, the loss at Boyacá meant that royal authority in the viceroyalty collapsed. The liberation of Nueva Granada was now reduced to an extended mop-up operation. With no money, the remains of the Spanish armies in the viceroyalty were immediately immiserated. Still, liberating the coast and the southern highlands took months and required picking off one corner at a time. It was not until October 1821 that Cartagena, now practically a ruin, was liberated. This enabled Bolívar's armies to press southward to Quito and down the spinal chord of the Andes, while his Venezuelan generals squeezed in on Caracas.

THE RESOURCE STRUGGLE

The contest for the loyalties of colonial subjects was important in shifting the tides of war, but it was only part of the struggle. The counterrevolution spurred a competition for resources to wage the war, a cycle that ravaged the class that once dominated the imperial and colonial orders: merchants. Each side scrambled for resources and paid less attention to the longer-term fate of the constituency that possessed them because it represented a narrow band of the social spectrum. For their part, merchants had the most liquid assets and their property was susceptible to predatory policies. Here was the dilemma: merchant capitalists were highly motivated to shape policy to protect their rents, but they were also vulnerable to exactions.

---

[50]Masur, *Simón Bolívar*, pp. 256–57; Boyacá, pp. 270–72, 274; Earle, *Spain and the Independence of Colombia*, pp. 133–44.

Merchant capital was cleaved between those who embraced commercial opportunities of open ports and those who clung to peninsular mercantilism. If there was a patina of unity it reflected the fear of social unrest and political upheaval. On September 30, 1814, the merchants of the port of Buenos Aires convened to discuss the state of affairs—after being cut off from the Andes, watching the Banda Oriental get torn up by rival armies, and being subjected to multiple war levies. It was an unhappy occasion. One merchant complained about "the political convulsions that simultaneously and successively visit these regions [and that] have caused among our capitalists great losses in the many places where they trade, slowing the regular conduct of business just when speed has become even more important for profits." This depressed merchant in effect depicted the multiple squeeze on merchant capitalists of the Spanish empire: as intensifying warfare imposed rising costs on those with the most fungible resources, those with the liquidity to fund war were being subjected to a rapidly changing commercial order of unfettered competition.[51] Merchants in the colonies pleaded for succor from the peninsula when armies gathered on the outskirts of cities. They banged on the doors of the hapless viceroy of Nueva Granada in mid-1812 to complain that the revolt in Cartagena had cut them off from the Caribbean while British merchants in Jamaica were flooding the Magdalena basin with their cheap wares, robbing the faithful subjects of their rightful control of domestic markets. They also protested the government's endless requests for loans and special levies.[52] Caraqueño merchants breathed a great sigh of relief after the fall of the first republic, worried when Bolívar returned, and then wiped their brows when the second republic imploded. The Caracas merchant guild voted unanimously on September 19, 1814, to declare the "most sincere and sacred" loyalty to Ferdinand when he returned to power.[53] The one mighty outpost of loyalty, right to the end, was Lima, where one strong group of consulado merchants never flinched in their commitment to ancien-régime economics. As late as the end of 1819, when San Martín's forces were on the move from the south and Bolívar's had taken the northern Andes, the officers of the merchant guild pleaded for Spain "to take whatever measures are necessary to preserve these dominions." But even in Lima, as we shall see, the breakup of the empire buckled the commitments of its merchant classes.[54]

[51]AGNBA, Sala IX, Consulado, 29/2/1, Actas 1814–16, September 30, 1814, p. 5; Anna, *Spain and the Loss of America*, pp. 151–55; Charles C. Griffin, "Economic and Social Aspects of the Era of Spanish-American Independence," *Hispanic American Historical Review* 29:2 (1949): 170–87.

[52]AGI, Estado, Santa Fé, 53/26, June 1812, Benito Pérez to Minister de Estado.

[53]AGI, Gobierno, Caracas, 917, September 19, 1814.

[54]AGI, Gobierno, Lima, 1550, December 26, 1819.

In the early days of the restoration, these declarations of piety filled the messages back to Spain. But there was a difference between supporting imperial restoration and backing, not to mention funding, the counterrevolution. In the years after 1814, merchant capitalists grew less enthusiastic about Ferdinand's grand plans. Fidelity had its limits; the interests in empire had to confront two looming problems for which they ultimately had no solution. First, how would merchants preserve the mercantilist, protectionist barriers to entry of foreign merchants and merchandise when the political structures to enforce these rules were in shambles? Second, as the war ramped up thanks to Ferdinand's decision to reconquer the colonies, how would merchants contend with repeated demands for revenues by both sides? In the end, the breakdown of the empire meant that the government could not defend merchants from competition. Worse, it unleashed political rivals' demands for revenues. The mercantilist pact of balancing public revenues and private rents was thrown into irretrievable disequilibrium. When the political foundation that upheld colonial extractive systems collapsed, it brought down the layered interests that had thrived off it.

Conflict over trade had long preceded the revolts, but as the cycle of decomposition intensified so did the battle for commercial freedom—and control. When Ferdinand came back to power in 1814, he was determined not just to bring the curtain down on open trade but to roll back concessions to colonial commerce since the 1790s. This idea of economic restoration conjured exclusivist rules that had long since lapsed in the metropolis itself. Seized with near xenophobic fears of foreign merchants' parasitic exploitation of Spain's temporary weakness, the Cádiz guild slapped down requests by foreigners, even those long based in the metropolis, to trade.[55] But what about the colonies? How could the regime pacify the colonies *and* curb commercial autonomy? Martín de Garay, undeterred by his failure to get his king to soften his political position on the colonies, tried to get him to rethink his intransigence on economic policy. He focused on the causes of the malaise in the colonies, insisting that earlier concessions to freer trade from the 1790s onward were made out of necessity: peninsular commerce was too anemic then, and certainly too anemic now, credibly to force the colonists to trade only with Spain. To do so would make the pacification effort even more difficult, and more dependent on military success. It would be better to make the concessions to colonists than attempt to enforce an unenforceable policy. Nor was Garay alone. As the Council of the Indies pointed out in a long report to the king in December 1815, free trade would go

---

[55] AGI, IG, 2320, Expedientes del consulado, July 21, 1813.

a long way toward winning back the loyalty of colonists while at the same time solving the fiscal problems of the metropolis. In a new colonial pact, the council argued, merchants in the fringe would gain more rents from greater trade, and thus could afford to pay more taxes to the royal treasury. All that was required was tinkering with the old rent-for-revenue pact within empire. The Council of State issued its own *consulta* in early 1817 and came to the same conclusion that "our primitive laws," especially in matters of commerce, required updating. The king might as well make a virtue out of necessity: "among the opportune and effective measures we might take to end the Rebellion, none offers more hope than trade." Besides, the consulta added, warfare and restrictions on commerce had impoverished the colonies and only made them more rebellious. What better way to restore the old peace than by giving them new means to enhance their fortunes, pay royal levies, and therefore express fidelity to the king?[56]

Metropolitan merchants, threatened with the loss of what was left of their exclusive domains and rents, fought back. In effect, they argued, Spanish reconstruction after the war—indeed recovering Spanish grandeur, appealing to the king's fantasy of restoring Philip II's imperium—depended on the preservation of monopoly and exclusive rights to generate the rents that could be ploughed back into Spain. Without mercantilism, all the latent centrifugal forces would break out and Spain would be relegated to a subordinate place in the European concert. The Marquis of Casa Irujo, one of the fiercest exponents of monopoly, urged the king not to let British merchants promote "mercantile avarice," for what they called "liberty" would only breed "license." What is more, "foreign trade has been the precursor and vehicle of the revolutions" in the Americas. The British, led by Castlereagh, had been trying to secure access to Spanish and colonial markets as a quid pro quo for driving the French out of the peninsula. To the Marquis, this was evidence enough that foreigners had designs on the empire and wanted to subject Spain to the status of permanent subordinate in the European concert; colonists who wanted open trade were simply dupes of Spain's rivals and had conflated their passions for private fortunes with the interests of Spain's enemies. As for those who argued that open trade would smooth colonial feathers, another high-ranking

---

[56] AGI, Estado, Caracas, 71/9, no. 19, March 6, 1817, Oficio de Martín de Garay; AGI, Estado, Americas, 86A(2), no. 40, December 3, 1815, "Borrador de la Consulta del Consejo de Indias"; Estado, Americas, 88/11, see February 8 1817, report in "R.O. reservado al presidente del Consejo de Indias"; AGI, IG, 1568, February 22, 1917, "Pacificación de América"; Hamnett, *La política española*, pp. 232–33; Anna, *Spain and the Loss of America*, pp. 161–64.

official argued that free trade in the empire was tantamount to rewarding insurgents for their disloyalty. As the debate in Madrid heated up, the Cádiz guild bombarded the king's ministries and councils with petitions, arguing that the colonies must remain the exclusive domain for Spanish commerce.[57]

Commercial networks were more than just funnels for rents; they were sinews of revenues. From the moment Ferdinand returned to Madrid, he had to govern under the burdens of high debts and empty coffers. "Spain," observed one report in late 1814, "is behind in her credit because she is completely discredited."[58] One might think that this would have forced Madrid to accept commercial reform: Garay kept insisting that free trade would generate the revenues that would spare the king from borrowing more. He noted that so long as the king was bent on funding military expenditures, he would not be able to escape the money crunch. There was a fundamental incompatibility between restoring an old model of empire and resolving the financial crisis of the monarchy. He created a *Junta de economía* to monitor the books, noting to the king that sovereign debts "are the principal cause of decadence of the kingdom... passing on to future generations our actual expenses, and pushing us to the precipice over which we now run the risk of plunging." His jeremiads were fruitless. The king was not above spending money he did not have for broader counterrevolutionary goals. Instead, his debts soared—by 1819 they surpassed 1.7 million reales; and in January 1820, the index of depreciation on his bonds sank to 83 percent. Garay urged plan after plan for fiscal and commercial recovery, only to be rebuffed.[59]

The Cádiz consulado was aware of how the king's penury was a source of leverage. It mustered all its waning financial muscle to assure Ferdinand that peninsular merchants could bankroll the restoration, provided that they continued to possess their ancient trading privileges. Intent on a military strategy for pacification, but with empty coffers, Ferdinand was easily tempted by Cádiz merchants' offers to pay for Morillo's expedition. The merchants had put together 30 million reales to pay for the reconquest. Moreover, as the war ground on, Cádiz squeezed more and more liquidity from mercantile ranks to fund the losing

---

[57]AGI, Estado, Americas, 89/88, September 21, 1818 Representación de Marqués de Casa Irujo al Rey; 86A (7), December 31, 1816, "Memoria sobre si es o no conveniente el comercio de los extranjeros en nuestras Americas"; Consulados, 81, "Informe del Consulado al Ministerio de Hacienda satisfaciendo el decreto de 12 de noviembre de 1816." Michael P. Costeloe, "Spain and the Latin American Wars of Independence: The Free Trade Controversy," *Hispanic American Historical Review* 61:2 (1981): 209–34.

[58]AGI, IG, 1708, October 24, 1814, "Informe de la Junta del Crédito Público."

[59]AGI, IG, 1707, "Real decreto para el establecimiento del sistema general de hacienda," June 1, 1817; Hamnett, *La política española*, pp. 241–44.

effort. In late 1818, the king asked peninsular merchants to lend him an additional 10 million reales to fund the expeditions in South America, 4 million from Cádiz alone.[60] So, with the metropolitan merchants financing the counterrevolution, Ferdinand could not violate their demands for a quid pro quo to keep foreigners out of colonial markets. Mutual dependency threw both sides into each other's arms to cling to a system that crumbled with every effort to shore it up.

The clash within the king's circle came to a head in September 1818. Chile and much of Venezuela had been reconquered; Nueva Granada was being subdued; and the River Plate was cracking up. The king's strategy appeared to be working, which reinforced the convictions of the king and his hard-line advisors that reforms were not only unnecessary, but that they placated the very interests that had to be subdued. In that month, several reformists were dismissed. A minister of state who had been touting free trade as a balm for the colonies, José García de León y Pizarro, found himself sacked. The Marquis of Casa Irujo took over as minister and scuppered British proposals to mediate between Spain and the colonies, blocking all efforts to alter the commitment to a commercial hard line. To the last, the Cádiz merchants were relentless in their campaign, reminding the sovereign and his officials that the most loyal subjects in the realm were the monopoly merchants and the most disloyal were the colonists, and that the only way to restore the fiscal and commercial balance was to protect the agreement to monopolize mercantile rents in return for royal revenues. As Timothy Anna has noted, it was ironic that hawkish hard-liners, the Spanish military, and the old merchants of the peninsula consolidated their control of policymaking at precisely the time when they could least afford to mount any further offensive against insurgents in America.[61]

The compound pressures of borrowing peninsular merchants' money *and* restricting the trading rights with colonies did not sit well with all merchants in Spain, even in Cádiz. The weakness of the archaic bloc became more evident as it tightened its grip on royal decision making. Indeed, while the merchant guild was busy lobbying in Madrid, it was also engaged in rear-guard action against homegrown defectors. One guild officer based in reconquered Cartagena noted that even if Cádiz wanted to preserve the traditional monopolistic trading system with the gateway to the Magdalena River, the whole guild enforcement system

---

[60]AGI, IG, 2321, "Copia de dos exposiciones elevadas á S.M. por la Juna de Diputados Consulares," November 5, 1818.

[61]AGI, Estado, Americas, 86A/40 (9c), "Consulado de Cádiz representación al rey," January 5, 1819; Costeloe, "Free Trade Controversy," p. 230; Anna, *Spain and the Loss of America*, p. 208.

had collapsed. Moreover, it was impossible even to get Cádiz merchants to respect the rules in the devastated fringe, suggesting that old monopolistic merchants were themselves violating the rules that the guild was supposed to—but found impossible to—apply.[62] Ysidro de Angulo, whose status as a *natural* was unquestionable, grew tired of having to contribute to the king's financial requests to cover the reconquest of the colonies while he himself could not trade freely with these colonies. What he lacked were both merchandise and ships to carry it, and accordingly requested rights to conduct his business using foreign vessels. He noted in his appeal that he had always given loans and *donativos* generously, and that he disapproved of "the disgraceful insurrection of our ungrateful children in our Americas," but business was business, and it could not be done without some rule bending. His request for permission to deal with foreign shippers was unceremoniously declined.[63]

Peninsular defection from the system paled beside the destruction of the old mercantile regime in the colonies. There, as Garay and others had been warning, open trade was less a matter of voluntary policy than a survival strategy for fringe economies. For without effective authority, and with elites cleaved by social and political conflict, the enforcement mechanisms of Spanish mercantilism simply collapsed. It was *sauve qui peut* among merchants who scrambled to trade with any partner available. This was not always as welcome as the apostles of free trade may have thought. Merchants in Caracas informed the Cádiz consulado in 1813 that the British were flooding their markets from bases in Curaçao.[64] In Nueva Granada, trade also became uncontrolled. As early as 1812, merchants complained that they were unable to compete. From reconquered Cartagena came repeated protests that while it was possible to wipe out the rebellion, it was impossible to wipe out rampant illegal commerce. Indians and runaway slaves were doing a swift business buying merchandise offshore or, worse, from small ports up and down the Guajira peninsula and selling it to retailers and vendors who were desperate to replenish their stocks. The honorable merchants in the port— or what was left of them—simply could not compete with these rogue traffickers who contributed to "the contagion of insurrection" by flaunting commercial laws. Even Santa Marta, the staunch outpost of the counterrevolution, informed Spain in 1818 that merchants faced more than just a drop in trade as a result of the wars; they also encountered

[62] AGI, Gobierno, Santa Fé, July 29, 1818, Juan Guillermo Ros to Secretario de Estado.
[63] AGI, IG, 2321, October 14, 1819, Ysidro de Angulo.
[64] AGI, Estado, Americas, 63/34, March 7, 1813, Oficio de José Vázquez Figueroa.

intensified competition from local and foreign merchants who did not respect the rules.[65] Buenos Aires merchants—who were spared reconquest—including those who had led the charge for more open trade before 1810, often regretted the new system to which they had subjected themselves. Juan José Anchorena, one of the city's most puissant merchants, groaned that "the importation of all overseas effects and the exports of our own staples are being monopolized by foreigners, and therefore national merchants have their hands tied." Manuel Aguirre, who carried the flag for neutral trade from 1794 to 1807, now lamented the full-scale aperture: "I am ashamed when I think about this, and I confess that even in my own *patria* governed by her own sons, I consider myself beaten down and humiliated before foreigners, to whom I must concede the justice of recognizing their superiority."[66] Even in Lima, where the old guard stood squarely behind mercantilist exclusions, merchants noted that they could not hold back contraband from Panama and Buenos Aires—which many of the lesser merchants procured in the teeth of royal regulations.[67]

Money Wars

The destruction of mercantilist trading systems undermined the cohesion of merchant capital; but what finally smashed the pillars of the old economic order was the desperation to borrow—or steal—resources from colonial merchants to bankroll counterrevolutionary and insurgent warfare. Colonial merchants were especially vulnerable because they sat on top of the most fungible and concentrated pools of capital, wealth that could be ploughed into munitions and salaries for soldiers (when they were paid). It was the scramble for money that ultimately brought the dominant class of empire to its knees and tilted the fortunes of war in favor of revolutionaries.

In some respects, the royalists began the war in the strongest position, for they had access to metropolitan war subsidies and the prospect of borrowing money abroad as a sovereign power. After all, British financiers, albeit not always happily, bankrolled the Spanish state during and

---

[65] AGNB, Anexo, Comercio, t. I, September 15, 1812, p. 160, and September 22, 1818, pp. 223–24; AGI, Estado, Santa Fe, 53/42, Francisco de Montalvo to Minister de Estado, November 13, 1816.

[66] AGNBA, Sala IX, Consulado, Actas 29/2/1, 1814–16, September 30, 1814, p. 11, and September 1, 1815, p. 48.

[67] AGI, Consulado, 346, February 15, 1817, Antonio de Elizalde to Cádiz; Marks, "Power and Authority in Late Colonial Peru," pp. 292–303.

after the Napoleonic Wars. These were advantages that—despite the appeals of Belgrano from Buenos Aires and Bolívar from Bogotá—colonists did not have. Supporting rebels meant angering the Spanish monarchy and thus disrupting the reactionary equipoise in Europe. So, what proved decisive for Anglo-American rebels in 1776—French subsidies and loans, backed by French and Spanish armies—was unavailable to South American patriots after 1810.

Still, Spain could not fund the war from peninsular sources alone. True, Cádiz merchants were willing to sponge liquidity to finance the *reconquista*. But as Pablo Morillo discovered, a drawn-out struggle far from home meant that he had to turn to local sources to support the counterrevolution. At first, his solution was simple, if politically counterproductive. Once he occupied Caracas, he began expropriating the properties and estates of rebels and auctioning them, even in the face of creditors' protests. By the time he reconquered Santa Fé, Morillo had refined this tactic: shortly after entering the capital, he rounded up republicans and told them to hand over whatever they had in return for an amnesty (to which he did not always hold himself).[68]

Under the circumstances, Morillo was relatively controlled—and tried to uphold a basic distinction between soaking rebel families and exempting loyalists, foisting the burdens of his campaign on the former as much as possible. Boves, his predecessor, had less time for such nuances. He went for anyone who had money and made pillaging an effective means to finance his unruly army. But Boves's financial tactics presaged measures that Morillo would be increasingly compelled to adopt. In effect, the more intractable the war got, the more the royalists switched from selective confiscations to collective ones.[69]

Voluntary or not, royalist demands eventually exhausted their sources. Matters grew especially troublesome after 1817, whereupon collective confiscation and repudiations of debts became financial mainstays of the regime. The war groaned on indefinitely. Martín de Garay was struggling to keep the royal house's credit ratings from collapsing and issued—in May 1817—an appeal to all the guilds of the colonies, through the master house in Cádiz, for a special tax that would pay off old debts. This set off a round of protests in the colonies. In Caracas, Juan Bernardo Larrain reported to the consulado in 1817 that the royal administration was in complete upheaval and that he could not make heads or tails of government accounts. He tried to figure out which merchants owed how much

---

[68]Restrepo, *Historia de la Revolución de Colombia*, v. 2, p. 102; Earle, *Spain and the Independence of Colombia*, pp. 115–23.

[69]Restrepo, *Historia de la Revolución de Colombia*, v. 3, p. 13; Veitch, "Repudiations and Confiscations by the Medieval State," p. 31.

to the government in taxes or unpaid loan promises, to no avail. By this point whatever distinction once existed between the public royal treasury in the colonies and the private purse of the merchant guild had evaporated. The weakness of the colonial state forced the government to transform the consulado into the fiscal arm of the state. Both, as a result, lost control together. The idea of balancing ledgers was a joke. Two weeks later the guild got word from the Count of La Granja that members were facing an additional request for 500,000 pesos to support the army and the fight against Bolívar's rekindled campaign in the east and Páez's guerrillas in the west. By this point, the merchants had had enough. "This House," the guild members snapped back, "has decided to resist this arbitrary resolution" and "the violence that would be provoked by stripping the knowledge and administration of such privileged funds upon Your Majesty's recommendation." Several months later, undeterred, Cádiz asked Caracas merchants why they were not forthcoming with money, only to be informed that there "were insuperable inconveniences" and a glut of royal demands "for us to subsidize the public credit."[70]

It was not just the embattled merchant communities that felt the fiscal pinch turn into a crunch. Even those relatively unscathed by the conflict got hit. In Lima, deeply loyal and reclaiming the highland silver axis for itself, the merchants faced growing demands. At first, the special levies, taxes, and "exceptional" loans were accepted as the price to be paid for keeping their monopoly rights intact. Still, they found room to warn, as they did in 1813, that their businesses were suffering and thus their ability to subsidize the treasury was limited. That year, Cádiz's envoy to Lima informed the peninsular headquarters that a special committee had to be erected to handle the wave of bankruptcies. But by 1817, war levies were starting to eclipse merchants' abilities to pay. Reporting to Cádiz in April, Antonio de Elizalde noted that levies were rising sharply as legal traffic was plummeting. A month later, a group of merchants sent a special plea to the king. The spread of insurrection from Buenos Aires to Chile and the paralysis in the highlands prompted a wave of defaults. Lima's merchants, the petitioners lamented, "have been forced to suspend their operations which they once conducted in these regions," which left them prostrate and unable to pay their dues. After sending over 7 million reales to pay the costs of the war against Buenos Aires and another 2 million reales to the peninsula, they were now exhausted. They confessed that this was not just a disaster for our trade, "but for the State in general." Thus when Garay's emergency appeals to the guilds came in, Spain's loyal merchants in Peru were forced to admit

---

[70]AGI, Gobierno, Caracas, 918, October 3, 1817; AGI, Consulados, 346, June 12, 1817, Juan Bernardo Larrain.

that "in spite of their great desire which we all share to help the Treasury in these fatal needs. . . . [we] have deliberated this request . . . and this market, with well-known bankruptcies, is completely paralyzed; even though we wish to make even greater efforts, we are simply unable." This, of course did not stop Lima's capitalists from denouncing, in ever more apocalyptic terms, the prospect of free trade. Open ports would eviscerate fiscal support for the monarchy; free trade would lead inexorably to monarchical and imperial collapse—the very outcome Madrid was trying to avoid: "it would break all the mutual ties that sustain the Peninsula and the Americas." In the balance between private interests and the reasons of state, loyal capitalists and benevolent kings had to look out for each other now more than ever. In other words, the specter of revolution threatened not just particulars but what kept them united as part of a moral community: the nation. "The merchants of Lima hope that you will be the principal and first protector of our requests, not for the mere sake of the particular or private good, but for the enthusiasm with which we must save the Nation. Right now we are applying our services in favor of the Monarchy for the pacification of these Dominions. This love for our glories and greatness is our bedrock so that you may defend the Rights which are menaced."[71]

For all the platitudes about love of country it was the need for money that put Peruvian rulers in a bind that exposed the impossibility of restoring ancien-régime economics without a cohesive merchant bloc willing to fund it. Lima's economic and political cohesion unraveled quickly. While the peninsula was calling in as many remittances as possible, and merchants coped with commercial upheavals, the viceroyalty wavered. After the Spanish defeat at Maipú in Chile (April 5, 1818), the southern flank opened up. The viceroy who had replaced Abascal in 1816, Joaquín de la Pezuela, tried to put together a naval squadron to defend the Peruvian coast and build an additional army to reconquer Chile. In October 1818, he circulated a special appeal for funds. But his requests for money from local merchants drew mainly declarations of pious penury. He recounted to the Duke of San Carlos, the ambassador to London who was trying to broker the loan of warships and munitions to Peru, how frustrating it was to need a sudden infusion of resources from a market that was unable to step forth with even the most limited support. He added that with the fall of Chile and Morillo's setbacks in Venezuela, the crown might have to reassess its strategy for reconquest—for the costs

---

[71]AGI, Consulado, 345, October 15, 1813, Zacarías Pereyra to Consulado; 346, April 29, 1817, May 3, 1817, June 25, 1818, and November 10, 1818; Archivo General de la Nación (Lima; hereafter AGNL), Real Tribunal de Comercio de Lima (RTCL), Legajo 6, undated letter, 1817.

were outpacing the resources of even the most committed loyalists. By July 1818, the viceroy was desperate enough to propose opening Lima's port, Callao, to direct trade with foreigners as a revenue measure. By the end of 1818, he was warning Madrid directly that the state of affairs in Lima was very precarious: he was unable to fund the state, his armies were suffering from mass desertions, and, while "the opinion of Indians and Cholos are still favorable to the king, the multitude of Slaves is now openly decided for the rebels, from whose hands they hope for their liberty." So, in February 1819, Pezuela had to levy a forced loan on the city's capitalists of one million pesos. It provoked howls of protest. "We will have 150 lawsuits instead of a million pesos," bellowed one petition. At the end of 1819, the viceroy again suggested that Lima's longstanding official commitment to commerce with Spain alone be reconsidered. At least this would enable Pezuela to defend the monarchy from revolutionaries by reviving trade, albeit in foreign hands. Lima's metropolitan merchants, of course, got wind of these sorts of proposals and were furious, sending direct appeals to Cádiz and Madrid, demanding that their traditional rights be upheld just as their deep loyalty was untarnished. They warned the viceroy that these sorts of ideas would visit ruin upon not just merchants "but on all our Nation." Well before San Martín's expedition arrived off the Peruvian coast, the royalist coalition was coming apart in Lima.[72]

The struggle for resources ultimately doomed Morillo's pacification campaign. The original plan was to deliver a swift, terminal drubbing to the rebels. Once this failed, the commander got bogged down in a withering and costly counterinsurgency, which meant that he had to sustain a large standing army with battalions spread across Venezuela and Nueva Granada. And since his pleas to Madrid to send money and reinforcements went unrequited, he was compelled to turn to local pools of capital to fund the war. In other words, the very constituency he was supposed to be rescuing from the maw of revolution found itself caught in the jaws of a failing counterrevolution. This was not the original plan. The pacification was supposed to be brief enough to be covered by other imperial sources. But the assumption that merchants had the wherewithal to sustain it was, at best, wishful, as was the view that merchant capital would be loyal to the end to the king and imperial restoration.

---

[72]AGI, Gobierno, Lima, 74/29, July 29, 1818, Joaquín de la Pezuela to San Carlos, and 74/30, November 12, 1818, Pezuela to Secretario de Estado, and 1550, December 26, 1819, Secretario de Estado to Pezuela; AGI, Gobierno, Lima, 1551, June 16, 1818, Consular letter to king and Legajo 15, July 2, 1818, Consulado to Pezuela; Marks, "Power and Authority in Late Colonial Peru," chap. 5, esp. pp. 304–14.

Morillo's problems mounted from the moment he retook Nueva Granada. He could only continue to assault rebels through increasingly coercive fiscal demands on loyalists. It was not only Cartagena's merchants who felt the pinch. Panama's and Santa Marta's merchants also dug into their pockets and came up increasingly empty. As Morillo's soldiers entered "liberated" towns, they seized cattle, food, and jewelry, anything to feed, clothe, and pay the royal troops. When, in September 1817, Morillo simply seized the Cartagena consulado's treasury, the merchants appealed to Spain "for him to abstain from proceeding in such a violent way, completely breaching the authority which he is supposed to represent."[73] By the time Morillo had to rush back to Venezuela to take care of the insurgency there, fiscal shortages had become a permanent state of affairs, and he found it impossible to pursue the guerrillas and stop their naval movements, especially in the mouth of the Orinoco. In early 1818, he convoked a junta of notables in Caracas to come up with more funds. The only thing forthcoming was a unanimous declaration of bankruptcy and a plea for Spain to authorize transfers from Veracruz and Havana to fund the war, "for we have brought the economy to a point of intolerable privation." Morillo informed Madrid that he was running short of resources and that this was standing in the way of the campaign's goals: "the awful shortages in the Treasury, the impossibility of sustaining the war in this devastated land means that I cannot cover the subsistence of my fighters." In Madrid, Garay considered the request for subventions from Mexico and Cuba, but found it necessary to inform Morillo that he could not accede to the request. Morillo reconvened his junta of notables and delivered the bad news to a gloomy gathering. Meanwhile, in the town of Pital, José Antonio Barreyro complained to the government that he could not come up with a meager fifty pesos and that the local collectors were taking away his cows. Eventually, Morillo came to recognize that he was defending an "absurd system."[74]

REVENUES FOR REBELS

It is important not to leave the impression that the rebels won the war by being better fiscal handlers or by enjoying more support from merchant classes. Indeed, both sides encountered the same fiscal algorithm of

---

[73] AGNB, Anexo, Emprestitos, III, ff. 528–36; AGI, Gobierno, Santa Fe, 961, November 22, 1816, and January 31, 1818.

[74] AGI, Estado, Caracas, 69/41, 16/01/18, Pablo Morillo to Secretano de Estado, and 69/42, February 7, 1818, Martín de Garay to Minister de Estado; AGNB, Anexo, Emprestitos, III, November 25, 1818, f. 537; Stoan, *Pablo Morillo*, pp. 156–71.

civil war. As the struggle ground to a stalemate, it was impossible for merchants to bet on any sure winner. Faced with a more polarized struggle, rebels actually lost financial support because their commitments to honor obligations were no more credible. The consequence: the absence of voluntary financial support drove both sides to confiscate. In some cases, like Caracas or Cartagena, these first "republics" collapsed on their own feeble fiscal foundations. Near the end of 1813, as Antonio Nariño was pursuing straggling royalists deep into southern Nueva Granada, the rebels could have defeated them convincingly were Nariño not forced to stall for lack of money. This allowed them to escape, regroup, and eventually turn the tide of the war.[75] To win, rebels relied on the same alienating techniques to raise funds as did the royalists. Forced loans were a commonplace. The patriot government in Nueva Granada issued appeal after appeal and eventually order after order to local officials to beat the bushes for money. In November 1813, the mayor of the small town of Chipasque handed over 335 pesos to regional tax collectors, adding an explanation for the meager sum in a very rustic Spanish: "la causa principal de averse Recaudado tanpoca contidad consiste en que mayor parte de este vecindario se alla constitu-ido en la mayor miseria Redeados de familia y quiza cin Alvitrio Alguno para poder ecistir." Joaquin Heredia, a retailer in the capital, wrote that "I paid President Nariño two hundred pesos, and to Sr. Alvarez another one hundred, and Mr Bolívar first twenty-five, then one hundred.... While our business is suspended, the troops of Mr Bolívar robbed a very large sum of goods and money I had in my chest."[76]

The one exception—Buenos Aires—proved this more general rule: in Buenos Aires, the government barely scraped by on forced loans, extra-ordinary taxes, and increasingly worthless bonds. But, it is worth remem-bering, the porteño government faced the weakest counterrevolution, and no royalist army ever got there to back it up—unlike Peru, Nueva Granada, and Venezuela. This did not spare Buenos Aires the scourge of debt. From early 1811, the autonomous government borrowed from "the powerful subjects" upon the promise of future revenues. And from the start, creditors and fiscal administrators chewed their nails off wondering whether revenues would come in sufficient quantities to make promises credible. Merchants wondered openly whether they had thrown good—and increasingly scarce—money after a losing, and thus insolvent, cause. Debts did mount, at times frighteningly, until local governors devised a

---

[75] AGNB, Anexo, Enprestitos, t. I, November 5, 1812; Restrepo, *Historia de la Revolución de Colombia*, v. 1, pp. 313–14.

[76] AGNB, Anexo, Emprestitos, t. I, f. 476, November 10, 1813, t. III, f. 384, April 16, 1816.

system of printing notes, thereby socializing the costs of their shortfalls across the market. Indeed, from a relatively early stage, the city experimented with public credit systems, like issuing paper money, because of one crucial advantage: it was a natural hoarder at the mouth of a major commercial gateway and thus able to cream revenues off the rents that funneled through the entrepôt.[77] But most of the colonies did not have the physical advantages of Buenos Aires and had to endure devastating waves of revolutionary and counterrevolutionary struggles.

As with the royalists, revolutionaries' slope from tax collecting to confiscation to outright plunder was well greased. Coercive means to generate revenues did not stop at the less powerful peasants and shopkeepers; the upper echelons of the merchant capital got hit, too. Consider what the merchants of Santa Fé de Bogotá faced in mid-1819, before and after the Battle of Boyacá. In March, the local governor convened the city's top merchants and insisted to the gathering that they had to cough up 22,000 pesos each month to fund the city's defenses. What was left of the merchant guild assembled to figure out a scheme in the midst of its "misery," admitting that this was going to be a tall order that would fall on "the powerful individuals among whom the 'loan' [as exactions came to be called euphemistically] must be spread." A few months later, the Battle of Boyacá changed the political landscape. No sooner did Bolívar defeat the royalists than he marched into the capital and proceeded to issue his own fiscal demands in the form of summonses of fixed amounts to all the merchants of the city. One merchant replied, "I just have no money left." Another, after getting a summons for 1,000 pesos, pleaded, "I am not trying to trick you because my story is well known to all the inhabitants of this city, and I hope with this knowledge Your Excellency accepts the amount of 100 pesos." Bolívar penned instructions to his officers at the bottom of the letter: "if this money is not delivered in the amount and time prescribed, proceed with the embargo of assets to cover the full amount." The merchant appealed the decision. Bolívar replied charitably: "for equity lower his fee to five hundred pesos and the rest should be consigned immediately to the public Treasury." Paying levies under threats of imprisonment became the primary means of revenue generating. The *trapiche* owner José Gregorio Caycedo, who endured "violent plunders" and "suffered imprisonment twice at the hands of the Spanish" for his loyalties, had to plead to Bolívar to release him from house arrest and potential jail for being unable to pay 3,000 pesos. The

---

[77]AGNBA, Sala IX, Consulado, 4/6/16, November 22, 1811; Actas, 29/2/1, September 30, 1814; Adelman, *Republic of Capital*, pp. 91–97.

Liberator accepted 900 pesos, 48 mules, 66 bulls, and 2 cows instead and instructed his deputies to release the patriot.[78]

Finally, wherever patriots fought, they also financed their struggles by forcing merchants to accept scrip in return for money, supplies, and the constant demand for livestock. Under the rubric "emprestitos," officials from Caracas to Cuzco scribbled promissory notes redeemable by public authorities within a certain lapse of time. Most merchants knew only too well that these were worthless, though they tried to use these instruments to pay their taxes or to make payments to producers or other merchants. In this fashion, paper money of a sort began to circulate throughout South America, even though it was ungoverned by any real authority and quickly depreciated. By November 1820, the new "Republic of Colombia" handed out paper in return for merchants' "loans," whose promise to pay was backed by "the belongings of the State"—whatever those might be. In 1821, the province of Antioquia issued ninety-five bonds to raise money. Most were printed; some were written out by hand. In the National Archives in Bogotá there are several bundles of small notes signed by the Liberator Simón Bolívar, instruments he used to pay for requisitioned materiel.[79]

The scramble for access to pools of merchant capital ravaged the very political economy that counterrevolutionaries claimed they were sheltering from the revolution, or which revolutionaries claimed to be liberating from the venal oppressive hand of the Spanish regime. But there was one way in which the rebels had a decisive advantage: relying on local troops, with access to the countryside as a means of subsistence, especially in waging of guerrilla wars, exempted the rebels from expenses that Morillo, Pezuela, Elío, and other Spanish commanders could not avoid. But there was a deeper advantage that patriots had in the struggle for money. Fighting these wars meant adapting to the contours of colonial capitalism, calibrating the needs of the fighting machines as much as possible to the productive topography of each region. Once Ferdinand decided to mount a counterrevolution to pacify his colonies and ditch conciliation, he alienated many of the agents he needed to have on his side to win the war. Indeed, as his advisor Martín de Garay insisted, it was hard to have it all ways: mount a counterrevolution in America without being able to pay for it, and expect the colonists to foot the bill while denying them rights as loyalists. It was

---

[78]AGNB, Anexo, Emprestitos, t. III, March 26, 1819, ff. 545–55, August 21, 1819, f. 564, and August 24, 1819, f. 568, and November 22, 1819, f. 609.
[79]AGNB, Anexo, Emprestitos, t. III, May 1821, ff. 629–32.

only a matter of time before the imperium finally broke up, not as a result of international war but because of a civil war it sired.

CONCLUSION

The wars in South America, and the contradiction into which Ferdinand plunged his empire, eventually brought down his regime. Like so many distant colonial wars, this one ended by ravaging the metropolis itself and prompted the king to turn to one last, desperate effort to vindicate himself, his policies, and the virtues of imperial restoration. He fastened his gaze on Buenos Aires. In a bold gambit to send a massive expedition to the River Plate, hoping that invading Buenos Aires would force the Argentine armies to withdraw from Peru to protect their fissiparous capital, Ferdinand began assembling an army in Cádiz in 1819. Porteños began to quake at the thought of facing Venezuela's fate—knowing that they had few defenses. Under the circumstances, and given Ferdinand's unswerving devotion to his own ambitious plans, his audacity was at least consistent with his goals. (Of course, Ferdinand could not restrain himself from fantasizing about a simultaneous invasion of Portugal while his forces in the River Plate could take Brazil after—in theory anyway— a quick pacification of Buenos Aires.) But his audacity was disastrous, bringing down his pseudo-absolutist regime and kicking the legs out from under what remained of royalism in Spanish South America.

Money was at the heart of the problem. Many of Spain's naval vessels were found to be unseaworthy. Worse, no sooner did the soldiers begin to gather in Cádiz to assemble "The Great Expedition" to Buenos Aires than grumbling began among the troops. The food, supplies, clothing, and conditions were not just poor—they were appalling. Disease began to spread. And as the soldiers convened in larger numbers (the army was supposed to reach 14,000 men-in-arms), the material situation deteriorated rapidly. Sedition spread among the ranks of junior officers (some of whom still nursed ideals of restoring the liberal 1812 constitution). There was simply not enough money to cover the expenses of an army large enough to recapture the River Plate. Of course, the merchants of Cádiz kept promising to cover some of the costs, bent as they were on defending their last hopes of imperial grandeur and personal profits. The very same ships that were used to transport troops could be filled with South American staples and return to Cádiz, where they could thence be shipped to the rest of Europe and make the fortune necessary to cover the cost of the expedition. This was the idea, in any case. If their loyalty to the ancien régime could not be questioned, their realism certainly could. Events, meanwhile, took their own course: on January 1, 1820, a group of officers led by Major Rafael Riego staged a revolt, proclaiming the need for a constitutional monarchy along the lines of the 1812 charter. The unrest spread quickly to other military command centers around Spain. By March, the one pillar of state against which Ferdinand consistently leaned, the army, crumbled. He had no option but to accept the Constitution on March 7.[80]

The fall of the ancien régime in the peninsula quickly realigned forces in the colonies. The king issued a declaration to the colonies, announcing his fidelity to the revived constitution and apologizing for his missteps. It was a remarkable statement from a reactionary sovereign. But it did nothing to embolden support for him—by rebels and royalists alike—for it simply acknowledged the validity of patriotic grievances while stoking the fears of quivering loyalists. He blamed himself for not being aware of "the state of public opinion" in the empire when he abrogated the 1812 charter. And for this he was apologetic, promising to mend his ways. And there he stopped, with the promise of the status quo ante, round about 1812. The king: "Spanish Americans: I have sworn to the Constitution, and this idea alone should suffice to put an end to all your complaints, calm your doubts, and bolster your hopes. The representation ensured in that document, the per-fect equality in rights with all *naturales* of the Peninsula... do not allow you to doubt that your demands will be attended to." The king could not have offered a less effective message. In some deep way he still did not understand "public opinion" and failed to realize that the Cortes had hardly distinguished itself as a legitimate source of imperial sovereignty in the eyes many colonists, and had openly backtracked on the very principle the king was reiterating as the cornerstone of a new empire: equality. To this was added the new Overseas Governing Council's decision to try to assuage colonial nerves by promising to support and advocate "the complete cast-ing into oblivion of what has happened—*un absoluto olvido de lo pasado*." This simply presumed that both sides had legitimate grievances and were guilty of misdeeds and that peace could be achieved through bilateral amne-sia (not unlike postdictatorial amnesties of the twentieth century). In fact, each side saw itself as *the* aggrieved one and the other as *the* incubus of its mis-fortunes. As healing calls go, Ferdinand's were flops and revealed that, to the end, he did not fathom the nature of the war he had waged. Certainly his dis-course was less compelling than Simón Bolívar's, one that acknowledged—nay embraced—suffering and pain rather than trivializing it, exalting violence as a cathartic process in the making of something radically new, not Spanish in America, but American.[81]

---

[80]AGI, IG, 1568, November 5, 1820, Juan Tabat to Gobernación de Ultramar; Anna, *Spain and the Loss of America*, pp. 208–21.

[81]AGI, IG, 1568, Fernando VII, "Españoles de Ultramar."

Spanish rule in South America took another four years to complete its denouement. But it was more or less inevitable. When the Spanish military rose up against the king, Pablo Morillo was still able to defend significant quarters in Venezuela and Nueva Granada, in spite of the setback at Boyacá. When he got word of the shakeup in Spain Morillo was shocked. But he quickly surmised that restoring the 1812 constitution and offering to placate colonists rather than pacify them would help address the grievances he had been ordered to suppress militarily. Now he could offer "rights" instead of aiming rifles. The new cabinet in Madrid gave orders to Morillo to negotiate a six-month truce while Spanish envoys tried to negotiate a pact with the colonies. Thus, the very same people Morillo's armies had been bloodying for years were suddenly asked to sit down and talk—and to forget what the fighting had been all about. Páez, however, was quick to disabuse Morillo of any fantasy of reconciliation. Writing to the Spanish commander, the guerrillero noted that "Liberty and Independence has been our general cry. Liberty and Independence have been precious objects because they have lavished the blood of their sons." The conflict, and the sense of irrevocable separation of colony from metropolis, were too far advanced to be reversed.[82] Still, ever the loyal soldier, if deeply humiliated commander, Morillo agreed to a truce with Bolívar on November 25. Two days later Morillo and Bolívar met in Santa Ana, in the interior of western Venezuela, to discuss the terms of an armistice. But there was not really much to talk about: the ancien régime had collapsed under the weight of debts and charges of brutality, and for all intents and purposes had brought the empire down with it. Those who had remained loyal to the royalist cause knew they were to be betrayed and began to flee. Morillo himself boarded a ship from Puerto Cabello on December 27, 1820, and turned his back forever on South America, leaving the dispersed Spanish armies bereft of a commander.[83]

With Morillo gone, little stood in the way of patriotic armies approaching Peru from Chile. The battle for the line had been settled, ending the mobile stalemate between loyalists and royalists. But the fall of Peru—the last chapter of the denouement of the Spanish empire—was steeped in as much ambiguity as the fall of the empire.[84] In a sense, the implosion in the metropolis replicated itself at the heart of the ancient

---

[82]AGI, IG, 1568, June 17, 1820, Morillo to Madrid, and July 13, 1820, Páez to Morillo.

[83]Stoan, *Pablo Morillo*, pp. 218–27; Ullrick, "Morillo's Attempt to Pacify Venezuela," pp. 561–63.

[84]Gustavo Montoya, *La independencia del Perú y el fantasma de la revolución* (Lima: Instituto de Estudios Peruanos, 2002), pp. 70–77, 84–85; Fisher, "The Royalist Regime in the Viceroyalty of Peru," pp. 55–84, and Timothy E. Anna, *The Fall of Royal Government in Peru* (Lincoln: University of Nebraska Press, 1979), pp. 133–62.

306 • Chapter Seven

viceroyalty: it was propelled by a cumulative crumbling of the old system and prolonged by persistent loyalty to it. In September 1820 the drama came to a head when on the fourth, news arrived of the liberal revolt in Spain and the viceroy received instructions to proclaim the constitution. Six days later, San Martín's expedition of 4,000 troops plus a small naval escort arrived south of Lima at Pisco. On the fifteenth, Viceroy Pezuela tried to drum up enough pomp and ceremony to make the reinstated constitution look like a triumphal act, hoping also to stop the rebel advance. In keeping with the inverted logic of imperial decline, it was less San Martín that threatened the identification of sovereignty with imperium than its hollowing out from within. In Lima, it was hard to be enthusiastic about the new model of imperial legitimacy. Limeños had spent almost fifteen years devoted to, and paying for, the defense of the status quo ante. They were now being told that their sacrifices for the state, in the name of the state, had been in vain. Not surprisingly, it was the nexus of money and fidelity, interest and loyalty, that exposed the contradictions. The officers of the city's merchant guild pleaded to Spain for help, to defend Lima from the forces of revolution lying at the city's outskirts. Instead, the viceroy asked for an emergency 100,000-peso loan to defend the city. This was the last straw: Viceroy Pezuela was spurned one final ignominious time.[85] With the support of a clique of outraged merchants, a group of Spanish officers mounted a *golpe de estado* and deposed Pezuela in January 1821. One of the commanders, José de la Serna, declared himself the royalist successor. He would be South America's last. Chaos loomed across the capital. The coup scandalized many limeños who feared fratricidal warfare behind the royalist lines, and they were shocked at the example of insubordination. Losing all confidence in the city, and encircled by Chilean and Argentine armies, de la Serna fled to the highlands where estate owners and merchants clung to the vestiges of the ancien régime to prepare their stance. San Martín entered a fallen city on July 28, 1821; indeed, he had timed it for the fait accompli, the internal collapse of imperium, to be complete.[86]

It was harder to put in place the foundations of a new, postcolonial order than it was to watch the destruction of its predecessor. San Martín, himself bereft of money, could not even give chase to the fleeing viceroy and "free" the highlands. The merchants who withheld support from Pezuela were no more inclined to fund the Argentine liberator they once

---

[85] AGI, Consulados, 346, March 17, 1820, Lima, Joaquín de la Pezuela.
[86] Montoya, *La independencia del Perú*, pp. 84–95; Fisher, "The Royalist Regime in the Viceroyalty of Peru," pp. 65–72; Anna, *The Fall of Royal Government in Peru*, pp. 160–91; Marks, "Power and Authority in Late Colonial Peru," pp. 461–79.

despised. Frustrated, San Martín set sail in July 1822 for Guayaquil to confer with Bolívar. What transpired in this gathering remains a source of some speculation, but what is certain is that the Argentine withdrew from the campaign and went into permanent retreat, leaving the final stage of the war to the Venezuelan commander. Somewhat embittered, San Martín made his way back home to the River Plate, only to find more civil conflict there. Despondent, he eventually left the hemisphere whose independence he had fought for to take refuge in Europe.

Bolívar was also prone to disenchantment with his own cause. But for the moment, the prospect of toppling the remains of Spanish authority in the Andean highlands was enough to fuel his resolve. Bolívar landed in the port of Callao in September 1823 and made his way into Lima, a city seething with backstabbing and intrigue, and arrogated dictatorial powers to himself to staunch the infighting and wage the final year's fighting against the *serrano* royalists. On December 9, 1824, Bolívar's principal lieutenant, General Antonio José de Sucre, defeated de la Serna's 7,000-man army at the Battle of Ayacucho.[87] The few remaining pockets of loyalty were eventually wiped out, and the ancient highlands, the core of the colonial mercantilist system, finally fell. Still even these final skirmishes were bitter and bloody. The final battle took place in the port of Callao, as Spanish troops clung to their last toehold, Spain's gateway to its once massive South American empire. Besieged and bombarded, thousands perished in the fighting. This was the last human toll of almost fifteen years of struggle over home rule and empire. The news of the victory, however, went almost unnoticed. By then freed colonists were embroiled in a prolonged conflict over what should fill the void of empire.

---

[87]Montoya, *La independencia del Perú*, pp. 116–17; AGI, Estado, Lima, 75/31, March 21, 1924, Gobierno de Callao-José Ramón Rodil-Min de Guerra.

8   Crossing the Rubicon

In February 1814, hundreds of slaves in Bahia fled their workplaces and descended upon whaling stations full of weapons just north of the capital, Salvador. Within days, the insurrection spread as the rebels joined forces with runaways from nearby quilombos. They began marching toward the heartland sugar belt of the Recôncavo burning houses and killing whites, mulattos, and even slaves they met en route. On the shores of the River Joanes, a combined force of cavalry and militiamen squared off against the rebels—who resisted bullets with spears, arrows, and rocks. The battle lasted an hour. In the end, fifty-eight rebel-slaves died. Four were executed, and many others died either in prison or in penal colonies. Successfully crushed, the conspiracy nonetheless rekindled old fears among local whites. The merchants and notables of Bahia addressed a petition to the Prince Regent, Dom João, arguing that the "insolence" of slaves reflected the weakness of the local governor, the Count dos Arcos, who was accused of being too liberal to blacks. "Nobody with good sense can doubt that the fate of this captaincy will be the same as that of the island of Saint Domingue," they cried. Local elites, in effect, were pleading for a greater presence and strength of the state to preserve social order, "for serious steps to be taken" lest loyal subjects "become the victims of rebellion and tyranny." What they could not predict was how the dynasty's very efforts to extend state authority from 1815 to 1822 ended by shattering the Portuguese empire.[1]

Reconstituting the Portuguese empire after the Napoleonic Wars took place against the backdrop of an emerging Atlantic state system. As the cycle of interimperial rivalries that had smashed the formal ties among British, French, and Spanish capitals and their principal colonies in the

---

[1] "Slaves Rebel in the Captaincy of Bahia," in Robert Edgar Conrad, ed., *Children of God's Fire: A Documentary History of Black Slavery in Brazil* (Princeton: Princeton University Press, 1983), p. 401–5. The petition called for more patrols, a stronger military, firmer courts, more immigration of Portuguese families, and the end of the slave trade because slaves "constitute an enormous number." For more on slave unrest in Bahia, see João José Reis, *Rebelião escrava no Brasil: A história do levante dos malês em 1835* (São Paulo: Companhia das Letras, 2003), pp. 81–93.

Americas now came to a close, the old empire-focused state system gave way to a new one. What emerged was a "concert" of conservative victors determined to manage the frictions between competitive states in order to defuse its dangerous revolutionary consequences. The challenge was to fashion an interstate structure that was simultaneously an alternative to empire that kept the dynastic features of kingdoms and aristocracy.

Portuguese rulers saw themselves as uniquely positioned for greatness—for unlike their European rivals, their prize colony remained ever loyal, the empire intact. The issue was how to ensure Brazil's effective contribution to dynastic grandeur. If the rulers in Rio de Janeiro sought to chart an alternative trajectory for Atlantic empire and dynastic continuity—if not greatness—the dissolution of imperium became harder to avoid. One of the arguments of this chapter is that dissolution was the effect of efforts to reconstitute the empire by integrating it on new foundations. Brazil would secede from Lisbon, like its Spanish American neighbors from Madrid, as a response to imperial rulers' efforts to establish a new framework for an older imperial system. But there were important contrasts. When Brazil seceded from Portugal, the process was less contested; the incision between revolution and counterrevolution was much less bloody—indeed difficult to locate at all. This contrast has inspired historians to treat the dissolution of the Portuguese empire as more or less inevitable, and therefore less contestable. Oliveira Lima, for instance, maintains that Brazil had acquired a sense of national selfhood through the eighteenth century, and saw it ripen in 1808 and mature in ensuing years. When independence did come in 1822, it was a foregone conclusion. The years from 1814 to 1822 added up to a necessary transition period, allowing for the maturing of a national identity within an older colonial mold in order to dismantle it. But this is not the only inevitabilist account. Fernando Novais has argued that Brazilian independence was not the result of decolonization and the withering of the imperial state. Rather, for Novais, the contradictions of the Portuguese Atlantic were not governed by the teleology of a colony becoming a nation, but by the crisis of an ancien régime wedded to mercantilism, absolutism, and primitive accumulation. In the hothouse of the age of revolutions, the forces of modernity were bound to sweep aside the archaic structures that integrated the Luso-Brazilian Atlantic. What both interpretations share is the emphasis on structural causes of imperial breakup—which at once explain Brazil's emergence and its comparative uniqueness in Latin America.[2]

---

[2] For a classic account, see Oliveira Lima, *O movimento da independencia, 1821–1822*, 5th ed. (Rio de Janeiro: Topbooks, 1997). See Fernando A. Novais, "As dimensões da independencia," in Carlos Guilherme Mota, ed., *1822: Dimensões* (São Paulo: Editôra Perspectiva, 1972), pp. 15–26, for a synthetic statement.

Colonial secession and imperial dissolution were not such predictable outcomes in 1814, when the dominant sentiment among members of the ruling elites was loyalty to empire and monarchy. The rush to account for national "exit" from empire can miss the passages through loyalty and voice. The debates over state sovereignty, unleashed by imperial and revolutionary wars, and the sovereignty of private property rights, given freer rein by the spread of market forces and discourses of political economy, altered the mode and meaning of collective conflict in ways that the ancien-régime empire could simply not resolve. In 1808, Brazil de facto, and eventually de jure, got home rule. But who would rule at home? How would they rule? These became contentious issues that did not go away with each effort to reconstitute the empire. Indeed, they heightened the jostling within the empire and over the boundaries of private rights and public powers without necessarily tilting "Brazil" to secede as an act of self-determination. In this fundamental sense, Brazil, like Spanish America, became independent as a consequence, and not the cause, of unresolved conflicts of empire.

As with the irresolution of empire, so too with its successor. As sovereignty became more contested, it raised fundamental questions about loyalty to, voice in, and exit from "what?" Not only was secession from Portugal not simply automatic or preordained, it was far from clear what in fact was seceding: Brazil, or a collection of provinces that refused to comply with Lisbon's efforts to restore its centrality in empire? What is important is that a unitary, nationalized Brazil was not imagined and did not declare itself into existence by people who identified as such in order to bring down the old order. In many ways, Brazil came into existence because of the frailties and contradictions of earlier models of sovereignty—ones that patrician classes, slave owners, planters, and merchants eventually, and even reluctantly, repudiated. With "exit" in 1822, the ruling classes then had to confront the challenge of what to be loyal to now that they were free of formal European control.

A New Dependency

The withdrawal of French troops from Portugal created a vacuum. As the European powers began to establish a reactionary concert in 1814–15, the ministry in Rio de Janeiro began to reflect some of these international conservative trends. A clique led by Count Araújo as navy and colonies minister, and Fernando José de Portugal (soon to be the Marquis of Aguiar) as foreign minister held sway over decision making. Less inclined to embrace deep structural reforms as Linhares had, Araújo and Portugal saw the new international alignments as an opportunity to restore Portuguese sovereignty and greatness. As the forces of persistence settled over the Congress of Vienna, and Europe's powers agreed to squelch the democratic forces that were blamed for regicide and revolution in Paris, the Luso-Brazilian government cozied up to Austria and Russia, in part to wean the regime from the historic dependence on Britain. João himself supported this—and had to find a way keep an arm's length from British pressure, which included urgings to return to Portugal. This is important to note because the first instinct of Portuguese court members was to seize the opportunity presented by the incoming reactionary tide in Europe to invigorate a bygone autocratic system. In this sense, there was less difference in the political inclination between the Spanish and Portuguese post-Napoleonic reactions; what differed was their room to maneuver, which, as it turned out, was much more limited in the Portuguese empire. These limitations had the paradoxical effects of simultaneously confining what the regime could do to reconstitute itself while preventing a full-blown explosion of counterrevolutionary and revolutionary elements in the colonies. But it came close.

Establishing new external foundations for sovereignty was one pressing challenge; realigning the internal fundaments of empire was another. Like Spain, Portugal was eager to recover the prestige lost by the fall to French occupants—prestige that could be clawed back by reinvigorating the empire. There was an immediate problem: how could restoring the empire's grandeur not come at the expense of the colony that had recently become its new center, Brazil? To make matters worse for Lisbon, there was lingering resentment about the 1810 treaties signed with Britain and the dependency on London for financial and military succor. The Braganza house was also anxious to thwart metropolitan liberals who used the occasion of the restoration of Portuguese freedom from French occupants—and the distance of the monarch in Brazil—to press for constitutional limits to the crown's authority. Finally, once Ferdinand was restored to the throne in Madrid, João also had to contend with Spanish hunger to restore not only the territorial integrity of the empire in contentious borderlands like the River Plate, but even temptations to occupy Portugal itself in the absence of a ruling dynast.

A "new mold of structural dependency," to use the words of the Portuguese historian Valentim Alexandre, blunted the political ambitions of those who wanted to restore the old regime. As a result, the very weakness of the regime, its dependency on Brazilian and British merchants for funding, exposure to liberal lobbying at home, and the need for common support against Spanish aggression stood in the way of vindictive absolutism of the sort unveiled by Ferdinand in 1814. Ironically, deliverance of the Portuguese monarchy from French armies appeared to rescue the monarchy and to lean the historical trajectory toward continuity with the old regime. In fact, the efforts to restore the ancien régime on new grounds within a conducive international environment were constrained by the very limited instruments for the dynasty to reintegrate its empire. Once again, the fates of old, transitional, and new regimes were not just foretold in the inertial forces of feudality and tradition. External forces, especially the shifting balance of commercial power and interstate conflict, shaped the choices of domestic and local colonial actors.[3]

Any temptation to reinvent autocracy in the Portuguese Atlantic, or even restore Lisbon's centrality in empire, ran headlong into realities of Portuguese dependency on Britain. The British, having led the expedition to drive the French from Portugal, effectively accomplished after the joint Anglo-Portuguese victory at Salamanca in 1812, were also important bankrollers of the regime, having extended emergency subsidies and financed the military reconquest of the peninsula. As we saw in chapter 6, London drove a hard trading bargain as compensation in the treaties of 1810. Free trade and British penetration of colonial markets created immediate unease in Lisbon and Rio de Janeiro. To make matters worse, the British also increased pressure on the Braganza dynasty to curb the Atlantic slave trade in keeping with the provisions of Article 10 of the friendship treaty, which aimed to clamp down on slave trading, especially north of the Congo River. After the Second Treaty of Paris in November 1815, Britain, Russia, Austria, and Prussia all committed to the "entire and definitive abolition" of the slave trade. Britain intensified its pressure on the Braganza court to follow suit, culminating in 1815 with a new treaty banning slavers from operating above the equator. The Count of Aguiar was forced to concede to Lord Strangford in mid-1813 that the list of British terms added up to a major blow to Portuguese sovereignty. He added that while Britain enjoyed unobstructed access to Portuguese and Brazilian markets, the same was not true of Luso-Brazilian trade into British markets. Strangford shot back, pointing out that a deal was a deal and that the prince's ministers had signed the 1810 trade treaty voluntarily. This vulnerability to British pressure on the government severely compromised its ability to cope with centrifugal strains on the empire.[4]

---

[3]Alexandre, *Os sentidos do império*, p. 284. On the personalities of the cabinet, see Oliveira Lima's classic, *D. João VI*, pp. 150–51.

[4]ANRJ, J C Caixa 361, pacote 2, f. 19, Count of Aguiar to Lord Strangford, July 19, 1813; see also f. 20, report by Felix Manoel da Silva, July 25, 1813. On the British pressure to abolish the slave trade, see Bethell, *The Abolition of the Brazilian Slave Trade*, pp. 8–15; Robert E. Conrad, *World of Sorrow: The African Slave Trade to Brazil* (Baton Rouge: Louisiana State University Press, 1986), pp. 56–58.

Dependency was not absolute; it, too, had its limits. London had wanted the dynasty repatriated to the metropole as part of the more general restorationist drive in Europe and to ensure that Portugal would not be engulfed in local feuding. Authorities in Portugal clamored for the court to return to its rightful place at the historic center; the landed aristocrats wanted to restore their proximity to royalty; merchants wanted to shape commercial policy. João refused. But he had to do something in order to appear as if he were doing more than nothing to restore imperial grandeur. His circle devised a compromise that would seek to give autocracy a new lease on life while laying out the groundwork for a new spatial model of sovereignty. The prince announced in late 1815 a Carte de Lei, which changed the structure of sovereignty of the Portuguese empire. "Brazil" became a kingdom in its own right—and was folded in as an equal to the other two kingdoms of the realm, Portugal and Algarves. Accordingly, in December 1815, the monarchy pronounced that henceforth Brazil would be elevated to the status of kingdom, along with the kingdom of Portugal; Brazil's sovereignty was inscribed in the very affirmation of the imperium. In effect, what many Spanish colonists had been advocating became a reality in the Luso-Brazilian Atlantic. This was a blueprint straight out of Rodrigo de Souza Coutinho's memorials since the 1790s: a commonwealth of Portuguese kingdoms to create a more perfect and virtuous Atlantic empire. Portuguese America, as Barman has noted, became, henceforth, synonymous with Brazil. This appeared to fortify the empire by creating a commonwealth—and in some sense was the sort of thing that many moderates in Madrid and colonists in the Americas, fatigued with civil war and protracted fighting, had been urging on Ferdinand. There was, however, a fundamental difference: there was no call for a constitution or a new model of representation within empire. In this sense, this was a reform fully in keeping with the autocratic spirit of the age—which simply displaced the problem of sovereignty to the issue of *how* Brazil might be integrated as a "kingdom" as a condition of its equality within empire. In short order, this issue would explode and lead to a much more intense resistance against Rio de Janeiro than was ever mounted against Lisbon.[5]

INTEGRATION AND SECESSION

The 1815 charter was a compromise between metropolitan demands to be relocated at the center and Brazil's importance to imperial survival. But by extending the purview of an autocratic state, the compromise

---

[5]Barman, *Brazil*, p. 53.

simply displaced the problems to regions and captaincy generals of what was now a partnership of integrated kingdoms under the same dynastic house. How were these "provinces" going to fit, especially as parts of an autocracy that tied them closer to Rio de Janeiro than they ever had been to Lisbon—and did so without the basic means of representation? The compromise designed to integrate Brazil even more effectively into a world empire by making it a full partner and extending the powers of the dynastic state across its parts set in train a series of regional upheavals that threatened to tear Brazil apart and bring the regime to its knees.

Creating a Brazilian kingdom meant integrating five subregions into a single dynastic polity centered in Rio de Janeiro. Most Brazilian regions had had meager contact with the capital and relied on local systems of representation which, while hardly parliamentary, had enabled colonists to voice collective concerns to authorities. This had begun to shift after 1808, and became more intense after 1815 when the government created new judicial and executive officers, answerable to Rio de Janeiro, posted in erstwhile autonomous captaincies. This was hardly a juggernaut of centralization. But making a kingdom out of the colonies posed a basic question. Now that the crown had relocated itself to create a new capital in the colony to reconstitute the sovereignty of the empire, and elevated Brazil to a single "kingdom," how would the subregions align or identify with a new capital? Just as centralization and curbing regional autonomy had provoked resistance to the imperial reforms in the 1780s, and was a source of upheaval in Spanish America after 1814, it inevitably created a riptide of revolt in Brazil, too. In the south and north of Brazil, powerful movements exploded, calling for a whole new local constitutional order that would curb or destroy the powers of monarchy and roll back intrusions from central state authority, even those dressed in the cause of the "Brazilian" nation.[6]

The biggest single threat to the ancien régime erupted in 1817 in Recife, and led to one of the few revolts that aimed to topple the dynasty altogether. On March 6, 1817, a group of military officers affiliated with Masonic lodges sparked an uprising in the city's barracks under the banner of "Religion, Patria, and Liberty." They expelled the highly unpopular royal governor and proclaimed a republican junta in charge. Their demands were backed by local planters, who complained that sugar prices (faced with soaring Cuban cane production) and cotton prices (faced with rising American output) had plummeted while taxes on exports and imports rose to pay for war. In the meantime, the cost of slaves was rising. With diminishing returns and rising costs, planters

---

[6]Ibid, pp. 44–45, 53.

turned to merchants, many of them Portuguese—for whom they racked up as much resentment as debt. Moreover, local interests had long been subjected to the monopoly of the Pernambuco Company, which was in the hands of a few peninsular merchants and a constant thorn in the side of amicable relations between Lisbon and its Brazilian captaincy. Indeed, a powerful antimonopoly, antiprivilege discourse lay behind the demands for equality, especially equal rights to participate in capitalist enterprise free of the state burdens imposed by Rio de Janeiro or the private burdens of Portuguese merchants. The result was, as Carlos Guilherme Mota has noted, a surge of rustic ideas about the entitlements of the "miserable plebe," freedom from usury, folded into a set of demands to protect the "sons of the earth" (*filhos da terra*)—a nativist and localist mélange that resisted the emerging centralized political and economic order. To this was combined a more patrician sense among lettered circles in Recife that the virtues and benefits of the Enlightenment were being thwarted by the autocratic ways of the government's envoys to the northeast. The syncretism led rebels to argue that only a republican, federalist system could preserve the natural rights to enjoy property, and only the enjoyment of property could restore moral order to public affairs.[7]

The Republic of Pernambuco, as it became called, promised religious toleration, equal rights for all citizens, and determined defense of private property and slavery, all of which was inscribed in a constitution passed by the local assembly on March 29, borrowing heavily from the charter of the United States. This was the first constitution written in Brazil and aimed, among other things, to repudiate autocracy. The example of freedom of representation and freedom from Rio de Janeiro's control spread to neighboring Alagoas, Ceará, Paraíba, and Rio Grande do Norte. The accent on equality emboldened plebeian populations of Pernambuco and not a few slaves—for whom the promise of freedom meant something altogether more radical—to rally to the republican cause, which only added to the confusion, as this was the last thing the local elites wanted. Indeed, the specter of a republican uprising turning into a slave revolt sent shivers of fear down the spines of local notables, many of whom had not declared their affinity for either side. Soon, the uprising gave way to internecine struggles and countercoups. Two and a half months after starting, the rebellion was crushed; Admiral Rodrigo Lobo talked the rebels into withdrawing from Recife, only to coordinate their encirclement and eventual capture. The army arrested around two-hundred rebels and executed twenty of them, dismembering their bodies

---

[7] Carlos Guilherme Mota, *Nordeste 1817* (São Paulo: Editora da Universidade de São Paulo, 1972), pp. 20–23, 82–91.

before gawking spectators. Many more died in battle or subsequent mop-up operations. Many secretly grumbled that the government was too heavy-handed in its dealings and rather than try to assuage local grievances only suppressed them. Indeed, the victims of the repression soon became martyrs for a much more powerful movement in the north in the 1820s.[8]

While the brief uprising in Pernambuco failed, it undermined the façade, promoted relentlessly by the monarchy itself, that all was well in the Brazilian kingdom. This was not how wealthy Bahians saw the situation. As the news about Recife got out, many in Salvador began to prepare for a full-scale secessionist war and the specter of its racialization. When the republic's emissary to Bahia, José Inacio Ribeiro de Abreu e Lima, known as "Padre Roma," arrived to solicit support for his cause, the province's governor had him arrested and summarily executed. The Bahian barracks were put under an intense watch for any signs of sedition. Paradoxically, even though it was Bahian regulars who were used to suppress the Pernambuco uprising, the crown increasingly distrusted its own military, fearing the secret circulation of nativist and liberal ideas.[9]

The northeast was not the only source of the problem for Rio de Janeiro's efforts to re-center a kingdom for a revitalized empire. Indeed, the uprising of Pernambuco had been stoked by rising taxes and dwindling military morale on account of the decision by the court to plunge Brazil into a ruinous war in the River Plate. When Ferdinand VII came back to power in Madrid in 1814, rulers in Rio de Janeiro figured that Spain would be willing to sue for peace in order to restore calm in the colonies. This rekindled expansionist fantasies in the Brazilian capital, which had been in remission since Britain compelled the Rio de Janeiro aggrandizers to sign an armistice in October 1811 on the heels of the first invasion of the Banda Oriental. At the same time, Buenos Aires dispatched an envoy to Rio de Janeiro with a secret offer to Brazil: if Brazil were to invade and occupy the east bank of the River Plate, Buenos Aires would abstain from interfering and would eventually recognize Brazil's territorial sovereignty over the Banda Oriental. For revolutionary Buenos Aires, worried about a Spanish reconquest and beset by internal feuding, a deal with Rio de Janeiro seemed like a price worth paying for survival. What Buenos Aires wanted was to eliminate the federalist armies of José Gervasio Artigas and thus cripple the loose federalist

[8]Glacyra L. Leite, *A Inurreição Pernambucana de 1817* (São Paulo: Ed. Brasiliense, 1984), for a fine overview; Mota, *Nordeste 1817*, pp. 54–55, 156–62.

[9]*Idade d'Ouro do Brasil*, April 11, 1817; F.W.O. Morton, "The Military and Society in Bahia, 1800–1821," *Journal of Latin American Studies* 7:2 (1975): 260.

alliance of all the littoral provinces, led by the Oriental commander who opposed Buenos Aires' centralist designs. In effect, as Artigas's revolution spread across the River Plate provinces, broadcasting appeals to republicanism, federalism, abolition of slavery, and the dismantling of the landed mercantile alliance, it drew out the ire of both Buenos Aires and Rio de Janeiro. It also deepened the power vacuum across the River Plate.[10]

The vacuum inspired hubris in Rio de Janeiro. In late 1815, the news arrived that Argentine forces had been trounced in the Andes at the battle of Sipe Sipe. What was devastating to Buenos Aires was an opportunity for Rio de Janeiro. The Brazilian temptation to recover grandeur by invading the rebellious borderlands was too tempting to pass up—and it sucked the monarchy into the vortex of revolutionary war. With Britain desperately trying to keep its Iberian allies from going to war with each other and destabilizing the fragile European balance, João ordered an army of 5,000 seasoned soldiers under General Carlos Federico Lecor to cross into the River Plate. Portuguese armies descended on Montevideo in September 1816. Within thirty-six days, Artigas's forces had been routed by the well-planned, mobile, and skilled Portuguese cavalry and infantry.[11]

Bolstering Brazilian sovereignty by expanding its dominions immediately got the government in Rio de Janeiro in a tangle with the British. The Count of Palmella (charged with managing battered relations with London) defended the expansion southward by claiming that Portugal had the right to invade because Spain was so inept in handling its own colonies. Buenos Aires had been sowing the seeds of sedition all across the borderlands, "drawing supporters from our territory to Artigas' columns, and promoting the uprising of Slaves." It was "the threat to Brazil of the Jacobin principles espoused in the Spanish Provinces" that justified the occupation of the right bank of the River Plate. Still, in an effort to placate irate British officials, Palmella signed a convention in July 1817 that conceded to the British navy the right to board and search any Portuguese vessel suspected of carrying slaves on the high seas. This concession would later infuriate slave-trading magnates and would be held up as part of the thick dossier cataloguing how the government betrayed the interests of Brazilian capitalists.[12]

The conflict with London paled beside the mess that Rio de Janeiro created along its borderlands. In the calculus of war, losses soon eclipsed

---

[10]John Street, "Lord Strangford and the Río de la Plata, 1808–1815," *Hispanic American Historical Review* 33:4 (1953): 479–510; idem, *Artigas,* pp. 279–82.

[11]Street, *Artigas,* pp. 295–98.

[12]ANTT, MNE, Caixa 38, f. 3, "Extractos dos oficios do Conde Palmella."

gains. If Ferdinand would not brook dissent in the colonies, he was certainly not going to tolerate Portuguese exploitation of the civil war in the River Plate, and he prepared an army to invade Portugal itself. The British meanwhile accused the government in Rio de Janeiro of perfidy. What is more, establishing a toehold in Montevideo was one thing; controlling the countryside, where the insurgency was widespread, was quite another. Like Pablo Morillo in Venezuela, like so many occupying armies fighting local guerrillas, Portuguese commanders found their troops bogged down in constant, costly skirmishes. Artigas ordered all of Montevideo to evacuate, feeling that the city was not necessary to defend the Banda Oriental. Regrouping his forces, he prepared for an insurgency against occupants: "My plan has always been to sustain the war in the open country in view of the resources there." The gaucho guerrilla forces were soon able to hem the Portuguese armies to Montevideo and a sliver along the coast; the Portuguese armies responded with a scorched-earth counterinsurgency campaign that did nothing to endear them to the local population and only dragged the campaign into brutal and indecisive depths. To top off the sequence of miscalculations, the helmsman of João VI (who became king in 1816 after his mother, Queen Maria, finally passed away), the Count of Araújo, died in June 1817, creating a power vacuum at the very heart of the government. Pretty soon, Rio de Janeiro lost control of the war that it had started. But as Araújo's successors realized, it was easier to slide into war than get out of it without defeating the original purpose: aggrandizing the dynasty. The war dragged on; the government dipped into the financial till to pay its bills; and inflation began to take off.[13]

In this context, on the heels of a scary revolt in the northeast and an unpopular war in the southern borderlands, the regime stepped up theatrics to promote itself to the subject population. In February 1818, Rio de Janeiro spent three days celebrating the tenth anniversary of the court's arrival to the capital. There were special performances in the royal theater, and balls for the royal family, the nobility, and diplomats. Honorific titles were doled out, as dozens of financiers and military officers became knights, counts, and marquis. But the courtly culture was also meant for mass consumption. Large crowds gathered before the royal palace, applauding when the ruling family appeared on the balcony to wave at their loyal vassals. On the other side of the square,

---

[13]Street, *Artigas*, pp. 313–29. On the diplomacy behind the war, see Alexandre, *Os sentidos do imperio*, pp. 338–46. The war was so costly that when Rio de Janeiro learned that Ferdinand was preparing a major expedition to pacify the River Plate as it had in northern South America, the government prepared to evacuate from the Banda Oriental and let Spanish armies pick up where they had left off.

the magnificent offices of the Royal Commercial Council (the Junta do Comércio) were decked out, holding up one end of a magnificent display. Two columns towered over the crowd, each with a giant crown with the letters S.M.J.VI embossed on their façades. Large archways stretched across the square, bearing bas-reliefs of the history of the monarchy in Brazil, from João's arrival in Guanabara Bay, to his receipt of the keys to the capital supported by a mythic image of America, to João sitting on a pedestal holding the coats of arms of the three "kingdoms": Brazil, Portugal, and the Algarves. On the frontal frieze of the largest archway, massive letters trumpeted his inaugural recognition of the end of Brazil's colonial status: "AO LIBERTADOR DO CÓMERCIO." The festivities culminated with a king's benevolent gesture, releasing 31 prisoners held in the capital's jails and feeding 239 others who were still shackled.[14]

It is hard to say just how much of the applause was heartfelt and how much was opportunistic festivity. Either way, the view from the balconies of the choreographed displays was taken as gestures of popular loyalty to the regime. However, behind ministerial doors, it was becoming clear that loyalties were more ambiguous, for if the theatrics were undoubtedly royalist, they were also celebrating the degree to which Brazilian sovereignty had been reordered around a new political and economic metropolis: Rio de Janeiro. This was what provincial forces were contesting to the point of picking up arms. Elsewhere, where the quest to extend autocracy to its territorial limits drove the government into a headlong confrontation with contentious borderlanders, the resistance was even harder to contain. The public triumphalism in the capital was, as a result, in sharp contrast with difficult arm wrestling between the king's officials and the economic moguls over the mounting price of political ambition.

BREAKING UP THE BLOC

If the Braganza dynasty had to struggle to keep provincial secessionists at bay, another challenge to persistence came from within the ruling power circle. Restoration of monarchy and empire after the revolutionary and Napoleonic wars could not mask the fundamental tensions among the ruling classes of the Portuguese empire. Each turn of events— "liberating" the metropole, making concessions to Britain, suppressing dissent, and going to war in the south—seemed to exacerbate disputes over taxation, commercial competition, and command of the slave trade. Whereas the re-centering of the ancien régime in Brazil appeared to

---

[14]*Gaceta do Rio de Janeiro*, February 16, 1818.

rescue the empire, it displaced the costs of bankrolling the regime to merchants of the new kingdom while exposing them to ever more risks and uncertainties of a new economic order.

Some of the imperial tension developed out of the long-term effects of the Napoleonic Wars on commercial networks developed over the previous century. It had become harder and harder to keep the triangular circulation of commodity and credit flows between merchants of Portugal, Africa, and South America. And with adjustments, it became harder and harder to graft economic interests onto a political framework. Consider the problems of José Dias da Silva Guimaraens, an entrepôt merchant who ran a swift business between Pernambuco and Buenos Aires carrying slaves, sugar, rice, and aguardiente to the River Plate in return for flour, hides, and jerked beef to northern Brazil. This business, developed over generations, now thrived as ports opened after 1808. But if freer trade for colonial commerce was a bonanza to many, the political convulsions in Europe could also mean bust in the colonies. By 1812, the wars in the peninsula created headaches. One of Guimaraens's partners in Pernambuco, José Baptista Ferreira, failed to honor a letter of exchange when he could not recover bills owed to him from Portuguese debtors, and this soon led to a wave of defaults on money owed to Guimaraens, who was then unable to pay his suppliers for their advanced staples. In this case, and so many others, the wars in Europe snapped through the lines of credit that extended back and forth across the Atlantic, issuing waves of defaults and throwing Guimaraens and others to the mercy of the merchant courts.[15]

While the upheaval was taking its toll on networks of merchant capital, especially those with corners in the crippled metropolis, the state was forced to adjudicate in ways that tried to shore up Portuguese merchants in Brazil and Portugal. Faced with the havoc in commercial relations provoked by the wars in Portugal, one judge was forced to issue a decision that absolved metropolitan merchants of any responsibility for their mishaps. According to the commercial jurist José Apolhinar de Mattos, the meaning of a merchant's obligation was deeply rooted in the notion that "credit is the honor of one's signature," and that "all merchant contracts should be considered essentially = good faith." [sic]. The invasion and "sacking" of Lisbon was not the fault of metropolitan capitalists, "but were accidents, and for obvious reasons they were not anticipated in the Laws," and so the Lisbon debtors could not be held responsible. The same principle, derived from commercial jurisprudence, which relied on notions of subjective good faith and "honorable conduct" as measures of liability,

---

[15] ANRJ, J C, Caixa 377, pacote 3, f. 3, José Francisco da Costa (1812).

stopped short of covering colonial merchants as well, presumably because they did not suffer the direct effects of the French invasion. For Anselmo José Antunes, a Bahian merchant who was trying to recover money owed to him from Lisbon, there was no consolation in Mattos's principles.[16] Indeed, by 1814, the commercial tribunals in Lisbon and Brazil were flooded with appeals from creditors—especially in Brazil. Plaintiffs complained that a small group of privileged Portuguese merchants were being exempted from paying their bills owed to honorable creditors in Brazil. Why shouldn't the judges absolve all debtors of their payments since no one was "responsible" for war? That way, the Brazilian merchants could not be forced to pay their obligations. There was some logic to this position, even though it would have destroyed the credit system that upheld the commercial networks, and so it was rejected.[17] Decisions such as these stoked the feeling that the rules were stacked in favor of metropolitan capital. What was also clear was that the metropolis had become the weak link in the chain of commercial relations across the Iberian Atlantic. At best, ties to the metropolis were now redundant; at worst, they were a liability.

While Portuguese defaults reverberated through the South Atlantic, so did the effects of greater competition as a result of the monarchy's decision to throw open Brazilian ports to British merchants. In December 1809, a group of merchants in Rio de Janeiro petitioned the government, thanking the prince for allowing "us merchants to conduct our business under the healthy laws of this Monarchy." The supplicative opening gave way to a litany of grievances—none of which was ascribed to João's policies but which, in the view of the petitioners, nonetheless required that he reciprocate the merchants' loyalty with some protection from competition. They signaled "the general upheaval of the universe which has condemned us to total decadence, and reduced our trade to importing English merchandise." To make matters worse, English merchants were not satisfied with simply selling to the large houses that once controlled the importing system but set up shop directly, handling their own merchandise and dealing it to retailers—down to petty street marketers—on consignment and credit. The petitioners invoked law after law to argue that this explosion of competition threatened "the common good of

---

[16]ANRJ, JC, Caixa 377, pacote 3, f. s.n., Anselmo José Antunes (no date).

[17]ANTT, JC, Maço 15, Caixa 169, f. 6, September 12, 1814; f. 10, June 7, 1814. For a discussion of how the wars devastated the commercial networks to the peninsula, see Pedreira, "From Growth to Collapse," pp. 846–53, while cutting loose those within the Americas and across to Africa, see Maria Lígia Prado and Maria Cristina Z. Luizetto, "Contribução para o estudo do comércio de cabotagem no Brasil, 1808–1822," *Anais do Museo Paulista*, 30 (1980–81): 159–96.

Trade" and that the monarchy had to expunge proliferating retailers from the market since they ducked taxes and violated the honorable traditions of the Brazilian trading community. The complaint eventually went to court and got a rejection from the magistrate, who argued that "this demand is inadmissible as it is against the liberal principles of free trade [*franqueza do comercio*] and industry which we have currently adopted." This did not go over well among merchants. When they received the January 1808 open ports decree, they understood "the letter and spirit of the new liberal system of Economic Administration, and that the real intention was to restore the natural justice of civic contracts, bringing an end to ancient legislation, which are clearly incompatible with the current circumstances." The problem was not with liberal rules of political economy but a higher law of the sovereign: the defense of the commonwealth. "His essential objective," the plaintiffs argued in referring to the monarchy, "is to promote the common good of his subjects [*vassallos*] and facilitate the means so that they may live well from their useful, and loyally applied work." They did not object to opening the ports to friendly traders. They objected to opening the streets to unfettered and uncontrolled competition. This degraded the labors of honest upstanding merchants, exposed their honorably supported credit to the vicissitudes of the marketplace, and threatened to subject trading to a new form of "monopoly": a vulgar class of hawkers whose conduct would determine the price of merchandise. If commerce was to be subjected to new laws of political economy, which liberated Brazilian merchants to trade with a freer range of partners, surely the guidelines were themselves subject to moral laws of economy, which bound the sovereign to protect the interests of loyal subjects. On the list of dignitaries who signed the petition was none other than José da Silva Lisboa, the man most responsible for making Enlightenment political economy the framework for commercial policy of the ancien régime.[18]

Grievances and complaints only grew after the war in the south erupted again. Merchant houses appealed more loudly to the court for reprieve, some even hinting that the sovereign was falling short of his duties to protect the welfare of his subjects. The tone of appeals pushed deference to its limits, so that their echo sounded rather more like insubordination. In late 1817, 111 of Rio de Janeiro's biggest merchants sent a plea to the crown to do something about "contrabandists" and petty merchants who increased the risks of conducting business. Finally, in July 1821 the secretary of the Royal Trade Junta, José Albaro Fragoso,

---

[18]ANRJ, JC, Caixa 379, pacote 1, s.n., February 6, 1810; *Gazeta do Rio de Janeiro*, April 29, 1815, for a report on the influx of English cotton textiles.

rejected the appellants' case that unfettered trade violated the laws of 1749 and 1751 and the interests of the commonwealth. This inspired merchants to condemn "the arguments of the representative which are all contrary to the principles of Political Economy." Fragoso had conflated free trade with speculation, they charged, and threatened not just to legalize the ruin visited upon the supplicants but to undermine "the interests of the Public Cause." By letting the market fall prey to the "liberty of vagabond *Feirantes* [market traders]," such misguided policy put control of trade in the hands of men without *credito*. Here was the nub of their complaint. Big merchant houses of the cities earned their status because of their reputations for honoring contracts, and therefore built up "credit," understood as a credible commitment to pay up when the circulation of commodities from hinterlands to markets could finally clear. Until then, it was the reputation of men with "credit" that kept the network of exchanges based on promises going. Neither the interests of merchant capitalism nor the reasons of state could justify debasing reputations in the name of "indefinite liberty."[19]

If new principles of free trade were supposed to replace vestiges of mercantilism and put the empire on sounder economic footing, merchants nonetheless invoked understandings of political economy that implied that the monarchy was expected to uphold the social hierarchy of merchants, stratified by rank and integrated by honorable conduct. Higher laws, intoned the petition of 1817, dictated that the monarchy was bound to protect the "honorable citizenry" not "ignorantes sem cabedal nem credito," and uphold "merchants en grosso," not individual liberties. Thus the communitarian rhetoric normally used to redouble the bonds of reciprocity between the sovereign and his subjects was flipped to argue that some basic rights were being violated by a government more intent on its particular survival than the general interest.

THE SLAVE TRADE AND THE TRIUMPH OF PERIPHERAL CAPITAL

To make matters even worse, Brazilian merchants not only were forced to shoulder the burdens posed by defaulting metropolitan houses and cope with ramped-up competition, they also faced increasing pressure on one of the lifelines of the empire: the slave trade to Africa. The French occupation of Portugal basically knocked Lisbon out of the circuitry of slaves—indeed the city's role in the Atlantic slave trade had been waning for generations in favor of more powerful houses operating out of Rio

---

[19] ANRJ, J C, Caixa 379, pacote 3, f. s.n., petition, November 29, 1817; f. 62, July 7, 1821.

de Janeiro in particular. But in signing the 1810 treaty with Britain, followed by additional assurances, the monarchy committed itself, at least on paper, to complicating the lives of merchants who used their bilateral ties to African partners as a way of reinforcing their own local power in the South American hinterlands.

It is important to underscore that the actual numbers of slaves flowing into Pernambuco, Bahia, and Rio de Janeiro did not decline after 1810 but rose steadily. What mattered was the symbolic sense that the monarchy could not defend the legitimate interests of slave-trading merchants under pressure from the British. This had been a latent source of disenchantment with the ruling system during the Napoleonic Wars. But with the liberation of Portugal, it no longer seemed right to many Brazilians that they continue to pay the price of dependence on Britain to restore metropolitan sovereignty. Especially after 1815, when British antislaving patrols cruised off the coast of West Africa and boarded Brazilian bottoms with greater frequency, slave importers grumbled about the government's impotence. This was especially troublesome for merchants and planters in the north, whose supply of slaves depended on commerce with the Gold Coast, while Angolan and Mozambican slaves were shipped primarily to Minas Gerais and Rio de Janeiro. The *Providencia*, belonging to the Bahian Ignacio Antunes Guimaraens, was loaded with 417 captives when it was caught off the Mina Coast by the British navy in mid-1813. The merchant pleaded to the government for help—to no avail. One of Bahia's largest slave traders, Joaquim José de Andrade e Silva Menizes, complained of being hit hard twice, first by the French occupation of Portugal, which left him holding worthless bills of exchange, and then by a series of British seizures off the African coast of his loaded slaving vessels. Bankrupt, he threw himself upon the mercy of the courts, only to have his assets liquidated in 1818 after a prolonged suit with his creditors. The complaints of Brazilian merchants grew so loud that the government was finally compelled to create a "mixed commission" with British representatives in Sierra Leone to handle the conflicts from seizures and, if possible, soften the penalties imposed on merchants who had violated laws approved by their own rulers.[20]

The inability of the government to curb what were seen as overzealous British naval operations was a sharp contrast to the realization that

---

[20]ANRJ, JC, Caixa 416, pacote 3, s.n., May 25, 1816; Caixa 378, pacote 1, s.n., September 1812; *Gazeta do Rio de Janeiro*, January 17, 1818; ANTT, JC, Maço 62, Caixa 204, f. 2, "Atuos de justificação para qualificar navíos de comercio de escravos"; Fragoso and Florentino, *O arcaísmo como projeto*, p. 42; Miller, *Way of Death*, p. 643; Mieko Nishida, "Manumission and Ethnicity in Urban Slavery: Salvador Bahia, 1808–1888," *Hispanic American Historical Review*, 73:3 (1993): 364–65.

Brazilian merchants did not have to rely anymore on metropolitan participation. Gone was the fiction that the metropolis had a vital commercial role in the empire; Brazil was economically sovereign. Requests to comply with rules that were aimed at catering to interests located in Portugal were seen increasingly as burdens to Brazilian interests. This was how slave traders framed the assaults on their business. When Antonio de Araújo de Azevedo got permission to trade for slaves in the ports of Amrbis, Loge, and up the Zaire River, he was told that he would have to conform to Article 10 of the 1810 treaty. In response to charges that the government was letting the British have their way so that they would invest in the metropolis, Azevedo was assured that his majesty was dedicated to promoting greater bilateral trade between Brazil and Africa to promote the "commerce of the Interior of this Country [the slave hinterlands of Africa] which is in need of promotion."[21] Even African outposts pleaded to the court to allow Brazilian merchants to operate freely in ports along the littoral and dispense with any concern for Portuguese merchants. While Portuguese traders might lose their coastal privileges as slave exporters or factors, the empire's traffic as a whole would rise. In any event, as one petition noted, Portuguese traders were the victims of their own fondness for old protectionist measures and were unable to keep up with Brazilians who swapped staples at more competitive prices in return for slave cargos. Another report from São Tomé noted that the only way the empire would be able to reverse the filter of British manufactures into Portuguese domains in Africa was to let Brazilians have free rein, especially in the Bights. In fact, as Joseph Miller has shown, Brazilian merchants were fanning out north and south of the old bailiwicks in Luanda and Benguela as far as Mozambique. By the 1820s, when Brazil cut its ties from the metropolis, Rio de Janeiro's commercial presence was more dominant than ever in the largest source of captives: Angola.[22]

One effect of the pressures and adaptations of the slave trade was to reinforce Rio de Janeiro's commercial control over the slave trade at the expense of other Brazilian ports. What started as a commercial system with many sinews connecting a variety of ports on both sides of the Atlantic was quickly compressing into one large channel between Rio de Janeiro and the central coast of Africa. The implosion of the metropolis and the British pressure on trading above the equator drove the burgeoning commerce into African coastal routes that then converged into a transatlantic voyage to Rio de Janeiro, and from there entrepôt coastal

---

[21]AHU, CU, Códice 551, f. 229, November 18, 1814.
[22]ANRJ, JC, Caixa 361, pacote 1, s.n., September 3, 1813; pacote 2, f. 28, December 24, 1811; Miller, *Way of Death*, pp. 514–30.

traders carried slaves to other Brazilian ports. As a result, after 1814 the slave trade can be likened to the shape of a trunk lying across the south Atlantic. One end rested on central Africa, the other on central Brazil, with extended African roots at one end reaching ports from the Gold Coast to the Cape, and limbs at the Brazilian end branching out from Rio de Janeiro. Not surprisingly, after 1815 merchants and planters in the provinces grew increasingly impatient with what they perceived as an even more pernicious form of monopoly than the one once benignly wielded by Lisbon. If the old metropolis had never quite been able to enforce its commercial hegemony over the colonies, this was not the case for the new capital of the empire, Rio de Janeiro. Rio de Janeiro had a grip over the slave trade that Pombal could only have fantasized about for Lisbon in the eighteenth century.

The consolidation of Rio de Janeiro as a hub of merchant capital based on the slave trade had a double effect. It magnified the economic independence of Brazil at a time when the monarchy was going to be pressed to rebuild the old metropolis. But it also sharpened the internal differences within Brazil, especially between a dominant *fluminense* faction of Brazilian merchants and lesser, dependent factions based in the provinces. Bahian planters and merchants moaned that the constraints on the slave trade, coupled with declining prices of sugar, were forcing them to switch to cotton exports. It was in part the feeling that Rio de Janeiro was submitting Pernambuco to a more exploited colonial status that provoked the uprising of 1817. In effect, the break in the old colonial system yielded to a new model of dependency of Brazilian and African ports on the new imperial capital and its merchant capitalists. The new geography of dependency also fueled growing resentment over the powers of the new center. The result was the following paradox: while the merchant class of Rio de Janeiro was growing increasingly powerful, it created frictions with provincial dependencies while becoming more estranged from the state.[23]

Fiscal Collapse

The creation of a new bloc of merchant capitalists in Rio de Janeiro presented opportunities—and ultimately limits—to the court's efforts to perpetuate the ancien régime. The propinquity of merchant and

---

[23]ANRJ, JC, Caixa 416, pacote 3, s.n., October 17, 1818. For an example of a Pernambucan complaint, see ANRJ, JC, Caixa 179, pacote 1, f. 24, January 8, 1814. The suppression of the revolt did not put an end to provincial griping. See f. 70, February 17, 1818. For a general discussion of this new model of dependency, see Florentino, *Em costas negras*, pp. 89–122.

monarchs in one entrepôt city intensified the bargaining over rents and revenues. For as Rio's merchants saw their commercial rents swell, the king's ministers fretted about the fiscal solvency of the regime. The two sides engaged in a complicated wrangle over the division of the spoils, which ended up eroding the strength of the empire even as merchants professed their loyalty to the monarchy.

The fiscal state of affairs in the Portuguese empire was not as parlous as Spain's, but it was pretty bad. As early as 1808, the president of the royal treasury examined his accounts, found them bereft of funds, looked at his ability to send out tax collectors in search of revenues, and found none, and decided to strike two birds with a single stone: he proceeded to auction off positions as tax collectors to the highest bidders.[24] Once over the immediate crunch of financing the relocation of the royal court, ministers went about trying to generate a more continuous and reliable source of revenue by taxing trade. Much of the responsibility for soaking up a share of commercial rents fell to the Mesas de Inspeção, which functioned often as arms of the commercial guild, in the main commercial centers. A royal decree went out in July 1809 mandating the officers of the Mesas—who often came from the self-same ranks of merchants who were being asked to contribute—to impose a 6 percent surcharge on all Brazilian exports to Europe, Africa, and Asia. Partial evidence suggests that revenues did indeed rise. But tax collecting quickly locked merchants into a tug-of-war with Mesas officers. Three fiscal "inspectors" issued a long, detailed report to the government in May 1817 cataloguing the ineffectiveness of the tax-collecting system. The revenue machinery ground to such a halt that the government had to resort to desperate measures. Tax farming crept back into the picture. In Maranhão, after much resistance to enforcing the levies or remitting them to Rio de Janeiro, the collection system got so bad that local officials entrusted the job to the English house of Robert Hasketh and Company.[25]

In the absence of an effective revenue system capable of tapping rents for revenues, the crown tried to borrow money abroad and had little choice but to go back to British financiers. London had buoyed the regime through its transition to Brazil and continued to provide "subsidiary aid" to keep the old metropolis afloat during the war and even after the liberation. What the government in Rio de Janeiro wanted, however, was a larger loan to consolidate its debts and smooth out the payments while revamping the revenue machinery. As chapter 6 has shown, Portuguese

---

[24]ANRJ, JC, Caixa 770, pacote 2, f. 23, November 20, 1808.
[25]ANRJ, JC, Mesa de Inspeção, Caixa 178, pacote 2, for revenue data from Porto Alegre, Pará, and Ceará. For a comprehensive report, see s.n., May 6, 1817. On Hasketh, see pacote 1, ff. 16, 36.

pleas for large loans fell on deaf ears. After 1812, however, money was also needed to plow into the rebuilding of Portugal. The government, feeling too insecure about its ability to raise funds in Brazil, went back to British sources, this time hoping that official support from Whitehall would win them favor with London's financial magnates.

Circumstances, however, had changed—and not in favor of the prospective borrowers. Ironically, the success of the Anglo-Portuguese expedition in driving out the French actually removed the urgency to bail out the court in Brazil. Moreover, the British financiers were themselves smarting from the accumulated costs of their own war and subsidies to Iberian allies. By the time the envoy to London, the Count of Funchal, met with the foreign secretary, Lord Castlereagh, in early 1812 to discuss the prospect of a new loan he got a distinctly chilly reception. Lord Wellington turned out to be even more hostile to the idea. They pointed to the Braganza court's inability to force its subjects to comply with the commercial treaty and dismantle remaining monopolies (especially in the trade of Portuguese wines), as well as the endemic violations by Brazilian slave traders, as evidence that the debtors signed deals in bad faith. British traders added to the hostility. Knowing that Funchal was pushing for another loan, they raised a hue and cry over the obstacles to doing business in Portugal and Brazil, making it hard for Castlereagh to offer any help (even if he had been more disposed) without alienating the merchants who were bankrolling Britain's own war effort. Without Whitehall's blessing then, Funchal approached Alexander Baring, one of the city's most prominent monied men, directly. Baring informed the Portuguese envoy that floating a loan would not be well received. Everyone knew how hard it would be to squeeze payments from Brazil to cover loans designed to rebuild the old metropolis. And investors knew how penurious Portugal was, and thus how improbable that it could drum up the money to honor its debts. In effect, the Portuguese empire's dependency on British military and financial support also meant that the British, especially once the threat of alignment with France was gone, could draw limits on their backing. Funchal, after fruitless meetings, blamed the British for their intransigence: "One characteristic property of this business and which makes it so difficult, is the commitment of all Parties against the Slave Trade with a blindness and ardor which equals the Religious Fanaticism of by-gone days." Funchal missed the irony that it was the domestic military costs of crushing slave and popular insurrections in the north and south of Brazil that hiked the fiscal deficits and increased the regime's financial burdens.[26]

---

[26] ANTT, MNE, Caixa 733, Count of Funchal to Galveas, November 18, 1812, Funchal to unknown, April 1, 1813.

Absent an external source of financial support, the regime turned to Brazilian merchants. Appealing to merchants for ad hoc loans was a longstanding expediency and became more frequent, almost quotidian, for the rest of the years of the Portuguese empire in Brazil. Usually these were issued as "special" requests to cover immediate pressing needs, like the appeal for "voluntary donations" in November 1810 to cover the costs of an expedition to Algeria to rescue trapped Portuguese subjects. By the end of the year, the monarchy thanked its vassals for coughing up almost 9 million milreis. The list of donors was a veritable who's who of Brazil's potentates, and the royal gratitude was thus also designed to redouble the mythic bonds between a dynasty that looked out for its imperiled vassals while enabling wealthy subjects to display their loyalty through contributions to public causes.[27] Calls for special loans, however, evolved quickly from invitations to voluntary contributions to the royal treasury to ever more coerced "loans." The shift coincided with the deterioration of tax collecting and the escalating costs of war—to suppress insurgents in the north and wage a savage war against Artigas and the Banda Oriental in the south. No sooner did General Lecor throw his forces against Artigas's cavalries in late 1816 than the *Gazeta do Rio de Janeiro*, the official broadsheet, announced "that many capitalists, merchants, property-owners, and people of all classes have been asked to subscribe spontaneously to cover the needs of the State in its current urgent circumstances. All amounts were welcome!" This was April 1817. A month later, news arrived in Rio of the uprising in Pernambuco. The injunctions for "spontaneous" contributions intensified. In May 1817, the *Gazeta* started to publish the lists of contributors, many of whom were rewarded for their support with noble titles. The most magnanimous of all, the Baron of Rio Seco, gave up 1.2 million milreis alone by the end of the year. Ennoblement of elites thereby became a compensatory mechanism for the state's fiscal weakness, thickening the patina of aristocracy over Brazilian merchants and planters.[28]

There was not, however, an inexhaustible source of funds and, therefore, a limit to which patents of nobility could enlist money for the state treasury. Professions of loyalty and gratitude began to yield diminishing returns. There was, however, one more recourse. Another tried, if not always true, remedy for fiscally strapped regimes whose ability to make good on debt was so low that borrowing was not an option was monetizing the shortfall. Indeed, in the 1790s, *all* parties involved in the revolutionary and Napoleonic wars had to print money to cover their

---

[27]*Gazeta do Rio de Janeiro*, November 24, 1810.
[28]*Gazeta do Rio de Janeiro*, April 2 and October 15, 1817.

costs. The royal mint began issuing paper money in 1797—notes without any backing in specie held in state coffers. The effect was immediate inflation, pumped with further emissions in 1798, 1799, 1805, and 1807. By the time the court evacuated Lisbon, money markets were awash with depreciating paper notes, and a reliable medium of exchange went scarce.

The Americanization of the court and the spreading political violence in the hinterlands meant increasing emissions—bringing us full circle to the initial experiment in public banking in Brazil, which, as chapter 6 has shown, was less a business than a burden on capitalists. The enthusiasm waned as it became clear that the Banco do Brasil was issuing notes without full metallic backing, swamping the market with depreciating paper money. The crown then devised a system to cater to aristocratic wannabes: buyers of three shares would earn the title of Hábito de Cristo; owners of twenty shares would get commended with the Order of Christ; and buying thirty shares would get investors a knighthood. In effect, the government made investment in the private bank a sluiceway for ennoblement of the Brazilian elite. What is more, buying shares would push any investor up the officer rank of the militia; all shareholders were promoted to captain; four shares got the rank of lieutenant; and so on. Deep pockets that could afford ten shares exempted the investor from any field service in the event of war while elevating him to the top officer rank. But doling out noble titles only wound up depreciating them; only the truly status-hungry found the rewards appealing. A supine royal press applauded the bank's great strides. In early 1817, the Bahian paper *Idade d'Ouro do Brasil* celebrated the "glorious reputation and solidity of that happy establishment."[29] But the regime's propaganda machinery could not hide uncomfortable realities from those who were being asked to foot the bills, domestic or foreign. It was clear enough, for instance, to Funchal in London that the sorry state of the bank and the government's books was not news to British financiers and was undermining his appeal for a loan. One of his assistants bemoaned the "imperious orders for forced loans" in Brazil because "I confess, it means that the British Government looks at me with repugnance as I try to enter into new Contracts for new Loans."[30]

[29]In early 1816, the bank had opened a branch in Bahia. *Idade d'Ouro do Brasil*, March 25, 1817; Franco, *Historia do banco*, pp. 33–49. The rhetoric and promise were lofty enough to inspire Portuguese subjects to clamor for their own bank, to help revive the metropolitan economy, and, one senses, to counter the power of Brazilian magnates over the crown. See ANTT, J C, Maço 67, Caixa 213, s.n., February 20, 1816, João Fletcher.

[30]ANTT, MNE, Caixa 731, Rafael da Cruz Guerreira to Funchal, April 7, 1812.

Then, when warfare erupted in northern and southern Brazil in 1816–17, the precarious public financing scheme began to collapse. The king's close advisor, Tomás Antonio Vilanova Portugal, urged resorting to drastic measures. To stanch the efflux of specie from Brazil he prohibited all shipments or transfers of metal money from Rio de Janeiro, created a special account in the bank for gold and silver reserves, and ordered the immediate cessation of monetary printing. Designed to restore the value of paper currency by showing good faith efforts to try to back notes with specie reserves, the measures were supposed to contract the local supply of money. This is not what happened, for while the regime spoke of fiscal and financial probity, it was busy printing money to fund its wars and largesse. Between 1814 and 1820, the supply of banknotes quadrupled and added to the creeping unpopularity of the regime's economic policies. Finally, in February 1821, the government was forced to intervene directly and place the bank under the mantle of the royal mint, removing all its autonomy and dispensing with the fiction that it was designed to protect private financial property rights. A month later, the king commissioned João Pereira de Almeida, later the Baron of Ubá, to examine the sorry state of the bank and devise recommendations for its future. When the sobering report came in, its author claimed that it was nearly impossible to know exactly how bad the situation was, as account keepers had more or less given up keeping track of the books.[31]

It is easy to pin the blame for financial mismanagement on a reckless regime. After all, here was a system in which the government was the regulator of the exchange business and its largest borrower at the same time. But the original deal with private financiers did provide the latter with some undeniable—and ultimately irresistible—opportunities. Aside from getting their knighthoods, the directors discounted each other's notes at the bank without charge and paid no interest on private loans they took out on the bank's account. This money could then be converted into resources to expand their own commercial networks down the social pyramid, by advancing unstable funds to procure staples or help market commodities on credit. Basically, big shareholders elevated their social status to aristocracy while they converted the bank into their own bottomless source of private credit that enabled them to reinforce their commercial hegemony over lesser merchants and producers. The bank was not expected to produce regular ledgers, the directors did not hold themselves to accounting standards that would have publicized

---

[31]Johnson, "A Preliminary Inquiry," p. 244; J. J. Sturz, *A Review, Financial, Statistical and Commercial, of the Empire of Brazil and Its Resources* (London: Effingham Wilson, 1837), pp. 2–4; Ribeiro Fragoso, *Homens de grossa aventura*, pp. 200–203, for a discussion of how the bank abandoned its mandate to serve the private credit market.

the legerdemain, and, in the words of one analyst reporting on the state of the Brazilian economy in the 1830s, the capital did not have "a well-conducted periodical press which could open the eyes of the people to the robbery that was about to be committed to them." One corner of the financial revolution that reinforced any stable public credit system—public accountability through a free press—was missing on account of the government's commitment to ancien-régime ways, which stifled the "financial revolution" it so needed to survive. Thus it was that efforts to reconstitute the old order by extending dynastic autocracy throughout Brazil reached their limits.[32]

Therefore, even before tensions erupted between Lisbon and Rio de Janeiro, the relationship between the merchant elite and the royal authorities was growing strained. Many felt that the regime was too willing to sacrifice commercial interests of Brazil to British and Portuguese demands. There were those who felt robbed by the government's inability to make good on its debts; others were simply tired of the calls for "voluntary donations." Finally, soaring inflation, especially after 1814, took its toll on the general legitimacy of the regime. Ennoblement and promotions in the militia could not always compensate for sharp material losses. Indeed, as a satirical press began to take off around 1820, the image of the paupered baron was a common figure of ridicule. What is important is that the nexus of private power-holders and royal authorities that once supported the imperial ancien régime was breaking up. Indeed, just as power tilted from the Old to the New World, it also shifted from political to economic brokers. The emergence of a powerful bloc of merchant capitalists in Rio de Janeiro posed a limit to the autonomy of the royal regime—a limit the regime was reaching before 1820. The political economy radiating out of the Brazilian capital also limited the influence of metropolitan interests over imperial policy. Starting in 1820, when metropolitan interests insisted on greater command over imperial domains, the latent fissures of the regime broke open, setting the stage for the denouement of the Portuguese empire in the New World.

Denouement

The regime reached an inflexion point by 1820. The ruling bloc within Brazil was coming undone while the kingdom could command only threadbare loyalty in its distant provinces. If troubles within Brazil were difficult enough to handle, it is important to recall that it was still in

---

[32]Sturz, *A Review*, p. 4.

many ways ruled by an Old World dynasty tied to metropolitan interests and claims. With the passing years, the compromise implicit in the 1815 charter between Old and New World loyalties, between looking backward and looking forward, became harder to juggle. In Lisbon and other Portuguese cities, political factions struggled to recompose authority and recover from the humiliation of French victory and royal flight. They were also at each other's throats and were looking for some outside ally to join one or the other side. By 1820, Portuguese leaders yearned to restore the peninsula's centrality in the empire, while fighting to establish local political hegemony.

The liberation of Portugal eventually created increasing pressure to restore the old order. Some members of the court, notably those who still thought of Lisbon as the natural home of the dynasty, grumbled that it was becoming too acclimated to the new surroundings. Especially as the war in southern Brazil began to bog down, royal advisors worried that imperial authority was getting caught in what were provincial, "American" conflicts, and that his majesty needed to restore an essentially "European" worldwide optic on the empire. In February 1820, Rio de Janeiro learned that Artigas's guerrillas had invaded Rio Grande do Sul and that slaves were joining his insurrection en masse. Count Palmella for one, thought that the mishandling of the war in the Banda Oriental would not have happened if the monarchy had been allowed to keep its eyes trained on the great power politics of Europe. Certainly, avoiding a wasteful war in the borderlands would have spared the regime a direct conflict with Madrid and diplomatic tensions with London. In fact, Palmella's "metropolitanism" led him to conclude that the Portuguese regime would be better-off sacrificing the interests of Brazilian slave traders by joining the British war against the slave trade, thereby restoring the natural alliance with (and capital flows from) London.[33]

While the court was torn between Brazilian and metropolitan orientations to empire, political forces in the metropolis also recovered strength—and therefore tilted the balance in the court to the Europeanists. In particular, liberals, nationalists, and imperial reformers embraced a discourse that aimed to reverse the decay and decline of the empire. They saw the comfort of the court in Rio de Janeiro as the principal hurdle to Portuguese revitalization, and upstart Brazil, slavery, and the pretensions of the recently enriched and ennobled potentates in Rio de Janeiro as the obstacles to imperial greatness. Portugal, it is worth saying, was struggling

---

[33]*Gazeta do Rio de Janeiro*, February 29, 1820; Alexandre, *Os sentidos do império*, pp. 349–350; Barman, *Brazil*, pp. 62–64.

to recover after the war. Its industries smarted from the loss of imperial markets. Its agriculture faced competition from cheap imported food-stuffs. And its commercial houses were shadows of their former selves. These material woes only contributed to the symbolic and ideological concerns that Portugal was sliding into perpetual poverty and secondary status in the European power game. In the wake of the war with France, Portuguese leaders in the metropolis constructed a sense of nationhood out of a threat that the old imperial grandeur would be forever lost. And what was distinctive about this emerging metropolitan nationalism was the way in which it counterposed Portuguese interests to those of its colony, Brazil. Therefore, much as the crown resolved the crisis of the ancien régime in 1807 by leaving for Rio de Janeiro, it left unresolved the matter of where the empire would be centered. What metropolitan forces could agree on—notwithstanding the rest of their disagreements— was that the empire could not be centered in Brazil without ceasing to be a *Portuguese* empire. They demanded more and more vociferously that the king return to Lisbon, his rightful home and the natural hub of the Portuguese realm.

Events unfolded in a way that overwhelmed King João's preference for solving problems with solutions that required the least amount of effort. In early 1820, Portugal was abuzz with intrigue and disappointment at the monarch's lethargic response to their demands. Then, after the eruption of the Liberal Revolt in Spain in January 1820, which forced Ferdinand to sign the 1812 constitution, Portuguese liberals and nation-alists grew louder in their talk. The commander of the Portuguese army, General Beresford, worried that the example of the military conspiracy in Spain would inspire officers on his side of the border. Impatient with the king's refusal to take charge of the situation and introduce reforms, Beresford decided to sail to Rio de Janeiro himself to urge the monarch to take command of his own metropolis, leaving the Portuguese army acephalous. A few months after Beresford set foot in Rio de Janeiro in May 1820, a garrison in Porto rose up and declared its fealty to the liberal cause of constitutionalism and reform in the metropolis. The insurrection within the army spread quickly and swept most political forces into a common front, culminating in the proclamation of a con-stitution (copied from the Spanish model), the creation of a provisional government, the summoning of a parliament (Cortes) to write a perma-nent charter, and the return of João to Lisbon. On October 17, 1820, the news of liberal revolution in Portugal arrived to a dumbfounded court in Rio. The official press publicized nothing of the upheaval; the strictures of the old censorious order still clung to the belief that they could con-trol public opinion. But the alignments that had been cobbled together after 1808 and given a semblance of unity in 1815 crumbled. In order to prevent the breakdown from cascading into a breakup, the king and his twenty-two-year-old son, Pedro, swore an oath to the new constitutional system, ordered elections to the Cortes, and presided over several days of festivities. Meanwhile, João began to pack his bags. He promised to leave Pedro behind as the regent.[34]

If João had hoped that his return to Lisbon and his acceptance of a new representative order would restore old loyalties, his decisions in fact emboldened the advocates of metropolitan restoration to push their re-centering aspirations with even more force. What rulers did not grasp was that giving life to electoral activity and lifting restrictions on the press gave sudden, vertiginous autonomy to public opinion—and its highly contingent repercussions. As in the Spanish Atlantic, political norms had changed dramatically since 1808, becoming more public—it was much harder to restore the order *ex ante* 1808 without also adjusting to what had become commonplace in politics since then. The press may have been censored in Brazil, but it still played a role in forging "public opinion." The same held for Portuguese newspapers and rumor mills—which had the additional freedom of being so distant from royal authority. As the metropolitan and Brazilian sides would diverge, the newspapers in the principal cities could not help but catalogue the reasons for discrepancy—and eventually whip up the sense that Brazilian independence was a legitimate act of self-preservation. If the press became one crucial actor in the publicness of politics, so did spreading electoral activity. "Representatives" chosen by "the people" filled local assemblies and eventually the new imperial parliament in Portugal. In 1821, printing presses in Brazil went into overdrive, pumping out newspapers and broadsheets to report on metropolitan "absolutism" and forge a public opinion as the gauge of the common good. According to Kirsten Schultz, in 1821–22 there issued forth as many publications in Brazil as in the preceding dozen years combined—yielding to a "war among journalists" as Isabel Lustosa has so brilliantly described. The press created a guide for what the people wanted for rulers who committed themselves to ruling in the interests of the ruled. As in the Spanish Atlantic then, the principles of representation and public good, which had been devised to modernize the monarchies, became divisive forces for the empires. As politics became more public, it made the task of creating consensus around bargaining over interests more difficult, more

---

[34]*Gazeta do Rio de Janeiro*, February 24, 1821; Barman, *Brazil*, pp. 66–69. It is worth noting that João even considered sending his son, Dom Pedro, to Lisbon in his stead, but then worried that liberals would happily coronate the heir instead as the new Portuguese emperor. For a summary of events in the metropolis, see Alexandre, *Os sentidos do império*, pp. 465–90.

contingent, and ultimately less controllable by rulers since they had to play by rules that they no longer monopolized.[35]

Forced to return to Lisbon, the king could not resist the temptation to take one last bite out of Brazil's financial structure to cover his own needs. The money would come in handy to placate Portuguese liberals. To be sure, the king announced that he wished he could pay the government's creditors, who held 15 billion reis (about 3 million pounds sterling) by the middle of the year. Creditors "will not be in the circumstance of having to wait for too long to realize their repayments," the king promised. Few put stock in the promise.[36] But not long after this pronouncement of royal magnanimity, news leaked out that as the king and his retinue boarded vessels to set sail for Lisbon in April 1821, he made sure that his officers emptied the coffers of the bank. The royal jewels, which had been deposited as a lure for private investment, were smuggled aboard the ships, along with the entire store of bullion amassed since the finance minister slapped on the monetary controls in 1817. When the news got out that the king had plundered his own bank, the arriviste aristocrats of Rio de Janeiro followed suit and hastened to withdraw their deposits or cash in their worthless shares; a mad rush ensued. Those who were not in the know were left holding empty promissory notes. In August 1821, the bank announced that it would have to suspend all exchanges, burn worthless paper notes, and bury the monetary system that it had killed.[37]

The fate of the Banco do Brasil, whipped up by the press for whom the news provided ample fuel for stories of skulduggery, contributed to the sense of decay and corruption of the ancien-régime empire. The transfer of the court to the New World and the creation of new financial and fiscal machinery were supposed to fuse the public cause of the Portuguese empire with the interests of Rio de Janeiro's capitalist classes. Instead, the rulers' policies contributed to a decisive and irreversible split between a struggling imperial monarchy and a powerful bloc of magnates in Brazil. One popular lyric, composed shortly after the king had set sail and the news of his financial shenanigans got out, linked the unpopularity of the imperial regime with the instruments it had so degraded.

> Lá vão no Banco opinar
> Piolhos, patos, leões.
> Hão de talentos mostrar

---

[35]Schultz, *Tropical Versailles*, pp. 248–49. Isabel Lustosa, *Insultos impressos: A guerra dos jornalistas na independência, 1821–1823* (São Paulo: Companhia das Letras, 2000).

[36]*Diario do Rio de Janeiro*, June 3, 1821.

[37]Ibid., August 3, 1821.

E, no fim das discussões,
Morder, roer, devorar.
Não ha destino prefixos:
Foi o foco da riqueza,
Porém, sujeito a caprichos,
Depois de tanta grandeza,
Vem a ser pátio de bichos.[38]

In this context, the divergence between Brazil and Portugal, two "united" kingdoms each with metropolitan ambitions of its own, may have been overdetermined, but it was provoked by the way in which the two sides responded to signals from the other side in the year following the Porto uprising. For Brazilian leaders, there was little in principle that was offensive in the proclamations of the 1820 revolutionaries. Like the Portuguese garrisons, those based in Brazil led the drive to put the regime on some liberal foundations. Through early 1821, troops in Belém, Piauí, Maranhão, and Bahia, and eventually Rio de Janeiro, rose up, demanding that the monarchy embrace the revolutionary principles. Dom Pedro helped defuse the tension and assumed the mantle of regent as an interim measure until the new constitution could be approved. While soldiers returned to their barracks, political life shifted dramatically to the streets, salons, and taverns of Brazil's provinces—which had been invited to elect deputies to the Cortes.[39]

There was a festive atmosphere to the electoral season. It could be said that the election of provincial deputies—forty-five of them from Brazil's regions—was what brought the diversity of the dominions under a carapace of "nationhood." As in Spain, the constitutional Cortes was generally seen as *the* national forge since the monarchy itself had seen its legitimacy drain away. In the name of remaking the nation, however, new principles and practices of representation wound up creating Atlantic cleavages. It was the metropolitan demands that the king return, and especially that Brazil be content with returning to the Iberian shadow, that irked many Brazilians. The immediate spark was, as in Spain, over the practice, not the principle, of representation. It was fine that the "people" be entitled to elect delegates to an assembly, but the presumption that it had to meet in Portugal was not as self-evident to Brazilians as it was to Portuguese. What is more, the two sides wrangled over who got to be a member of the electorate that was represented. As in Spain, metropolitan liberals drew the line of eligible voters around

---

[38]Franco, *Historia do Banco*, pp. 80–112.
[39]Barman, *Brazil*, pp. 70–71.

a circle that left out nonwhites and thus threatened to stack the Cortes with delegates from the peninsula. For Brazil, nonwhites constituted the majority and would have reduced Brazil's collective share of the votes in the assembly to a fraction of Portugal's. In the end, Brazil elected forty-five deputies; Portugal, one hundred. It did not help that the Cortes convened in Portugal before Brazilian delegates even began to arrive and began promulgating laws designed to restore Portuguese centrality in the empire. The most formidable bloc of delegates was supposed to come from São Paulo, and they were not expected to arrive until May 1822, more than a year after the assembly started approving new laws. One galling measure, for instance, was the approval of a list of new military governors to rule the Brazilian provinces as if they were imperial viceroys, rolling back established practices of local governance. When the Brazilian delegates did start arriving, they were ridiculed and insulted. One infamous Portuguese liberal described Brazil as a "land of monkeys and niggers from the coast of Africa, and of bananas." By October 1822, Brazilian deputies, outnumbered anyway, took flight from Lisbon and refused to swear allegiance to the new constitution that was promulgated earlier that year.[40]

The news of metropolitan "abuses" got back to Brazil and stoked the sense that where there was once a single empire, now there really were just two kingdoms destined to go their separate ways. The Brazilian press fanned the flames of outrage, broadcasting the most salacious news and choice symbolic affronts. The *Gazeta do Rio de Janeiro* lambasted the Cortes's attitude toward Brazilian representatives and described Brazilians as boiling "with a noble indignation." The Cortes's laws promised only to create a "system of anarchy and slavery" for Brazilians. At the same time, the paper announced that Brazilians, who had displayed their ability to exercise home rule in 1808, were determined to remain "a brother" to Portugal. In keeping with the family metaphor, the *Gazeta* charged that the Cortes was threatening to break up natural sibling bonds.[41] José da Silva Lisboa's own broadsheet, *O conciliador do reino unido*, celebrated the monarchy for having transformed an empire into a "united kingdom" dedicated to the principle of good government for *all* subjects of the realm: "The Art of Good Government," noted the conservative thinker, "consists in making the people rich and prosperous: constituting them as religious, obedient, well-behaved and polite."

---

[40]For a full study of this process, see Márcia Regina Berbel, *A Nação como Artefato: Deputados do Brasil nas Cortes Portuguesas, 1821–1822* (São Paulo: Hucitec, 1999); Leslie Bethell, "The Independence of Brazil," in Bethell, ed., *Cambridge History of Latin America*, v. 3, pp. 182–84.

[41]*Gazeta do Rio de Janeiro*, January 8, 15 and 24, 1822.

Echoing his earlier invocations of Montesquieu's notion of *doux commerce*. Silva Lisboa claimed that "all individuals are softly [*docemente*] bound by the golden belt of Subordination to Legitimate Authority, all embracing the shield of *good faith*, in order to enjoy the Civil Liberties limited by Good Reason, which sustains the General Security of people and property." Yet even Silva Lisboa, arch defender of the monarchy and its political economy, was forced to concede that the principal threats to this felicitous order came not from the kingdom of Brazil but that of Portugal, whose subjects appeared to have forgotten the principles that once made it great. Indeed, Silva Lisboa framed his principles of monarchy for the New World as a realm of Christian equality and civic freedom inspired by Edmund Burke. Following Burke, he envisioned Brazil as a host for a more perfect combination of public sagacity and private virtue, a model that would stand historically as the nemesis of the French Revolution.[42]

The final problem was that as Rio de Janeiro and Lisbon locked horns over the centeredness of the empire, Brazilian provinces took the opportunity to declare their own autonomy from either capital. Since the convocation of the Cortes according to instructions issued in March 1821 had gone out to "provinces" of the empire, treated as relatively sovereign parts of a larger nation, this signified an important shift in Brazilian political geography. What were once captaincies subordinated to a centralized (if incomplete) autocracy in Rio de Janeiro had become autonomous political machines endowed with rights to send their own deputies to a supra-Atlantic congress. In effect, the rather weak centripetal system contrived in 1815 started to splinter as Spanish America had, intensifying a dispute over which body of government was the rightful custodian of the sovereign rights of the people. Local provincial assemblies, Juntas de Govêrno, declared one by one that they were; the 1821 instructions gave them the power to elect envoys to the Cortes. Many local authorities repudiated efforts on the part of ministers in Rio de Janeiro to keep a handle on Brazilian affairs. This threatened Rio de Janeiro with the prospect of a decentralized order, one that threatened to dissolve if the assemblies went the way of their in Spanish American neighbors. The full implications of the rise of provincial power will be explored in the next chapter. For the moment, however, Brazilian disintegration was contained because transatlantic disintegration proved even

---

[42]*O conciliador do reino unido*, I. This sheet was published through most of 1821 to smooth over the conflicts until it shut down, recognizing the futility of the effort. There were no dates to the numbers. For a synthesis of Silva Lisboa's thoughts, see *Memoria dos beneficios politicos do Governo de El Rey Nosso Senhor D. João VI* (Rio de Janeiro: Impressão Regia, 1818); and Schultz, *Tropical Versailles*, pp. 197–208.

more unavoidable. Paradoxically, Portuguese effrontery, the treatment by metropolitan deputies of "Brazilian" as somehow inferior and less consequential to the nation, created a sense of unity among the fissiparous Brazil delegations. It was not a sense of Brazilian nationalism that galvanized New World unity. Rather, the aversion to *europeus* overwhelmed suspicion of *cariocas*. Each time the Portuguese Cortes threatened to restore Brazilian provinces to their colonial status, it humiliated provincially elected deputies. This made it easier for Rio de Janeiro to proclaim its defense of the sovereign rights of the colonies. One by one the provincial juntas, which worried that they did not have access to the military resources necessary to ward off a Portuguese invasion, rallied to Rio de Janeiro's leadership, less out of nationalist conviction than provincial preservation.[43]

Metropolitan condescension and its imperial logic engendered its reactive nemesis. Parliamentary activity compressed the colonies into a single coalition that eventually embraced not just home rule within empire but complete sovereignty from it. Notably, there was relatively little antimonarchical sentiment on either side of the Atlantic; dissolution of the ancien-régime empire cannot be explained by the appeal of republicanism—which accounted for a powerful strain of the secessionist struggles in Spanish South America. Indeed, the presence of Pedro, his Austrian wife, Leopoldina, and their assiduous efforts to nurture filial bonds with Brazilian subjects led many to believe that it was the Braganza heir who was best suited to defend Brazilian interests and identities. Part of the press campaign that played up the metropolitan abuses also urged Pedro to resist the Cortes's instructions for him to return to Lisbon. He should stay in Brazil as a Brazilian ruler. Thus, just as the Cortes was breaking up the fraternal bonds between Brazil and Portugal, they were also shattering the filial ties between Pedro and João, son and father. In this fashion the apostles of Brazilian secession could argue that it was Brazil, not Portugal, that stood behind the principle of dynastic integrity as the model for the political community. The official discourse that championed Brazilian sovereignty therefore did so in the name of continuity of the ancien régime. Indeed, in some respects this formulation set the stage for a political move that would sacrifice the Portuguese empire in order to save the ancien régime.[44]

---

[43]Berbel, *A Nação como Artefato*, pp. 48–50; Barman, *Brazil*, pp. 93–95. The unity, however, should not be exaggerated, for even as Brazil separated, provincial sources warned that simply replacing Lisbon's yoke with one forged in Rio was not more integrative. See the Bahian paper *Semanario civico*, Septemper 26, 1822.

[44]*Despertador Brasiliense*, I, published without dates in 1821; *Gazeta do Rio de Janeiro*, January 24, 1822.

Had Pedro not declared his intention to stay in Brazil, and had the entire dynasty been associated with Lisbon's aggressive injunction to restore its primacy, it is quite possible that anti-Portuguese sentiment might have spilled into antimonarchical feeling. As it was, Pedro's highly celebrated promise that "I will stay" was a popular gesture across the provinces. Pedro kept up his popular injunctions. "The time has come," the prince exclaimed, "to stop tricking men." He unveiled a list of grievances including "Portugal's" exploitation of the Banco do Brasil (that it was his father that plundered the bank's chest was a subtlety that went unreported). To culminate three centuries of abuse and exploitation, metropolitan interests left Brazil "burdened with an enormous National debt." Pedro's intentions in announcing Brazil's grievances and sovereign rights aimed to preserve the royal order and put the primary menace to its stability—Portugal—on notice. Talk of this sort stoked more audacious calls for home rule. In the words of one editorial, self-rule would ensure the "bases of the kingdom's future greatness and prosperity, and free it from all elements of disorder and anarchy."[45] In the words of an appeal to the Prince Regent in the *Revérbero Constitucional Fluminense*: "Do not disdain the founding of a new Empire . . . Prince, all nations receive a single chance to establish their own government which, once missed, does not return. The Rubicon is crossed; hell is behind, and in front the temple of immortality."[46]

The rhetoric coming from Brazil provoked Portugal to make its final, counterproductive move. The Cortes's metropolitan delegates decreed that Brazil's laws violated imperial law, charged Brazilian ministers with treason, and ordered that an army be raised in the metropolis to restore calm and obedience on the other side of the Atlantic. Whether the regime could have afforded to even try reconquering Brazil is beside the point—the conflict had clearly escalated to a semiotic fever, bitter enough to cleave the empire in two. Certainly, the Portuguese Cortes might have desisted from such saber-rattling had they paid closer attention to the futility of Spanish "pacification" efforts. Either way, when Pedro learned that Portugal was prepared to coerce Brazil into submission, he declared the country formally free of the metropolis on September 7, 1822. There was little opposition to independence in Brazil, though there was a great deal of friction over just how much the provinces had to succumb to a new Rio de Janeiro–centered order. Indeed, by severing "Brazil" from Portugal, he reoriented the provinces back to Rio de Janeiro. The fact

---

[45] *Gazeta do Rio de Janeiro*, August 6, 1822; *Diario do Rio de Janeiro*, August 7, 1822. The Banco do Brasil became a potent symbol of metropolitan abuse and mismanagement even before the prince issued his catalogue. See *O Correio do Rio de Janeiro*, April 24, 1822.

[46] Cited in Barman, *Brazil*, p. 91.

that it was the monarch himself who declared independence took the "revolutionary" sting out of breakup. The few isolated Portuguese troops were invited to renounce their loyalty to Lisbon and stay (some did) or board waiting vessels and leave for good. On the whole, the demilitarization of the secession struggle went smoothly. On December 1, Dom Pedro I was publicly crowned as the emperor of Brazil amid much pomp and ceremony. Now he, his ministers, and the power bloc in Rio de Janeiro could turn their attention to consolidating a regime to hold provinces in a unitary order that combined the principles of representation, sovereignty, and the defense of merchant capitalism's pillars of slavery and staple exports for the Atlantic world.[47]

Brazilian independence, the birth of an autonomous public opinion, and internal debate over who would rule at home flowed, therefore, into a movement not for a rupture with an aristocratic, monarchical past, but for its redemption through exit from empire.

CONCLUSION

Structural breaks in the Iberian Atlantic were not of a piece. In contrast to the Spanish Atlantic, where the Cádiz merchant elite used its propinquity to and dependency on the imperial monarchy to draw the line against concessions to colonial claims, the opposite happened in the Portuguese Atlantic. The Americanization of the dynasty, followed by efforts to bolster the prestige of the Braganza monarchy, associated the fate of the ancien régime with colonial, not metropolitan, capital. As long as this reconfiguration persisted, the very idea of Brazilian "independence" was redundant. In the Spanish dominions the effort to restore metropolitan power over the colonies unleashed centrifugal pressures and eventually full-blown civil wars. In Brazil, provinces may have resented the puissance of the new capital of the empire, but their ability to contest centralism remained blunted by two intrusive variables. First, the relocation of the power bloc to the Americas made it harder for local grievances to evolve into a "nationalist," American movement against "imperial" hegemony. Second, the condescension in Portugal after 1820 treated the provincial delegates as a "Brazilian" whole—exit from the Portuguese empire could be understood as simultaneously a declaration of Brazilian and provincial sovereignty.

---

[47]The sequence is told episodically by Lima, *O movimento da independência*. While this account captures the intricacies and centrality of the court's leadership, it stresses the conjuncture between the return of João and the declaration of independence as the birth of an immanent sense of national selfhood.

What kept Brazil from breaking up were also the conditions that shaped the nature of the breakup of the old Portuguese empire. For, as King João soon discovered, the power bloc in Rio de Janeiro that squashed hinterland secessions also had the means to cut its ties with the metropolis and carry with it all of Brazil's provinces (even precariously). This reduced the prospect that a conflict across the Atlantic world might degenerate into a civil war within the New World. By contrast to the fitful and violent process of achieving independence in Spanish America—and, for that matter, in the United States and Saint Domingue—the formal transition to independence in Brazil did not involve large-scale militarization of political conflict.

The absence of a militarized politics in Brazilian secession from the old metropolis did not mean that the reordering was bereft of political violence. The warfare in the south and north dragged the peripheries into swamps of bloodshed. What was at stake in the hinterlands was not just the matter of who would rule at home but how they would rule. Brazilian independence, and the definition of territorial sovereignty, did not settle this. On the contrary: breaking with the old metropolis exemplified the possibilities that other changes were possible. Nor did secession take care of what it meant to be Brazil. Independence was therefore less the end of an ineluctable process of national formation than a formative start. Indeed, the regime and the public spaces like the press, cafés, and plazas that would shape its legitimacy, as well as the economic forces that would yield the resources for its construction, had to turn their energies away from castigating an external foe to promoting an idea of Brazil and a state that would serve as its handmaiden. There would be, as the new ruler and ruling classes would discover, much more consensus over what Brazil had ceased to be, a colony, than the principles that should govern the new state-nation.

9   Revolution and Sovereignty

It has been said that historians are creatures of habit. Certainly, since the American Revolution, we have often taken for granted that consolidating nationhood as a surrogate for empire involved deliberative lawmaking. Drafting and approving a constitution represented the last episode in an epic passage beginning when colonial peoples shattered the association of imperium with sovereignty; constitutions, after all, have been—are—meant to resolve underlying questions about the principles of rulership, questions opened up by revolutionary upheaval.[1]

Habits can also breed false certainties. For all the importance of constitution making to close the transition from an old era to a new one, some assumptions have been allowed to pass unexamined. One in particular has concerned this book: the durable presumption that nations matured within colonial molds and challenged archaic imperial structures in favor of new ones. This has been a mainstay of nationalist historiographies, which give to national actors and identities agentic powers in making the world anew and—in their mind's eye—by toppling doomed empires in favor of national successors. All it took was freed people to embrace the institutions that most perfectly molded to their national aspirations; hence the sequenced hyphen of the *nation*-state, as if the former gave birth to the latter.

But what happens when we look at history differently, and do not suppose the existence of the nation, either as social formation or as idyll, before empires crumbled and the fires of revolution began to spread across colonial hinterlands? What happens, to return to the metaphor of the labyrinth, when we do not know the end? What would the story look like if the future was much less clear than its teleologists proclaim?

Lawmaking, as this chapter will show, did not dissolve the heritages of imperial and revolutionary pasts into shared national destinies in the Iberian Atlantic. There was no swelling national esprit waiting to be released from colonial thralldom; no compelling model of sovereignty

---

[1]David A. Lupher, *Romans in a New World: Classical Models in Sixteenth-Century Spanish America* (Ann Arbor: University of Michigan Press, 2003); Pagden, *Peoples and Empires*, esp. pp. xxi–xxii.

waited in the wings for the legislator to promulgate into existence once empire was irretrievably lost. As colonies seceded from empires, a specific brand of constitutionalism took hold. Lawmakers saw themselves as the makers of states as well as nations. Indeed, their challenge was to make states as foundations for nationhood, reterritorializing sovereignty in previously colonial spaces to be filled with nations in the making. When the delegates of the liberated territories of Venezuela gathered at Angostura in 1819 to approve a charter that would enshrine newly won rights into a fundamental law, Simón Bolívar reminded them that colonists were now free, but they lacked basic virtues that prepared them for citizenship because as Spanish colonists they had never been apprenticed in the art of governance and the mores of the civitas. Bolívar's worries echoed across the lettered elites of South America. Neither the American model of laws nor French declarations of basic rights were appropriate cornerstones for constitutionalism in South America. Turning to Montesquieu, Bolívar made the case against universal theories of lawmaking: "Does not *L'Esprit des Lois* state that laws should be suited to the people for whom they are made?"[2]

Bolívar and other constitutionalists advocated a particular spirit of lawmaking. Most of the founders of new South American states agreed that constitutions in these former colonial societies had to create virtues and rights where few had existed under empire. They were not simply diffusing the universal features of the Enlightenment to deprived, rights-starved corners of the Atlantic world. Theirs may have been struggles that formed part of a more general drive to human betterment, but they could not so easily erase the traits of historical inheritances without constitutions that would create citizens through state power rather than defend them from state encroachments. If North American colonists or French *citoyens* had to be armed with legal weaponry to uphold their existing rights against arbitrary and intrusive rule, South American lawmakers felt they could not premise their charters on the defense of rights that Iberian rulers had never instilled in the first place. Having made the long passage from loyalty, to voice, to exit, former colonists had circled back to the question of loyalty. The issue would be: loyalty to what if the future had to be premised on freedoms with no precedents?

With no historical precedents—mythic or institutional—to rely upon, the framers of statehood ran headlong into the intractable problem of sovereignty once its fundamental features and limitations were revealed. Gone or going were the anciens régimes. Their demise exposed the very foundations of political power and cast a sharp light on the limits of state structures that

---

[2]Bolívar, "The Angostura Address," in Bushnell, ed., *El Libertador*, pp. 31–53.

are more often hidden from view as long us they are not questioned. This leaves the normal course of debating sovereignty to the issue of who within the political order was invested with which powers. But these were not normal times—they came at the end of a long process of collapse and emergency. These were the conditions, as Walter Benjamin and Giorgio Agamben have noted, in which the properties of political order itself are challenged. This is not to say that membership in the political community and access to powers that govern it were not relevant; it's just that these powers became contingent when the principles and "originary structures" were questioned, challenged, and resisted. Restoring rule with a new originary structure of sovereignty was the aspiration of constitutionalists. It was also the means used to restore sovereignty. Herein lay the drama of the 1820s. It was a decade in which the centrifugal crisis of ancien régime empires bore down on fledgling post-colonial systems, ravaging the remnants of old orders, and leaving their deep imprints on their successors.[3]

NEW AND OLD IN THE ATLANTIC WORLD

In the wake of the revolutionary and Napoleonic wars, leaders across the Atlantic world grappled with the challenge of building a postrevolutionary state system. Having appealed to "the people" to wage war against imperial rivals, ruling classes made nation-states the evolved cognates of empire. Indeed, European elites embraced many of the ideas of national sovereignty, if only to preserve what the French Revolution came close to destroying—their ennobled privileges. The predominant thrust of the 1820s was to stabilize the concert of nation-states by rescuing incumbent elites from their propensity to rivalry and interstate conflict—whose eighteenth-century escalations had nearly destroyed the old regimes.[4]

Restoration had ambivalent effects on the Iberian Atlantic. The selfsame determination on the part of European elites to remake anciens régimes after revolution limited what they could do when it came to integrating former colonies within the transatlantic state system.[5] Foreign capitals recoiled from validating Iberian American sovereignty because

---

[3]Giorgio Agamben, *Homo Sacer: Sovereign Power and Bare Life* (Stanford: Stanford University Press, 1998), pp. 11–12.

[4]C. A. Bayly, *The Birth of the Modern World, 1780–1914* (Oxford: Basil Blackwell, 2004), pp. 125–28; Mayer, *The Persistence of the Old Regime*, for a strong claim that nationalism revitalized pre-revolutionary mores. Eric Hobsbawm, *The Age of Revolution, 1789–1848* (London: Weidenfeld and Nicolson, 1962), esp. chap. 7 on nationalism.

[5]Waddell, "International Politics and Latin American Independence," pp. 200–210; Masur, *Simón Bolívar*, pp. 72–82; Caio de Freitas, *George Canning e o Brasil (Influência da diplomacia inglêsa na formação brasileira)* (São Paulo: Companhia Editora Nacional, 1958), v. 1.

of their commitment to the politics of European restoration, which included supporting aristocracies, monarchies, and the remnants of the anciens régimes in Iberia. There were some sympathizers, like Jeremy Bentham, who saw the region as a good field for utopian plans. Along with James Mill, Bentham actively shared ideas for a great code to systematize and rationalize the legal systems of Spanish America in correspondences with Rivadavia, Bolívar, and Guatemala's José del Valle.[6] In general, however, earnest colonial supplicants failed in European capitals. Foreign secretaries, from Wellesley to Castlereagh, were tone deaf to colonial arguments. Faced with the choice of backing colonial claims draped in reasoned self-interest, or supporting metropolitan reactionaries who shamelessly played antirepublican and antirevolutionary cards at every turn, European powers aligned with the interests of Lisbon and Madrid. What stood in the way of European recognition of Iberian American states was the resilient model of Iberian sovereignty as imperia, states still envisioned as powers on the European scene because they were empires. Fortunes only began to shift after Castlereagh's suicide in August 1822, when George Canning took over the task of managing the interstate order and the place of the British empire in it.[7]

While British governments dithered over whether to support Iberian American statehood, other powers were no less ambivalent. The Russian tsar, Austria's Metternich, and the French government were all livid that Canning was willing to defect from the reactionary concert and had turned his back on the shaky monarchies in Lisbon and Madrid. Behind closed doors, however, France was inclined to try to win some Iberian American favor to buttress enduring jealousies of Anglo-American power. The United States had its own reasons for neighborly ambivalence. Washington certainly did not want powerful southern neighbors at a time when its gaze was fastened on the west and southern borderlands; on the other hand, it did not want the unruliness of Iberian American affairs to induce European meddlers looking for informal dependencies. The dilemma was: it was in the interest of state builders in the United States to have "good neighbors" while securing their own revolution at home by taking advantage of weak adjacent states. The compromise was President Monroe's message in December 1823 denouncing European interference in sovereign American affairs. But his government was not willing to throw its weight behind Iberian American state builders in large part because just the right amount of instability in the rest of the

---

[6] See also Miriam Williford, *Jeremy Bentham on Spanish America* (Baton Rouge: Louisiana State University Press, 1980).

[7] Wendy Hinde, *George Canning* (Oxford: Basil Blackwell, 1973), pp. 345–54, 365–70.

Americas would ensure that Washington could emerge as the unrivaled power in the New World.[8]

Transatlantic commercial interests were more receptive to demands for colonial autonomy—especially when Lisbon and Madrid stuck by old mercantilist policies. There was a notion that behind the walls of Iberian mercantilism lay societies of teeming consumers eagerly waiting cheaper goods—and this certainly motivated European and North American approaches to Iberian America as much, if not more, than the aversion to republicanism and revolution.[9] South American independence rekindled foreign interest in commercial prospects. Not surprisingly, British merchant capital seized upon the opportunities presented by Iberian American independence. Acknowledging the promise of a new commercial marriage between mining and agrarian Iberian America with manufacturing Britain, Canning wrote to Wellington in November 1822 declaring that "the American questions are out of all proportion more important to us than the European, and that if we do not seize and turn them to our advantage in time, we shall rue the loss of an opportunity never, never to be recovered."[10] Commercial interests could not agree more. The British Committee of Merchants in particular sent delegations and missions to the Iberian colonies to report back on the prospects for business; it lobbied parliamentarians; and it used the emerging commercial press to make the case for enlightened self-interest while indulging in unabashed El Dorado imagery to do so.[11]

In the end, it was the need to secure commercial treaties that forced the British cabinet to recognize independent states across the region. In late 1824, Canning began dispatching representatives to the main

---

[8]James E. Lewis, Jr., *The American Union and the Problem of Neighborhood: The United States and the Collapse of the Spanish Empire, 1783–1829* (Chapel Hill: University of North Carolina Press, 1988); Piero Gleijeses, "The Limits of Sympathy: The United States and the Independence of Spanish America," *Journal of Latin American Studies* 24:3 (1992): 481–505; Waddell, "International Politics and Latin American Independence," pp. 205–10; C.W. Crawley, "International Relations, 1815–1830," in his *New Cambridge Modern History,* v. 9, pp. 669–83.

[9]Indeed, as the Spanish and Portuguese regimes imploded, merchants large and small, mainly from the United States and Britain, zeroed in on Iberian American markets. On the British invasion of the River Plate in 1806–7, see Klaus Gallo, *De la invasión al reconocimiento: Gran Bretaña y el Río de la Plata, 1806–1826* (Buenos Aires: A-Z Editora, 1994), pp. 55–69.

[10]Hinde, *George Canning,* p. 345; O'Brien, "The Impact of the Revolutionary and Napoleonic Wars," pp. 335–95.

[11]John Luccock, *Notes on Rio de Janeiro* (London, 1820); Francis Bond Head, *Rough Notes Taken during Some Rapid Journeys across the Pampas and among the Andes* (London, 1826), p. 13; D.C.M. Platt, *Latin America and British Trade, 1806–1914* (London: Adam and Charles Black, 1972), pp. 4–12, 21–29.

Spanish American capitals with instructions to work out trade deals with fledgling states. A year later, in defense of his policies against critics who accused him of abandoning Spain, Canning insisted that he gained much more, Spain's "Indies." He declared to the House of Commons that "I called the New World into existence to redress the balance of the Old." It is safe to say that the habits of looking at the Americas through the realpolitik lens of European rivalries had not altogether vanished.[12] That commercial opportunism corroded the bonds of principled support for imperial allies is even clearer when it came to the biggest of all markets, Brazil.[13]

The commercial interests that motivated the recognition of state power in South America at the end of the cycle of Atlantic revolutions changed the historic relationship between interests and institutions that once dovetailed under empire. With freer trade—reinforced by treaties with Atlantic powers, which were seen as a modest price to pay for legal recognition of sovereignty—the option of restoring old models of accumulation waned for good. Whether by ideological conviction in the blessings of free trade, or self-interested pursuit of new market opportunities, states neither could nor would protect mercantilist rentier networks. The 1820s brought final closure on the reciprocal exchange of ancien-régime revenues for the protection of merchant capital's rents. Thereafter, the relations between capital and public power, private interests and public institutions, had to be negotiated on different terms.

NATIONAL INTERESTS

Merchant capital had to cope with some radical changes in the commercial circuitry of the Atlantic economies. To start with, the traffic between colonies and old metropolises never recovered. Portuguese houses went into a tailspin after 1808. They might have revived, and some of the old infra-Portuguese commerce might have bounced back, had the Portuguese

---

[12]Kaufmann, *British Policy*, p. 220; Gabriel Paquette, "The Intellectual Context of British Diplomatic Recognition of the South American Republics, c. 1800–1830," *Journal of Transatlantic Studies* 2:1 (2004): 85–87.

[13]George Canning to Sir Charles Stuart, October 10, 1825, in C. K. Webster, ed., *Britain and the Independence of Latin America, 1812–1830: Select Documents from the Foreign Office Archives* (Oxford: Oxford University Press, 1938), p. 289; John J. Johnson, "United States-British Rivalry in Latin America, 1815–1830," *Jahrbuch für Geschichte von Staat, Wirtschaft un Gesellschaft Lateinamerikas* 22 (1985): 341–91; Manchester, *British Preëminence in Brazil*, pp. 205–10; de Freitas, *George Canning e o Brasil*, 2 vols.; John Murray Forbes, *Once años en Buenos Aires (1820–1831)* (Buenos Aires: Emecé, 1956), pp. 214–19.

and Brazilian rulers not been compelled to sign preferential trading agreements with Britain. Also damaging was the shredding of ancient trading ties up and down the littoral from Buenos Aires to Rio de Janeiro, controlled by merchant houses in the coastal entrepôts, whose lifeblood was the caravans of silver that traveled overland from Potosí and slaves imported from Angola. Of these networks, none emerged unscathed; and not a few became relics like the empires they once enriched.[14]

Old commercial channels of the Spanish Atlantic went into permanent paralysis. By independence there was little commercial substance holding the old parts of the empire together. The value of total trade (imports and exports) between the colonies and Spain in 1820—a year in which Spanish merchantmen could finally sail without being threatened by foreign warships—barely exceeded a third of the value it registered in 1792 when, it could be legitimately argued, the commercial benefits of eighteenth-century reforms were bearing real dividends. Of course, the largest single plummet came from the dramatic decline in shipments of precious metals; by 1827, when the wars were finally over, some trade survived, but was reduced to just a few staples like spices, hardwoods, and sugar from Cuba (the latter accounting for half of all imports from Spanish America). It would be hard to exaggerate the effects of smashing the silver-lined mercantilist system on the powers of incumbency. Much of the effort to rebuild state systems in the wake of revolution had to grapple with how to close the specie gap.[15]

The fall of the old orders threw open markets and quickly undermined the relatively insulated worlds of guild commerce. British merchants arrived in Bogotá, Rio de Janeiro, and Buenos Aires as agents of Liverpool and London houses—with access to deeper pockets of credit, a new way of conducting business, and a determination to replace the complex and expensive system of retailing. Incumbent importers, who once thrived behind mercantilist restrictions (no matter how poorly enforced they were) to mark up their transactions, now faced stiff competition. Where competitors and prices were once closely monitored by guild officials, these colonial associations could no longer interfere in market transactions with sanctions. By the late 1820s, many merchants were reeling from competitive pressures.[16]

---

[14]Pedreira, "From Growth to Collapse," pp. 854–59.

[15]Cuenca Esteban, "Statistics of Spain's Colonial Trade," p. 409; Fontana Lázaro, "Colapso y transformación del comercio exterior español," pp. 7–8; Fisher, "Commerce and Imperial Decline," pp. 469–79; idem, *Trade, War and Revolution*, p. 85.

[16]AGNBA, Tribunal de Comercio (hereafter TC), A-1, *Ruperto Albarellos v. Juan Bayta Romero* (1829).

Open trade was a source of opportunity, but as merchants soon realized, with opportunities came risks. Hammered by the multiplication of forced loans occasioned by war, and weakened by the lifting of restrictions on business, colonial guilds could not enforce the kinds of rules that once reined in competition and kept trading—especially at the top of the commercial system—within a gentlemanly circle of well-connected magnates. The tradition of infra-elite bargaining within corporate bodies and guilds gave way to challenges to merchants' ability to command prices for goods and collect interest on loans. In May 1821, the governor of Rio Grande do Norte, José Ignacio Borges, informed authorities in Rio de Janeiro that all was not well between farmers, including the owners of large estates, and the merchants, to whom producers had racked up large debts. Cotton producers, for instance, struggled to sell their staples at penurious prices while having to buy their necessities at usurious rates. They "work in good faith," Borges noted, "and nothing should be impossible for them with justice." Yet, men of money were exploiting their privileges: "capital put in commercial circulation always leads to direct possession of products flowing to the market." These are verities, argued the governor, known only to those "ignorant in matters of Political Economy." But they were also abusive, he insisted. Echoing the weekly petitions that crossed his desk, Borges described the actions of merchants as "malicious." At the very least—and enclosing a petition of twenty prominent subjects of the capital, Natal—the government in Rio de Janeiro should give producers freedom to sell and buy from whom they please to release them from thralldom to merchant classes.[17]

Realities of market choices did not make life any easier. As commercial transactions became more unpredictable, the prospect of a loss hiked the cost of that which integrated American hinterlands with European and African consumers: merchant credit. Credit, ranging from advances on goods awaiting future payment to the everyday use of bills of exchange (which operated as a kind of promissory note from one merchant to the next), activated the cycle of production and consumption. Locking American frontier lands into the Atlantic system, their *mise en valeur*, credit was in the hands of an increasingly beleaguered class of merchants. The problems manifested themselves in the chain reactions that one merchant failure issued upon a whole network of debtors and creditors. When one British merchant, Thomas Armstrong, forced a creole trader in Buenos Aires, Victoriano Bolaños, to pay off his debts in

---

[17]ANRJ, JC, Mesa da Inspeção, Caixa 178, pacote 2, f. 59; Adelman, *Republic of Capital*, pp. 94–105.

1824, he set off a cascade of litigation. Having emptied his pockets to pay Armstrong, Bolaños reneged on his other debts, was dragged to the debtors' prison, and left his creditors scrambling to recover—without success—their losses. And this was a modest setback compared to the effects of failure to pay debts by one of the largest commercial partnerships in Buenos Aires. When Juan Pedro Aguirre and Guillermo Ford faced imprisonment for defaulting, the who's who of the Argentine business elite formed a bloc to prevent creditors from seizing the partners' assets—rendering a firm of this size (Ford's obligations, tallied by the courts, exceeded one million pesos) insolvent threatened to bring down the whole credit system of the city.[18]

In the Brazilian capital the shift from a regulated and protected economy designed to bolster mercantile rents to a more competitive, unfettered market presented an amalgam of opportunities and disruptions. Merchants began to complain loudly about the influx of foreign traders and the proliferation of petty merchants whose retailing techniques undermined the collusive, rentier habits of the dominant class. One group of merchants decried their arriviste competitors "who have occasioned the multiplication of failures that have swept our class and endanger the market." They made clear, however, that their calls for help were not pleas to restore old monopolies but simply to protect what is good about commerce "for the interests of the Public Cause." The menace was coming from those who speculate and endanger the morality of exchange by putting self-interest first. What they wanted was controlled competition and bridled markets. This kind of parsing characterized the commercial language in this transitional period, arguing not for a restoration of the old mercantilist rackets but managing and protecting self-interest in the name of a common concern. As *O Correio do Rio de Janeiro* observed in mid-1822, national merchants were getting squeezed by foreign merchants waving their treaty rights and loading warehouses with goods for sale on consignment. "From this abuse is born grave dangers to national [merchants] who can neither sell or must do so at a loss, on account of the prices charged by Foreigners." The paper called for a national "commission" to investigate the "damages" and recommend measures to restore the moral foundations of Brazilian merchant capitalism.[19]

---

[18]AGNBA, TC, E-67 (1820–25), Francisco Elias sobre que se entregue un documento de clarificación de crédito contra el estado (1824); F-83 (1824–28), Moratorias declaradas por los acreedores de Juan Pedro Aguirre y Guillermo Ford (1828); Price, "Credit in the Slave Trade and Plantation Economies," pp. 293–96.

[19]ANRJ, JC, Caixa 379, pacote 3, 62, July 7, 1821; *O Correio do Rio de Janeiro*, June 20, 1822.

Incumbents were not without other kinds of tools, informal devices to give elites some stamina. Credit instruments functioned on the basis of trust—assurances that the transactors would honor their commitments. Partnerships among friends and family members to share information, spread risks, and rely on personal mechanisms to pressure associates to live up to their part of deals helped build commercial alliances to smooth out transactions. In 1822, four Italian merchants, each with a special niche (one was a baker, another owned a warehouse, and so on), pooled some capital and formed their "ethnic" alliance to buy hides and wheat to export from Buenos Aires, procure sugar and Paraguayan tea from the north to ship to Mendoza and Chile, and in general to rely on each other's specialty "to speculate on the staples [*frutos*] of the country" to turn a profit. A few years later, José Manuel Coronel in Buenos Aires and Damaso del Campos in Montevideo joined together to sell salt in Montevideo, import cotton, and make uniforms for the military. Instead of simply contracting with each other, they created a legal "society" to be able to hold respective sides of bargains. Yet, the surges and plunges of markets flooded courts with aggrieved partners.[20] Where partnerships and commercial alliances—consummated by the ultimate infra-elite bonding agent, intermarriage—proved most effective in preserving incumbency was in Rio de Janeiro. As Manolo Florentino and João Fragoso have noted of the mercantile elite of the Brazilian capital, the latticework of partnership and intermarriage intensified as risks mounted—in part to defray the effects of competition with collusion, but also to ensure that a failure in one business transaction could be made up with deals elsewhere. In effect, partnerships and familial integrations managed risks by diversifying enterprises within associations and kin networks, reinforcing Rio de Janeiro's merchant class at the top of the social pyramid.[21]

The political break from empire had divergent effects. Where change undermined conventional ways of promoting trust and enforcing bargains, merchants' ability to centralize commercial affairs came apart. The effects can be seen in the changing economic geography of South America. Most regions lost their cohering centers or were torn between waning and emerging hubs. In Peru, the crisis of Andean mining augmented a shift to coastal sectors and revealed an abrasive relationship

---

[20]AGNBA, TC, C-22 (1825–27), Pedro Cadelago and Santiago Marchi y Cia (1825); AGNBA, TC, C-23 (1828–32), *José Manuel Coronel v. Damaso del Campos* (1828); Lugar, "The Merchant Community of Salvador," pp. 133–39.

[21]Florentino, *Em costas negras*, pp. 134–56; Fragoso, *Homens de grossa aventura*, pp. 171–82.

between the interests of the Pacific littoral and the highland provinces. Similar fissures opened up in Colombia: coastal cities like Cartagena, Mompox, and Santa Marta were devastated; indeed much of the nineteenth century witnessed a chronic struggle for littoral hegemony among the entrepôts. The "invasion corridors" like the Valley of Cúcuta and between the llanos and the eastern Cordillera were ravaged; the mainstays of rural enterprise, slaves and cattle, for all intents and purposes were no more. Wherever the fighting was fierce, regions that relied on forced labor and imported African slaves to sustain industries and estates went into decline.[22]

The shift to the new order could also cut other ways: in some quarters and families, new opportunities gave the members of the merchant class renewed integrative powers. Indeed, the River Plate region provides the starkest examples of how colonial economic spaces fractured and acquired new centers. The old viceregal economy began to reorient away from its historic dependence on silver to a new reliance on agrarian produce from the Pampas. Hides, jerked beef, tallow, and eventually wool filled the warehouses and kept the wharves of Buenos Aires and Montevideo busy. Along with this emerging Pampean prosperity, some of the provinces of the interior had to adjust, with much more uneven effects. For the provinces that relied on highland markets, the collapse of silver mining brought penury. The cotton textile factories of Misiones had to face imported competitors, as did those of the Andean interior provinces. The damage and gains were hardly instantaneous: the economic geography of the old viceroyalty began its fifty-year reorientation to the region's new location in the Atlantic system.[23]

The regional effects of the shift to new markets and new opportunities were equally marked in Brazil, though these changes were more drawn out because mercantilist vestiges had been eroding for some time. As in the River Plate, the effects of new opportunities were uneven. Some areas' local and international markets boomed—especially the export economies of Rio de Janeiro and São Paulo. Indeed, Rio de Janeiro became a flourishing hub for a regional and transatlantic economy, a process that simply gathered strength with independence. This in turn spurred adjacent districts. After the decline of gold and diamond mining in Minas Gerais,

---

[22]Paul Gootenberg, *Between Silver and Guano: Commercial Policy and the State in Postindependence Peru* (Princeton: Princeton University Press, 1989), esp. chap. 3 on "merchant nationalism"; Brungardt, "The Economy of Colombia," pp. 164–93.

[23]Samuel Amaral, "Del mercantilismo a la libertad: Las consequencias económicas da la independencia argentina," in Leandro Prados de la Escosura and Samuel Amaral, eds., *La independencia americana: Consequencias económicas* (Madrid: Alianza, 1993), pp. 203–7; Halperín Donghi, *Historia argentina*, pp. 151–57.

the province diversified its staple production to include tobacco, cattle, dairy products, and eventually coffee—a process that began in the 1780s but intensified especially after 1808 with the relocation of the court and the booming coastal markets around Rio de Janeiro.[24] The southward shift in the Brazilian center of economic gravity changed the fortunes of the old northeastern provinces. In the Recôncavo parishes around the Bay of All Saints, tobacco and sugar exports began to decline after the Napoleonic Wars; smaller cane farmers and tobacco growers substituted cassava (the base for *farinha de mandioca*) and other consumables for old staples; the local market eclipsed the export market. One report on the state of Bahian agriculture on the eve of independence noted how the rising price of slaves and sagging price of sugar were like hands choking the necks of planters.[25]

In general, independence did not provoke a decisive economic shift from a crumbling, unviable old order to a robust and uplifting new one; there was no maturing capitalist class or spirit bursting to be free from the confines of Iberian feudality or imperial mercantilism. This was no "bourgeois revolution" mounted by colonial elites looking for a better deal out of the rapidly changing Atlantic economies. As a result, the lifting of colonial fetters on trade and industry did not spark a uniform and sudden surge in economic growth; the new opportunities were not the heralds of unambiguous prosperity. A schism opened up between the more abrupt decline of some sectors and fortunes and the rather more drawn-out, gradual emergence of some regional and export markets. The new model did not immediately fill the vacuum left by the demise of the old one. There was no integrative economic structure upon which to attach nascent political structures.

THE AFRICAN EXCHANGE

We need to widen the scope of constraints and inducements on state formation in South America, for the fortunes of incumbency were as much shaped by discourses and practices of free labor as free trade. The effects of the political caesura also transformed the commerce between Africa and

---

[24]Renato Pinto Venancio, "Comércio e fronteira em Minas Gerais colonial," in Júnia Ferreira Furtado, org., *Diálogos Oceânicos* (Belo Horizonte: Universidade Federal de Minas Gerais, 2001), pp. 181–92; Laird W. Bergad, *Slavery and the Demographic and Economic History of Minas Gerais, Brazil, 1720–1888* (Cambridge: Cambridge University Press, 1999), pp. 216–17.

[25]ANRJ, JC, pacote 3, s.n., October 17, 1818; Barickman, *Bahian Counterpoint*, pp. 44–70, 147–61; Schwartz, *Sugar Plantations*, pp. 252–53, 301–12, 442–51. For a set of useful case studies, see Szmrecsányi and Amaral Lapa, orgs., *História econômica da independência e do império*.

South America, with countervailing consequences. The traffic in slaves had been booming since the 1780s, had given so much commercial vitality to colonial hinterlands, and had reinforced the social incumbency of merchant capital. After 1810 the South Atlantic networks underwent dramatic changes, and some of them were severed for good. The reasons for these changes cannot be adduced to an underlying economic logic. Eric Williams's declaration that "the rise and fall of mercantilism is the rise and fall of slavery" does not hold up to South American evidence.[26] The slave trade to South America adapted less to independent changes in market forces and more to the history of struggles for state sovereignty that provided the legal foundations for commercial transactions. It is important, however, to acknowledge the more general insight of Williams's thesis: when it came to holding and trading slaves, incumbent elites depended on control of state policy. The revolutionary upheaval associated with the crisis of empire spawned new principles of legitimacy and loyalty that determined the fate of the slave trade and fortunes of merchant capital.[27]

The manner and timing with which insurgent regimes of Spanish America cut the lifelines between the source of labor in Africa and its application to the expansion of agrarian frontiers in the Americas exemplify the autonomy of political choices over economic interests. There were, to be sure, ideological convictions at stake. But abolitionist sentiment was much more frail and contingent in the Iberian Atlantic, particularly after the Haitian Revolution. More decisive was the way in which antislavery was adopted as a way to bring along allies to the secessionist cause after 1810. As we have seen, abolishing the slave trade helped insurgents' appeal to slaves as recruits to armies. It also helped curry the favor of British authorities who were making abolition of the traffic in captives a condition of legal recognition. The holdout was Peru, where authorities did not finally halt the slave trade until 1847, though San Martín shut the import of slaves in 1821 and the earlier closure of slave traffic through Montevideo and Buenos Aires cut Peru from its traditional entrepôts. For all intents and purposes, the slave trade to Spanish South America was severed after 1810 (see fig. 5).

The end of the slave trade was part of a more general demise of slavery. Spanish South America proved as inhospitable to restored slave societies as they were hostile to restored imperial monarchies.[28] While Chile was the

[26] Marques, *Os sons do silêncio*; Williams, *Capitalism and Slavery*, p. 136; Fragoso and Florentino, *O arcaísmo como projeto*, pp. 24–25.

[27] For a good survey of the debate, see Holt, "Explaining Abolition," pp. 371–78.

[28] John V. Lombardi, *The Decline and Abolition of Negro Slavery in Venezuela, 1820–1854* (Westport, CT: Greenwood, 1971), pp. 36, 43; Halperín Donghi, *Historia argentina*, pp. 100, 146; Peter Blanchard, *Slavery and Abolition in Early Republican Peru* (Wilmington, DE: Scholarly Resources, 1992), pp. 56–57; Helg, *Liberty and Equality*, pp. 162–64.

Slave Imports to the Americas
1811 to 1830

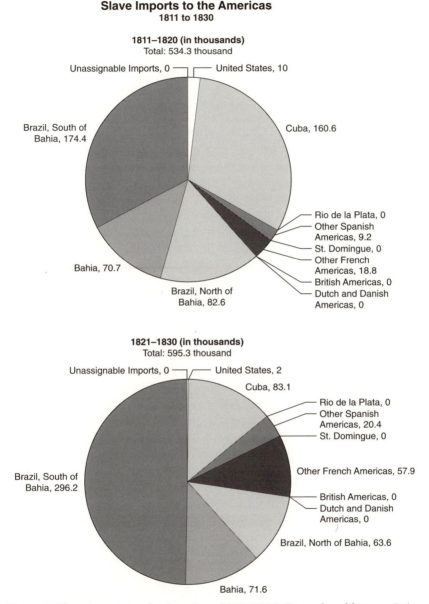

1811–1820 (in thousands)
Total: 534.3 thousand

Unassignable Imports, 0 — United States, 10
Brazil, South of Bahia, 174.4
Cuba, 160.6
Rio de la Plata, 0
Other Spanish Americas, 9.2
St. Domingue, 0
Other French Americas, 18.8
British Americas, 0
Dutch and Danish Americas, 0
Bahia, 70.7
Brazil, North of Bahia, 82.6

1821–1830 (in thousands)
Total: 595.3 thousand

Unassignable Imports, 0 — United States, 2
Cuba, 83.1
Rio de la Plata, 0
Other Spanish Americas, 20.4
St. Domingue, 0
Other French Americas, 57.9
British Americas, 0
Dutch and Danish Americas, 0
Brazil, South of Bahia, 296.2
Brazil, North of Bahia, 63.6
Bahia, 71.6

Figure 5. Slave imports to the Americas, 1811–1830. Reproduced by permission from David Eltis, *Economic Growth and the Ending of the Transatlantic Slave Trade* (Oxford: Oxford University Press, 1987), p. 249.

first to abolish slavery after independence (in 1823), and the Congress of Cúcuta emancipated all slaves born after 1821, other republics only formally ended slavery when it was being extinguished anyway. The transition varied in legal form and speed; in many places it was slow, partial, albeit inexorable. The age of slave societies in Spanish South America was over, even if in some quarters societies with slaves still held out.[29]

The trade in captives between Brazil and Africa could not escape the conflagration. In mid-1823, a British warship captured a Portuguese slave vessel, ironically called the *Sinceridade*, in the harbor of one of the Cape Verde islands with a cargo of captives destined for Brazil. Escorted to Sierra Leone, where the captain would be judged by the "Mixed Commission" in charge of violators of the accords that banned slave trading above the equator, the slaves were released, the ship was impounded, and the investors watched their profits wane into losses. Abolitionism also had some domestic champions. José Bonifacio de Andrada e Silva, Dom Pedro's advisor and unofficial head of the "Luso-Brazilian" bloc that sought to combine Enlightenment ideas with the merits of political gradualism, prepared to address the Brazilian Constituent Assembly on the matter of slavery in late 1823. Like Bolívar, he felt that creating a new state was an opportunity to put it on more solid moral foundations. He decried the slave trade's barbarous nature as not only an affliction on Africans (and therefore a violation of natural laws), but also a vice that perpetuated Brazil's own cultural ill-preparedness for true liberty. Importing slaves stood in the way of Brazilian efforts to create "a homogeneous nation, without which we will never truly be free, respectable and happy"; it also reproduced retardant habits among whites because they were dependent on servile labor and not "independent" subjects producing wealth and opulence from their own work and enterprises—cultural mores that stood in the way of their maturing into citizens. Ending the slave trade was a way of signaling a more profound break with colonial inheritances; so long as Brazil imported slaves, the umbilical relationship to the past, and to Portugal (for whom José Bonifacio spared few words of praise since "no nation ever sinned more against humanity than the nation of Portugal"), endured. Never far from José Bonifacio's thoughts was the awareness that closing the slave trade would also sway British public opinion, and therefore the foreign secretary, in support of Brazilian sovereignty. Bonifacio's position was

---

[29] Blackburn, *The Overthrow of Colonial Slavery*, pp. 342–75.

TABLE 1
Decadal Imports of Slaves in Brazil, 1801–30 (thousands of slaves)

	1801–10	1811–20	1821–30
Brazil, north of Bahia	57.6	82.6	63.6
Bahia	75.4	70.7	71.6
Brazil south of Bahia	108.3	174.4	296.2

Source: David Eltis, *Economic growth and the Ending of the Transatlantic Slave Trade* (Oxford: Oxford University Press 1987), p. 249.

not rare in Brazil; but it was a decisive minority and never really dented the political consensus in favor of slavocracy.[30]

In spite of the pressures on the South Atlantic slave trade, there was less a crisis in the "commercial marriage" (to use Joseph Miller's bons mots) between Africa and Brazil than a maturing of some underlying processes: it relocated to more southern routes and became more and more concentrated on the bilateral exchange between southern Brazil and Angola. While authorities in Rio de Janeiro managed to defer an effective end to the slave trade until the early 1850s, the routes that skirted or crossed the equator had to contend with British naval patrols. Shipments to Pernambuco and Bahia felt the heat of the constraints on slave imports from West Africa and had to rely on Rio de Janeiro as an entrepôt. This commercial dependency was a recipe for resentment—but it was also a bonanza for Rio de Janeiro. What Luiz Felipe de Alencastro has described for the sixteenth and seventeenth centuries—the origins of a "Atlântico Fluminense" (a Rio de Janeiro–centrism)—intensified in the age of revolution. Between Africa, especially Angola, and Rio de Janeiro there emerged a historically unprecedented flow; slave shipments nearly doubled (see table 1). To many staple producers in Minas Gerais, Angola was simply an extension of the thriving Rio de Janeiro markets to which they shipped their produce.[31]

---

[30]ANTT, JC, Maço 62, Caixa 203, November 10, 1823; Kennedy, "Bahian Elites," pp. 433–38; Lugar, "The Merchant Community of Salvador," pp. 82, 177–91; José Bonifacio de Andrada e Silva, "Perhaps No Nation Ever Sinned More against Humanity than Portugal," in Conrad, ed., *Children of God's Fire*, pp. 418–19; more on José Bonifacio, see Barman, *Brazil*, pp. 76–77, 85–96.

[31]Miller, *Way of Death*, pp. 290, 517–30, 601–43; Alencastro, *O trato dos viventes*. In 1824, Portuguese settlers in Angola sparked a rebellion that sought to integrate the African colony as a province of Brazil. It failed. José Honório Rodrigues, *Brazil and Africa* (Berkeley: University of California Press, 1965), pp. xv, 40; Miller, *Way of Death*, pp. 290, 526–30; Manuel dos Anjos da Silva Rebelo, *Relações entre Angola e Brasil (1808–1830)* (Lisboa: Agência-Geral do Ultramar, 1968), pp. 224–49.

Political independence that freed Rio de Janeiro from Lisbon's meddling, combined with the clamps on the slave trade north of the equator, fastened the grip of large slave traders in the capital over the mercantile hierarchy of the country. By 1822, almost half the merchant class of the capital was engaged in slave trading as part of their commercial business; two-thirds of all Luso-Brazilian slave traders made the capital their hub. Indeed, it seems clear that British economic penetration into Brazilian markets infused credit to help make up for the demise of the silver trade from Potosí and the closure of Spanish American ports to captives. British interests were thus more complementary than competitive with Brazilian merchants who ran cargos from Angola. The soaring supply of slaves channeled through the capital became a critical driving force for agrarian expansion into new exporting frontiers of Brazil, especially the emerging coffee belts of the Paraíba Valley.[32]

The collapse of anciens-régimes had disparate effects on the systems of accumulation they once thrived on. Where the political rupture had led to war and revolution, labor systems were disrupted or destroyed—with important implications for the material foundations of new regimes. In this regard, we can make some observations about the different passages from changing political structures, economic incentives, and social interests to collective choices and their outcomes. The contrasts between Brazil and Spanish South America come into relief, for the braided continuity of the monarchy and the slave trade in Brazil, compared to the break with both in the Spanish Atlantic, would provide the backdrop to state-building efforts in the 1820s. The ability of constitutionalists to erect new regimes depended on the internal cohesion and resources of ruling classes just as the fortunes of ruling classes depended on the ability of lawmakers to effect their plans.

Social Upheaval

Warfare and political conflict also shook the internal alignments that reproduced the other social component of accumulation: labor. Patrician classes who once griped about abuses from Madrid and Lisbon soon objected to insubordination from below. *El Argos de Buenos Aires* printed a typically bemoaning letter about disobedient workers from one upset *estanciero*, for whom social upheaval was a legacy of freedom: "ordinary

---

[32]Florentino, *Em costas negras*, pp. 89, 121–24; Ribeiro Fragoso, *Homens de grossa aventura*, pp. 153–59; Francisco Vidal Luna and Herbert S. Klein, *Slavery and the Economy of São Paulo, 1750–1850* (Stanford: Stanford University Press, 2003), pp. 53–78.

itinerant peons, lazy in their work habits, enjoy the most pernicious license to abandon, without just motive, their houses and maybe even a miserable harvest [*la abundancia de un renglón*] which the customs of this country have now made into a prime necessity." Imperial and revolutionary warfare had compelled rival sides to make claims to the bodies—and loyalties—of subaltern peoples, claims they would not have otherwise been able to lay legitimately, and which in effect dispossessed the masters of slaves, the recruiters of Indian workers, and the bosses of plebeian folk who were impressed into colonial labor systems.[33]

War and work were at odds. One of the cornerstones of the colonial system—coerced labor—became harder and harder to sustain as the legal system it had produced and legitimated collapsed. From the grasslands to the highlands, the call to reject ancient "customs" of servitude, including the *mita*, which drove generations of Indians into the silver mines, was a cornerstone appeal to plebeians to rally behind the cause of sovereignty. Some joined the fighting machines; others took advantage of the moment to make a career out of resistance to bosses and masters. Even before Lima's elites declared their loyalty to San Martín, Indians had begun fleeing the mines in droves. Others seized the moment to begin invading landed estates. In the Central Andean valleys where republiquetas had filled the void of the crumbling viceroyalty, colonial property was divvied up among villagers. The roads radiating out of cities became dangerous; at night travelers were prey to bandoleros who took advantage of the government's weakness. Banditry ceased being a purely rural phenomenon and transcended the color lines that demarcated Indians from castas. As a concession to Indians, hoping to win their support and ratchet back the insurgency, republican authorities abolished the mita and obligatory Indian tribute payments in 1824. No doubt welcome, these decrees did not prevent some bandits from gathering into montonero guerrillas who would compose a political force that endured through much of the nineteenth century. For those to whom "three hundred years of oppression" was more than a rallying cry against imperium but a banner for resistance against colonial models of accumulation, secession afforded an unprecedented opportunity to change the ground rules of property relations.[34]

---

[33]Cited in Sergio Bagú, *El plan económico del grupo rivadaviano (1811–1827)* (Buenos Aires: Universidad Nacional del Litoral, 1966), p. 17.

[34]Charles Walker, "Montoneros, bandoleros, malhechores: Criminalidad y política en las primeras décadas republicanas," in Aguirre and Walker, eds., *Bandoleros* pp. 102–8; Alberto Flores Galindo, "Bandidos de la costa," in Aguirre and Walker, *Bandoleros*, pp. 60–67; Lynch, *The Spanish American Revolutions*, p. 278.

For slaves, the collapse of the imperial state also occasioned an opportunity to push back the terms of colonial exploitation. To a large extent, the institution of slavery was yet another victim of the violence that accompanied imperial crises. Armies were major recruiters of slaves, for whom service was a price worth paying for freedom. In an army's wake, slaves joined in droves or scattered to the hinterlands, never to be recovered. Flight, in its many manifestations, became rampant. When Rio de Janeiro declared independence, the potentates in Bahia shuddered. The quickly shifting political conjuncture brought with it a surge in fugitives; runaway communities (called quilombos) grew, fueling the rumor mill that violent uprisings by slaves and runaways were being plotted. In Minas Gerais and Rio de Janeiro, fugitive slave communities also proliferated. Quilombos strategically located themselves on the margins of market life in order to participate in—or prey on—it. The quilombo of Oitizeiro was the home of manioc farmers who sold their harvests in local markets and even to the plantations that once forced them to work in the fields. Occupational ventures of fugitives included contraband in food, but also traffic in arms and gunpowder that frequently wound up in the hands of the militias created by the changing political structure. Another mainstay for runaway slaves was banditry—many of the principal highways were the targets of small- and large-scale assaults. In Venezuela, where fugitives from cocoa and cattle estates became bandolero platoons, taking advantage of the conflict to make a career out of pillaging, sometimes with scant regard for the partisanship (or even race) of victimized communities, runaways transformed plundering into a mass business. Flight enabled ex-slaves to become predators on the market networks that once thrived on their servitude.[35]

Political shifts also motivated slaves to combat the system that enslaved them. After independence, as statesmen pondered over slavery and dragged their feet in debates about how to handle it, slaves kept up the fight against enslavement jurisprudence. Mobilized into fighting machines, armed ex-slaves were potent enough to compel rebel authorities to embrace their cause. Across the region, towns declared an end to the importation of slaves. Caracas was the first to ban the slave trade, by decree on August 14, 1810, and the prohibition in "the vile traffic of slaves" was a clause of the first Venezuelan constitution of December 1811. In May 1812, Buenos Aires' patriots abolished imports; Cartagena did the same in June 1812. In short order, the slave trade that had sustained

---

[35]Gomes, "Quilombos do Rio de Janeiro," pp. 263–90; Guimarães, "Mineração, quilombos e palmares," p. 142.

the labor markets of colonial societies was slammed shut. In this regard, as we shall see, the decision *not* to abolish the slave trade in Brazil would distinguish its political economy from its neighbors.[36]

Ending the traffic in slaves did not automatically bring the curtain down on legal slavery. State measures to free slaves were more halting, partial in their scope, and incomplete in their enforcement. As early as 1816, Bolívar was moved to advocate the abolition of slavery across South America, going beyond the promises to free any slave who joined his armies. At the Congress of Angostura in 1819, he sought to have the abolition of slavery inscribed into the foundational charter. He wound down his famous address with an injunction to make history anew in Venezuela by freeing her slaves. The freedom of the republic was completely entwined with the freedom of slaves. "It is unnecessary for me to persuade you of the fairness, necessity, and positive effects of this measure [the abolition of slavery], for you know the history of the helots, of Spartacus, and of Haiti; you also know that one cannot be simultaneously free and enslaved except by violating at one and the same time the natural law, the political laws, and the civil laws . . . I beg the confirmation of absolute freedom for the slaves, just as I would beg for my life and the life of the republic." He closed his address thus: "Grant to Venezuela an eminently popular government, eminently just, eminently moral, that will fetter oppression, anarchy, and rancor, a government where innocence, humanity, and peace will reign and where equality and freedom will triumph under the rule of law." For his part, San Martín did the same in Peru, signing laws in August and November 1821 declaring the freedom of all newborns and the end of the slave trade, setting in train the gradual eclipse of legal slavery.[37]

Abolitionism on paper was one achievement; materializing it was another. It often fell to slaves themselves to have owners, even the most well-meaning, honor the spirit of the laws. One patriot, Ildefonso Coronel of Guayaquil, bought a slave woman, fittingly named Angela Batallas, shortly after the city proclaimed itself the capital of the Republic of Guayas and soon declared his "love" for his slave. Batallas got an apartment of her own; her owner taught her to how to sign her name and promised her liberty. The relationship soured when she gave birth to a girl and thus threatened

---

[36]For overviews of the end of the slave trade, see James Ferguson King, "The Latin American Republics and the Suppression of the Slave Trade," *Hispanic American Historical Review* 24:3 (1944): 388–95; Blackburn, *The Overthrow of Colonial Slavery*, pp. 331–80.

[37]Bolívar, "The Angostura Address," in Bushnell, ed., *El Libertador*, p. 52; on Peruvian emancipation, see Christine Hünefeld, *Paying the Price of Freedom: Family and Labor among Lima's Slaves, 1800–1854* (Berkeley: University of California Press, 1994), pp. 194–97.

her master's standing in the local community. The parents wound up in court, wrangling over the status of the child and her mother—exposing the contested degrees of freedom within new republican legislation. Batallas and her lawyer made the connection between freed states and free slaves, and the significance of the union of two bodies as a gesture of their fundamental equality, explicit: "I do not believe that this tribunal will justify it, nor that the meritorious members of a Republic that, full of philanthropic and liberal sentiments, has given all necessary proofs of liberalism, employing their arms and heroically risking their lives to liberate us from the Spanish Yoke, would want to promise to keep me in servitude, even against the promise that Coronel made to me the first time he united himself with me." As the litigants wrestled in court, big events were unfolding in the city: Bolívar and San Martín were meeting in Guayaquil to discuss the fate of the liberation struggle. So, while Bolívar was preparing his forces for an assault on Peru, Batallas took matters into her own hands and paid the Liberator a visit. Like the famous meeting between San Martín and Bolívar, the encounter between the Liberator and the slave woman went unrecorded. But it did yield results: Bolívar issued an instruction to the court to do "justice for this unhappy slave." The public defender complied.[38]

The conflicts over colonial sovereignty did more than motivate individual acts of resistance against slavery; it also inspired collective ones. With the final triumph of secession, slaves mobilized to assault the remnants of legal bondage. Even in Brazil, where no concessions were made to close the slave trade or to free newborns, slaves found collective means to repudiate slavery. Quilombos and palenques swelling with refugees were prime staging grounds for insurgencies. Fears of uprisings were not far-fetched. During the skirmishing in Bahia at the time of independence, slaves mounted three revolts to abolish the laws of bondage. The ensuing political instability, and the difficulties keeping local and regional disciplinary forces invigilating plantations, perpetuated slave unrest: in the 1820s, there were ten slave uprisings—which created the backdrop of instability for the slave revolt in Salvador in 1835. Chronic and pervasive rebellion aggregated into a low-intensity "slave war" in Bahia. In many parts of Spanish America, such as the Pampas, the Llanos, and the Pacific coast, it would have been hard to distinguish between the social insurrection against colonial slavocrats and the political revolt against imperial bureaucrats.[39]

---

[38]For a discussion of this fascinating moment, see Townsend, "Half My Body Free."

[39]Schwartz, *Sugar Plantations*, pp. 484–87; João José Reis, "Salave Resistance in Brazil: Bahia, 1807–1835," *Luso-Brazilian Review* 25:1 (1988): 119–33; idem, *Rebelião escrava no Brasil*, pp. 94–122, Reis's count of Bahian uprisings is slightly lower than Schwartz's.

Across South America, the fracturing of state sovereignty broke the pillars that legalized and legitimated the social hierarchies premised on colonial exploitation and the preeminence of white letrado rule in the capital cities. The turmoil in plantations, estates, and mines fractured the blocs that tried to seize control of the old—and new—state systems. Social mobilization over plebeian freedom deepened the competition for, and increasingly mutually exclusive claims to, sovereign polities; in so doing, it shaped the critical passage of reassembling colonial remnants into successors.[40]

A New Synthesis

The leaders of revolutionary coalitions faced countervailing pressures. Urban elites were pushing hard to reconstitute a system of centralized, urban rule based on the colligative resources of merchant capital, while local alliances of marginalized magnates and plebeian folk, especially in the countrysides and secondary cities, advocated a model of sovereignty premised on local and regional autonomy and popular freedoms. Having put an end to the debate over membership and place in empire, South Americans embarked on the long—and still unresolved—struggle over citizenship and power in state-nations. The systems that emerged in the wake of independence were the products neither of a democratic compact based on a shared ideal of popular sovereignty nor an evolution of customary pacts among elites. Looking for a Lockean expression that we so automatically associate with founding moments of constitution writing, or a "Hispanic" triumph of homegrown norms of primordial vintage, misses what is so intriguing and important about Iberian American constitutional conflicts in the axial 1820s. Lawmakers improvised syncretic models shaped by circumstances and principles they derived from particular interpretations of their own histories.[41]

While lawmakers had a great deal to argue about, there was one thing they agreed on: what determined the viability of new states was their ability to stabilize political and social relations. Bolívar outlined this urgency, replete with philosophical principles, in the Angostura address

---

[40] It was Leon Trotsky's observation that the fracturing of state sovereignty was the cornerstone of the revolutionary process. See Charles Tilly, *From Mobilization to Revolution* (Reading, MA: Addison-Wesley, 1978), pp. 190–91.

[41] Guerra, *Modernidad e independencias*, pp. 51–52; Bayly, *The Birth of the Modern World*, p. 139, for a statement about "hybrid legitimacy" and claims that it was altogether the more general rule.

of 1819. While stability had to be the foundation of happiness, the identification of virtues and civic consciousness, not rights and liberties, had
to guide lawmakers' decisions. It was not that rights and liberties were not
relevant but that they required prior conditions to flourish: "If the principle of political equality is generally recognized, so also must be the
principle of physical and moral inequality. Nature makes men unequal in
intelligence, temperament, strength and character." This distinction,
between political equality and universal rights, and civic inequality and
particular aptitudes, was critical to Bolívar's approach to state building.
In effect, public institutions framed by basic laws had to induce a civic
consciousness that could sustain the activities of rights-bearing citizens;
in the right institutional environment, postcolonial nurture could overcome colonial nature. This was an important sequence for Bolívar and
many other constitutionalists of the 1820s. "Laws correct this disparity,"
argued Bolívar, "by so placing the individual within society that education, industry, arts, services and virtues give him a fictitious equality that
is properly termed political and social." Bolívar's reading of Montesquieu's
L'esprit des lois reinforced his insistence that laws had to be made out of
real, historical contexts and with specific political goals. "We must not
aspire to the impossible, lest, in trying to rise above the realm of liberty,
we again descend into the realm of tyranny. Absolute liberty invariably
lapses into absolute power, and the means between these two extremes is
supreme social liberty. Abstract theories create the pernicious idea of
unlimited freedom. Let us see to it," he told the Angostura delegates,
"that the strength of the public is kept within the limits prescribed by
reason and interest; that the national will is confined within the bonds
set by a just power."[42]

For all the convulsions of the next decade, the statement of principles
at Angostura remained remarkably consistent. The accent on virtue as a
condition for liberty came through in his 1826 draft of the constitution
for Bolivia, the acme expression of Bolívar's career as legislator. The
legislators of Alto Perú (renamed Bolivia in honor of the Liberator) were
caught between the forces of two "monstrous enemies": tyranny and
anarchy. What Bolívar drafted for their consideration and approval was
a charter that would help citizens survive in "an immense sea of oppression encircling a tiny island of freedom that is perpetually battered by
the forces of the waves and the hurricane that ceaselessly threatens to
submerge it." Like all good governments, this one would enjoy the regular contribution of the electorate—whose participation in choosing the

---

[42]Simón Bolívar, "Address Delivered at the Inauguration of the Second National
Congress of Venezuela in Angostura," in Bierck, ed., *Selected Writings*, pp. 182, 191.

legislature was a cornerstone of democracy. Political citizenship was limited, however, to those possessing the virtues of knowing "how to write down their votes, sign their names, and read the laws." Criminality, idleness, and ignorance were bars to membership in the civitas. Lest anyone think that this system restored the rule of aristocracies of the ancien régime, Bolívar was unequivocal: property was not a condition of the right "to exercise the august function of sovereign." Later he reiterated: "Knowledge and honesty, not money, are the requirements for exercising public authority."[43]

Knowledge and wisdom were essential to American statecraft in order to reconcile contingent necessities and universal aspirations. "The Art of Good Government," argued José da Silva Lisboa, "consists in making the people *rich and prosperous*," of combining interests and institutions in a new harmony. If it was a creative act, it could still be subjected to an appreciation of historical laws of political economy. Few writers articulated more clearly the relationship between the science of political economy and constitutionalism with the practice of virtuous lawmaking than the Bahian jurist Silva Lisboa, whose efforts to chart the principles of Brazilian constitutionalism got him ennobled as the Viscount of Cairú. We have seen him at work in previous chapters, as the translator of Edmund Burke's polemic against the French Revolution (and as father of Adam Smith's Portuguese translator of *The Wealth of Nations*), as the author of the monarchy's open ports decree, and as propagandist of imperial continuity. In the 1820s, Silva Lisboa's reflections came to a head in his majestic two-volume *Constituição moral e deveres do Cidadão*, published in 1824. Dedicated to Pedro I on the heels of his declaration of Brazilian independence, he lauded the new monarch for rescuing Brazil "from the contagion of infidelity propagated by Revolutions in both Hemispheres," and for preserving the political principles that upheld the moral fabric of Brazilian society.[44]

Silva Lisboa's understanding of moral sensibility was derived from the Greek notion of sympathy, which the Bahian took to have reached a mature and contemporary expression in Smith's *Theory of Moral Sentiments*, and insisted that natural man was a social being whose emotional life took shape in families, as a believer in God, and were thus rooted in these duties, "deveres." This is why ideas of abstract self-interest

---

[43]Simón Bolívar, "Message to the Congress of Bolivia," in Bushnell, ed., *El Libertador*, pp. 55–56, 63; Frank Safford, "Bolívar as Triumphal State-Maker and Despairing 'Democrat': Origins of Party Polarization in Colombia" (manuscript in author's possession).

[44]For an elegant recent study of Silva Lisboa's later thought, see Pedro Meira Monteiro, *Um moralista nos trópicos: O visconde de Cairú e o Duque de la Rochefoucauld* (São Paulo: Boitempo Editorial, 2004).

drove him to distraction (he had nothing but scorn for Mandeville and Bentham, for instance), and why he upheld these notions as having underpinned obnoxious revolutionary activity that threatened to undermine the moral fabric of society—and therefore deprive markets of what they are so good at: enabling moral, virtuous citizens to exchange goods for their personal as well as collective good. If good laws, and the moral constitution, are what nurtured these sentiments and protected them from *"moral egoistica,"* there was also a flip side: a theory of moral obligations. Part 3 of the second volume of *Constituição moral* offered a taxonomy of general principles and specific duties of all citizens, ranked according to age, class, and profession. But what was more implicit in his earlier writings, especially *Principios da Economia Política*, was now explicit: the ties between purposive individual economic activity, which only the market could encourage, and the importance of public institutions to uphold the sociability of interdependent citizens. Silva Lisboa tied these together in a series of articles published in the *Spectador Brasileiro* and the *Diario do Rio de Janeiro* that explored the economic laws—the *Regras Capitães*, in his words—that dovetailed with the moral constitution. This brought him full circle to themes he raised in the 1790s about commercial law, in a draft for a modern Commercial Code in 1826. In this recitation, the recently ennobled Viscount of Cairú argued that "commerce was the foundation of all human politics, and is the means through which to create peace and love among men." But it had to be grounded in "good customs" derived from generations of responsible conduct by exemplary merchants who met as God-loving gentlemen to exchange "reciprocal interests"—and in so doing exemplifying the traits of virtuous citizens.[45]

It is often said that Cairú's visions were tailor-made for monarchy, that his defense of moral economy was a singular apologia for the continuity of regalism. But this should not be pushed too far. Indeed, the ties between poverty, corruption, and vice, and the principles of statehood of the 1820s were picked up by *La Abeja Argentina* to make a thoroughgoing case for republicanism premised on a similar recombination of constitutionalism with political economy. Julián Segundo Agüero, its editor, and one of the principal figures in the constitutional debates in Argentina in the 1820s, detailed the importance of a republican political economy that relied on public institutions to foment industry, agriculture, and commerce—"the founts of wealth and public prosperity"—and thereby give people the means to possess property, apply their faculties,

---

[45]Cairú's articles were assembled in a pamphlet called *Leituras de economia politica ou direito economico* (Rio de Janeiro: Typographia Plancher-Seignot, 1827). His draft of the commercial code can be found in ANRJ, JC, Codice 700, "Projéto de Código do Comércio pelo Senador Barão de Cairú [*sic*]," April 24, 1826.

and work. To be free meant not to be dominated, to be immune from the arbitrary will of others, rulers as well as neighbors. The civitas had to be made of independent and resourceful citizens. And for three hundred years, according to Agüero, this is precisely what Spanish rulers had *not* done. Lawmakers had to make up for lost time to create the social and institutional conditions for rights-bearing citizens.[46]

Here was a vision of statehood that helped people to be free by enabling them to be virtuous while guarding them from avarice and passion. For this to occur, people had to participate in public affairs not as self-loving subjects but out of disinterested motives for the moral good of the whole, which was the condition for personal betterment. In this intellectual setting, leavened by readings of history, including the history of other revolutions and of the principal works of the Enlightenment, and molded by the prevailing anxiety about the social turmoil that accompanied independence, constitutions had specific, "positive" roles. If the American and French Revolutions gave themselves basic defensive principles inscribed in declarations of independence and rights, based on abstract and universal principles, South American lawmakers had different ideas in mind. Their constitutions were meant to create states where old regimes had little to bequeath. These states were not *defenders* of inalienable individual rights but the *creators* of habits, customs, and social exchanges that were supposed to foster private virtue, the necessary condition for citizenship. Rights may have existed in the abstract; but they required certain historical conditions to thrive. In a context in which freed societies had gone through the catharsis of secession from empires but still hovered on the precipice of civil war, constitutionalists aimed to rebuild centralist systems, reliant on strong executive authorities to diffuse conflicts, ensure stability, and inculcate the personal habits that were seen as the premises for the participation of an active citizenry.

We can call this model of sovereignty "unitarian," a familiar label at the time that described centralist movements in the nineteenth century. Centralism was, indeed, an important dimension of Bolívar, Silva Lisboa, and Agüero's prospectuses for statehood. But it was also much more than that; unitarianism was an effort to integrate historically particular exigencies with some covering laws about humanity. It was a dominant constitutionalist spirit when delegates gathered in Rio de Janeiro in 1823, in Buenos Aires in 1824, and in Cúcuta in 1821 to found the state of Gran Colombia out of Venezuela and Nueva Granada.

---

[46]Julián Segundo Agüero, "Prospecto," *La Abeja Argentina*, April 12, 1822, from Senado de la Nación, *Biblioteca de Mayo* (Buenos Aires: Senado de la Nación, 1960), v. 6, p. 5246.

There was, however, a rub: democracy. The notion of a citizenry endowed with rights to elect its rulers was not a principle that unitarians repudiated, for it was critical to the legitimacy of new public institutions. Older practices of representation, tied to the city and its well-to-do veci-nos who congregated in town councils, gave way to broader, rural, and subaltern representation—especially as the convocations of parliaments in Spain and Portugal were accompanied by calls for provinces to elect their delegates. This was a sign of the times that no one wanted to tear down. Still, could democracy have gone too far? *El Argos de Buenos Aires* aired the feeling of many *letrados* about the vote, noting that "the influence of vulgarity, of absurd preoccupations and plebeian misery should not be allowed to endanger the act upon which the happiness of the republic depends."[47]

What to do about the democratic comportment of an uncivic citizenry? One reflex was to draft hybrid charters to accommodate patrician ideals of creating citizens with a model that was seen as legitimately democratic, building on the political achievements of defeating metropolitan monarchies. Accordingly, suffrage laws were approved, and then embellished with restrictions. Where explicit curbs did not follow democratic declarations the art of electoral exclusion devolved to more prosaic practices. This was a way to have it both ways—call the nation sovereign without handing its fate over to "the people." So, in Argentina, where any "hombre libre" was a citizen (so even some foreigners could vote), voting rights could lapse under certain, somewhat wooly circumstances, such as becoming a domestic or lacking a "job that is lucrative or useful to the country." The idea of an "independent" citizenry able to vote was a cornerstone of Pedro I's constitution of 1824, in which all men over twenty-five could vote with no mention of race, and any married man over twenty-one could likewise vote. Literacy was not a requirement, but income (voters had to earn 200 milreis or more annually) and "independence" were thresholds (servants were barred, as were all ex-slaves). What is more, as Richard Graham has shown, effective restrictions were left to the enforcement powers of political bosses and their clientelist machinery. Cúcuta's delegates steered clear of general voting principles, but slapped specific property and income conditions on the vote (eventually a literacy restriction was added). Formal models of incomplete representation were reinforced by the precipitous ways in which electoral coalitions evolved into patronage networks—with all their mobilizing

---

[47]Alberto Palcos, *Rivadavia, ejecutor del pensamiento de May* (La Plata: Universidad Nacional La Plata, 1960), v. 1, p. 424.

and stultifying propensities. The broad egalitarian and nation-building drives of the age were tagged, therefore, with legal and practical restrictions to prevent popular electoral forces from overwhelming what were seen as delicate, still nascent political systems.[48]

Founding charters also included plenty of safeguards for political elites to use their authority to defend order, allowing power-holders to override basic rights by stripping them of unassailable properties. This was achieved in two ways. One was to create relatively centralized systems capable of ruling weak "provinces" or "states" with legalized discretionary powers to intervene in local affairs in the name of the public interest. In early 1826, the delegates began approving constitutional articles and elected Bernardino Rivadavia as the United Provinces of the River Plate's first national president. One of his first acts was to make Buenos Aires the federal capital, severing it legally from the province that bore the same name; not only was the centralist design taking rapid form, but it appeared to be coming at the direct expense of provinces. In Brazil there was a dust-up in the Constitutional Assembly until Pedro dissolved it and named a Council of State to draft a charter behind closed doors and which potentates could then execute into existence in short order. The charter to create a constitutional monarchy swept through municipal boards with only minor grumbling. Room for intervention in local affairs to keep the peace was reinforced by a second feature: instead of fulsome declarations of universal rights of citizens, early constitutions focused more on elaborate designs of the central state. As Emilia Viotti da Costa has reminded us, Brazil's charter nodded to the French Declaration of the Rights of Man of 1789, taking verbatim its second article, which stipulated that "the goal of all political association is the preservation of the natural and inalienable rights of men and these rights are liberty, property, security," while leaving out the last four words: "and resistance to oppression."[49]

---

[48]David Bushnell, "El sufragio en la Argentina y Colombia hasta 1853," *Revista del Instituto de Historia del Derecho Ricardo Levene* 19 (1968): 11–29; Marcela Ternavasio, "Nuevo régimen representative y expansion de la frontera política: Las elecciones en el estado de Buenos Aires, 1820–1840," in Antonio Annino, comp., *Historia de las elecciones en Iberoamerica* (Buenos Aires: Fondo de Cultura Económica, 1995), pp. 65–72; Bushnell, *The Making of Modern Colombia*, pp. 51–54; Richard Graham, *Patronage and Politics in Nineteenth-Century Brazil* (Stanford: Stanford University Press, 1990), pp. 103–8.

[49]Emilio Ravignani, "El Congreso Nacional de 1824–1827, la Convención Nacional de 1818–1829," in Levene, ed., *Historia de la nación*, esp. pp. 118–44; Ricardo Piccirilli, *Rivadavia y su tiempo* (Buenos Aires: Ed. Peuser, 1943), v. 1, pp. 308–12; Macauley, *Dom Pedro*, pp. 152–64; Barman, *Brazil*, pp. 123–25; Emilia Viotti da Costa, *The Brazilian Empire: Myths and Realities* (Chicago: University of Chicago Press, 1985), pp. 58–60.

What can be said of these charters is that they did not imagine their nations as confederations of rights-bearing people whose loyalties were tied to provinces or states that agreed to contract or bond together to form a nation. On the contrary, these were formerly colonial people who could only become nations by living under the institutional structures defined by positive constitutions. The political vacuum after independence was filled with "unitarian" projects, balancing acts, and hybrid constructs, acknowledging the sovereignty of the nation while addressing the historic necessity of delivering it from the state of nature, colonialism, and civil war to a new age.

INTERESTS OF STATE

The emerging constitutional model emphasized the mutuality of public order, personal wealth, and civic virtue. But what sorts of interests could serve as a bonding agent between citizens and state power to replace the defunct ones of the imperium? Could such interests reinforce the integrative efforts of constitutions and tame the passions unleashed by war and revolution? Here, too, unitarians looked to hybrid solutions. They cobbled together notions that had been touted by physiocrats, who treated the internalization of market relations and the ownership of property as mainstays of virtue and wealth, with new realities—that their countries had to "compete" for markets in the Atlantic world and get used to new media of exchange, like paper money. Underlying this synthesis was a commercial logic whose elements can be traced back to the 1790s, but which acquired more self-conscious and prescriptive features during the lawmaking decade of the 1820s.

A revealing outline of the triad of order, wealth, and virtue bound in a single model of virtuous and integrating interests can be found in Manuel Moreno's "Vista Política-Económica de la Provincia de Buenos Aires," a long series of articles published in Agüero's journal in 1822. For Moreno, societies could be likened to markets that comprised independent individuals who gathered to exchange goods. So, while independent in the sense that they were not forced, commercial agents were still dependent on the reiterated and reciprocated relations with others for their survival. Relying on one's own work and the work of others to sustain common good was simultaneously the road to riches—because it encouraged people to specialize in occupations for which they had comparative talents—and the right metaphor of the polite and respectful sociability of the republic. The opposite was producing for subsistence, which was the hazard of South American provinces, because it bred lassitude, isolated citizens from each other, and reproduced penury. Poverty, in this sense, was both the effect of a society's failure to engage people with each other to satisfy reciprocal needs, and what inhibited people from seeing that they could otherwise enhance and apply their talents. And yet, lawmakers had to beware of throwing open markets under the naïve conviction that people were universally and equally disposed to translate self-interest into the kind of other-regarding activity of commercial sociability. Indeed, self-interest was as dangerous as indolence, for without reining in the passions, unfettered markets were just as liable to introduce subjects to the temptations of greed. There was too much evidence, warned Moreno, that these provinces "have inclined themselves fatally to create a spirit of traffic and of speculation which does not produce an apparatus of wealth, but a true immorality, fraud, and disguised laziness." Again, this is where laws were supposed to operate as the guardians of virtuous exchange whose participatory conditions, as in politics, required that the passions be tamed in favor of enlightened self-interest. For this reason, Moreno described at length the role of "public credit" doing for commerce what constitutions were supposed to do for politics—and that the two combined, credit and constitutions, would lift the republics from centuries of darkness.[50]

This vision of statehood narrowed the gap between the rules governing market activity and those applied to governments. "Positive" constitutionalism deliberately blurred the line between private, acquisitive activity and the labors of states because Iberian empires had deprived colonial subjects of the virtue-enhancing powers of democratic property and representation. The role of the state had to focus less on defending people's liberties and properties and more on creating the conditions for people to enjoy them in the first place. This meant that in tandem with constitutions for foundling states were a whole series of laws to create the conditions for spreading market activity through "public credit."

When it came to money, more than principles were at stake. The Viscount of Cairú, Agüero, and other statemakers also spun virtues out of necessities. For one, the end of mercantilism, open imports, and the demise of the silver flows created shortages of liquidity. To boot, all governments faced mounting debts of war. In the 1820s, there was practically an obsession—and a fascination—with money. Money was simultaneously the measure of value, the medium of exchange, and the means to bankroll new states. There was, therefore, rather a lot riding on the new monetary system, which was discussed under the rubric of "public credit." According

---

[50]Manuel Moreno, "Vista Política-Económica de la Provincia de Buenos Aires," *La Abeja Argentina*, April 15, May 15, and June 15, 1822, in *Biblioteca de Mayo*, quotes from pp. 5251–52.

to Manuel Moreno, "today there is no institution more deserving of our attention than public credit." To be sure, the political economists who contributed to the legal debates of the 1820s were concerned with the ways in which all three functions of money reinforced each other. In the end, however, one function loomed especially large: how new financial instruments could be disposed to build political authority that would restore social stability, legality, and therefore healthy market life. Its virtuous possibilities distinguished the new order from its predecessor, for it could "not exist in countries in which public powers are absolute, and where these may destroy tomorrow what they created yesterday; where the passions, the interests, and the conveniences of public power can change, alter, and topple the social, political, and commercial order." In Moreno's view, public credit, created by a free state for a sovereign people, was the guardian of its own principles. Properly designed, public credit was a way to handle the state's debts without treading on private property rights while giving agents means to transact that only the state could provide as a public good. Principles, therefore, aligned interests.[51]

Interests could also support principles. The emergence of "national" debts was an opportunity for creditors to become stakeholders in the new model of sovereignty—and to mold it to financiers' wishes. Reciprocally, monied men could contribute to the state's efforts to internalize market relations by unleashing their command over private credit to spread habits of trade to the reterritorialized sovereignty of nations-in-the-making. One of the cornerstones of the financial systems of the 1820s was the idea of a "national" bank, the product of a state charter to handle the monetary affairs of the nation, indeed a way to monetize the national space by means of its principle legal power: the issuance of notes that could be used to trade, pay taxes, and buy public bonds. Banknotes would release the productive energies of citizens, buoy economies, and create the revenue base for state needs—eventually, therefore, eliminating all need of governments to finance their activities by borrowing against future revenues. Once in train, bank stocks would rise, people would have more confidence in its ability to defend the value of its notes, and they would be more willing to use them in their transactions, giving up old commodity money and thereby enabling the bank to issue yet more notes. This at least was the theory, which is easy in retrospect to dismiss as fanciful; but it should be remembered that the same kind of idea was current in the postrevolutionary decade of the 1780s in the United States for analogous reasons—and interests.[52]

---

[51]Ibid., pp. 5252–58.

[52]Riesman, "Money, Credit, and Federalist Political Economy," pp. 140–41; Carruthers, *City of Capital*, esp. pp. 9–26; Bordo and Capie, introduction to Bordo and Capie, eds., *Monetary Regimes in Transition*, pp. 1–12; Neal, *The Rise of Financial Capitalism*.

DISCREDITED STATES

Unitarians had uplifting ways to explain and justify their projects, combining the fates of states and fortunes of capital in such a way blurred the boundaries between the two. In the name of creating systems of national sovereignty, unitarians obscured some of the dangers of fusing market and political life. The risks of this formulation were less evident in the internal coherence of the arguments than in the assumptions upon which they rested. These assumptions—that public debt and private economic activity would create pools of capital deep enough to fund personal accumulation *and* the making of new states—became exposed, not by theory but by history.

The most audacious model of using new financial instruments to reinforce efforts to reconstruct a constitutional order took place in Buenos Aires. As a prelude to the constitutional debates of the mid-1820s, financiers and ministers in Buenos Aires began to erect the financial structures for public and private transactions to make the city the economic and political hub of the independent provinces of the River Plate. Under the umbrella of a unitarian government, the porteño administration, first of Martín Rodríguez as the governor of Buenos Aires and later of Bernardino Rivadavia, his influential minister of government and foreign affairs, who became the first president of the republic under the new constitution of 1826, began approving laws in 1821 to introduce fiscal discipline after over a decade of war-induced splurging, streamlining customs levies and introducing direct taxes. Rivadavia exemplified the new spirit of lawmaking. Heavily influenced by classical political economy (having translated James Mill's *Elements of Political Economy* into Spanish in 1823), he was a key figure behind the effort to reconstitute the old viceroyalty into a centralized republic, ruled by enlightened laws and lawmakers to instill the bountiful effects of the marketplace as a tamer of passions among the unruly folk of the former colony.

The unitarian linchpin was a central monetary authority to regulate domestic borrowing by overseeing discounting operations, accepting deposits, and acting as the main agent for the treasury; it also enjoyed the monopoly of issuing paper pesos. When Rodríguez's minister of finance, Manuel García, met with merchants to discuss the creation of a bank, he assured them that one of its missions was "to animate the prosperity of commerce." Nine merchants stepped forward to draft the outlines of such an institution. The Banco de Buenos Aires threw open its doors in September 1822. Juan Pedro Aguirre, a wealthy merchant and estate owner, Manuel Aguirre, a prominent trader, brother-in-law of the finance minister (Manuel García), and a leader of the Club of Merchants and Hacendados, and Sebastián Lezica, another puissant merchant, were all either presidents or directors of the bank—and willingly joined forces in an alliance with the unitarian state builders. The list of shareholders of the bank was a who's who of the city's commercial aristocracy.[53]

For all the heavyweights, the bank's mandate was a tall—and probably unrealistic—order. Wars had decimated old financial sinews; the ancient source of precious metals, the mines of Potosí, no longer pumped out caravans of silver. As a result, the bankers were constantly scrambling to make up for the gap between dream and reality. Furthermore, as both the emitter of banknotes and the handler of the treasury's needs, the bank was vulnerable to the government's requests to fund its fiscal shortfalls by monetizing the debt. The merchant-directors did not at first recoil at the government's repeated requests for loans and emissions— though in early 1823, the directors entrusted a committee of two of the richest men in South America, Juan José Anchorena and Diego Britain, to supervise the printing of money. In May that year, a meeting of over two hundred directors and shareholders agreed to approve another round of peso emissions to overcome the shortage of money and to inject more liquidity into the marketplace. As time passed, it became clearer that merchants had fixed themselves on the horns of a dilemma they were complicit in creating: they needed the state to build and legitimate a new centralized financial infrastructure but the very weakness of the state meant that rulers used public credit to legitimate their claims to power. Things got worse a year later when the new, now national, government decided it needed a financial analogue to consolidate the centralist order. The Banco Nacional, founded in early 1826, was even more beholden to the fiscal needs of the new constitutional regime. Porteño merchants became the stakeholders of an agency with contradictory powers and missions, the right to issue money, and the obligation to see the state through its revenue needs.[54]

If there were flaws in the design, circumstances brought them into sharp relief and turned what was supposed to be a virtuous cycle into a vicious one. Indeed, it is possible that the system might have worked despite its shortcomings. There was a new, centralized constitution. The economy was showing signs of rebounding after years of war. But in early 1825,

[53]ABPBA, Libros de Actas, v. 1, p. 1; Bagú, *El plan económico del grupo rivadaviano*, pp. 20–24, 37–38; Juan Carlos Nicolau, *La reforma económica-financiera en la Provincia de Buenos Aires (1821–1825)* (Buenos Aires: Fundación Banco de la Provincia de Buenos Aires, 1988), pp. 124–31; Miron Burgin, *The Economic Aspects of Argentine Federalism, 1820–1852* (Cambridge, MA: Harvard University Press, 1946), pp. 58–62.

[54]ABPBA, Libros de Actas, v. i, p. 36; Ministro de Hacienda, Correspondencia, 023-1-1, July 21, 1826, doc. 314, and August 8, 1826, doc. 326.

tensions arose with Brazil over the perennially contested borderlands of the Banda Oriental. In April, thirty-three Oriental patriots crossed the River Plate from San Isidro, Buenos Aires, with the goal of besieging Montevideo and liberating the Oriental Province occupied by Brazil. From late 1825 to late 1828, the neighbors plunged into a withering, wasteful, and ultimately unwinnable war that left all sides exhausted and impoverished. With an unfunded war, the bank was forced to print more money; inflation took off. Even the minister of finance had to admit in early 1826 to the directors of the provincial bank that "of late there has been a scandalous rise in the price of everything." With no reserves, and fearing that the naval blockade by Brazilian warships would destroy the commercial recovery, the unitarian government issued one great—and terminal—request for a loan of 6 million pesos. In early 1826, Rivadavia, only recently elected by the congress as the country's first president, spun the request in the most optimistic way possible: "all classes could possess in abundance the circulating medium or have the facility to acquire it, and could, by means of this loan to the Government invest securely, productively, and with no risk at all."[55] What was once a barely manageable debt of about 2 million pesos in late 1821 billowed into almost 11 million pesos of unpayable obligations by the end of the decade. In May 1826, the congress made de jure what was de facto: it approved a temporary and partial suspension of gold payments. The peso immediately plunged. The finance minister, Ramon de Basavilbaso, fretted to the city's merchants of all the "*males de inmensa trasendencia*." Merchants responded by refusing to lend more money to the government. The result was predictable: notes in circulation soared from 6.5 million in early 1828 to 15 million by mid-1830.[56]

By the late 1820s, conditions were so bad that merchants were flooding courts because they were unable to pay debts and, worse, because the instruments they used to conduct business were becoming worthless. Some stopped paying debts altogether. This of course put the banks themselves in a spot—as they were both agents for public borrowing through money emissions and lenders to private merchants. They could hardly afford to lose money now and resorted to tough tactics to get their money back. The national bank dragged Agustin Almeyda to court on charges of having failed to meet a payment on a loan and got the court to embargo Almeyda's properties and auction them off. More often, the debtor-creditor ties among private agents got mangled by

---

[55]ABPBA, Ministerio de Hacienda, Correspondencia, 023-1-1, doc. 723.

[56]Samuel Amaral, "Comercio y crédito en Buenos Aires (1822–1826)," *Siglo XIX* 5:9 (1990): 105–21; Halperín Donghi, *Historia argentia*, pp. 224–34; Burgin, *The Economic Aspects of Argentine Federalism*, pp. 50–54, 64–67.

the financial anarchy. Ruperto Albarellos, for instance, did not deny that he owed Juan Bayta Romero—a powerful porteño merchant—almost 5,000 pesos. But he blamed "a conjunction of circumstances" that paralyzed commerce and ruined businesses throughout the region. Was he, therefore, "guilty"? "Knowing," Albarellos pleaded in his defense, "that I have nothing to do with the oscillations of the value of money, nor with the ravages of speculation, nor in the bankruptcies of some, nor in the discredit of others and myself, it is therefore enough that I walk calmly to prison." If there was a centralizing, nation-building bloc of ministers and merchants that tried to fund its way to a new constitutional order, it imploded under the weight of its own aspirations.[57]

One might wonder whether the war with Brazil simply accelerated the inevitable or whether, on its own, it brought down the River Plate regime. Other Spanish American cases suggest that the revolutionary warfare that enfeebled incumbent merchant capital left republics caught in riptides of inflation. So, even if merchants could bankroll states, it was increasingly clear that it was more a question of whether they would. In Venezuela and Nueva Granada, Bolívar had resorted to forced loans to fund his armies and left behind "liberated" territories with no treasuries. In November 1820, the Republic of Colombia was doling out paper scrip called "loans," though none appears to have been redeemed. Six months later, it was still calling for loans to cover the "grave urgencies of capital," and backed up promises to pay with the "goods belonging to the State." But which—or better, what—state? Bonds circulating in the province of Antioquia were handwritten. When the Constitution of Cúcuta was formally inducted in January 1822, to bring Venezuela and Colombia together, its coffers were bare. Authorities immediately picked up where Bolívar had left off, turning to forced loans to sustain their affairs—which did little to make them more acceptable or legitimate to citizens, many of whom did not see the virtues of a great confederation. To Juan Manuel Restrepo, Bolívar's former minister and a protagonist in the nation-building enterprises of the 1820s, the financial straits of the nascent states were their principal—and ultimately insurmountable—hurdle. As Malcolm Deas has observed, Colombia was a country whose state was born poor and whose early political history carried the traits of penury.[58]

---

[57]AGNBA, TC, B-12 (1802–35), *Banco Nacional v. Agustin Almeyda* (1828); A-1 (1806–31), *Ruperto Albarellos v. Juan Bayta Romero* (1829).

[58]AGNB, Anexo, Emprestitos, III, docs. 625, 629, 632; Restrepo, *Historia de la Revolución de Colombia*, v. 4, pp. 376–85; Malcolm Deas, "The Fiscal Problems of Nineteenth-Century Colombia," *Journal of Latin American Studies* 14:2 (1982): 287–89.

In effect, after so many years of war, private coffers had been stripped so bare there was nothing left when the fledgling public treasurers came calling for financial support. One solution was to find foreign sources of money. Foreign merchants were as keen as domestic ones were in recombining blocs of constitutionalists and capitalists in a new virtuous order. According to the London *Morning Chronicle*, "there is no better way to dispose of surplus money than by investing in South America." The government of Gran Colombia, promoted by old contacts with Miranda and Bolívar, was a trailblazer in turning to international credit to finance national states. Bolívar had dispatched Francisco Antonio Zea in 1820; in 1822 the first loan was approved. Chile and Peru were next in line to get loans. By 1825, the boom was in full swing. A large share of loans, in spite of the frantic promotion of investment schemes in mining, land, and even fishing companies, were earmarked to pay public debts rather than invest in private assets. Of all the British loans flowing to Latin America between 1824 and 1827, valued at 25 million pounds sterling, fully 17 million were for the purchase of government securities and investment in sovereign statebuilding. The strapped government of Colombia turned to the firm of B. A. Goldschmidt and Company—which went out on a limb (the more cautious Baring Brothers and House of Rothschild stuck to the safer bets of Argentina and Brazil). Either way, foreign lenders eventually faced what domestic creditors were already familiar with; in early 1826, Bogotá suspended payments to the British merchant bankers and sent the house of Goldschmidt reeling. In fact, the crash had begun in late 1825 with a European banking crisis and coincided with the outbreak of war between two of the biggest debtors, Argentina and Brazil. The rest, however, were bound to default, and the end of the furious, if short-lived, cycle of foreign borrowing closed the option of financing state building with foreign money, at least until the 1870s.[59]

The virtues of the unitarian ideal also got inverted in Brazil. In a sense, Brazil was better positioned to make the best of its foreign credits because the costs of secession from Portugal were milder by comparison than those of the Spanish colonies, and because Brazilian merchants, especially those organized around the thriving slave trade, had deeper pockets. However, unlike the other former colonies for whom foreign credits were afterthoughts, this was a country born in foreign debt.

---

[59]Carlos Marichal, *A Century of Debt Crises in Latin America: From Independence to the Great Depression, 1820–1930* (Princeton: Princeton University Press, 1989), pp. 14, 27–41; Frank Griffith Dawson, *The First Latin American Debt Crisis: The City of London and the 1822–1825 Loan Bubble* (New Haven: Yale University Press, 1990), pp. 13–21.

It was encumbered by a secret agreement to pay part (2 million pounds sterling) of Lisbon's debt to London from the Napoleonic Wars in an effort to settle scores with Portugal and curry favor with the British. The government also agreed to compensate Portugal for any losses sustained by independence. In 1824, British lenders were preparing to contract 3 million pounds sterling. As Canning learned, the debt was guaranteed for "the whole of the revenue of Brazil is to be hypothecated for the payment of interest."[60] Were the revenues enough? Evidently not, as Brazil followed the other debtors into default. Even though Brazil had managed to dodge a war with the metropole, it still had local secessionist movements to extinguish. The shortfall was evident as early as 1818; tax collectors in the colony were warning authorities that there was nothing left in the way of money to remit to Lisbon because it was all being tied up paying for armies in Pernambuco and the Banda Oriental. As independence neared, the government supplemented its normal levies with calls for "free contributions" to meet "the urgencies of the State." How free these were is questionable: the official organ of the court, the *Diario do Governo*, began to publish in May 1823 the names of Rio de Janeiro's citizens who had promised to make contributions but had so far failed to deliver them. We do not know how effective shame was as a borrowing technique.[61]

Brazil's fiscal condition in the first years of independence differed only in degree when compared to that of the Spanish American republics. The same held for the financial infrastructure—which Silva Lisboa had once vaunted as the example of the monarchy's vision of a public credit system that fostered trade while giving monied ballast to the state. But creating the bloc of merchants and ministers to make the passage to national sovereignty was not easy. Merchants had bankrolled the Banco do Brasil, created in 1808, but they were at constant loggerheads with the government, which treated the bank as its financial arm. The manner in which the old imperial government had simply used the bank to print its way through fiscal deficits, and then made off with its reserves in April 1821, left shareholders—effectively the ennobled merchants of the capital—furious. José Antonio Lisboa had been named to look at the books and report to the bank's shareholders to restore confidence. His report admitted that there was serious cause for concern, but added that the magnates of the city had little option but to bail out the bank and stand behind the

---

[60] Henry Thornton to George Canning, January 7, 1824, in Webster, ed., *Britain and the Independence of Latin America*, v. 1, p. 235; Manchester, *British Preëminence in Brazil*, p. 200; Barman, *Brazil*, p. 141.

[61] ANRJ, JC, Mesa de Inspeção, Caixa 178, doc. 16, September 22, 1818, and doc. s.n., May 6, 1817; *Diario do Governo*, April 16, 1822, May 22, 1823.

government: the bank's "credit is so intimately tied to the interests of the Nation, and especially the inhabitants of Rio de Janeiro, that all feelings of shock that they might have would without doubt bring a general calamity, and bring with them the ruin and desolation of a great part of the Lusitanian Monarchy." If this message was supposed to breed optimism by pointing out that merchants had little choice since they were effectively stakeholders in public debts, it did not. The author earned the moniker of "traveling flea." The bank ceased its commercial operations; the government gave up using bonds and capital markets to cover its shortfalls.[62]

If the independent regime wanted to restore the bank as a virtuous instrument of the new order (as its rival in Buenos Aires had), this was not really an option. The merchants who had to be its stakeholders would not forget that joining in the financial racket with the state was full of risks. The economic effects of independence were beginning to be felt. Gonçalo Vicente, a businessman from Itaparica, pleaded to authorities to release him from their fiscal demands in early 1823. He had a large family and an honor to uphold. Besides, "there is only a small traffic and business left among just a few markets in this Recôncavo," he added.[63] João Maria de Costa, editor of the influential *Gazeta do Brasil*, acknowledged that the only way to erase bad memories was to reconstitute the bank as a private entity with an arm's length from the treasury and some drastic efforts to retire old banknotes from circulation. But just as Costa published his outline, Brazil's finances were going from bad to worse. In 1827, the war with Argentina had ground to a costly standstill, and the government was starved of funds. It turned to the tried and true mechanisms of indiscriminate confiscations through inflation. The bank remained essentially the money printer for the government, which made up for its deficits by swamping the market with depreciating milreis. By 1830, when the inflationary spiral finally began to taper off, the currency had lost half its value; by then, the bank was seen as irremediable, and Brazil's deputies began to discuss its liquidation.[64]

Independence may have severed ties with Portugal, but the constitutional monarchy of Pedro I did not break with earlier financial habits of using public credit to bolster a dominant bloc that would support the regime's state-building ambitions. Still, hitching a financial system to

---

[62]José Antonio Lisboa, *Reflexões sobre o Banco do Brasil Ofrecidas aos seus Accionistas* (Rio de Janeiro: Typographia Nacional, 1821), p. 14; Franco, *Historia do Banco*, pp. 95–128; Fragoso, *Homens da grossa aventura*, pp. 200–203.

[63]APB, Secção Colonial 4626, s.n., petition by Gonçalo Vicente, March 25, 1823.

[64]*Gazeta do Brasil*, October 31, 1827; *Diario do Rio de Janeiro*, December 14, 1829; Johnson J, "A Preliminary Inquiry," p. 244; Barman, *Brazil*, p. 140.

audacious state-building plans was not as explosive in Brazil as it was in neighboring republics. There was a wealthy merchant class capable of absorbing the state's spendthrifty habits and centralizing ambitions. The quid pro quo was that the government safeguarded the interests of merchant capital in Rio de Janeiro—by preserving the centralizing networks of private credit through the provinces by keeping them in line, and of course ensuring that slavery, the slave trade, and exports of slave-produced commodities continued to be the basis of Brazil's connection to the Atlantic economy. Inflation was a nuisance to be sure, but it was a price worth paying to sustain the political economy of the "new" era.

It was one of the important coincidences of the age that just as state builders turned to incumbent elites to fund the creation of new political systems, merchant capital was undergoing a severe crisis. Where merchants still had means, ran centripetal trading systems, and tapped into staple-producing hinterlands and labor systems, they could—albeit at a price—buttress unitarian dreams. But where the merchant bloc that once dominated colonial economies had been pounded by mounting bills and convulsed labor systems, there was little left to contribute to its successor.

E UNUM PLURIBUS

The pressures of creating and legitimating new constitutional systems splintered the blocs that laid claim to state power. In Brazil, the pressures exploded but ultimately were contained; in Spanish America they brought down the unitarian schemes. What determined the stamina of unitarian blocs was their ability to contain rival alignments composed of disaffected elite and popular sectors, dismayed or outright disgusted at unitarian models of sovereignty.

The shattering of fledgling orders cannot be reduced to a single cause. Class conflict clearly mattered. The merchant elites in the cities became symbols of an "oligarchy" that put its interests ahead of the nation's, even though it was precisely the nation-building plans of elite urbanites that fomented dissidence. At the same time, one cannot gainsay the force of local autonomist sentiments that had their wellsprings in the ways that local authorities filled the inaugural political voids of 1807–8. The fusion of economic and political opposition, sparked by pangs of social grievances, was combustible. As prices soared, credit disappeared, and centralizing decrees rolled out of the parliamentary gatherings, incumbents became the targets of public campaigns, flyers, posters, and, most ominously, fighting words from the military commanders of local militias and popular armies.

As the political conflicts of the 1820s unfolded, the legacies of more than ten years of creating new political mores and affinities came to the fore. One source of public opinion—the old vecinos of literary salons, the physiocratic press, and associational life of Bogotá, Buenos Aires, and Rio de Janeiro—had flourished in the late colonial years and filled the immediate vacuum when metropolitan authorities imploded. But there was another source of public opinion that was no less the progeny of how old systems had collapsed. As warfare spread, public opinions were also associated with a *pueblo* identified in screaming posters, military barracks, and rural canteens seething with unrest. It was, therefore, not just a mode of production but a mode of legitimation that was in crisis. There was a paradox to the clash of the 1820s: that provincial forces could marshal compelling alternative claims to sovereignty under the banner of federalism is what stiffened unitarian resolve to reintegrate colonies into centralist units. But in so doing, unitarians provoked violence that reoriented the forces of revolution inward, so that the fragments of imperium now trained the arsenal of state formation against domestic rivals. What was latent before 1820 now burst forth: nation builders "internalized" the revolutions that brought them to power.[65]

The splintering had its precedents. But it was contained by a shared animus toward Spain, stoked by Ferdinand's revanchist war. The triumph of patriot over royalist armies after the Battle of Boyacá revealed the incisions within the anti-imperial alliance and culminated in the secession of Venezuela in 1826 from the confederacy of Gran Colombia. Indeed, four days after Boyacá, the delegates at Angostura approved a constitution to put political authority in civilian hands, but it never stuck. If internal secessionism would have been hard to avoid, it coincided with a shifting role for the Liberator himself, whose indomitable ability to mobilize was giving way to a growing propensity to polarize. The harder Bolívar tried, the more he poured his energies into drafting ever more inspired charters for the Andean republics, and the more the freed peoples and their elected delegates at the congresses that were supposed to approve them recoiled at his utopian charters for "American" unity.

In this incendiary environment any wrong move could bring on a firestorm. And everyone made the wrong move. The leader of Venezuelans' calls for local autonomy was Bolívar's erstwhile ally, General José Antonio

---

[65]Pilar González Bernaldo, "Producción de una nueva legitimdad: Ejercicio y sociedades patrióticas en Buenos Aires entre 1810 y 1813," in Noemi Goldman et al., *Imagen y recepción de la Revolución Francesa en la Argentina* (Buenos Aires: Gel, 1990), pp. 27–51; Noemí Goldman, "Legalidad y legitimidad en el caudillismo: Juan Facundo Quiroga y La Rioja en el Interior Rioplatense (1810–1835)," *Boletín del Instituto de Historia Argentina y Americana Dr. Emilio Ravignani* 7 (1993): 31–57. On "internalization," see Mayer, *The Furies*, pp. 607–95.

Páez, whose loyalty among llaneros, Indians, and runaway slaves had made his armies such a formidable force. To many in Páez's rank and file, the fight had been for local sovereignty and freedom. Rule from Bogotá was almost as noxious as it was from Madrid. By 1826, Venezuelans, in a wave of municipal decrees starting in Valencia, openly repudiated centralism—prompting the congress to begin to impeach Páez and order him to Bogotá to stand trial for treason. With little to lose, and much of Venezuela on his side, Páez rebelled. Even the city council of Caracas—which had little affection for Páez's rustic, rough-edged ways—supported him. Town by town invoked the concept of an "Antigua Venezuela" with mythic ancient taproots in municipal sovereignty to repudiate the legitimacy of the government in Bogotá. Bolívar heard the news of the crumbling while he was in Peru and Bolivia (where he was penning his Caesarist masterpiece) and began his long trek back to Bogotá to salvage what he could. By the time he reached the city, there was not much left to rescue. He resorted to a constitutional convention—hoping, once more, that a great deliberative occasion would be the democratic catharsis to unite the crumbling nation—at Ocaña in 1828. By this point, he not only had lost his neighboring republics but was enmeshed in open feuding with another former ally, General Santander, with his own base of popular support that preferred the sound of the latter's liberalism and embrace of federalism for "Colombia." The Bolivarian delegation walked out on the convention; the absence of a quorum led the remaining deputies to dissolve the assembly. That was, more or less, the demise of Colombian unitarianism as a force majeure it never quite became. In October 1829, the Caracas town council approved a resolution in favor of adopting a "representative and federal" government for Venezuela. Hounded by enemies on all sides, Bolívar eventually gave up, withdrew from public affairs, and began his journey into exile. En route, he learned that his greatest ally and the victor at Ayacucho, General Sucre, had been assassinated by rebels, which inspired his immortally dejected words, "America is ungovernable. Those who serve the revolution plough the sea. The only thing to do in America is to emigrate." Consumed by tuberculosis, Bolívar died in Santa Marta on December 17, 1830.[66]

As they became nightmares, Bolívar's unitarian dreams yielded to provincial metonyms of race. In a retrospective essay penned in 1829, Bolívar concluded that the enemy of freedom was less imperium than its

[66]David Bushnell, *The Santander Regime in Gran Colombia* (Newark, DE: University of Delaware Press, 1954), pp. 287–359, for the best single narrative of the Colombian side of the implosion; Véronique Hébrard, *Le Venezuela indépendant: Une nation par le discours—1808–1830* (Paris: Editions L'Harmattan, 1996), pp. 297–374.

cultural heritages. He noted that the revolution had degenerated into civil war because "blood, death, and every crime were the patrimony resulting from a federation combined with the rampant appetite of a people who have broken their chains and have no understanding of the notions of duty and law and who cannot cease being slaves except to become tyrants." His supporters denounced southerners as backward "Indios" whose lack of virtue was what inspired their loyalty to Spain and the monarchy—and this discourse mutated easily into analogous denunciations when their leaders, among them the popular commanders Colonels José María Obando and José Hilario López, who embraced the federalist cause. They were deemed heirs to "the corruption of the *pueblo*."[67]

What held for regions where Indian and mestizo peasants supported local autonomy was also true of the heavily black districts and coalitions, seen as the cauldrons of a dangerous "pardocracia." When two hundred slaves and freedmen attacked the barracks of Petare in Venezuela, crying "Long live the king and death to whites," it only confirmed what letrado state builders were beginning to believe: freed people of color were thwarts to freedom. This convenient formulation soon came to affect the way leaders dealt with their own colored allies. Consider the example of José Padilla, the zambo corsair who rose to the rank of admiral, who delivered a warning shot over the constitutional bow when he declared that "this sword with which I gave days of glory to the fatherland, this same sword will support me against anyone who tries to lower my class and degrade my person." Padilla had become a leading liberal figure across the Colombian coast, especially in Cartagena, and swung his support behind Santander, believing that a federalist state would uphold local sovereignty and egalitarianism, and thus enable the blacks or mulattos to redress old grievances with less constraint from Bogotá. His affiliations put him at odds with Bolívar, who was growing ever more convinced that fusion of local and racialized claims would visit ruin on the nation. As Bolívar was losing all hope for a confederation of nation-states, he grew determined to curb what he saw as the threats to each nation-state. When he sought to tighten a grip on *santanderistas* of all stripes, revolts erupted across Colombia. Emboldened by *libertos* who

---

[67]Simón Bolívar, "A Glance at Spanish America," in Bushnell, ed., *El Libertador*, p. 96; For a thoughtful set of reflections on the image of Indians and the racialization of attitudes toward popular sectors, see Frank Safford, "Race, Integration, and Progress: Elite Attitudes and the Indian in Colombia, 1750–1870," *Hispanic American Historical Review* 71:1 (1991): 1–33; and Brooke Larson, *Trials of Nation Making: Liberalism, Race, and Ethnicity in the Andes, 1810–1910* (New York: Cambridge University Press, 2004), esp. pp. 33–40.

felt that the 1821 emancipation decree had not fully delivered them from
thralldom, Padilla led pardo opposition in Cartagena in 1828 to prevent
Bolívar's last-ditch efforts to rescue centralism at the Ocaña convention.
But its racial composition frightened local whites, who otherwise
dithered over whether to support federalism (they liked the idea of being
free from Bogotá's commercial and fiscal policies) or centralism (the popularity of federalist movements was proof of its own menace). As fears
of a race war spread along the coast, white elites appealed for "help."
The government engineered the capture of the zambo war hero and sent
him to Bogotá. After a hasty trial, he was shot and hanged before the
capital's crowds. This repressive turn by Bolívar (who soon thereafter
confessed that he was tormented by his own decision) prompted the
great epic historian—and his former minister—José Manuel Restrepo to
wonder whether the Liberator had not become his own nemesis. Without
betraying his own enlightened centralist faiths, Restrepo had to conclude
that Bolívar, far from swaying public opinion, simply delivered it to his
detractors. Restrepo's majestic *Historia de la Revolución de Colombia*
inscribed a paean to the futility of using democratic means to build
nations out of former Spanish colonies into the origins of Colombian liberal historiography.[68]

In the River Plate as well, the crumbling unfolded along similar lines,
with the obvious difference that there was a material and symbolic center to the new nation—the United Provinces of the Río de la Plata—the
city of Buenos Aires, and a great deal of the dissident insurgency swept
a pan-provincial alliance against porteño centralism. It took little time to
dismantle and destroy what had been so painstakingly pieced together.
No sooner did the Constitutional Congress create a national regime than
it began to fall apart. Provincial forces began rumbling even as the constitution rolled off the printing presses in December 1826. General
Manuel Dorrego of Buenos Aires warned centralists that "in a republican system, the masses are what give authority." One deputy from Salta
captured the discordant sentiment: sovereignty had reverted to the people and their provincial form when the monarchy fell. Accordingly, it had
to be built from the bottom up, as an amalgam of provinces to form the
nation, not the other way around. "The way to constitute the nation," he
proclaimed, "is to build it part by part; constituting it in fact [*de hecho*];
forming it; giving it the powers whose result will form the whole of the
constitution." What unitarians were doing was the opposite; using the

---

[68]Restrepo, *Historia de la Revolución de Colombia*, v. 5, p. 160; on the fear of pardocracia, see Helg, *Liberty & Equality*, pp. 165–67, 195–211; Lynch, *The Spanish American
Revolutions*, p. 265.

constitution as a de jure blueprint for nationhood. Provincial governors and deputies, many of whom had cut their teeth as commanders in the wars against peninsular forces, combined the vertical appeal to their warrior followers with widespread popular elections that had become the cornerstone of provincial politics to assemble a league of their own, emerging into a powerful alternative alliance against unitarians, and sealed their alliance in the Federal Pact in May 1827. This pact, along with Artigas's proclamations about popular sovereignty, have become the founding emblems of federalist constitutionalism in the River Plate.[69]

The combination of the wasteful war against Brazil, the failure of the London loan bubble to buoy state finances and economic prosperity, and the juggernaut of unitarianism motivated provincial forces into action. As with Venezuela and Colombia, the crisis led to a clashing within the military forces that had developed in the struggle against Spain, and were now training their guns and sabers at each other. The militaries, in effect, occupied the terrain that once, if fleetingly, belonged to political parties—practically ensuring that warfare would be the default retreat for political competition.

By the time the porteño government settled its conflict with Brazil in September 1828, it was too late; Rivadavia, disgraced by the debacle of the embarrassing armistice and economic collapse, resigned and fled the country, leaving behind a political vacuum to be filled by the governor of Buenos Aires—none other than General Manuel Dorrego. When Buenos Aires' armies, led by General Juan Lavalle, returned from war against Brazil, they found the unitarian government gone. Irate that the regime he had fought for had decomposed, Lavalle arranged Dorrego's assassination. News of the killing, and the military's effort to revive the unitarian order, spread like a brushfire. Country militiamen, gauchos, and Indians who sympathized with the anti-elite rhetoric rallied to the cry of rural bosses, led by the caudillo Juan Manuel de Rosas, to put down what they felt was an oligarchic, centralist restoration. Pampean taverns were flooded with lithographs of the martyred governor. Insurgents donned the red sash that soon became the symbol of federalist montonero power, before galloping into battle against the remnants of the unitarian armies. Rivadavia himself sought refuge in Montevideo and eventually took up translating Alexis de Tocqueville's *Democracy in America*, no doubt resonating to the French aristocrat's worries about popular democracy. The unitarians never recovered; two decades later, Domingo

---

[69]Palcos, *Rivadavia*, v. 2, p. 67; Ravignani, "El Congreso Nacional," pp. 65–87; José Rafael López Rosas, *Historia constitucional argentina* (Buenos Aires: Editorial Astrea, 1986), pp. 384–95.

Faustino Sarmiento called them "the mummies of the Argentine Republic."[70]

The successor, federalist regime was even more hybrid than its predecessor. On November 3, 1829, Juan Manuel de Rosas entered Buenos Aires to be received as a hero by war-weary citizens. The House of Representatives elected Rosas governor. It also granted him sweeping, extraordinary powers several months later, ushering in decades of counterconstitutional rule based on carefully staged elections, managed infraelite conflict, and calibrated pacts with neighboring provinces. The new authorities may have demolished the nation building and constitutional order of the unitarians. But they were not at all opposed to order. Armies, gendarmes, and justices of the peace patrolled the countryside to restore labor discipline. The new government also promised to restore value to money—"one of the primitive obligations upon which authority is constituted . . . for currency is intimately tied to the reestablishment and conservation of order." Rosas, a savvy estate owner and heir to the federalist movements that had swept the Pampas as the old viceroyalty broke up, drove the political and economic frontier deep into the hinterlands, heralding a shift to rural property and country politics.[71]

Federalism surged in Brazil as well and forced a retreat, albeit less decisive, of unitarian plans. While antecedents of federalism were more recent than in Spanish America, and electoral coalitions had had much less time to coagulate into ideological or party affiliations, the implosion of the empire had shifted power to the provinces. It must be recalled that the convocation of the Cortes in Portugal had inscribed in provincial authorities the right to elect deputies for the parliament in the restored metropolis; *juntas provisórias*, self-governing entities, popped up all over, beginning with Bahia's junta in early 1821.

As with the uprising of 1817 against the power in Rio de Janeiro, it was from the province of Pernambuco that the strongest stance against centralism resurfaced. In the local capital of Recife, federalists created a junta of federalist militiamen, former 1817 rebels, and some planters irate at their merchant creditors, many of whom were Portuguese. So even before independence, federalism was dividing the country and

---

[70]Pilar González Bernaldo, "Social Imagery and Its Political Implications in a Rural Conflict: The Uprising of 1828–29," in Szuchman and Brown, eds., *Revolution and Restoration*, pp. 177–207; Palcos, *Rivadavia*, v. 2, pp. 233–69; Domingo Faustino Sarmiento, *Facundo: Civilization and Barbarism*, trans. Kathleen Ross (Berkeley: University of California Press, 2003), p. 125.

[71]Ternavasio, "Nuevo régimen representative y expansion de la frontera política," pp. 78–80; ABPBA, Actas, Comisiones Especiales, 001-6-2, October 3, 1929; Adelman, *Republic of Capital*, pp. 109–40.

provinces; indeed, the years between independence and the approval of the constitution saw intensified jostling between federalists and centralists. Northeasterners were bursting with tension. In early 1824, as the emperor sought to impose his candidate for president of the province of Pernambuco, the wealthy merchant-planter and imperial stalwart Francisco Pais Barreto (later the Marquis of Recife), local federalists were horrified. The federalist firebrand Frei Caneca (Friar Mug, so nicknamed because he once sold mugs on the streets of Recife) denounced the constitution for failing to secure national sovereignty; only a charter that respected local electoral rights and autonomy would. Others charged that Pedro's dissolving of the Constituent Assembly and resorting to handpicked counselors to draft a charter had violated the provinces' rights to have their chosen delegates participate in lawmaking. Manoel de Carvalho Pais de Andrade insisted that "each Province must have its respective center, and each of these centers forms part of a great chain that will make Brazil invincible." In the words of *Typhis Pernambucano*, "Brazil became sovereign, not only in the whole, but in every one of its parts or provinces." Federalists moved to elect their own president and cobbled together a "Confederation of the Equator" including Paraíba do Norte, Rio Grande do Norte, and Ceará. In fact, this was less a secessionist alliance than a demand that Pedro drop his charter and convoke a legitimate, elected assembly of lawmakers to reunite the country. As in the River Plate, these were not declarations of independence from the capital but announcements of a legitimate autonomy, that the nation was made up of self-governing parts agreeing to contract together to form a whole. Still, Pedro would brook no compromise. He ordered the national army and navy to crush the rebels, which they accomplished by year's end. While the imperial navy blockaded Recife, the city's slaves and free blacks sang verses extolling Henri Christophe of Haiti: "Qual eu imito a Christovam, esse immortal haitiano. Eai! Imitai a seu povo, Oh meu povo soberano!"[72]

The federalist upsurge in Pernambuco horrified Rio de Janeiro's state builders. José da Silva Lisboa wrote a hysterical pamphlet decrying federalists as "incorrigible Jacobins" bent on destroying the integrity "OF THE EMPIRE OF BRAZIL." Echoing the racial metonyms with which other

---

[72]Graham, *Patronage and Politics in Nineteenth-Century Brazil*, pp. 136–48; Lugar, "The Merchant Community of Salvador," pp. 289–90; Barman, *Brazil*, pp. 120–22; Marcus Carvalho, "Rumores e rebeliões," *Liberdade: Rotinas e ruptures do escravismo no Recife, 1822–1850* (Recife: Ed. Universitária da Universidade Federal de Pernambuco, 2002), p. 197; Glacyra Lazzari Leite, *Pernambuco 1824* (Recife: Fundação Joaquim Nabuco, 1989), p. 100; Barbosa Lima Sobrinho, *Pernambuco: Da independência à Confederação do Equador* (Recife: Prefeitura da Cidade do Recife, 1998), p. 201.

unitarians tarred dissidence, he accused Manoel de Carvalho of taking refuge in "the Quilombos of Lamarão" and stirring slaves and freed blacks. The emperor, empowered by this sense of rectitude, might have been able to consolidate his centralist rule were it not for other regional threats. The southern provinces resonated to the federalist esprit that was sweeping the Platine borderlands. In early 1825, the provincial "uprising" in the Banda Oriental whipped other Brazilian provinces into the same kind of resistance to Rio de Janeiro as was afflicting Buenos Aires. The ultra-royalist Baron von Mareschal reported a conversation he had with Dom Pedro to the Austrian foreign minister, Count Metternich, relaying the emperor's sense of "the real danger with which he is menaced by the republican form of the rest of the Governments in South America... Bolívar's latest victories have inspired in him a veritable terror." Would Rio Grande do Sul join with the montonero forces of the Banda Oriental? This fear of contagion, and of the insurrection against the slavocrat regime as a whole, drove the government to war against Buenos Aires, which the court blamed for stoking insurgent republicans. The war was a disaster from the start. Alarmed, Dom Pedro himself rushed to the front to take command—only to fall ill and return home with his empress. Spreading mutinies eventually forced the emperor to agree to peace talks.[73]

In military terms, the Brazilians did worse than the Argentines. But politically, the regime survived, albeit scathed; the price of keeping the system of rulership in place was paid by the ruler himself—who eventually lost support of the patrician classes of Rio de Janeiro. Here we can see the shaded differences between the fate of unitarianism in Argentina and Brazil. In the former, a diffusive war apparatus became the vehicle of political polarization, whereas in Brazil, armies and navy were prevented from deteriorating into plundering machines. The contrast, however, needs to be nuanced for in fact the Brazilian army was a recurring source of turmoil. Recruits, most of whom were mulattos, seethed in their garrisons; the food was wretched and scarce, they went unpaid, and they were forced into losing battles against kinfolk with sympathetic ideas. Yet, the rampant desertion of foot soldiers and setbacks in the battlefield did not translate into internecine feuding within the high command because it was not made up of professionalized provincial chieftains who had cut their warrior teeth in localized guerrilla wars against peninsular armies; in many ways, the Brazilian army was a holdover from the

---

[73]José da Silva Lisboa, *Appello á Honra Brasileira contra a Facção dos Federalistas de Pernambuco* (Rio de Janeiro: Imprensa Nacional, 1824), pp. 1–5; Ron Seckinger, *The Brazilian Monarchy and the South American Republics, 1822–1831* (Baton Rouge: Louisiana State University Press, 1984), pp. 25–31; Macauley, *Dom Pedro*, pp. 204–11.

imperial era. Still, Dom Pedro, his military, and his ministers lost a great deal of face for the handling of the war and the terms of peace. During the 1828 elections, nativists, republicans, and federalists made hay at the expense of the court. Lingering calls by liberal federalists, like Antônio Borges da Fonseca, whose *Gazeta Paraibana* fulminated against the emperor for trampling on the sovereign rights of locals, sustained a relentless campaign in favor of deep, decentralizing reforms. The emperor's role in political life receded, and his advisors were increasingly discredited. Elites did not renege on their commitment to the slavocrat regime. But they grew fatigued by Pedro's repeated request for funds and his well-known indulgences in food and sex. They staged a bloodless coup d'état and forced the emperor to abdicate and leave the country in order to rescue the regime. In 1831, he set sail aboard a British man-of-war, leaving the state in the hands of a regency and his young son, Pedro II, as well as a clique that artfully reconstructed a political elite founded less on its social integration than a shared commitment to ideological unity—and continuity.[74]

Over the ensuing decades, central authorities engaged in protracted bargaining with local potentates and political bosses, gradually decentralizing the state in order to preserve it, creating, incrementally, a federalist empire in the new world. Out of the unum emerged an increasingly potent pluribus. For all the vaunted continuity of parliamentary monarchy and ministerial authority as the mainstays of nineteenth-century Brazilian constitutionalism, the ballast came from grassroots boss rule, which was as indifferent to the rule of law as it was zealous in its defense of autonomy from the capital.

Conclusion

The crucible decade of the 1820s saw patrician ideals and institutions clash with rival aspirations. The effort to replace empire with something else gave rise to the simultaneous advent of patriotic localisms and centralisms. As supreme lawmakers set about building new models of sovereignty to recombine political subjects and state powers, they paradoxically gave form to alternative notions of sovereignty. In the clashing that ensued, no stable or hegemonic model took root. In addition, each side drew strength in reaction to the other so that rival models of sovereignty

[74]José Murilo de Carvalho, *A construção da ordem* (Rio de Janeiro: Editora Universidade Federal de Rio de Janeiro, 1996), pp. 209–11; Seckinger, *The Brazilian Monarchy*, pp. 147–51; Macauley, *Dom Pedro*, pp. 236–52; Barman, *Brazil*, pp. 153–59.

gave way to two enduring, if antagonistic, traditions. Federalism owed its heritage as much to the revolutions that toppled imperium as did unitarian constitutionalism. Provinces, as much as nations, were the descendants of empires. Indeed, for many federalists rising up against Rivadavia, Bolívar, and Dom Pedro was consistent with the declarations of colonial home rule in 1808–10. It was centralists who appeared to be trying to restore old ways. By the same token, it had been the fear of the way local sovereignties had filled the immediate vacuum of imperial crises that emboldened unitarians to position themselves as the more truly national and integrative force. In effect, the emergency of the 1820s revealed the contingent nature of state power. It elevated these contingencies to matters of fundamental question and in so doing mobilized social actors into polarizing camps.[75]

The new, precarious compromises and combinations reflected the degree to which old institutions collapsed without automatic successors. They were also adaptations to much more leveled societies than anything imagined before the empires imploded. New models of representation, developed in the new circles of sociability, outside the privileged gathering points of urban well-to-doers, created novel political alliances and affiliations. Taverns, militia barracks, a popular press, and vibrant rumor mills created alternative ways to legitimate—or stigmatize—power-holders. This was certainly a political landscape that rulers—presidents, caudillos, or regents—had to conform to. It was also a force to be reckoned with by economic interests. The debacle of public credit schemes was not just a fiscal miscalculation; these financial arrangements rested on the backs of commercial magnates whose abilities to reproduce their own location atop the social hierarchies were increasingly contested. Finally, centralizing monetary authority also ran into the opposition of social classes, not all of which were made of plebeian genes, who were as suspicious of the formation—or in their view a re-formation—of a dominant merchant class as they were of the states they were supposed to bankroll. Clearly here the Brazilian elite coherence and access to autonomous and lucrative means of accumulation—the bounty of the slave trade—redoubled patrician fealty to the central state so long as state centralizers were ultimate guarantors of a slavocrat order. By contrast, in regions where the political rupture weakened and splintered

---

[75]See the important works of José Carlos Chiaramonte, "Legalidad constitucional o caudillismo: El problema del orden social en el surgimiento de los estados autonomos del litoral argentine en la primera mitad del siglo XIX," *Desarrollo Económico* 102:26 (1986): 175–96, and "La cuestión regional en el proceso de gestación del estado nacional argentine," in Waldo Ansaldi and José Luis Moreno, comps., *Estado y sociedad en el pensamiento nacional* (Buenos Aires: Cántaro, 1989), pp. 159–203.

elites it was much harder for state builders to erect integrated constitutional systems; in turn, the travails of lawmaking prevented states from nurturing the commercial habits and civic norms associated with virtuous citizenship.

From the 1820s there emerged some common traits of postcolonial societies that would distinguish them from colonial antecedents: the belief that there was a sovereign people, even if some fretted that it was not prepared for popular sovereignty, and the conviction that private economic activity had to be free of arbitrary intrusions, even if others worried that unbridled markets sowed avaricious habits. What could not be denied was that societies—not kings living in metropolitan palaces—were the source of power and repository of rights to decide on the legitimacy of institutional life. The problem was that societies that had not plunged into revolution as one did not emerge as one. The quest endured. Sovereignty from empire had been achieved. But how to give sovereignty new meaning remained as equivocal as ever.

Afterword

In a rebellion, as in a novel, the most difficult part to invent is
the end.

—Alexis de Tocqueville

This book has examined the ways in which models of sovereignty changed
during the age of revolutions, an age in which moral, economic, and historical inquiries became closely aligned with the image of the state as an
indivisible ideal reaching its territorial limits. The notion of indivisibility,
of association between statehood and sovereignty, was a trait passed on
from the imperium to its successors. In whatever form, its rulers imagined
the state as the instrument for creating moral communities of civic-minded
men (and some women), defined as subjects or citizens, who lived and
transacted together under the same legal norms and statutes.

If this was the ideal for imperialists and nationalists alike, the indivisibility of sovereignty was under assault. Interimperial contests, infra-imperial
conflict, and eventually the carnage of civil war ripped apart the Iberian
Atlantic empires and their colonial formations; warfare and revolution
remapped the legal geography of the Atlantic world by transforming the
ways in which subjects understood sovereignty and therefore statehood,
uncoupling what had endured and evolved for centuries under the mantle
of monarchy and imperium.

The ends of empire and the beginnings of successor regimes were violent sources of immense contingencies because they marked the demise
of incumbent power and the proliferation of alternatives. They also
revealed how imperfectly statehood and sovereignty aligned—how much
the defense of legitimate legal orders depended on bargains and pacts
within ruling elites and between rulers and ruled, whose basic variega-
tions dissolved into promulgated ideals of justice within the territorial
limits of a state's powers. Sovereignty may have been an ideal, but it was
also a compromise between internally heterogeneous peoples and places.
Sovereignty operated on various levels, therefore: as aspiration and as a
condition of how power should function.

Even as political theorists contrived ideas of statehood, the conflict
between European states ramped up—and they ramped up because they

took increasingly imperial forms. Indeed anciens régimes—Spain and Portugal no less than others—so closely identified imperium with sovereignty because it offered them and their subjects universalizing possibilities. These universalizing claims provided the ultimate legitimating trump cards for conquest, exploitation, and aggrandizement of rulers and ruling classes. The history told in this book is about how a world of competing empires used geographic expansion and capital accumulation as a source of legitimacy and a mainstay for a ruling bloc—and therefore plunged it into wars and revolutions that would sever the historic ties between Old World capitals and their New World colonies.

Along the way, subjects stuck by their sovereigns, remained loyal, and acquired voice as a means to defend what they thought best and most legitimate before they could imagine the world anew. This process cannot be waved away as simply precursive activity, as if it were all fated to give way to something new, more modern. The analysis of loyalty and voice is critical to our understanding of how and when empires collapsed. It is unhelpful to presume, as so many historians of empires have, that they were (and are) doomed structures. Being under assault through warfare or local insurgency in the eighteenth century did not by themselves cast light on the diminishing limits of state powers.

How and why they receded did so much to prepare the social and legal groundwork for what followed. One central argument of this book is that colonists in Spanish and Portuguese possessions in the Americas did not rise up against decadent empires because they imagined a newer, more virtuous model of sovereignty and thereby created a revolution that brought down the ancien régime. The downfall of empires occurred when the pacts and principles governing empire collapsed in the imperial cores to disclose the originary structures of political order. The crisis of legitimacy at the center radiated outward, creating concentric disputation and conflict, and brewing civil war at the fringes. Only once loyalty to and voice within older structures became too stigmatized to sustain—and in this regard, it was the efforts by restorationists in Portugal and Spain that did so much to pull the rug out from under their colonial allies—did the exit option gather force. The revolutions that made the world anew were the consequence, not the cause, of the end of imperial sovereignty.

More than a pedantic exercise in getting the sequence right, this history reveals some deeper ambiguities about the making of sovereign states in former Iberian colonies to illustrate the tensions that arose when the principles of sovereignty were highly contested—from inside and outside—without presuming that historic agents lived by teleological maxims or the benefits of hindsight they did not have.

One element that did survive the disruption was the belief that whatever came after empire had to resolve what anciens régimes had failed to do: reconstitute the association of sovereignty with statehood, now reimagined along national lines. What was so difficult to reconcile in the 1820s was that many members of South American societies aspired to a new order—but the ways in which they dismantled the old order had left them polarized, fractured, and mobilized into armed camps. It would have required the shared idyll of a "nation," the acceptance of a fictional indivisibility of sovereignty and statehood, or some social consensus about the virtues of market life to transcend the enmities born of civil war, when these very motivating forces were not what occasioned the struggle for sovereignty in the first place. Bolívar resolved the bequests of history by drafting a constitution for Bolivia as a partnership between legislators and censors with a single fundamental goal for the nation's citizens: "the moral development of man." The Viscount of Cairú argued for a similar formulation: the role of the state was to create the nation in its image. For Bolívar and Cairú, this spirit of lawmaking was the necessary condition of sovereignty after empire.

In trying to resolve the political form of the state in a way that would herd its members into a debate over sovereignty as a matter of determining who *within* the order was endowed with certain powers rather than a contest over the order itself brought the revolutions to a new phase—intensifying their force as they turned inward upon their prophets. The breakup of imperial sovereignty meant the proliferation of its progeny. There was more than one way—much to Bolívar and Cairú's dismay—to imagine the world anew. With empires smashed by rivalries they could not—by definition—avoid, no single vision of postcolonial sovereignty filled the vacuum left behind. Regional elites and their popular allies, and even the freed slaves and Indians who rallied to the secessionist cause in pursuit of their personal freedoms, were also heirs to a struggle against the old regime precisely *because* the nation was not prefigured by colonialism to herald its demise. *Because* the nation emerged in the wake of empire, it was open to multiple meanings and more than one "story of peoplehood." Frei Caneca in Brazil, José Artigas in the Banda Oriental, and Manuel Piar in Colombia were also central to the passage from the ancien régime. Their vision of federalist republics offered alternative models of sovereignty that did not map so coherently onto the centralized state-nations championed by unitarians. Theirs were more equivocal about nationhood as the aspiration of modern sovereignty and instead championed notions of sovereignty as a condition of freedom inscribed in local, popular cognates for monarchy and empire.

In the aftermath of revolutions, sovereignties multiplied across the former Iberian colonies. At times they coexisted in unstable hybrid models. At times they polarized and motivated decades of civil wars. No single brand of lawmaking or history writing took hold. The way in which these empires collapsed also deprived colonists of any means for reaching back to grasp doctrines of ancient rights or liberties in order to build something new. When North American colonists improvised a constitutional system in the wake of their own revolution, they relied on the resources of history to recombine fundamental law and governmental power; indeed the founders of "the" republic imagined themselves as more perfect heirs of English ideals than the parliamentary custodians they repudiated. This was not an option for South American colonists, whose notions of sovereignty had to promise something entirely different and therefore more questionable, in order to build something new. Constitutionalism in Iberian America had to be premised not on an ancient constitution as a colonial birthright, but on a charter that replaced empire with surrogates made of new cloth.

The history of the Iberian Atlantic was not at odds with the promissory meanings of sovereignty. The multitude of sovereignties that emerged from empire reveal not so much a failure of nation builders or revolutionaries as much as the difficulty of making history anew when the ambiguities of sovereignty could not be easily dissimulated in visions of nationhood or political power without the existence of previous deep-seated ideologies to justify them.

As Hannah Arendt once observed, the North American colonists had the singular good fortune of being able to have a revolution and crystallize a new system of power and a single source of law because there was so little that had to be changed. They also had the advantage of being first—and thus innocent of their consequences.[1] Not so the subjects of the Iberian Atlantic, for whom the knowledge of the consequences and alternatives of change was present at the moment of birth. For them, the next two centuries would be governed by the plenitude of possible futures and the challenge of changing so much.

---

[1] Arendt, *On Revolution*, esp. pp. 156–59.

Index